CAMBRIDGE
EDUCATIONAL SERVICES

AMERICA'S PREMIERE TESTING READINESS PROGRAM

Victory for the ACT® and SAT® Tests

STUDENT TEXT

ACT® • PLAN® • EXPLORE® • ACT Aspire™ • SAT® • PSAT/NMSQT® • PSAT™ 8/9 • PSAT™ 10 • WorkKeys® • GRE® • GMAT® • LSAT® • GED® • TASC™ • HiSET® • ITBS • MCAT® PRAXIS® Stanford • EOC and State Tests • Analytics • Classroom Texts • Teacher Curriculum • Professional Development • Web Courses • Question Writing Online Services • CollegePrep™ • Guidance Services • Motivation/Admissions Workshops • Learning Styles • Career Interest Inventory Non-Negotiable Skills™ • Essential Skills • Cambridge iFlara™ eBooks

Our Mission: Progress Through Partnership
Cambridge Educational Services partners with educators who share the significant mission of educational advancement for all students. By partnering together, we can best achieve our common goals: to build skills, raise test scores, enhance curriculum, and support instruction. A leading innovator in education for twenty years, Cambridge is the nation's premier provider of school-based test preparation and supplemental curriculum services.

Cambridge Publishing, Inc.
www.CambridgeEd.com

Fifth edition 2015

Printed in the United States of America
18 17 16 15 1 2 3 4 5

ISBN-13: 978-1-58894-245-6

TABLE OF CONTENTS

COURSE OVERVIEW

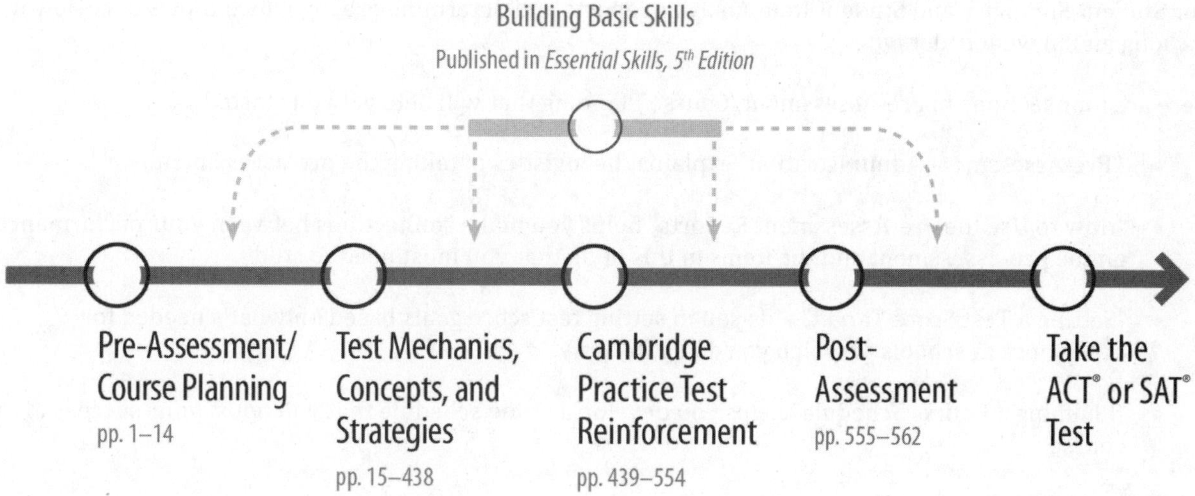

This course is organized into six parts, which are outlined in the chart above:

- **Pre-Assessment/Course Planning:** A diagnostic pre-assessment and score report helps you identify your starting point and prepare for the course.
- **Building Basic Skills:** This review material, found in *Essential Skills, 5th Edition,* serves as a refresher on topics you may not have studied in a while.
- **Test Mechanics, Concepts, and Strategies:** Your instructor will use items resembling those on the real tests to teach tested concepts and applicable strategies.
- **Practice Test Reinforcement:** Two full-length practice tests (one ACT test and one SAT test) allow you to practice your skills in a testing format.
- **Post-Assessment:** A diagnostic post-assessment helps you see how far you've come and recommended courses of action help you continue your study after the course.
- **Take the ACT and/or SAT Test:** After you complete the course, you will take the test, using everything you learn throughout this course to succeed on test day.

The following introduction will briefly explain how to use each part of this program.

Pre-Assessment/Course Planning

In order to know where to begin preparing for the real test, you have to find out what you already do well and what you could learn to do better. The pre-assessment serves this purpose. First, you will take a pre-assessment which is written, normed, and distributed by ACT, Inc. or by College Board and released for practice (we call this a previously administered test). Then, with the help of your instructor, you will examine your Student Summary and Student Item Analysis reports and determine exactly which topics to review for how long and in what order.

There are four sections in Pre-Assessment/Course Planning that will help get you started:

- "Pre-Assessment Administration" explains the logistics of taking the pre-assessment.
- "How to Use the Pre-Assessment Reports" helps you make connections between your performance on the pre-assessment and the items in this book that you most need to study.
- "Setting a Test Score Target" aids you in setting test score goals based on what's needed for acceptance at schools to which you'd like to apply.
- "Planning a Course Schedule" helps you develop a study schedule that will boost your success in the course.

Building Basic Skills

Essential Skills, 5th Edition serves as a companion to this *Victory* book. It provides targeted skill-building material to help you fill any skill gaps as you prepare for test day. Your instructor may cover this material in class or assign it as homework.

There are four chapters in *Essential Skills*:

- English and Writing
- Reading
- Mathematics
- Science

Each of these chapters (except the Writing an Essay section) is organized into three sections: basic, intermediate, and advanced. Each section addresses a group of skills essential for college and career success.

Test Mechanics, Concepts, and Strategies

Test Mechanics, Concepts, and Strategies make up the heart of this course. This part of the book contains items that have the same content, represent the same difficulty levels, and can be solved by using the same problem-solving skills and alternative test-taking strategies as the items you will encounter on test day.

There are seven chapters in Test Mechanics, Concepts, and Strategies, with each chapter representing a core component of the exams:

- ACT Reading and SAT Reading
- ACT English and SAT Writing and Language

- ACT Essay
- SAT Essay
- ACT Mathematics and SAT Math: Multiple-Choice
- SAT Math: Student-Produced Responses
- ACT Science

Each of the above chapters begins with a Course Concept Outline, which acts as a syllabus and lists the concepts that are tested for each item type. The items in each chapter are organized to correspond with their respective outline. For each concept in the outline, there is a group of items. Groups contain a greater number of items if the item type appears with great frequency on the real test and a lesser number of items if the item type appears with less frequency. Although the concepts are not grouped in this way on the real ACT and SAT tests, we organize the lessons in this manner to emphasize and reinforce concepts. After you learn the concepts, you will be able to hone your skills by applying this conceptual knowledge on the practice tests.

Practice Test Reinforcement

In the Practice Test Reinforcement portion of this book, there are two full-length practice tests, one a Cambridge practice test for the ACT test and the other a Cambridge practice test for the SAT test. In these tests, the items not only mimic the real tests in content and difficulty level, but they are also arranged in an order and with a frequency that simulates the real test.

You should complete the practice tests with the same time restrictions you will have on the real tests. You may complete these items in class or your instructor may assign them as homework. Either way, adhering to the time restrictions forces you to pace yourself as you would on the real test. If you complete both of the practice tests, any test anxiety you may have will be greatly reduced. Answers and explanations to the practice tests are located in Appendix A of this book.

Post-Assessment

In order to know how far you've come since the pre-assessment, you will take a second previously administered test. You will take this post-assessment under actual testing conditions. You will then receive a second Student Summary and Student Item Analysis report to help you determine final areas for review.

The Post-Assessment contains three sections to help you see how far you've come:

- "Post-Assessment Administration" explains the logistics of taking the post-assessment.
- "How to Use the Post-Assessment Reports" shows you how to use the Student Summary and Student Item Analysis reports you will receive to identify areas of study, as well as particular items in your textbook, upon which to focus as you continue to prepare for the real test.
- "Planning for Further Study" includes advice on how to make an effective and concrete action plan. You will learn how to maximize your remaining course time and prioritize material to be reviewed before you take the actual test.

Pre-Assessment/ Course Planning

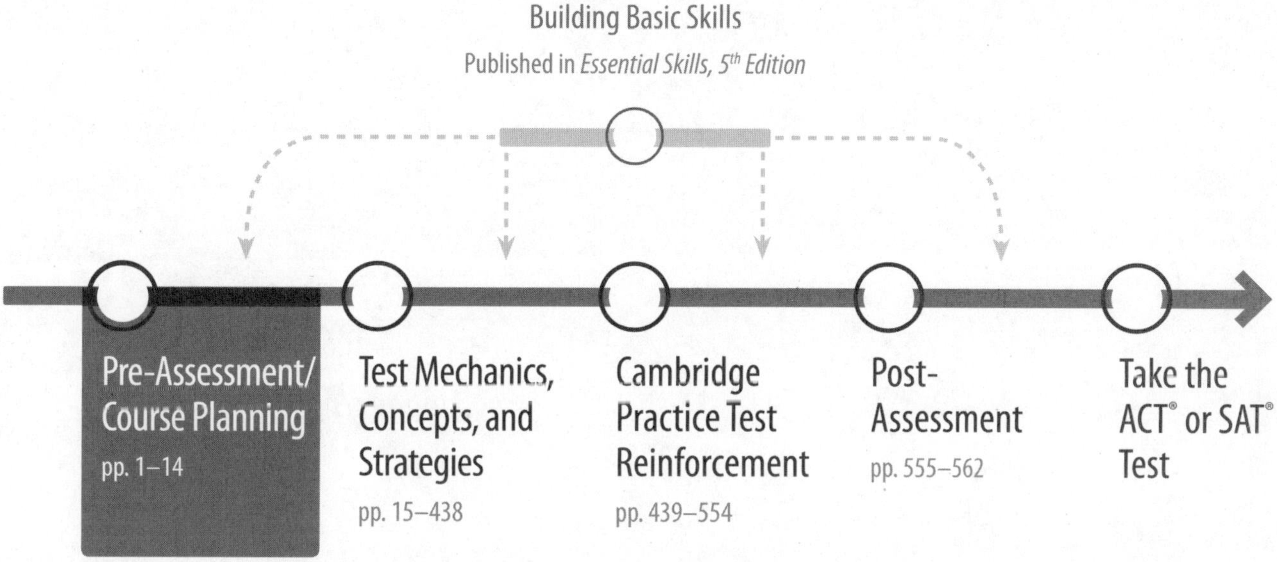

CAMBRIDGE
VICTORY FOR THE
ACT® AND SAT® TESTS

PRE-ASSESSMENT ADMINISTRATION

At the beginning of the course, you will take a pre-assessment. This pre-assessment is written, normed, and distributed by ACT, Inc. or by College Board and released for practice (we call this a previously administered test). When you take the pre-assessment, you should bring the following items to the classroom, in addition to anything else your teacher instructs you to bring:

1. Sharpened, soft-lead, No. 2 pencils
2. A calculator that is approved for use on the test. Most graphing calculators and all scientific and four-function calculators are permitted, but four-function calculators are not recommended. The following are not permitted:
   - Handheld or laptop computers, tablets, cell phones, or smart phones
   - Electronic writing pad or pen-input devices
   - Models that can access the internet, have wireless, Bluetooth, cellular, audio/video recording or playing, camera, or any other smart phone-type feature
   - Models with a QWERTY (typewriter) keypad
   - Models with paper tape
   - Models that make noise or "talk"
   - Models that must be plugged into an outlet
3. A watch (to pace yourself as you work through each test section)

If your program has ordered pre-assessment Student Summary reports, you will receive one of these reports with your pre-assessment results. This report will help you determine the areas in which you need the most study and enable you to target the skills that are necessary to lay a foundation for success in the course. You can then utilize the course time to prepare in those areas so that when you take the real test, you are ready to do your best. You will learn more about how to read and use the Student Summary report in the "How to Use the Pre-Assessment Reports" section on page 5.

How to Use the Pre-Assessment Reports

You and your teacher will use the results of your pre-assessment to recognize your individual strengths and weaknesses. Having this valuable information will allow you to create a realistic study plan for the course so that you can effectively manage your time.

You will receive the results of your pre-assessment in the form of a Student Summary and a Student Item Analysis. These reports provide details about your performance and will help you determine where to focus your efforts during the course by strategically targeting the skills that will help you to improve in your areas of weakness. Review the details of the sample Student Summary and Student Item Analysis reports on the next four pages so that you are familiar with their contents.

Sample Student Reports

On the following pages are sample ACT test and SAT test Student Summary and Student Item Analysis reports.

Student Summary for an ACT Test

The Student Summary report summarizes all your scaled scores based on your test performance. In addition, it shows how you performed within specific categories for each of the four subject tests (English, Mathematics, Reading, and Science). For example, English includes the categories Rhetorical Skills (RH) and Usage/Mechanics (UM).

CAMBRIDGE EDUCATIONAL SERVICES

(800) 444-4373
testprep@cambridgeed.com
www.cambridgeed.com

Site: SAMPLE SCHOOL
Student: SAMPLE STUDENT (20170050)
Grade: 11
ACT® Test: 0556B

Student Summary

TEST	SCORE	PERCENTILE
English	26	84
Mathematics	23	68
Reading	19	41
Science	21	57
Composite	22	63
STEM	23	
Writing	25	
ELA	22	

ENGLISH	RIGHT	WRONG	OMIT
Usage/Mechanics (UM)	32	8	0
Rhetorical Skills (RH)	28	7	0
TOTAL English	60	15	0

26 — 18 (Minimum Benchmark) — 36

MATHEMATICS	RIGHT	WRONG	OMIT
Pre-Algebra/Elem. Algebra (EA)	19	5	0
Int. Algebra/Coord. Geo. (AG)	10	8	0
Plane Geo./Trig. (GT)	9	9	0
TOTAL Mathematics	38	22	0

23 — 22 (Minimum Benchmark) — 36

READING	RIGHT	WRONG	OMIT
Social Studies/Sciences (SS)	8	12	0
Arts/Literature (AL)	10	9	1
TOTAL Reading	18	21	1

19 — 22 (Minimum Benchmark) — 36

SCIENCE	RIGHT	WRONG	OMIT
Conflicting Viewpoint (CV)	1	0	6
Data Representation (DR)	12	3	0
Research Summary (RS)	12	2	4
TOTAL Science	25	5	10

21 — 23 (Minimum Benchmark) — 36

English: The English test measures your ability to apply the conventions of standard written English to a piece of writing. Items are divided into two categories: Usage/Mechanics (Punctuation, Grammar and Usage, and Sentence Structure) and Rhetorical Skills (Strategy, Organization, and Style).

Mathematics: The Mathematics test measures your ability to apply the knowledge and skills taught in high school mathematics courses. Items are divided into three categories: Pre-Algebra/Elementary Algebra, Intermediate Algebra/Coordinate Geometry and Plane Geometry, Trigonometry.

Reading: The Reading test measures your ability to read and think carefully about four passage types typically encountered in a first-year college course (Prose Fiction, Humanities, Social Studies, and Natural Sciences). You are asked to comprehend and respond to the passages through a variety of item-types, including Main Idea, Explicit Detail, Vocabulary, Development, Implied Idea, Application, and Voice.

Science: The Science test measures your ability to apply scientific concepts and reasoning techniques. You will read six or seven passages and answer the questions that follow. There are three types of science passages: Data Representation, Research Summary, and Conflicting Viewpoints.

Writing: The optional Writing test measures your ability to develop a perspective on a given issue and evaluate other perspectives with a well organized and clearly written essay. You will have 40 minutes to write a response. The Writing test does not affect the composite score or scores on the individual subject tests.

Note: Numbers used for scores and percentiles in the report are for illustrative purposes only and do not necessarily represent a valid correlation.

The composite score is the average of the four subject scores. Colleges typically base about 45% of their admissions decision on the composite score. Other factors they consider include GPA, extracurricular involvement, and social service activities.

Percentile rank indicates what percent of students scored lower than the student's composite score. Here, 63% of test-takers scored at or below this student's composite score of 22.

The STEM score is an average of the Mathematics and Science scores, while the ELA score is an average of the English, Reading, and Writing scores.

There is no penalty for an incorrect answer, so be sure not to leave any questions blank. Here on the science section, the student could have increased her score by an average of 2 points simply by guessing.

The writing score is not included in the overall composite score and is reported on a scale of 1–36.

Student Item Analysis for an ACT Test

The Student Item Analysis provides a comprehensive breakdown of each item: how you answered each question, the correct answer, and its category (corresponding to the categories listed on the Student Summary).

CAMBRIDGE
EDUCATIONAL SERVICES®

(800) 444-4373
testprep@cambridgeed.com
www.cambridgeed.com

Site: SAMPLE SCHOOL
Student: SAMPLE STUDENT
Test Date: 09/03/15
ACT® Test: 0556B

Student Item Analysis

ENGLISH

Problem Number:	1	2	3	4	5	6	7	8	9	10	11	12	13	14	15	16	17	18	19	20	21	22	23	24
Category:	UM	RH	UM	RH	UM	UM	RH	UM	RH	RH	UM	RH	UM	UM	UM	UM	UM	RH	RH	RH	RH	UM	RH	UM
Correct Answer:	B	G	D	J	C	H	A	J	C	J	A	H	D	G	D	F	B	G	A	J	B	J	C	H
Your Answer*:	•	H	+	+	+	+	D	+	+	+	D	G	+	+	+	+	+	F	+	+	D	+	A	+

Problem Number:	25	26	27	28	29	30	31	32	33	34	35	36	37	38	39	40	41	42	43	44	45	46	47	48
Category:	UM	RH	UM	RH	UM	UM	RH	UM	RH	RH	UM	RH	UM	UM	UM	UM	UM	RH	RH	RH	RH	UM	RH	UM
Correct Answer:	B	G	D	J	C	H	A	J	C	J	A	H	D	G	D	F	B	G	A	J	B	J	C	H
Your Answer*:	+	H	+	+	+	+	D	+	A	+	D	G	+	+	+	+	+	F	+	+	D	+	A	+

Problem Number:	49	50	51	52	53	54	55	56	57	58	59	60	61	62	63	64	65	66	67	68	69	70	71	72
Category:	UM	RH	UM	RH	UM	UM	RH	UM	RH	RH	UM	RH	UM	UM	UM	UM	UM	RH	RH	RH	RH	UM	RH	RH
Correct Answer:	B	G	D	J	C	H	A	J	C	J	A	H	D	G	D	F	B	G	A	J	B	J	C	H
Your Answer*:	+	H	+	+	+	+	D	+	+	+	D	G	+	+	+	+	A	F	+	+	D	H	A	•

Problem Number:	73	74	75
Category:	UM	RH	UM
Correct Answer:	B	J	A
Your Answer*:	C	H	D

MATHEMATICS

Problem Number:	1	2	3	4	5	6	7	8	9	10	11	12	13	14	15	16	17	18	19	20	21	22	23	24
Category:	EA	AG	EA	EA	AG	AG	GT	EA	GT	EA	AG	EA	EA	EA	EA	GT	GT	GT	AG	GT	EA	EA	GT	GT
Correct Answer:	B	G	D	J	C	H	A	J	C	J	A	H	D	G	D	F	B	G	A	J	B	J	C	H
Your Answer*:	+	H	+	+	+	+	D	+	+	+	D	G	+	+	+	H	C	F	+	+	D	+	A	+

Problem Number:	25	26	27	28	29	30	31	32	33	34	35	36	37	38	39	40	41	42	43	44	45	46	47	48
Category:	AG	GT	EA	AG	EA	EA	AG	EA	GT	AG	EA	AG	AG	EA	EA	GT	GT	GT	AG	EA	GT	GT	AG	AG
Correct Answer:	B	G	D	J	C	H	A	J	C	J	A	H	D	G	D	F	B	G	A	J	B	J	C	H
Your Answer*:	+	H	+	+	+	+	D	+	•	+	D	G	+	+	+	+	+	F	+	+	+	+	A	+

Problem Number:	49	50	51	52	53	54	55	56	57	58	59	60
Category:	AG	GT	EA	EA	GT	EA	GT	AG	EA	AG	EA	AG
Correct Answer:	B	G	D	J	C	H	A	J	C	J	A	H
Your Answer*:	+	H	+	+	+	J	+	•	•	•	•	•

"•" = omitted + = correct response ? = scan error

ENGLISH:
UM = Usage Mechanics
RH = Rhetorical Skills

MATHEMATICS:
EA = Pre-Algebra/Elem. Algebra
AG = Int. Algebra/Coord. Geo.
GT - Plane Geo./Trig.

Only two of the last ten items were answered correctly. Consider whether this was due to the student running out of time or to the perceived increase in difficulty at the end of the test. (Note: only the problems in the math test are arranged in ascending order of difficulty.)

When you see the correct answer to an item that was missed, ask yourself why it was missed:

1. The concept was never learned.
2. It was a careless mistake.
3. It would have been answered correctly if the concept had been reviewed before the test.

It appears that the student ran out of time since the last five questions on the math test were left blank.

Student Summary for an SAT Test

The Student Summary report summarizes all your scaled scores based on your test performance. In addition, it shows see how you performed within specific categories for each of the three subject tests (Reading, Writing and Language, and Math). For example, Writing and Language includes the categories Standard English Conventions (SE) and Expression of Ideas (EI).

CAMBRIDGE EDUCATIONAL SERVICES®

(800) 444-4373
testprep@cambridgeed.com
www.cambridgeed.com

Site: SAMPLE SCHOOL
Student: SAMPLE STUDENT (20170050)
Grade: 11
SAT® Test: TEST 1 (09/01/2015)

SAT® Student Summary

SECTION SCORE	SCORE
Evidence-Based Reading and Writing (200–800)	630
Math (200–800)	660
Total Score (400–1600)	1290

READING (10–40)	RIGHT	WRONG	OMIT	SCORE
Literary Fiction (LF)	9	1	0	-
Natural Science (NS)	17	4	0	-
Social Studies (SS)	12	4	5	-
TOTAL Reading (10–40)	38	9	5	32

WRITING & LANGUAGE (10–40)	RIGHT	WRONG	OMIT	SCORE
Expression of Ideas (EI)	18	6	0	-
Standard English Conventions (SE)	13	7	0	-
TOTAL Writing & Language (10–40)	31	13	0	31

MATH (10–40)	RIGHT	WRONG	OMIT	SCORE
Math - No Calculator	15	5	0	-
Heart Of Algebra (HA)	7	1	0	-
Passport To Advanced Math (PA)	7	2	0	-
Additional Topics (AT)	1	2	0	-
Math - Calculator	30	8	0	-
Heart of Algebra (HA)	9	2	0	-
Problem Solving And Data (PS)	14	3	0	-
Passport To Advanced Math (PA)	5	2	0	-
Additional Topics (AT)	2	1	0	-
TOTAL Reading (10–40)	45	13	0	33

SUBSCORES (1–15)	RIGHT	WRONG	OMIT	SCORE
Command Of Evidence (R And WL)	13	4	1	11
Relevant Words In Context (R And WL)	12	4	2	10
Expression Of Ideas (WL)	18	6	0	11
Standard English Conventions (WL)	13	7	0	10
Heart Of Algebra (M)	16	3	0	13
Problem Solving And Data (M)	14	3	0	12
Passport To Advanced Math (M)	12	4	0	11

CROSS-TEST SCORES (10–40)	RIGHT	WRONG	OMIT	SCORE
History/Social Studies (H/S)	23	7	5	30
Science (S)	27	7	0	33

Throughout this report, **dashes (-)** represent subcategories that contribute to a total overall score but do not receive their own scores.

The section score is calculated from the Reading, Writing and Language, and Math test scores using a conversion factor. There are only two section scores becuase the Reading test score and the Writing and Language test score are combined into one section score. The **composite score** is sum of the two section scores.

The **Reading test** measures your ability to comprehend a broad range of texts based on passage types typically encountered in first-year college courses. Passage topics are listed above (LF, NS, and SS). The **Writing and Language test** measures your ability to revise and edit texts in various content areas. The skills tested are listed above (EI and SE). The **Math test** is comprised of two test sections, one that permits calculator use and one that does not. It measures your ability to apply what is taught in high school math courses. The skills tested are listed above (HA, PS, PA, and AT).

Within each subject test, some items are grouped to create a **subscore**, indicating how you preformed on certain types of items. The subject test abbreviations are listed next to each subcategory and include: R = Reading, WL = Writing and Language, and M = Math. Not all the items on each test are included in a subcategory. The **cross-test scores** measure your ability to apply various Reading, Writing and Language, and Math skills within Science (S) or History/Social Studies (H/S) contexts. A few items from each test contribute to the cross-test scores. To see which items contribute to each score, see the Item Analysis on the second page of this report.

The total score is the sum of the two section scores. Colleges typically base about 45% of their admissions decision on the composite score. Other factors they consider include GPA, extracurricular involvement, and social service activities.

There is no penalty for incorrect answers, so be sure not to leave any questions blank — even if you need to guess!

Subscores and cross-test scores indicate your performance on selected items in each test. Your instructor may use these scores to target specific topics and/or skills throughout your course.

Note: Numbers used for scores and percentiles in the report are for illustrative purposes only and do not necessarily represent a valid correlation.

Student Item Analysis for an SAT Test

The Student Item Analysis provides a comprehensive breakdown of each item: how you answered each item, the correct answer, and its category (corresponding to the categories listed on the Student Summary).

CAMBRIDGE
EDUCATIONAL SERVICES

(800) 444-4373
testprep@cambridgeed.com
www.cambridgeed.com

Site: SAMPLE SCHOOL
Student: SAMPLE STUDENT (20170050)
Grade: 11
SAT® Test: TEST 1 (09/01/2015)

SAT® Student Item Analysis

Reading

Item:	1	2	3	4	5	6	7	8	9	10	11	12	13	14	15	16	17	18	19	20	21	22	23	24	25	26
Category:	LF	LF	LF	LF	LF	LF	LF	LF	LF	LF	SS	SS	SS	SS	SS	SS	SS	SS	SS	SS	SS	NS	NS	NS	NS	NS
Correct:	A	B	D	B	A	C	D	A	B	C	A	D	D	B	A	B	C	A	A	B	D	C	A	B	C	D
Yours*:	+	+	+	+	+	+	+	+	+	B	C	+	+	+	+	+	D	+	+	+	+	+	+	+	+	C
Item:	27	28	29	30	31	32	33	34	35	36	37	38	39	40	41	42	43	44	45	46	47	48	49	50	51	52
Category:	NS	NS	NS	NS	NS	NS	NS	NS	NS	NS	NS	NS	NS	NS	NS	NS	SS	SS	SS	SS	SS	SS	SS	SS	SS	SS
Correct:	D	A	C	B	B	D	A	C	B	C	A	B	B	C	C	D	A	C	D	D	A	B	D	A	C	C
Yours*:	+	+	+	+	A	C	+	+	+	+	D	+	+	+	+	+	+	B	+	C	+	•	•	•	•	•

Writing and Language

Item:	1	2	3	4	5	6	7	8	9	10	11	12	13	14	15	16	17	18	19	20	21	22	23	24	25	26
Category:	EI	SE	EI	EI	SE	EI	SE	EI	EI	SE	SE	EI	SE	EI	EI	SE	EI	SE	EI	EI	SE	SE	EI	SE	EI	EI
Correct:	B	B	C	D	A	C	B	D	A	C	D	A	C	C	B	C	D	A	D	B	A	C	C	D	B	C
Yours*:	+	+	+	+	+	+	+	B	+	+	+	+	+	+	C	A	+	+	+	+	+	B	+	+	C	+
Item:	27	28	29	30	31	32	33	34	35	36	37	38	39	40	41	42	43	44								
Category:	SE	EI	SE	EI	EI	SE	SE	EI	SE	EI	EI	SE	EI	SE	EI	EI	SE	SE								
Correct:	D	A	A	D	C	B	A	D	C	C	B	A	C	D	D	A	B	C								
Yours*:	A	+	+	B	+	+	C	+	+	+	+	+	+	A	C	D	A	B								

Math—No Calculator

Item:	1	2	3	4	5	6	7	8	9	10	11	12	13	14	15	16	17	18	19	20
Category:	HA	PA	PA	HA	HA	PA	HA	PA	AT	HA	PA	HA	PA	PA	AT	HA	PA	PA	HA	AT
Correct:	D	B	B	C	A	D	A	C	B	B	C	D	A	B	100	50	2/3	150	.5	6/5
Yours*:	+	+	+	+	+	+	+	+	C	+	+	+	C	+	+	+	+	300	20	3/5

Math—Calculator

Item:	1	2	3	4	5	6	7	8	9	10	11	12	13	14	15	16	17	18	19	20	21	22	23	24	25	26
Category:	HA	PS	PS	HA	HA	PA	HA	PS	PS	PS	HA	PS	PS	PS	PA	HA	PS	PA	HA	PS	AT	PS	PS	PS	PA	PS
Correct:	B	C	A	D	D	B	C	A	D	A	C	C	B	D	A	B	B	A	C	D	A	B	C	A	D	B
Yours*:	+	+	+	+	B	+	+	+	+	+	+	+	+	+	+	+	C	+	+	+	+	+	+	+	+	A
Item:	27	28	29	30	31	32	33	34	35	36	37	38														
Category:	PS	HA	AT	AT	HA	PA	HA	PS	PA	HA	PS	PA														
Correct:	C	D	B	C	48	1/5	550	8.5	10	12/7	600	12														
Yours*:	+	+	C	+	+	2/5	+	+	+	2	51.5	30														

"•" = omitted   + = correct response   ? = scan error

READING:
LF = Literary Fiction
SS = Social Studies
NS = Natural Science

WRITING AND LANGUAGE:
EI = Expression of Ideas
SE = Standard English Conventions

MATH:
HA = Heart of Algebra
PS = Problem Solving and Data
PA = Passport to Advanced Math
AT = Additional Topics in Math

On each test section, the last few items were answered incorrectly or left blank. Consider whether this was due to the student running out of time or to the perceived increase in difficulty at the end of the test.

When you see the correct answer to an item that was missed, ask yourself why it was missed:

1. The concept was never learned.
2. It was a careless mistake.
3. It would have been answered correctly if the concept had been reviewed before the test.

SETTING A TEST SCORE TARGET

Your test score target is unique to you and depends on your future educational and career goals. Setting your test score target involves several steps (testing, researching, and taking action) which are outlined below.

Test

Your first step is to take the pre-assessment that is part of your Cambridge course. After you take this test, you will receive a score report that gives you a very accurate measure of where you stand. To begin the process of setting a test score goal, fill in your pre-test scores below. Use the table below that corresponds to the pre-assessment you took.

ACT TEST SECTION	SCORE
English	
Mathematics	
Reading	
Science	
Composite	
Writing	

SAT TEST SECTION	SCORE
Reading	
Writing and Language	
Math	
Composite	
Essay	

As you use these scores to make a plan for improvement throughout this course, remember that if you had a bad test day (for example, if you were ill or distracted by personal problems), your scores may not be reflective of your true abilities. Be sure to take this into account as you set a goal for your post-test and your real test.

Research

Now, make a list of colleges or universities that you are interested in attending and research the average test scores and GPAs of admitted students so you can get an idea of how you stack up. Fill in the score that you estimate you need for each school. If you are interested in applying for scholarships, make sure you also research the scores each school requires for scholarship eligibility.

School: ________________	Average ACT/SAT Test Score of Admitted Students: ____ Average GPA of Admitted Students: ____ Scholarship Score Requirement: ____ Estimated ACT/SAT Test Score Needed: ____ Additional Points Needed: ____
School: ________________	Average ACT/SAT Test Score of Admitted Students: ____ Average GPA of Admitted Students: ____ Scholarship Score Requirement: ____ Estimated ACT/SAT Test Score Needed: ____ Additional Points Needed: ____
School: ________________	Average ACT/SAT Test Score of Admitted Students: ____ Average GPA of Admitted Students: ____ Scholarship Score Requirement: ____ Estimated ACT/SAT Test Score Needed: ____ Additional Points Needed: ____
School: ________________	Average ACT/SAT Test Score of Admitted Students: ____ Average GPA of Admitted Students: ____ Scholarship Score Requirement: ____ Estimated ACT/SAT Test Score Needed: ____ Additional Points Needed: ____

Once you have this chart filled in for several schools, you should have a good idea of the difference between your pre-test score and the score you will need to get into your schools of interest. Fill in this information below:

Estimated Score Needed: __________ **Additional Points Needed:** __________

Action

How do you translate these numbers into an action plan? See your Student Item Analysis report. This report gives you valuable information for every question on the pre-assessment. You'll see your answer, the correct answer, and the type of question that was asked. With a little analysis, you can see exactly where your weaknesses are and make a plan to address them. Also, make sure to review the "Planning a Course Schedule" section on the next page.

PLANNING A COURSE SCHEDULE

The most important component of an effective study plan is having it written down. A written study plan is more concrete than one you simply draw on from memory. So, when creating your plan, write out a day-by-day schedule for reviewing all materials necessary for success in the course. This written format of your plan will provide a clear and dependable guide for study. The schedule should be prioritized according to the time you need to devote to each of the different subjects and based on the amount of time that you have.

Consider how you can plan your study time so that it corresponds with the course topics. In addition to assignments given in class, you may wish to devote extra study time to your particular areas of weakness. Use the calendar template that follows to develop a plan of action with your teacher, determining what topics you will study each day and allotting time to study those sections of the book and complete the relevant exercises. Remember that it is not necessary for you to do everything all at once. Instead, picking a few things to focus on each week will help you better manage your time.

Use the following empty calendar as a template, filling in your assignments and study plan for each day. Your teacher can help you set goals for each subject.

MONTH: ______________

Sunday	Monday	Tuesday	Wednesday	Thursday	Friday	Saturday

Test Mechanics, Concepts, and Strategies

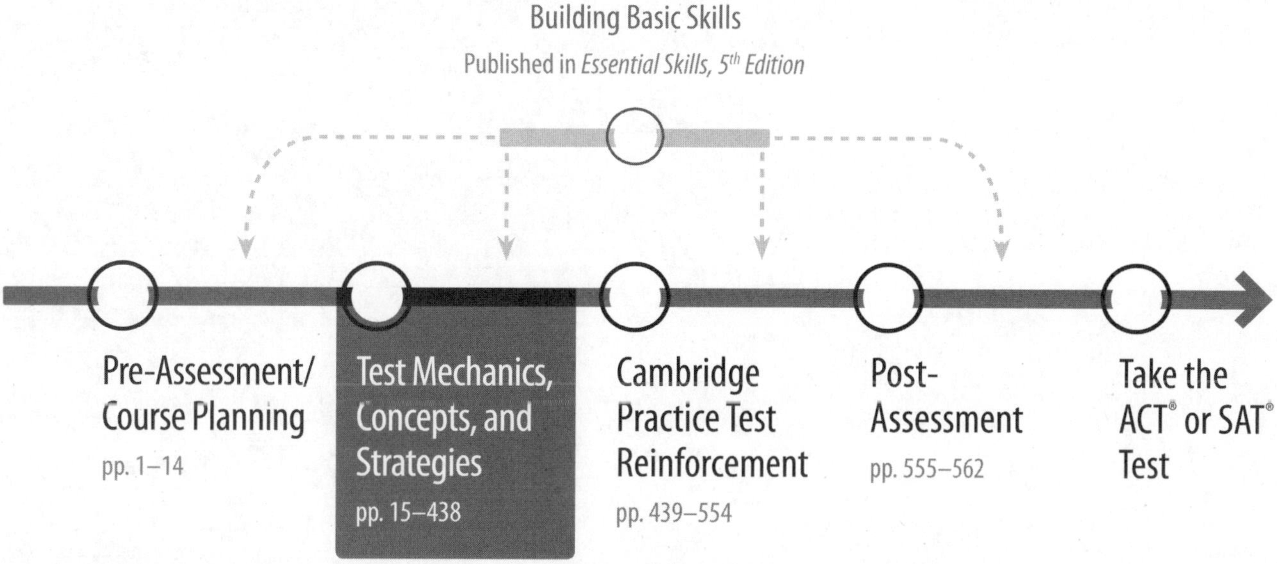

CAMBRIDGE
VICTORY FOR THE
ACT® AND SAT® TESTS

ACT Reading and SAT Reading

Course Concept Outline

I. Lesson | Preliminaries[1]

A. Lesson Features

B. What Is Tested

C. Directions

D. Item Profiles

E. Facts about Passages

1. Three Passage Topics, Unfamiliar Subjects
2. Passages Test Comprehension, Not "Speed-Reading"

II. Lesson 1 | Information and Ideas (p. 21)

A. Item-Types (p. 21)

1. Main Idea (Items #1–2, p. 22)
2. Explicit Detail (Items #3–5, p. 22)
3. Implied Idea (Items #6–9, pp. 22– 23)
4. Application (Items #10–11, p. 23)

B. Item-Type Strategies (p. 24)

1. Main Idea Clues (Item #12, p. 24)
2. Explicit Detail Clues (Item #13, p. 25)
3. Implied Idea Clues (Items #14–15, p. 25)
4. Application Clues (Item #16, p. 25)

---

[1] Some concepts in this Course Concept Outline are not illustrated through examples in your student text but may be covered by your instructor in class. They are included here to provide a complete outline of your course.

LESSON 1 | INFORMATION AND IDEAS

ACT READING AND SAT READING

The passages and items in this section accompany the in-class review of the skills and concepts tested by the ACT Reading Test and the SAT Reading Test. You will work through the items with your instructor in class. Answers are on page 565.

Item-Types

DIRECTIONS: Each passage or pair of passages is followed by a set of items. Choose the best answer to each question based on what is stated or implied in the passage or passages and in any accompanying graphics.

Items #1–11 refer to the following passage.

The following passage discusses the presidential election of 1796.

To broaden their voting appeal in the presidential election of 1796, the Federalists selected Thomas Pinckney, a leading South Carolinian, as running mate for the New Englander John Adams. But Pinckney's Southern friends chose to ignore their party's intentions and regarded Pinckney as a presidential candidate, creating a political situation that Alexander Hamilton was determined to exploit. Hamilton had long been wary of Adams' stubbornly independent brand of politics and preferred to see his running mate, who was more pliant and over whom Hamilton could exert more control, in the president's chair.

The election was held under the system originally established by the Constitution. At that time, there was but a single tally, with the candidate receiving the largest number of electoral votes declared president and the candidate with the second largest number declared vice president. Hamilton anticipated that all the Federalists in the North would vote for Adams and Pinckney equally in an attempt to ensure that Jefferson would not be either first or second in the voting. Pinckney would be solidly supported in the South while Adams would not. Hamilton concluded that if it were possible to divert a few electoral votes from Adams to Pinckney, Pinckney would receive more than Adams, yet both Federalists would outpoll Jefferson.

Various methods were used to persuade the electors to vote as Hamilton wished. In the press, anonymous articles were published attacking Adams for his monarchical tendencies and Jefferson for being overly democratic, while pushing Pinckney as the only suitable candidate. In private correspondence with state party leaders, the Hamiltonians encouraged the idea that Adams' popularity was slipping, that he could not win the election, and that the Federalists could defeat Jefferson only by supporting Pinckney.

Had sectional pride and loyalty not run as high in New England as in the deep South, Pinckney might well have become Washington's successor. New Englanders, however, realized that equal votes for Adams and Pinckney in their states would defeat Adams; therefore, eighteen electors scratched Pinckney's name from their ballots and deliberately threw away their second votes to men who were not even running. It was fortunate for Adams that they did, for the electors from South Carolina completely abandoned him, giving eight votes to Pinckney and eight to Jefferson.

In the end, Hamilton's interference in Pinckney's candidacy lost him even the vice presidency. Without New England's support, Pinckney received only 59 electoral votes, finishing third to Adams and Jefferson. He might have been president in 1797, or as vice president a serious contender for the presidency in 1800; instead, stigmatized by a plot he had not devised, he served a brief term in the United States Senate and then dropped from sight as a national influence.

Main Idea Ⓐ Ⓢ

1. The main purpose of the passage is to

   A) propose reforms of the procedures for electing the president and vice president.
   B) condemn Alexander Hamilton for interfering in the election of 1796.
   C) describe the political events that led to John Adams' victory in the 1796 presidential election.
   D) contrast the political philosophy of the Federalists to that of Thomas Jefferson.

2. Which of the following titles best describes the content of the passage?

   A) The Failure of Alexander Hamilton's Plan for Thomas Pinckney to Win the 1796 Presidential Election
   B) The Roots of Alexander Hamilton's Distrust of John Adams and New England's Politics
   C) Important Issues in the 1796 Presidential Campaign as Presented by the Federalist Candidates
   D) The Political Careers of Alexander Hamilton, John Adams, and Thomas Pinckney

Explicit Detail Ⓐ Ⓢ

3. According to the passage, which of the following was true of the presidential election of 1796?

   A) Thomas Jefferson received more electoral votes than did Thomas Pinckney.
   B) John Adams received strong support from the electors of South Carolina.
   C) Alexander Hamilton received most of the electoral votes of New England.
   D) Thomas Pinckney was selected by Federalist party leaders to be the party's presidential candidate.

4. According to the passage, Hamilton hoped to exploit all of the following features of the political situation EXCEPT

   A) articles published in newspapers to create opposition to John Adams.
   B) South Carolina's loyalty to Thomas Pinckney.
   C) private contact with state officials urging them to support Thomas Pinckney.
   D) John Adams' reputation as a stubborn and independent New Englander.

5. The passage supplies information that answers which of the following questions?

   A) How many electoral votes were cast for John Adams in the 1796 presidential election?
   B) Under the voting system originally set up by the Constitution, how many votes did each elector cast?
   C) Who was Jefferson's running mate in the 1796 presidential election?
   D) What became of Alexander Hamilton after his plan to have Thomas Pinckney elected president failed?

Implied Idea Ⓐ Ⓢ

6. The passage implies that some electors voted for John Adams because they were

   A) in favor of a monarchy.
   B) persuaded to do so by Hamilton.
   C) afraid South Carolina would not vote for Pinckney.
   D) anxious to have a president from their geographical region.

7. Which of the following can be inferred from the passage?

   A) Thomas Pinckney had a personal dislike for Jefferson's politics.
   B) The Federalists regarded themselves as more democratic than Jefferson.
   C) The Hamiltonians contacted key Southern leaders to persuade them to vote for Adams.
   D) Electors were likely to vote for candidates from their own geographical region.

8. It can be inferred that had South Carolina not cast any electoral votes for Jefferson, the outcome of the 1796 election would have been a

A) larger margin of victory for John Adams.
B) victory for Thomas Jefferson.
C) victory for Thomas Pinckney.
D) defeat of the Federalist presidential candidate.

9. It can be inferred from the description of Hamilton's plan that a key element of the strategy was to

A) prepare Pinckney for a run for the presidency in the 1796 election.
B) avoid revealing that the plan had been devised by Hamilton.
C) amend the Constitution so that electors would vote for both a president and for a vice president.
D) personally discredit Pinckney for being inconsistent on various issues.

Application Ⓐ Ⓢ

10. The electors who scratched Pinckney's name from their ballots behaved most like which of the following people?

A) A newspaper publisher who adds a special section to the Sunday edition to review the week's political events
B) A member of the clergy who encourages members of other faiths to meet to discuss solutions to the community's problems
C) An artist who saves preliminary sketches of an important work even after the work is finally completed
D) A general who orders his retreating troops to destroy supplies they must leave behind so the enemy cannot use them

11. Hamilton's strategy can best be summarized as

A) divide and conquer.
B) retreat and regroup.
C) feint and counterattack.
D) hit and run.

Item-Type Strategies

Items #12–16 refer to the following passage.

The following passage discusses the cultural heritage of the Aleuts.

The Aleuts, residing on several islands of the Aleutian Chain, the Pribilof Islands, and the Alaskan Peninsula, have possessed a written language since 1825, when the Russian missionary Ivan Veniaminov selected appropriate characters of the Cyrillic alphabet to represent Aleut speech sounds, recorded the main body of Aleut vocabulary, and formulated grammatical rules. The Czarist Russian conquest of the proud, independent sea hunters was so devastatingly thorough that tribal traditions, even tribal memories, were almost obliterated. The slaughter of the majority of an adult generation was sufficient to destroy the continuity of tribal knowledge, which was dependent upon oral transmission. Consequently, the Aleuts developed a fanatical devotion to their language as their only cultural heritage.

The Russian occupation placed a heavy linguistic burden on the Aleuts. Not only were they compelled to learn Russian to converse with their overseers and governors, but they had to learn Old Slavonic to take an active part in church services as well as to master the skill of reading and writing their own tongue. In 1867, when the United States purchased Alaska, the Aleuts were unable to break sharply with their immediate past and substitute English for any one of their three languages.

To communicants of the Russian Orthodox Church, knowledge of Slavonic remained vital, as did Russian, the language in which one conversed with the clergy. The Aleuts came to regard English education as a device to wean them from their religious faith. The introduction of compulsory English schooling caused a minor renaissance of Russian culture as the Aleut parents sought to counteract the influence of the schoolroom. The harsh life of the Russian colonial rule began to appear more happy and beautiful in retrospect.

Regulations forbidding instruction in any language other than English increased its unpopularity. The superficial alphabetical resemblance of Russian and Aleut linked the two tongues so closely that every restriction against teaching Russian was interpreted as an attempt to eradicate the Aleut tongue. From the wording of many regulations, it appears that American administrators often had not the slightest idea that the Aleuts were clandestinely reading and writing in their own tongue or that they even had a written language of their own. To too many officials, anything in Cyrillic letters was Russian and something to be stamped out. Bitterness bred by abuses and the exploitations that the Aleuts suffered from predatory American traders and adventurers kept alive the Aleut resentment against the language spoken by Americans.

Gradually, despite the failure to emancipate the Aleuts from a sterile past by relating the Aleut and English languages more closely, the passage of years has assuaged the bitter misunderstandings and caused an orientation away from Russian toward English as their second language, but Aleut continues to be the language that molds their thought and expression.

Main Idea Clues Ⓐ Ⓢ

12. The author is primarily concerned with describing

A) the Aleuts' loyalty to their language and American failure to understand the language.

B) Russian and American treatment of Alaskan inhabitants both before and after 1867.

C) how the Czarist Russian occupation of Alaska created a written language for the Aleuts.

D) American government attempts to persuade the Aleuts to use English as a second language.

Explicit Detail Clues Ⓐ Ⓢ

13. According to the passage, the most important reason for the Aleuts' devotion to their language was

A) the invention of a written version of their language.
B) the introduction of Old Slavonic for worship.
C) the disruption of oral transmission of tribal knowledge.
D) the institution of compulsory English education.

Implied Idea Clues Ⓐ Ⓢ

14. Which of the following statements about the religious beliefs of the Aleuts can be inferred from the passage?

A) Prior to the Russian occupation, they had no religious beliefs.
B) American traders and adventurers forced them to abandon all religious beliefs.
C) At no time in their history have the Aleuts had an organized religion.
D) The Russians forced Aleuts to become members of the Russian Orthodox Church.

15. The passage implies that

A) the Cyrillic alphabet was invented for the Aleut language.
B) all of the Cyrillic characters were used in writing the Aleut language.
C) Russian and the Aleut language have some similar speech sounds.
D) English is also written using the Cyrillic alphabet.

Application Clues Ⓐ Ⓢ

16. Distributing which of the following publications would be most likely to encourage Aleuts to make more use of English?

A) Russian translations of English novels
B) English translations of Russian novels
C) An English-Russian bilingual text devoted to important aspects of Aleutian culture
D) An Aleut-English bilingual text devoted to important aspects of Aleutian culture

Further Use of Information and Ideas Strategies Ⓐ Ⓢ

Items #17–21 refer to the following passage.

The following passage is an excerpt from Mark Twain's *Life on the Mississippi, Part 2*.

At the end of what seemed a tedious while, I had managed to pack my head full of islands, towns, bars, "points," and bends; and a curiously inanimate mass of lumber it was, too. However, inasmuch as I could shut my eyes and reel off a good long string of these names without leaving out more than ten miles of river in every fifty, I began to feel that I could make her skip those little gaps. But of course my complacency could hardly get started enough to lift my nose a trifle into the air, before Mr. Bixby would think of something to fetch it down again. One day he turned on me suddenly with this settler:

"What is the shape of Walnut Bend?"

He might as well have asked me my grandmother's opinion of protoplasm. I reflected respectfully, and then said I didn't know it had any particular shape. My gunpowdery chief went off with a bang, of course, and then went on loading and firing until he was out of adjectives.

I had learned long ago that he only carried just so many rounds of ammunition, and was sure to subside into a very placable and even remorseful old smoothbore as soon as they were all gone. That word "old" is merely affectionate; he was not more than thirty-four. I waited. By and by he said:

"My boy, you've got to know the *shape* of the river perfectly. It is all there is left to steer by on a very dark night. Everything else is blotted out and gone. But mind you, it hasn't the same shape in the night that it has in the daytime."

"How on earth am I ever going to learn it, then?"

"How do you follow a hall at home in the dark? Because you know the shape of it. You can't see it."

"Do you mean to say that I've got to know all the million trifling variations of shape in the banks of this interminable river as well as I know the shape of the front hall at home?"

"On my honor, you've got to know them *better* than any man ever did know the shapes of the halls in his own house."

"I wish I was dead!"

"Now I don't want to discourage you, but..."

"Well, pile it on me; I might as well have it now as another time."

"You see, this has got to be learned; there isn't any getting around it. A clear starlit night throws such heavy shadows that, if you didn't know the shape of a shore perfectly, you would claw away from every bunch of timber, because you would take the black shadow of it for a solid cape; and you see you would be getting scared to death every fifteen minutes by the watch. You would be fifty yards from shore all the time when you ought to be within fifty feet of it. You can't see a snag in one of those shadows, but you know exactly where it is, and the shape of the river tells you when you are coming to it. Then there's your pitch-dark night; the river is a very different shape on a pitch-dark night from what it is on a starlit night. All shores seem to be straight lines, then, and mighty dim ones, too; and you'd *run* them for straight lines, only you know better. You boldly drive your boat right into what seems to be a solid straight wall (you knowing very well that in reality there is a curve there), and that wall falls back and makes way for you. Then there's your gray mist. You take a night when there's one of these grisly, drizzly, gray mists, and then there isn't any particular shape to a shore. A gray mist would tangle the head of the oldest man that ever lived. Well, then different kinds of *moonlight* change the shape of the river in different ways."

17. When the narrator compares Bixby's question to asking his "grandmother's opinion of protoplasm" (line 16), he means that

A) the question is inane.
B) the speaker is very old.
C) he does not know the answer.
D) his grandmother would be able to respond.

18. Comparing the chief to a gun (lines 18–20) points out the chief's

A) accuracy.
B) peppery temper.
C) love of hunting.
D) violent past.

19. The narrator's reaction to Bixby's insistence on needing to know the river at night is one of

A) despair.
B) elation.
C) puzzlement.
D) anger.

20. Bixby is shown to be extremely

A) knowledgeable.
B) rude.
C) condescending.
D) fearful.

21. According to the passage, which of the following is true?

A) A riverboat should always be within 100 feet of the shore.
B) On a clear, starlit night, the shoreline is easy to see.
C) On a pitch-dark night, the pilot cannot discern the curve of the shoreline.
D) The river's shape gives no hint of underwater snags.

Items #22–30 refer to the following passage.

The following passage discusses the concept of democratic citizenship.

The concept of democratic citizenship can be traced back to the classical Greeks, who believed that uniquely human capacities could be completely developed only through full participation in the political community of the city state. Aristotle argued that outside of the *polis* man must be either beast or god; human capacities could not be developed apart from political community. The Greek notion of citizenship required direct participation of citizens in deliberations on public issues. The status of citizen in the early Greek *polis* was limited to the few who possessed the economic means and the leisure to devote their attention to public matters. The classical Greek concept of citizenship emphasized the predominance of public obligations over the pursuit of private interests.

The liberal view of democratic citizenship that developed in the seventeenth and eighteenth centuries was fundamentally different from that of the classical Greeks. The pursuit of private interests with as little interference as possible from government was seen as the road to human happiness and progress rather than the public obligations and involvement in the collective community that were emphasized by the Greeks. Freedom was to be realized by limiting the scope of governmental activity and political obligation and not through immersion in the collective life of the *polis*. The basic role of the citizen was to select governmental leaders and keep the powers and scope of public authority in check. On the liberal view, the rights of citizens against the state were the focus of special emphasis.

Over time, the liberal democratic notion of citizenship developed in two directions. First, there was a movement to increase the proportion of members of society who were eligible to participate as citizens—especially through extending the right of suffrage—and to ensure the basic political equality of all. Second, there was a broadening of the legitimate activities of government and a use of governmental power to redress imbalances in social and economic life. Political citizenship became an instrument through which groups and classes with sufficient numbers of votes could use the state's power to enhance their social and economic well-being.

Within the general liberal view of democratic citizenship, tensions have developed over the degree to which government can and should be used as an instrument for promoting happiness and well-being. Political philosopher Martin Diamond has categorized two views of democracy as follows. On the one hand, there is the "libertarian" perspective that stresses the private pursuit of happiness and emphasizes the necessity for restraint on government and protection of individual liberties. On the other hand, there is the "majoritarian" view that emphasizes the "task of the government to uplift and aid the common man against the malefactors of great wealth." The tensions between these two views are very evident today. Taxpayer revolts and calls for smaller government and less government regulation clash with demands for greater government involvement in the economic marketplace and the social sphere.

22. The author's primary purpose is to

A) study ancient concepts of citizenship.
B) contrast different notions of citizenship.
C) criticize modern libertarian democracy.
D) describe the importance of universal suffrage.

23. According to the passage, all of the following would characterize the liberal idea of government, but not the Greek idea of government, EXCEPT

A) the emphasis on the rights of private citizens.
B) the activities that government may legitimately pursue.
C) the obligation of citizens to participate in government.
D) the size of the geographical area controlled by a government.

24. A majoritarian would be most likely to favor legislation that would

A) eliminate all restrictions on individual liberty.
B) cut spending for social welfare programs.
C) provide greater protection for consumers.
D) lower taxes on the wealthy and raise taxes on the average worker.

25. The evolution of the liberal view discussed in the third paragraph is characterized by

A) increased fragmentation of the citizenry into smaller and smaller groups.
B) a return to the classical view of the priority of the *polis* over the individual.
C) the use of government power by citizen groups to solve social problems.
D) the control of routine government functions by special interest groups.

26. From the discussion in the fourth paragraph of the libertarian and majoritarian views of citizenship, one can conclude that

A) the libertarian view is most clearly aligned with the original liberal view, while the majoritarian view is most closely aligned with the classical view.
B) the libertarian view is most closely aligned with the classical view, while the majoritarian view is most closely aligned with the original liberal view.
C) the libertarian view represents the original liberal view, while the majoritarian view represents the more developed liberal view.
D) both the libertarian view and the majoritarian view represent a totally new variation on the original liberal view.

27. Which of the following titles best fits the passage?

A) The Shift from Citizenship as Public Participation to Citizenship as Private Interest
B) The Decreasing Influence of Public Participation in Democratic Government
C) Continuing Tension between Classical and Liberal Views of Democratic Government
D) Aristotle's Theories on Citizenship and the Role of the *Polis*

28. Which of the following statements most accurately captures the different notions of citizenship found in ancient Greece and the liberal democracies of the seventeenth and eighteenth centuries?

A) Liberal democracies subverted the ideal of Greek democracy by transferring to the government control over the individual.
B) Classical Greek democracy preached perfection in the public sphere while liberal democracy rejected the idea of perfection.
C) Liberal democracies inverted the logical priority of the public sphere over the citizen and placed the individual above the state.
D) Classical Greek democracy was restricted to wealthy men with sufficient leisure to participate in public affairs while liberal democracy emphasized universal suffrage.

29. At the beginning of the passage, the author sets out to

A) describe all aspects of the Greek view of democratic citizenship.
B) trace the history of various views of democratic citizenship.
C) elaborate on Aristotle's concept of the *polis*.
D) provide a definition of what a political community is.

30. Given the description of the Greek concept of citizenship, which of the following activities would have been considered inappropriate?

A) Service in the military
B) Showing irreverence
C) Acting as a juror
D) Participating in public debate

LESSON 2 | PASSAGE DEVELOPMENT

ACT READING AND SAT READING

The passages and items in this section accompany the in-class review of the skills and concepts tested by the ACT Reading Test and the SAT Reading Test. You will work through the items with your instructor in class. Answers are on page 565.

Item-Types

DIRECTIONS: Each passage or pair of passages is followed by a set of items. Choose the best answer to each question based on what is stated or implied in the passage or passages and in any accompanying graphics.

Items #1–14 refer to the following passage.

This passage is adapted from an article about literary genres.

When we speak casually, we call *Nineteen Eighty-Four* a novel, but to be more exact we should call it a political fable. This requirement is not refuted by the fact that the book is preoccupied with an individual, Winston Smith, who suffers from a varicose ulcer, or by the fact that it takes account of other individuals, including Julia, Mr. Charrington, Mrs. Parsons, Syme, and O'Brien. The figures claim our attention, but they exist mainly in their relation to the political system that determines them. It would indeed be possible to think of them as figures in a novel, though in that case they would have to be imagined in a far more diverse set of relations. They would no longer inhabit or sustain a fable, because a fable is a narrative relieved of much contingent detail so that it may stand forth in an unusual degree of clarity and simplicity. A fable is a structure of types, each of them deliberately simplified lest a sense of difference and heterogeneity reduce the force of the typical. Let us say, then, that *Nineteen Eighty-Four* is a political fable, projected into a near future and incorporating historical references mainly to document a canceled past.

Since a fable is predicated upon a typology, it must be written from a certain distance. The author cannot afford the sense of familiarity that is induced by detail and differentiation. A fable, in this respect, asks to be compared to a caricature, not to a photograph. It follows that in a political fable there is bound to be some tension between a political sense dealing in the multiplicity of social and personal life, and a fable sense committed to simplicity of form and feature. If the political sense were to prevail, the narrative would be drawn away from fable into the novel, at some cost to its simplicity. If the sense of fable were to prevail, the fabulist would station himself at such a distance from any imaginary conditions in the case that his narrative would appear unmediated, free or bereft of conditions. The risk would be considerable: a reader might feel that the fabulist has lost interest in the variety of human life and fallen back upon an unconditioned sense of its types, that he has become less interested in lives than in a particular idea of life. The risk is greater still if the fabulist projects his narrative into the future: the reader cannot question by appealing to life conditions already known. He is asked to believe that the future is another country and that "they just do things differently there."

In a powerful fable, the reader's feeling is likely to be mostly fear: he is afraid that the fabulist's vision of any life that could arise may be accurate. The fabulist's feeling may be more various. A fable such as *Nineteen Eighty-Four* might arise from disgust, despair, or world-weariness induced by evidence that nothing, despite one's best efforts, has changed and that it is too late now to hope for the change one wants.

Development Ⓐⓢ

1. In the first sentence of the passage the author

A) lists the main features of a political narrative.
B) corrects a misunderstanding about terminology.
C) distinguishes formal from casual literary works.
D) compares *Nineteen Eighty-Four* to folk tales.

2. Which of the following best explains why the author mentions that Winston Smith suffers from a varicose ulcer?

A) To demonstrate that a political fable must emphasize type over detail
B) To show that Winston Smith has some characteristics that distinguish him as an individual
C) To argue that Winston Smith is no more important than any other character in *Nineteen Eighty-Four*
D) To illustrate one of the features of the political situation described in *Nineteen Eighty-Four*

3. The author develops the passage primarily by

A) defining and clarifying a concept.
B) pointing out a logical inconsistency.
C) tracing the connection between a cause and an effect.
D) illustrating a general statement with examples.

4. The author's primary concern is to

A) demonstrate that *Nineteen Eighty-Four* should be considered a political fable and not a novel.
B) prove that a novel is, as a rule, more interesting than a political fable about the same topic.
C) show that Winston Smith is the same character whether he appears in a political fable or in a novel.
D) outline a procedure by which literary works that are political fables can be distinguished from those that are novels.

Textual Evidence ⓢ

5. The author of the passage would most likely agree that

A) the characters of a literary work cannot function effectively in both a novel and fable.
B) readers are more likely to describe literary works casually rather than precisely.
C) Winston Smith would function better as the main character in a novel than in a political fable.
D) in order to qualify as a fable the author of a literary work must set the action in some future time.

6. Which of the following citations provides direct support for the correct answer to the preceding question?

A) Lines 17–20 ("A fable is a structure . . . typical")
B) Lines 25–30 ("Since a fable . . . photograph")
C) Lines 46–51 ("The risk is greater . . . there")
D) Lines 52–60 ("In a powerful fable . . . wants")

7. The author expresses the opinion that Julia, Mrs. Parsons, Syme, and O'Brien cannot function as characters in a novel. Which of the following text citations provides the reasoning to support that conclusion?

A) Lines 3–10 ("This requirement . . . determines them")
B) Lines 10–17 ("It would indeed . . . simplicity")
C) Lines 34–37 ("If the political . . . simplicity")
D) Lines 41–46 ("The risk would be considerable . . . life")

Voice Ⓐ Ⓢ

8. The author treats the suggestion that *Nineteen Eighty-Four* might be considered a novel with an attitude of

A) harsh condescension.
B) ironic surprise.
C) bitter disappointment.
D) scholarly respect.

9. The author's statement that Nineteen Eighty-Four was written out of a sense of despair can best be described as

A) apprehensive.
B) speculative.
C) resigned.
D) intrepid.

Information and Ideas Review Ⓐ Ⓢ

10. In drawing an analogy between a fable and a caricature (lines 28–30), the author would most likely regard which of the following pairs of ideas as also analogous?

A) The subject of a caricature and the topic of a fable
B) The subject of a caricature and the main character in *Nineteen Eighty-Four*
C) The subject of a fable and the artist who draws the caricature
D) The artist who draws the caricature and a novelist

11. Which of the following would be the most appropriate title for the passage?

A) "A Critical Study of the Use of Characters in *Nineteen Eighty-Four*"
B) "*Nineteen Eighty-Four*: Political Fable Rather Than Novel"
C) "*Nineteen Eighty-Four*: Reflections on the Relationship of the Individual to Society"
D) "The Use of Typology in the Literature of Political Fables"

12. According to the passage, which of the following is a characteristic of a political fable?

A) It is widely popular at its time of development.
B) The reader is unlikely to experience fear as his reaction to the political situation described.
C) Its time frame must treat events that occur at some point in the future.
D) Its characters are defined primarily by their relationship to the social order.

13. The "tension" that the author mentions in line 31 refers to the

A) necessity of striking a balance between the need to describe a political situation in simple terms and the need to make the description realistic.
B) reaction the reader feels because he or she is drawn to the characters of the fable as individuals but repulsed by the political situation.
C) delicate task faced by a literary critic who must interpret the text of a work while attempting to describe accurately the intentions of the author.
D) danger that too realistic a description of a key character will make the reader feel that the fable is actually a description of his own situation.

14. The author uses the phrase "another country" in line 50 to describe a political fable in which

A) the political events described occur in a place other than the author's country of origin.
B) a lack of detail makes it difficult for a reader to see the connection between his own situation and the one described in the book.
C) too many minor characters create the impression of complete disorganization, leading the reader to believe he is in a foreign country.
D) the author has allowed his personal political convictions to affect his description of the political situation.

Item-Type Strategies

Items #15–23 refer to the following passage.

The following passage is about the history of healthcare services.

Considerable advances have been made in healthcare services since World War II. These include better access to healthcare (particularly for the poor and minorities), improvements in physical plants and facilities, and increased numbers of physicians and other health personnel. All have played a part in the recent increase in life expectancy. But there is mounting criticism of the large remaining gaps in access, unbridled cost inflation, the further fragmentation of service, excessive indulgence in wasteful high-technology "gadgeteering," and breakdowns in doctor-patient relationships. In recent years, proposed panaceas and new programs, small and large, have proliferated at a feverish pace and disappointments have multiplied at almost the same rate. This has led to an increased pessimism—"everything has been tried and nothing works"—that sometimes borders on cynicism or even nihilism.

It is true that the automatic "pass through" of rapidly spiraling costs to government and insurance carriers produced for a time a sense of unlimited resources and allowed a mood to develop whereby every practitioner and institution could "do his own thing" without undue concern for the "Medical Commons." The practice of full-cost reimbursement encouraged capital investment and now the industry is overcapitalized. Many cities have hundreds of excess hospital beds; hospitals have proliferated a superabundance of high-technology equipment; and structural ostentation and luxury were the order of the day. In any given day, one-fourth of all community beds are vacant; expensive equipment is underused or, worse, used unnecessarily. Capital investment brings rapidly rising operating costs.

Yet, in part, this pessimism derives from expecting too much of healthcare. Care is often a painful experience accompanied by fear and unwelcome results; although there is room for improvement, it will always retain some unpleasantness and frustration. Moreover, the capacities of medical science are limited. Humpty Dumpty cannot always be put back together again. Too many physicians are reluctant to admit their limitations to patients; too many patients and families are unwilling to accept such realities. Nor is it true that everything has been tried and nothing works, as shown by the prepaid group practice plans. However, typically such undertakings have been drowned by a veritable flood of public and private moneys that have supported and encouraged the continuation of conventional practices and subsidized their shortcomings on a massive, almost unrestricted scale. Except for the most idealistic and dedicated, there were no incentives to seek change or to practice self-restraint or frugality. In this atmosphere, it is not fair to condemn as failures all attempted experiments; it may be more accurate to say that many never had a fair trial.

Development Clues Ⓐ Ⓢ

15. The author cites the prepaid plans (lines 47–50) as

A) counterexamples to the claim that nothing has worked.
B) examples of healthcare plans that were overfunded.
C) evidence that healthcare services are fragmented.
D) experiments that yielded disappointing results.

16. Which of the following best describes the logical structure of the selection?

A) The third paragraph is intended as a refutation of the first and second paragraphs.
B) The second and third paragraphs are intended as a refutation of the first paragraph.
C) The second and third paragraphs explain and put into perspective the points made in the first paragraph.
D) The first paragraph describes a problem, the second its causes, and the third a possible solution.

17. Why does the author use the invented term "gadgeteering" (line 12) to refer to wasteful spending on technology?

A) The term suggests an unimportant device of limited utility, thereby emphasizing the wastefulness of the expenditure.
B) The foreign-sounding word suggests a device of theoretical complexity created by a mind of great sophistication.
C) The clever turn of phrase is consistent with advances in healthcare such as better access for more people.
D) The technical jargon hints of great sophistication that can be achieved only at a great financial cost.

Textual Evidence Clues Ⓢ

18. In the first paragraph, the author states that "considerable advances have been made in healthcare services." Which of the following text citations support the author's conclusion?

A) Lines 2–8 ("These include . . . expectancy")
B) Lines 8–13 ("But . . . relationships")
C) Lines 28–35 ("Many cities . . . unnecessarily")
D) Lines 43–50 ("Humpty Dumpty . . . plans")

Voice Clues ⒶⓈ

19. In the third paragraph, the author

A) harshly criticizes those who imagine that improvements to the healthcare system cannot satisfy all expectations.
B) supports various plans to improve the healthcare system but notes that most will probably fail.
C) cautions against expecting too much of the healthcare system but encourages attempts to improve it.
D) discourages people from expecting good outcomes from the healthcare system and suggests that they reconcile themselves to its weaknesses.

Information and Ideas Review ⒶⓈ

20. According to author, the "pessimism" mentioned in line 17 is partly attributable to the fact that

A) there has been little real improvement in healthcare services.
B) expectations about healthcare services are sometimes unrealistic.
C) large segments of the population find it impossible to get access to healthcare services.
D) advances in technology have made healthcare service unaffordable.

21. It can be inferred that the sentence "Humpty Dumpty cannot always be put back together again" means that

A) the cost of healthcare services will not decline.
B) some people should not become doctors.
C) medical care is not really essential to good health.
D) medical science cannot cure every ill.

22. With which of the following descriptions of the system for the delivery of healthcare services would the author most likely agree?

A) It is biased in favor of doctors and against patients.
B) It is highly fragmented and completely ineffective.
C) It has not embraced new technology rapidly enough.
D) It is generally effective but can be improved.

23. The author's primary concern is to

A) criticize physicians and healthcare administrators for investing in technologically advanced equipment.
B) examine some problems affecting delivery of healthcare services and assess the severity of those problems.
C) defend the medical community from charges that healthcare has not improved since World War II.
D) analyze the reasons for the healthcare industry's inability to provide quality care to all segments of the population.

Further Use of Reading Strategies Ⓐ Ⓢ

Items #24–30 refer to the following passage.

The following passage is adapted from a scientific article about galaxies.

Galaxies come in a variety of sizes and shapes: majestic spirals, ruddy disks, elliptically shaped dwarfs and giants, and a menagerie of other, more bizarre forms. Most currently, popular theories suggest that conditions prior to birth—mass of the protogalactic cloud, its size, its rotation—determine whether a galaxy will be large or small, spiral or elliptical; but about 10 percent of all galaxies are members of rich clusters of thousands of galaxies. The gravitational forces of fields of nearby galaxies constantly distort galaxies in the crowded central region of rich clusters. In addition, rich clusters of galaxies are pervaded by a tenuous gas with a temperature of up to 100 million degrees. Galaxies are blasted and scoured by a hot wind created by their motion through the gas. In crowded conditions such as these, environment becomes a more important determinant of the size and shape of a galaxy than heredity. In fact, if our galaxy had happened to form well within the core of a cluster such as Virgo, the sun would probably never have formed, because the sun, a second- or third-generation star located in the disk of the galaxy, was formed from leftover gas five billion years or so after the initial period of star formation. By that time, in a rich cluster, the galaxy may well have already been stripped of its gas.

As a galaxy moves through the core of a rich cluster, it is not only scoured by hot gas; it encounters other galaxies as well. If the collision is one-on-one at moderate to high speeds of galaxies of approximately the same size, both galaxies will emerge relatively intact, if a little distorted and ragged about the edges. If, however, a galaxy coasts by a much larger one in a slow, grazing collision, the smaller one can be completely disrupted and assimilated by the larger.

Under the right conditions, these cosmic cannibals can consume 50 to 100 galaxies. The accumulative effect of these collisions is to produce a dynamic friction on the large galaxy, slowing it down. As a result, it gradually spirals in toward the center of the cluster. Eventually, the gravitational forces that bind the stars to the in-falling galaxy are overwhelmed by the combined gravity of the galaxies in the core of the cluster—just as the ocean is pulled away from the shore at ebb tide by the moon, the stars are pulled away from their in-falling parent galaxy. If there is a large galaxy at the center of the cluster, it may ultimately capture these stars. With the passage of time, many galaxies will be torn asunder in the depths of this gravitational maelstrom and be swallowed up in the ever-expanding envelope of the central cannibal galaxy.

Galactic cannibalism also explains why there are few if any bright galaxies in these clusters other than the central supergiant galaxy. That is because the bright galaxies, which are the most massive, experience the greatest dynamical friction. They are the first to go down to the gravitational well and be swallowed up by the central galaxies.

Over the course of several billion years, 50 or so galaxies may be swallowed up, leaving only the central supergiant and the 51st, the 52nd, etc., brightest galaxies. Given time, all the massive galaxies in the cluster will be absorbed, leaving a sparse cluster of a supergiant galaxy surrounded by clouds of small, dim galaxies.

24. It can be inferred from the passage that the physical features of a galaxy that does not belong to a rich cluster are determined primarily by the

A) size and rotation of the protogalactic cloud.
B) intensity of light emanating from the galaxy.
C) temperature of the interstellar gas.
D) age of the protogalactic cloud.

25. The author implies that the currently accepted theories on galaxy formation are

A) completely incorrect and misguided.
B) naive and out-of-date.
C) speculative and unsupported by observation.
D) substantially correct but in need of modification.

26. According to the passage, a cluster with a central, supergiant galaxy will

A) contain no intermediately bright galaxies.
B) have 50–100 galaxies of all sizes and intensities.
C) consist solely of third- and fourth-generation stars.
D) produce only spiral and disk-shaped galaxies.

27. In which of the following text excerpts does the author of the passage describe the environmental factors that determine the features of a galaxy?

A) Lines 4–9 ("Most currently . . . galaxies")
B) Lines 30–37 ("If the collision . . . larger")
C) Lines 42–54 ("As a result . . . cannibal galaxy")
D) Lines 57–61 ("That is because . . . galaxies")

28. According to the passage, as a galaxy falls inward toward the center of a cluster, it

A) collides with the central core and emerges relatively intact.
B) absorbs superheated gases from the interstellar medium.
C) is broken apart by the gravitational forces of the core.
D) is transformed by collisions into a large, spiral galaxy.

29. The passage provides information that will answer which of the following questions?

A) What is the age of our sun?
B) What proportion of all galaxies are found in clusters?
C) Approximately how many galaxies would be found in a rich cluster?
D) What type of galaxy is ours?

30. The tone of the passage can best be described as

A) lighthearted and amused.
B) objective but concerned.
C) detached and unconcerned.
D) cautious but sincere.

LESSON 3 | VOCABULARY

ACT READING AND SAT READING

The passages and items in this section accompany the in-class review of the skills and concepts tested by the ACT Reading Test and the SAT Reading Test. You will work through the items with your instructor in class. Answers are on page 565.

Vocabulary Clues Ⓐ Ⓢ

DIRECTIONS: Each passage or pair of passages is followed by a set of items. Choose the best answer to each question based on what is stated or implied in the passage or passages and in any accompanying graphics.

Items #1–10 refer to the following passage.

The following passage is an excerpt from a history of the political career of Thomas Jefferson, the author of the "Declaration of Independence."

"Heartily tired" from the brutal, almost daily conflicts that erupted over questions of national policy between himself and Alexander Hamilton, Thomas Jefferson resigned his position as Secretary of State in 1793. Although his Federalist opponents were convinced that this was merely a strategic withdrawal to allow him an opportunity to plan and promote his candidacy for the presidency should Washington step down in 1796, Jefferson insisted that this retirement from public life was to be final.

But even in retirement, the world of politics pursued him. As the election grew nearer and it became apparent that Washington would not seek a third term, rumors of Jefferson's presidential ambitions grew in intensity. Reacting to these continuous insinuations in a letter to James Madison, Jefferson allowed that while the idea that he coveted the office of chief executive had been originated by his enemies to impugn his political motives, he had been forced to examine his true feelings on the subject for his own peace of mind. In so doing, he concluded that his reasons for retirement—the desire for privacy, and the delight of family life—coupled with his now failing health were insuperable barriers to public service. The "little spice of ambition" he had in his younger days had long since evaporated and the question of his presidency was forever closed.

Jefferson did not actively engage in the campaign on his own behalf. The Republican party, anticipating modern campaign tactics, created grass roots sentiment for their candidate by directing their efforts toward the general populace. In newspapers, Jefferson uniformly advocated equal rights among the citizens while Adams was portrayed as the champion of rank, titles, heredity, and distinctions. Jefferson was not certain of the outcome of the election until the end of December. Under the original electoral system established by the Constitution, each presidential elector cast his ballot for two men without designating between them as to office. The candidate who received the greatest number of votes became the president; the second highest, the vice president. Jefferson foresaw on the basis of his own calculations that the electoral vote would be close. He wrote to Madison that in the event of a tie, he wished for the choice to be in favor of Adams. In public life, the New Englander had always been senior to Jefferson; and so, he explained, the expression of public will being equal, Adams should be preferred for the higher honor. Jefferson, a shrewd politician, realized that the transition of power from the nearly mythical Washington to a lesser luminary in the midst of the deep and bitter political divisions facing the nation could be perilous, and he had no desire to be caught in the storm that had been brewing for four years and was about to break. "This is certainly not a moment to covet the helm," he wrote to Edward Rutledge. When the electoral vote was tallied, Adams emerged the victor. Rejoicing at his "escape," Jefferson was completely satisfied with the decision. Despite their obvious and basic political differences, Jefferson genuinely respected John Adams as a friend and compatriot. Although Jefferson believed that Adams had deviated from the course set in 1776, in

Jefferson's eyes he never suffered diminution; and Jefferson was quite confident that Adams would not steer the nation too far from its Republican tack. Within two years, Jefferson's views would be drastically altered as measures such as the Alien and Sedition Acts of 1798 convinced him of the need to wrest control of the government from the Federalists.

1. In line 1, the word "heartily" most nearly means
   A) sincerely.
   B) vigorously.
   C) zealously.
   D) completely.

2. In line 10, the word "public" most nearly means
   A) communal.
   B) open.
   C) official.
   D) popular.

3. In line 10, the word "final" most nearly means
   A) last.
   B) closing.
   C) ultimate.
   D) conclusive.

4. In line 17, the word "allowed" most nearly means
   A) permitted.
   B) admitted.
   C) tolerated.
   D) sanctioned.

5. In line 31, the word "anticipating" most nearly means
   A) expecting.
   B) presaging.
   C) awaiting.
   D) inviting.

6. In line 34, the word "uniformly" most nearly means
   A) precisely.
   B) consistently.
   C) militantly.
   D) eternally.

7. In line 35, the word "champion" most nearly means
   A) victor.
   B) opponent.
   C) colleague.
   D) defender.

8. In line 48, "senior to" most nearly means
   A) older in age than.
   B) higher in rank than.
   C) more experienced than.
   D) grander than.

9. In line 53, the word "luminary" most nearly means
   A) bright object.
   B) famous person.
   C) office holder.
   D) candidate.

10. In line 66, the word "diminution" most nearly means
    A) foreshortening.
    B) shrinkage.
    C) abatement.
    D) degradation.

Items #11–20 refer to the following passage.

This passage is adapted from Edgar Allan Poe's "The Oval Portrait."

The portrait was that of a young girl. It was a mere head and shoulders, done in what is technically termed a vignette manner; much in the style of the favorite heads of Sully. The arms, the bosom, and even the ends of the radiant hair, melted imperceptibly into the vague yet deep shadow, which formed the background of the whole. The metallic yellow frame was a valuable oval, richly gilded and filigreed in exquisitely fine detail. As a thing of art, nothing could be more admirable than the painting itself. But it could have been neither the execution of the work, nor the immortal beauty of the countenance, which had so suddenly and so vehemently moved me. Least of all could it have been that my fancy, shaken from its half slumber, had mistaken the head for that of a living person. I saw at once that the peculiarities of the design, of the vignetting, and of the frame, must have instantly dispelled such ideas—must have prevented even its momentary entertainment. Thinking earnestly upon these points, I remained, for an hour perhaps, half sitting, half reclining, with my vision riveted upon the portrait. At length, satisfied with the true secret of its effect, I fell back within the bed. I had found the spell of the picture in an absolute *life likeness* of expression, which at first startling, finally confounded, subdued, and appalled me. With deep and reverent awe, I replaced the candelabrum in its former position. The cause of my deep agitation being thus shut from view, I sought eagerly the volume which discussed the paintings and their histories. Turning to the number which designated the oval portrait, I there read the vague and quaint words which follow:

"She was a maiden of rarest beauty, and not more lovely than full of glee. And evil was the hour when she saw, and loved, and wedded the painter. He, passionate, studious, austere, and having already a bride in his Art; she all light and smiles and frolicsome as the young fawn; loving and cherishing all things: hating only the Art which was her rival; dreading only the palette and brushes and other untoward instruments which deprived her of her lover. It was thus a terrible thing for this lady to hear the painter speak of his desire to portray even his young bride. But she was humble and obedient, and sat meekly for many weeks in the dark high turret-chamber where the light dripped upon the pale canvas only from overhead. But he, the painter, took glory in his work, which went on from hour to hour from day to day. And he was a passionate and moody man, who became lost in reveries; so that he *would* not see that the light which fell so ghastly in that lone turret withered the health and the spirits of his bride, who languished visibly to all but him. Yet she smiled on and still on, uncomplainingly, because she saw that the painter (who had great renown) took a fervid and burning pleasure in his task, and wrought day and night to depict her who so loved him, yet who grew daily more dispirited and weak. And, in sooth, some who beheld the portrait spoke of its resemblance in low words, as of a mighty marvel, and a proof not less of the power of the painter than of his deep love for her, whom he depicted so surpassingly well. But at length, as the labor drew nearer to its conclusion, there were admitted none into the turret; for the painter had grown wild with the ardor of his work, and turned his eyes from the canvas rarely, even to regard the countenance of his wife. And he would not see that the tints which he spread on the canvas were drawn from the cheeks of her who sat beside him. And when many weeks had passed, but little remained to do, save one brush upon the mouth and one tint upon the eye, the spirit of the lady again flickered up as the flame within the socket of the lamp. And then the brush was given, and the tint was placed; and for one moment, the painter stood entranced before the work which he had wrought but in the next, while he yet gazed, he grew tremulous and very pallid, and aghast, and crying with a loud voice, 'This is indeed *Life* itself!' turned suddenly to regard his beloved—*She was dead!*"

11. It can be inferred that the word "vignette," as it is used in line 3, primarily refers to

A) a noteworthy incident or event.
B) a particular style of brushstroke.
C) a short musical composition.
D) a picture with no definite border.

12. In line 9, "gilded" is best understood to mean

A) sponsored.
B) overlaid with gold.
C) entangled.
D) overfilled.

13. In line 9, "filigreed" is best understood to mean

A) inspiring greed or avarice.
B) characterized by lack of taste.
C) delicately ornamented.
D) without foundation.

14. As it is used in line 13, the word "countenance" most nearly means

A) face.
B) approval.
C) pretense.
D) motif.

15. In context, "designated" (line 33) most nearly means

A) delegated.
B) indicated.
C) appointed.
D) delivered.

16. In line 43, "deprived her of" most nearly means

A) emptied her of.
B) entitled her to.
C) precluded her from.
D) robbed her of.

17. As it is used in line 55, the word "languished" most nearly means

A) unwound.
B) flickered.
C) wasted away.
D) fomented.

18. In line 58, "renown" is best understood to mean

A) fame.
B) aptitude.
C) obscurity.
D) perseverance.

19. It can be inferred that the word "ardor," as it is used in line 68, primarily refers to

A) difficulty.
B) passion.
C) sincerity.
D) indifference.

20. As it is used in line 79, the word "wrought" most nearly means

A) covered with metal.
B) displayed prominently.
C) worked with great care.
D) operated remotely.

Items #21–30 refer to the following passage.

This passage is adapted from Arthur Conan Doyle's "The Adventure of the Devil's Foot."

In recording from time to time some of the curious experiences and interesting recollections, which I associate with my long and intimate friendship with Mr. Sherlock Holmes, I have continually been faced with difficulties caused by his own aversion to publicity. To his sombre and cynical spirit all popular applause was always abhorrent, and nothing amused him more at the end of a successful case than to hand over the actual exposure to some orthodox official, and to listen with a mocking smile to the general chorus of misplaced congratulation. It was indeed this attitude upon the part of my friend and certainly not any lack of interesting material which has caused me of late years to lay very few of my records before the public. My participation in some of his adventures was always a privilege, which entailed discretion and reticence upon me.

It was in the spring of the year 1897 that Holmes's iron constitution showed some symptoms of giving way in the face of constant hard work of a most exacting kind, aggravated perhaps by occasional indiscretions of his own. In March of that year Dr. Moore Agar, of Harley Street, whose dramatic introduction to Holmes I may some day recount, gave a positive injunction that the famous private agent lay aside all his cases and surrender himself to complete rest if he wished to avert an absolute breakdown. The state of his health was not a matter in which he himself took the faintest interest, for his mental detachment was absolute, but he was induced at last, on the threat of being permanently disqualified from work, to give himself a complete change of scene and air. Thus, it was that in the early spring of that year we found ourselves together in a small cottage near Poldhu Bay, at the further extremity of the Cornish peninsula.

It was a singular spot, and one peculiarly well suited to the grim humor of my patient. From the windows of our little whitewashed house, which stood high upon a grassy headland, we looked down upon the whole sinister semicircle of Mounts Bay, that old death trap of sailing vessels, with its fringe of black cliffs and surge-swept reefs on which innumerable seamen have met their end. With a northerly breeze it lies placid and sheltered, inviting the storm-tossed craft to tack into it for rest and protection.

Then came the sudden swirl round of the wind, the blustering gale from the southwest, the dragging anchor, the lee shore, and the last battle in the creaming breakers. The wise mariner stands far out from that evil place.

On the land side our surroundings were as sombre as on the sea. It was a country of rolling moors, lonely and dun-colored, with an occasional church tower to mark the site of some old-world village. In every direction upon these moors were traces of some vanished race, which has passed utterly away, and left as its sole record strange monuments of stone, irregular mounds which contained the burned ashes of the dead, and curious earthworks which hinted at prehistoric strife. The glamour and mystery of the place, with its sinister atmosphere of forgotten nations, appealed to the imagination of my friend, and he spent much of his time in long walks and solitary meditations upon the moor. The ancient Cornish language had also arrested his attention, and he had, I remember, conceived the idea that it was akin to Chaldean, and had been largely derived from the Phoenician traders in tin. He had received a consignment of books upon philology and was settling down to develop this thesis when suddenly, to my genuine sorrow, and to his unfeigned delight, we found ourselves, even in that land of dreams, plunged into a problem at our very doors which was more intense, more engrossing, and infinitely more mysterious than any of those which had driven us from London. Our simple life and peaceful, healthy routine were violently interrupted, and we were precipitated into the midst of a series of events which caused the utmost excitement not only in Cornwall but throughout the whole west of England.

Many of my readers may retain some recollection of what was called at the time "The Cornish Horror," though a most imperfect account of the matter reached the London press. Now, after some thirteen years, I will give the true details of this inconceivable affair to the public.

21. In line 10, "orthodox" is best understood to mean

A) conventional.
B) original.
C) eccentric.
D) personal.

22. The word "recount" (line 26) most nearly means to

A) compile data.
B) calculate.
C) reimburse.
D) narrate a story.

23. As it is used in line 26, the word "injunction" most nearly means

A) command.
B) embargo.
C) ruling.
D) reprimand.

24. In line 38, "singular" is closest in meaning to

A) separate.
B) remote.
C) ill-defined.
D) remarkable.

25. As it is used in line 46, the word "placid" most nearly means

A) flat.
B) calm.
C) mute.
D) uniform.

26. It can be inferred that the word "atmosphere," as it is used in line 65, primarily means

A) vapor.
B) state.
C) impression.
D) lair.

27. It can be inferred that the word "arrested," as it is used in line 69, primarily means

A) caught.
B) imprisoned.
C) detained.
D) charged.

28. In line 75, "unfeigned" most nearly means

A) affected.
B) legitimate.
C) insincere.
D) authentic.

29. In line 86, "recollection" refers to a(n)

A) imprint.
B) memory.
C) opinion.
D) report.

30. As it is in line 87, the word "imperfect" most likely means

A) injured.
B) impoverished.
C) incomplete.
D) restricted.

Items #31–40 refer to the following passage.

This passage is adapted from an essay entitled "Customs and Opinions of Ancient Nations" in an introductory sociology textbook.

Nature being everywhere the same, men must necessarily have adopted the same verities, and fallen into the same delusions, in regard to those things which are the immediate objects of sense, and the most striking to the imagination. They simply have ascribed the noise and effects of thunder to some superior being inhabiting the air. The people bordering upon the ocean, seeing great tides inundate their coasts at the time of the full moon, must naturally have imputed to the moon the vicissitudes which attended her cyclical phases.

Among animals, the serpent must have appeared to them to be endowed with superior intelligence; because, seeing it sometimes cast its skin, they had reason to think it became young again. It might, then, by this process of rejuvenation always remain youthful and therefore immortal. In Egypt and Greece, it was the symbol of immortality. The larger serpents found in proximity to fountains deterred the timorous from approaching them; hence they were imagined to be guardians of hidden treasure. Serpents were also found to be mischievous animals, but as they were supposed to possess something divine, nothing less than a deity was imagined capable of destroying them.

Dreams too much have introduced the same superstitions all over the earth. If while awake, I am uneasy for my wife's or son's health, and in my sleep I see them in the agonies of death, should they die a few days later, it cannot be denied the gods sent me this warning. If my dream is not fulfilled? It was a fallacious representation, with which the gods wished to terrify me. Or a woman applies to the oracles to know whether her husband will die within the year. One answers yes, the other no. It is certain that one of them must be correct, and she will proclaim all over the city the wisdom of the one whose prognostication was fulfilled.

The origin of good and evil is a more philosophical question. The first theologians must have put the same question which we all do from the age of fifteen or so: Why is there any evil in the world? It was taught in India, that Adimo, the daughter of Brahma, brought forth from the navel, the just from her right side and the unjust from her left; it was from this left side that evil was originally introduced. We know of Pandora of the Greeks. This is the finest of all the allegories which antiquity has handed down to us.

So too all peoples have provided for the expiation of wrongdoing, for where was the man or woman who had not been guilty of some injury against society? Who had not profaned the gods? Who had not debased himself? Where was the person whose natural instinct did not prompt a feeling of remorse? Water cleanses the body and our apparel, and fire purifies metal. It was natural then that water and fire should purge the soul of its guilt, and in every temple were found holy water and sacred fire.

Men plunged themselves into the Ganges, the Indus, and the Euphrates when it was the noon moon. This immersion expiated their sins. If they did not purify themselves in the Nile, it was only for fear that the penitents might have been devoured by crocodiles. However, the priests who purified themselves on the people's behalf immersed themselves in large tubs of water. The Greeks had in all of their temples sacred baths as well as sacred fires, which were universal symbols for all men of the purity of their souls.

31. As it is used in line 2, the word "verities" refers to

A) methods.
B) truths.
C) histories.
D) falsehoods.

32. In context, "inundate" (line 9) most nearly means to

A) dehydrate.
B) capitulate.
C) overflow.
D) emphasize.

33. In line 11, the word "vicissitudes" refers to

A) changes in fortune.
B) mental confusion.
C) alteration of plans.
D) fierceness or aggression.

34. It can be inferred that the word "rejuvenation," as it is used in line 16, primarily refers to the

A) ending of life.
B) appearance of illusion.
C) personification of characteristics.
D) restoration of youth.

35. The word "proximity" (line 19) is used to indicate

A) agility.
B) probability.
C) relevance.
D) nearness.

36. Based on its use in line 34, it can be inferred that the word "oracles" primarily refers to

A) public speeches or debates.
B) people believed to foretell the future.
C) organizations or coalitions.
D) people making a donation.

37. As it is used in line 38, the word "prognostication" refers to a

A) delay.
B) responsibility.
C) prediction.
D) perception.

38. Based on its use in line 48, it can be inferred that the word "allegories" primarily refers to

A) unsupported assertions.
B) symbolic stories about human existence.
C) musical compositions.
D) pledges of allegiance.

39. In line 56, "remorse" is closest in meaning to

A) shame.
B) arrogance.
C) humility.
D) compassion.

40. Based on the use of the word "immersion" in line 63, "immerse" most nearly means to

A) absorb excess liquid.
B) confront one's emotions.
C) rise up from or come into view.
D) completely cover with liquid.

Items #41–50 refer to the following passage.

This passage is adapted from an introductory textbook on the history of American music.

Harmonica, mouth organ, French harp, harp—there are dozens of appellations in American English for this simple instrument, evidence of the local and regional level of its widespread appeal. The ubiquitous little music maker may seem homely when compared with more cultivated species, but the hardy perennial has taken root in our musical landscape, and has been owned and played by more Americans than any other instrument. This wildflower has long been mistaken for a weed by stodgy and established musical experts; consequently, there has been little scholarly writing devoted to it.

Like many familiar domestic blooms, the harmonica is an Old World transplant. The ancestral rootstock of the free-reed family, to which the mouth harp belongs, comes from Asia where according to myth, the Chinese female sovereign Nyn-Kwa invented the *sheng* or mouth organ about 3000 BC. Written descriptions of the instrument date from a thousand years later, and examples and representations of *sheng* have been found at grave sites in central China dating from the 5th century BC. Although its invention has been credited to several people, the first patent for the familiar mouth harmonica was filed in Berlin by Friedrich Buschmann in 1821. Within ten years of its invention, the European mouth organ was being produced commercially in Austria, Switzerland, and the German kingdom of Saxony.

In the second half of the nineteenth century, German manufacturers began the mass production of harmonicas with an eye to the huge export market. Towards the end of the century, German factories were producing up to ten million instruments a year, and more than half were sold in the United States. Popularity of the instrument peaked between the world wars, when it was used for music education in public schools, on the vaudeville stage, and on early blues and "hillbilly" recordings. In the late 1940s, electric "city" blues bands featured amplified harmonicas as lead instruments, and their records, though less popular in black communities since the mid-1960s, continue to be a strong influence on popular music both here and abroad.

With millions of mouth organs imported each year for over a century, the harmonica is the most popular musical instrument in our nation's history. Why, then, the dearth of literature on the harmonica? One explanation is the type of sound produced by the instrument. In reed instruments such as the saxophone or oboe, a flexible sliver of reed is vibrated against something. Once the reed is vibrating, the length of a resonating column of air is varied to produce different pitches. Free-reed instruments, like the harmonica, have reeds that vibrate without touching anything else. As the vibrations of the free reeds are unhindered, the resulting sounds are dense with overtones, producing a timbre alternately described as mellifluous or irritating, according to the tastes of the listener. However, the same may also be said of a "serious" instrument such as the violin. A more likely explanation is the simplicity and cost of the harmonica. Small and cheap, it has been the instrument of choice for children, working people, and vagabonds. Thus, the social status of the most visible harp players has not encouraged the attention of students of "serious" music.

Fortunately, critical neglect has not prevented harmonica players from making good music. Much of the music endemic to the US Harmonica tune books from the 1920s suggest the instrument's repertory embraced familiar dance tunes, popular songs, and sentimental favorites of the preceding half-century. Prominent among early recordings are entertaining solo pieces in which harmonica virtuosos imitate the sounds of animals, crying babies, electric pumps, and railroads. Train whistles and fox chases pervaded the recorded harmonica repertory.

Other virtuoso pieces make use of "note bending" to make sounds and play pitches which are, in theory, impossible to play on the instrument. The technique, as yet unexplained by acoustic physicists, makes possible the distinctively fluid phrasing and wailing sound of the blues harmonica. By deflecting air with the mouth, the player can "bend" or flatten a note, almost to the tonal value of the next lower-pitched reed. This technique was widely employed by blues players of the 1920s. In some solo recordings, the player sings a line, then uses the mouth harp to play an improvised instrumental response.

It is difficult to generalize about an instrument used in making so many different kinds of music, except to say the differences in style between individuals are stronger than most regional characteristics. There is an intimate relationship between player and harp; the resulting music reflects experience, outlook, and even mood more than with most instruments. While limited in range, the harmonica can speak with a very personal voice. Perhaps its versatile adaptability is the real key to the small instrument's large role in the musical life of America.

41. Based on its use in line 2, it can be inferred that "appellations" most nearly means

A) names.
B) appearances.
C) destinations.
D) manifestations.

42. It can be inferred that the word "perennial," as it is used in line 7, primarily refers to something that is

A) original.
B) rude in behavior.
C) continuous.
D) annoying.

43. As it is used in line 11, the word "stodgy" most nearly means

A) substantial.
B) boring.
C) unaffected.
D) lively.

44. In line 18, "sovereign" most nearly means

A) ruler.
B) traveler.
C) explorer.
D) supplicant.

45. It can be inferred that the word "timbre," as it is used in line 61, primarily refers to

A) a nervous characteristic.
B) the wood of growing trees.
C) a short, simple song.
D) the quality of sound.

46. In line 73, "endemic" most nearly means

A) widespread or rapid growth.
B) characteristic of a particular region.
C) a long poetic composition.
D) external to one's country or origin.

47. In line 75, "repertory" most nearly refers to a(n)

A) musical play or production.
B) entire collection of works.
C) place where something is kept safe.
D) history of development.

48. Based on its use in line 79, it can be inferred that "virtuosos" primarily refers to

A) students.
B) amateurs.
C) experts.
D) entertainers.

49. In line 94, "improvised" most nearly means

A) skillful or accomplished.
B) made up or performed spontaneously.
C) immediately pertinent.
D) dramatic monologue.

50. Based on its use in line 105, "versatile" can be defined as all of the following EXCEPT

A) adaptable.
B) multipurpose.
C) resourceful.
D) inflexible.

Items #51–60 refer to the following passage.

This passage is adapted from a lecture entitled "Memory and Learning."

Long-term learning—positive and negative—is made possible by the fact that the mind is able to remember virtually all it was ever aware of, including the most trivial details. However, there are several conditions to this process of retention.

One condition is that such memory (learning) is situational. It is determined in part by the nature of the situation in which the learning occurs. Students "pay attention" in school and learn things tied to a concrete, not abstract, teaching/learning situation; they learn something solely for the purpose of earning a grade. Consequently, since most school situations have no counterparts outside of school, a student often develops amnesia and is unable to recall information learned in another context. Memory is like a filing system, in which an item is stored to be retrieved with a code keyed to that specific situation. If the situation eliciting that particular code is not encountered again, the filed item remains untouched and unused. It is important to remember the filed item is not transient; it does not fade or die. It is merely dormant during the time it is not in use.

A second condition of "memory" learning is it appears to be bound to the state of arousal that existed for the original learning. The ability to remember, therefore, depends to some degree on the ability to recreate or re-enter the formative state of arousal: the feeling, tone, or affective quality that characterized the brain at the time of learning. Thus, since there is always some subjective element, some aura of feeling that accompanies all we ever learn, it is simply not enough to consider what so-called objective content or skill is being taught. Classroom ambience affects students' feelings, so teachers should take care to make the classroom feel safe, comfortable, and pleasant. Teachers should also be more aware of their facial expressions, body language, and behavior as even a temporary lapse into boredom or irritation can place the students in a situation which makes learning unnecessarily onerous.

51. In context, "virtually" (line 3) most nearly means

A) nearly.
B) completely.
C) exclusively.
D) superficially.

52. As it is used in line 10, the word "concrete" most nearly means

A) insubstantial.
B) significant.
C) particular.
D) durable.

53. In line 12, "consequently" most nearly means

A) in addition.
B) regardless.
C) for the reason.
D) as a result.

54. As it is used in line 17, the word "retrieved" most nearly means

A) repeated.
B) recovered.
C) withdrawn.
D) deleted.

55. Based on the use of the word "eliciting" in line 18, it can be inferred that "elicit" most nearly means to

A) make unlawful.
B) evoke.
C) offer.
D) misplace.

56. It can be inferred that the word "transient," as it is used in line 21, most nearly means

A) easily seen through.
B) altered.
C) temporary.
D) transferrable.

57. In line 29, "affective" most nearly means

A) useful.
B) stern.
C) aloof.
D) emotional.

58. It can be inferred that the word "aura," as it is used in line 32, most nearly means

A) of or relating to the ear or sense of hearing.
B) of, in, or pertaining to air.
C) distinctive and persuasive quality or atmosphere.
D) an observable luminous phenomenon.

59. In line 35, "ambience" primarily refers to a(n)

A) mood or feeling associated with a place.
B) appropriate behavior for an occasion.
C) skill, talent, or special ability.
D) highly structured learning situation.

60. In line 42, "onerous" most nearly means

A) effortless.
B) costly.
C) burdensome.
D) mistaken.

Items #61–70 refer to the following passage.

This passage is adapted from an essay entitled "Antarctic Exploration" in an introductory earth sciences textbook.

At 3:29 p.m. on November 28, 1929, a heavily laden Ford Trimotor bounced down the rough ice runway of 'Little America' and clawed its way through an Antarctic overcast—embarking on an epic flight that was anything but routine. The little plane, called the Floyd Bennett, weighed only 6,000 pounds. With its four-man crew, extra gasoline, food, and survival gear, it was carrying more than seven tons. The plane's three engines put out 975 horsepower; cruising speed was just over 100 miles per hour. For navigating the desolate wastes, there were two drift meters and a sun-compass. The only other scientific instrument aboard was a bulky 100-pound aerial camera. Eighteen hours and 37 minutes (and 1,600 miles) later, the Floyd Bennett touched back down on the Little America landing strip, mission completed. Richard E. Byrd and his crew were the first to conquer the South Pole by air, and their historic journey, the consummation of years of work and meticulous planning, had opened a new era of scientific exploration.

Simply establishing the Little America base camp a year earlier was a triumph of logistics. Byrd's men unloaded and hauled several hundred tons of food, fuel, and equipment (including three airplanes) over the crumbling ice barrier on dog sleds. The dismantled all-metal Ford Trimotor was stored that winter in a hangar made of snow blocks. After the long months of darkness set in, Byrd and his companions began final planning for their aerial assault on the South Pole. The 1,600-mile-long flight involved unprecedented features. For hundreds of miles, they would fly over a barren, rolling surface, then climb a mountain rampart 14,000 feet high, with a 10,500-foot pass, and continue the journey across a 10,000-foot plateau. Factors of speed, horsepower, rate of climb, and other engineering problems entailed endless hours of tedious and complicated calculations.

Excavated from its snow cave in early November, the Floyd Bennett was reassembled in temperatures that reached 50 degrees below zero. Without photographer Ashley McKinley and his equipment and survival gear, the plane could fly to the South Pole and back with no problem. To Byrd, McKinley's task was the crux of the plan: to photograph every mile of the flight and to make a permanent record available to science. Since the extra weight would make a nonstop trip impossible, it would be necessary to cache gasoline and food near the base of the mountain range that bordered the high Antarctic plateau. The aircraft would then land and refuel during the return leg of the flight. Even so, weight and fuel consumption calculations were critical. The Floyd Bennett had to be light enough by the time it reached the Queen Maud Mountains to climb 11,000 feet and slip through the pass at the head of the Axel Heiberg glacier.

On November 19, Byrd and his crew flew 400 miles to reconnoiter the jagged mountain barrier, then landed to establish their forward camp. On November 28, a geological party radioed that the weather over the mountains was excellent, so that afternoon the Floyd Bennett headed south toward the pole. As the plane neared the Axel Heiberg glacier with its 10,500-foot pass, the men sighted another glacier which seemed low enough and wide enough to cross. The decision had to be made quickly: to tackle the Axel Heiberg, altitude known but air currents unknown—the bordering peaks might be so high that air currents would dash the plane to the ground—or to take the unknown glacier, which looked feasible?

Byrd opted for the unknown glacier. As powerful air currents tossed the plane about, the pilot fought to gain altitude. Suddenly, the wheel turned loosely in his hands. The pass loomed ahead, but the Floyd Bennett would go no higher. If gasoline were jettisoned, it would be impossible to reach the pole and return. If food were thrown overboard, all lives would be endangered in the event of a forced landing. "A bag of food overboard," ordered Byrd. The plane responded immediately and began to climb, but the fast-approaching glacier was higher. Byrd gestured and another 150-pound bag of food careened through the trapdoor of the aircraft. Byrd reported "those were the slowest minutes we ever spent. Finally, we reached the pass. We ambled over—a few hundred yards to spare."

The vast Antarctic plateau ranged from 11,000 to 7,000 feet, sloping toward the South Pole. Cruising at only 90 miles per hour against a brisk headwind, Byrd navigated carefully over the jumbled terrain. At 1:14 a.m. on November 29, the big moment had come. The crew dropped an American flag.

Flying at 2,500 feet over the snow, the plane then angled back over the original line of flight to cross again over the pole and make certain the feat was accomplished. Then, the aircraft veered north toward Little America. Byrd's navigation was unerring.

Several hours later, the weary crew spotted the Axel Heiberg glacier in the distance. This time the lightened plane soared through the pass with no difficulty. After landing and refueling, Byrd and his crew resumed the flight. At 10:10 a.m., the Floyd Bennett touched down at Little America. "We were deaf from the roar of the motor," according to Byrd, "tired from the strain of the flight, but we forgot all that in the tumultuous welcome of our companions."

The welcome echoed far beyond the cluster of huts at Little America. Congratulations poured in from all over the world. Byrd was a national hero. His dramatic adventure had captured the imagination of millions of Americans, and Antarctica was etched on the national consciousness.

61. As it is used in line 11, the word "desolate" most nearly means

A) without human inhabitants.
B) hopeless.
C) marked by indulgence.
D) densely populated.

62. It can be inferred that the word "aerial," as it is used in line 14, most nearly means

A) pertaining to radio.
B) a small area between things.
C) of, in, or produced by the air.
D) a level piece of ground.

63. In context, "consummation" (line 19) most nearly means

A) antithesis.
B) completion.
C) conservation.
D) utilization.

64. In line 23, "logistics" refers to

A) defense of an encampment.
B) analysis of data.
C) planning and coordination of operation details.
D) the formal principles of knowledge.

65. In line 27, "dismantled" most nearly means

A) violently shattered.
B) deprived of courage.
C) taken apart and stripped of essential parts.
D) dismissed or discharged.

66. The word "rampart" is used in line 34 to refer to

A) extravagance or absence of restraint.
B) a low place in mountain range.
C) a way of entrance or exit.
D) a wall-like ridge or dirt embankment.

67. In line 60, "reconnoiter" most nearly means to

A) restore.
B) explore.
C) climb.
D) contemplate.

68. Based on the use of the word "jettisoned" in line 79, it can be inferred that "jettison" most nearly means to

A) throw overboard.
B) burn or extinguish.
C) overflow.
D) illuminate.

69. In line 86, "careened" most nearly means

A) exploded.
B) wedged.
C) lurched.
D) poked.

70. In line 118, "etched" most nearly means

A) misused.
B) engraved.
C) irritated.
D) erased.

Items #71–80 refer to the following passage.

This passage is adapted from a discussion on the application of science and technology in the field of meteorology.

We can think of science as the attempt to comprehend the workings of nature, and of technology as the practical application of this knowledge. There are three major steps in applying science and technology: experimental observation, analysis, and utilization.

There are two aspects of the experimental observation phase. One is the observation of natural phenomena as they occur. The second is the observation of controlled experiments. The former has necessarily been the way of the past. However, with sounding rockets and satellites, the second became feasible and is being more extensively used.

The observation of natural phenomena as they occur involves the development of sensors to observe important phenomena and the collection of results into a data inventory that is readily accessible to all. For example, in meteorology, this involves a ground activity of assembling temperature, humidity, wind velocity and direction, and other weather data. This information is observed at myriad locations throughout the world and forwarded regularly to central data collection stations. The development of a wide variety of sensors will be used for continued weather satellite observations to provide an even wider variety of data—daily and on a global scale. A very significant meteorological observation activity now underway is the Global Atmospheric Research Program (GARP). This activity involves a large number of countries throughout the world, cooperating to gather weather data of unprecedented scope on a global scale to help in the understanding of weather systems and phenomena throughout the world and the major factors that control their origin, development, and movement.

The observation of controlled experiments involves the development and use of techniques for conducting both passive and active experiments with natural phenomena and observation of the results. An example of the passive approach is the barium cloud experiment, in which a sounding rocket was used to disperse a quantity of fine barium powder high above the atmosphere in the earth's magnetic field. In this case, the natural phenomena were undisturbed, and the barium cloud was used to chart with considerable definition the earth's magnetic-field lines. An example of an active experiment is the injection of silver iodide pellets in cloud formations to induce rainfall.

In the analysis phase, basic relationships and trends are discerned and a better understanding of the phenomena evolves. From the observed relationships and growing understanding, theories are developed and models of the phenomena are postulated. These theories and models are intended to help understand the complex cause and effect interactions among the many variables involved. Definitive experiments are then sought to test the validity of the theories and models. Such experiments often entail further observations to obtain critical elements of data. It is via progressive iterative steps between experimental observation and analysis that models evolve sufficiently for use on an operational basis. Using meteorology as an example, we currently have general models of weather system behavior. Although these models are limited to very crude weather forecasting, continued satellite observations—together with programs like GARP—can lead to improvements in our global weather models, our understanding, and our ability to predict it.

In the utilization phase, all of the understanding from observations made and models analytically developed is employed to predict what can or will happen under a specified set of conditions. Weather prediction is a typical example of how models are used in conjunction with current observation to develop forecasts for public use. It is the combination of an ability to monitor and forecast events, together with an understanding of the basic mechanisms which cause predicted events—be they natural events or those created by man—that eventually will lead to global systems for management of our resources and control of our environment in ways that best suit the needs of man.

71. In context, "phenomena" (line 9) refers to

A) unobservable events or facts.
B) observable events or facts.
C) unrecorded events or facts.
D) recorded events or facts.

72. In context, "data" (line 17) refers to

A) unobservable events or facts.
B) observable events or facts.
C) unrecorded events or facts.
D) recorded events or facts.

73. As used in line 17, the word "inventory" refers to a(n)

A) discovery or finding.
B) secure place of storage.
C) division for classification.
D) organized list of collected information.

74. In line 18, "accessible" most nearly means

A) easily used.
B) valuable.
C) capable of being estimated.
D) unobtainable.

75. It can be inferred that the word "disperse," as it is used in line 43, most nearly means to

A) separate or divide.
B) distribute or scatter.
C) set on fire.
D) replace or drive out.

76. Based on the use of the word "discerned" in line 52, it can be inferred that "discern" most nearly means to

A) ignore.
B) analyze.
C) identify.
D) eliminate.

77. In line 60, "validity" is best understood to mean

A) error.
B) illusion.
C) accuracy.
D) strength.

78. As it is used in line 61, the word "entail" most nearly means to

A) cause to be ineffective.
B) plan or carry out with great care.
C) indicate or set apart.
D) cause or involve by necessity.

79. It can be inferred that the word "iterative," as it is used in line 63, most nearly means

A) extreme or outermost.
B) involving repetition.
C) traveling from place to place.
D) obligatory or necessary.

80. In line 78, "conjunction" most nearly means

A) contradiction.
B) combination.
C) exclusion.
D) estimation.

LESSON 4 | DATA PRESENTATIONS

ACT READING AND SAT READING

The passages and items in this section accompany the in-class review of the skills and concepts tested by the SAT® Reading Test. You will work through the items with your instructor in class. Answers are on page 566.

Different Types of Data Presentations

Table Charts Ⓢ

DIRECTIONS: Each passage or pair of passages is followed by a set of items. Choose the best answer to each question based on what is stated or implied in the passage or passages and in any accompanying graphics.

Items #1–2 refer to the following table.

Summer 2014 Temperatures, Major United States Cities (degrees Fahrenheit)

	June		July		August		September	
	Median High	Peak High	Median High	Peak High	Median High	Peak High	Median High	Peak High
Atlanta	87	93	89	91	87	94	80	87
Boston	76	89	81	91	79	90	72	92
Chicago	80	93	82	91	81	91	74	87
Detroit	79	91	83	91	81	91	73	93
Houston	89	92	91	96	90	97	87	92
Los Angeles	77	82	81	91	83	91	82	102
Miami	88	92	89	95	88	94	87	92
New York	76	88	80	90	78	89	72	92
Seattle	71	80	76	90	77	93	70	83
Washington, DC	84	96	88	98	86	96	79	94

1. For how many cities shown were the summer monthly median high temperatures greatest in August?

A) Two
B) Three
C) Five
D) Six

2. Which of the following conclusions can be inferred from the data?

A) The lowest peak high temperature for the entire summer was recorded in Los Angeles.
B) The difference between Atlanta's highest and lowest monthly peak high temperature for the summer was less than that for Washington, D.C.
C) The city with the greatest range in monthly median high temperatures for the summer of 2014 was Detroit.
D) The city with the highest peak temperature for the summer of 2014 was Houston.

Bar Graphs Ⓢ

Item #3 refers to the following graph.

Percentage of Students
Failing State-Mandated Tests

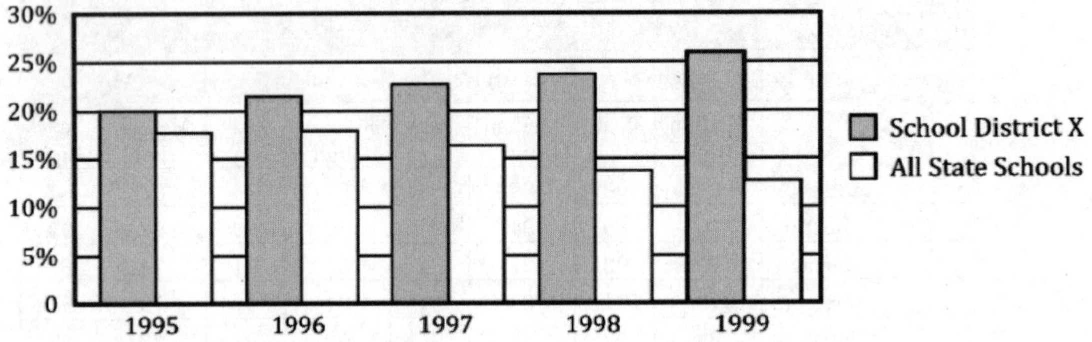

3. Which of the following statements is supported by the data in the graph?

A) The percentage of students in School District X failing state-mandated tests increased to more than 25% in 1999.
B) The percentage of students in all state schools failing state-mandated tests increased from 1996 to 1999.
C) The percentage of students failing state-mandated tests in School District X dropped in each of the years between 1996 and 1999.
D) The number of schools in District X with students failing state-mandated tests exceeded the number of schools statewide in each year shown.

Line Graphs Ⓢ

Items # 4–5 refer to the following graph.

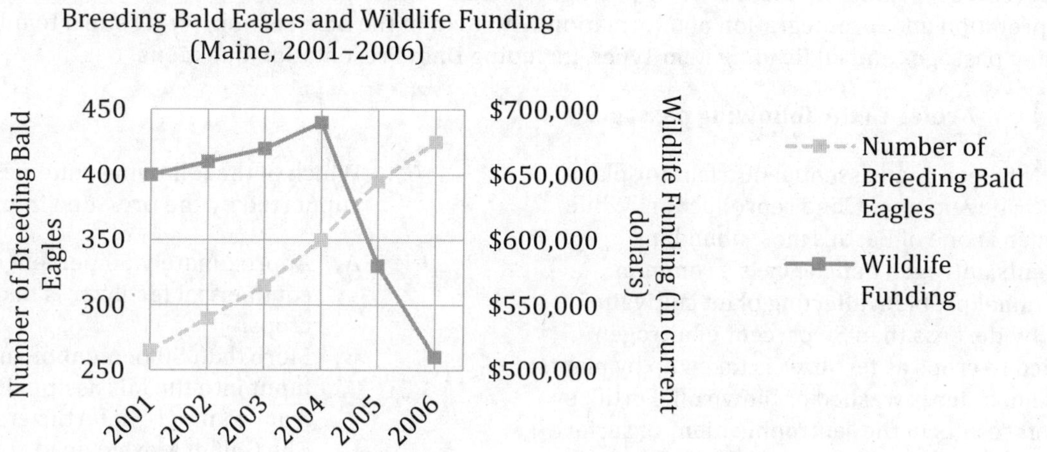

4. Which of the following conclusions is supported by the graph?
   A) The wildlife funding increased linearly from 2001 to 2003.
   B) The wildlife funding increased by the same percentage each year from 2001 to 2003.
   C) The number of breeding bald eagles increased linearly from 2001 to 2006.
   D) The number of breeding bald eagles increased by the same percentage annually from 2001 to 2006.

5. For which year did the wildlife funding show the greatest rate of increase over the previous year?
   A) 2002
   B) 2003
   C) 2004
   D) 2005

Data Presentations and Items Illustrated Ⓢ

Each of the following passages with data presentations represents short excerpts from full-length Reading passages. We'll begin with these shorter passages and associated graphics to focus on items requiring data interpretation and/or integration of information with text. In the next section, we'll return to full-length Reading passages and all Reading item-types, including Data Presentation questions.

Items #6–7 refer to the following passage.

Nitrogen is an essential nutrient for plant growth, development, and reproduction. While nitrogen is one of Earth's most abundant elements, nitrogen deficiency is a common nutritional problem affecting plant cultivation worldwide. Less than 50 percent of nitrogen applied to crops as fertilizer is taken up by plants; the remainder is washed or blown off. Fertilizer run-off results in the "eutrophication" of surface waters: a process in which a body of water is enriched by the addition of excessive nutrients, causing excessive algae growth and subsequent oxygen depletion. Many species cannot survive in these conditions, and large "dead zones" appear from decaying matter undergoing anaerobic degradation. An increase in the use of nitrogen and phosphorus fertilizers in the Mississippi River Basin has been implicated as a cause of hypoxia in the Gulf of Mexico dead zone, an area of over 5,000 square miles along the Louisiana-Texas coast at the mouth of the Mississippi River.

Estimate of Annual Nitrogen Input into Mississippi River Basin	
Source of Nitrogen	Metric Tons (millions)
Commercial Fertilizer	5.87
Livestock Manure	3.45
Soybeans and Alfalfa	1.03
Atmospheric Wet Deposition	0.51
Human Domestic Waste	0.63
Industrial Point Sources	0.11
Total, all sources	11.60

6. Which of the following statements is supported by the provided information?

A) Approximately 50 percent of applied commercial fertilizer is taken up by crops.
B) More than 50 percent of annual nitrogen input into the Mississippi River Basin is from commercial fertilizers.
C) The Gulf of Mexico dead zone is caused by the application of approximately 5.87 million metric tons of commercial fertilizer annually in the Mississippi River Basin.
D) More than 50 percent of applied commercial fertilizer is released into the Mississippi River Basin annually.

7. Based on the information provided, it can be inferred that "hypoxia" refers to

A) oxygen depletion of a body of water.
B) excessive nutrient enrichment of a body of water.
C) run-off of fertilizer into a body of water.
D) nitrogen deficiency in plants.

Item #8 refers to the following passage.

We think of invasive non-native plants as overgrowing an entire ecosystem, but plants can also change entire ecosystems by modifying ecosystem traits and processes. In the arid Southwest, the deep roots of Mediterranean salt cedars deplete soil water, costing western states more than $1,000 annually per acre in water and flood control losses. On the island of Hawaii, the nitrogen-fixing fire tree has invaded nitrogen-poor areas. As there are no native nitrogen fixers, native Hawaiian plants have adapted to the nitrogen-poor soil. However, introduced species cannot tolerate it, so a wave of invasive plants are taking over areas that are prepared by the fire tree. In Florida, Australian paperbark trees, with spongy outer bark and highly flammable leaves and litter, have increased the frequency of fire, allowing paperbark to convert over 500,000 acres of native wetlands to forest, causing significant monetary impact. With recent years being the driest on record, much of Florida is experiencing drought conditions. Not only does this encourage the paperbark to spread, it also cuts off airboat access to many areas, including the Everglades, preventing paperbark removal by contractors hired to eliminate it.

Monetary Impact Estimates of Paperbark in Florida
(Millions of Dollars)

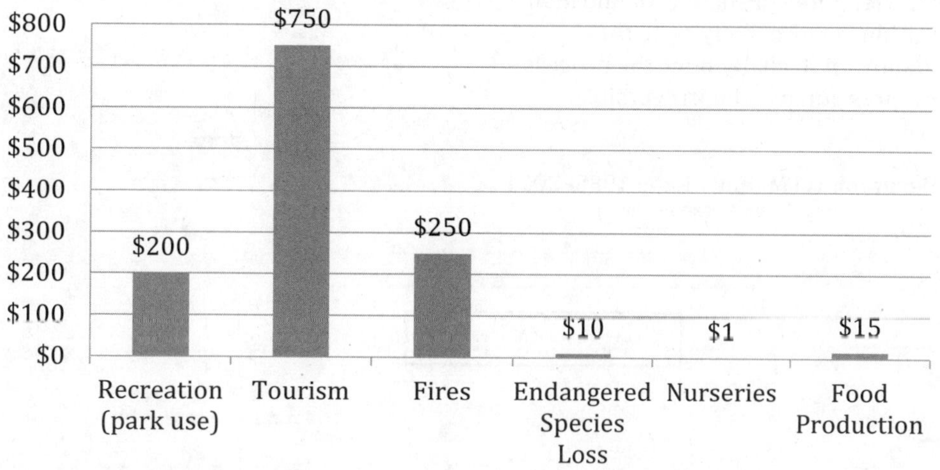

8. Which of the following claims is NOT supported by the graph?

A) The paperbark in Florida has caused recreation and tourism losses of over 900 million dollars.
B) The damage caused by the paperbark in Florida extends beyond native wetlands to include nurseries and agriculture land.
C) Invasive species such as the paperbark and fire tree have caused approximately 10 million dollars of damage to endangered species.
D) The paperbark is estimated to have cost approximately 250 million dollars in Florida due to fires caused by its highly flammable leaves and litter.

Item #9 refers to the following passage.

Historically, the socialization process in America has been characterized by the interaction of structured groups that share both a sense of mission about the nation's future and codes of behavior rooted in common principles. Communities were bound by religious beliefs, ethnic backgrounds, and strong family relationships. However, this configuration of socializing institutions no longer functions as it once did. Mobility is one factor in the changing picture. Many Americans change residence each year, but they do not "pack" their culture; they simply move, breaking old community ties. However, recent decreases in mobility rates puts greater emphasis on a second factor in the breakdown of the socialization process: depersonalization. Emerson once wrote that an institution is the lengthened shadow of one man. Today's institution is more likely to be the lengthened shadow of itself. By now, the process of social decompression may be irreversible.

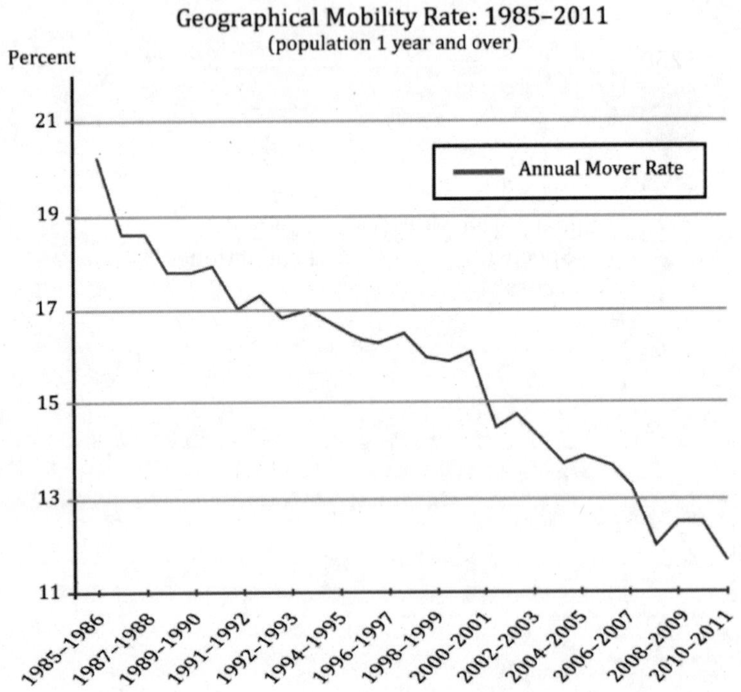

9. The graph supports the author's assertion that

A) mobility rates of Americans have remained constant in recent years.
B) mobility rates of Americans have decreased in recent years.
C) mobility rates were a major factor historically in the socialization process in America.
D) depersonalization is a major factor in the breakdown of the socialization process.

Items #10–11 refer to the following passage.

For indigenous people of the United States, the continuance of cultural values and traditions depends on the transmission of language, but many languages are dying and many more have become extinct. Of the 85–100 indigenous languages that used to exist in California, half are gone. As for the other half, the vast majority have five or fewer speakers, all over 70 years old. During the 1998–1999 school year, California voters approved Proposition 227, an English-focused education initiative that dismantled most bilingual education in California public schools. However, as ethnic populations have continued to increase in California, many school districts, parents, and community organizations have launched dual-immersion programs. Not only do these programs help keep California the most linguistically diverse area of North America, English-language learners in dual immersion programs progress much more quickly than in other forms of instruction. The languages are silent at home and in the community, and so the most effective way to get a critical mass of new fluent speakers of an endangered language is through the school; the same institution that was used to destroy those very languages in the past.

Percentage of English Learners Enrolled in Bilingual Education in California

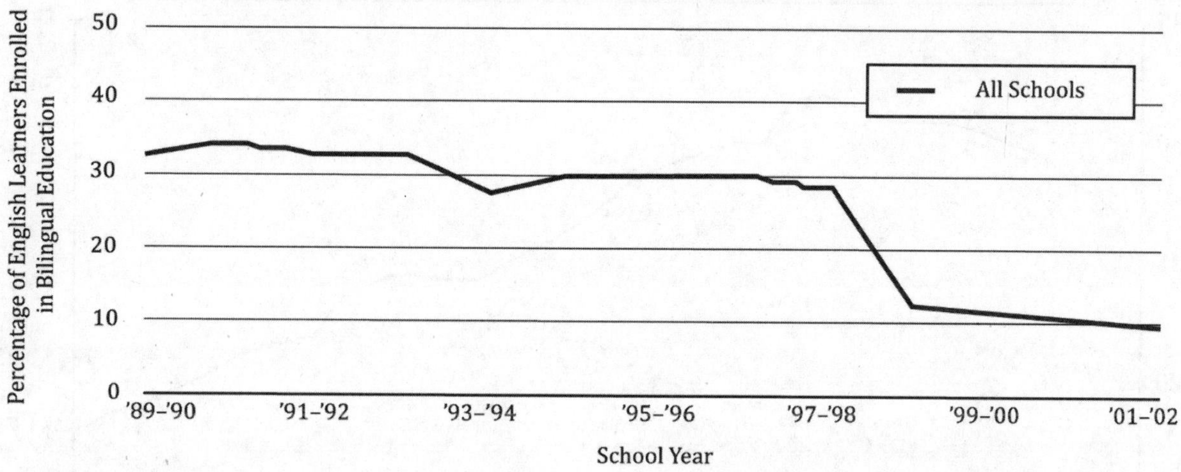

10. As used in line 18, the word "linguistically" refers to

A) languages.
B) indigenous populations.
C) ethnic cuisines.
D) educational programs.

11. Which of the following claims is supported by the data in the graph?

A) In California, the percentage of English learners enrolled in bilingual education has historically always been higher in elementary schools than in elementary, middle, and high school combined.
B) In California, the percentage of English learners enrolled in bilingual education in all schools decreased by over 50 percent following the passage of Proposition 227.
C) Following the passage of Proposition 227, the enrollment of English learners in dual immersion programs in California public schools has remained approximately constant.
D) Following the passage of Proposition 227, the number of dual immersion programs has steadily increased in all California public schools.

Items #12–13 refer to the following passage.

In 1964, the Surgeon General announced that cigarette smoking was a significant health hazard, yet smoking still kills over 480,000 people annually in the United States, including over 40,000 deaths from secondhand smoke exposure—more deaths each year than from AIDS, alcohol, cocaine, heroin, homicide, suicide, motor vehicle crashes, and fires combined. We have made gains in preventing and controlling tobacco use with massive education campaigns and litigation, as well as substantial price hikes designed to curb smoking. A clear negative relationship exists between the price of cigarettes and consumption levels. Today, the percentage of adult smokers in the United States is at its lowest level in over 40 years. Yet nearly 1 in 5 Americans still smokes and thousands of young people start every day. Keeping cigarette prices high is a key strategy in both encouraging smokers to quit and discouraging young people from ever trying tobacco products.

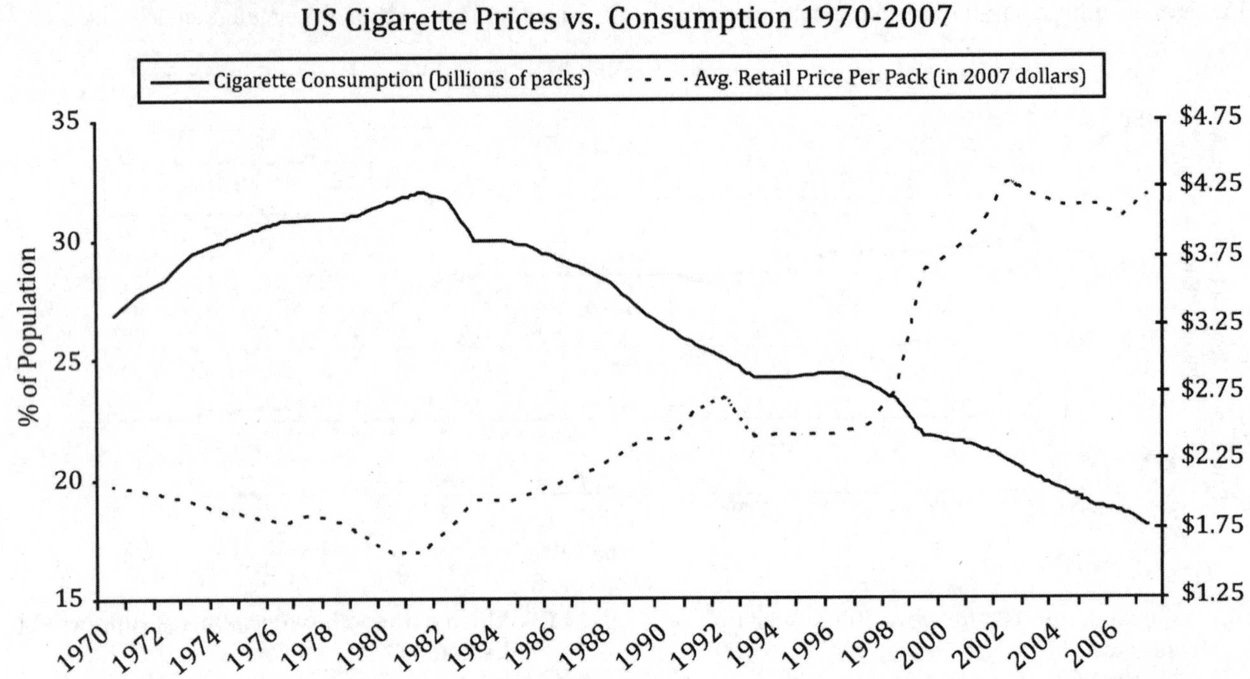

12. The passage is most likely an excerpt from a speech made by

A) a governor proposing an increase in state sales tax on cigarettes.
B) a member of a quit-smoking support group.
C) a high school health teacher warning students about the dangers of tobacco use.
D) a cigarette company spokesman testifying before Congress.

13. Which of the following statements from the passage is supported by the data in the graph?

A) Smoking still kills over 480,000 people annually in the United States.
B) The percentage of adult smokers in the United States is at its lowest in over 40 years.
C) A clear negative relationship exists between the price of cigarettes and consumption levels.
D) Thousands of young people start smoking every day.

Items #14–15 refer to the following passage.

Many volcanoes are associated with the movement of tectonic plates. Where the plates move apart, such as along mid-ocean ridges, a rift forms and allows magma to escape from deep within the earth. Although the temperature of the magma is about 1200°C, it solidifies into a mixture of minerals and volcanic glass due to the cold deep ocean water. The resulting basalt formations are slowly broken down due to weathering. Once believed to be a chemical process, evidence suggests that microbial organisms may partly be responsible for weathering. Microscopic examinations of weathered basalts show pits, channels, and other patterns that are unlike chemical weathering. These weathered rocks also contain large amounts of carbon, phosphorus, and nitrogen, byproducts of biological activity, as well as traces of nucleic acids. In a recent study, the surfaces of weathered basalt drilled from various depths below the seafloor of a mid-Pacific Ocean rift were investigated and the percentage microbial of total weathering (biotic plus abiotic) was determined.

Weathering in Mid-Pacific Ocean Rift Weathered Basalt Samples

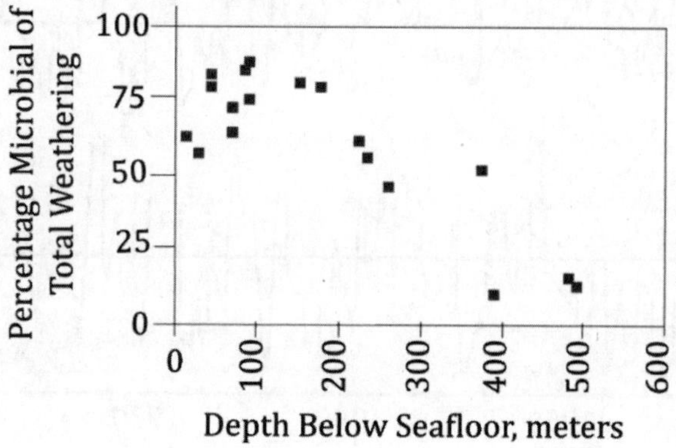

14. Which of the following conclusions is supported by the study's findings?

A) For basalt samples from depths less than 250 meters below the rift, microbial weathering is less than chemical weathering.
B) For basalt samples from depths less than 300 meters below the rift, microbial weathering is greatest while total weathering is lowest.
C) For basalt samples from depths greater than 400 meters below the rift, chemical weathering is greatest while total weathering is lowest.
D) For basalt samples at a depth of 500 meters below the rift, microbial weathering accounts for approximately 10% of total weathering.

15. Which of the following statements is consistent with the results of the study?

A) Microbial activity in the seafloor below mid-oceanic rifts appears to decrease with increasing depth.
B) Chemical processes in the seafloor below mid-oceanic rifts appear to decrease with increasing depth.
C) The amount of microbial weathering of basalt samples appears to decrease with increasing depth below mid-oceanic rifts.
D) Basalt samples from beneath mid-oceanic rifts indicate that weathering from microbial activity is greater than from chemical processes.

Items #16–17 refer to the following passage.

Like tropical reef corals, deep-sea corals have hard skeletons built from calcium and carbonate ions extracted from seawater. Oxygen and oxygen isotopes in carbonate ions can be used to determine the water temperature when the skeleton was formed. The absolute abundance of an isotope is difficult to measure, so studies focus on the ratio of the rare oxygen isotope ^{18}O to the common isotope ^{16}O, commonly denoted as $\delta^{18}O$. Some corals live for decades or centuries, so their skeletons contain a natural record of climate variability, like tree rings and ice cores. The information gathered would be useful in determining the extent to which global warming may be a problem.

Coral $\delta^{18}O$ and Sea Surface Temperatures

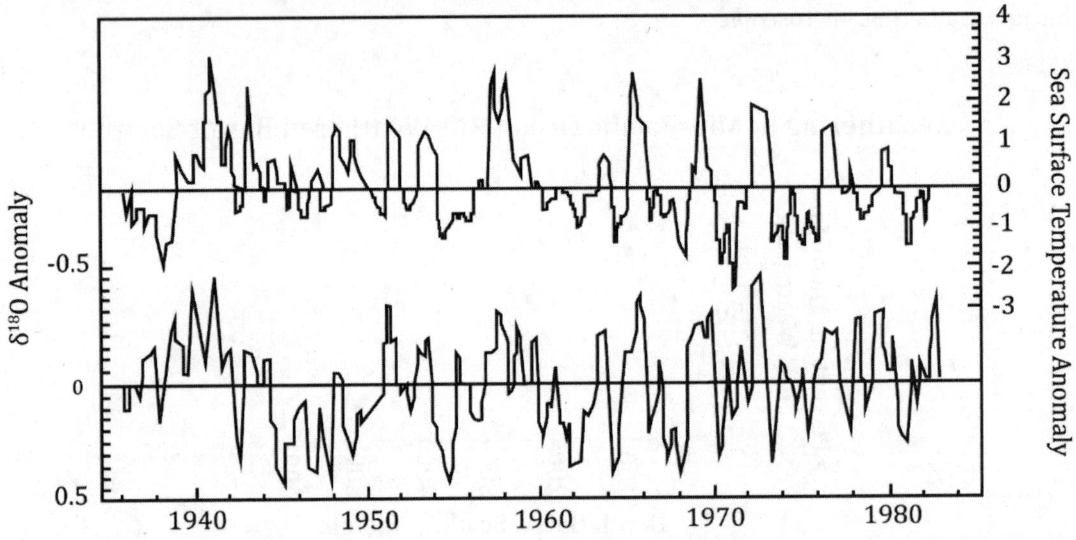

16. As used in the graphic, "anomaly" most nearly means

A) oddity.
B) deviation.
C) anonymous.
D) peculiar.

17. It can reasonably be inferred from the passage and graphic that studies demonstrating a decrease in the ratio of the ^{18}O isotope to the ^{16}O isotope in coral for a certain period would most strongly support the conclusion that

A) global warming had intensified for those years.
B) climate variations for the period were insignificant.
C) the water temperature in the surrounding area had decreased.
D) the water temperature in the surrounding area had increased.

Items #18–20 refer to the following passage.

In 1986, a Wall Street Journal article first used the phrase "glass ceiling" to refer to an invisible, but impenetrable, barrier preventing women from reaching the highest level of business. Subsequent research confirmed the existence of such a barrier. In 2014, over ninety-five percent of Fortune 500 CEOs were male. Where there are women in high places, their compensation is lower than that of men in comparable positions. Nor is the glass ceiling likely to disappear soon. There are relatively few women in the "pipeline," the positions most likely to lead to the top. Furthermore, the glass ceiling doesn't apply only to women. In the same Fortune 500 companies, two-thirds of senior executives (one-step below CEO) were white men, and while 19% were white women, less than 3% were African Americans, 4% were Latinos, and 8% were Asian Americans. In short, the world at the top of the corporate hierarchy does not look anything like America.

Figure 1: Female CEOs in Fortune 500 Companies

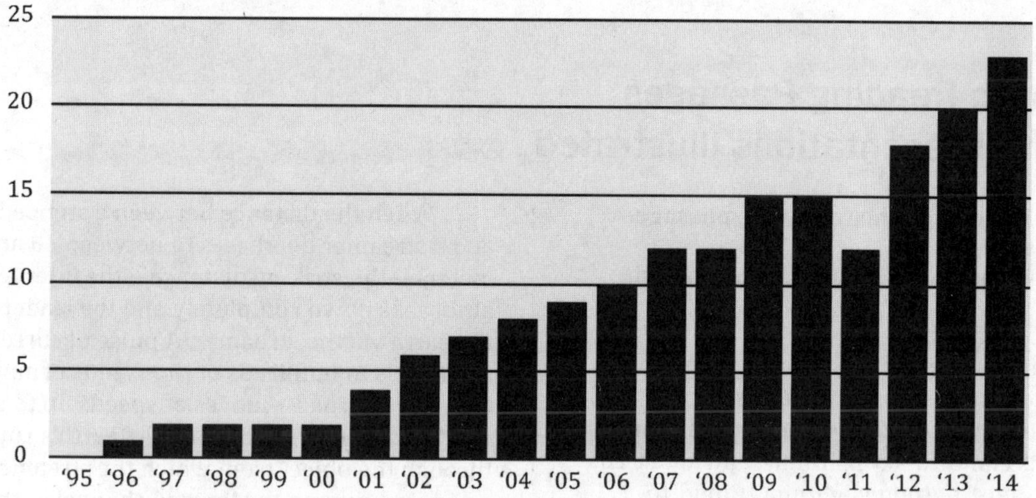

Figure 2: Fortune 500 Senior Executives, 2014

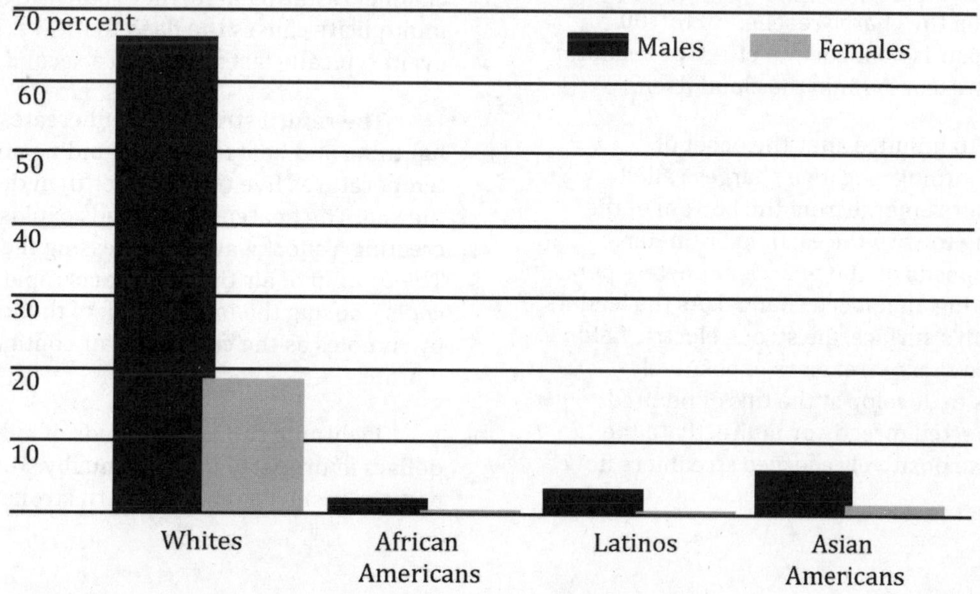

18. The author regards the existence of the "glass ceiling" (line 2) as

A) well documented.
B) theoretically possible.
C) relatively unlikely.
D) entirely speculative.

19. The author includes Figures 1 and 2 to support the statements in

A) lines 8–10 and lines 6–7, respectively.
B) lines 10–11 and lines 14–16, respectively.
C) lines 6–7 and lines 17–19, respectively.
D) lines 17–19 and lines 8–10, respectively.

20. Which of the following statements is supported by the provided information?

A) The number of female Fortune 500 CEOs has risen steadily since 1995.
B) In 2014, nineteen percent of Fortune 500 CEOs were women.
C) In 2014, the percentage of white male Fortune 500 CEOs was even greater than the percentage of white male Fortune 500 senior executives.
D) In 2014, approximately one percent of Fortune 500 senior executives were female Latinos.

Full-Length Reading Passages with Data Presentations Illustrated Ⓐⓢ

Items #21–30 refer to the following passage.

The following passage is adapted from an article on lightning.

Lightning is an electrical discharge of immense proportions. Some 80 percent of lightning occurs within clouds, an extremely small percentage is cloud-to-sky lightning, and about 20 percent is cloud-to-ground lightning. Cloud-to-ground lightning begins when complex meteorological processes cause a tremendous electrostatic charge to build up within a cloud. Typically, the bottom of the cloud is negatively charged. When the charge reaches 50 to 100 million volts, air is no longer an effective insulator, and lightning occurs within the cloud itself.

Ten to 30 minutes after the onset of intracloud lightning, negative charges called stepped leaders emerge from the bottom of the cloud, moving toward the earth in 50-meter intervals at speeds of 100 to 200 kilometers per second, creating an ionized channel. As the leaders near the earth's surface, the strong electric fields of the leaders cause streamers of positively charged ions to develop at the tips of pointed objects connected directly or indirectly to the ground. These positively charged streamers flow upward.

When the distance between a stepped leader and a streamer decreases to between 30 and 100 meters—the striking distance—the intervening air breaks down completely and the leader joins the earth via the streamer. A pulse of current thousands to hundreds of thousands of amperes—the return stroke—moves at speeds up to one-third the speed of light from the earth's surface, through the object from which the streamer emanated, and up the ionized channel to the cloud's charge center. The ionized channel remains in the air and additional negative charges called dart leaders move quickly down the channel resulting in further return strokes. This multiplicity causes the flash to flicker. The entire event typically lasts less than a second.

The return stroke current creates visible lightning and heats the surrounding air to temperatures five times hotter than the surface of the sun. The heated air expands explosively, creating a shockwave compressing the nearby air. The column of air then contracts rapidly as it cools, causing the initial crack of thunder, followed by rumbles as the column of air continues to vibrate.

Lightning causes hundreds of millions of dollars in property losses annually. Most direct damage results from the return stroke current high temperatures or arcing at the point of ground contact. If the lightning current is carried by an enclosed conductor (e.g., within a jacketed cable, through a concrete wall, or beneath a painted surface), entrapped moisture in the conductor is instantly converted into high-pressure steam that can cause the cable, wall, or painted object to explode. Arcing frequently ignites combustibles and causes the majority of forest fires.

New developments in detection technologies, implementation of early warning systems, and measures to educate the public have led to declines in lightning-related fatalities in the United States. However, lightning still causes on average about 50 deaths each year.

Weather-Related Fatalities

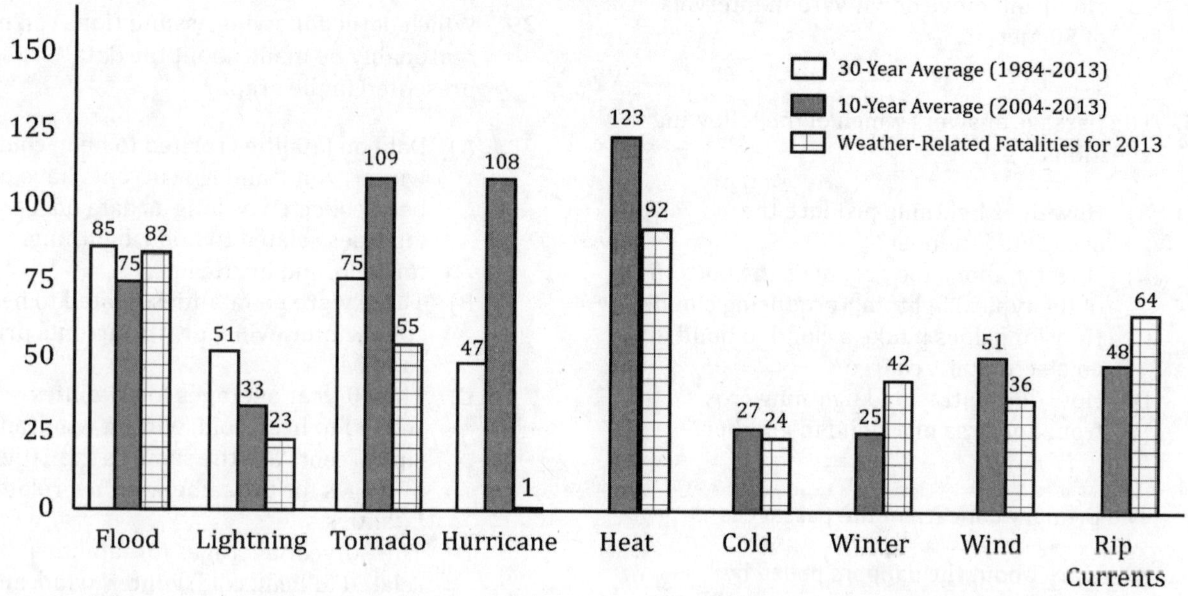

21. In line 14, the word “intracloud” most nearly means

A) between clouds.
B) within a cloud.
C) from cloud to sky.
D) from leader to cloud.

22. The passage defines “striking distance” as the distance between

A) the ground and the cloud.
B) a stepped leader and a dart leader.
C) a dart leader and a return stroke.
D) a streamer and a stepped leader.

23. According to the passage, the flickering appearance of a lightning strike is created by

A) the stepped movement of leaders.
B) multiple return strokes.
C) water being vaporized.
D) arcing at ground contact.

24. According to the passage, which of the following is NOT true of stepped leaders?

A) They develop 10 to 30 minutes after intracloud lightning.
B) As they traverse the distance from cloud to ground, they create an ionized channel.
C) Their powerful positive charge causes streamers to develop in grounded objects.
D) They emerge from the bottom of the cloud and move downward in intervals of 50 meters.

25. The passage answers which of the following questions?

A) How does lightning produce the associated thunder?
B) How far above the ground is the bottom of the typical lightning-producing cloud?
C) How long does it take a cloud to build up an electrostatic charge?
D) How does intracloud lightning cross from one area of a cloud to another?

26. The primary concern of the passage is to

A) warn about the dangers posed by lightning strikes.
B) describe the sequence of events that make up a lightning strike.
C) support the commonly held view that lightning strikes the ground.
D) prove that lightning occurs because of a charge imbalance between a cloud and the ground.

27. What topic might the author logically address in a continuation of the passage?

A) Precautions that minimize lightning damage and fatalities
B) Basic principles governing electricity
C) Identifying different types of clouds
D) History of scientific theory about lightning

28. The last sentence of the last paragraph refers to data in the graph representing

A) the number of lightning-related fatalities in 2013.
B) the number of weather-related fatalities in 2013.
C) the 30-year average for lightning-related fatalities (1984–2013).
D) the 10-year average for lightning-related fatalities (2004–2013).

29. Which of the following assumptions can most reasonably be made about the data presented in the graph?

A) Data on fatalities related to heat, cold, winter, wind, and rip currents have not been collected as long as data on fatalities related to flood, lightning, tornado, and hurricane.
B) There were no fatalities related to heat, cold, winter, wind, or rip currents prior to 2004.
C) The 30-year averages for fatalities related to heat, cold, winter, wind, and rip currents are the same as the 10-year averages for the same weather-related fatalities.
D) The 30-year averages for fatalities related to heat, cold, winter, wind, and rip currents is zero.

30. Which of the following conclusions is supported by the graph?

A) Lighting continues to be a major weather-related killer in the United States.
B) Lightning-related fatalities have decreased every year since 1983.
C) The number of lightning-related fatalities in 2013 was less than two-thirds the average for the previous 10 years.
D) The number of lightning-related fatalities in 2013 was less than half the average for the previous 30 years.

Items #31–44 refer to the following passage.

The following passage is adapted from an article about galaxies.

Galaxies come in a variety of sizes and shapes: majestic spirals, ruddy disks, elliptically shaped dwarfs and giants, and a menagerie of other, more bizarre forms. Current popular theories suggest that conditions prior to birth—such as the mass of the protogalactic cloud, its size, and its rotation—determine whether a galaxy will be large or small, spiral or elliptical; but about ten percent of all galaxies are members of rich clusters of thousands of galaxies.

In the crowded central region of these rich clusters, galaxies are constantly distorted by gravitational forces of the fields of nearby galaxies. Additionally, the clusters are pervaded by a tenuous gas of temperatures up to 100 million kelvin. The motions of the galaxies through this gas create hot winds that blast and scour the galaxies. In such crowded conditions, the environment becomes a more important determinant of the size and shape of a galaxy than heredity. In fact, had our galaxy formed in the core of a rich cluster such as Virgo, our Sun would never have formed. The Sun, a second- or third-generation star located in the disk of the Milky Way, was formed from leftover gas five billion years or so after the initial period of our galaxy's star formation. By that time, in the center of a rich cluster, a galaxy would have already been stripped of its gas.

In addition to being scoured by hot gas, as a galaxy moves through the core of a rich cluster, it encounters other galaxies. If the collision is between two similarly sized galaxies moving at moderate to high speeds, both galaxies emerge relatively intact, if a little distorted and ragged at the edges. However, if the collision is a slow, grazing one between a small galaxy and a much larger galaxy, the smaller one can be completely disrupted or assimilated by the larger one. The accumulative effect of such collisions produces a dynamic friction on the larger galaxy, slowing it down. As a result, the larger galaxy spirals gradually toward the center of the cluster.

Eventually, the gravitational forces binding the stars to the inward falling galaxy are overwhelmed by the combined gravity of the galaxies at the cluster core and pulled from the parent galaxy—just as the ocean is pulled by the moon from the shore at ebb tide. If there's a large galaxy at the cluster core, it will ultimately capture these stars. With time, many galaxies will be torn asunder in such a gravitational maelstrom and swallowed up in the ever-expanding envelope of the central supergiant galaxy.

Galactic cannibalism also explains why there are few, if any, luminous galaxies in rich clusters other than the central supergiant galaxy. Luminous galaxies, being the most massive, experience the greatest dynamical friction and are the first to be devoured by a central supergiant galaxy. Under the right conditions and over several billion years, these cosmic cannibals can consume 50 to 100 galaxies, leaving a sparse cluster consisting of the central supergiant galaxy surrounded by clouds of small, dim galaxies.

Characteristics of Galaxy Clusters

Property	Rich Clusters	Groups/Poor Clusters
Number of Galaxies per Cluster or Group	1,000–10,000 galaxies	10–1,000 galaxies
Radius	1-10 Mpc	< 1 Mpc
Radial Velocity Dispersion	400–1,400 km/s	100–500 km/s
Mass	10^{14}–$10^{15} \times M_\odot$	10^{12}–$10^{14} \times M_\odot$
Luminosity	10^{11}–$10^{12} \times L_\odot$	10^{10}–$10^{12} \times L_\odot$
Proportion of All Galaxies	10%	55%

*$M_\odot$ is the mass of the Sun; $L_\odot$ is the luminosity of the Sun.

31. In line 3, the word "menagerie" most nearly means

A) odd mixture.
B) open environment.
C) uniform collection.
D) simple structure.

32. It can be inferred from the passage that the physical features of a galaxy that does not belong to a rich cluster are determined primarily by the

A) size and rotation of the protogalactic cloud.
B) gravitational forces of nearby galaxies.
C) temperature of the interstellar gas.
D) age of the protogalactic cloud.

33. In line 15, the word "tenuous" most nearly means

A) slender.
B) thin or rarefied.
C) of slight importance.
D) lacking in clarity.

34. The passage's author implies that the currently accepted theories on galaxy formation are

A) naive and out-of-date.
B) speculative and unsupported by observation.
C) substantially correct but in need of modification.
D) accurate and adequate to explain all known observations.

35. According to the passage, a rich cluster with a central, supergiant galaxy will

A) contain no intermediately luminous galaxies.
B) have 50–100 galaxies of all sizes and intensities.
C) produce only spiral and disk-shaped galaxies.
D) be surrounded by galaxies of all sizes and shapes.

36. Which of the following contributes to the outcome of a collision between two galaxies?

A) The relative velocities of the galaxies
B) The relative sizes of the galaxies
C) The relative velocities and ages of the galaxies
D) The relative velocities and sizes of the galaxies

37. According to the passage, as a galaxy falls inward toward the center of a rich cluster, it

A) collides with the central core and emerges relatively intact.
B) is broken apart by the gravitational forces of the core.
C) is transformed by collisions into a large, spiral galaxy.
D) captures unattached stars that have been ejected from the galaxy's core.

38. Which of the following questions can be answered best without the support of the table?

A) How many galaxies are in a rich cluster?
B) What proportion of all galaxies are found in rich clusters?
C) What is the age of the Sun?
D) What is the shape of our galaxy?

39. Which of the following questions CANNOT be answered based on the information provided in the table?

A) How many galaxies are in a rich cluster?
B) What proportion of all galaxies are found in rich clusters?
C) What proportion of all galaxies are found in groups/poor clusters?
D) What is the luminosity of the Sun?

40. The table supports the author's claim that

A) the gas pervading rich clusters has temperatures of up to 100 million kelvin.
B) the Sun is a second- or third-generation star.
C) as much as 10% of galaxies exist in rich clusters.
D) a supergiant galaxy at the center of a rich cluster can consume up to 50 to 100 galaxies.

41. According to the information provided in the table, which of the following characteristics has some overlap between rich clusters and groups/poor clusters of galaxies?

A) Number of galaxies
B) Mass
C) Radius
D) Luminosity

42. Which paragraph in the passage best explains the data overlap in the table as determined in the previous item?

A) Paragraph 2
B) Paragraph 4
C) Paragraph 5
D) None of the paragraphs explains the data overlap in the table as determined in the previous item.

43. According to the table, galaxy groups/poor clusters

A) are most likely as rare as rich clusters.
B) can be larger than rich clusters.
C) can be more luminous than rich clusters.
D) have less radial velocity dispersion than rich clusters.

44. The difference in mass between rich clusters and groups/poor clusters is best explained by the difference in

A) the number of galaxies in each type.
B) the proportion of all galaxies in each type.
C) the luminosities for each type.
D) the age of each type.

LESSON 5 | PAIRED PASSAGES

ACT READING AND SAT READING

The passages and items in this section accompany the in-class review of the skills and concepts tested by the SAT® Reading Test. You will work through the items with your instructor in class. Answers are on page 566.

DIRECTIONS: Each passage or pair of passages is followed by a set of items. Choose the best answer to each question based on what is stated or implied in the passage or passages and in any accompanying graphics. Ⓐ Ⓢ

Items #1–4 refer to the following two passages.

The following passages discuss the nature of comedy.

Passage 1

Comedy appeals only to the intelligence, for laughter is incompatible with emotion. Depict some fault, however trifling, in such a way as to arouse sympathy, fear, or pity, and it is impossible to laugh. On the other hand, a vice—even one that is, generally speaking, of an odious nature—can be made ludicrous by a suitable contrivance. So long as it leaves our emotions unaffected, it is funny. This is not to say that the vice itself is ludicrous but only that the vice, as embodied in a particular character, is ludicrous. The only requirement is that it must not engage our feelings.

Passage 2

Absentmindedness is always comical. Indeed, the deeper the absentmindedness the higher the comedy. Systematic absentmindedness, like that of Don Quixote, is the most comical thing imaginable; it is the comic itself, drawn as nearly as possible from its very source. Take any other comic character, however unconscious he may be of what he says or does: he cannot be comical unless there is some aspect of his person of which he is unaware, one side of his nature which he overlooks. On that account alone does he make us laugh.

1. The author of Passage 1 implies that laughter

A) is not an emotional reaction.
B) counteracts feelings of dread.
C) can correct a vice.
D) is triggered only by a vice.

2. The author of Passage 1 discusses vice primarily in order to

A) advise the reader on how to avoid certain behavior.
B) make it clear that comedy does not engage the emotions.
C) provide an example that the reader will find amusing.
D) demonstrate that emotions are more powerful than intelligence.

3. In context, "deeper" (line 14) means

A) complete.
B) complex.
C) courageous.
D) futile.

4. Which of the following best describes the logical connection between the views expressed in the two passages?

A) Passage 2 provides examples that show that the views of Passage 1 are incorrect.
B) Passage 2 redefines a key term that is used by the author of Passage 1.
C) The two passages reach the same conclusion based on different evidence.
D) The two passages discuss different aspects of the topic.

Items #5–6 refer to the following two passages.

The following passages discuss different theories about the earth's history.

Passage 1

The history of Earth has been punctuated by catastrophic events. Valleys were formed by dramatic plunges of fragments of the earth's crust; mountains rose in gigantic upheavals of land; rocks formed when one worldwide ocean precipitated out great masses of different materials. The mix of observed animal and plant fossils can be explained only by events such as massive fires or floods that wiped out living forms that were then replaced by other species.

Passage 2

Great changes result from gradual processes over long periods of time. Valleys form as constantly flowing water from streams cuts through the sides and bottom of the land. Rocks and mountains are formed, destroyed, and reformed by ongoing volcanic processes and weathering. Different fossil types in successive rock layers represent changes that occur among related organisms due to long-term evolutionary processes.

5. The use of the word "punctuated" in line 1 suggests events that are

A) observable but gradual.
B) powerful but controlled.
C) known but mysterious.
D) sudden and well defined.

6. The two passages develop differing viewpoints about the

A) observable features of the earth.
B) time that is spanned by Earth's history.
C) forces that have shaped the earth.
D) importance of studying geology.

Items #7–8 refer to the following two passages.

The following passages suggest two plausible scenarios for an *E. coli* outbreak.

Passage 1

An *E. coli* outbreak at a county fair sickened hundreds of people. Epidemiologists concluded that individuals with culture-confirmed cases of *E. coli* infection were exposed on August 28 by consuming beverages sold by vendors supplied with water from Well 6. A dye study performed in late September showed a hydraulic connection between the septic system of a nearby 4-H dormitory and Well 6. Tests of a cattle manure storage area suspected as a possible contamination source did not show a hydraulic connection with Well 6 nor with the presence of the relevant strain of *E. coli*. Therefore, the outbreak was caused by leakage from the dormitory septic system.

Passage 2

Manure runoff from the nearby cattle barn cannot be ruled out as a cause of the outbreak because exact environmental conditions, including drought followed by heavy rain, could not be replicated during the later study. Additionally, manure in the storage area was removed daily. Thus, it can never be known if manure-contaminated water percolated from the manure storage area to Well 6.

7. In line 22, the word "percolated" most nearly means

A) boiled.
B) infected.
C) tested.
D) seeped.

8. Which of the following best describes the relationship between the two passages?

A) The two speakers agree that *E. coli* caused the illnesses but believe that two different strains were involved.
B) The two speakers agree that *E. coli* caused the illnesses but disagree about the source of the contamination.
C) The two speakers agree that the same strain of *E. coli* caused the outbreak and agree that the dormitory septic system was the source.
D) Speaker 1 maintains that *E. coli* was the cause of the outbreak of illness, but Speaker 2 thinks that some other agent might have been involved.

Items #9–23 refer to the following two passages.

The following passages are excerpts from fiction written about the relationship between people and the wilderness.

Passage 1

Shortly after sunrise, just as the light was beginning to come streaming through the trees, I caught the big bright eyes of a deer gazing at me through the garden hedge. The expressive eyes, the slim black-tipped muzzle, and the large ears were perfectly visible, as if placed there at just the right distance to be seen. She continued to gaze while I gazed back with equal steadiness, motionless as a rock. In a few minutes she ventured forward a step, exposing her fine arching neck and forelegs, then snorted and withdrew.

Trembling sprays indicated her return, and her head came into view; several steps later, she stood wholly exposed inside the garden hedge, gazed eagerly around, and again withdrew, but returned a moment afterward, this time advancing into the middle of the garden. Behind her I noticed other pairs of eyes.

It then occurred to me that I might possibly steal up to one of them and catch it, not with any intention of killing it, but only to run my hand along its beautiful curving limbs. They seemed, however, to penetrate my conceit and bounded off with loud, shrill snorts, vanishing into the forest.

I have often tried to understand how so many deer, wild sheep, bears, and grouse—nature's cattle and poultry—could be allowed to run at large through the mountain gardens without in any way marring the beauty of their surroundings. I was, therefore, all the more watchful of this feeding flock, and carefully examined the garden after they left, to see what flowers had suffered; I could not, however, detect the slightest disorder, much less destruction. It seemed rather that, like gardeners, they had been keeping it in order. I could not see one crushed flower, nor a single blade of grass that was bent or broken down. Nor among the daisy, gentian, or bryanthus gardens of the Alps, where the wild sheep roam at will, have I ever noticed the effects of destructive feeding or trampling. Even the burly, shuffling bears beautify the ground on which they walk, decorating it with their awe-inspiring tracks, and writing poetry on the soft sequoia bark in boldly drawn hieroglyphics. But, strange to say, man, the crown, the sequoia of nature, brings confusion with all his best gifts and with the overabundant, misbegotten animals that he breeds, sweeps away the beauty of the wilderness like a fire.

Passage 2

The night was intolerable for Antoine. The buffalo were about him in countless numbers, regarding him with vicious glances. It was only due to the natural offensiveness of man that they gave him any space. The bellowing of the bulls became louder, and there was a marked uneasiness on the part of the herd. This was a sign of an approaching storm.

Upon the western horizon were seen flashes of lightning. The cloud that had been a mere speck had now become an ominous thunderhead. Suddenly the wind came, and lightning flashes became more frequent, showing the ungainly forms of the animals like strange monsters in the white light. The colossal herd was again in violent motion. It was a blind rush for shelter, and no heed was paid to buffalo wallows or even deep gulches. All was in the deepest of darkness. There seemed to be groaning in heaven and earth—millions of hoofs and throats roaring in unison.

As a shipwrecked sailor clings to a mere fragment of wood, so Antoine, although almost exhausted with fatigue, stuck to the saddle of his pony. As the mad rush continued, every flash displayed heaps of bison in death's struggle under the hoofs of their companions.

When he awoke and looked around him again it was morning. The herd had entered the strip of timber which lay on both sides of the river, and it was here that Antoine conceived his first distinct hope of saving himself.

"Waw, waw, waw!" was the hoarse cry that came to his ears, apparently from a human being in distress. Antoine strained his eyes and craned his neck to see who it could be. Through an opening in the branches ahead, he perceived a large grizzly bear lying along an inclined limb and hugging it desperately to maintain his position. The herd had now thoroughly pervaded the timber, and the bear was likewise hemmed in. He had taken his unaccustomed refuge after making a brave stand against several bulls, one of which lay dead nearby, while he himself was bleeding from several wounds.

Antoine had been assiduously looking for a friendly tree, by means of which he hoped to escape from captivity. His horse, by chance, made his way directly under the very box-elder that was sustaining the bear and there was a convenient branch just within his reach. He saw at a glance that the occupant of the tree would not interfere with him. They were, in fact, companions in distress. Antoine sprang desperately from the pony's back and seized the cross-limb with both his hands.

By the middle of the afternoon the main body of the herd had passed, and Antoine was sure that his captivity had at last come to an end. Then he swung himself from his limb to the ground, and walked stiffly to the carcass of the nearest cow, which he dressed, and prepared himself a meal. But first he took a piece of liver on a long pole to the bear!

9. The word "sprays" (line 12) refers to

A) minute droplets.
B) light mist.
C) thin legs.
D) small branches.

10. In context, "steal up" (line 20) means

A) acquire unlawfully.
B) prepare for action.
C) promise faithfully.
D) approach undetected.

11. In the first two paragraphs, the author of Passage 1 is primarily concerned with

A) recounting an experience.
B) exploring a theory.
C) teaching a lesson.
D) offering an opinion.

12. In context, "conceit" (line 23) means

A) arrogance.
B) selfishness.
C) fanciful notion.
D) dissatisfaction.

13. According to the passage, the deer and the sheep are alike in that they both

A) are wary of human beings.
B) inhabit remote Alpine gardens.
C) feed without causing destruction.
D) live untamed in wilderness regions.

14. The "boldly drawn hieroglyphics" (lines 43–44) are probably

A) claw marks.
B) park signs.
C) rare flowers.
D) hoofprints.

15. The author compares the deer to gardeners (lines 34–37) in order to

A) encourage the reader to learn more about deer.
B) refute the idea that deer are aggressive.
C) illustrate the similarity between deer and humans.
D) emphasize that deer are not destructive.

16. In context, "wallows" (line 64) means

A) shallow depression.
B) deep cave.
C) rugged cliff.
D) low hill.

17. By "the natural offensiveness of man" (line 52), the author of Passage 2 probably refers to man's

A) frequent rudeness.
B) disagreeable odor.
C) uncontrolled aggression.
D) distasteful behavior.

18. All of the following are true of the comparison drawn in the third paragraph of Passage 2 EXCEPT

A) Antoine, like a shipwrecked sailor, is in a desperate situation.
B) The herd of buffalo are like the storm-driven sea.
C) Antoine's pony supports him the way that debris might support a shipwrecked sailor.
D) The environment is filled with dangerous creatures that threaten a sailor the way the buffalo threaten Antoine.

19. The tone of the first two paragraphs of Passage 2 is

A) frivolous.
B) suspenseful.
C) animated.
D) reserved.

20. The phrase "unaccustomed refuge" (line 89) suggests that the bear

A) preferred open areas to confined spaces.
B) rarely climbed a tree for safety.
C) did not often encounter buffalo.
D) was fearful of the presence of a human.

21. In context, "dressed" (line 107) means

A) adorned.
B) clothed.
C) bound.
D) prepared.

22. The mood of Passage 2 moves from

A) joy to despair.
B) hopelessness to hope.
C) happiness to gloom.
D) apprehension to courageousness.

23. The information provided in Passage 2 most directly challenges Passage 1 in its description of

A) wild animals as gentle and nondestructive.
B) human beings as able to survive dangerous threats.
C) gardens as suitable habitats for wild animals.
D) bears as being unable to climb trees.

Items #24–33 refer to the following two passages.

Passage 1 is adapted from Henry David Thoreau's *Walden* (1854) in which the author discusses his life of solitude in the New England woods. Passage 2 is adapted from *Public Opinion*, published in 1922 by Walter Lippman, a noted journalist and commentator.

Passage 1

I am sure that I never read any memorable news in a newspaper. If we read of one man robbed or murdered or killed by accident, or one house burned, or one vessel wrecked, or one steamboat blown up, or one cow run over on the railroad, or one mad dog killed, or one lot of grasshoppers in the winter—we never need read of another. One is enough. If you are acquainted with the principle, what do you care for a myriad instances and applications? All news, as it is called, is gossip, even though many people insist on hearing it. If I should pull the bell-rope of the local church to sound a fire alarm, almost everyone in the entire area would stop everything and come running, not mainly to save property from the flames but to see the blaze, especially if it were the parish church itself on fire.

After a night's sleep, the news is as indispensable to most people as breakfast: "Pray tell me everything important that has happened anywhere on this globe." They read over coffee and rolls that a man has had his eyes gouged out the previous evening on the Wachito River. There was such a rush the other day at the railway office to learn the foreign news by the last arrival, that several large squares of plate glass were broken—news that I seriously think a ready wit might have written a year or twelve years earlier with surprising accuracy. As for Spain, for instance, if you know how to throw in Don Carlos and the Infanta or Don Pedro and Seville and Granada from time to time in the right proportions—they may have changed the names a little since I last saw the papers—and serve up a bull-fight when other entertainments fail, it will be true to the letter and give as good an idea of the exact state of ruin of things in Spain as the most succinct and lucid reports under this head in the newspapers. And as for England, almost the last significant scrap of news from that quarter was the revolution of 1649; and if you have learned the history of her crops for an average year, you never need attend to that thing again, unless your speculations are of a merely pecuniary character. If one may judge who rarely looks into the newspapers, nothing new does ever happen in foreign parts, a French revolution not excepted.

Passage 2

There is an island in the ocean, where in 1914 a few Englishmen, Frenchmen, and Germans lived. The island was not served by telegraph, and the British mail steamer came once every sixty days. By September, it had not yet come, and the islanders were still talking about the latest newspaper, which told about the approaching trial of Madame Caillaux for the shooting of Gaston Calmette. It was, therefore, with more than usual eagerness that the whole colony assembled at the quay on a day in mid-September to hear from the captain what the verdict had been. Instead, they learned of the start of the war and that for over six weeks those of them who were English and those of them who were French had acted as if they were friends with those of them who were Germans, when in fact they were enemies.

Their plight was not so different from that of most of the population of Europe. They had been mistaken for six weeks; on the continent, the interval may have been only six days or six hours, but there was an interval. There was a moment when the picture of Europe on which business was conducted as usual, and it did not correspond in any way to the Europe that was about to make a jumble of so many lives. There was a time for which each person was still adjusted to an environment that no longer existed. All over the world as late as July 25th, people were making goods that they would not be able to ship and buying goods that they would not be able to import. Careers were planned, enterprises were contemplated, and hopes and expectations were entertained, all in the belief that the world as known was the world as it was. Authors were writing books describing that world. They trusted the picture in their heads. Then, over four years later, on a Thursday morning, came the news of an armistice, and people gave vent to their unutterable relief that the slaughter was over. Yet, in the five days before the real armistice came, though the end of the war had been celebrated, several thousand young men died on the battlefields.

Looking back, we can see how indirectly we know the environment in which we live. We can see that the news of it comes to us sometimes quickly, sometimes slowly, but whatever we believe to be a true picture, we treat as if it were the environment itself. It is harder to remember that about the beliefs upon which we are now acting, but in respect to other peoples and other ages, we flatter ourselves that it is easy to see when they were in deadly earnest about ludicrous pictures of the world. We insist, because of our superior hindsight, that the world as they needed to know it and the world as they did know it were often two quite contradictory things. We can see, too, that while they governed and fought, traded and reformed in the world as they imagined it to be, they produced results, or failed to produce any, in the world as it was. They started for the Indies and found America.

24. The newspaper report that a man has had his eyes gouged out is included by the author of Passage 1 as an example of

A) a local event that affects people's lives directly.
B) an insignificant incident that does not affect the reader.
C) an unusual occurrence that merits special coverage.
D) an international incident that warrants detailed description.

25. The author of Passage 1 mentions Don Carlos and the Infanta in order to

A) demonstrate a thorough familiarity with current events in Spain.
B) familiarize the reader with recent events that occurred in Spain.
C) explain how events in Europe affect people all over the world.
D) illustrate the point that news from Spain repeats itself.

26. The attitude of the author of Passage 1 towards the news is one of

A) ridicule.
B) admiration.
C) indifference.
D) confidence.

27. As used in this context, "attend to" (line 41) means

A) be present at.
B) be ignorant of.
C) be concerned with.
D) grow weary of.

28. The author adds "especially if it were the parish church" (line 16) in order to

A) emphasize that people are fascinated by the bizarre.
B) prove that citizens do not care about public property.
C) show that residents take an interest in local events.
D) stress the importance of the church to community.

29. According to the author of Passage 2, the people on the island "acted as if they were friends" (line 61) because they

A) originally came from European countries.
B) were isolated from the rest of the world.
C) disagreed over the outcome of the trial.
D) did not realize that war had started.

30. The "plight" to which the author refers in line 64 was

A) incorrect reporting about the progress of the war.
B) lack of accurate information about current conditions.
C) an inability to obtain reports on a regular basis.
D) slanted war news from the European front.

31. In lines 103–107, the author implies that people of another time

A) accomplished something significant based upon wrong information.
B) failed to realize that the information available was wrong.
C) could have foreseen that America lay between Europe and India.
D) realized only in hindsight that they had landed in America.

32. Which of the following best summarizes the different points of view of the two passages?

A) The author of Passage 2 believes that news is important while the author of Passage 1 believes it is irrelevant.
B) The author of Passage 1 believes that news is unreliable while the author of Passage 2 believes that it is accurate.
C) The author of Passage 1 believes that newspapers provide critical information while the author of Passage 2 believes newspapers are too slow.
D) The author of Passage 1 believes that news coverage could be improved while the author of Passage 2 believes that it is already adequate.

33. If the two authors had been able to write about the internet, they likely would

A) say that their points apply to the news content on the worldwide web.
B) acknowledge that the new media makes reporting more relevant and more reliable.
C) insist that newspapers remain a better source of information than electronic media.
D) conclude that global news coverage gives readers a more accurate view of the world.

LESSON 6 | ADDITIONAL PRACTICE

ACT READING AND SAT READING

The items in this section accompany the in-class additional practice for the ACT and SAT Reading Test sections. You will work through the items with your instructor in class. Answers are on page 566.

DIRECTIONS: Each passage or pair of passages is followed by a set of items. Choose the best answer to each question based on what is stated or implied in the passage or passages and in any accompanying graphics. Ⓐ Ⓢ

Items #1–10 refer to the following passage.

This passage is adapted from an article about the history of alcoholism.

The present-day view of alcoholism as a physical disease was not a scientific discovery; it is a medical thesis that has developed only slowly over the past 200 years and amidst considerable controversy. Historically, the moral perspective has been that excessive use of alcohol is a willful act, one that leads to intoxication and other sinful behavior; but in the early nineteenth century, Benjamin Rush, a founder of American psychiatry, proposed that "the habit of drunkenness is a disease of the will." By the late nineteenth century, physicians generally viewed the habitual use of drugs such as opiates, tobacco, and coffee as a generic disorder stemming from biological vulnerability, either inherited or acquired.

Prohibition represented a triumph of the older morality over a modern medical concept. Where physicians who championed the disease concept of alcoholism emphasized the need for treatment, the Temperance Movement stressed that alcohol itself was the cause of drunkenness and advocated its control and eventually its prohibition. Scientific interest in alcoholism, dampened by Prohibition, revived toward the middle of the twentieth century, not because of any new scientific findings, but because of humanitarian efforts to shift the focus from blame and punishment to treatment and concern.

The early 1960s witnessed a growing acceptance of the notion that, in certain "vulnerable" people, alcohol use leads to physical addiction—a true disease. Central to this concept of alcoholism as a disease were the twin notions of substance tolerance and physical dependence, both physical phenomena. Substance tolerance occurs when increased doses of a drug are required to produce effects previously attained at lower dosages; physical dependence refers to the occurrence of withdrawal symptoms, such as seizures, following cessation of a drinking bout.

In 1972, the National Council on Alcoholism outlined criteria for diagnosing alcoholism. These criteria emphasized alcohol tolerance and physical dependence and treated alcoholism as an independent disorder, not merely a manifestation of a more general and underlying personality disorder.

In 1977, a World Health Organization report challenged this disease model by pointing out that not everyone who develops alcohol-related problems exhibits true alcohol dependence. This important distinction between dependence and other drug-related problems that do not involve dependence was not immediately accepted by the American Psychiatric Association. The early drafts of the 1980 edition of its *Diagnostic and Statistical Manual of Mental Disorders* described a dependence syndrome for alcohol and other drugs in which tolerance and dependence were important, but not essential criteria for diagnosis, but at the last moment, the inertia of history prevailed, and tolerance and dependence were both included not as necessary to diagnose dependence, but as sufficient indicators in and of themselves.

It was not until 1993 that the American Psychiatric Association modified this position. In the fourth edition of the *Manual*, tolerance and withdrawal symptoms are the first two of seven criteria listed for diagnosing alcohol and other drug dependence, but the clinician is not required to find whether either is present, or in what degree, in order to make the diagnosis.

Today, there is almost universal agreement among doctors that alcoholism is a disease, but we should not forget that the moral perspective on alcoholism is still very much alive. It perhaps does not surprise us that the Reverend D. E. Todd wrote an essay entitled, "Drunkenness a Vice, Not a Disease" in 1882, but we should be concerned that the book *Heavy Drinking: The Myth of Alcoholism as a Disease* was published in 1988. Even as late as the mid-1970s, sociologists were reporting that the term "alcoholic" was commonly used in the United States as a synonym for "drunkard," rather than as a designation for someone with an illness or a disorder. Apparently, in the minds of those outside the health profession, the contradictory notions of alcoholism as a disease and alcoholism as a moral weakness can coexist quite comfortably.

1. The author's primary concern is to

A) refute the notion that drunkenness is a serious social problem.
B) argue that alcoholism is less serious than it was 200 years ago.
C) explain the evolution of the idea that alcoholism is a disease.
D) give an example of the way that medical terminology changes over time.

2. According to the passage, members of the Temperance Movement

A) agreed with doctors that alcohol abuse was a serious problem.
B) agreed with doctors that the solution to alcohol abuse was treatment.
C) agreed with doctors that drunkenness should be treated as a disease.
D) disagreed with doctors that alcoholism was a serious problem.

3. The author mentions Benjamin Rush in order to

A) mark the beginning of the evolution of the disease concept of alcoholism.
B) highlight the seriousness of habitual use of certain drugs.
C) discredit a central tenet of the religious view of alcoholism.
D) encourage physicians to treat alcoholism as a physical disease.

4. It can be inferred that the concepts of tolerance and dependence helped to establish the disease model of alcoholism because they

A) prove that alcoholism is not a manifestation of a fundamental personality disorder.
B) are necessary but not sufficient findings to diagnose alcoholism.
C) demonstrate that alcohol abuse is similar to abuse of opiates and other drugs.
D) are evidence of physical addiction which is an affliction of the body.

5. The author regards the essay, "Drunkenness a Vice, Not a Disease" as

A) misguided and dangerous.
B) incorrect and harmful.
C) insightful and beneficial.
D) outdated and harmless.

6. The author implies that all of the following are true EXCEPT

A) historically, alcoholism has been regarded as a weakness of the will rather than a disease.
B) in modern times, the medical community has disagreed over the exact definition of alcoholism.
C) the medical profession may make terminological distinctions that are not understood by the general population.
D) the long-held view that alcoholism is a moral problem has finally been totally discredited.

7. According to the passage, the draft versions of the 1980 *Diagnostic and Statistical Manual of Mental Disorders* were similar to the 1993 version in that they

A) listed tolerance and dependence as both necessary and sufficient conditions for the diagnosis of alcoholism.
B) did not specify tolerance and dependence as essential elements of alcoholism.
C) suggested that alcoholism might be a generic, personality disorder.
D) argued that viewing alcoholism as a disease might actually encourage drunkenness.

8. With which of the following statements would the author most likely agree?

A) Shifting public opinion will force physicians to return to the view that alcoholism is a moral weakness.
B) A physician should not make a finding of alcoholism in a patient in the absence of either tolerance or dependence.
C) The determination to classify a problem as a disease depends in part on whether it is susceptible to medical treatment.
D) New scientific findings on the workings of tolerance and dependence warranted a shift to the disease model of alcoholism.

9. The graph below shows the responses to a recent survey that asked people in relevant categories whether they considered alcoholism to be (1) a disease or (2) a moral weakness. The data provided in the graph could be used by the author to support which of the following statements made in the passage?

Is Alcoholism a Disease or a Moral Weakness?

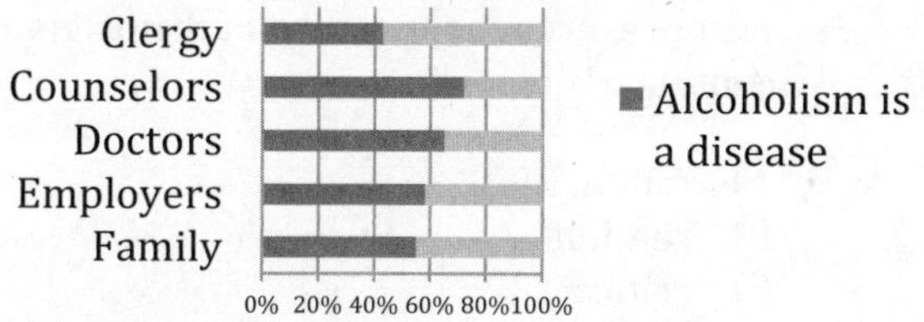

A) Lines 72–73 ("Today . . . disease")
B) Lines 74–75 ("the moral . . . alive")
C) Lines 76–78 ("Reverend . . . 1882")
D) Lines 80–83 ("Even . . . 'drunkard'")

10. The graph below shows the responses to a 2015 survey that asked people in relevant categories to what extent they considered alcoholism to be a disease and to what extent a moral weakness. Responses were recorded as percentages, and the graph gives the average of the data. (Bars do not total 100% because respondents sometimes mentioned various other factors such as "heredity"). The data provided by the graph could be used by the author to support which statement from the text?

Percentage of Alcoholism That Is a Disease and Percentage of Alcoholism That Is a Moral Weakness

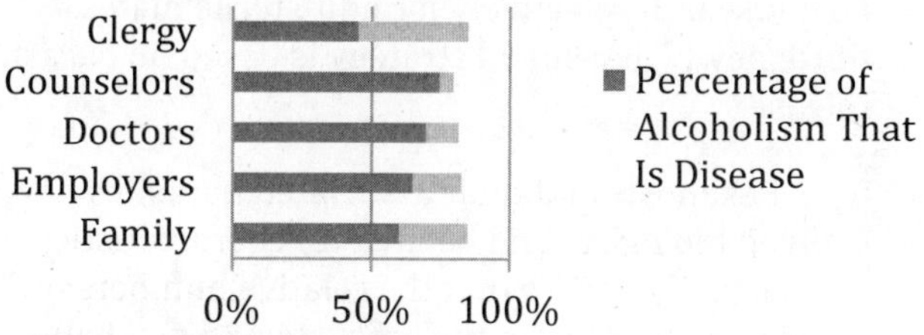

A) Lines 5–8 ("Historically . . . behavior")
B) Lines 11–15 ("By the . . . acquired")
C) Lines 49–50 ("Not everyone . . . dependence")
D) Lines 85–88 ("Apparently . . . comfortably")

Items #11–20 refer to the following passage.

This passage is adapted from an article about pest control and eradication methods.

Traditional strategies for controlling insect-pests tend to rely on the use of nonselective insecticides that cause extensive ecological disruption. The alternative sterile insect technique, in which members of the target species are irradiated to cause sterility, has enjoyed some modest success. When released into an infested area, the sterile insects mate with normal insects but produce no offspring. Unfortunately, the irradiation weakens the insects, making it less likely that they will mate; and, in any event, sterile insects do not search selectively for non-sterile mates. A third, newly developed strategy is based on parasite release.

Pest hosts and their associated parasites have evolved biological and behavioral characteristics that virtually ensure that the relative numbers of hosts and parasites in the ecosystem they inhabit remain within relatively narrow limits—even though coexisting populations may fluctuate up to 100-fold during a single season. The close numerical relationships are entirely consistent with nature's balancing mechanisms, which permit closely associated organisms to live together in harmony. Thus, in natural populations, the ratios of parasites to hosts are not high enough to result in dependable control. However, it is possible to mass-rear parasites so that they can be released at strategic times and in numbers that result in parasite-to-host ratios sufficient to control host populations.

Biosteres tryoni, for example, has a strong affinity for medfly larvae. Let us assume that a new medfly infestation is discovered. It is likely to have originated from a single female and, even in an area with a good surveillance program, to be in the third reproductive cycle. The rate of population increase is tenfold per generation; so at the time the infestation comes to light, about 1,000 males and 1,000 females are emerging and will produce a total of approximately 80,000 larvae. Reproduction will be concentrated in an area of about one-square-mile, but scattered reproduction will occur anywhere within a 25-square-mile area. At first glance, the odds of controlling the infestation by parasite release seem low; but with new techniques for mass-producing parasites, it is possible to release one million males and one million females into the infested area. This would mean an average of 62 females per acre, and the average female parasitizes about 30 host larvae during its lifetime.

Additionally, the parasites actively search for host habitats by using the kairomone signals emanating from infested fruit. Even assuming that only 10 percent of the released females are successful and, further, that they parasitize an average of only 10 larvae, they could still parasitize one million larvae. Only 80,000 larvae are available, however; so the actual ratio would be 12.5 : 1. A ratio as low as 5 : 1 results in 99 percent parasitism.

This method of pest eradication presents no health or environmental problems and is actually cheaper. The cost of mass-rearing and distributing *B. tryoni* is about $2,000 per million. So even if six million parasites of both sexes are released during a period corresponding to three medfly reproductive cycles, the total cost of the treatment would be $12,000—compared to $25,000 for a single insecticide spray application to the same 25-square-mile area.

11. The author implies that the sterile insect release strategy is not completely effective because

A) some sterile insects mate with other sterile insects.
B) weakened sterile insects refuse to mate with healthy insects.
C) the cost of producing a sufficient number of sterile insects is prohibitive.
D) sterile insects are incapable of producing offspring.

12. Which of the following words, when substituted for "strategic" in line 28, would best preserve the meaning of the original sentence?

A) military
B) random
C) critical
D) ill-advised

13. According to the passage, *Biosteres tryoni* is effective in controlling medfly infestations because

A) female *B. tryoni* feed on adult medflies.
B) male and female *B. tryoni* parasitize medfly larvae.
C) male and female *B. tryoni* mate with medflies.
D) female *B. tryoni* parasitize medfly larvae.

14. It can be inferred that if *B. tryoni* were not attracted by kairomone signals from medfly-infested fruit, the parasite release strategy would be

A) less effective because some *B. tryoni* would remain in areas not infested.
B) less effective because none of the *B. tryoni* would parasitize medfly larvae.
C) equally as effective because *B. tryoni* do not damage fruit crops.
D) more effective because some *B. tryoni* would fail to reproduce.

15. In the development of the passage, the author

A) explains a scientific theory and then offers evidence to refute it.
B) cites statistics to compare the relative effectiveness of different strategies.
C) speculates on the probable course of scientific developments.
D) states a general principle and then provides an example of its application.

16. Which of the following statements about medfly reproduction can be inferred from the passage?

A) The medfly is capable of reproducing asexually.
B) A typical generation contains 10 times as many females as males.
C) A new generation of medfly is produced once a year.
D) Only about 25 percent of larvae reach adulthood.

17. The author calculates the cost of treating a 25-square-mile area with six million parasite insects in order to demonstrate that

A) treatment with parasites would be more effective than treatment using insecticide spray applications.
B) use of parasite insects as a means of pest control would be cheaper than spraying the same area.
C) the cost of using sterile insects to treat pest infestation is more expensive than the cost of insecticide spraying.
D) a ratio of parasitic insects to target insects of as low as 12.5:1 would achieve 99% percent eradication.

18. In the final paragraph, the phrase "even if" (line 63) indicates that the author is

A) making an unproved assumption about the effectiveness of parasite pest control programs.
B) providing evidence of the ecological harm done by indiscriminate use of pesticides.
C) responding to a point about program cost that was specifically developed in the previous paragraph.
D) considering the strongest possible objection against the cost of the parasite release strategy.

19. The author is primarily concerned with

A) criticizing the use of nonselective insecticides.
B) defending the use of parasite release programs.
C) explaining the workings of a new pest-control method.
D) refuting the suggestion that parasite release is costly.

20. It can be inferred that the author regards the release of parasites to control pests as

A) reasonably effective.
B) prohibitively expensive.
C) environmentally reckless.
D) highly experimental.

Items #21–35 refer to the following passage.

This passage is adapted from an article about the immune system.

Have you ever wondered why you become feverish when you are suffering from the flu? Your body's immune system is simply doing its job. Because the presence of certain organisms in the body is harmful, the immune system will attempt to bar their entry or, failing that, to seek out and destroy them.

At the heart of the immune system is the ability to distinguish between self and non-self. The body's defenses do not normally attack tissues that exhibit a self-marker.* Rather, immune cells and other body cells coexist peacefully. But when immune defenders encounter cells or organisms carrying molecules that say "foreign," the immune troops muster quickly to eliminate the intruders.

Any substance that is capable of triggering an immune response is called an antigen. An antigen can be a virus, a bacterium, a fungus, or a parasite; tissues or cells from another individual, except an identical twin, also act as antigens; even otherwise harmless substances such as ragweed pollen or cat hair can set off a misguided response known as an allergy, in which case the substance is called an allergen. An antigen announces its foreignness by means of intricate and characteristic shapes called epitopes, which protrude from its surface.

The immune system controls the production, development, and deployment of white cells called lymphocytes and includes the bone marrow, the thymus (a multi-lobed organ behind the breastbone), and the blood and lymphatic vessels. Like all other blood cells, cells destined to become immune cells are produced in the bone marrow and are called stem cells. Some stem cells develop into lymphocytes while others develop into phagocytes.

The two most important classes of lymphocytes are B cells, so called because they mature in the bone marrow, and T cells, which migrate to the thymus. T cells directly attack their targets, which include body cells that have been commandeered by virus or warped by malignancy. (This is called cellular immunity). B cells, in contrast, work chiefly by secreting antibodies into the body's fluids. (This is known as humoral immunity).

The other group of stem cells is the phagocytes; they are large white cannibal cells. A special group of phagocytes, called macrophages (literally, "big eaters"), also have the ability to "display" the antigen after it has been digested.

To fend off the threatening horde, the body has devised astonishingly intricate defenses. Microbes attempting to enter the body must first find a chink in its armor. The skin and the mucous membranes that line the body's portals not only interpose a physical barrier, but they are also rich in scavenger cells and antibodies. Next, invaders must elude a series of non-specific defenses—cells and substances equipped to tackle infectious agents without regard to their antigenic peculiarities. Many potential infections are stopped when microbes are intercepted by patrolling scavenger cells or disabled by enzymes.

Microbes that breach the non-specific barriers are then confronted by weapons that are specifically designed to combat their unique characteristics. This immune system response includes both cellular and humoral components.

The cellular response is initiated by a macrophage. The macrophage digests an antigen and then displays antigen fragments on its own surface. This gives the T cells their marching orders. Some T cells become killer cells and set out to track down body cells that have become infected. Other T cells become communication cells and secrete substances that call other kinds of immune cells, such as fresh macrophages, to the site of the infection. Others coordinate the movements of the various groups of cells once they arrive on the scene. Still, others secrete substances that stimulate the production of more T cell troops.

Humoral immunity is primarily the function of B cells, although some help from T cells is almost always needed. B cells, like macrophages, eat antigens. Unlike macrophages, however, a B cell can bind only to an antigen that specifically fits its antibody-like receptor, so the B cell exhibits an antigen fragment that attracts the attention of a T cell. The B cell and T cell interact, and the helper T cell stimulates the B cell to produce clones of itself—each with the highly specific antibody-like receptor. These clones then differentiate into plasma cells and begin producing vast quantities of identical antigen-specific antibodies. Released into the bloodstream, the antibodies lock onto their matching antigens. The antigen-antibody complexes are then cleansed from the circulatory system by the liver and the spleen.

These seemingly chaotic but actually very well-orchestrated maneuvers continue until the attack has been repulsed. At that point, specialized T cells, called suppressors, halt the production of antibodies and bring the immune response to a close.

When viewed from a clinical perspective, this process manifests itself in the three classic symptoms of redness, warmth, and swelling. Redness and warmth develop when small blood vessels in the vicinity of the infection become dilated and carry more blood. Swelling results when the vessels, made leaky by yet other immune secretions, allow soluble immune substances to seep into the surrounding tissue. But all of this subsides as the controller T cells begin their mop-up activities. And with that, your illness has run its course.

*Self-markers are distinctive molecules that are carried by virtually all body cells.

21. The passage can best be described as a

A) refutation of an ancient medical idea.
B) definition of a biological concept.
C) description of a biological process.
D) technical definition of a medical term.

22. According to the third paragraph, an "allergen" differs from an "antigen" in that an allergen

A) does not trigger an immune response.
B) does not exhibit unique epitopes.
C) is not ordinarily harmful.
D) does not announce its foreignness.

23. The passage implies that without the ability to distinguish self from non-self cells, the immune system would

A) function effectively except against the most powerful threats.
B) still be able to identify various epitopes.
C) no longer require both T cells and B cells.
D) be rendered completely ineffective.

24. Which of the following best explains why tissue that is transplanted from an identical twin is not attacked by the immune system?

A) The transplanted tissue has the same self-identifying molecules as the body.
B) The transplanted tissue triggers an allergic, not antigenic, reaction.
C) The transplanted tissue has no unique identifying self or non-self markers.
D) The body's immune system recognizes the transplanted tissue as foreign but ignores it.

25. According to lines 32–45, all of the following statements are true of T cells and B cells EXCEPT

A) they are two different types of lymphocytes.
B) B cells mature in the bone marrow, T cells in the thymus.
C) both classes of cells are produced by the bone marrow.
D) either class can differentiate into a macrophage.

26. As used in this context, "humoral" (line 44) means

A) comical.
B) latent.
C) fluid.
D) dangerous.

27. The author refers to phagocytes as "cannibal cells" (line 47) because they

A) are large in size.
B) digest human tissue.
C) display the antigen.
D) eat other cells.

28. According to the passage, the body's first line of defense against microbes is

A) enzymes.
B) scavenger cells.
C) skin and mucous membranes.
D) a macrophage.

29. The body's "non-specific defenses" (line 58) ignore

A) antigenic epitopes.
B) foreign substances.
C) physical antibodies.
D) scavenger cells.

30. According to lines 69–104, cellular and humoral responses are similar in that both

A) require the presence of a macrophage.
B) commence with one cell's digesting another.
C) are carried out exclusively by one type of cell.
D) necessitate the presence of B cells.

31. The passage mentions all of the following as functions of the T cells EXCEPT

A) directing cellular activity.
B) communicating with other cells.
C) terminating an immune response.
D) secreting antibodies into the blood.

32. In line 100, "well-orchestrated" most nearly means

A) effective.
B) desperate.
C) musical.
D) coordinated.

33. It can be inferred that without the presence of suppressor T cells

A) B cells would be unable to clone themselves.
B) non-specific defenses would become ineffective.
C) immune reactions would continue indefinitely.
D) macrophages would not respond to an infection.

34. Which of the following best describes the function of the final paragraph?

A) It alerts the reader to the topic that will follow.
B) It provides further details on functions of immune cells.
C) It highlights issues that need further research.
D) It answers the question raised in the first paragraph.

35. The passage relies upon an extended metaphor of an immune response as a

A) transaction between business partners.
B) battle between warring camps.
C) struggle against oppressive rule.
D) debate between political candidates.

TEST MECHANICS

ACT READING AND SAT READING

ACT Reading Overview

The ACT Reading test consists of four reading selections, each approximately 700 words in length, and each followed by 10 items. You read a passage and answer the items based on what is stated or implied in the reading selection.

You'll have one passage from each of the following four categories: Literary Fiction, Social Science, Humanities, and Natural Science. In most cases, the passage will be about a topic with which you are not familiar. The test-writers choose unusual topics so that the Reading Test will be one of reading skill and not of knowledge. Of course, you may find a topic that you know something about, but even so, your knowledge is probably not going to help you very much, though familiarity with a topic may be of some help.

The time limit for the 40 items on the Reading Test is 35 minutes. Given the time limit, you obviously need to work quickly. The exam, however, is not a test of "speed-reading." Instead, the exam is a test of reading *comprehension*.

SAT Reading Overview

The Reading test is one of the two sections of the Evidence-Based Reading and Writing component of the SAT test. The other section is the Writing and Language test (see the Writing and Language section of this book for additional information). The Reading test consists of five reading selections followed by several items. You read the selection and answer the items based on what is stated or implied in the selection.

Reading selections (also called "passages") come in different lengths (ranging from 500 words to 750 words) with varying numbers of items (10 to 11 items per passage). Sometimes, selections use paired passages on the same topic and pose questions asking you to compare and contrast the two points of view presented.

The reading passages are selected from three general content areas: Literary Fiction, Social Studies, and Natural Sciences. There will be 1–2 graphics in one of the Social Studies passages and one of the Natural Sciences passages. You will have to use information from the graphics and the passage to answer corresponding items.

In most cases, the passage will be about a topic with which you are not familiar. The test writers choose unusual topics so that Reading items will be a test of reading skill and not of knowledge. Of course, you may find a topic that you know something about, but even so, your knowledge is probably not going to help you very much.

The SAT Reading test is 65 minutes with a total of 5 passages (4 single passages and 1 set of paired passages) and 52 questions. Given the time limit, you obviously need to work quickly. The exam, however, is not a test of speed-reading. Instead, the exam is a test of reading *comprehension.*

ACT Reading and SAT Reading Anatomy

DIRECTIONS: Each passage or pair of passages is followed by a set of items. Choose the best answer to each question based on what is stated or implied in the passage or passages and in any accompanying graphics.

Items #1–4 are based on the following passage.

This passage is adapted from a government publication about the history of alcohol abuse.

The movement to prohibit alcohol began in the early years of the nineteenth century with the formation of local societies in New York and Massachusetts to promote temperance in consumption of alcohol. Many of the temperance societies were affiliated with Protestant evangelical denominations and met in local churches. As time passed, most temperance societies modified their goal to call for complete abstinence from all alcoholic beverages.

In 1919, largely in response to the lobbying efforts of the Anti-Saloon League, the Eighteenth Amendment to the Constitution was passed banning the production, transportation, and sale of all alcoholic beverages. The amendment, also known as the Prohibition Amendment, provided for concurrent enforcement by both federal and state law. By January 1920, in addition to the federal Volstead Act, the nation had laws in thirty-three states prohibiting alcohol entirely.

Prohibition, however, proved unworkable as bootleggers and speakeasies quickly organized to satisfy the public's continuing thirst for alcohol. Thirteen years later, the "Noble Experiment," doomed by the impracticality of enforcement, ended with the repeal of the Prohibition Amendment.

*The directions make Reading items sound easy: read this and answer the items. So, the directions aren't very helpful, and you can ignore them from now on. (***NOTE:** *Graphics will only be included in SAT Reading tests, so only SAT Reading directions will reference graphics.)*

Passages will include an introductory note telling you where the passage comes from. A note may provide some useful information, so read it.

Typically, Reading passages discuss an unfamiliar topic. Even if you know something about Prohibition, that information may or may not be helpful since you'll be asked about this particular passage and not about your general knowledge of the topic.

This particular passage is organized chronologically. The first paragraph talks about the "early years of the nineteenth century;" in other words, the early 1800s.

The second paragraph starts with 1919. Then, the passage briefly traces the events leading up to Prohibition.

The third paragraph explains why Prohibition failed: people wanted to drink, so bootleggers and illegal clubs satisfied that demand. Eventually, Prohibition was repealed.

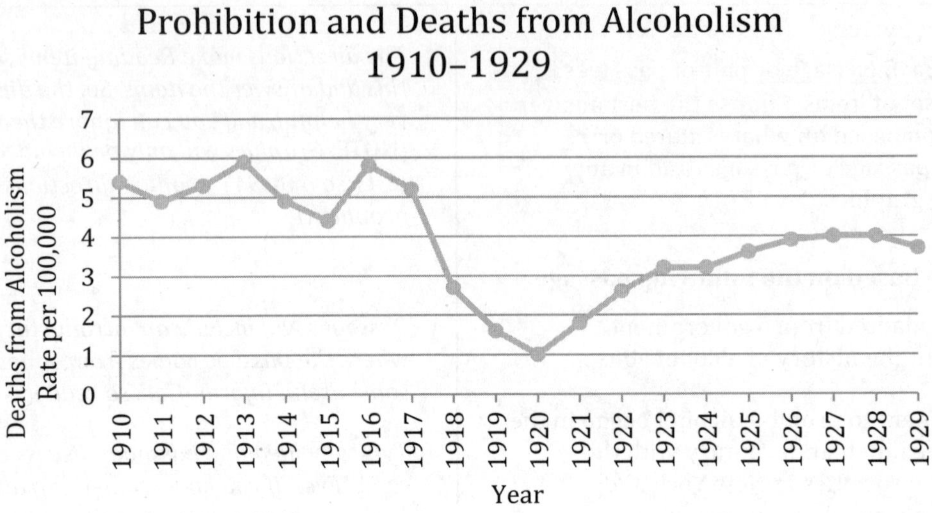

1. The passage is primarily concerned with the

   A) social problems caused by alcohol abuse.
   B) founding of anti-alcohol temperance societies.
   C) origins of Prohibition and its subsequent failure.
   D) efforts to enforce Prohibition legislation.

2. According to the passage, in the early nineteenth century, temperance societies originally

   A) encouraged moderation in alcohol use.
   B) demanded the repeal of the Eighteenth Amendment.
   C) supported efforts to enforce the Volstead Act.
   D) refused to align with religious groups.

3. In line 17, the word "concurrent" means

   A) unsuccessful.
   B) shared.
   C) practicable.
   D) intermittent.

1. **(C)** *This is a common type of reading item: the item asks you to identify the main idea of the passage. The passage discusses the origins and failure of Prohibition.*

2. **(A)** *This item asks about something that is specifically stated in the passage. The author clearly states that the temperance societies were originally founded to "promote temperance" as opposed to complete prohibition.*

3. **(B)** *This item asks you for the definition of a term in the context of the passage. The passage states that the federal government and the states were given "concurrent" authority and that the states, as well as the federal government, passed laws against alcohol. So, "concurrent" must mean something like "joint" or "shared."*

4. Based on information from the graph, which of the following sentences placed as the second sentence in the final paragraph would offer the most persuasive argument that Prohibition was unsuccessful in stopping the consumption of alcohol?

A) The number of deaths from alcoholism dropped sharply at the start of Prohibition but quickly rebounded and remained at pre-Prohibition highs for the remainder of the years during which alcohol was illegal.
B) The number of deaths per 100,000 from alcoholism was lowest at the start of Prohibition but grew throughout the 1920s as bootlegging, speakeasies, and other violations of the law became increasingly widespread.
C) The average number of gallons of alcohol consumed by individuals dropped at the start of Prohibition and remained fairly stable for the remainder of the Roaring Twenties.
D) Annual deaths per 100,000 due to alcoholism for the 1920s was lower than for the period 1910 to 1919, indicating that the national policy to completely stop consumption of alcohol was successfully implemented.

4. (B) *This item would only appear on an SAT test, not an ACT test. It requires that you interpret the information in the graphic and apply it to the passage. According to the graph, the rate of deaths per 100,000 was the lowest in 1920. However, the rate increased through the remaining years of Prohibition. Therefore, (B) is the most persuasive argument that Prohibition was unsuccessful.*

ACT Reading Pacing

The ACT Reading Test has 40 items and a 35-minute time limit. The fact that there are four passages of approximately equal length, each with the same number of items, and a 35-minute time limit leads naturally to the conclusion that you should spend eight minutes and 45 seconds on each passage—and that's a pretty good plan. The following table summarizes the timing for this approach.

TASK	ALLOTTED TIME	REMAINING TIME
Read the first selected passage	2.5 minutes	32.5 minutes
Answer the accompanying items	6.25 minutes*	26.25 minutes
Read the second selected passage	2.5 minutes	23.75 minutes
Answer the accompanying items	6.25 minutes*	17.5 minutes
Read the third selected passage	2.5 minutes	15 minutes
Answer the accompanying items	6.25 minutes*	8.75 minutes
Read the fourth selected passage	2.5 minutes	6.25 minutes
Answer the accompanying items	6.25 minutes*	0 minutes

*Approximately 37 seconds per item

For reasons discussed in the "Personalize the Passage Order" in the Game Plan section, you might choose to start with the last passage given. It's up to you.

SAT Reading Pacing

The SAT Reading test has 52 items and a 65-minute time limit. The fact that there are five passages (four single passages and one set of paired passages) of approximately equal length, each with approximately the same number of items, and a 65-minute time limit leads naturally to the conclusion that you should spend 13 minutes on each passage—and that's a pretty good plan. The following table summarizes the timing for this approach.

TASK	ALLOTTED TIME	REMAINING TIME
Read the first selected passage	2.6 minutes	62.4 minutes
Answer the accompanying items	10.4 minutes*	52 minutes
Read the second selected passage	2.6 minutes	49.4 minutes
Answer the accompanying items	10.4 minutes*	39 minutes
Read the third selected passage	2.6 minutes	36.4 minutes
Answer the accompanying items	10.4 minutes*	26 minutes
Read the fourth selected passage	2.6 minutes	23.4 minutes
Answer the accompanying items	10.4 minutes*	13 minutes
Read the fifth selected passage	2.6 minutes	10.4 minutes
Answer the accompanying items	10.4 minutes*	0 minutes

*Approximately 60 seconds per item

For reasons discussed in the "Personalize the Passage Order" in the Game Plan section, you might choose to start with the last passage given. It's up to you.

ACT Reading and SAT Reading Time Trial

(3 items; 3 minutes)

DIRECTIONS: The passage below is followed by a set of items. Read the passage and choose the best answer for each item. You may refer to the passage as often as necessary to answer the items.

Passage I

Natural Science: This passage is an excerpt from an essay about the possible reasons for the extinction of salmon runs in New England rivers.

Folklore holds that Atlantic salmon were once so abundant in New England rivers that early colonists walked across the backs of the fish as they ran up the rivers in spring. Then, according to the received wisdom, at the turn of the nineteenth century, increasing pollution in the rivers and the construction of large dams across rivers caused salmon to become severely depleted. If this theory were accurate, then there should be ample archaeological evidence that salmon played a major role in the diets of the aboriginal peoples of New England. But in site after site, although bones of many other fish species have been recovered, no salmon bones have been found. It's more likely that the accounts of salmon were embellished by early writers.

In fact, salmon did not begin to colonize New England streams until a period of climatic cooling known as the Little Ice Age (C.E. 1550–1800). At the end of this period, the climatic warming created less favorable environmental conditions for salmon. Thus, their range retracted. The idea that initial colonization did not occur until this time, and then only as a temporary range expansion, explains the lack of salmon in prehistoric sites and the depletion of the fish at the end of the eighteenth century.

While authorities such as D. W. Lufkin have stated that "the circumstances leading to the demise of *Salmo salar* are relatively simple to identify" and have cited dams, pollution, logging practices, and over-fishing, causes behind its demise are more complex, with ecological and climatological bases. If pollution and dams were the major cause of the extinctions, then why were the runs not made extinct on the Penobscot, a heavily dammed and polluted river in Maine? Why did salmon runs become extinct downstream of the dams on the Connecticut River? The general lack of success in salmon restoration programs over the last two centuries suggests a fundamental ecological cause for impoverished salmon runs in New England rather than an anthropogenic one.

1. The primary purpose of the passage is to:

A. propose a long term plan for restoring salmon runs to the rivers of New England.
B. undermine the theory that human activity caused the extinction of salmon runs in New England rivers.
C. demonstrate that anthropogenic factors are often more powerful than natural ones in shaping the environment.
D. provide evidence that the disappearance of *Salmo salar* was caused by the damming and pollution of the rivers.

2. The author cites the lack of salmon bones in archaeological digs as evidence that:

F. the salmon population in New England rivers declined sharply after the end of the Little Ice Age.
G. aboriginal Americans, who consumed other fish species, refused to eat the abundant salmon.
H. salmon were not available to aboriginal Americans before the time of the arrival of the first colonists.
J. anthropogenic factors were largely responsible for the extinction of the salmon runs.

3. It can be inferred that D. W. Lufkin would most likely:

A. agree with the author that the primary causes of the depletion of salmon stocks are climatological.
B. accept the author's contention that early reports about the abundance of salmon were greatly exaggerated.
C. reject the author's thesis and insist that the causes of salmon extinction are anthropogenic.
D. disagree with the author that salmon stocks have declined precipitously since the end of the eighteenth century.

ACT Reading and SAT Reading Game Plan

Quickly Preview the Test Section, but Skip the Directions

Last-minute adjustments to the test format are theoretically (but not practically) possible, so check the test section before you start to work, especially the number of passages, the number of items, and the time limit. And yes, the test-writers always tell you to read the directions carefully. But they don't tell you that you have to read them during the test. Instead, become familiar with them before test day. That way, you won't waste 30 seconds or more (enough time to answer an item) re-reading directions you are already familiar with.

Personalize the Passage Order

Remember that you don't have to do the items in the order in which they are presented in the booklet. For some sections, like the math section, doing problems in order (more or less) makes good sense. But in the Reading test, it is a sound strategy to make a choice about the order in which you're going to work through the section. You may decide to do the reading passages in the order presented, or you may want to change the order.

What factors should you consider? First, you may find a topic that seems familiar to you. Of course, you can't expect that you'll already know the answers to the items, but familiarity may be an advantage. Second, you'll feel more comfortable with some topics than with others. Do you like biology but hate literature or like social science but hate ecology? Then do the passages with topics that you like first.

When you choose your passages, you should number them in the margin of your test booklet. Then, you'll formulate an order for the remaining passages and number all the passages "1" through "5."

Read Any Introductory Notes

Passages will include an introductory note telling you where the passage comes from and maybe some other information. Sometimes, this information is useful for getting a better understanding of the passage. Therefore, before starting on a passage and items, always read any introductory notes.

Preview the Passage

Before you begin reading a particular passage, take 15 to 30 seconds to preview key sentences. Key sentences are the first and last sentences of the passage and the first sentence of each paragraph. Why preview? First sentences are often topic sentences, so reading a series of topic sentences will tell you what the author is trying to say, and it can give you an outline of the development of the passage. Sometimes, though not always, the last sentence is a conclusion. Note that for short, single-paragraph passages, you will probably skip this step.

To see how this can work, preview the following passage about solar energy, in which only the key sentences are visible.

At the present time, 98 percent of world energy consumption comes from sources such as fossil fuels.

Our energy consumption amounts to about one ten-thousandth of the energy we receive from the sun.

It is often stated that the growth rate will decline or that energy conservation measures will preclude any long-range problem.

The only practical means of avoiding the problem of thermal pollution is the use of solar energy.

To see what you can learn from just a few sentences, think about these questions:

What's the passage about?

- Gas mileage.
- Space exploration.
- Solar energy.

What is a common attitude about energy conservation?

- That it doesn't work.
- That it might work.
- That it will probably work.

What's the author's view on solar energy?

- It doesn't work.
- It's unnecessary.
- It's absolutely essential.

And the answers are that the passage is about solar energy, which the author believes to be necessary, even though a lot of people think conservation could solve all our problems.

Preview the Item Stems

Additionally, before reading a particular passage, you <u>may</u> find it helpful to preview the item stems, which are presented either as questions or incomplete statements. If a stem mentions a key word or phrase, make a mental note and look for it as you read the selection. See what you would learn from the following items, in which only the item stems are visible.

1. According to the passage, the most important disadvantage of nuclear energy is

A)
B)
C)
D)

Previewing would tell you to look for certain information in your reading. The first stem uses the phrase "most important disadvantage of nuclear energy." So, you know that the passage will discuss disadvantages of nuclear energy. When you find the "most important" one, mark that reference so that you can answer this item.

2. According to the author, shifting climate patterns will have all of the following effects EXCEPT

A)
B)
C)
D)

The second stem tells you that the author discusses "shifting climate patterns," probably in some detail since the passage mentions multiple effects. Each time you find one of the effects, mark it so that when you answer this item you can eliminate those choices that mention such effects. ("EXCEPT" means to look for the one NOT mentioned in the passage.)

3. The author's attitude toward scientists who deny that average temperatures are rising can best be described as

A)
B)
C)
D)

The third stem lets you know that the passage discusses average temperatures and a theory advanced by some scientists. If you find that reference in your reading, you'll have the answer to this item.

4. Which of the following best describes the main point of the passage?

A)
B)
C)
D)

Finally, the last stem tells you to look for the main idea. That, in and of itself, is not particularly helpful because you're always reading for the main idea—even if you don't get a question that asks about it. So, some stems are not very helpful while others are.

Read the Passage

Keep the following points in mind when reading a passage:

- Read the passage quickly but carefully. You'll probably need about two to three minutes to read a single passage or a pair of passages. This is about 300 to 350 words a minute.
- Read the passage for important themes. Many of the items will ask about important themes of the passage, such as the main point, the purpose of a particular paragraph, or the author's intention.
- Do not try to memorize details. If you need detailed information, you can always go back to the passage to find it. This is an "open-book" test.
- Pause at the end to mentally summarize your reading. One of the most helpful reading techniques is to summarize in your own words what you have just read. What is the main point? What did the author do in the first paragraph? In the second paragraph? What did the author prove?

Answer the Items

Keep the following points in mind when answering the accompanying items:

- Identify the question being asked. Passage items fall into one of nine categories such as "Main Idea," "Explicit Detail," and "Vocabulary." Specific item-types have characteristic kinds of answers. If you identify the category first, it will be easier to find the right answer. You'll learn more about the nine item-types later in the Reading Lesson.
- Answer the question being asked. One of the most common mistakes made by examinees is to read the item stem carelessly and then answer the "wrong" question. That is, they respond to what they think they read rather than what is actually on the page. Since wrong answers often sound plausible, if you make this mistake, you're probably going to find a pretty good answer—to the wrong question.
- Read the answer choices carefully. In the Reading Lesson you'll learn how to recognize the nine Reading item-types and what the correct answer to each should look like. Reading comprehension doesn't stop at the end of the last sentence of the passage. It continues all the way through to the last word of the last answer choice to the last item.
- Pay attention to thought-reversers. Thought-reversers are words in the item stem like "NOT," "BUT," and "EXCEPT." These words turn the question upside down. What is normally the right answer is now a wrong answer, and what is normally a wrong answer is the right answer.
- Do not spend too much time on any one item. Remember that you get one point for the hardest question and one point for the easiest. With Reading items, the easiest ones can theoretically be the last in the group and the hardest ones can be the first. So, if you sense that you're spinning your wheels, make an educated guess and then move along.

QUIZ

ACT READING

This section contains a Reading quiz. Complete the quiz under timed conditions. Answers are on page 567.

(18 items; 15 minutes)

DIRECTIONS: Each passage below is followed by a set of items. Read the passage and choose the best answer for each item. You may refer to the passage as often as necessary to answer the items.

Passage I

Social Science: This passage discusses the economic structure of current healthcare policy.

The healthcare economy is replete with unusual and even unique economic relationships. One of the least understood involves the peculiar roles of producer or "provider" and purchaser or "consumer" in the typical doctor-patient relationship. In most sectors of the economy, the seller attempts to attract a potential buyer with various incentives of price, quality, and utility, and the buyer makes the decision. When the buyer has no choice because there is effectively only one seller and the product is essential, the government usually asserts a monopoly and places the industry under price and other regulations. Neither of these conditions prevails in most of the healthcare industry.

In the healthcare industry, the doctor-patient relationship is the mirror image of the ordinary relationship between producer and consumer. Once an individual has chosen to see a physician—and even then there may be no real choice—it is the physician who usually makes all significant purchasing decisions: whether the patient should return "next Wednesday," whether X-rays are needed, whether drugs should be prescribed, etc. It is a rare and sophisticated patient who will challenge such professional decisions or raise in advance questions about price, especially when the ailment is regarded as serious.

This is particularly significant in relation to hospital care. The physician must certify the need for hospitalization, determine what procedures will be performed, and announce when the patient may be discharged. The patient may be consulted about some of these decisions, but ultimately it is the doctor's judgments that are final. Little wonder, then, that in the eyes of the hospital, the physician is the real "consumer." Consequently, the medical staff represents the "power center" in hospital policy and decision-making, not the administration.

Although usually there are in this situation four identifiable participants—the physician, the hospital, the patient, and the payer (generally an insurance carrier or government)—the physician makes the key decisions for all of them. The hospital becomes an extension of the physician; the payer generally meets most of the bona fide bills generated by the doctor/hospital; and for the most part the patient plays a passive role. In routine or minor illnesses, or just plain worries, the patient's options are, of course, much greater with respect to use and price. In illnesses that are more serious, however, such choices tend to evaporate, and it is for these illnesses that the bulk of the healthcare dollar is spent. We estimate that 75 to 80 percent of healthcare expenditures are determined by physicians, not patients. For this reason, economy measures directed at patients or the public are relatively ineffective.

1. In line 1, the phrase "replete with" most nearly means:

    A. filled with.
    B. restricted by.
    C. enriched by.
    D. damaged by.

2. The author's primary purpose is to:

F. speculate about the relationship between a patient's ability to pay and the treatment received.
G. criticize doctors for exercising too much control over patients.
H. analyze some important economic factors in healthcare.
J. urge hospitals to reclaim their decision-making authority.

3. It can be inferred that doctors are able to determine hospital policies because:

A. it is doctors who generate income for the hospital.
B. most of a patient's bills are paid by health insurance.
C. hospital administrators lack the expertise to question medical decisions.
D. a doctor is ultimately responsible for a patient's health.

4. According to the author, when a doctor tells a patient to "return next Wednesday," the doctor is in effect:

F. taking advantage of the patient's concern for his health.
G. instructing the patient to buy more medical services.
H. warning the patient that a hospital stay might be necessary.
J. advising the patient to seek a second opinion.

5. The author is most probably leading up to:

A. a proposal to control medical costs.
B. a discussion of a new medical treatment.
C. an analysis of the causes of inflation in the United States.
D. a study of lawsuits against doctors for malpractice.

6. The tone of the passage can best be described as:

F. whimsical.
G. cautious.
H. analytical.
J. inquisitive.

7. With which of the following statements would the author be most likely to agree?

A. Few patients are reluctant to object to the course of treatment prescribed by a doctor or to question the cost of the services.
B. The payer, whether an insurance carrier or the government, is less likely to acquiesce to demands for payment when the illness of the patient is regarded as serious.
C. Today's patients are more informed as to what services and procedures they will need from their healthcare providers.
D. The more serious the illness of a patient, the less likely it is that the patient will object to the course of treatment prescribed or question the cost of services.

8. The author's primary concern is to:

F. define a term.
G. clarify a misunderstanding.
H. refute a theory.
J. discuss a problem.

Passage II

Humanities: This passage discusses Leif Ericsson's and Biarni's voyages to North America.

In the summer of 999, Leif Ericsson voyaged to Norway and spent the following winter with King Olaf Tryggvason. Substantially the same account is given by both the Saga of Eric the Red and the Flat Island Book. Of Leif's return voyage to Greenland, the latter says nothing. But according to the former, it was during this return voyage that Leif discovered America. The Flat Island Book, however, tells of another and earlier landfall by Biarni, the son of a prominent man named Heriulf. It makes this trip Leif's inspiration for the voyage to the new land. In short, like Leif, Biarni and his companions discovered three countries in succession before reaching Greenland. To come upon each new land takes one "doegr" more than the last until Biarni comes to land directly in front of his father's house in the last-mentioned country.

Most later writers have rejected this narrative, and they may be justified. Possibly, Biarni was a companion of Leif when he voyaged from Norway to Greenland via America. Or it may be that the entire tale is but a garbled account of that voyage and Biarni is another name for Leif. It should be noted, however, that the stories of Leif's visit to King Olaf and Biarni's to that king's predecessor are in the same narrative in the Flat Island Book. So there is less likelihood of duplication than if they were from different sources. Also, Biarni landed on none of the lands he passed, but Leif apparently landed on one, for he brought back specimens of wheat, vines, and timber. Nor is there any good reason to believe that the first land visited by Biarni was Wineland. The first land was "level and covered with woods," and "there were small hillocks upon it." Later writers do not emphasize forests particularly in connection with Wineland, though they are often noted incidentally; and of hills, the Saga says of Wineland only "wherever there was hilly ground, there were vines."

Additionally, if the two narratives were from the same source, we should expect a closer resemblance of Helluland. The Saga says of it: "They found there hellus" (large flat stones). According to the Biarni narrative, however, "this land was high and mountainous." The intervals of one, two, three, and four "doegr" in both narratives are suggestive. But mythic formulas of this kind may be introduced into narratives without altogether destroying their validity. It is also held against the Biarni narrative that its hero is made to come upon the coast of Greenland exactly in front of his father's home. But it should be recalled that Heriulfsness lay below two high mountains that served as landmarks for navigators.

I would give up Biarni more readily were it not that the story of Leif's voyage, contained in the supposedly more reliable Saga, is almost as amazing. But Leif's voyage across the entire width of the North Atlantic is said to be "probable" because it is documented in the narrative of a preferred authority. Biarni's is "improbable," or even "impossible," because the document containing it has been condemned.

9. The author's primary concern is to demonstrate that:

A. Leif Ericsson did not visit America.
B. Biarni might have visited America before Leif Ericsson.
C. Biarni did not visit Wineland.
D. Leif Ericsson visited Wineland first.

10. The passage provides information that defines which of the following terms?

I. Doegr
II. Hellus
III. Heriulfsness

F. I only
G. II only
H. I and II only
J. II and III only

11. It can be inferred from the passage that scholars who doubt the authenticity of the Biarni narrative make all of the following objections EXCEPT:

A. Biarni might have accompanied Leif Ericsson on the voyage to America, and that is why a separate, erroneous narrative was invented.
B. the similarity of the voyages described in the Saga and in the Flat Island Book indicates that there was but one voyage, not two voyages.
C. it seems very improbable that a ship, having sailed from America to Greenland, could have found its way to a precise point on the coast of Greenland.
D. both the Saga of Eric the Red and the Flat Island Book make use of mythic formulas, so it is probable that the same person wrote them both.

12. The author mentions the two high mountains (lines 52–53) in order to show that it is:

F. reasonable for Biarni to land precisely at his father's home.
G. possible to sail from Norway to Greenland without modern navigational equipment.
H. likely that Biarni landed on America at least 100 years before Leif Ericsson.
J. probable that Leif Ericsson followed the same course as Biarni.

13. All of the following are mentioned as similarities between Leif Ericsson's voyage and Biarni's voyage EXCEPT:

A. both visited Norway.
B. on the return voyage, both visited three different lands.
C. both returned to Greenland.
D. both sighted Wineland.

14. It can be inferred that the author regards the historicity of the Biarni narrative as:

F. conclusively proved.
G. almost conclusively proved.
H. possibly true.
J. highly unlikely.

15. In the final paragraph, the author suggests that some authorities who regard the Saga as authentic are guilty of which of the following errors in reasoning?

A. Oversimplification
B. Logical contradiction
C. False analogy
D. Circular reasoning

16. According to the passage, Heriulf is:

F. Leif Ericsson's son.
G. one of Leif Ericsson's sailors.
H. Biarni's father.
J. King Olaf Tryggvason's son.

17. According to the author, most authorities regard the Biarni narrative as:

A. conclusively demonstrated.
B. probably true.
C. probably untrue.
D. an attempted fraud.

18. Biarni's home was in:

F. Norway.
G. Greenland.
H. Wineland.
J. Flat Island.

QUIZ

SAT READING

Complete this quiz under timed conditions. Answers are on page 567.

(17 items; 15 minutes)

DIRECTIONS: Each passage below is followed by a set of items. Read the passage and choose the best answer for each item. You may refer to the passage as often as necessary to answer the items.

Passage I

Items #1–10 refer to the following passage.

This passage discusses the 1796 presidential election between Thomas Jefferson and John Adams.

"Heartily tired" from the brutal, almost daily, conflicts that erupted between himself and Alexander Hamilton, Thomas Jefferson resigned his position as Secretary of State in 1793. His Federalist opponents were convinced that this was merely a strategic withdrawal to allow him an opportunity to plan and promote his candidacy for the presidency should Washington step down in 1796. Jefferson, however, insisted that this retirement from public life was to be final.

But even in retirement, the world of politics pursued him. As the election grew nearer and it became apparent that Washington would not seek a third term, rumors of Jefferson's presidential ambitions grew in intensity. He reacted to these continuous insinuations in a letter to James Madison. Jefferson admitted that while his enemies had originated the idea that he coveted the office of chief executive, he had been forced to examine his true feelings on the subject for his own peace of mind. In so doing, he concluded that his reasons for retirement—the desire for privacy and the delight of family life—coupled with his now failing health were insuperable barriers to public service. The "little spice of ambition" he had in his younger days had long since evaporated and the question of his presidency was forever closed.

Jefferson did not actively engage in the campaign on his own behalf. The Republican Party, presaging modern campaign tactics, created a grass roots sentiment for their candidate by directing their efforts toward the general populace. In newspapers, Jefferson was presented as "the uniform advocate of equal rights among the citizens" while Adams was portrayed as the "champion of rank, titles, heredity, and distinctions."

Jefferson was not certain of the outcome of the election until the end of December. Under the original electoral system established by the Constitution, each presidential elector cast his ballot for two men without designating between them as to office. The candidate who received the greater number of votes became the president; the second highest, the vice president. Based on his own calculations, Jefferson foresaw that the electoral vote would be close. He wrote to Madison that in the event of a tie, he wished for the choice to be in favor of Adams. The New Englander had always been his senior in public office, he explained, and the expression of public will being equal, he should be preferred for the higher honor. Jefferson, a shrewd politician, realized that the transition of power from the nearly mythical Washington to a lesser luminary in the midst of the deep and bitter political divisions facing the nation could be perilous. He had no desire to be caught in the storm that had been brewing for four years and was about to break. "This is certainly not a moment to covet the helm," he wrote to Edward Rutledge. When the electoral vote was tallied, Adams emerged as the victor. Rejoicing at his "escape," Jefferson was completely satisfied with the decision. Despite their obvious and basic political differences, Jefferson genuinely respected John Adams as a friend and compatriot. Although he believed that Adams had deviated from the course set in 1776, Jefferson never felt a diminution of confidence in Adams' integrity and was confident he would not steer the nation too far off its Republican tack. Within two years, Jefferson's views would be drastically altered as measures such as the Alien and Sedition Acts of 1798 convinced him of the need to wrest control of the government from the Federalists.

1. The phrase "heartily tired" (line 1) is most probably a quotation from

A) Alexander Hamilton.
B) Thomas Jefferson.
C) George Washington.
D) John Adams.

2. The "escape" mentioned in line 61 refers to the fact that Jefferson

A) was no longer Secretary of State.
B) would not be burdened with the problems of the presidency.
C) fled the country following the election.
D) was hoping that the votes would be recounted.

3. According to the passage, the Republican Party appealed primarily to

A) wealthy landowners.
B) ordinary people.
C) prosperous merchants.
D) high society.

4. The author states that all of the following were reasons Jefferson resigned as Secretary of State EXCEPT

A) Jefferson disliked Madison.
B) Jefferson wanted to spend time with his family.
C) Jefferson was weary of the demands of public service.
D) Jefferson wished for greater privacy.

5. The author is primarily concerned with revealing

A) the feud between Alexander Hamilton and Thomas Jefferson.
B) the difference between the Federalists and the Republicans.
C) the strategies used by early American political parties.
D) Thomas Jefferson's character and personality.

6. The author relies on which of the following in developing the selection?

I. Personal correspondence
II. Newspapers
III. Voter registration rolls

A) I only
B) II only
C) I and II only
D) I and III only

7. One reason for Jefferson's retirement was his disagreement with

A) Alexander Hamilton.
B) George Washington.
C) James Madison.
D) Edward Rutledge.

8. In the context of the passage, the phrase "covet the helm" (lines 58–59) means

A) to aspire to be president.
B) to desire to purchase a boat.
C) to wish to be left in peace.
D) to hope to become wealthy.

9. The passage suggests that two years after the 1796 election, Jefferson would

A) ally himself with Alexander Hamilton.
B) ally himself with John Adams.
C) disagree with John Adams.
D) disagree with Edward Rutledge.

10. The newspaper depicted Jefferson and Adams as

A) conservative and liberal, respectively.
B) liberal and conservative, respectively.
C) conservatives.
D) liberals.

Passage II

Items #11–17 refer to the following passage.

This passage discusses human social evolution and adaptation.

Man, so the truism goes, lives increasingly in a man-made environment. This puts a special burden on human immaturity, for it is plain that adapting to such variable conditions must depend on opportunities for learning, or whatever the processes are that are operative during immaturity. It must also mean that during immaturity, man must master knowledge and skills that are neither stored in the gene pool nor learned by direct encounter. Rather, they are contained in the culture pool—knowledge about values and history, skills as varied as an obligatory natural language or an optional mathematical one, as mute as levers or as articulate as myth telling.

Yet, it would be a mistake to leap to the conclusion that because human immaturity makes possible high flexibility, anything is possible for the species. Human traits were selected for their survival value over a four- to five-million-year period with a great acceleration of the selection process during the last half of that period. There were crucial, irreversible changes during that final man-making period: the recession of formidable dentition, a 50-percent increase in brain volume, the obstetrical paradox—bipedalism and strong pelvic girdle, larger brain through a smaller birth canal—an immature brain at birth, and creation of what Washburn has called a "technical-social way of life," involving tool and symbol use.

Note, however, that hominidization consisted mainly of adaptations to conditions in the Pleistocene. These preadaptations, shaped in response to earlier habitat demands, are part of man's evolutionary inheritance. This is not to say that close beneath the skin of man is a naked ape, that civilization is only a veneer. The technical-social way of life is a deep feature of the species adaptation. But we would err if we assumed that man's inheritance placed no constraint on his power to adapt. Some of the preadaptations can be shown to be presently maladaptive. Man's inordinate fondness for fats and sweets no longer serves his individual survival well. Furthermore, the human obsession with sexuality is plainly not fitted for survival of the species now, however well it might have served to populate the upper Pliocene and the Pleistocene. Nevertheless, note that the species typically responds to these challenges by technical innovation rather than by morphological or behavioral change. Contraception dissociates sexuality from reproduction. Of course, we do not know what kinds and what range of stresses are produced by successive rounds of such technical innovation. Dissociating sexuality and reproduction, for example, surely produces changes in the structure of the family, which in turn redefines the role of women, which in turn alters the authority pattern affecting the child, etc. Continuing and possibly accelerating change seems inherent in such adaptation. This, of course, places an enormous pressure on man's uses of immaturity, preparing the young for unforeseeable change—the more so if there are severe restraints imposed by human preadaptations to earlier conditions of life.

11. The primary purpose of the passage is to

A) refute some misconceptions about the importance of human immaturity.
B) introduce a new theory of the origins of the human species.
C) describe the evolutionary forces that formed the physical appearance of modern humans.
D) discuss the importance of human immaturity as an adaptive mechanism.

12. It can be inferred that the obstetrical paradox is puzzling because

A) it occurred very late during the evolution of the species.
B) evolutionary forces seemed to work at cross purposes to each other.
C) technological innovations have made the process of birth easier.
D) an increase in brain size is not an ordinary evolutionary event.

13. Which of the following statements can be inferred from the passage?

A) Human beings today are less sexually active than were our ancestors during the Pleistocene era.
B) During the Pleistocene era, a fondness for fats and sweets was a trait that contributed to human survival.
C) Mathematics was invented by human beings during the latter half of the Pleistocene era.
D) The use of language and tools is a trait that is genetically transmitted from one generation to the next.

14. As it is used in line 32, the word "preadaptations" refers to traits that

A) were useful to earlier human beings but have since lost their utility.
B) appeared in response to the need to learn a natural language and the use of tools.
C) humans currently exhibit but that developed in response to conditions of an earlier age.
D) are disadvantageous to creatures whose way of life is primarily technical and social.

15. The author mentions contraception to demonstrate that

A) human beings may adapt to new conditions by technological invention rather than by changing their behavior.
B) sexual promiscuity is no longer an aid to the survival of the human species.
C) technological innovation is a more important adaptive mechanism than either heredity or direct encounter.
D) conditions during the upper Pliocene and Pleistocene eras no longer affect the course of human evolution.

16. With which of the following statements would the author LEAST likely agree?

A) The technical-social way of human life is an adaptive mechanism that arose in response to environmental pressures.
B) The possibility of technical innovation makes it unlikely that the physical appearance of humans will change radically in a short time.
C) Technological innovations can result in changes in the social structures in which humans live.
D) The fact that humans have a technical-social way of life makes the species immune from evolutionary pressures.

17. The author is most probably addressing which of the following audiences?

A) Medical students in a course on human anatomy
B) College students in an introductory course on archaeology
C) Psychologists investigating the uses of human immaturity
D) Biologists trying to trace the course of human evolution

STRATEGY SUMMARY

ACT READING AND SAT READING

Reading Strategies

Understanding the three levels of reading comprehension and how they relate to the nine SAT Reading and ACT Reading item-types will help you to identify quickly the question that is being asked by a particular item.

Information and Ideas

The first group of Reading items, Information and Ideas items, tests your general understanding of the passage, your understanding of specific details in the passage, and your ability to evaluate the passage.

Main Idea items ask about the central theme that unifies the passage(s). The first sentence of a paragraph—often the topic sentence—may provide a summary of the content of that paragraph. Also, the last sentence of a paragraph usually provides concluding material that may also be helpful in understanding the general theme of the passage.

- *Which of the following is the main point of the passage?*
- *The primary purpose of the passage is to . . .*

Explicit Detail items ask about details that are specifically mentioned in the passage. This type of item differs from a Main Idea item in that explicit details are points provided by the author in developing the main idea of the passage. Explicit Detail items provide "locator words" that identify the required information in the passage.

- *The author mentions which of the following?*
- *According to the passage, . . . ?*

Implied Idea items don't ask about what is specifically stated in the passage; rather, Implied Idea items ask about what can be logically inferred from what is stated in the passage. For example, the passage might explain that a certain organism (X) is found only in the presence of another organism (Y). An accompanying Implied Idea item might ask the following question: "If organism Y is not present, what can be inferred?" Since the passage implies that in the absence of Y, X cannot be present, the answer would be "X is not present." Since this type of item generally builds on a specific detail, "locator words" for identifying information in the passage are often provided in the item stem.

- *The passage implies that . . .*
- *The author uses the phrase " . . . " to mean . . .*

Application items are similar to Implied Idea items, but they go one step further: examinees must apply what they have learned from the passage to a new situation.

- *With which of the following statements would the author most likely agree?*
- *The passage is most probably taken from which of the following sources?*

Passage Development

This group of Reading items deals with the structure of the passage. Development, Textual Evidence, and Voice items all test your ability to understand the underlying structure and tone of the passage. Since this is an "open-book" test, returning to the selection is always an option. Therefore, if something is highly technical or difficult to understand, do not dwell on it for too long—come back later if necessary.

Development items ask about the overall structure of the passage or about the logical role played by a specific part of the passage.

- *The author develops the passage primarily by . . .*
- *The author mentions . . . in order to . . .*

Textual Evidence items ask which phrases or sentences in the passage support a particular conclusion or claim. These items only appear on the SAT test.

- *Which of the following sentences provides direct support for . . . ?*
- *Which of the follow phrases supports the author's claim that . . . ?*

Voice items ask about the author's attitude toward a specific detail or the overall tone of the passage.

- *The tone of the passage can best be described as . . .*
- *The author regards . . . as . . .*

Vocabulary

The third category of Reading item is Vocabulary. The nature of the Vocabulary items indicates two points. First, the correct answer choice will make sense when it is substituted for the referenced word. Second, the correct answer choice may not be the most commonly used meaning of the word.

Vocabulary items test the understanding of a word or phrase in context.

- *The word "-------" in line ## means . . .*
- *In line ##, what is the best definition of the word "-------"?*

Data Presentations

The final category of Reading item is Data Presentations. Some Reading passages include a graphic or data presentation, and Reading questions may ask how the information in the data presentations relates to the information presented in the passage.

Data Presentations items test the understanding of graphics or data corresponding to the reading selection. These items only appear on the SAT test.

- *Which of the following best summarizes the information presented in the graph?*
- *According to the data presentation, which of the following is true about . . . ?*

General Strategies

Reading strategies are not an exact science. Practice is essential to master the following techniques:

1. **Preview the Passage:** Read the first and last sentence of each passage in the test section. After reading the first sentence of each passage, label each passage as either "Easy" or "Hard" based on your initial understanding of the material and your level of interest. Analyze the easier passages first.

2. **Preview Each Paragraph:** There is usually an introductory paragraph from the excerpted passages that identifies the author and provides a brief description of the selection. First, read this introductory material to gain clues as to the author's point of view. Then, preview the first and last sentences of each paragraph, as they often provide paragraph summaries.

3. **Preview the Item Stems:** Skim the item stems, making note of stems that mention key words or phrases. Look for those words or phrases as you read the passage.

4. **Read the Passage:** Ask what the author is attempting to describe. Also, read the first sentence in each paragraph prior to reading the entire selection. This step is optional, depending on the ease of the selection, your personal preference, and the time available. Bracket difficult material, either mentally or with some sort of a mark, and then simply revisit it if necessary or if time permits. Instead of wasting time re-reading, attempt to understand the context in which the author introduces a particular concept.

5. **Code in Groups:** If you are taking a paper-and-pencil test, circle the answers to the items in the test booklet and transcribe the answers to all the items for a passage to the answer sheet after finishing each passage. This approach helps increase accuracy and makes checking your work easier and more efficient. Transcribe the answers to the answer sheet together as a group. Only when the time limit approaches should you transcribe each answer individually.

ACT English and SAT Writing and Language

Course Concept Outline

---

[1] Some concepts in this Course Concept Outline are not illustrated through examples in your student text but may be covered by your instructor in class. They are included here to provide a complete outline of your course.

LESSON 1 | STANDARD ENGLISH CONVENTIONS

ACT ENGLISH AND SAT WRITING AND LANGUAGE

The passages and items in this section accompany the in-class review of the skills and concepts tested by the SAT® Writing and Language Test. You will work through the items with your instructor in class. Answers are on page 568.

Grammar and Usage

Subject-Verb Agreement Ⓐ Ⓢ

DIRECTIONS: Each passage is followed by a set of items. For each item, you will select the choice that improves the passage's expression of ideas or corrects errors in sentence structure, usage, or punctuation. A passage or a question may be accompanied by one or more graphics that you will consider as you make editing decisions.

Some items will direct you to an underlined portion of a passage, and others will direct you to a location in a passage or ask you to think about the passage as a whole.

For each item, choose the answer to each question that most effectively improves the quality of writing in the passage or that makes the passage follow the conventions of standard written English. Choose the "NO CHANGE" option if you think the best choice is to leave the relevant portion of the passage as it is.

1. The professor <u>were traveling</u> in Europe when she received notice of her promotion.

A) NO CHANGE
B) was traveling
C) travels
D) is traveling

Material Inserted Between Subject and Verb Ⓐ Ⓢ

2. The professor voted Teacher of the Year by the students <u>were traveling</u> in Europe when she received notice of her promotion.

A) NO CHANGE
B) was traveling
C) travels
D) is traveling

3. Most teachers, unless they have an appointment to a prestigious university, <u>earns</u> relatively less as teachers than they might in business.

A) NO CHANGE
B) earned
C) earn
D) will be earning

4. Many nutritionists now believe that a balanced diet and not large doses of vitamins <u>are</u> the best guarantee of health.

A) NO CHANGE
B) is
C) was
D) will be

5. Television comedies in which there is at least one really detestable character captures the interest of viewers.

A) NO CHANGE
B) did capture
C) captured
D) capture

6. The opposition to smoking in public places are prompting many state legislatures to consider banning smoking in such locations.

A) NO CHANGE
B) is prompting many state legislatures to consider
C) are prompting many state legislatures considering
D) is prompting many state legislatures considering

7. Diplomats sent to an unstable region or a genuinely hostile territory usually is assigned an aide or chauffeur who function also as a bodyguard.

A) NO CHANGE
B) are assigned an aide or chauffeur who function
C) are assigned an aide or chauffeur who functions
D) is assigned an aide or chauffeur that function

Inverted Sentence Structure Ⓐ Ⓢ

8. Though this is the wealthiest country in the world, within a few blocks of the White House, there is scores of homeless people who live on the streets.

A) NO CHANGE
B) there could be
C) there are
D) are there

9. Just a few miles from the factories and skyscrapers stand a medieval castle that looks exactly as it did in the twelfth century.

A) NO CHANGE
B) stood
C) is standing
D) stands

Compound Subjects Ⓐ Ⓢ

10. John, his wife, and the rest of his family plans to attend the award dinner hosted by the company to honor the employees with the most seniority.

A) NO CHANGE
B) plan
C) having planned
D) they plan

11. Either the governor or one of his close aides prefer not to have the senator seated at the head table where he would be conspicuous.

A) NO CHANGE
B) was preferring
C) does prefer
D) prefers

12. Surrounded by layers of excelsior, none of the crystal goblets were broken when the workers dropped the crate.

A) NO CHANGE
B) got broke
C) had broken
D) broken

Pronoun Usage

Pronouns Must Have Antecedents Ⓐ Ⓢ

13. During her rise to fame, she betrayed many of her friends, and because of it, very few people trust her.

A) NO CHANGE
B) and in spite of it
C) and even though
D) and because of her behavior

14. In New York City, they are brusque and even rude but quick to come to one another's assistance in a time of crisis.

A) NO CHANGE
B) the people there are
C) people are
D) some are

Antecedents Must Be Clear Ⓐ Ⓢ

15. Ten years ago, the United States imported ten times as much French wine as Italian wine, but today Americans are drinking more of it.

A) NO CHANGE
B) of them
C) French wine
D) Italian wine

Pronoun-Antecedent Agreement Ⓐ Ⓢ

16. Although a police officer used to be a symbol of authority, today they receive little respect from most people.

A) NO CHANGE
B) they received
C) he or she receives
D) police officers can receive

17. Mrs. Martinez was an effective administrator who attempted to assign each volunteer a task particularly suited to their talents and training.

A) NO CHANGE
B) his or her
C) your
D) there

18. After three years of college education, one should be allowed to apply to graduate school, because by that time you are ready to choose a profession.

A) NO CHANGE
B) a profession can be chosen
C) your profession is ready to be chosen
D) one is ready to choose a profession

19. If one wishes to apply for a scholarship, you must submit a completed application by March 1.

A) NO CHANGE
B) one must have submitted the application already
C) a completed application must be submitted
D) your application must be submitted

Pronouns Must Have Proper Case Ⓐ Ⓢ

20. The judges were unable to make a final decision on a single winner, so they divided the first prize between John and he.

A) NO CHANGE
B) he and John
C) John and himself
D) John and him

21. Although Peter had been looking forward to the debate for weeks, a sore throat prevented him taking part.

A) NO CHANGE
B) prevented taking his part
C) prevented his taking part
D) prevented he from taking part

Adjectives versus Adverbs

Adjectives Modify Nouns; Adverbs Modify Verbs, Adjectives, and Other Adverbs Ⓐ Ⓢ

22. The company's mission statement took into consideration the significant changes that were made in the field of technology.

A) NO CHANGE
B) significantly changes
C) significant changed
D) significantly changed

23. When asked about the chance that the defenders might concentrate their forces at the beachhead, the general responded tart that he was fully aware of all the possibilities.

A) NO CHANGE
B) tartly that he was full
C) tart that he was full
D) tartly that he was fully

Linking Verbs Ⓐ Ⓢ

24. When the door burst open, Kevin looked up angry from his desk.

A) NO CHANGE
B) was looking up angry
C) looked up angrily
D) looks up angrily

25. The director explained that the scene required Edmund to look distraughtly on hearing the news of his sister's death.

A) NO CHANGE
B) looking distraughtly
C) to have looked distraughtly
D) to look distraught

Watch for Adjectives Posing as Adverbs Ⓐ Ⓢ

26. Some psychologists maintain that a child who has seen violence on television is more likely to react violent in situations of stress.

A) NO CHANGE
B) to react violently
C) to react with violent
D) reacting violently

27. The recent created commission has done nothing to address the problem except to approve the color of its stationery.

A) NO CHANGE
B) recent creation
C) recently created
D) created recently

28. The track meet begins at 10:00 a.m., so the team needs to depart from the school at a reasonable early hour.

A) NO CHANGE
B) at a reasonably early hour
C) during a reasonable early hour
D) at a reasonably hour that is early

Double Negatives Ⓐ Ⓢ

29. Not hardly a sound could be heard in the auditorium when the speaker approached the dais to announce the result of the contest.

A) NO CHANGE
B) No sounds could not be heard
C) Hardly a sound could be heard
D) Sounds couldn't not be heard

30. Although she had been hired by the magazine to write book reviews, she knew scarcely nothing about current fiction.

A) NO CHANGE
B) as if she knew anything
C) she didn't know nothing
D) she knew scarcely anything

Nouns and Noun Clauses Ⓐⓢ

31. The reason Harriet fired her secretary is because he was frequently late and spent too much time on personal phone calls.

A) NO CHANGE
B) although
C) that
D) because of the fact

32. The reason the manager changed pitchers was because he knew that the opposing side had a left-handed batter.

A) NO CHANGE
B) The reason that pitchers were changed by the manager was because
C) The reason the manager changed pitchers which
D) The manager changed pitchers because

33. I read in a magazine where scientists believe they have discovered a new subatomic particle.

A) NO CHANGE
B) in which
C) that
D) about

Faulty or Illogical Comparisons Ⓐⓢ

34. The company offers plastic key cards so that employees can carry them in their wallet.

A) NO CHANGE
B) can carry them in their wallets
C) can carry it in their wallet
D) can carry it in their wallets

35. The great pianist Vladimir Horowitz played the music of the Romantic Era better than any pianist in history.

A) NO CHANGE
B) the best of any pianist in history
C) better than any other pianist in history
D) better compared to any other pianist in history

36. Like Neil Simon, many of Tennessee Williams' plays reflect a culture familiar to the playwright.

A) NO CHANGE
B) Many of Tennessee Williams' plays, like Neil Simon's,
C) Many of Tennessee Williams' plays, like Neil Simon,
D) As with the plays of Neil Simon, many of Tennessee Williams' plays

37. Educators are now expressing their concern that American school children prefer watching television to books.

A) NO CHANGE
B) prefer television to reading books
C) prefers television to books
D) prefer watching television to reading books

38. The novels of Nathaniel Hawthorne contain characters who are every bit as sinister and frightening as the master of cinematic suspense, Alfred Hitchcock.

A) NO CHANGE
B) as those of the master
C) like the master
D) like those of the master

Verb Tense

Principal Parts of Verbs Ⓐⓢ

39. After the broken glass and other debris were cleaned up, we realized that the thief had took not only the necklace but a valuable ring as well.

A) NO CHANGE
B) had taken
C) was took
D) was taken

40. Everyone was very surprised when Sylvia brought her grandfather to music class and asked him to perform several Spanish songs on the guitar.

A) NO CHANGE
B) because Sylvia bringing
C) that Sylvia brang
D) for Sylvia to bring

41. The sheriff called off the search for the escaped convict because he doubted that the convict can successfully cross the river because the current was so swift.

A) NO CHANGE
B) the convict successfully crossed the river because the current was so swift
C) the convict would have been successful in crossing the river, the current being so swift
D) a successful attempt to cross the river was made by the convict because the current was so swift

When to Use the Perfect Tenses ⒶⓈ

42. Elaine is the favorite to win the final event because she had always run well at the 100-meter distance.

A) NO CHANGE
B) has always run
C) always ran
D) will always run

43. My computer crashed several times before I finally figured out that I had loaded a corrupted copy of the program.

A) NO CHANGE
B) had finally figured out that I loaded
C) had finally figured out that I had loaded
D) finally had figured out that I loaded

44. At the current rate of consumption, we have exhausted our supply of firewood before the weather turns warm.

A) NO CHANGE
B) had exhausted
C) will exhaust
D) will have exhausted

The Subjunctive Mood ⒶⓈ

45. The will is going to be read at 3:00 p.m., so the lawyer has asked that all family members are present in the office at that time.

A) NO CHANGE
B) are presently
C) are going to be present
D) be present

46. A dangerous situation could arise if the override switch were left open and the water drops below 50 percent of capacity.

A) NO CHANGE
B) dropped
C) allowed to drop
D) allows to drop

Sequence and Verb Tense ⒶⓈ

47. The teacher began to discuss the homework assignment when he will be interrupted by the sound of the fire alarm.

A) NO CHANGE
B) had been interrupted by
C) was interrupted by
D) interrupted

48. The conductor announced that the concert would resume as soon as the soloist replaces the broken string on her violin.

A) NO CHANGE
B) replaced
C) will replace
D) would replace

49. Many patients begin to show symptoms again after they stopped taking the drug.

A) NO CHANGE
B) will stop taking
C) stop to take
D) stop taking

50. The winter was so severe that several of Hillary's prize rose bushes had sustained serious damage from the frost.

A) NO CHANGE
B) are in danger of sustaining
C) will sustain
D) sustained

Diction

Wrong Preposition Ⓐⓢ

51. In contrast of the prevailing opinion, the editorial lays the blame for the strike on the workers and their representatives.

A) NO CHANGE
B) Contrasting
C) In contrast to
D) In contrast with

52. Although ballet and modern dance are both concerned in movement in space to musical accompaniment, the training for ballet is more rigorous than that for modern dance.

A) NO CHANGE
B) concerned with
C) concerning
D) concerned to

Wrong Word Choice Ⓐⓢ

53. By midnight the guests still had not been served anything to eat, so they were ravishing.

A) NO CHANGE
B) they are ravenous
C) they had been ravishing
D) they were ravenous

54. The raise in the number of accidents attributable to drunk drivers has prompted a call for stiffer penalties for driving while intoxicated.

A) NO CHANGE
B) raising
C) rise
D) rising

Gerund versus Infinitive Ⓐⓢ

55. The idea of trying completing the term paper by Friday caused Ken to cancel his plans for the weekend.

A) NO CHANGE
B) complete
C) to complete
D) to completing

56. Psychologists think that many people eat satisfying a need for affection that is not otherwise fulfilled.

A) NO CHANGE
B) to satisfy
C) to have satisfied
D) satisfy

Sentence Structure

Run-On Sentences Ⓐⓢ

57. The armor plating on the new tank protects more vulnerable areas than the armor on the old tank, it costs about three times as much to manufacture and install.

A) NO CHANGE
B) areas than the armor on the old tank, because it costs
C) areas than the armor on the old tank, and it costs
D) areas than the armor on the old tank, which costs

58. The filibuster continued late into the night some senators slept sitting upright in the chairs while others slumped over their desks.

A) NO CHANGE
B) As the filibuster continued late into the night, some
C) The filibuster continued late into the night with some
D) The filibuster, which continued late into the night, some

Comma Splices Ⓐⓢ

59. The weather forecast predicted heavy rain, the baseball game was postponed until the following day.

A) NO CHANGE
B) rain while the
C) rain, so the
D) rain the

60. The devastation caused by the flood was so complete, it was impossible to tell that the pile of debris had once been a house.

A) NO CHANGE
B) so complete, and it
C) so complete that it
D) so completely, it

Fragments Ⓐⓢ

61. The audience, dazzled by the sequined costumes and brilliant lights and applauded wildly.

A) NO CHANGE
B) brilliant lights, applauded
C) brilliant lights applauding
D) brilliant lights had applauded

62. Most of the delegates, who were from smaller villages and rural areas and so opposed any plans to improve conditions in the large cities.

A) NO CHANGE
B) rural areas and so opposed to
C) rural areas, they opposed
D) rural areas, opposed

Problems of Coordination and Subordination Ⓐⓢ

63. Carlos telephoned to say that weather had delayed his plane, but he will not be able to attend the meeting.

A) NO CHANGE
B) plane, so he will
C) plane, but he would
D) plane because he will

64. By the fifth inning, Cindy was showing signs of fatigue and walked three consecutive batters, so the coach refused to take her out of the game.

A) NO CHANGE
B) batters, when
C) batters, moreover
D) batters, but

65. Because the wetlands were protected by federal law, the owners were not able to build the shopping center that they had planned.

A) NO CHANGE
B) However
C) Moreover
D) So that

66. Victoria was nominated to the office of club president, or it is doubtful that she would serve even if elected.

A) NO CHANGE
B) president so
C) president, though
D) president, in that

67. The driving snow made the roadway slippery and reduced visibility to no more than a few feet, and fortunately there were no accidents despite the heavy volume of traffic.

A) NO CHANGE
B) but fortunately there were no
C) if fortunately there were no
D) so fortunately there were no

68. The land surrounding Las Vegas is characterized by parched red dunes and flats with dry ravines, but it is almost entirely lacking in vegetation.

A) NO CHANGE
B) or it is
C) and it is
D) whereas it is

69. Kari stopped applying to schools and she learned of her acceptance at her first choice.

A) NO CHANGE
B) so she learned
C) but she learned
D) when she learned

70. Although the American relay team did not qualify for the finals, the anchor runner dropped the baton shortly after the hand-off.

A) NO CHANGE
B) When the American relay team did not qualify for the finals, the
C) The American relay team did not qualify for the finals because the
D) Not qualifying for the finals, the American relay team's

Faulty Parallelism Ⓐ Ⓢ

71. To abandon their homes, leave behind their families, and traveling across the ocean required great courage on the part of the immigrants who moved to America.

A) NO CHANGE
B) travel across the ocean
C) to travel across the ocean
D) while traveling across the ocean

72. The review praised the wit, charm, and interpreting of the recitalist but never once mentioned her voice.

A) NO CHANGE
B) interpretation of the recitalist
C) interpreted the recitalist
D) interpretive of the recitalist

73. To acknowledge that one has something to learn is taking the first step on the road to true wisdom.

A) NO CHANGE
B) taken the first step
C) to taking the first step
D) to take the first step

Incomplete Split Constructions Ⓐ Ⓢ

74. The students are critical of the dean because he is either unfamiliar or doesn't care about the urgent need for new student housing on campus.

A) NO CHANGE
B) more unfamiliar than or
C) unfamiliar with or
D) unfamiliar about or

75. Baseball has and probably always will be the sport that symbolizes for people in other countries the American way of life.

A) NO CHANGE
B) has been
C) has been and
D) have been and

Misplaced Modifiers Ⓐ Ⓢ

76. Letters were received by the editor of the newspaper that complained of its editorial policy.

A) NO CHANGE
B) Letters were received by the editor of the newspaper having complained of its editorial policy.
C) The editor of the newspaper received letters complaining of the newspaper's editorial policy.
D) Letters were received by the editor complaining of the newspaper's editorial policy by the editor.

77. Riding in a coach and wearing the crown jewels, the crowd cheered the royal couple.

A) NO CHANGE
B) cheering for the royal couple was done by the crowd
C) the royal couple was cheered by the crowd
D) the royal couple's cheering was done by the crowd

78. Wrapped in several layers of newspaper, packed carefully in a strong cardboard carton, and bound securely with tape, the worker made sure that the fragile figurines would not be broken.

A) NO CHANGE
B) Wrapped in several layers of newspaper, packed carefully in a strong cardboard carton, and then binding the carton securely with tape, the worker made sure that the fragile figurines would not be broken.
C) The worker, wrapping the figurines in several layers of newspaper, packing them carefully in a strong cardboard carton, and securely binding the carton with tape, made sure that they would not be broken.
D) To make sure that the figurines would not be broken, the worker wrapped them in several layers of newspaper, packed them carefully in a strong cardboard carton, and securely bound the carton with tape.

Unintended Meanings Ⓐ Ⓢ

79. Mary Lou was awarded the gold medal because she scored more points than any child participating in the field day.

A) NO CHANGE
B) more points than any other child participating
C) the most points than any child participating
D) more points than all of the children participating

80. Appearing in his first American tour, the British singer's album rose to the top of the charts.

A) NO CHANGE
B) While appearing
C) While he was appearing
D) While it appeared

Punctuation

Commas Ⓐ Ⓢ

81. I think that Doré's illustrations of Dante's *Divine Comedy* are excellent; but my favorite drawing is "Don Quixote in His Library."

A) NO CHANGE
B) are excellent, but my favorite drawing is "Don Quixote in His Library."
C) are excellent in that my favorite drawing is "Don Quixote in His Library."
D) are excellent even though "Don Quixote in His Library" is my favorite drawing.

82. Practically all nitrates are crystalline and readily soluble, and they are characterized by marked decrepitation when heated on charcoals by a blowpipe.

A) NO CHANGE
B) crystalline and readily soluble and
C) crystalline, and readily soluble, and
D) crystalline and readily soluble and,

83. The door was ajar and the house had been ransacked, but it did not seem as though any of his possessions were missing.

A) NO CHANGE
B) was ajar and the house, had been ransacked, but
C) was ajar, and the house had been ransacked but
D) was ajar, the house had been ransacked but

84. Since many diseases and insects cause serious damage to crops, special national legislation has been passed to provide for the quarantine of imported plants; and under provisions of various acts, inspectors are placed at ports of entry to prevent smugglers from bringing in plants that might be dangerous.

A) NO CHANGE
B) crops special national legislation has been passed to provide for the quarantine of imported plants and under provisions of various acts
C) crops special national legislation has been passed to provide for the quarantine of imported plants; and under provisions of various acts
D) crops, special national legislation has been passed to provide for the quarantine of imported plants and under provisions of various acts

85. A full train crew consists of a motorman, a brakeman, a conductor, and two ticket takers.

A) NO CHANGE
B) A full train crew consists of a motorman, a brakeman, a conductor and, two ticket takers.
C) A full train crew consists of a motorman, a brakeman a conductor and two ticket takers.
D) A full train crew consists of a motorman a brakeman a conductor, and two ticket takers.

86. The procedure requires that you open the outer cover plate, remove the thermostat, replace the broken switch, and then replace the thermostat.

A) NO CHANGE
B) plate remove the thermostat, replace the broken switch; and
C) plate remove, the thermostat replace the broken switch, and
D) plate remove the thermostat replace the broken switch and

87. After Peter finished painting the bird feeder he and Jack hung it from a limb of the oak tree.

A) NO CHANGE
B) the bird feeder, he and Jack hung it
C) the bird feeder; he and Jack hung it
D) the bird feeder, he and Jack, hung it

88. When Pat explained to his mother that ten was the highest mark given on the entrance test she breathed a sigh of relief.

A) NO CHANGE
B) mother, that ten was the highest mark given on the entrance test,
C) mother that ten was the highest mark given on the entrance test,
D) mother that ten was the highest mark given on the entrance test;

89. Tim hopes to score well on the exam because he plans to go to an Ivy League school.

A) NO CHANGE
B) Tim hopes to score well on the exam: he plans to go to an Ivy League school.
C) Tim hopes to score well on the exam, because he plans to go to an Ivy League school.
D) Tim hopes to score well on the exam he plans to go to an Ivy League school.

90. In this impoverished region with its arid soil a typical diet may contain only 800 calories per day.

A) NO CHANGE
B) In this impoverished region with its arid soil; a typical diet may contain only 800 calories per day.
C) In this impoverished region, with its arid soil, a typical diet may contain only 800 calories per day.
D) In this impoverished region with its arid soil, a typical diet may contain only 800 calories per day.

91. Begun in 1981 and completed in 1985 the bridge provided the first link between the island and the mainland.

A) NO CHANGE
B) Begun in 1981 and completed in 1985, the bridge
C) The bridge begun in 1981 and completed in 1985
D) Begun—in 1981 and completed in 1985—the bridge

92. To slow the bleeding Van tied a pressure bandage around the lower portion of the leg.

A) NO CHANGE
B) To slow the bleeding—Van tied a pressure bandage around the lower portion of the leg.
C) To slow the bleeding, Van tied a pressure bandage around the lower portion of the leg.
D) To slow the bleeding, Van tied a pressure bandage, around the lower portion of the leg.

93. Niagara Falls, which forms part of the border between the United States and Canada, was the site of a saw mill built by the French in 1725.

A) NO CHANGE
B) Niagra Falls forms part of the border between the United States and Canada
C) Niagra Falls, which forms part of the border between the United States and Canada—
D) Niagra Falls, which forms part of the border between the United States and Canada; it

94. Secretary of State Acheson, however, made a reasoned defense of the treaty.

A) NO CHANGE
B) Secretary of State Acheson, however, he made a reasoned defense of the treaty.
C) Secretary of State Acheson; however, made a reasoned defense of the treaty.
D) Secretary of State Acheson however made a reasoned defense of the treaty.

95. Until the end of the eighteenth century, the only musicians in Norway, were simple peasants who traveled about the countryside.

A) NO CHANGE
B) the eighteenth century, the only musicians in Norway were simple peasants
C) the eighteenth century, the only musicians in Norway were simple peasants,
D) the eighteenth century the only musicians in Norway were simple peasants—

96. Prizes will be awarded in each event, and the participant, who compiles the greatest overall total, will receive a special prize.

A) NO CHANGE
B) event; and the participant, who compiles the greatest overall total, will receive
C) event, and the participant who compiles the greatest overall total will receive
D) event, and the participant who compiles the greatest, overall, total will receive

97. Since learning of the dangers of caffeine, neither my wife nor I have consumed any beverage, containing caffeine.

A) NO CHANGE
B) caffeine neither my wife nor I have consumed any beverage,
C) caffeine—neither my wife nor I have consumed any beverage—
D) caffeine, neither my wife nor I have consumed any beverage

98. After months of separation, Gauguin finally joined Van Gogh in Arles in October of 1888, Gauguin left a few weeks later.

A) NO CHANGE
B) in Arles in October of 1888; Gauguin, however, leaving a few weeks later
C) in Arles in October of 1888, it was three weeks later when Gauguin was gone
D) in Arles in October of 1888, but a few weeks later Gauguin left

99. By the middle of June, the foliage on the trees and the underbrush was lush and green and so thick that it was impossible to see very far, into the woods.

A) NO CHANGE
B) By the middle of June the foliage on the trees and the underbrush was lush and green; and it was so thick that it was impossible to see, very far, into the woods.
C) By the middle of June the foliage, on the trees and the underbrush, was lush and green and so thick that it was impossible to see very far, into the woods.
D) By the middle of June, the foliage on the trees and the underbrush was lush and green and so thick that it was impossible to see very far into the woods.

100. Students who plan to graduate with joint majors, must declare their intention and identify the two areas of study by the end of their junior years.

A) NO CHANGE
B) Students who plan to graduate with joint majors must declare
C) Students, who plan to graduate with joint majors, must declare
D) Students—who plan to graduate with joint majors—must declare

Semicolons Ⓐ Ⓢ

101. He grew up on a farm in Nebraska; he is now the captain of a Navy ship.

A) NO CHANGE
B) He grew up on a farm in Nebraska, he is now the captain of a Navy ship.
C) He grew up on a farm in Nebraska he is now the captain of a Navy ship.
D) He grew up on a farm in Nebraska; while he is now the captain of a Navy ship.

102. The Smithtown players cheered the referee's decision; the Stonybrook players booed it.

A) NO CHANGE
B) The Smithtown players cheered the referee's decision the Stonybrook players booed it.
C) The Smithtown players cheered the referee's decision, the Stonybrook players booed it.
D) The Smithtown players cheered the referee's decision: the Stonybrook players booed it.

103. When John entered the room; everyone stood up.

A) NO CHANGE
B) room, everyone
C) room, everyone,
D) room everyone

104. Clem announced that the prize would be donated to Harbus House; a well-known charity.

A) NO CHANGE
B) would be donated to Harbus House a well-known
C) would be donated to, Harbus House, a well-known
D) would be donated to Harbus House, a well-known

105. The nineteenth-century composers Wagner and Mahler did more than just write music, they conducted their own works.

A) NO CHANGE
B) music, in that they conducted
C) music; they conducted
D) music, with their conducting of

Colons ⒶⓈ

106. The seemingly tranquil lane has been the scene of many crimes including: two assaults, three robberies, and one murder.

A) NO CHANGE
B) including two assaults, three robberies, and one murder
C) including two assaults three robberies and one murder
D) including: two assaults three robberies and one murder

107. In addition to test scores, college admissions officers take into consideration many other factors such as: grades, extracurricular activities, and letters of recommendation.

A) NO CHANGE
B) factors such as grades, extracurricular activities, and letters of recommendation
C) factors: such as grades, extracurricular activities, and letters of recommendation
D) factors such as grades extracurricular activities and letters of recommendation

End-Stop Punctuation ⒶⓈ

108. Peter notified Elaine. The guidance counselor, that he had been accepted.

A) NO CHANGE
B) Peter notified Elaine the guidance counselor, that he had been accepted.
C) Peter notified Elaine, the guidance counselor that he had been accepted.
D) Peter notified Elaine, the guidance counselor, that he had been accepted.

Dashes Ⓐ Ⓢ

109. Peanuts—blanched or lightly roasted, add an interesting texture and taste to garden salads.

A) NO CHANGE
B) Peanuts—blanched or lightly roasted—add an interesting texture and taste to garden salads.
C) Peanuts blanched or lightly roasted—add an interesting texture and taste to garden salads.
D) Peanuts, blanched or lightly roasted—add an interesting texture and taste to garden salads.

110. The rug gets its striking colors from the weaver's skilled use of dyes—both natural and synthetic to create shades in subtle variations.

A) NO CHANGE
B) dyes both natural and synthetic to create
C) dyes—both natural—and synthetic to create
D) dyes—both natural and synthetic—to create

Quotation Marks Ⓐ Ⓢ

111. The first chapter of *The Scarlet Letter* is "The Custom House."

A) NO CHANGE
B) The first chapter of *The Scarlet Letter* is The Custom House.
C) The first chapter of *The Scarlet Letter* is *The Custom House.*
D) The first chapter of "*The Scarlet Letter*" is "The Custom House."

Apostrophes Ⓐ Ⓢ

112. According to legend, King Arthurs court consisted of twenty-four knights, each of whom was chosen by Arthur for a special talent or virtue.

A) NO CHANGE
B) King Arthurs' court
C) King Arthur's court
D) Kings Arthurs's court

113. In the turmoil of our modern times, it is important to try to keep in mind the fundamental moral values that structure our society.

A) NO CHANGE
B) modern times'
C) modern time's
D) modern times's

114. While she addressed the barbell, the weightlifters face had an expression of deep concentration.

A) NO CHANGE
B) the weightlifters' face
C) the weightlifters's face
D) the weightlifter's face

Punctuating for Clarity Exercise Ⓐⓢ

DIRECTIONS: Item #115 requires punctuation of the paragraph.

115. On Monday Mark received a letter of acceptance from State College He immediately called his mother herself a graduate of State College to tell her about his acceptance When he told her he had also been awarded a scholarship she was very excited After hanging up Mark's mother decided to throw a surprise party for Mark She telephoned his brother his sister and several of his friends Because the party was supposed to be a surprise she made them all promise not to say anything to Mark Mark however had a similar idea a party for his mother to celebrate his acceptance at her alma mater He telephoned his brother his sister and several of his parents' friends to invite them to a party at his house on Saturday night and he made them all promise to say nothing to his mother On Saturday night both Mark and his mother were surprised

LESSON 2 | EXPRESSION OF IDEAS

ACT ENGLISH AND SAT WRITING AND LANGUAGE

The passages and items in this section accompany the in-class review of the skills and concepts tested by the ACT English and SAT Writing and Language Tests. You will work through the items with your instructor in class. Answers are on page 569.

Strategy

Appropriate Supporting Material Ⓐ Ⓢ

DIRECTIONS: Each passage is followed by a set of items. For each item, you will select the choice that improves the passage's expression of ideas or corrects errors in sentence structure, usage, or punctuation. A passage or a question may be accompanied by one or more graphics that you will consider as you make editing decisions.

Some items will direct you to an underlined portion of a passage, and others will direct you to a location in a passage or ask you to think about the passage as a whole.

For each item, choose the answer to each question that most effectively improves the quality of writing in the passage or that makes the passage follow the conventions of standard written English. Choose the "NO CHANGE" option if you think the best choice is to leave the relevant portion of the passage as it is.

Items #1–5 are based on the following passage.

[1]

[1] In my mind, one of the most pressing issues facing America today is healthcare. [2] One aspect of the problem is lack of access to a doctor. [3] Many people just cannot afford to pay for a visit to a doctor. [4] They avoid going to the doctor until they are really sick. [5] If they were treated in the first place, they wouldn't get so sick. [6] This practice not only causes human suffering but is wasteful. [7] Health insurance for surgery is also an issue. [8] Many people do not get adequate health insurance with their jobs and cannot afford to pay for it. [9] The inability to pay for health

insurance also creates an unfair distribution of healthcare in America.

[2]

[10] An even more important aspect of the healthcare problem in America is the choices that people make for themselves. [11] Take smoking for example. [12] Scientific evidence proves that smoking causes lung cancer and other diseases. [13] Yet many people continue to smoke, and young people continue to start smoking. **1** [14] There are other health problems such as being overweight and using drugs that may also come from private choices.

[3]

2 [15] Some government assistance is needed for those who cannot afford medical care or health insurance. [16] The most important thing is for people to be concerned with their own health. [17] If we take care of ourselves by eating better, exercising more, and avoiding destructive choices, we will all live longer, healthier, and happier lives.

1. The author is considering inserting the following factual statement between sentences 13 and 14:

> Nicotine, which is found in tobacco, is one of the most addictive chemicals known to science.

Would this statement add to the development of the paragraph?

A) Yes, because the paragraph identifies smoking as a serious problem.
B) Yes, because the sentence explains why young people start to smoke.
C) No, because scientific evidence is irrelevant to the author's point.
D) No, because the addictive mechanism behind smoking is not relevant.

Effective Opening, Transitional, and Concluding Sentences Ⓐ Ⓢ

2. Which of the following revisions to sentences 15 and 16 best clarifies the author's position?

A) NO CHANGE
B) Some government assistance is needed for those who cannot afford medical care or health insurance and people need to be concerned with their own health.
C) The most important thing is for people to be concerned with their own health and for them to ask for government assistance.
D) Even though some government assistance is needed for those who cannot afford medical care or health insurance, the most important thing is for people to be concerned with their own health.

Main Idea Ⓐ Ⓢ

3. In context, which of the following best describes the main purpose of the essay?

A) To expose faulty reasoning
B) To evaluate a theory set forth earlier
C) To provide specific illustrations
D) To propose a solution to a problem

Audience Ⓐ Ⓢ

4. In writing this passage, the author was most probably addressing

A) a convention of surgeons.
B) a group of concerned citizens.
C) a meeting of insurance executives.
D) a conference of tobacco executives.

Organization

Paragraph-Level Structure Ⓐ Ⓢ

5. What should be done to sentence 7 to strengthen the organization of the essay?

A) NO CHANGE
B) Begin a new paragraph.
C) Switch sentence 6 with sentence 7.
D) OMIT sentence 7.

Passage-Level Structure Ⓐ Ⓢ

Item #6 is based on the following passage.

[1]

Each year, my family plants a vegetable garden. Both my parents work, and so it is the job of the children to tend the garden.

[2]

Work starts several weeks before the growing season actually begins. We put little pots of soil containing seeds that must sprout before they are planted outdoors on the sun porch. Then, my father prepares the ground with a rototiller. When the danger of frost is past, it is time to plant.

[3]

For the first few weeks, we water the seed beds regularly and pull weeds by hand. Once the plants are established, the leaves of the good plants block the sunlight so weeds can't grow. However, there are other jobs such as staking tomatoes and tending to running vines.

[4]

Then the blossoms appear and are pollinated by bees and other insects. As small vegetables appear, the blossoms drop off. They continue to grow and later in the summer begin to ripen. Up to this point, tending the garden has been a chore, but now it becomes a pleasure. Each afternoon, we pick the ripe ones and wash them so that they are ready for cooking. I suppose that I feel proud that I have helped to feed my family. I have to admit that my greatest enjoyment is the taste of the freshly picked vegetables.

6. The overall organization of the passage can best be described as

A) chronological development.
B) explanation of two sides of an issue.
C) generalization of a statement with illustrations.
D) posing a question and then answering it.

Items #7–12 are based on the following passage.

[1]

[1] On my vacation to Alaska, I took a trip to Porcupine. In 1905, Porcupine was a thriving town of 2,000 people, retail stores, and a post office. [2] Hardly any of the town remains today, but there is still gold there, and our guide showed us how to pan for gold. [3] It's easy to learn how, and anyone can do it. 7

[2]

[4] The technique of panning depends on the weight of gold. [5] It's about 20 times heavier than water, so the gold stays at the bottom of a stream and gets caught in the sand in slow-flowing water around bends and along the edge of the stream. 8 [6] It can also get stuck in small crevices of rock and even wedged into pieces of wood.

[3]

[7] You need to find where the gold is. There's no sense in panning for gold in a stream where there isn't any, so go to a stream where people have found gold before. [8] Then concentrate on those areas that are most likely to trap the little bits of gold.

[4]

[9] Keep moving the pan until about half the original material has been carried away. [10] Lift the pan out of the water, tilt it toward the side with the riffles 10 (the small ridges), and swirl until the water is gone. [11] Repeat this process until nearly all the material is gone.

7. Which of the following sentences inserted after sentence 3 would best introduce the remaining paragraphs of the essay?

A) Gold is one of the most valuable substances on earth.
B) Just follow these simple instructions.
C) I try to do a lot of different things on my vacations.
D) Did you even know that there was a gold rush in Alaska?

8. The best placement for sentence 6 would be

A) where it is now.
B) before sentence 4.
C) after sentence 4.
D) as the first sentence of paragraph 3.

9. Which of the following sequence of paragraphs is most logical?

A) NO CHANGE
B) 6, 4, 5
C) 5, 4, 6
D) 5, 6, 4

10. Is the parenthetical note following the word "riffles" in paragraph 4 appropriate?

A) Yes, because it clarifies a technical term for the reader.
B) Yes, because it presents an idea that is essential to the passage.
C) No, because it distracts the reader from the directions for panning.
D) No, because the author does not cite a source for the definition.

[5]

[12] To start panning, put a few handfuls of material into your gold pan. [13] Then submerge the pan in the water of the stream. [14] Hold the pan under the surface and move it in a circular motion so that the lighter material sloshes over the edge. [15] You have to be careful not to be too aggressive or you'll send your gold downstream along with the silt and other debris.

[6]

[16] Use a small stream of water suction pipette (or even a spray bottle with a concentrated setting on the nozzle) to sort the gold from the remaining debris. [17] Pick up the flecks with a tweezers or your fingers and place them in a small glass container such as a test tube or a medicine bottle.

[7]

11 [18] Panning takes practice, patience, and luck, but even a little bit of gold is a big thrill. [19] You're probably not going to find a lot of gold.

11. The best placement for sentence 18 would be

A) where it is now.
B) after sentence 19.
C) before sentence 4.
D) before sentence 16.

12. Suppose the author had been assigned to write a brief essay on an interesting travel destination. Assuming that all of the following statements are true, would this essay successfully fulfill the assignment?

A) Yes, because many gold-seekers came to Porcupine during the nineteenth century.
B) Yes, because panning for gold would be a fun activity on a trip.
C) No, because very little remains today of the town of Porcupine.
D) No, because most people have never before heard of Porcupine.

Style

Conciseness Ⓐ Ⓢ

DIRECTIONS: Items #13–20 have a single part of a sentence underlined or the entire sentence underlined. Identify the rephrasing that best expresses the meaning of the underlined material. The answer choice "NO CHANGE" indicates that the underlined material is correct as written.

13. Angela is hoping to save enough for a trip to Europe, during which the small village where her grandparents were born will be visited.

A) NO CHANGE
B) the small village where her grandparents had been born will be visited
C) she will visit the small village where her grandparents were born
D) there will be a visit to the small village where her grandparents were born

14. Finally and at long last the old dog opened his eyes and noticed the intruder.

A) NO CHANGE
B) Finally
C) So finally
D) Yet at long last

15. The speaker declared that alternative ways of utilizing waterfront land ought to be explored.

A) NO CHANGE
B) alternatives of use for
C) alternative utilizations of
D) alternate uses of

16. Since only the ruling party is allowed to vote, its members are able to maintain the existing status quo.

A) NO CHANGE
B) remaining status quo
C) existed status quo
D) status quo

17. Each year, the geese make their annual migration from Northern Canada to their winter habitats in the United States.

A) NO CHANGE
B) migration
C) annually migration
D) annual

18. Although the committee met for over two weeks and issued a 50-page report, its findings were of little importance or consequence.

A) NO CHANGE
B) importance or significance
C) importance and consequence
D) consequence

Clarity of Meaning Ⓐ Ⓢ

19. Along with an end to featherbedding and no-show jobs, the new head of the Transit Authority has eliminated many other inefficient employment practices.

A) NO CHANGE
B) In addition to eliminating featherbedding and no-show jobs
C) Not only did he end featherbedding and no-shows jobs
D) Besides featherbedding and no-show jobs coming to an end

Idiomatic Expression Ⓐ Ⓢ

20. Being that the hour was late, we agreed to adjourn the meeting and reconvene at nine o'clock the following morning.

A) NO CHANGE
B) Since
C) Because that
D) During

Additional Practice Ⓐ Ⓢ

Items #21–26 are based on the following passage.

[1]

My first real job was working at the Burger Barn. Before that, I **21** did odd jobs for neighbors such as mowing lawns and shoveling snow and was paid by them. **22** The Burger Barn is a typical fast food restaurant, serving food such as hamburgers and french fries. The only experience that most people have with a fast food restaurant is as a customer. They order and pay for **23** it and then either sit down or go home to eat. A lot more goes on behind the counter.

[2]

There are rules for everything. The oil for the french fries must be exactly 375 degrees, and the fries must cook until the timer sounds. The patties must be cooked until they are well done. All counters, floors, and utensils must be cleaned and disinfected every evening.

[3]

There must be so many orders of fries under the warming lamp and a certain number of burgers on the grill. **24** However, paper products and condiments must be restocked every half hour, and employees receive five-minute breaks every two hours with 20 minutes for lunch during a six-hour shift. To outsiders, these rules **25** may seem silly, but they are necessary to make sure that the food we serve is safe to eat and that during evening rush we can serve as many as 150 people. The evening rush is from 5:30 p.m. to 7:00 p.m. **26**

21. A) NO CHANGE
B) did odd jobs for neighbors such as mowing lawns and shoveling snow who paid me for them
C) was paid by neighbors for doing odd jobs such as mowing lawns and shoveling snow
D) received pay by neighbors for odd jobs such as mowing lawns and shoveling snow

22. A) NO CHANGE
B) The Burger Barn is a typical fast food restaurant in that it serves
C) Typically, a fast food restaurant such as the Burger Barn serves
D) A fast food restaurant such as your typical Burger Barn serves

23. A) experience
B) restaurant
C) food
D) people

24. A) However
B) In addition
C) Therefore
D) Perhaps

25. A) NO CHANGE
B) may seem silly, since they are necessary to make sure
C) are necessary to make sure, even though they may seem silly,
D) are necessary, even though they may seem silly, and make sure

26. In context, which of the following would be the most appropriate revision of the last sentence of the essay?

A) Delete it because it does not contribute to the development of the essay.
B) Delete it because definitions are not appropriate in an essay.
C) Place it in quotation marks because it is a definition.
D) Move it to the beginning of the final paragraph.

Items #27–30 are based on the following passage.

[1]

[1] In the past several years, lawyers have increasingly been in the negative public spotlight. 27 [2] A group of students hires a lawyer to sue their school because they don't like the mascot. [3] A driver sues a take-out restaurant because he was scalded by the hot coffee he spilled while driving. [4] A prison inmate goes all the way to the Supreme Court because the jail uses the wrong kind of peanut butter.

[2]

[5] All of these examples make lawyers seem like publicity-hungry, money-grubbing parasites. [6] Seemingly outrageous cases, 28 certainly, are often incorrectly reported by the media.

[3]

[7] Take the famous peanut butter case as an example. [8] Since inmates aren't permitted to have cash, they have accounts with the prison commissary where they buy items like soap, stationery, and snacks. [9] An inmate ordered a jar of crunchy-style peanut butter but got creamy-style instead. [10] Then the commissary repeatedly refused to fix the mistake. [11] The inmate properly returned the merchandise, but the commissary didn't credit his account. [12] So the inmate sued the commissary for the price of the peanut butter. [13] The inmate won, so the prison appealed and lost.

[4]

[14] When you hear the actual facts of the peanut butter case, you can see that the inmate had a legitimate beef. [15] This is true of most of the other cases you hear about as well.

27. Which of the following would be the most suitable sentence to insert immediately after sentence 1?

A) Lawyers go to school for an additional three years after graduating from college.
B) Every night, the news has stories of how people have been hurt or injured that day.
C) I have often thought about becoming a lawyer after I graduate from college.
D) It seems as though every day we hear of another frivolous lawsuit.

28. A) NO CHANGE
B) more or less
C) however
D) fortunately

29. Which of the following changes in the organization of the third paragraph is most needed?

A) NO CHANGE
B) Start a new paragraph with sentence 9.
C) Put sentence 10 after sentence 11.
D) Start a new paragraph with sentence 12.

30. Which of the following would be most appropriate for the writer to do in a fifth paragraph to be added to the essay?

A) Explain why the media gets the facts of cases wrong.
B) Analyze the legal arguments in the "peanut butter case."
C) Refute the contention that prison inmates have legal rights.
D) Present cases where people falsely claimed to be seriously injured.

Items #31–35 are based on the following passage.

[1]

[1] I have been an amateur astronomer for years. [2] My first telescope was a gift from my uncle. **31** [3] He taught astronomy at the local college. [4] I was only nine years old.

[2]

[5] One of the advantages of astronomy as a hobby is **32** <u>that you did not have to be</u> an expert to enjoy it. [6] With even an inexpensive telescope, you can step outside on a clear night and see thousands of stars.

[3]

[7] How many are there?

[4]

[8] We know that our solar system is part of a much larger system of hundreds of billions of stars. **33** [9] <u>As such</u>, this system is the Milky Way Galaxy, a huge disk of stars and gas. **34** [10] A light year is the distance traveled by light in a year, almost 10 million, million kilometers. [11] We also know that ours is not the only galaxy in the universe. [12] As far as the largest telescopes in the world can see, there are galaxies in every direction. [13] The nearest large galaxy to the Milky Way is the Andromeda Galaxy, which is about two million light years away. [14] Andromeda is a giant spiral galaxy, much like our own in size, shape, and number and type of stars. [15] This nearby sister galaxy provides us an opportunity to get a good view of a galaxy much like our own. **35**

31. What is the best way to deal with sentence 3?

A) NO CHANGE
B) Connect it to sentence 2 with the word "who" replacing "He."
C) Place it before sentence 2.
D) Connect it to sentence 2 with the word "and."

32. A) NO CHANGE
B) that you do not have to be
C) that you not being
D) which you did not have to be

33. A) NO CHANGE
B) Actually
C) As a matter of fact
D) OMIT the underlined phrase

34. The best placement for sentence 10 would be

A) where it is now.
B) between sentences 11 and 12.
C) between sentences 12 and 13.
D) between sentences 13 and 14.

35. Which of the following, if placed after sentence 15, would be the most effective concluding sentence for the essay?

A) However, astronomy may not be suitable for very young children.
B) Finally, you can learn more about galaxies by becoming an amateur astronomer yourself.
C) Therefore, think about the Andromeda Galaxy the next time you look at the night sky.
D) In effect, we get to see ourselves as others would see us.

Items #36–40 are based on the following passage.

[1]

[1] My favorite American artist is Georgia O'Keeffe. 36 [2] Her parents were dairy farmers, but Georgia knew she was going to be an artist from early on. [3] She studied and taught art in Chicago, Virginia, Texas, and South Carolina.

[2]

[4] After years of teaching, Georgia did a series of abstract charcoals. [5] She sent the drawings to a friend who in turn showed them to Alfred Stieglitz, a well-known photographer and gallery owner in New York. [6] Stieglitz exhibited the drawings without first consulting Georgia. [7] This angered her, and she went to New York with the intention of removing the drawings. [8] After meeting Stieglitz, 37 however, she agreed to let him show her work.

[3]

[9] This incident began a relationship that was to result in their marrying. [10] Georgia painted cityscapes inspired by the spectacular view from their 30th-floor apartment.
[11] Stieglitz and O'Keeffe also spent a lot of time in the Adirondack Mountains, 38 where she created many paintings of the Lake George area.

36. Which of the following would be the most suitable sentence to insert immediately after sentence 1?

A) Georgia graduated from the Chatham Episcopal Institute in 1905.
B) In 1985, she was awarded the National Medal of Arts.
C) She was born in Wisconsin in 1887.
D) My favorite European artist is Vincent Van Gogh.

37. A) NO CHANGE
B) naturally
C) you see
D) certainly

38. A) NO CHANGE
B) where many of the paintings of the Lake George area were created by her
C) where the Lake George area was to be featured in many of her paintings
D) where many paintings were created by her of Lake George

[4]

[12] After 12 years, Georgia had had enough of the city as a subject and felt the need to travel again and took a trip to New Mexico. [13] She was inspired by the mountains and deserts of the region and the mysterious aura of the place. [14] She referred to landscape as "the faraway" and would travel dusty roads in a Model A Ford to find scenes to paint. [15] After Stieglitz's death in 1946, Georgia established permanent residence in New Mexico, **39** so she could paint her famous images of sun-bleached skulls.

[5]

[16] With eyesight failing, she spent her final years in Santa Fe. **40** [17] She died on March 6, 1986, at the age of 98, and her ashes were scattered over her "faraway."

39. A) NO CHANGE
B) and she painted
C) though she painted
D) where she painted

40. The author uses the phrase "faraway" in sentence 17 to

A) set up a contrast between the discussion of O'Keeffe's landscapes and her cityscapes.
B) reinforce the idea that O'Keeffe felt a strong personal connection to New Mexico.
C) show the tragedy of O'Keeffe's death after a lengthy career as an artist.
D) remind the reader that O'Keeffe knew from an early age that she wanted to be an artist.

Items #41–45 are based on the following passage.

[1]

[1] Uranus is a strange planet. [2] It lies tipped over on its side. [3] Instead of spinning like a top, it rolls like a ball along the path of its orbit. **42** [4] The geographic poles are located on either side, one pointing toward the Sun and the other pointing away. [5] The clouds in the Uranian atmosphere move in the same direction that the planet rotates.

[2]

[6] The moons of Uranus are equally as strange. [7] Miranda, the one closest to the planet, has huge markings where terrains of totally different types appear to have been jammed together. [8] On Ariel, the next moon out, the landscape has huge faults; however, there is no evidence of any geologic activity on Ariel. [9] Umbriel, the third moon, seems to be painted with a dark substance. **43** [10] On one side is the "doughnut," it being a bright, round indentation caused by the impact of a large object. [11] Between the orbit of Miranda and the planet's surface are up to one hundred charcoal-colored rings, ringlets, and bands of dust.

[3]

[12] Like the clouds in the planet's atmosphere, they circle Uranus in the same direction as the planet rotates. [13] That is, they orbit over the top and bottom of the planet rather than around the sides, as the clouds in the Earth's atmosphere do.

[4]

[14] Scientists are confident that they will discover additional planets in our Solar System. **45** [15] Until they do it, Uranus will remain the strangest of all.

41. The sentence that best states the main idea of the passage is

A) sentence 1.
B) sentence 5.
C) sentence 6.
D) sentence 8.

42. A) NO CHANGE
B) Located on either side, the geographic poles are pointing, one toward the Sun and the other away.
C) On either side, the geographic poles are located pointing toward the Sun or away.
D) The geographic poles are pointing toward and away from the Sun with one being on each side.

43. A) Nevertheless, on one side is the "doughnut," it being a bright, round indentation caused by the impact of a large object.
B) On one side is the "doughnut," it being a bright, round indentation caused by a large object.
C) On one side is the "doughnut," a bright, round indentation caused by the impact of a large object.
D) On one side is the "doughnut," it being a bright; round indentation caused by the impact of a large object.

44. Which of the following revisions would most improve the organization of paragraphs two and three?

A) Make a new paragraph following sentence 7.
B) Make a new paragraph following sentence 9.
C) Make sentence 11 the first sentence of paragraph three.
D) Make sentence 12 the last sentence of paragraph two.

45. A) NO CHANGE
B) Until the discovery, Uranus
C) Until others are discovered, Uranus
D) Regardless of it, Uranus

Items #46–50 are based on the following passage.

[1]

46 [1] Do you like music, art, sports or some similar activity? [2] Then you would enjoy stamp collecting. [3] Stamps offer a look at the major cultural trends that shape our world. [4] Plus, they honor individual artists, musicians, athletes, and others who have made important contributions to their fields.

[2]

[5] It's easy to start a stamp collection. [6] Simply save stamps from letters, packages, and postcards, and ask friends and family to save stamps from their mail. [7] Neighborhood businesses that get a lot of mail might save their envelopes for you, too.

[3]

[8] At some point in your collecting, you'll find an old stamp and wonder whether it might be valuable. 47 [9] <u>That depends on how rare the stamp is and what condition it</u> is in. 48

46. The function of sentence 1 is to

A) ask a rhetorical question to get the reader's attention.
B) tell the reader the order in which topics will appear.
C) inform the reader what position the author will take.
D) show puzzlement about various cultural activities.

47. A) NO CHANGE
B) Value depends on how rare the stamp is and what condition it
C) Collected depends on how rare the stamp is and what condition it
D) That depends on how rare the stamp is and what condition they

48. Which of the following would be the most suitable sentence to insert immediately after sentence 9?

A) The value of items such as paintings and books as well as stamps depends on how rare they are.
B) Commemorative stamps are issued by the Post Office to celebrate a particular event such as the first moon landing.
C) You can get an idea of how rare the stamp is by consulting a buyer's guide at your local library.
D) The most valuable stamps are usually sold at auction to wealthy collectors.

[4]

[10] Then, as to condition, a cancelled stamp is one which has been through the postal system and bears a postmark. **49** [11] Cancelled stamps are usually the least valuable. [12] An unused stamp has no cancellation but may not have any gum on the back. [13] A stamp in mint condition is the same as it was when purchased from the post office. [14] Mint stamps are usually worth more than unused stamps.

[5]

[15] You probably will not find a rare stamp on an envelope that has just been through the mail, but you might find one in the attic or garage in a box with old records and papers. **50** [16] Even if you don't find a stamp that is worth a lot of money, you are sure to have a good time looking for them.

49. A) NO CHANGE
B) Cancelled stamps are usually the less valuable.
C) Cancelled stamps are usually less valuable than the others.
D) Of other stamps, cancelled ones are usually less valuable.

50. A) NO CHANGE
B) Even if you don't find a stamp that is worth a lot of money, you are sure to have a good time looking for one.
C) Even if you don't find a stamp that is worth a lot of money, you are sure to have a good time looking for it.
D) Even though you don't find a stamp that is worth a lot of money, you are sure to have a good time looking for them.

Items #51–55 are based on the following passage.

[1]

[1] My favorite opera is *La Bohème* by Puccini. 51 [2] Why is *La Bohème* my favorite? [3] The action of the opera takes place on the Left Bank of Paris in the 1830s. [4] The Left Bank is where the struggling artists and students lived. [5] Four of the main characters in the opera are a painter, a philosopher, a musician, and, most important for me, a poet. [6] The sets include a sidewalk café and a garret room. 53 [7] They even have a passionate romance with a tragic ending.

[2]

[8] The opera is based on *Scènes de la Vie de Bohème* written by Henri Murger. [9] When Murger wrote this novel, he himself was a poor writer living in the Latin Quarter in the 1840s. [10] The book is a collection of short, funny stories about Henri and his friends.

[3]

[11] The individual scenes, on which the novel is based, first appeared as a series of stories in a Parisian newspaper. [12] The group of struggling artists that made up Henri's group loved to eat and drink in cafés, but they hardly ever had any money to pay the check. 54 [13] They were all very poor, but they will make the most of the present without worrying about the future.

[4]

[14] Legend has it that someone once came to visit Murger in his tiny apartment and found Murger in bed. [15] When the visitor suggested that Murger get dressed to go to a café, Murger said that he couldn't because he'd lent his only pair of pants to a friend. 55 [16] I like to think of this story and imagine myself as Murger, being that he is the struggling writer.

51. The function of sentence 2 is to

A) pose a question that the writer will answer.
B) invite the reader to answer to the question.
C) signal the writer's confidence about the topic.
D) imply that "favorite" is a matter of personal choice.

52. If the writer wanted to add that the Left Bank is also called the Latin Quarter, that purpose could best be accomplished by inserting

A) "The Latin Quarter is another name for the Left Bank." after sentence 3.
B) "The Latin Quarter and the Left Bank are the same thing." after sentence 3.
C) "(also called the Latin Quarter)" after "Left Bank" in sentence 4.
D) "The Left Bank is also called the Latin Quarter." after sentence 4.

53. A) NO CHANGE
B) As a matter of fact, they even have
C) It is even that they have
D) The opera even has

54. A) NO CHANGE
B) They were all very poor, but struggling artists will make
C) They were all very poor, but they made
D) They were all very poor, but. They will make

55. A) NO CHANGE
B) I like to think of this and imagine myself as Murger, being that he is
C) I like to think of this story and imagine myself as Murger,
D) I like to think of this story and imagine myself as Murger; being that he is

Items #56–60 are based on the following passage.

[1]

[1] In 1928, a National Flag Conference adopted the National Flag Code. [2] The Code established principles of flag etiquette based upon the practices of the military. [3] These principles were eventually enacted into law. [4] The Flag Code law does not impose penalties for misuse of the United States Flag, but it is the guide for the proper handling and display of the Stars and Stripes. [5] Generally, you should display the flag only from sunrise to sunset on buildings and on stationary flagstaffs in the open. [6] You can, however, display the flag twenty-four hours a day if it is properly illuminated during the hours of darkness. [7] It is appropriate to display the flag on any day of the year but especially on important holidays such as Memorial Day, Independence Day, and Veterans Day. **58** [8] The flag should not be displayed on days when the weather is inclement, unless they're all-weather flags.

[2]

59 [9] When raising the flag, it should be hoisted briskly. [10] When you take it down, it should be lowered ceremoniously. [11] Take care not to let it touch the ground. [12] It should be neatly folded and carefully stored away.

56. The main idea of the essay is expressed by

A) sentence 1.
B) sentence 8.
C) sentence 15.
D) sentence 18.

57. The overall development of the thesis would be made clearer by beginning a new paragraph with

A) sentence 2.
B) sentence 3.
C) sentence 5.
D) sentence 6.

58. A) NO CHANGE
B) The flags should not be displayed on days when the weather is inclement, unless they're all-weather flags.
C) The flag should not be displayed on days when the weather is inclement, unless it's an all-weather flag.
D) The flag should not be displayed on days the weather is inclement, unless they're all-weather flags.

59. A) NO CHANGE
B) When raising, the flag should be hoisted briskly.
C) When the flag is rising, it should be done briskly.
D) When raising the flag, you should hoist it briskly.

[3]

[13] It is all right to clean and mend your flag. [14] However, when it becomes so worn that it no longer serves as a proper symbol of the United States, it should be replaced. [15] The old flag should be destroyed, preferably by burning.

[4]

[16] You may think that displaying the flag just means buying a flag and hanging it on a pole. **60** [17] <u>Because the Flag Code covers many other points that you probably don't know about, this will surprise you.</u> [18] If you really want to show your patriotism by displaying the flag, then you should be familiar with the rules of flag etiquette.

60. A) NO CHANGE
B) The Flag Code covers many other points that may surprise you.
C) Because the Flag Code covers many other points that may surprise you.
D) You may be surprised that the Flag Code covers many other points.

LESSON 3 | WORDS IN CONTEXT

ACT ENGLISH AND SAT WRITING AND LANGUAGE

The passages and items in this section accompany the in-class review of the skills and concepts tested by the ACT English and SAT Writing and Language Tests. You will work through the items with your instructor in class. Answers are on page 569.

Contextual Meaning—Basic Technique Ⓐ Ⓢ

DIRECTIONS: In each of the following items, a word or phrase is underlined. Following each sentence or sentences are alternative suggestions for rewriting the underlined part. If you think the original is correct, choose NO CHANGE. Otherwise, choose the best alternative.

1. To compensate for the funds that will no longer be available due to a decline in the value of the endowment's portfolio, the university will need to find an <u>anticipated</u> sum from another source if it hopes to avoid cutting back on student services.

A) NO CHANGE
B) equivalent
C) unofficial
D) inconsequential

2. The mobster's efforts to appear mentally unstable in order to avoid criminal prosecution were <u>contrived</u>, and the unconvinced judge ordered the trial to begin immediately.

A) NO CHANGE
B) classical
C) altruistic
D) tenacious

3. Awed by the credentials of the reviewing committee, the doctoral candidate was intimidated and set forth the central thesis of the paper <u>tentatively</u>.

A) NO CHANGE
B) decisively
C) recklessly
D) imperially

4. Unlike gold, paper money has no <u>monetary</u> value; it is merely a representation of wealth.

A) NO CHANGE
B) financial
C) economic
D) intrinsic

5. Although Barbara argues strongly that current policies are unjust, she does not <u>presume</u> any particular changes.

A) NO CHANGE
B) advocate
C) recite
D) remember

6. As science progresses, observations that at one time seemed to conflict with one another can sometimes be <u>re-established</u> by a more advanced theory.

A) NO CHANGE
B) detected
C) observed
D) reconciled

7. Marxist revolution directly challenged the bourgeois order, and Communism explicitly endeavored to destroy traditional religion and to believe itself as an alternative faith.

A) NO CHANGE
B) enshrine
C) signal
D) illuminate

8. Since the evidence of the manuscript's authenticity is inconclusive, its publication will be postponed until a team of scholars has examined it and declared it to be genuine.

A) NO CHANGE
B) infallible
C) indubitable
D) redoubtable

9. If we continue to consume our fossil fuel supply without restraint, then someday it will be depleted.

A) NO CHANGE
B) limited
C) useless
D) reserved

10. Though critics complained about the confused structure of the novel, it was necessitated by the story itself with its spies, double spies, and triple spies, all operating for and against various governments and one another.

A) NO CHANGE
B) fragmented
C) fractious
D) byzantine

Precise Meaning Ⓐ Ⓢ

11. Using an infusion of capital and a clever idea for marketing computers, Eddie enlarged a small neighborhood store into a citywide chain of electronic boutiques.

A) NO CHANGE
B) transferred
C) transformed
D) enhanced

12. With the evidence accepted from careful study of numerous x-rays, scientists are beginning to form a picture of the atomic structure of the cell.

A) NO CHANGE
B) gleaned
C) enticed
D) elicited

13. The critic thought the film was completely unrealistic; he termed the plot false and the acting unbelievable.

A) NO CHANGE
B) unimaginative
C) insincere
D) contrived

14. Dedicated wildlife photographers willingly travel great distances and gladly endure considerable hardship to share with audiences their attention to the natural world.

A) NO CHANGE
B) preference for
C) expectations of
D) enthusiasm for

15. The term "Indian" is a misnomer for the Native American, first introduced by Columbus, repeated by his contemporaries, and perpetuated by later historians.

A) NO CHANGE
B) instigated
C) perpetrated
D) articulated

16. As the heir of the Samurai, the Japanese soldier had a worthy heritage, but the Allies initially underestimated the capabilities of the Japanese armed forces. Then, following early Japanese victories, the Allies overestimated them. Thus was born the myth of the Japanese super-soldier, a myth nurtured by Japanese propaganda and spread by suspicious war correspondents who wrote about their invincibility.

A) NO CHANGE
B) credulous
C) credible
D) callow

Items #17–18 refer to the following paragraph.

In the nineteenth century, the popular imagination transformed the West into a land of adventure where cowboys **17** sanctified the bravery and strength of the rugged individual. In the twentieth century, movies, television, and literary fiction **18** perpetrated the cowboy myth of the West.

17. A) NO CHANGE
B) actualized
C) presupposed
D) epitomized

18. A) NO CHANGE
B) renounced
C) exhumed
D) perpetuated

19. The decline and virtual disappearance of African American jockeys and horse trainers at the turn of the twentieth century presented a sharp reversal from previous decades. Following the Civil War, black jockeys and trainers dominated southern race tracks as they had during the equestrian era, and the top riders competed against white jockeys in the North. Black jockeys won fifteen of the first twenty-eight Kentucky Derbies beginning in 1875.

A) NO CHANGE
B) post-war
C) antebellum
D) war-like

20. After two days of heavy fighting, the unit had been truncated. Of the original 50 soldiers, only 35 were still actively fighting when reinforcements arrived.

A) NO CHANGE
B) decimated
C) fragmented
D) detracted

21. Deer are now more numerous than when the first European settlers arrived to this continent, and their ghostly forms are often seen at dusk gliding by in the roadside brush.

A) NO CHANGE
B) spiritual
C) deceased
D) magical

22. Josef Stalin, who ruled the Soviet Union as a dictator until his death in 1953, believed that history was fiction, an infinitely divisible text to be shaped to the needs of the State.

A) NO CHANGE
B) plastic
C) meaningless
D) expandable

23. The city can ticket the cars with diplomatic plates, but then the diplomats claim diplomatic immunity from the laws of this country. Thus, the diplomats can park anywhere with recklessness.

A) NO CHANGE
B) impunity
C) indulgence
D) caution

24. In the Middle Ages, scientists thought the world was well-ordered and harmonious; today, scientists are more likely to see the world as pre-determined.

A) NO CHANGE
B) disruptive
C) accidental
D) chaotic

25. Before the eighteenth century, European artists and writers had relied for their livelihood on the generosity of their masters. They were paid lavishly in exchange for painting and writing.

A) NO CHANGE
B) overlords
C) patrons
D) peers

Tone Ⓐ Ⓢ

26. The almost daily reports that we hear about some grimy politician make us despair of the possibility of actually achieving the lofty goals set forth in the Declaration of Independence and the Constitution.

A) NO CHANGE
B) low-life
C) scum ball
D) corrupt

27. In his private life he was quite a skinflint, but he gave large sums of money to charities, so most people thought of him as a philanthropist.

A) NO CHANGE
B) tightwad
C) miser
D) penny-pincher

28. Albert Camus' emotional and intellectual honesty led to exile from all of the communities to which he belonged because he refused to endorse simplistic solutions. He refused to take a my-way-or-the-highway moral position in the face of the complexities of human experience.

A) NO CHANGE
B) a yes-or-no
C) a black-and-white
D) an absolutist

29. The Battle of Saratoga was the turning point of America's Revolutionary War because with that victory the American cause seemed sufficiently doable for France to enter into an alliance to help the Americans.

A) NO CHANGE
B) winnable
C) manageable
D) viable

30. When construction of the new State House is completed, the Governor will host a grand celebration featuring federal officials, visitors from other states, and foreign dignitaries.

A) NO CHANGE
B) big blow-out
C) wild party
D) gigantic wingding

Conciseness ⒶⓈ

31. Musical theater, which for so long enjoyed a golden era, fell into a dark age as young composers, intimidated by the great masters, slavishly copied the work of their predecessors who had come before them and failed to produce works with originality.

A) NO CHANGE
B) their predecessors
C) the composers who had preceded before them
D) the composers who preceded before them

32. Because the poet was uncomfortable in the society of others, he lived a reclusive existence by himself, alone in the house in which he was born.

A) NO CHANGE
B) as a recluse
C) an existence by himself, alone
D) a reclusive existence, alone

33. For several years, the city had tried unsuccessfully to lure a professional baseball team to their vacant stadium, which had stood empty since the Red Shirts had moved to another city.

A) NO CHANGE
B) stadium, which had stood vacant
C) vacant stadium, which had stood unoccupied
D) vacant stadium, which had stood

34. Mardi Gras in Mobile is the annual Carnival celebration in Mobile, Alabama. In fact, it is the oldest annual Carnival celebration in the United States, having started in 1703, fifteen years before New Orleans was founded. However, owing to the fact that it is better known, the New Orleans celebration is more famous.

A) NO CHANGE
B) owing to the fact that it is best known
C) because of the fact that it is better known
D) DELETE the underlined part

35. Recent studies of the testimony of eyewitnesses who actually saw an event take place suggest that personal memory is actually unreliable, easily reshaped, and too easily contaminated by suggestion and conversation.

A) NO CHANGE
B) eyewitnesses who saw an event
C) people who witnessed an event and saw it take place
D) eyewitnesses

Idiomatic Expression ⒶⓈ

36. Johnny Appleseed is an American folk hero whose real name was John Chapman. He is known for sowing apple trees through Pennsylvania, Ohio, Indiana, and Illinois, advocating conservation, and being a missionary.

A) NO CHANGE
B) in
C) inside
D) throughout

37. Because the junior varsity was not present on campus when the infractions occurred, the Dean announced that the members of the team would be accepted from the week-long ban on participation in sports.

A) NO CHANGE
B) expected
C) excluded
D) deleted

38. Addressing Harvard Divinity Schools, Emerson questioned common assumptions of organized religion—a challenge that elicited charges of heresy among his critics, prompting officials to banish him from speaking at Harvard for three decades.

A) NO CHANGE
B) erase
C) ban
D) delete

39. Oceans, plants, petroleum, and soil all store carbon, but right now, by burning fossil fuels, humans are <u>adding</u> carbon to the atmosphere in the form of carbon dioxide faster than natural processes can remove it.

A) NO CHANGE
B) supplanting
C) protracting
D) raising

40. As a food source, pecans are a natural choice for pre-agricultural society. They can provide two to five times more calories per unit weight than wild game and require no preparation. As wild forage, the fruit of the <u>first</u> growing season is commonly still edible when found on the ground. Hollow tree trunks, found in abundance in pecan stands, offer ideal storage of pecans by humans and squirrels alike.

A) NO CHANGE
B) previous
C) introductory
D) erstwhile

LESSON 4 | DATA PRESENTATIONS

ACT ENGLISH AND SAT WRITING AND LANGUAGE

The passages and items in this section accompany the in-class review of the skills and concepts tested by the SAT Writing and Language Test. You will work through the items with your instructor in class. Answers are on page 569.

DIRECTIONS: Each passage is followed by a set of items. For each item, you will select the choice that improves the passage's expression of ideas or corrects errors in sentence structure, usage, or punctuation. A passage or a question may be accompanied by one or more graphics that you will consider as you make editing decisions.

Some items will direct you to an underlined portion of a passage, and others will direct you to a location in a passage or ask you to think about the passage as a whole.

For each item, choose the answer to each question that most effectively improves the quality of writing in the passage or that makes the passage follow the conventions of standard written English. Choose the "NO CHANGE" option if you think the best choice is to leave the relevant portion of the passage as it is.

Data Presentations and Items Illustrated Ⓢ

Item #1 refers to the following passage.

Experts in the field of virtual reality believe that widespread virtual reality use has the potential to change not only our leisure behaviors but also how we think and live. [1] <u>An average of 4.0 million people visit Yosemite every year,</u> putting enormous environmental strain on the park. Next generation virtual reality headsets can produce an experience that rivals the actual drive through Yosemite, thus not only sparing the park, but also making it available to those who couldn't otherwise afford to go.

Yosemite Park Visitors	
Year	Number of Visitors
2013	3.7 million
2012	4.0 million
2011	4.1 million
2010	4.0 million
2009	3.9 million
2008	3.6 million
2007	3.6 million
2006	3.4 million
2005	3.4 million

1. Which choice best begins the sentence with accurate data from the table?

A) NO CHANGE
B) The number of visitors to Yosemite Park has steadily increased over the last nine years,
C) Though peaking at 4.1 million people in 2010, millions of people still visit Yosemite every year,
D) Millions of people visit Yosemite every year.

Item #2 refers to the following passage.

Crude oil from shale formations has put the US closer to energy independence than it's been since 1989. However, the current US shale-oil boom may not last. Though shale wells start strong, output decreases by as much as 70% in the first year alone. Additional wells are needed to offset decline in older wells. According to some estimates, as many as 6,000 new wells per year are needed to maintain current production. Some experts argue that rather than being a panacea for energy independence, shale is the last gasp of the oil industry. **2** Predictions suggest that US oil production will peak in 2017 and fall to 2013 levels within two years.

United States Oil Production by Geological Formation, in Barrels per Day

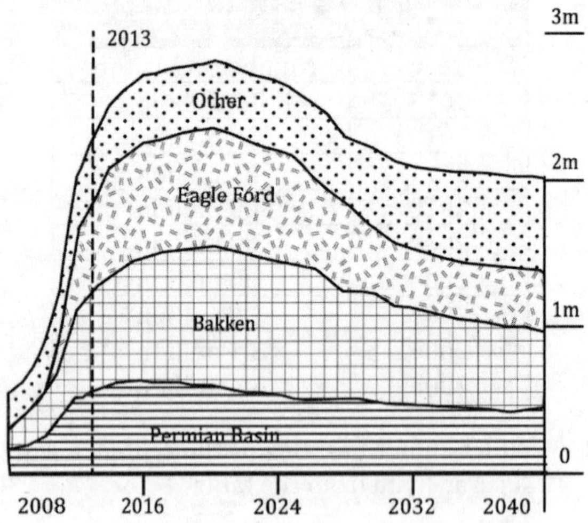

2. Which choice most logically ends the paragraph with accurate data from the graph?

A) NO CHANGE
B) Predictions suggest that US oil production will peak in 2020 and fall to 2013 levels within 10 years.
C) However, predictions suggest US oil production will continue to increase for the foreseeable future.
D) However, predictions suggest that US oil production will peak in 2020 before a continuous decline for the next 30 years.

Items #3–4 refer to the following passage.

In 1964, the Surgeon General announced that cigarette smoking was a significant health hazard, yet smoking still kills over 480,000 people annually in the United States, including over 40,000 deaths from secondhand smoke exposure—more deaths each year than from AIDS, alcohol, cocaine, heroin, homicide, suicide, motor vehicle crashes, and fires combined. **3** Despite gains in preventing and controlling tobacco use with massive education campaigns, litigation, and substantial cigarette price hikes, the percentage of adult smokers in the US is at its highest level in over 40 years. **4** Yet nearly 1 in 5 adults and teens still smokes, so we need to increase access to cessation programs and raise taxes on cigarettes.

Smoking in the United States, 1965–2011

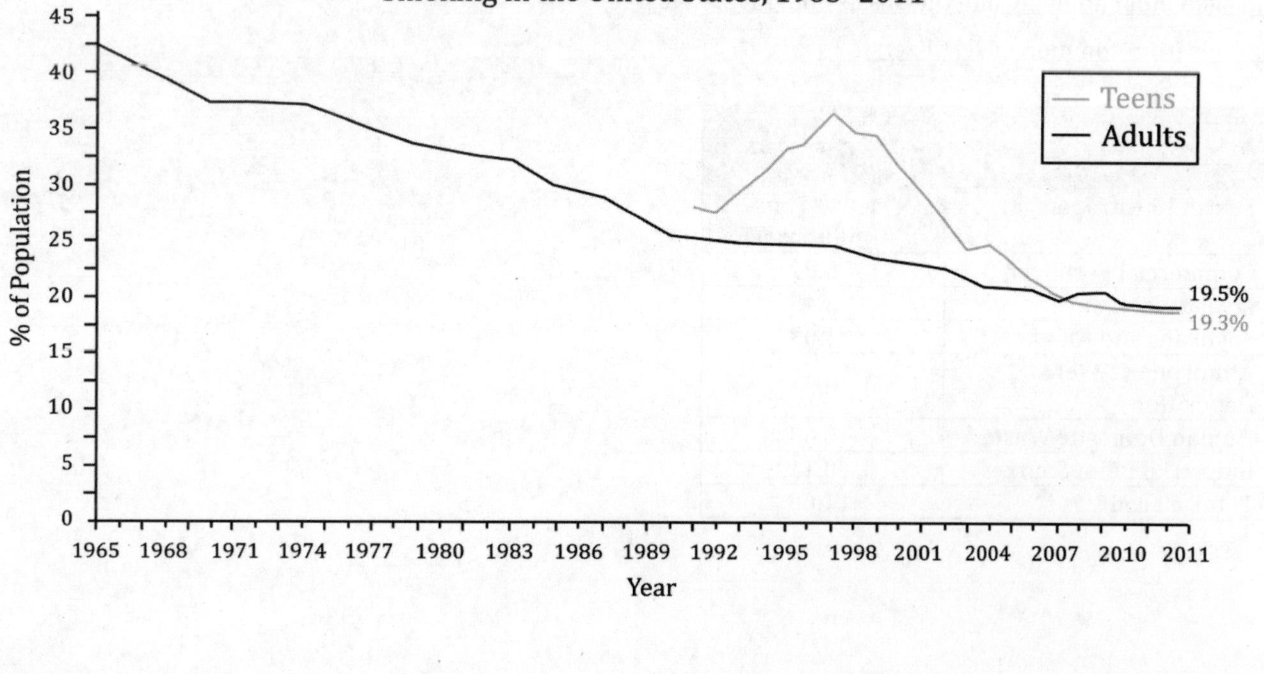

3. Which choice is logically consistent with the data in the graph?

A) NO CHANGE
B) Despite gains in preventing and controlling tobacco use with massive education campaigns, litigation, and substantial cigarette price hikes, the percentage of adult smokers in the US is at its lowest level in over 40 years.
C) We have made gains in preventing and controlling tobacco use with massive education campaigns, litigation, and substantial cigarette price hikes.
D) Gains in preventing and controlling tobacco use with substantial cigarette price hikes is demonstrated by a clear negative relationship between the price of cigarettes and the percentage of the population that smokes.

4. Which choice best begins the sentence with accurate evidence from the graph and logically concludes the paragraph?

A) NO CHANGE
B) Yet nearly 1 in 10 Americans still smokes, so
C) Though only 1 in 5 adults and teens still smokes,
D) Nearly 1 in 5 American adults still smokes and nearly 1 in 5 American students still smokes, so

Item #5 refers to the following passage.

Nitrogen is an essential nutrient for plant growth, development, and reproduction. While nitrogen is one of Earth's most abundant elements, nitrogen deficiency is a common nutritional problem affecting plant cultivation worldwide. Less than 50 percent of nitrogen applied to crops as fertilizer is taken up by plants; the remainder is washed or blown off. Fertilizer run-off results in the "eutrophication" of surface waters: a process in which a body of water is enriched by the addition of excessive nutrients, causing excessive algae growth and subsequent oxygen depletion. Many species cannot survive in these conditions, and large "dead zones" appear from decaying matter undergoing anaerobic degradation. An increase in the use of nitrogen and phosphorus fertilizers in the Mississippi River Basin has been implicated as a cause of hypoxia in the Gulf of Mexico dead zone, an area of over 5,000 square miles along the Louisiana-Texas coast at the mouth of the Mississippi River. 5 More than 11.6 million metric tons of nitrogen input annually into the Mississippi River Basin is from commercial fertilizers.

Estimate of Annual Nitrogen Input into Mississippi River Basin	
Source of Nitrogen	Metric Tons (millions)
Commercial Fertilizer	5.87
Livestock Manure	3.45
Soybeans and Alfalfa	1.03
Atmospheric Wet Deposition	0.51
Human Domestic Waste	0.63
Industrial Point Sources	0.11
Total, all sources	11.60

5. Which sentence presents accurate data from the table?

A) NO CHANGE
B) More than 50 percent of applied commercial fertilizer is released into the Mississippi River Basin annually.
C) More than 50 percent of nitrogen input annually into the Mississippi River Basin is from commercial fertilizers.
D) The Gulf of Mexico dead zone is caused by the annual application of approximately 5.87 million metric tons of commercial fertilizer in the Mississippi River Basin.

Item #6 refers to the following passage.

We think of invasive non-native plants as overgrowing an entire ecosystem, but plants can also change entire ecosystems by modifying ecosystem traits and processes. In the arid Southwest, the deep roots of Mediterranean salt cedars deplete soil water, costing western states more than $1,000 annually per acre in water and flood control losses. On the island of Hawaii, the nitrogen-fixing fire tree has invaded nitrogen-poor areas. As there are no native nitrogen fixers, native Hawaiian plants have adapted to the nitrogen-poor soil. However, introduced species cannot tolerate it, so a wave of invasive plants are taking over areas that are prepared by the fire tree. In Florida, Australian paperbark trees, with spongy outer bark and highly flammable leaves and litter, have increased the frequency of fire, allowing paperbark to convert over 500,000 acres of native wetlands to forest. With recent years being the driest on record, much of Florida is experiencing drought conditions. Not only does this encourage the paperbark to spread, it also cuts off airboat access to many areas, including the Everglades, preventing paperbark removal by contractors hired to eliminate it. The monetary impact of the paperbark in Florida is estimated to be 6 less than one billion dollars in total.

Monetary Impact Estimates of Paperbark in Florida	
Recreation (park use)	200 million
Tourism	750 million
Fires	250 million
Endangered Species Loss	10 million
Nurseries	1 million
Food Production	15 million

6. Which choice completes the sentence with accurate data from the graph?

A) NO CHANGE
B) less than one billion dollars.
C) more than one billion dollars in recreation and tourism losses alone.
D) more than one billion dollars in total.

Items #7–8 refer to the following passage.

In the past, the socialization process in America has been characterized by the interaction of structured groups that share both a sense of mission about the nation's future and codes of behavior rooted in common principles. Communities were bound by religious beliefs, ethnic backgrounds, and strong family relationships. However, this configuration of socializing institutions no longer functions as it once did. Mobility is one factor in the changing picture. **7** One-fifth of Americans change residence each year, but they do not "pack" their culture; they simply move, breaking old community ties. **8** However, recent decreases in mobility rates put greater emphasis on a second factor in the breakdown of the socialization process: depersonalization. Emerson once wrote that an institution is the lengthened shadow of one man. Today's institution is more likely to be the lengthened shadow of itself. By now, the process of social decompression may be irreversible.

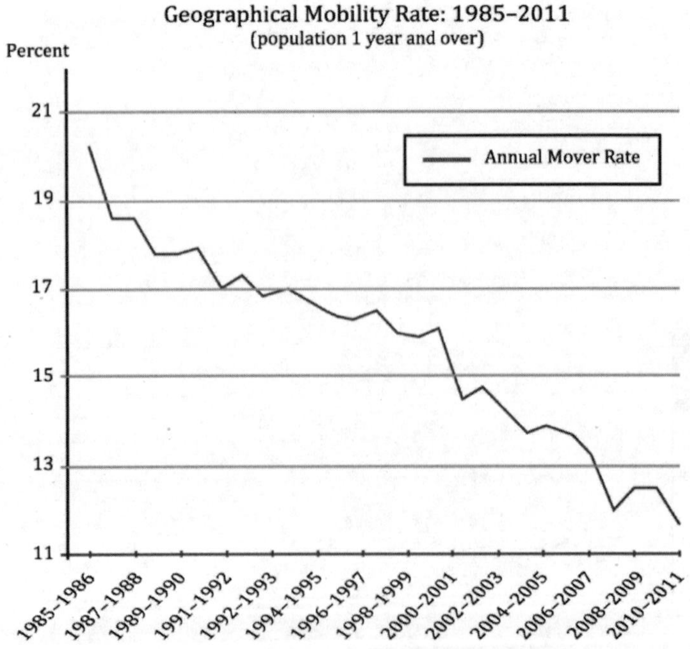

7. Which choice logically incorporates accurate data from the graph?

A) NO CHANGE
B) Historically, as many as one-fifth of Americans change residence each year, but they do not "pack" their culture; they simply move, breaking old community ties.
C) Historically, as many as one-fifth of Americans changed residence each year, but they did not "pack" their culture; they simply moved, breaking old community ties.
D) Ten percent of Americans changed residence in 2011, but they did not "pack" their culture; they simply moved, breaking old community ties.

8. Which choice for the beginning of the sentence is supported by the graph?

A) NO CHANGE
B) However, recent increases in
C) These relatively high
D) Unchanging

Item #9 refers to the following passage.

For indigenous people of the United States, the continuance of cultural values and traditions depends on the transmission of language, but many languages are dying and many more have become extinct already. Of the 85–100 indigenous languages that used to exist in California, half are gone. As for the other half, the vast majority have five or fewer speakers, all over 70 years of age. During the 1998-1999 school year, California voters approved Proposition 227, an English-focused education initiative that dismantled most bilingual education in California public schools. The percentage of English learners enrolled in bilingual education **9** decreased by less than 50 percent following its passage. However, as ethnic populations have continued to increase in Californian, many school districts, parents, and community organizations have launched dual-immersion programs. Not only do these programs help keep California the most linguistically diverse area of North America, English-language learners in dual immersion progress much more quickly than in other forms of instruction. The languages are silent at home and in the community, and so the most effective way to get a critical mass of new fluent speakers of an endangered language is through the school, the same institution that was used to destroy those very languages in the past.

9. Which choice completes the sentence with accurate data based on the graph?

A) NO CHANGE
B) decreased by over 50 percent following its passage.
C) had already decreased by over 50 percent prior to its passage.
D) remained approximately constant following its passage.

Percentage of English Learners Enrolled in Bilingual Education in California

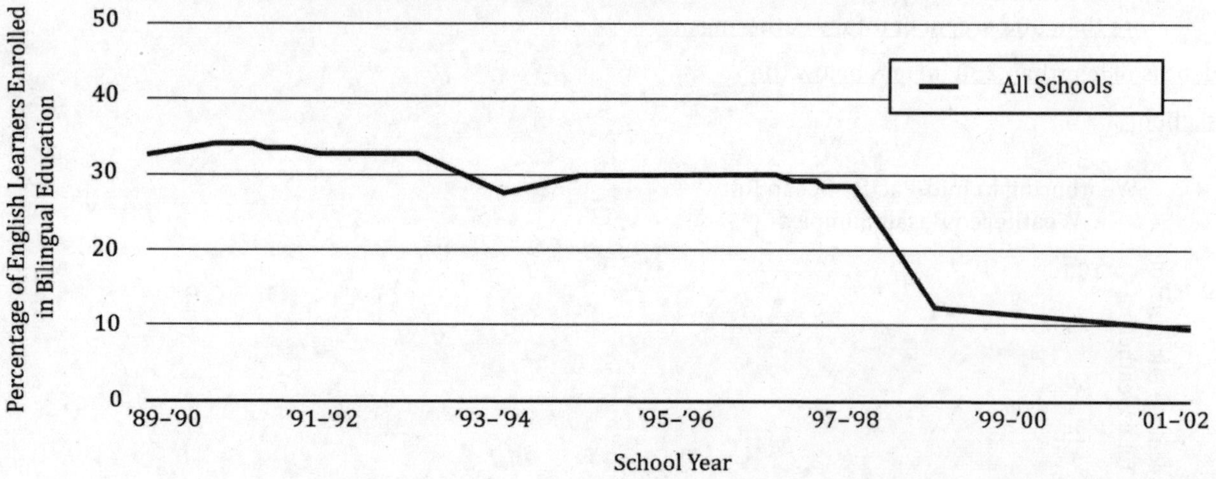

Items #10–11 refer to the following passage.

Many volcanoes are associated with movement of tectonic plates. Where the plates move apart, as along mid-ocean ridges, a rift forms and allows magma to escape from deep within the earth. Though the temperature of the magma is about 1200°C, it solidifies into a mixture of minerals and volcanic glass due to the cold deep ocean water. The resulting basalt formations are slowly broken down due to weathering. Once believed to be a chemical process, evidence suggests that microbial organisms may partly be responsible for weathering. Microscopic examinations of weathered basalts show pits, channels, and other patterns that are unlike chemical weathering. These weathered rocks also contain large amounts of carbon, phosphorus, and nitrogen (which are byproducts of biological activity), as well as traces of nucleic acids. A recent study of the surfaces of weathered basalt drilled from various depths below the seafloor of a mid-Pacific Ocean rift demonstrated that the percentage of total weathering caused by microbial activity generally **10** <u>increased with decreasing depth</u>. According to the results, microbial weathering accounted for **11** <u>more than 50 percent of total weathering at depths of less than 250 meters below the seafloor.</u>

Weathering in mid-Pacific Ocean Rift Weathered Basalt Samples

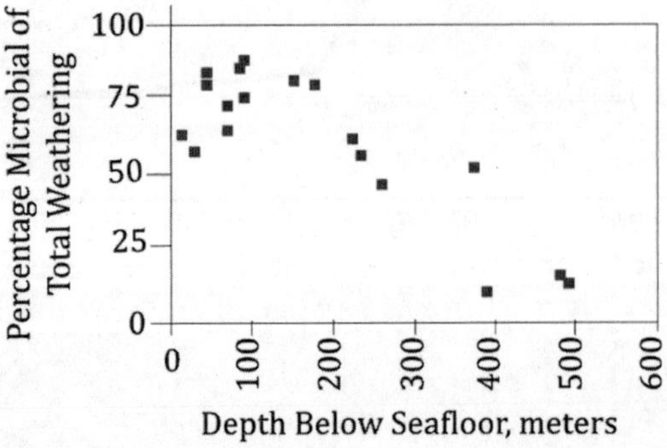

10. Which choice completes the sentence with an accurate description of the relationship illustrated in the graph?

A) NO CHANGE
B) increased with increasing depth.
C) decreased with decreasing depth.
D) decreased with increasing depth.

11. Which choice completes the sentence with accurate data based on the graph?

A) NO CHANGE
B) more than 50 percent of total weathering at depths of more than 250 meters above the seafloor.
C) less than 50 percent of total weathering at depths of more than 250 meters below the seafloor.
D) between 10 percent and 50 percent of total weathering regardless of depth.

Items #12–13 refer to the following passage.

Like tropical reef corals, deep-sea corals have hard skeletons built from calcium and carbonate ions extracted from seawater. Oxygen and oxygen isotopes in carbonate ions can be used to determine the water temperature when the skeleton was formed. The absolute abundance of an isotope is difficult to measure, so studies focus on the ratio of the rare oxygen isotope ^{18}O to the common isotope ^{16}O, commonly denoted as $\delta^{18}O$. This ratio is **12** <u>not</u> related to water temperature during formation of carbonates, so **13** <u>higher ratios mean lower temperatures</u>. Some corals live for decades or centuries, so their skeletons contain a natural record of climate variability, like tree rings and ice cores. The ratio can be used as a proxy for data that cannot be obtained by direct measure. The information gathered would be useful in determining the extent to which global warming may be a problem.

12. Which choice completes the sentence with an accurate description based on the graph?

A) NO CHANGE
B) inversely
C) directly
D) rarely

13. Which choice ends the sentence with an accurate description based on the graph?

A) NO CHANGE
B) higher ratios mean higher temperatures
C) the ratio does not affect temperatures
D) lower ratios mean lower temperatures

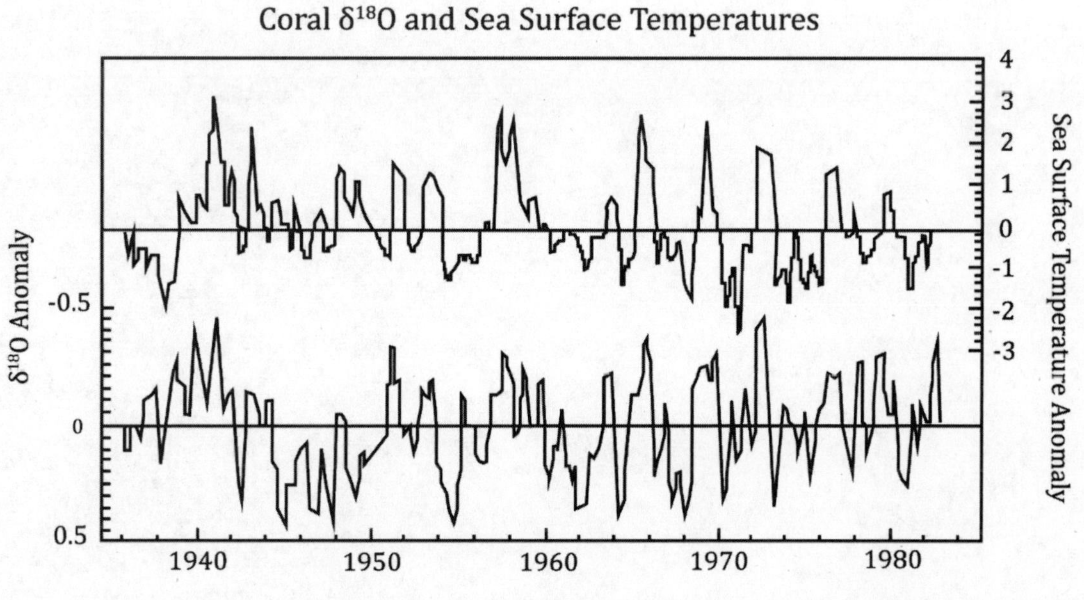

Items #14–15 refer to the following passage.

In 1986, a Wall Street Journal article first used the phrase "glass ceiling" to refer to an invisible, but impenetrable, barrier preventing women from reaching the highest level of business. Subsequent research confirmed the existence of such a barrier. In 2014, **14** approximately 23 percent of Fortune 500 CEOs were female. Where there are women in high places, their compensation is lower than that of men in comparable positions. Nor is the glass ceiling likely to disappear soon. There are relatively few women in the "pipeline," the positions most likely to lead to the top. Furthermore, the glass ceiling doesn't apply only to women. In the same Fortune 500 companies, two-thirds of senior executives (one-step below CEO) were **15** white, one-third were women, and more than 3% were African Americans, 4% were Latinos, and 8% were Asian Americans. In short, the world at the top of the corporate hierarchy does not look anything like America.

14. Which choice completes the sentence with accurate data from Figure 1?

A) NO CHANGE
B) 23 out of 25 Fortune 500 CEOs were male.
C) between 50 and 75 percent of Fortune 500 CEOs were male.
D) over 95 percent of Fortune 500 CEOs were male.

15. Which choice creates a logical sentence with accurate data from Figure 2?

A) NO CHANGE
B) white, less
C) white men, and while 19% were white women, less
D) white men, and of the 19% that were women, less

Figure 1: Female CEOs in Fortune 500 Companies

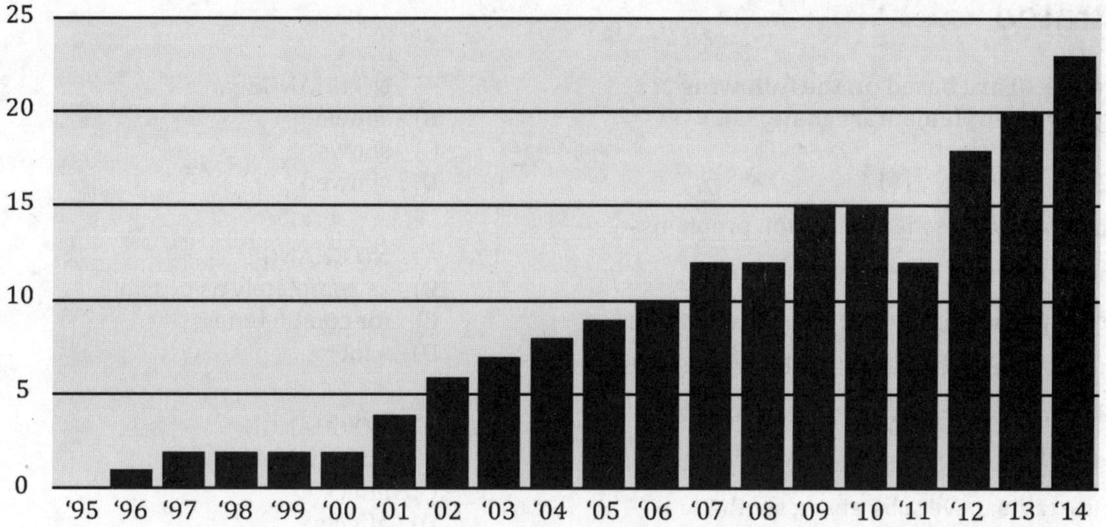

Figure 2: Fortune 500 Senior Executives, 2014

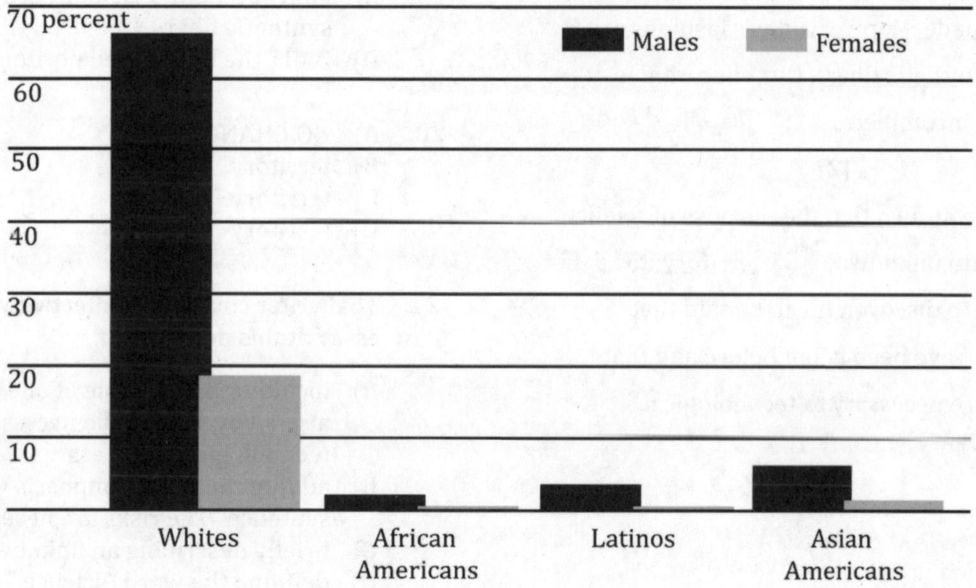

Full-Length Passages Illustrated Ⓐ Ⓢ

Items #16–30 are based on the following passage and supplementary material.

[1]

The history of modern pollution problems **16** show that most have resulted from negligence and ignorance. We have an appalling tendency to interfere with nature before all of the possible consequences of our actions have been studied **17** into completeness. We produce and distribute radioactive substances, synthetic chemicals and fibers, and many other potent compounds before fully comprehending their **18** effects on living organisms. **19** Synthetic means manmade. Many of today's fashions are made with synthetic fibers. Our education is dangerously incomplete.

[2]

It will be argued that the purpose of science is to move into unknown **20** territory; to explore, and to discover. It can be said that similar risks have been taken before and that these risks are necessary to technological progress. **21**

16. A) NO CHANGE
B) shown
C) shows
D) showed

17. A) NO CHANGE
B) as completely as possible
C) for completeness
D) a lot

18. A) NO CHANGE
B) effectiveness
C) affect
D) affects

19. A) NO CHANGE
B) Synthetic fibers are manmade.
C) Many of today's fashions are made with synthetic fibers.
D) OMIT the underlined portion.

20. A) NO CHANGE
B) territory:
C) territory,
D) territory

21. The writer could most effectively bolster the essay at this point by:
A) including an example of one of the risks argued by some to be necessary for technological progress.
B) adding rhetorical emphasis with the sentence "The risks are necessary."
C) briefly describing an unknown territory.
D) defining the word "science."

[3]

These arguments overlook **22** an important element. In the past, risks taken in the name of scientific progress were restricted to a small place and brief period. The effects of the processes we now strive to master are **23** not either localized nor brief. Air pollution covers vast urban areas. Ocean pollutants have been discovered in nearly every part of the world. In the United States, synthetic chemicals have been found in the groundwater of **24** every state. Synthetic chemicals spread over huge stretches of forest and farmland may remain in the soil **25** for decades and years to come. Radioactive pollutants will be found in the biosphere for generations. The size and **26** persistent of these problems have grown with the expanding power of modern science.

US Groundwater Contaminants

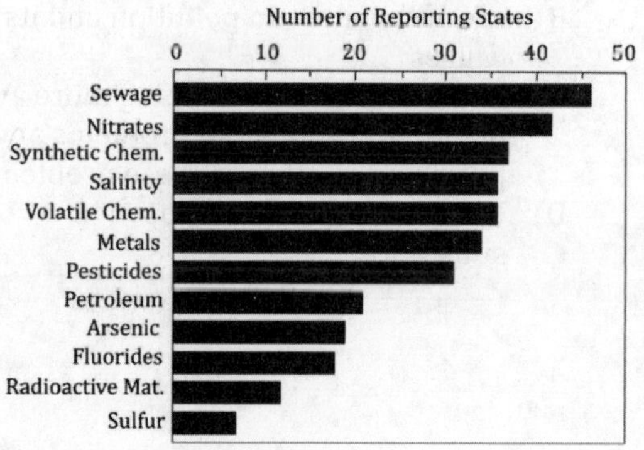

22. A) NO CHANGE
B) a important
C) importance
D) important

23. A) NO CHANGE
B) either
C) not neither
D) neither

24. Which choice completes the sentence with accurate data from the graph?

A) NO CHANGE
B 35 states.
C) over 35 states.
D) approximately 37 percent of states.

25. A) NO CHANGE
B) for decades
C) for years to come in decades
D) for decades and years

26. A) NO CHANGE
B) persistence
C) persevering
D) persisting

[4]

One might also argue that the hazards of modern pollutants are small **27** comparison for the dangers associated with other human activity. No estimate of the actual harm done by smog, fallout, or chemical residues can obscure the reality that the risks are being taken before being fully understood.

[5]

The importance of these issues lies in the failure of science to predict and **28** control. Human intervention into natural processes. The true measure of the danger is represented by the hazards we will encounter if we enter the new age of technology without first evaluating our responsibility to the environment.

27. A) NO CHANGE
B) consideration for
C) comparing with
D) compared to

28. A) NO CHANGE
B) control human
C) control; human
D) control and human

Items #29–30 ask about the preceding passage as a whole.

29. Choose the order of paragraph numbers that will make the essay's structure most logical.

A) NO CHANGE
B) 2, 4, 3, 1, 5
C) 1, 3, 2, 4, 5
D) 5, 1, 2, 3, 4

30. This essay was probably intended for readers who:

A) lack an understanding of the history of technology.
B) are authorities on pollution and its causes.
C) are interested in becoming more aware of our environmental problems and the possible solutions to these problems.
D) have worked with radioactive substances.

Items #31–48 are based on the following passage and supplementary material.

[1]

In the course of billions of years, millions of stars may **31** sometimes occasionally be concentrated into a region, or regions, only a few light years across, **32** and in these crowded conditions colliding with one another. Some of these collisions **33** would occur at high speeds, in which case the stars are torn partially or completely apart. Other collisions are gentle **34** bumps, but the stars coalesce. The bigger the star **35** becomes, the more likely it is to be hit again and the faster it grows until it reaches instability, collapses on itself, **36** and forms a black hole.

31. A) NO CHANGE
B) sometimes, occasionally
C) occasionally
D) off and on

32. A) NO CHANGE
B) colliding
C) and in these crowded conditions, they collide
D) which causes them to collide

33. A) NO CHANGE
B) will occur
C) to occur
D) occur

34. A) NO CHANGE
B) bumps, since the stars
C) bumps, and the stars coalesce
D) bumps, with the stars coalescing

35. A) NO CHANGE
B) becomes the more
C) becomes the more,
D) becomes; the more

36. A) NO CHANGE
B) and a black hole is formed
C) and when this happens a black hole is formed
D) and thus a black hole is formed at this very moment

[2]

When most of the stars and gas in the core of a galaxy **37** has been swallowed up by the black hole, the nucleus of the galaxy settles down **38** to a relative quiet existence. This is probably the state of the nucleus of our own galaxy, but every hundred million years or so it may flare **39** for a brightness 100 times its present level when a globular cluster or especially large gas cloud **40** of enormous size spirals into the nucleus.

[3]

Once formed, a central "seed" black hole grows mainly through the accretion of gas accumulated in the **41** nucleus; gas obtained from disrupted stars, from supernova explosions, or from stars torn apart by the gravitational field of the black hole. Perhaps an entire galaxy can collide with another **42** galaxy, and the result would be the transfer of large amounts of gas from one galaxy **43** to each other.

37. A) NO CHANGE
B) have been
C) will have been
D) would have been

38. A) NO CHANGE
B) to a relatively
C) for a relative and
D) relatively

39. A) NO CHANGE
B) by
C) up to
D) OMIT the underlined portion.

40. A) NO CHANGE
B) of great enormity
C) which is huge
D) OMIT the underlined portion.

41. A) NO CHANGE
B) nucleus and gas
C) nucleus. Gas
D) nucleus gas

42. A) NO CHANGE
B) galaxy to result in
C) galaxy. Such a collision could result in
D) galaxy with the results that

43. A) NO CHANGE
B) to the other
C) an other
D) and another

[4]

A comparison of the masses of galaxies with the masses of the supermassive black holes at their centers shows **44** no relationship. Furthermore, the speed of the outer stars of a galaxy also exhibits **45** a weak correlation with the mass of the supermassive black hole at its center. **46** Very massive black holes are at the center of galaxies with very massive center bulges and relatively fast moving outer stars. While most scientists agree that both of these correlations happen early in the evolution of a galaxy and its central black hole, they continue to debate on the question of which came first, the galaxy or the black hole.

Figure 1

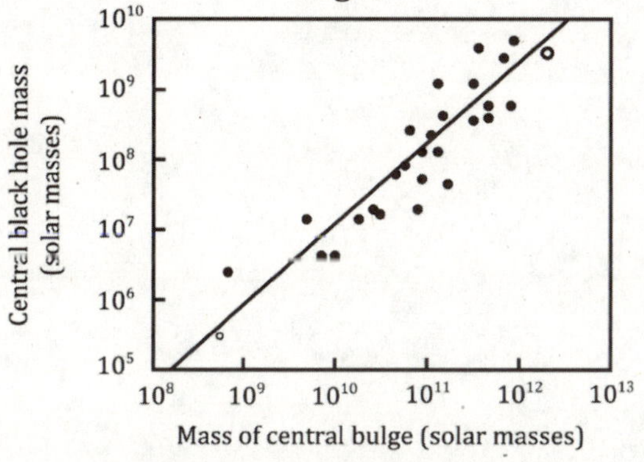

Figure 2

Mass Relationships

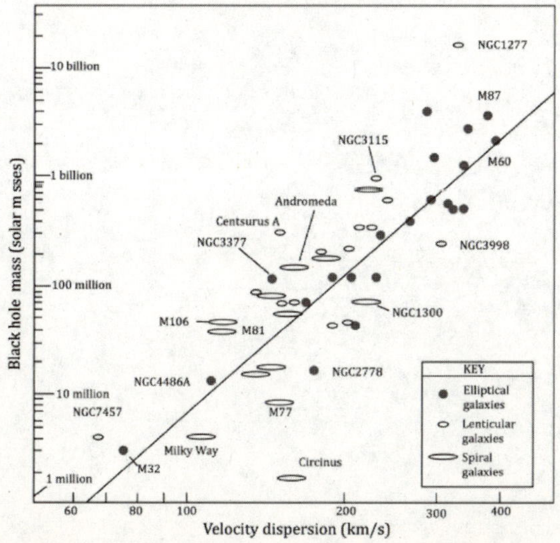

Figure 3

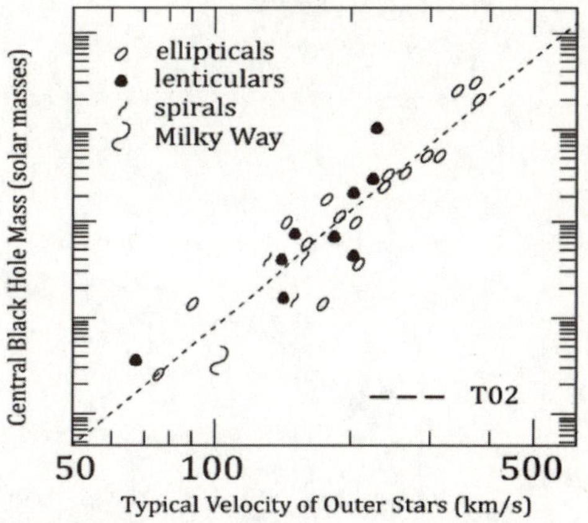

44. Which choice completes the sentence with an accurate description based on the appropriate graph?

A) NO CHANGE
B) an indirect correlation: the greater the mass of the black hole, the smaller the mass of the center bulge of the galaxy.
C) a direct correlation: the greater the mass of the center bulge of a galaxy, the more massive the black hole at its center.
D) a direct correlation: the greater the mass of a black hole, the greater the velocity of the outer stars of the galaxy.

45. Which choice is an accurate description of the data in Figure 2?

A) NO CHANGE
B) a strong
C) an inverse
D) no

46. Which choice is the most logical and accurate sentence based on its position in the paragraph and the information given in the graphs?

A) NO CHANGE
B) Very massive black holes are at the center of massive galaxies with fast moving outer stars.
C) At the center of galaxies with massive center bulges and fast moving outer stars are massive black holes.
D) OMIT the underlined sentence.

Items #47–48 ask about the preceding passage as a whole.

47. Which of the following represents the most logical sequence for the paragraphs?

A) 1, 2, 3, 4
B) 1, 3, 2, 4
C) 2, 3, 4, 1
D) 3, 1, 2, 4

48. The author's intended audience is most likely:

A) astronomers.
B) young children.
C) high school students.
D) physicists.

LESSON 5 | STRATEGIES

ACT ENGLISH AND SAT WRITING AND LANGUAGE

The passages and items in this section accompany the in-class review of the skills and concepts tested by the SAT® Writing and Language Test. You will work through the items with your instructor in class. Answers are on page 570.

Additional Practice Ⓐ Ⓢ

DIRECTIONS: Each passage is followed by a set of items. For each item, you will select the choice that improves the passage's expression of ideas or corrects errors in sentence structure, usage, or punctuation. A passage or a question may be accompanied by one or more graphics that you will consider as you make editing decisions.

Some items will direct you to an underlined portion of a passage, and others will direct you to a location in a passage or ask you to think about the passage as a whole.

For each item, choose the answer to each question that most effectively improves the quality of writing in the passage or that makes the passage follow the conventions of standard written English. Choose the "NO CHANGE" option if you think the best choice is to leave the relevant portion of the passage as it is.

[1]

Republican candidate George W. Bush won the presidential election held on November 7. While votes were cast for other **1** candidates, with Ralph Nader receiving over two million votes, no candidate other than Bush or Gore received a significant number of electoral votes. The election was not finally decided until December 12 after various recounts, court appeals, and a Supreme Court decision. By 8:00 p.m. EST on election day, all major television news networks declared that Gore had won Florida's 25 electoral votes. The prediction was based on exit polls asking **2** voters which candidates they had selected, in the actual vote tally, Bush took an early lead in Florida. By 10 p.m. EST the networks put Florida back into the "undecided" column.

1. A) NO CHANGE
B) candidates with Ralph Nader receiving over two million votes
C) candidates with Ralph Nader, receiving over two million votes
D) candidates, with Ralph Nader receiving over two million votes

2. A) NO CHANGE
B) voters which candidates they had selected, in the actual vote tally Bush
C) voters which candidates they had selected in the actual vote tally, Bush
D) voters which candidates they had selected. In the actual vote tally, Bush

[2]

At approximately 2:30 a.m., with some 85% of the votes counted in Florida and Bush leading Gore by more than 100,000 votes, the networks declared that Bush had carried Florida and therefore, based on voting results from other states, had been elected president. 3 Similarly, most of the remaining votes to be counted in Florida were located in just three 4 counties, Broward, Miami-Dade, and Palm Beach, counties that are heavily Democratic. As these additional votes were reported, Gore began to gain on Bush. By 4:30 a.m., after all votes were counted, Gore had narrowed Bush's margin to just over 2,000 votes, and the networks 5 retracted their predictions that Bush had won Florida and the presidency.

3. Which of the following would be the most effective transition between the two sentences?

A) NO CHANGE
B) Therefore
C) Instead of
D) However

4. A) NO CHANGE
B) counties Broward, Miami-Dade, and Palm Beach;
C) counties: Broward, Miami-Dade, and Palm Beach,
D) counties, Broward Miami-Dade and Palm Beach,

5. Select the choice that best fits the meaning of the sentence.

A) NO CHANGE
B) denied
C) falsified
D) invalidated

6. Which of the following best introduces the reader to the topic of Paragraph 2?

A) A state with a large number of electoral votes can determine the outcome of an election.
B) The news coverage of the election turned out to be flawed.
C) The mistakes made by the networks that evening demonstrate that no process is foolproof.
D) The primary goal in any journalistic undertaking is providing the public with accurate information.

[3]

By the time a mandatory recount was completed later in the week, Bush's lead had dwindled to about 300 votes. A count of overseas military ballots later boosted his margin to about 900 votes. Eventually, after a US Supreme Court decision, Bush was declared the winner and became the president of the United States.

[4]

The faulty journalism resulted from excessive speed and competition, combined with overconfidence in experts and polls. The desire to be first and the goal of offering viewers unique insights led the networks to make calls unwisely based on sketchy and sometimes mistaken information.

[5]

[1] Ultimately, the business imperative to win high ratings overrode journalistic standards. **7** [2] Ratings (that is, the size of the audience) determines the price of commercials. **8** [3] What results being a speed trap in which all of the networks are doing their complicated calculations under maximum competitive pressure in minimum time, usually making their projections minutes apart. [4] Better ratings mean that networks can charge advertisers higher prices for commercial time. **9** [5] The revenue from commercials determines the bottom-line profits of the corporations that own the network.

Presidential Candidate	Nationwide Popular Vote		Electoral Vote
	Count	Percent	
George W. Bush (Republican)	50,456,002	47.87%	271
Al Gore (Democrat)	50,999,897	48.38%	266

7. Sentence 2 would be most effectively placed

A) where it is now.
B) before sentence 1.
C) after sentence 3.
D) after sentence 4.

8. A) NO CHANGE
B) What results were
C) Results are
D) What results is

9. Which of the following is the best way of joining sentences 4 and 5?

A) time, and the
B) time and the
C) time, the
D) time and, the

10. Paragraph 5 would be most effectively placed

A) where it is now.
B) after the first paragraph.
C) after the second paragraph.
D) after the third paragraph.

11. The writer wishes to add a sentence to the first paragraph to distinguish the outcome in Florida from the national vote. Using the data provided in the table, which of the following would correctly complete the following sentence?

Ironically, though Bush won Florida's popular vote, its 25 electoral votes, and the presidency, Al Gore received

A) more of the popular vote nationwide.
B) more of the electoral vote nationwide.
C) a larger portion of the electoral vote than Bush.
D) a smaller portion of the popular vote than Bush.

TEST MECHANICS

ACT ENGLISH AND SAT WRITING AND LANGUAGE

ACT English Overview

The items used by the ACT English Test fall into one of two categories: Usage and Mechanics or Rhetorical Skills. The Usage and Mechanics category (UM) includes all of the items that you would normally associate with a writing test, such as choosing proper verb tense and pronoun usage, while the Rhetorical Skills category (RH) includes items that ask about the development of a selection, such as crafting topic sentences and selecting effective transitions. You'll see specific examples of both types in the "Anatomy" section that follows.

For example, you might be asked to correct an error.

Example:

The recently created wildlife refuge, which includes nearly 30 small ponds for migrating geese and ducks, <u>were</u> made possible by substantial gifts from an anonymous donor to the Wildlife Protection Fund.

A. NO CHANGE
B. was
C. have been
D. being

The correct answer is (B) because the sentence should read "refuge...was," not "refuge...were." *A verb must agree in both number and person with its subject.* You must be aware of this grammatical rule in order to answer the question correctly, but you would not be asked to state the rule that explains it.

SAT Writing and Language Overview

The SAT Writing and Language Test consists of 44 questions. You'll have 35 minutes to read the passages and answer the questions. It doesn't seem like a lot of time, but you are being tested on what you should already know so you won't have to spend a lot of time on each question. You are not being tested on spelling or the exact rules of grammar. Rather, you are being tested on your understanding of the rules of grammar and writing and your ability to apply those rules.

For example, you might be asked to correct an error.

Example:

The recently created wildlife refuge, which includes nearly 30 small ponds for migrating geese and ducks, [1] <u>were</u> made possible by substantial gifts from an anonymous donor to the Wildlife Protection Fund.

1. A) NO CHANGE
B) was
C) have been
D) being

The correct answer is (B) because the sentence should read "refuge...was," not "refuge...were." *A verb must agree in both number and person with its subject.* You must be aware of this grammatical rule in order to answer the question correctly, but you would not be asked to state the rule that explains it.

The answer to the example should be fairly obvious. "Were" does not agree with the singular "refuge;" the correct answer is "was." This is a typical item for testing the principle of subject-verb agreement. The material that intervenes between the subject and verb ("which includes nearly 30 small ponds for migrating geese and ducks") is intended to confuse the ear. To be clear, it is not intended to be a dirty trick; it's just a way of testing whether students can identify subjects and verbs and ensure that they agree (this principle will be studied in greater detail later in the Writing and Language Lessons).

The items used by the Writing and Language Test fall into one of two categories: Standard English Conventions or Expression of Ideas. The Standard English Conventions category (SE) includes all of the items that you would normally associate with a writing test, such as choosing proper verb tense and pronoun usage, while the Expression of Ideas category (EI) includes items that ask about the development of a selection, such as crafting topic sentences and selecting effective transitions. You'll see specific examples of both types in the "Anatomy" section that follows.

ACT English Anatomy

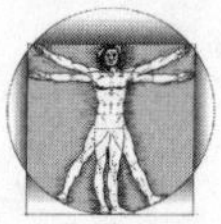

DIRECTIONS: In the passage below, certain parts of the sentences have been underlined and numbered. In the right-hand column, you will find different ways of writing each underlined part; the original version is indicated by the "NO CHANGE" option. For each item, select the choice that best expresses the intended idea, is most acceptable in standard written English, or is most consistent with the overall tone and style of the passage.

There are also items that ask about a section of the passage or the passage as a whole. These items do not refer to an underlined portion of the passage; these items are preceded by statements that are enclosed in boxes.

Read the passage through once before you begin to answer the accompanying items. Finding the answers to certain items may depend on looking at material that appears several sentences beyond the item. So, be sure that you have read far enough ahead before you select your answer choice.

The directions for the English Test are fairly long, and it would take you a while to read them during the test. You'd be wasting valuable time that could be used to answer questions. By the time you get to the test, you'll know what to do in the English Test, so skip the directions altogether.

Coastal Polynyas in Antarctica

Although you might not think it, the Antarctic waters are rich in nutrients. The lack of ice, combined [1] with shallow coastal waters, provides the top layers of

1. A. NO CHANGE
B. ice combined
C. ice combined,
D. ice—combined

1. **(A)** *This item tests punctuation. When you insert an aside or clarifying remark, you need to set off that material from the main part of the sentence, usually with commas—one at the start and one at the end of the material. The original sentence is correctly punctuated.*

the ocean with added sunlight, so polynyas (large open areas of waters surrounded by sea ice) [2] offer ideal conditions for phytoplankton blooms. Because the ice around polynyas is thin in the early spring when the long days begin, they are the first areas to get strong sunlight. The open waters retain more heat, further thinning ice cover and leading to early, intense, and

2. The writer is considering deleting the information in parentheses. If the writer removed this material, the essay would primarily lose:

F. a transition from the first paragraph to the second paragraph.
G. further examples of the animals that depend upon krill for food.
H. a definition of a term that might be unfamiliar to the reader.
J. additional information about the climate of Antarctica.

2. **(H)** *The writer includes the parenthetical material to define a key term that might otherwise be unfamiliar to the reader.*

short-lived plankton blooms. These blooms feed krill, a tiny, shrimp-like animal [3], which in turn are eaten by Adelie penguins, seals, whales, and other seabirds and animals.

3. A. NO CHANGE
B. tiny, shrimp-like animals
C. a tiny animal like a shrimp
D. an animal like a tiny shrimp

3. **(B)** *The original sentence lacks parallelism. In the main part of the sentence, the writer is talking about krill in the plural: "krill...which in turn are eaten." But in the appositive phrase, the writer uses the singular "animal." In order to be parallel to the plural noun "krill," "animal" must be changed to "animals."*

Because [4] relatively small in area, coastal polynyas play an important role. In eastern Antarctica, more than 90 percent of all Adelie penguin colonies live next to coastal polynyas. Polynya productivity explains, to a great extent, the increase and decrease in penguin population.

4. F. NO CHANGE
G. Although
H. Therefore
J. Furthermore

4. **(G)** *"Because" is a word used to introduce an explanation, so the reader expects the information in the independent clause to be the outcome of the information provided in the dependent ("because") clause. The writer, instead, intends to contrast the two ideas in the sentence: even though polynyas are small in area, they are very important to Adelie penguins.*

SAT Writing and Language Anatomy

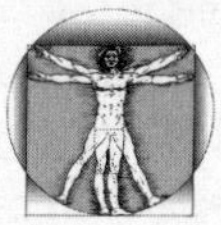

DIRECTIONS: Each passage is followed by a set of items. For each item, you will select the choice that improves the passage's expression of ideas or corrects errors in sentence structure, usage, or punctuation. A passage or a question may be accompanied by one or more graphics that you will consider as you make editing decisions.

Some items will direct you to an underlined portion of a passage, and others will direct you to a location in a passage or ask you to think about the passage as a whole.

For each item, choose the answer to each question that most effectively improves the quality of writing in the passage or that makes the passage follow the conventions of standard written English. Choose the "NO CHANGE" option if you think the best choice is to leave the relevant portion of the passage as it is.

Poverty in America

The defining characteristic of poverty is a lack of money. [1] A family is characterized as poor when its annual income [2] <u>is below a certain dollar</u> amount, calculated by the US Federal Government to be the minimum a family of their size would need to maintain a minimally decent standard of living.

The directions for the Writing and Language Test are fairly long, and it would take you a while to read them during the test. You'd be wasting valuable time that could be used to answer questions. By the time you get to the test, you'll know what to do in the Writing and Language Test, so skip the directions altogether.

1. Which of the following would, if added after the first sentence of the passage, help to clarify for the reader the scope of the passage?

A) While the defining characteristic of poverty is a lack of money, the incidence of poverty is not uniform throughout the United States.
B) Lacking money is a defining characteristic of poverty, but some people in poverty have more money than other people in poverty.
C) Poverty is primarily lacking money, and it is spread throughout the United States, affecting rural livers as well as young people.
D) The lack of money can affect anyone anywhere and is the cause of poverty in the United States.

1. **(A)** *(A) represents an improvement over the original because it tells the reader that the discussion will also include information about the distribution of poverty.*

2. A) NO CHANGE
B) being under a certain dollar amount,
C) is under a certain specific dollar amount,
D) is a certain dollar amount

2. **(A)** *The original sentence is correct. (B) and (C) are awkward and wordy by comparison. (D) destroys the structure of the sentence.*

In certain areas of rural America, poverty is the rule rather than the exception. **3** As much as 50 percent of the families may earn less than the poverty level, and **4** some may manage to survive by subsisting somehow or other on amounts even less than half the official poverty level income.

Poverty is particularly prevalent among those under age 18. According to the Census Bureau, **5** there are more people under the age of 18 living in poverty than people in any other age group.

Fig. 1 People in Poverty by Characteristic: 2013

	Group	Total	Number Below Poverty	Percent in Group below poverty (%)
Age	Under age 18	73,625,000	14,659,000	19.9
	Aged 18 to 64	194,833,000	26,429,000	13.6
	Aged 65 and older	44,508,000	4,231,000	9.5

Adapted from United States Census Bureau Poverty Data

3. A) NO CHANGE
   B) As many as
   C) So many as
   D) So much

3. **(B)** *Since families come in discrete units, the correct idiom is "many," not "much."*

4. A) NO CHANGE
   B) some folks may manage to survive by subsisting somehow
   C) some may manage to subsist somehow or other
   D) some may subsist

4. **(D)** *This is a words-in-context item, and it illustrates a couple of aspects of words-in-context items. First, the successively edited answer choices show that there is excess verbiage in the original, so eliminate (A). There is also low-level usage, "folks," in (B) and "somehow or other" in (C), so they can be eliminated. (D) is the most concise answer choice, and it is most consistent with the tone of the passage.*

5. Complete the sentence correctly based upon the information in Figure 1.

   A) NO CHANGE
   B) nearly 1 out of 5 persons under the age of 18 lives in poverty, a higher percentage than any other age group
   C) by the time these people reach age 65 most will no longer be poor
   D) of the total number of people living in poverty, nearly 1 out of 5 is under 18

5. **(B)** *For this item you need to analyze and draw information from the graphic in order to correctly revise the passage. According to the table, the greatest number of people below poverty are aged 18 to 64. However, as the table shows, the percentage of people living in poverty under age 18 is the greatest, 19.9%. Therefore, (B) is the correct answer.*

ACT English Pacing

The English Test consists of five passages, each approximately 300 words in length and with 15 corresponding items, for a total of 75 items. The time limit is 45 minutes. So, a fairly simple and easy-to-follow plan is to allocate nine minutes to each of the five passages:

TASK	ALLOTTED TIME	REMAINING TIME
Read first passage	1.5 minutes	43.5 minutes
Answer accompanying items	7.5 minutes*	36 minutes
Read second passage	1.5 minutes	34.5 minutes
Answer accompanying items	7.5 minutes*	27 minutes
Read third passage	1.5 minutes	25.5 minutes
Answer accompanying items	7.5 minutes*	18 minutes
Read fourth passage	1.5 minutes	16.5 minutes
Answer accompanying items	7.5 minutes*	9 minutes
Read fifth passage	1.5 minutes	7.5 minutes
Answer accompanying items	7.5 minutes*	0 minutes

*Approximately 30 seconds per question

This schedule describes what would happen in a perfect world; but, of course, the ACT test does not take place in a perfect world. Some items are going to take longer than others, particularly those that ask about the overall development of the passage. This means that you'll need to spend less time on the simple grammar items, building up a time reserve for those more difficult items that are coming. And the more difficult items are usually placed at the end of a passage because that's where it makes sense to ask, "What is the main idea?" and "How could the passage be improved?" The schedule actually gives you a feedback loop that lets you know whether you need to skip some items. For example, if you are nearing the "36 minutes left in the section" mark and still have two or three items to do on the first passage, then skip any Rhetorical Skills items and go straight away to the next passage. The Rhetorical Skills items take longer, and there will be some simple grammar items waiting to be cherry-picked in the next passage.

SAT Writing and Language Pacing

The SAT Writing and Language Test consists of four passages, each approximately 400–450 words in length and each with 11 corresponding items, for a total of 44 items. The time limit is 35 minutes. So, a fairly simple and easy-to-follow plan is to allocate 8 minutes and 45 seconds to each of the four passages and the questions that follow:

TASK	ALLOTTED TIME	REMAINING TIME
Read first passage	3.25 minutes	31.75 minutes
Answer accompanying items	5.5 minutes*	26.25 minutes
Read second passage	3.25 minutes	23 minutes
Answer accompanying items	5.5 minutes*	17.5 minutes
Read third passage	3.25 minutes	14.25 minutes
Answer accompanying items	5.5 minutes*	8.75 minutes
Read fourth passage	3.25 minutes	5.5 minutes
Answer accompanying items	5.5 minutes*	0 minutes

*Approximately 30 seconds per question

This schedule describes what would happen in a perfect world; but, of course, the SAT test is not administered in a perfect world. Some items are going to take longer than others, particularly those that ask about the overall development of the passage or refer to informational graphics. This means that you'll need to spend less time on the simple grammar items, building up a time reserve for those more difficult items that are coming. And the more difficult items are usually placed at the end of a passage because that's where it makes sense to ask "What is the main idea?" and "How could the passage be improved?" The schedule actually gives you a feedback loop that lets you know whether you need to skip some items.

ACT English and SAT Writing and Language Time Trial

(8 items; 5 minutes)

DIRECTIONS: Each passage is followed by a set of items. For each item, you will select the choice that improves the passage's expression of ideas or corrects errors in sentence structure, usage, or punctuation. A passage or a question may be accompanied by one or more graphics that you will consider as you make editing decisions.

Some items will direct you to an underlined portion of a passage, and others will direct you to a location in a passage or ask you to think about the passage as a whole.

For each item, choose the answer to each question that most effectively improves the quality of writing in the passage or that makes the passage follow the conventions of standard written English. Choose the "NO CHANGE" option if you think the best choice is to leave the relevant portion of the passage as it is.

Passage I

The Orchid Family

The orchids are the most diverse plant family with 20,000 to 30,000 species in over 800 genera. This represents about 10% of all flowering plant species. DNA research [1] suggesting that the orchids are among the most ancient flowering plant families, as old as 90,000,000 years. They are still evolving rapidly into new species. For example, many endemic species in the genus *Telipogon* are found in the Andes Mountains in areas that were

1. A) NO CHANGE
   B) suggest
   C) suggests
   D) to suggest

buried under glaciers [2] as recent as 10,000 years ago. Orchids are found on all continents except Antarctica. Like all monocots, including [3] lilies orchids are flowering plants that have only one seed leaf and typically [4] lacks woody tissue. All orchids have a single reproductive structure, called the column, which [5] is forming by the fusion of the male stamens and female style. These structures are separate in the flowers of most other families. Orchids also have a modified third petal called a [6] lip, and produce enormous numbers of very tiny seeds.

The vast majority of orchid species are native to the tropics, and [7] its numbers increase with proximity to the equator. The [8] most richest diversity of orchid species is found in the lush tropical forests of equatorial South America, Southeast Asia, and New Guinea. New species are constantly being discovered in these areas.

2. A) NO CHANGE
B) as recently as
C) so recently as
D) recently

3. A) NO CHANGE
B) lilies orchids,
C) lilies, orchids,
D) lilies, orchids

4. A) NO CHANGE
B) lacking
C) lack
D) lacked

5. A) NO CHANGE
B) forming
C) are formed
D) is formed

6. A) NO CHANGE
B) lip and produce
C) lip and produce,
D) lip, and produces

7. A) NO CHANGE
B) their
C) one's
D) your

8. A) NO CHANGE
B) more richer
C) richest
D) richly

ACT English and SAT Writing and Language Game Plan

Don't Read the Directions

By the time you get to the test, you'll know what to do when you see the English or Writing and Language Test just by the way it looks. Let the appearance of the items on the page be all the direction you need, and get started on reading the first passage immediately.

Start Each Set of Items by Reading the Passage

You really need to read the passage before you start answering questions because some items will not make sense without the proper context. Since the passages are about 400 words in length, you can finish a read-through in a little more than a minute. Read primarily for overall development so that you'll understand the logic in the author's presentation, and don't worry overly much about the details. Later, you can study the specific parts of the passage in which the various items appear.

Read Any Items with Underlined Parts, Looking for Errors

When an item asks about rewriting an underlined part, begin by reading the sentence, looking for an error. If you can spot an error, then you're more than halfway home. Later in the English and Writing and Language Lessons, you'll cover the important principles of writing and grammar that are tested, and there is a list of these principles provided in the Course Concept Outline (p. 119). You can treat this outline as a checklist of important things to look for in English and Writing and Language items.

Work Backwards from the Answer Choices

If you are having difficulty locating the right answer, use the answer choices to help you. Compare each answer choice with the original, and explain to yourself what the important difference is between the two of them. This can help you see an error that you may have overlooked. Additionally, you can compare choices to each other, asking yourself in what way one choice is better or worse than another one. Again, this technique can help you uncover a hidden error and make the right choice.

Don't Look for Spelling or Capitalization Errors

These topics are not tested, so don't waste your time looking for errors of this sort. Even if you think you've found a spelling mistake, there is nothing you can do with the information. The correct response is correct because it "follows the requirements of standard written English."

Make Educated Guesses

You should be able to eliminate some answer choices on most items because they introduce new errors that are not found in the original. Or, a choice may fail to correct an error that you know to be in the underlined part of the sentence. You should always guess, even if you are unable to eliminate any answer choices, because there is no penalty for guessing on the ACT and SAT tests. However, your chances improve if you are able to eliminate even one answer choice.

Don't Be Afraid to Pick "No Change"

Choose "NO CHANGE" if you think that the original is correct as written. Many students automatically refuse to pick "NO CHANGE" because they figure that there must be something wrong with the original—even if they are unable to say what. But this reasoning is faulty. "NO CHANGE," when it is an option, is statistically as likely to be correct as is one of the other three choices.

QUIZ

ACT ENGLISH

This section contains an ACT English quiz. Complete the quiz under timed conditions. Answers are on page 570.

(29 items; 20 minutes)

DIRECTIONS: In the passages below, certain parts of the sentences have been underlined and numbered. In the right-hand column, you will find different ways of writing each underlined part; the original version is indicated by the "NO CHANGE" option. For each item, select the choice that best expresses the intended idea, is most acceptable in standard written English, or is most consistent with the overall tone and style of the passage.

There are also items that ask about a section of the passage or the passage as a whole. These items do not refer to an underlined portion of the passage; these items are preceded by statements that are enclosed in boxes.

Read the passage through once before you begin to answer the accompanying items. Finding the answers to certain items may depend on looking at material that appears several sentences beyond the item. So, be sure that you have read far enough ahead before you select your answer choice.

Passage I

The Influence of the Southwest on Artists

Georgia O'Keeffe, <u>who's</u> [1] death <u>at age ninety-eight</u> [2] closed one of the most fertile chapters of

1. A. NO CHANGE
B. which
C. that
D. whose

2. F. NO CHANGE
G. at the old age of ninety-eight
H. at the age of ninety-eight years
J. when she was ninety-eight years old

American creativity and flourished 3 as a maverick in her life and work. Since other 4 painters spent a season or two in the country trying to come to terms with the scenes and settings of the Southwest—O'Keeffe stayed a lifetime. When the canvases of other artists, working in the region 5 faded from view and then were neglected in the chronicle of American visual history, 6 her stylized images made an indelible and permanent 7 impression on countless eyes.

Between 1900 and 1945, the region now called New Mexico both fascinated and also it perplexed 8 two generations of American artists. Despite their successes, 9 many of those artists wearied of the industrial world of the east. The vast expanse of the West offered a promise for inspiration. 10 For these artists, life and art, so

3. A. NO CHANGE
B. creativity, and flourished
C. creativity—flourished
D. creativity, flourished

4. F. NO CHANGE
G. Because other
H. In that other
J. Other

5. A. NO CHANGE
B. artists working in the region,
C. artists working in the region
D. artists, who worked in the region

6. F. NO CHANGE
G. got neglected then in the chronicle of American visual history
H. were also then neglected in the American visual history chronicle
J. then they were also totally neglected in the chronicle of American visual history

7. A. NO CHANGE
B. indelible
C. indelible—and permanent—
D. indelible but permanent

8. F. NO CHANGE
G. and perplexed
H. while perplexing
J. but perplexed

9. A. NO CHANGE
B. Despite their having many successes
C. In spite of their having their successes
D. Ensuring successes,

10. F. NO CHANGE
G. America's West, with its vast expanse, offered an inspiring promise.
H. America's vast expanse of the West offered a promise for inspiration.
J. Offering a promise of inspiration to the artists was the vast expanse of the American West.

separate in New York and Paris, seemed inextricably bounded [11] in Southwestern cultures. Painters of every persuasion were convinced [12] that sampling this mysterious phenomenon will strengthen [13] and enrich their own work. Most were touched by what D. H. Lawrence called the "spirit of the place." Besides the scenic beauty bathed in clear golden light. The [14] rich traditions of New Mexico's Indian and Hispanic people who were living there [15] became frequent subjects of the artists who traveled to Taos and Santa Fe.

11. A. NO CHANGE
B. inextricably bound
C. inextricable bounding
D. inextricably bounding

12. F. NO CHANGE
G. could be convinced
H. will be convinced
J. are convincing

13. A. NO CHANGE
B. would strengthen
C. strengthens
D. strengthening

14. F. NO CHANGE
G. light, the
H. light the
J. light: the

15. A. NO CHANGE
B. who lived there
C. living there
D. OMIT the underlined portion.

Items #16–17 ask about the preceding passage as a whole.

16. Is the author's quote of D. H. Lawrence in the last paragraph appropriate?

F. Yes, because the author is talking about how this spirit inspired artists, and the quote strengthens his argument.
G. No, because the author has already made his point about the spirit, and the quote is redundant.
H. No, because the author does not make it clear that Lawrence is an authority on the subject.
J. Yes, because it is always a good idea to end an article with a quotation.

17. How might the author have developed the essay so that it was more interesting?

A. The author could have told an anecdote about D. H. Lawrence.
B. The author could have eliminated all mention of Georgia O'Keeffe.
C. The author could have discussed the settling of New Mexico.
D. The author could have been more specific about the other artists who went to the Southwest.

Passage II

Chippewa Chief Demands Timber Payment

Early in November 1850, the work of a logging detail from Fort Gaines in the Minnesota Territory was interrupted by a party of Chippewa warriors who demanded payment for the timber. The loggers refused, so [18] the Indians, acting at the direction of Chief Hole-in-the-Day [19] confiscated the government's oxen. The loggers had established their camp on Chippewa lands without his authorizing it [20]. Therefore [21], in a move designed to force reimbursements for the timber, Hole-

18. F. NO CHANGE
G. The loggers refused—
H. The loggers refused:
J. The loggers refused so

19. A. NO CHANGE
B. that acted at the direction of Chief Hole-in-the-Day,
C. acting at the direction of Chief Hole-in-the-Day,
D. (acting at the direction of Chief Hole-in-the-Day),

20. F. NO CHANGE
G. without his authorization
H. without their authorizing it
J. without his authorization of it

21. A. NO CHANGE
B. Henceforth
C. Since
D. On the contrary

in-the-Day was ordering [22] his braves to seize the oxen.

Captain John Todd, the commanding officer at Fort Gaines, demanded that the cattle had to be returned to them [23]. The chief's reply was firm, and at the same time, it was friendly [24]. In his message to Captain Todd, Hole-in-the-Day explained that he had delayed to seize [25] the cattle until he could meet Todd in council and had sent a messenger to the officer requesting a conference at Crow Wing. When Todd did not come, he acted, additionally [26] he later decided that since the army had not paid for timber cut the previous winter, he intended to keep the oxen until the tribe was reimbursed by [27] all the timber taken for the fort. Hole-in-the-Day concluded by saying, "Do not think hard of me, but I do as others would—the timber is mine." [28]

22. F. NO CHANGE
G. gave orders that
H. orders
J. ordered

23. A. NO CHANGE
B. the return of the cattle
C. the cattle's returning
D. that they return the cattle

24. F. NO CHANGE
G. but, at the same time, it was friendly
H. yet friendly
J. at the same time—friendly

25. A. NO CHANGE
B. delayed to have seized
C. delayed to seized
D. delayed seizing

26. F. NO CHANGE
G. acted but additionally
H. acted. Additionally,
J. acted additionally,

27. A. NO CHANGE
B. reimbursed for
C. reimbursed
D. was reimbursed for

28. Is the author's use of the quote in the final paragraph appropriate?

F. Yes, because it neatly summarizes the main point of the essay.
G. No, because the chief's thoughts were irrelevant to the events.
H. Yes, but the author should have included a quotation from Captain Todd.
J. No, because quotations have no place in expository writing.

Item #29 asks about the preceding passage as a whole.

29. Which of the following best describes the overall character of the essay?

A. Description of a scene
B. Narration of events
C. Comparison of two theories
D. Argument for a change

Quiz

SAT Writing and Language

This section contains a Writing and Language quiz. Complete the quiz under timed conditions. Answers are on page 570.

(34 items; 25 minutes)

DIRECTIONS: Each passage is followed by a set of items. For each item, you will select the choice that improves the passage's expression of ideas or corrects errors in sentence structure, usage, or punctuation. A passage or a question may be accompanied by one or more graphics that you will consider as you make editing decisions.

Some items will direct you to an underlined portion of a passage, and others will direct you to a location in a passage or ask you to think about the passage as a whole.

For each item, choose the answer to each question that most effectively improves the quality of writing in the passage or that makes the passage follow the conventions of standard written English. Choose the "NO CHANGE" option if you think the best choice is to leave the relevant portion of the passage as it is.

Passage I

The Con Game Is No Game

[1]

Most people have a certain crime 1 that one believes should be ranked as the worst of all crimes. For some, 2 its' murder; for others, it may be selling drugs to children. I believe, 3 moreover, that the worst of all crimes may be the confidence scheme.

[2]

The confidence scheme may seem an 4 odd choice for the worst crime since con games are usually 5 nonviolent. Although, it is a crime that ranks high in heartlessness. Con artists are the most

1. A) NO CHANGE
B) that they believe
C) which one believes
D) that you believe

2. A) NO CHANGE
B) they are
C) it's
D) its

3. A) NO CHANGE
B) however
C) further
D) therefore

4. A) NO CHANGE
B) obvious
C) irrelevant
D) apt

5. A) NO CHANGE
B) nonviolent, though
C) nonviolent, but
D) nonviolent, and

devious, the most harmful, and the most disruptive members of society because **6** they break down **7** honesty, and trust, the most important bonds of the social order.

[3]

The con games themselves are **8** simplistic almost infantile. They work **9** on account of a con artist can win complete confidence, talk fast enough to keep the victim slightly confused, **10** and dangling enough temptation to suppress any suspicion or skepticism. Traditionally, the primary targets of these criminals **11** will be the elderly and **12** women. (And they prefer to work in large crowds.) In the past several years, however, as access to the web has become more widespread, the demographics have changed. **13**

6. A) NO CHANGE
B) it breaks
C) of its breaking
D) of them breaking

7. A) NO CHANGE
B) honesty, and trust the
C) honesty and trust, the
D) honesty and trust the

8. A) NO CHANGE
B) simplistic; almost infantile
C) simplistic, almost infantile
D) simplistic, yet almost infantile

9. A) NO CHANGE
B) on account of a con artist's ability to
C) owing to a con artist's ability to
D) because a con artist can

10. A) NO CHANGE
B) and dangles
C) and has dangled
D) and dangle

11. A) NO CHANGE
B) to be
C) are
D) is

12. A) NO CHANGE
B) women, and the con artists prefer to work in large crowds.
C) women, preferring, of course, to work in large crowds.
D) women (who prefer to work in large crowds).

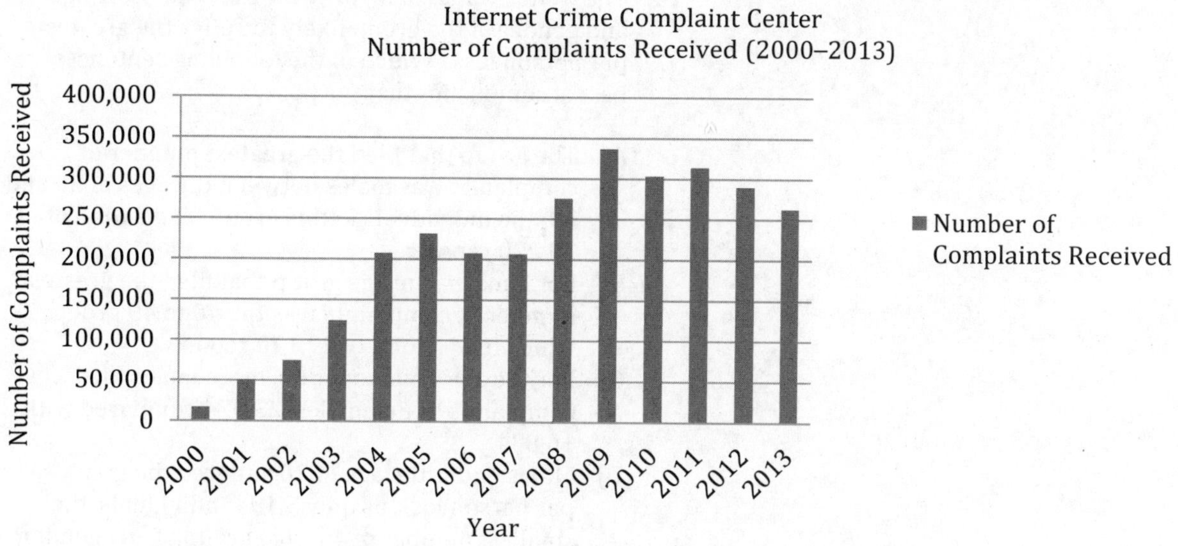

Internet Crime Complaints (2013)

Age (in years)	Number of Reports by Males	Total Loss Reported by Males	Number of Reports by Females	Total Loss Reported by Females
Under 20	5,194	$103,298,649	3,602	$2,364,515
20–29	24,549	$42,144,452	23,483	$23,619,502
30–39	28,391	$71,022,425	26,389	$41,784,048
40–49	26,668	$89,559,205	29,170	$70,355,407
50–59	29,220	$93,705,383	26,239	$83,858,340
Over 60	23,074	$87,244,816	16,834	$72,884,870

13. The author wishes to include a sentence using data from the graphs to prove this point. Which of the following would best accomplish this purpose?

A) In 2013, for the age group 20 to 59, the number of complaints filed by males and the number filed by females have been similar, while the number filed by people age 60 and over has been less than other groups in that range.

B) In 2013, the total dollar value of the loss reported by males over 60 was greater than the total dollar value of the loss reported by females over 60.

C) The total number of complaints received by the Internet Crime Complaint Center in 2013 was 262,813, but ten years earlier, the number reported in 2004 was only 207,492.

D) The total number of complaints received by the Internet Crime Complaint Center declined from 336,655 in 2009 to 262,813 in 2013, though one year, 2011, did show an increase.

14. The writer wants to identify for the reader the age and gender of the group likely to suffer the greatest per person loss. Which of the following sentences best accomplishes that purpose?

A) The group that filed the greatest number of complaints was males between the ages of 50 and 59; the individuals in this group filed a total of 29,220 reports.
B) For females, the age group that filed the greatest number of complaints was the 40 to 49 group, which filed a total of 29,170 reports.
C) For the age group over 60, more males filed complaints than females, 23,074 compared with 16,834.
D) Males under the age of 20 suffered the greatest per person loss, as only 5,194 individuals, the smallest number of any age group of any gender, suffered a total loss of $103,298,649, the largest of any group.

15. The writer wants to conclude the essay by answering a possible objection that internet fraud will become less important in the future based on the data for years 2012 and 2013. Which of the following sentences would most effectively accomplish this goal?

A) Between the years 2000 and 2005, the number of complaints filed with the Center increased, but the decline in that number in 2006 and 2007 strongly suggests that the importance of the internet is declining.
B) From 2007 to 2009, the number of complaints filed with the Center increased to a high of 336,655 but declined thereafter to a total of 262,813 in 2013.
C) In 2013, the total number of complaints filed with the Center was 262,813, which cumulatively resulted in hundreds of millions of dollars in losses.
D) Between 2000 and 2011, the number of annual complaints filed with the Center declined twice, but then increased, so the pattern suggests that the declines reported in 2012 and 2013 are likely to be reversed.

Items #16–18 ask about the preceding passage as a whole.

16. Which of the following is most probably the author's opinion rather than a fact?

A) The most disruptive members of society are con artists.
B) The majority of con games are nonviolent.
C) The targets of con games are mostly the elderly and women.
D) The con artists succeed when they win the complete confidence of their targets.

17. What would be the most logical continuation of the essay?

A) A description of some confidence games
B) An account of the elderly as crime victims in society
C) An account of the author's experience with con artists
D) An explanation of crowd psychology

18. What would strengthen the author's contention that con games rank first in heartlessness?

A) Statistics to show the number of people who were taken in by the con artist
B) A discussion of the way the police handle the problem
C) An example that shows how the con artist breaks down honesty and trust
D) An example to illustrate that con games are nonviolent and simple

Passage II

Elizabeth I's Intellect Ruled Supreme

[1]

Elizabeth I had a sensuous and indulgent nature that she inherited from her mother, Anne Boleyn **19** (who was beheaded by Henry VIII). Splendor and pleasure **20** is the very air she breathed. She loved gaiety, laughter, and wit. Her vanity **21** remained even, to old age. The vanity of a coquette.

[2]

The statesmen **22** who she outwitted believed, almost to the end, that Elizabeth I was little more than a frivolous woman **23** who was very vain. However, the Elizabeth they saw was far from **24** being all of Elizabeth, the queen.

19. A) NO CHANGE
B) (having been beheaded by Henry VIII)
C) beheaded by Henry VIII
D) OMIT the underlined portion.

20. A) NO CHANGE
B) is,
C) were
D) were,

21. A) NO CHANGE
B) remains, even to old age, the
C) remains, even to old age the
D) remained, even to old age, the

22. A) NO CHANGE
B) that she outwitted
C) whom she outwitted
D) who she was outwitting

23. A) NO CHANGE
B) and she was also very vain
C) known for her great vanity
D) OMIT the underlined portion.

24. A) NO CHANGE
B) to be
C) having been
D) OMIT the underlined portion.

The willfulness of her father, Henry VIII, and the triviality of Anne played over the surface of a nature 25 so hard like steel—a purely intellectual temperament. Her vanity and caprice carried no weight 26 whatsoever in state affairs. The coquette of the presence chamber 27 had became the coolest and hardest of politicians at the council board.

[3]

It was this part that gave her marked 28 superiority over the statesmen of her time. No 29 more nobler a group of ministers ever gathered round the council board than those of Elizabeth, but she was the instrument of none. She listened and she weighed, but her policy, as a whole, was her own. It was the policy of good sense, 30 not genius, she endeavored to keep her throne, to keep England out of war, 31 and she wanted to restore civil and religious order.

25. A) NO CHANGE
B) as hard as
C) so hard as
D) as hard like

26. A) NO CHANGE
B) no matter what
C) whatever, at all
D) whatever, despite everything

27. A) NO CHANGE
B) became
C) used to become
D) becomes

28. A) NO CHANGE
B) superiority in regard to
C) superiority about
D) superior quality to

29. A) NO CHANGE
B) nobler a group,
C) nobler a group
D) more nobler of a group,

30. A) NO CHANGE
B) not genius she
C) not genius. She
D) —not genius, she

31. A) NO CHANGE
B) wanting
C) and wanting
D) and

Items #32–34 ask about the preceding passage as a whole.

32. What might logically have preceded this essay?

A) Some biographical background on Elizabeth I
B) A discussion of the wives of Henry VIII
C) A discussion of the politics of Tudor England
D) A discussion of the policies of Elizabeth's ministers

33. This essay is most probably taken from a

A) scholarly work on Renaissance England.
B) biography of Elizabeth I.
C) diary kept by one of Elizabeth's ministers.
D) political science textbook.

34. Which of the following would most strengthen the essay?

A) Knowing who the ministers were and what their policies were
B) Examples of Elizabeth's dual nature
C) A discussion of Henry VIII's policies
D) A discussion of the role of the woman in Tudor England

STRATEGY SUMMARY

ACT ENGLISH AND SAT WRITING AND LANGUAGE

General Strategies

1. After you have memorized the directions, they can be safely ignored; therefore, do not waste valuable test time by re-reading instructions.
2. Read the entire selection for comprehension of the overall meaning. Look for possible errors. Mentally note how to correct possible errors.
3. Study the answer choices, looking for one that matches your anticipated answer.
4. Compare the answer choices. What makes them different from one another?
5. Do not choose answer choices that introduce new errors or change the meaning of the selection.
6. Use the additional strategies presented below when searching for errors.

Strategies for ACT Usage and Mechanics and SAT Standard English Conventions

Check for Grammatical Errors

1. Look for obvious subject-verb agreement problems. The test-writers may try to obscure agreement by inserting material between the subject and the verb, inverting the sentence structure so that the verb precedes the subject, or introducing compound subjects.
2. Check for proper pronoun usage. Remember that all pronouns must have antecedents. The pronoun must clearly refer to the antecedent and must agree in case, number, and person.
3. Be alert to the proper usage of adjectives and adverbs. Recall that adjectives modify nouns, while adverbs modify verbs. Also, adjectives, not adverbs, follow linking verbs. Lastly, watch out for adjectives posing as adverbs. Sometimes, adjectives can be transformed into adverbs by adding "-ly," so it is important to identify whether the modifier is an adjective or an adverb.
4. Watch for double negatives. Even though double negatives are sometimes used colloquially, they are not grammatically correct.
5. Check for proper noun clause introductions. A noun clause is a group of words that functions as the subject of a sentence and must be introduced with "that." Remember that "because" and "why" should not be used to introduce noun clauses.
6. Watch for illogical comparisons. Comparisons can only be made between similar objects. Be alert to the use of the comparative form of an adjective (for comparing two objects) and the superlative

form of an adjective (for comparing three or more objects). Remember that some adjectives and adverbs express the highest degree of quality; therefore, they cannot be improved upon.

7. Check for improper verb and mood shifts. The same verb tense and mood should be used within a sentence or paragraph unless there is a valid reason for a change. Also, be alert to the improper usage of verb tenses in general. Make sure that the verb tense within a sentence or a paragraph is logical.

8. Make sure that the choice of verb tense in a sentence reflects the sequence and the duration of the events described.

9. Check for diction errors such as wrong prepositions, improper word choice, and gerund-infinitive switching.

Check for Sentence Structure Errors

1. Check to see if the sentence is a run-on.

2. Be aware of comma splice errors in sentences.

3. Check to see if the sentence is a fragment.

4. Make sure the sentence contains logical coordinating conjunctions.

5. Watch for faulty parallelism in a sentence. Recall that whenever elements of a sentence perform similar or equal functions, they should have the same form.

6. Be alert for sentence structures in which a thought that is interrupted by intervening material is completed later in the sentence. Check that the interrupted thought is correctly completed. A simple way to check for this type of error is to read the sentence without the intervening material—the sentence should make sense, be grammatically correct, and represent a complete thought.

7. Look for misplaced modifiers. Modifiers should be placed as close as possible to what they modify. Errors in placement of modifiers create ambiguous and illogical constructions.

8. Be alert to misplacements or omissions of certain elements of a sentence. These errors lead to unintended meanings. Make sure the intended meaning of the sentence follows from its logical structure.

Check for Punctuation Errors

1. Check to see if commas are used correctly in the sentence. The following list summarizes the most important uses and misuses of commas:

   (a) Use a comma before a coordinating conjunction joining two clauses.

   (b) Use commas for clarity.

   (c) Use commas to separate three or more words in a series.

   (d) Use commas to mark the end of an introductory phrase.

   (e) Use pairs of commas to set off appositive, parenthetical, and nonrestrictive elements.

(f) A comma should not be used to separate a subject from its verb.

(g) Commas should not be used to set off restrictive or necessary clauses or phrases.

(h) A comma should not be used in place of a conjunction.

2. Check for correct semicolon usage. The following list summarizes the appropriate uses of semicolons:

   (a) Use a semicolon to separate two complete ideas.

   (b) Use a semicolon to separate a series of phrases with commas.

   (c) Use a semicolon to separate independent clauses.

   (d) Do not use semicolons to separate dependent clauses.

3. Check for correct end-stop punctuation. Make sure that any material ending with a period is a complete sentence.

4. Check for correct usage of dashes. The following are the rules for situations requiring the use of a dash:

   (a) Use a dash for emphasis or to set off an explanatory group of words.

   (b) Use a dash before a word or group of words that indicates a summation or reversal of what preceded it.

   (c) Use a dash to mark a sudden break in thought that leaves a sentence unfinished.

5. Check for correct apostrophe usage. Apostrophes are most commonly used to show possession. They are also used when a noun is used to modify another noun or a gerund.

6. Check to see if a punctuation mark is needed to clarify the sentence.

Strategies for ACT Rhetorical Skills and SAT Expression of Ideas

Check to See if the Strategy Used by the Writer Is Appropriate

1. Make sure that all supporting material is appropriate to the selection.

2. Be alert to opening, transitional, and concluding sentences. Check to see if they are effective or if they need improvement.

3. Read the selection for the main ideas and identify the main purpose of the entire passage.

4. Look for diction, purpose, and tone clues that identify the writer's audience.

Check for Organization Errors

1. Check the sentence-level structure. Sentences should be in a logical and appropriate order within the paragraph.

2. Check the paragraph-level structure. Paragraphs should be divided logically and unified around a central theme.

3. Check the passage-level structure. Passages should follow an identifiable pattern of development, with paragraphs appearing in a logical order.

Check for Stylistic Problems

1. Make sure that the sentences are concise and to the point.

   (1) Look for awkward sentences or weak passive verbs.

   (2) Look for needlessly wordy sentences.

2. Check for ambiguous sentences. Such sentences run two or more ideas together and require further clarification to separate and connect the disparate ideas.

3. Check for idiomatic usage.

Strategies for Words in Context

1. Look for precision of meaning.
2. Look for consistent tone within sentences and paragraphs.
3. Look for needlessly wordy sentences.
4. Look for idiomatic usage.

Strategies for SAT Data Presentations

1. Be alert for statements that misinterpret information presented graphically.
2. Be alert for statements that incorrectly evaluate the relevance or context of information presented graphically.

ACT Essay

Course Concept Outline

I. Lesson | Preliminaries[1]

- A. Lesson Features
- B. What Is Tested
- C. Directions
- D. Item Format
- E. Scoring
  1. Essay Scoring Guide
  2. Test Scores

II. Lesson | Essay (p. 217)

- A. Preliminaries
  1. What Is Tested
  2. Directions
  3. Item Format
  4. Scoring
     a) Essay Scoring Guide
     b) Test Scores
- B. Composing the Essay
  1. Pre-Writing
  2. Beginning the Writing Process

[1] Some concepts in this Course Concept Outline are not illustrated through examples in your student text but may be covered by your instructor in class. They are included here to provide a complete outline of your course.

LESSON | ESSAY

ACT ESSAY

The following essay topic will be used during the Essay Lesson to illustrate proper essay development and writing skills. Follow along with your instructor to outline and develop sample responses to the prompts. Sample essay responses begin on page 571.

DIRECTIONS: You have 40 minutes to plan and write an essay. Read the prompt carefully and make sure you understand the instructions. A successful essay will have the following features: it will evaluate each of the perspectives given in the prompt; it will state and develop a personal perspective; it will explain the relationship between the given perspectives and your personal perspective; it will present ideas with logical reasoning and clear, persuasive examples; and, finally, it will include clear and effective language in accordance with the conventions of standard written English.

Technological advances have enhanced our capacity to communicate. Email, twitter, Instagram, and social messaging sites have made the sharing of information and networking with others exponentially more efficient. Whether the 'other' is our neighbor next door, or someone or some group halfway around the planet, the ability to connect has been almost infinitely improved. However, critics claim that while we now communicate more quickly, we also interact more superficially, and the ease of interaction has, in many cases, rendered us more isolated. Although technology has made communication easier, are we, in fact, lonelier with more digital and less face-to-face interaction? As more and more communication happens online, it is important to assess the psychological effects of such connections.

Read and consider the perspectives below. Each perspective suggests a particular way of thinking about the impact of technology on human interaction.

Perspective 1

Despite the efficiency of moving information, so much of what is shared is facile and empty of real depth. We are now in a "fast food" age of information: quick turnaround with only "empty calories" of communication.

Perspective 2

Though we connect more easily with one another, there is a feeling that we are becoming ever more isolated and estranged from each other. We have a need for closer contact with the people we know.

Perspective 3

Technological advances have made it far easier to communicate in today's world. We can literally reach out and touch individuals, groups, and societies in an instant and be connected immediately.

Essay Task

Write a unified, coherent essay in which you evaluate multiple perspectives on the impact of technology on human interaction. In your essay be sure to:

- Analyze and evaluate the perspectives given
- State and develop your own perspective
- Explain the relationship between your perspective and those given

Your perspective may be in full agreement with any of the others, in partial agreement, or wholly different. Whatever the case, support your ideas with logical reasoning and detailed, persuasive examples.

TEST MECHANICS

ACT ESSAY

Overview

The Writing Test will assess in broad terms your ability to develop and express your ideas in writing. It is not intended to evaluate whether you'd be a good novelist or how well you'd write if given time to do research and write several drafts. In short, you will produce an on-demand piece of writing that will likely be of rough draft quality.

The Writing Test is also not intended to test your mastery of any body of knowledge. The topic will be sufficiently broad so that arguments and explanations can be drawn from personal experience; for example, the topic might ask you to express your opinions about sports, music, psychology, current events, or even modern technology such as "tweeting" or video games.

The essay topic will be described as a "prompt." The word "prompt" was chosen because it indicates that the topic is really just an *excuse* or *opportunity* for you to write something. The test could just as easily say, "During the next thirty minutes, write an essay on anything of interest to you." However, the readers would then have to deal with essays on an unwieldy number of topics; the prompt keeps everyone more or less on the same page.

Essays are scored *holistically*, which means they are given a grade based on the overall impression created. Bonus points are not awarded for a well-turned phrase, and specific points are not deducted for specific grammatical mistakes. However, consistently poor grammar that interferes with meaning will affect the essay score. You will receive three types of scores for your essay. First, the overall essay score is reported on a scale of 1–36. Second, you will receive additional scores reported within four domains: Ideas and Analysis, Development and Support, Organization, and Language Use and Conventions, on a scale of 2–12 for each domain (the scores of two readers are combined to determine each domain score). Third, the Essay score is combined with your English Test and Reading Test scores to produce an English Language Arts (ELA) score on a scale of 1–36. The Essay score is NOT included in your composite score.

Anatomy

DIRECTIONS: You have 40 minutes to plan and write an essay. Read the prompt carefully and make sure you understand the instructions.

The Electoral College

In light of the results of the 2000 presidential election, our indirect method of selecting our president through the Electoral College (all Electoral College votes are declared to the winning candidate in each of the 50 states) has come into question. Direct popular election is the method most often presented as the fairest way to choose a president. Adoption of this process would mean, simply, that the candidate who received the most votes would become president. Some argue that the Electoral College could be kept and votes in the states could be designated to a candidate in a proportional method, so a person who received 60% of a state's votes would receive 60% of its electoral votes. Those who favor this method argue this is the fairest way to choose who will lead the country, but would changing the constitution to address a situation that was problematic in only one recent election be an extreme and unwise change? No matter which side you may choose, this conversation is an important one for our nation's future.

Perspective 1

Direct election of the president by popular vote is the fairest way to choose our chief executive. Such a change in our process of selecting the president would reinforce our view that America is a government of the people, by the people, and for the people.

Perspective 2

The Electoral College has served the United States for over 250 years. Radical change is not always the best course. A tweaking of the selection process would provide candidates a percentage of the votes earned in each state.

Perspective 3

Changing the constitution is never to be done lightly. The founding fathers thought long and hard about this step. We should think long and hard about such a change to our constitution and the possible consequences of such a decision.

Essay Task

Write a unified, coherent essay in which you evaluate multiple perspectives on the impact of direct popular election of the President of the United States. In your essay be sure to:

- Analyze and evaluate perspectives given
- State and develop your own perspective
- Explain the relationship between your perspective and those given

Your perspective may be in full agreement with any of the others, in partial agreement or wholly different. Whatever the case, support your ideas with logical reasoning and detailed, persuasive examples.

Notice that the prompt does not test a specific body of knowledge. For example, it does not ask, "What were the causes of World War II?" or "What is the best recipe for chocolate cake?" Also, notice that the prompt is constructed so you can provide a very successful response based simply on the perspectives listed and your own personal experience. Finally, notice that the prompt points you in the right direction. It asks you a question, and all you need to do is respond to the question and meet the requirements outlined above. These requirements will be discussed in more detail later in the ACT Essay Lesson.

Pacing

There is one essay prompt with a 40-minute time limit. During the 40 minutes, you must read the prompt, formulate a position, outline your argument or analysis, write your essay, and proofread your essay. Here is a suggested breakdown for those tasks:

TASK	TIME TO EXECUTE	TIME REMAINING
Read the prompt.	1 minute	39 minutes
Evaluate the given perspectives.	2 minutes	37 minutes
Formulate your perspective.	2 minutes	35 minutes
Outline your essay.	2 minutes	33 minutes
Write the introduction.	4 minutes	29 minutes
Write the first paragraph.	7–8 minutes	21–22 minutes
Write the second paragraph.	7–8 minutes	13–15 minutes
Write the third paragraph.	7–8 minutes	5–8 minutes
Write the conclusion.	3 minutes	2–5 minutes
Proofread your essay.	2–5 minutes	0 minutes

If you follow this approximate schedule, it is likely your essay will score at least a 22. After all, your essay will include an introduction that evaluates the given perspectives and states your perspective, three supporting paragraphs (each of which will provide a specific reason in support of your perspective), and a brief conclusion that clearly expresses your point of view. Obviously, if your essay is also expressed in clear and precise language, and if it does not include any major grammatical errors, you will likely receive an even higher score.

Time Trial

(1 prompt; 11 minutes)

DIRECTIONS: Write an outline for your essay. Then write an introductory paragraph.

Planned Obsolescence

Many technology manufacturers follow a policy of planned obsolescence. Obsolescence describes the condition of no longer being used or useful. Planned obsolescence means that manufacturers make products that are designed to wear out and be replaced quickly. New smartphone applications only function on the latest version of a phone. High repair costs encourage consumers to buy a new laptop instead of fixing a broken one. Spare parts for a computer are no longer available after a few years. Planned obsolescence cuts costs for the manufacturer and the consumer, but what are the risks for both parties when the consumer must frequently replace a product? With the prevalent role of technological devices in our society, planned obsolescence has a strong financial impact on our lives.

Perspective 1

Planned obsolescence can be unfair to consumers, forcing them to spend more money than necessary on products that do not offer significant improvements to the older ones. Manufacturers should deliver high quality, long-lasting products. From the manufacturer's perspective, flimsy products could also encourage consumers to buy from a company with a more durable product.

Perspective 2

Some industries, such as the automotive industry, are focusing on creating new products that are more environmentally friendly than what is currently available. Planned obsolescence could encourage consumers to buy these newer products and ultimately have a positive impact on the environment.

Perspective 3

Planned obsolescence cuts manufacturing costs and encourages companies to design better products in a shorter period of time. This allows for greater innovation in products and ultimately gives the consumer a superior product.

Essay Task

Write a unified, coherent essay in which you evaluate multiple perspectives on the impact of planned obsolescence. In your essay be sure to:

- Analyze and evaluate perspectives given
- State and develop your own perspective
- Explain the relationship between your perspective and those given

Your perspective may be in full agreement with any of the others, in partial agreement or wholly different. Whatever the case, support your ideas with logical reasoning and detailed, persuasive examples.

Game Plan

Use a Pencil

Write your essay in pencil. Do not use a pen. Any essay written in pen will automatically receive a "0."

Respond to the Specific Prompt

Write on the topic that is presented. If you write an essay that is off-topic, your essay will automatically receive a "0" because it will be considered "not responsive." Also, remember to evaluate each of the given perspectives, present your own perspective, and describe how your perspective relates to each of the given perspectives. Following all the required steps outlined in the prompt is an easy—and essential—way to earn points.

Write Legibly

Write clearly and legibly. If you write an essay that is illegible, your essay will automatically receive a "0." Readers cannot give a grade to what they cannot read. So, if your handwriting is hard to read, take a little extra time and try printing.

Don't Copy the Prompt

Do not copy the prompt onto the lined paper. The readers know the topic, and it is already written on the page. If you copy the prompt onto the lined paper, it looks like you're simply trying to fill up space.

Don't Skip Lines

Do not skip lines when writing your essay on the lined paper. You should be able to make your essay legible without skipping lines. If you skip lines, it looks like you're trying to "pad" your essay to make it look longer.

Be Specific

When writing your essay, be specific. Avoid vague generalizations. For example, here are a few sentences that are weak because they are too vague:

> *"Perfection in house painting is very time-consuming and requires a lot of hard work. You just can't do it in a short time; you've got to invest a lot of effort."*

If you include specific details, the same point can be made much more persuasively. For example, here is the same argument about house painting but made with specific details:

> *"House painting requires attention to details. You have to prepare the surface by scraping away all old and loose paint and carefully washing it. You have to put down hundreds of strips of masking tape to protect those areas that should not receive paint, like glass panes, trim to be painted a second color, and fixtures. You have to apply a primer, then a base coat, and then the finish coat. Finally, you have to apply the second color and clean up all the mistakes. A perfect paint job would take 6 months or longer, and the cost would be prohibitive. That is why when you look closely you will always see imperfections."*

As you can see, this response is much more compelling because the point of view is supported by specific details. Specific details are frequently the difference between an essay that receives a Development and Support score of 4 or 6 and an essay that receives a Development and Support score of 8 or 10.

QUIZ

ACT ESSAY

This section contains an ACT Writing quiz. Complete the quiz under timed conditions. Sample essay responses begin on page 573.

(1 Essay Prompt; 40 minutes)

DIRECTIONS: You have 40 minutes to plan and write an essay. Read the prompt carefully and make sure you understand the instructions.

Fracking

The quest for finding additional sources of energy is almost never-ending, and our demand for fossil fuels has dominated our energy consumption. Fracking (hydraulic fracturing) which "pries" fossil fuel resources from the earth's crust, is one recent development at the forefront of promising innovations making our country energy sufficient. While this process offers great promise in delivering fuel to the world, some critics point to the environmental damage that can be caused by fracking, including pollution and destabilization of the earth's crust. Also, critics say that the success of fracking will bring a halt to the development of renewable energy sources as alternatives to fossil fuel. Although fracking would greatly increase our access to fossil fuel, is it a sustainable solution, given the environmental risks? As other sources of fossil fuels diminish, policymakers must address the benefits and risks of fracking.

Perspective 1

Dependence on fossil fuel must stop. We need to find alternative sources that are reliable, renewable, and safe. Human ingenuity and imagination must be put to the test to find such sources as quickly as possible for our survival.

Perspective 2

Fracking holds promise for greater energy sufficiency in the US. However, the process also has environmental risks that pose tremendous dangers to human, plant, and animal life.

Perspective 3

Fossil fuels are necessary for our societies to function. Methods of extracting fossil fuels from the earth's crust are crucial because there are still great quantities of fossil fuel beneath the earth's surface.

Essay Task

Write a unified, coherent essay in which you evaluate multiple perspectives on the impact of fracking. In your essay be sure to:

- Analyze and evaluate perspectives given
- State and develop your own perspective
- Explain the relationship between your perspective and those given

Your perspective may be in full agreement with any of the others, in partial agreement or wholly different. Whatever the case, support your ideas with logical reasoning and detailed, persuasive examples.

STRATEGY SUMMARY

ACT ESSAY

General Strategies

1. Begin with the prompt.
2. Write only on the assigned topic. Writing on any other topic will result in a score of "0."
3. Remember to evaluate the given perspectives, develop your own perspective, and describe how your perspective relates to the given perspectives.
4. Do not try to do too much. Try to limit the scope of your topic to a reasonable effort.
5. Organize your thoughts and write an outline before beginning the essay. Do not spend more than two minutes writing the outline.

   a) Familiarize yourself with the essay prompt and the given perspectives.

   b) Develop your own perspective.

   c) Develop a thesis.

   d) Identify three to four important points.

   e) Decide on the order of presentation of the major points.
6. Organize ideas into paragraphs.

   a) Begin with an introduction.

   b) Create three to four body paragraphs.

   c) End with a conclusion.
7. Write using correct grammar.
8. Write clearly, concisely, and legibly.
9. Punctuate and spell correctly.
10. Spend a few minutes proofreading your essay.

SAT Essay

Course Concept Outline

I. Lesson | Preliminaries[1]

A. Lesson Features

B. What Is Tested

C. Directions

D. Item Format

E. Scoring

II. Lesson | Essay (p. 231)

A. Composing the Essay

1. Pre-Writing (Essay prompt, p. 231)
2. Beginning the Writing Process
3. The Introduction
4. The Body
5. The Conclusion
6. Revising

B. Essay Writing Strategies

1. Begin with the Prompt
2. Write Only on the Assigned Source Text
3. Do Not Try to Do Too Much

---

[1] Some concepts in this Course Concept Outline are not illustrated through examples in your student text but may be covered by your instructor in class. They are included here to provide a complete outline of your course.

LESSON | ESSAY

SAT ESSAY

The following essay topic will be used during the SAT Essay Lesson to illustrate proper essay development and writing skills. Follow along with your instructor to outline and develop sample responses to the prompts. Sample essay responses begin on page 575.

DIRECTIONS: The Essay Test measures your ability to read and understand a passage and write an essay that analyzes the passage. In your essay, demonstrate that you have carefully read the passage, write a clear and logical analysis, and use language precisely.

You have 50 minutes to read the passage and write an essay in response to the provided prompt.

Read the passage below and think about how Melanne Verveer uses

- evidence (facts, examples, etc.) to support claims.
- reasoning to develop the passage and to connect claims and evidence.
- rhetorical or persuasive elements, such as language choices or emotional appeals, to increase the impact of the ideas expressed.

Adapted from "The Political and Economic Power of Women," a speech given by US Ambassador-at-Large for Global Women's Issues Melanne Verveer. Verveer gave the speech at the Center for International Private Enterprise in Washington, DC on June 20, 2011.

1 Today I want to talk to you about the political and economic power of women in a spirit of realistic optimism. Political and economic realities are intertwined. Progress in one dimension reinforces progress in the other. These are the two principal elements of empowerment.

2 Women's political participation has been slowly improving. In the last ten years, for example, the rate of participation in parliaments has grown from 13% to almost 18%. Clearly the figure ought to be much better, especially when exceptional women like Germany's Angela Merkel and Liberia's Ellen Johnson Sirleaf have demonstrated the strong qualities that women bring to political leadership.

3 Let me state this reality another way: women are half of the population yet hold one-fifth of the positions in national governments. They are significantly outnumbered in the chambers of parliaments and provincial councils, and more often than not missing from the negotiating tables where conflicts are to be resolved. All too often decisions that affect women, their families, and societies are made without women having a voice.

4 In the South Pacific where I recently participated in a policy dialogue initiated by the United States that was joined by women leaders from twelve of the Pacific Islands, female political participation is marginal at best. In Papua New Guinea, for example, there is one female parliamentarian out of 109 members. There has been legislation pending there to add 22 reserved seats for women but it remains pending.

5 Why should we care? For one, democracy without women is a contradiction in terms. Many of you may be familiar with the World Economic Forum's Gender Gap Report. It looks at the equality of women and men in a given country in four areas: access to education, health survivability, political participation, and economic security. Where the gap is closer to being closed (and in no country is it closed)—in countries where it has been narrowed and the disparities between women and men are not as great—those countries are more economically competitive and prosperous.

6 In publishing the study over the last several years, the WEF has documented greater progress in access to education and health care than in economic and political participation. The gap in political participation has been the toughest to close.

7 When women are discriminated against in the political arena, their experiences, talents, and perspectives are shut out of political decisions, and democracies and the prospects for a better world are shortchanged. Moreover, according to the World Bank, increases in female participation in government leadership correlate with decreases in corruption.

8 I have seen first-hand the differences women make when they are empowered politically. In India, approximately 40% of the elected representatives in the village and municipal councils are women. Thanks to a quota that was adopted many years ago, today more than a million women across the subcontinent have been elected at the local level to serve on panchayats—village councils or municipal councils—beyond the seats reserved for women. Their success has been described as a silent revolution in democracy in India. Research studies show that the women-led councils deliver much-needed public services more effectively. From sanitation to education, they target public resources to benefit the community and are responsible for considerable gains at the local level.

9 Women must also be at the table in peacemaking, peace negotiations, and work on post-conflict reconstruction. Ten years ago, the UN Security Council adopted Resolution 1325 linking women, peace, and security—recognizing that women have a key role to play at all levels of conflict resolution. Women suffer unspeakable horrors like sexual gender-based violence in times of conflict that must be addressed. Women can also help avoid conflict, end it, and recover from it.

10 The United States, in both Republican and Democratic administrations, has played a leadership role on 1325 and its successor resolutions. We need to continue to ensure women gain the skills and access to opportunities to participate in peace processes, political transitions, new constitutions, and the electoral process. The US support for quotas for women in Afghanistan and Iraq, which was chiseled into their constitutions, helped pave the way for women to participate in their parliaments and provincial councils.

11 One night in Kabul, I was meeting with a group of Afghan women to discuss their role in their country's transition in the peace and reconciliation process. One of the women made a plea that I've not forgotten. She said, "Don't look at us as victims but as the leaders that we are."

Write an essay explaining how Melanne Verveer develops her argument that women should have a greater role in the political arena. In your essay, analyze how Verveer uses one or more of the elements listed above (or other elements) to make her argument more logical and persuasive. Be sure to focus on the most relevant aspects of the passage.

Your essay should not discuss whether you agree with Verveer's claims but rather discuss how Verveer develops her argument.

TEST MECHANICS

SAT ESSAY

Overview

The optional Essay Test will assess in broad terms your ability to analyze a source text and use evidence from that source text in your written analysis. It is not intended to evaluate whether you'd be a good novelist or how well you'd write if given time to do research and write several drafts. In short, you will produce an on-demand piece of writing that will demonstrate your ability to write a clear analysis of a source text.

The Essay Test is also not intended to test your mastery of any body of knowledge. You are being tested on your ability to draw conclusions from a source text by using critical reasoning and evidence from the text. You won't be writing a response on whether you agree or disagree with the author; rather you will be focusing on how the author builds his or her argument to convince an audience.

The essay topic will be described as a "prompt." The word "prompt" was chosen because it indicates that the topic is really just an *excuse* or *opportunity* for you to write something. The prompt itself is consistent from test to test, but the source text will differ. The source texts examine ideas, trends, and debates on a wide array of topics. However, you won't need any prior knowledge of the topic to successfully write the essay.

Essays are scored based upon three traits: reading, analysis, and writing. Each of these traits will be scored by two readers on a scale of 1 to 4 for a total score for each trait ranging from 2 to 8. The scores for the Essay Test will not be factored into the composite score and will be reported separately.

Anatomy

DIRECTIONS: The Essay Test measures your ability to read and understand a passage and write an essay that analyzes the passage. In your essay, demonstrate that you have carefully read the passage, write a clear and logical analysis, and use language precisely.

Write your essay on the provided lines on your answer sheet. You will receive no other paper on which to write except for the Planning Page of the answer booklet. You will have enough space if you write on every line, avoid wide margins, and keep your handwriting to a reasonable size. Make sure to write or print so that your essay is legible.

You have 50 minutes to read the passage and write an essay in response to the provided prompt.

Read the passage below and think about how John F. Kennedy uses

- evidence (facts, examples, etc.) to support claims.
- reasoning to develop the passage and to connect claims and evidence.
- rhetorical or persuasive elements, such as language choices or emotional appeals, to increase the impact of the ideas expressed.

Adapted from former US President John F. Kennedy's Commencement Address at American University, June 10, 1963.

1 I have chosen this time and this place to discuss a topic on which ignorance too often abounds and the truth is too rarely perceived—yet it is the most important topic on earth: world peace.

2 What kind of peace do I mean? What kind of peace do we seek? Not a Pax Americana enforced on the world by American weapons of war. Not the peace of the grave or the security of the slave. I am talking about genuine peace, the kind of peace that makes life on earth worth living, the kind that enables men and nations to grow and to hope and to build a better life for their children—not merely peace for Americans but peace for all men and women—not merely peace in our time but peace for all time.

3 I speak of peace because of the new face of war. Total war makes no sense in an age when great powers can maintain large and relatively invulnerable nuclear forces and refuse to surrender without resort to those forces. It makes no sense in an age when a single nuclear weapon contains almost ten times the explosive force delivered by all the Allied air forces in the Second World War. It makes no sense in an age when the deadly poisons produced by a nuclear exchange would be carried by wind and water and soil and seed to the far corners of the globe and to generations yet unborn.

4 Today the expenditure of billions of dollars every year on weapons acquired for the purpose of making sure we never need to use them is essential to keeping the peace. But surely the acquisition of such idle stockpiles—which can only destroy and never create—is not the only, much less the most efficient, means of assuring peace.

5 I speak of peace, therefore, as the necessary rational end of rational men. I realize that the pursuit of peace is not as dramatic as the pursuit of war—and frequently the words of the pursuer fall on deaf ears. But we have no more urgent task.

6 Let us examine our attitude toward peace itself. Too many of us think it is impossible. Too many think it unreal. But that is a dangerous, defeatist belief. It leads to the conclusion that war is inevitable—that mankind is doomed—that we are gripped by forces we cannot control.

7 I am not referring to the absolute, infinite concept of peace and good will of which some fantasies and fanatics dream. I do not deny the value of hopes and dreams, but we merely invite discouragement and incredulity by making that our only and immediate goal.

8 Let us focus instead on a more practical, more attainable peace based not on a sudden revolution in human nature but on a gradual evolution in human institutions—on a series of concrete actions and effective agreements which are in the interest of all concerned. There is no single, simple key to this peace—no grand or magic formula to be adopted by one or two powers. Genuine peace must be the product of many nations, the sum of many acts. It must be dynamic, not static, changing to meet the challenge of each new generation. For peace is a process—a way of solving problems.

9 With such a peace, there will still be quarrels and conflicting interests, as there are within families and nations. World peace, like community peace, does not require that each man love his neighbor—it requires only that they live together in mutual tolerance, submitting their disputes to a just and peaceful settlement. And history teaches us that enmities between nations, as between individuals, do not last forever. However fixed our likes and dislikes may seem, the tide of time and events will often bring surprising changes in the relations between nations and neighbors.

10 So let us persevere. Peace need not be impracticable, and war need not be inevitable. By defining our goal more clearly, by making it seem more manageable and less remote, we can help all peoples to see it, to draw hope from it, and to move irresistibly toward it.

Write an essay explaining how John F. Kennedy develops his argument that world peace is a necessary and attainable pursuit. In your essay, analyze how Kennedy uses one or more of the elements listed before the passage (or other elements) to make his argument more logical and persuasive. Be sure to focus on the most relevant aspects of the passage.

Your essay should not discuss whether you agree with Kennedy's claims but rather discuss how he develops his argument.

Notice that the prompt does not test a specific body of knowledge or ask for your personal opinion. For example, it does not ask, "What were Kennedy's greatest accomplishments as a politician?" or "Do you agree with Kennedy that world peace is attainable?" Also, notice that the prompt is constructed so that your response is based solely on your analysis of the source text. Finally, remember that the prompt will always follow the same format; it is only the source text that will change.

Pacing

There is one essay prompt with a 50-minute time limit. During the 50 minutes, you must read the prompt, read the source text, analyze the source text, outline your response, write your essay, and proofread your essay. Here is a suggested breakdown for those tasks:

TASK	TIME TO EXECUTE	TIME REMAINING
Read the prompt.	1 minute	49 minutes
Read the source text.	6 minutes	43 minutes
Analyze the source text and outline your essay.	9 minutes	34 minutes
Write the introduction.	3 minutes	31 minutes
Write the first paragraph.	8 minutes	23 minutes
Write the second paragraph.	8 minutes	15 minutes
Write the third paragraph.	8 minutes	7 minutes
Write the conclusion.	3 minutes	4 minutes
Proofread your essay.	4 minutes	0 minutes

If you follow this approximate schedule, it is likely your essay will get at least an average score. After all, your essay will include an introduction that states your position, three supporting paragraphs of text analysis, and a brief conclusion. Obviously, if your essay is also expressed in clear and precise language, and if it does not include any major grammatical errors, you will likely receive an even higher score.

Time Trial

(1 prompt; 20 minutes)

DIRECTIONS: Write an outline for your essay. Then write an introductory paragraph.

Read the passage below and think about how Muñoz uses

- evidence (facts, examples, etc.) to support claims.
- reasoning to develop the passage and to connect claims and evidence.
- rhetorical or persuasive elements, such as language choices or emotional appeals, to increase the impact of the ideas expressed.

Adapted from "Bringing the Tech Revolution to Early Learning" by Cecilia Muñoz. Originally posted on www.ed.gov/blog in August 2014.

1 Why do I advocate for "early tech"? I'll give you three good reasons: my granddaughters Ella, Clara, and Zayla. I've seen the way technology has helped them to take charge of their own learning and opened doors to subjects and activities that really catch their interest.

2 It's nothing short of amazing to think about how far we've come in the past ten years. Our children—and our grandchildren—pick up a device and instantly know how it works. They shift seamlessly from a hand-held device to a laptop or desktop and back again.

3 Whether we've seen it firsthand in our families, read about it in the papers, or heard about it from our friends and co-workers, we know that technology can be a great tool for early learning. That's why America's early learning community—and anyone who wants to help build a brighter future for the next generation—must make smarter use of these cutting-edge resources, provide better support for the teachers who use them, and help ensure that all our young children have equitable access to the right technology. "Early tech" can be an incredible tool to increase access and quality, when we understand how to use it for good.

4 Today, devices can not only bring the world to our students, but they also can bring what children create to the world. Kids can generate their own media through digital still and video cameras and recording applications and, if they want, share it with students around the world. Our kids have the power to learn so much from their own creativity—creativity that technology supports and encourages.

5 In short, technology can spark imagination in young children, remove barriers to play, and provide appropriate learning platforms as tools for reflection and critical thinking. It also offers children the ability to reflect easily by erasing, storing, recalling, modifying, and representing thoughts on tablets and other devices.

6 As an educator, I'm excited by the almost limitless potential of really good technology to teach children new skills and reinforce what they already know. Tablets, computers, and handheld devices, like smartphones and mp3 players, can be powerful assets in preschool classrooms when they're integrated into an active, play-based curriculum. The National Association of Educators of Young Children, a leading organization that promotes early childhood education, agrees: technology and interactive media should be used intentionally to support learning and development.

7 What's more, recent research has found that when used properly, technology can support the acquisition of what are called "executive functioning skills," such as collaboration, taking turns, patience, and cooperative discussion of ideas with peers.

8 Technology can also dramatically improve communication and collaboration between each child's school and home. With the click of a mouse or the touch of a screen, teachers can connect with parents, updating them about a student's academic progress or providing information about an upcoming school event.

9 While we know its power to transform preschool classrooms, systemic and cultural barriers have prevented the early learning field from fully embracing technology. Preschools often have limited funding and few good hardware and software choices. At times, early learning teachers and directors have actually had less exposure to technology than their students have. They fear that technology won't be developmentally appropriate and that devices will distract students from rich, play-based classroom experiences. Teachers have told me they are daunted by the task of selecting the right apps and devices.

10 We need to change this way of thinking—and the systems behind it. Center directors, school principals, and other early learning leaders must step up and lead by example, facilitating the successful use of technology, particularly in preschool settings. Teachers shouldn't—and can't—be alone in this endeavor. They need fearless principals and administrators who will advocate for pre-service and in-service learning that supports teacher understanding of how to use technology in early learning settings.

11 At the same time, we need more models of how technology works in early learning classrooms. Technology strengthens and deepens classroom instruction. It can extend and support a child-centric, play-based curriculum just as other manipulatives do, including wooden blocks, magic markers, or a classroom pet—but in a format that can be accessible far beyond the classroom. But, in order to make effective use of these new strategies, teachers need to see them in practice—and that currently isn't happening in enough places.

12 We have, quite literally, tens of millions of reasons for taking action in all our precious children and grandchildren. Each and every one of them deserves a great start in life—and that's exactly what "early tech" helps to provide.

Write an essay explaining how Muñoz develops her argument that technology should be introduced in early learning classrooms. In your essay, analyze how Muñoz uses one or more of the elements listed above (or other elements) to make her argument more logical and persuasive. Be sure to focus on the most relevant aspects of the passage.

Your essay should not discuss whether you agree with Muñoz's claims but rather discuss how Muñoz develops her argument.

Game Plan

Read the Source Text Carefully

To answer the prompt correctly you have to read the source text. Do not skim the passage or rush through it. The Essay Test is assessing your reading comprehension as well as your ability to write an analysis about the source text. Make sure you fully comprehend the author's argument before you start writing.

Use Textual Evidence

Remember, this prompt is asking you to analyze the author's writing, not asking you your opinion on the topic. Make sure that you use specific quotes from the text to support your analysis. Cite specific facts the author uses and explain how the author uses those facts to support his or her argument. Or point out examples in the text that the author uses to make his or her point. Although your essay should address *what* the source-text author is saying, you should, most importantly, focus on the *way* in which the author says things.

Use a Pencil

Write your essay in pencil. Do not use a pen.

Write Legibly

Write clearly and legibly. Readers cannot give a grade to what they cannot read. So, if your handwriting is hard to read, take a little extra time and try printing.

Don't Copy the Prompt

Do not copy the prompt onto the lined paper. The readers know the topic, and it is already written on the page. If you copy the prompt onto the lined paper, it looks like you're simply trying to fill up space.

Don't Skip Lines

Do not skip lines when writing your essay on the lined paper. You should be able to make your essay legible without skipping lines. If you skip lines, it looks like you're trying to pad your essay to make it look longer.

Quiz

SAT Essay

This section contains an SAT Essay quiz. Complete the quiz under timed conditions. Sample essay responses begin on page 577.

(1 Essay Prompt; 50 minutes)

DIRECTIONS: The Essay Test measures your ability to read and understand a passage and write an essay that analyzes the passage. In your essay, demonstrate that you have carefully read the passage, write a clear and logical analysis, and use language precisely.

You have 50 minutes to read the passage and write an essay in response to the provided prompt.

Read the passage below and think about how Mariale Hardiman uses

- evidence (facts, examples, etc.) to support claims.
- reasoning to develop the passage and to connect claims and evidence.
- rhetorical or persuasive elements, such as language choices or emotional appeals, to increase the impact of the ideas expressed.

Adapted from "Does in-school arts education matter?" by Mariale Hardiman of Johns Hopkins University. Published on the Art Works Blog on August 20, 2014.

1 As I reflect on my experience and research regarding how the arts may be a means to improve students' academic outcomes and creativity, I must admit to my own transformation; thus, an apt title for this blog might be "How I Became a Reformed Educator."

2 Before joining the faculty at Johns Hopkins, I was principal of a large K-8 school in Baltimore, a position that came with the pressure of improving test scores or facing troubling repercussions that would affect the entire school community. So our school focused on the tested subjects and, as a result, the arts went by the wayside. We were not alone in this approach. Across the country, high-stakes testing has triggered a well-documented "narrowing of the curriculum," resulting in diminished opportunities for the arts and other non-tested subjects.

3 It didn't take long for our targeted work to pay off. The school received yearly performance awards for improved and sustained achievement. Yet, I saw that something was amiss in our academic climate. I came to realize that the vitality that I was seeking for the school could only be accomplished through robust arts programs. With the support of some arts advocates, I expanded visual and performing arts positions and also trained classroom teachers to use the arts as a tool to teach and reinforce content instruction.

4 As predicted, a focus on the arts transformed the school—students were more engaged in learning, arts and classroom teachers shared ideas, and parents noted a more creative approach to assignments. In short, learning became more visible. Interestingly, teachers began to note that students recalled information better when taught through arts-integrated lessons.

5 A few years later, I had the opportunity to test this idea when I became a faculty member at Johns Hopkins School of Education. I led research and curriculum-writing teams to design arts-integrated fifth-grade science

units and matched control units. We conducted two randomized control trials to test the effects of arts integration on long-term retention of academic content. The preliminary study tested two sets of units in four fifth-grade classrooms in a single school; the pilot study tested four units in 16 classrooms across six schools. We used pre, post, and two-month delayed tests to measure initial learning and retention of content.

6 As predicted, results from our preliminary study showed no differences between conditions in initial learning but significantly better retention in the arts-integrated condition. Analyzing results by levels of achievement revealed that increases in retention were greatest for students at the lowest levels of reading achievement.

7 Although the findings of our preliminary study are promising, more research is needed to determine the effects of arts integration on memory and on other important learning outcomes such as creative thinking and problem solving. We hope that our process for rigorously testing arts integration will encourage other researchers to contribute to this work. Just as I saw the transformative power of the arts in my K-8 school, I believe that arts integration has the potential to transform educational practices and policies in unique and substantial ways.

Write an essay explaining how Mariale Hardiman develops her argument that, despite a narrowed curriculum, arts education is necessary for the development of better learners and a more robust classroom experience. In your essay, analyze how Hardiman uses one or more of the elements listed above (or other elements) to make her argument more logical and persuasive. Be sure to focus on the most relevant aspects of the passage.

Your essay should not discuss whether you agree with Hardiman's claims but rather discuss how Hardiman develops her argument.

STRATEGY SUMMARY

SAT ESSAY

General Strategies

1. Begin by reading the source text and the prompt.
2. Write an analysis of the source text. Do not write about topics outside of the prompt.
3. Remember to analyze the author's argument and use textual evidence to back up your analysis. Do not write about your own opinion of the topic.
4. Do not try to do too much. Try to focus on the most important features or aspects of the source text.
5. Organize your thoughts and write an outline before beginning the essay. Do not spend more than nine minutes analyzing the passage and writing the outline.
   a) Familiarize yourself with the source text and the essay prompt.
   b) Analyze the author's argument.
   c) Develop a thesis.
   d) Identify three to four important points or features of the author's writing.
   e) Decide on the order of presentation of the major points.
6. Organize ideas into paragraphs.
   a) Begin with an introduction.
   b) Create three to four body paragraphs.
   c) End with a conclusion.
7. Write using correct grammar.
8. Write clearly, concisely, and legibly.
9. Punctuate and spell correctly.
10. Spend a few minutes proofreading your essay.

ACT Mathematics and SAT Math: Multiple-Choice

Course Concept Outline

I. Lesson | Preliminaries[1]

A. Lesson Features

B. What Is Tested

C. Item Profiles

D. General Strategies

1. A Note about Figures
2. Important Facts about the Answer Choices
   a) Answer Choices Are Arranged in Order
   b) Wrong Choices Correspond to Conceptual Errors
3. "Signal" Words Require Special Attention
4. Answer the Question Being Asked
5. Additional Helpful Hints
   a) Practice Previewing
   b) Test Prep Shortcuts
   c) The Gudonov Principle
   d) Alternative Solution Strategies

II. Lesson 1 | Problem Solving and Advanced Arithmetic (p. 251)

A. Arithmetic (p. 251)

1. Simple Manipulations—Just Do It! (Items #1–2, p. 251)

[1] Some concepts in this Course Concept Outline are not illustrated through examples in your student text but may be covered by your instructor in class. They are included here to provide a complete outline of your course.

LESSON 1 | PROBLEM SOLVING AND ADVANCED ARITHMETIC

ACT MATHEMATICS AND SAT MATH: MULTIPLE-CHOICE

The items in this section accompany the in-class review of the problem solving and advanced arithmetic skills and concepts tested by the ACT Mathematics and SAT Math: Multiple-Choice tests. You will work through the items with your instructor in class. Answers are on page 579.

Arithmetic

Simple Manipulations—Just Do It! Ⓐ

1. $\frac{8}{9}-\frac{7}{8}=?$

A) $\frac{1}{72}$
B) $\frac{1}{8}$
C) $\frac{1}{7}$
D) $\frac{15}{72}$

2. $\sqrt{1-\left(\frac{2}{9}+\frac{1}{36}+\frac{1}{18}\right)}=?$

A) $\frac{1}{5}$
B) $\sqrt{\frac{2}{3}}$
C) $\frac{5}{6}$
D) 1

Complicated Manipulations—Look for Shortcuts

Simplifying Ⓐ

3. $\frac{1}{2}\bullet\frac{2}{3}\bullet\frac{3}{4}\bullet\frac{4}{5}\bullet\frac{5}{6}\bullet\frac{6}{7}\bullet\frac{7}{8}=?$

A) $\frac{1}{56}$
B) $\frac{1}{8}$
C) $\frac{28}{37}$
D) $\frac{41}{43}$

Factoring Ⓐ

4. $86(37)-37(85)=?$

A) 0
B) 1
C) 37
D) 85

5. Which of the following is a prime factorization of 120?

A) (2)(2)(15)
B) (2)(3)(4)(5)
C) (2)(2)(3)(10)
D) (2)(2)(2)(3)(5)

Approximation Ⓐ

6. $-4.01(3.2)+0.2(0.4)=?$

A) −12.752
B) −4.536
C) 0.432
D) 1.251

7. Which of the following fractions is the largest?

A) $\frac{111}{221}$
B) $\frac{75}{151}$
C) $\frac{333}{998}$
D) $\frac{113}{225}$

The "Flying-X" Method Ⓐ

8. If $z=\frac{x+y}{x}$, then $1-z=?$

A) $\frac{1-x+y}{x}$
B) $\frac{x+y-1}{x}$
C) $\frac{1-x-y}{x}$
D) $-\frac{y}{x}$

Decimal-Fraction Equivalents Ⓐ

9. $0.125 \bullet 0.125 \bullet 64=?$

A) 0.125
B) 0.5
C) 0.625
D) 1

10. $\frac{0.111 \bullet 0.666}{0.166 \bullet 0.125}$ is approximately equal to which of the following?

A) 6.8
B) 4.3
C) 3.6
D) 1.6

Common Problem Solving Items

Percents ⒶⓈ

11. A jar contains 24 white marbles and 48 black marbles. What percent of the marbles in the jar are black?

A) 25%
B) $33\frac{1}{3}\%$
C) 60%
D) $66\frac{2}{3}\%$

12. A group of three friends shared the cost of a voice recorder. If Andy, Barbara, and Donna each paid \$12, \$30, and \$18, respectively, then Donna paid what percent of the cost of the voice recorder?

A) 10%
B) 30%
C) $33\frac{1}{3}\%$
D) 50%

13. Twenty students attended Professor Rodriguez's class on Monday and 25 students attended on Tuesday. The number of students who attended on Tuesday was what percent of the number of students who attended on Monday?

A) 20%
B) 25%
C) 80%
D) 125%

14. If the population of a town was 20,000 in 1997 and 16,000 in 2007, what was the percent decline in the town's population?

A) 50%
B) 25%
C) 20%
D) 10%

Items #15–17 refer to the following table:

CAPITOL CITY FIRES	
Year	Number of Fires
2002	100
2003	125
2004	140
2005	150
2006	135

15. The number of fires in 2002 was what percent of the number of fires in 2003?

A) 25%
B) $66\frac{2}{3}\%$
C) 80%
D) 100%

16. The number of fires in 2006 was what percent of the number of fires in 2005?

A) 90%
B) 82%
C) 50%
D) 25%

17. What was the percent decrease in the number of fires from 2005 to 2006?

A) 10%
B) 25%
C) 50%
D) 82%

Ratios Ⓐ Ⓢ

18. A groom must divide 12 quarts of oats between two horses. If Dobbin is to receive twice as much as Pegasus, how many quarts of oats should the groom give to Dobbin?

A) 4
B) 6
C) 8
D) 9

19. If the ratio of John's allowance to Lucy's allowance is 3:2, and the ratio of Lucy's allowance to Bob's allowance is 3:4, what is the ratio of John's allowance to Bob's allowance?

A) 2:5
B) 1:2
C) 3:4
D) 9:8

Proportions and Direct-Inverse Variation Ⓐ Ⓢ

20. If 4.5 pounds of chocolate cost $10, how many pounds of chocolate can be purchased for $12?

A) $4\frac{3}{4}$
B) $5\frac{2}{5}$
C) $5\frac{1}{2}$
D) $5\frac{3}{4}$

21. At Star Lake Middle School, 45 percent of the students bought a yearbook. If 540 students bought yearbooks, how many students did <u>not</u> buy a yearbook?

A) 243
B) 540
C) 575
D) 660

22. In the equation $y = kx$, k is the constant of variation. If y is equal to 6 when $x = 2.4$, what is the constant of variation?

A) 0.4
B) 2.5
C) 3.4
D) 3.6

23. A train traveling at a constant speed, k, takes 90 minutes to go from point P to point Q, a distance of 45 miles. What is the value of k, in miles per hour?

A) 20
B) 30
C) 45
D) 60

24. The cost of picture framing depends on the outer perimeter of the frame. If a 15-inch-by-15-inch picture frame costs $35 more than a 10-inch-by-10-inch picture frame, what is the cost of framing, in dollars per inch?

A) $3.50
B) $2.75
C) $2.25
D) $1.75

25. Walking at a constant speed of 4 miles per hour, Jill took exactly 1 hour to walk home from school. If she walked at a constant speed of 5 miles per hour, how many minutes did the trip take?

A) 48
B) 54
C) 56
D) 72

26. Ms. Peters drove from her home to the park at an average speed of 30 miles per hour and returned home along the same route at an average speed of 40 miles per hour. If her driving time from home to the park was 20 minutes, how many minutes did it take Ms. Peters to drive from the park to her home?

A) 7.5
B) 12
C) 15
D) 24

Complicated Problem Solving Items—Bridge the Gap Ⓐⓢ

27. If the senior class has 360 students, of whom $\frac{5}{12}$ are women, and the junior class has 350 students, of whom $\frac{4}{7}$ are women, how many more women are there in the junior class than in the senior class?

A) $(360-350)\left(\frac{4}{7}-\frac{5}{12}\right)$

B) $\dfrac{(360-350)\left(\frac{4}{7}-\frac{5}{12}\right)}{2}$

C) $\left(\frac{4}{7}\bullet\frac{5}{12}\right)(360-350)$

D) $\left(\frac{4}{7}\bullet 350\right)-\left(\frac{5}{12}\bullet 360\right)$

28. If the price of candy increases from 5 pounds for $7 to 3 pounds for $7, how much less candy (in pounds) can be purchased for $3.50 at the new price than at the old price?

A) $\frac{2}{7}$
B) 1
C) $1\frac{17}{35}$
D) 2

29. Diana spent $\frac{1}{2}$ of her weekly allowance on a new book and another $3 on lunch. If she still had $\frac{1}{6}$ of her original allowance left, how much is Diana's allowance?

A) $18
B) $15
C) $12
D) $9

30. A club doing a fundraiser stored items to be sold at the school. A heavy rain caused flooding and damaged a portion of the stored items. The club estimated that $\frac{2}{3}$ of the items could be salvaged, in which case the cost per salvageable item would be $0.72. If it later turned out that $\frac{3}{4}$ of the items were salvageable, then what was the actual cost per salvageable item?

A) $0.56
B) $0.60
C) $0.64
D) $0.68

31. In a clinical trial of an experimental drug, four out of five patients were given the drug while the other one out of five was given a placebo. Of the patients given the drug, 95 percent showed significant improvement; the other 5 percent did not show significant improvement. Of the patients given the placebo, 20 percent showed significant improvement; the others did not. What percent of the patients who showed significant improvement were given the placebo?

A) 4%
B) 5%
C) 8%
D) 16%

Advanced Arithmetic Items

Properties of Numbers Ⓐ Ⓢ

32. If n is the first number in a series of three consecutive even numbers, which of the following expressions represents the sum of the three numbers?

A) $n+2$
B) $n+4$
C) $n+6$
D) $3n+6$

33. If n is any odd integer, which of the following expressions must also be odd?

I. $n+n$
II. $n+n+n$
III. $n \cdot n \cdot n$

A) I only
B) III only
C) II and III only
D) I, II, and III

34. If n is a negative number, which of the following expressions must be positive?

I. $2n$
II. n^2
III. n^5

A) II only
B) III only
C) I and II only
D) II and III only

35. If $0 < x < 1$, which of the following expressions is the largest?

A) $2x$
B) x^2
C) x^3
D) $x+1$

36. If $-1 < x < 0$, which of the following expressions is the largest?

A) -1
B) x
C) $2x$
D) x^3

Scientific Notation Ⓐ

37. Which of the following is equivalent to 12,040,000,000,000?

A) 1.204×10^{-14}

B) 1.204×10^{-13}

C) 1.204×10^{12}

D) 1.204×10^{13}

38. The world's population in 2014 was estimated to be 1,000 times Bulgaria's population of 7.2×10^6. What was the approximate population of the world in 2014?

A) 7.2×10^3

B) 7.2×10^6

C) 7.2×10^7

D) 7.2×10^9

39. Which of the following is equivalent to $\dfrac{(4 \times 10^7)(6 \times 10^{12})}{8 \times 10^9}$?

A) 1.25×10^{10}

B) 2×10^{10}

C) 3×10^{10}

D) 2×10^{28}

40. A sound wave travels at approximately 1,125 feet/second. If a person hears a sound two and a half minutes after it happens, how far away, in feet, is the person from the source of the sound?

A) 1.6875×10^1

B) 2.8125×10^3

C) 2.8125×10^4

D) 1.6875×10^5

Sets: Union, Intersection, and Elements ⒶⓈ

41. In a certain school, each of the 72 music students must participate in the marching band, the orchestra, or both. If only music students participate, 48 students in total participate in the marching band, and 54 students in total participate in the orchestra, how many students participate in both programs?

A) 6
B) 18
C) 24
D) 30

42. All *S* are *M*.
No *P* are *M*.

Which of the following conclusions can be logically deduced from the two statements above?

A) All *S* are *P*.
B) All *M* are *S*.
C) Some *M* are *P*.
D) No *P* are *S*.

Absolute Value ⒶⓈ

43. How many integers are in the solution set of $|1 - 3x| < 5$?

A) None
B) One
C) Two
D) Three

44. Which of the following expressions represents the distance in altitude between the highest elevation on earth at the peak of Mount Everest (2,549 feet above sea level), and the lowest elevation on earth at the lowest point in Death Valley (282 feet below sea level)?

A) $|2{,}549-282|$
B) $|282-2{,}549|$
C) $|-282-2{,}549|$
D) 2,549 - 282

Matrices Ⓐ

45. What is the matrix solution of $2\begin{bmatrix} 5 & -1 \\ -3 & 7 \\ 1 & 0 \end{bmatrix} - \begin{bmatrix} -6 & 0 \\ 4 & 2 \\ 11 & -1 \end{bmatrix}$?

A) $\begin{bmatrix} 4 & -2 \\ -2 & 16 \\ 13 & -1 \end{bmatrix}$

B) $\begin{bmatrix} 16 & -2 \\ -14 & 10 \\ -20 & 2 \end{bmatrix}$

C) $\begin{bmatrix} -2 & -2 \\ 2 & 18 \\ 24 & -2 \end{bmatrix}$

D) $\begin{bmatrix} 16 & -2 \\ -10 & 12 \\ -9 & 1 \end{bmatrix}$

46. Which of the following is the matrix product $\begin{bmatrix} -2 & 0 \\ 3 & 5 \end{bmatrix} \cdot \begin{bmatrix} 1 & 2 \\ -1 & 0 \end{bmatrix}$?

A) $\begin{bmatrix} -2 & -4 \\ -2 & 6 \end{bmatrix}$

B) $\begin{bmatrix} -2 & 0 \\ -3 & 0 \end{bmatrix}$

C) $\begin{bmatrix} -1 & 2 \\ 2 & 5 \end{bmatrix}$

D) $\begin{bmatrix} -1 & -4 \\ -3 & -5 \end{bmatrix}$

47. The following matrix shows how many people in a certain company work in each of three departments:

accounting	marketing	human resources
35	22	60

The following matrix shows the fractions of each department that take public transportation:

accounting	0.2
marketing	0.5
human resources	0.75

Based on the given information, approximately how many people working in the three departments take public transportation to work?

A) 7
B) 11
C) 45
D) 63

48. The numbers of male and female students taking each subject at High School X are shown by the following matrix [S]:

$$\begin{array}{r} \\ \text{male} \\ \text{female} \end{array}\begin{array}{c} \begin{array}{ccc}\text{math} & \text{English} & \text{history}\end{array} \\ \begin{bmatrix} 120 & 164 & 100 \\ 140 & 180 & 110 \end{bmatrix}\end{array}$$

The estimates of the fractions of female and male students who will receive A's are shown in the following matrix [A]:

$$\begin{array}{cc}\text{male} & \text{female}\end{array}$$
$$\begin{bmatrix} 0.25 & 0.4 \end{bmatrix}$$

Based on the given matrices, how many students are expected to earn an A in English?

A) 41
B) 69
C) 72
D) 113

Complex Numbers Ⓐⓢ

49. $(3+i)(4-3i)=?$

A) $12-3i^2$
B) $9-5i^2$
C) $9-5i$
D) $15-5i$

50. $\frac{1}{2-i}=?$

A) -2
B) -1
C) $\frac{2+i}{5}$
D) $\frac{2-i}{5}$

Problem Solving and Advanced Arithmetic Alternative Strategies

"Test-the-Test" Ⓐⓢ

51. Which of the following is the larger of two numbers, the product of which is 600 and the sum of which is five times the difference between the two?

A) 10
B) 15
C) 20
D) 30

52. If $\frac{1}{3}$ of a number is 3 more than $\frac{1}{4}$ of the number, then what is the number?

A) 18
B) 24
C) 30
D) 36

53. If $\frac{3}{5}$ of a number is 4 more than $\frac{1}{2}$ of the number, then what is the number?

A) 20
B) 28
C) 35
D) 40

54. If both 16 and 9 are divided by n, the remainder is 2. What is n?

A) 4
B) 5
C) 6
D) 7

55. The sum of the digits of a three-digit number is 16. If the tens digit of the number is 3 times the units digit, and the units digit is $\frac{1}{4}$ of the hundreds digit, then what is the number?

A) 446
B) 561
C) 682
D) 862

56. If the sum of five consecutive integers is 40, what is the smallest of the five integers?

A) 4
B) 5
C) 6
D) 7

57. After filling the car's fuel tank, a driver drove from point P to point Q and then to point R. She used $\frac{2}{5}$ of the fuel driving from P to Q. If she used another 7 gallons to drive from Q to R and still had $\frac{1}{4}$ of a tank left, how many gallons does the tank hold?

A) 8
B) 12
C) 18
D) 20

"Plug-and-Chug" Ⓐⓢ

58. If n is any integer, which of the following is always an odd integer?

A) $n-1$
B) $n+1$
C) $n+2$
D) $2n+1$

LESSON 2 | ALGEBRA

ACT MATHEMATICS AND SAT MATH: MULTIPLE-CHOICE

The items in this section accompany the in-class review of the algebra skills and concepts tested by the ACT Mathematics and SAT Math: Multiple-Choice tests. You will work through the items with your instructor in class. Answers are on page 579.

Manipulating Algebraic Expressions

Basic Algebraic Manipulations Ⓐ Ⓢ

1. If $a^3+b=3+a^3$, then $b=?$

A) 3^3
B) $3\sqrt{3}$
C) 3
D) $\sqrt[3]{3}$

2. Which of the following expressions is equivalent to $4a+3b-(-2a-3b)$?

A) $2a$
B) $12ab$
C) $2a+6b$
D) $6a+6b$

Evaluating Expressions Ⓐ Ⓢ

3. If $x = 3$, what is the value of x^2+2x-2?

A) 4
B) 6
C) 9
D) 13

4. If $x=2$, then $\frac{1}{x^2}+\frac{1}{x}-\frac{x}{2}=?$

A) $-\frac{3}{4}$
B) $-\frac{1}{4}$
C) 0
D) $\frac{1}{4}$

5. If $\frac{1}{3}x=10$, then $\frac{1}{6}x=?$

A) $\frac{1}{15}$
B) $\frac{2}{3}$
C) 2
D) 5

6. If $p=1$, $q=2$, and $r=3$, what is the value of $\frac{(q \cdot r)(r-q)}{(q-p)(p \cdot q)}$?

A) −3
B) −1
C) 0
D) 3

Manipulating Expressions Involving Exponents Ⓐ Ⓢ

7. $\dfrac{9\left(x^2y^3\right)^6}{\left(3x^6y^9\right)^2} = ?$

A) 1
B) 3
C) x^2y^3
D) $3x^2y^3$

8. $2\left(4^{-\frac{1}{2}}\right) - 2^0 + 2^{\frac{3}{2}} + 2^{-2} = ?$

A) $-2\sqrt{2} - \dfrac{1}{4}$
B) $2\sqrt{2} - \dfrac{1}{4}$
C) $2\sqrt{2}$
D) $2\sqrt{2} + \dfrac{1}{4}$

Factoring Expressions Ⓐ Ⓢ

9. Which of the following expressions is equivalent to $\dfrac{x^2 - y^2}{x + y}$?

A) $x^2 - y^2$
B) $x^2 + y$
C) $x - y$
D) $x + y^2$

10. Which of the following expressions is equivalent to $\dfrac{x^2 - x - 6}{x + 2}$?

A) $x^2 - \dfrac{x}{2} - 3$
B) $x - 3$
C) $x - 2$
D) $x^2 - 2$

11. Which of the following is the factorization of $6x^2 + 4x - 2$?

A) $(2x + 2)(3x - 1)$
B) $(3x - 1)(2x - 2)$
C) $(6x + 3)(x - 1)$
D) $(6x + 1)(x - 3)$

Logarithmic Expressions Ⓐ

12. Evaluate $\log_5 125 + \log_2\left(\dfrac{1}{2}\right)$.

A) -1
B) 0
C) 1
D) 2

13. If $\log_b x = m$ and $\log_b y = n$, then what is $\log_b xy$?

A) $m + n$
B) bmn
C) bxy
D) $m - n$

Evaluating Sequences Involving Exponential Growth Ⓐ Ⓢ

14. In a geometric sequence of positive numbers, the fourth term is 125 and the sixth term is 3,125. What is the second term of the sequence?

A) 1
B) 5
C) 10
D) 25

15. City University projects that a planned expansion will increase the number of enrolled students every year for the next five years by 50 percent. If 400 students enroll in the first year of the plan, how many students are expected to enroll in the fifth year of the plan?

A) 600
B) 675
C) 1,350
D) 2,025

16. Jimmy's uncle deposited $1,000 into a college fund account and promised that at the start of each year, he would deposit an amount equal to 10 percent of the account balance. If no other deposits or withdrawals were made and no additional interest accrued, what was the account balance after three additional annual deposits were made by Jimmy's uncle?

A) $1,030
B) $1,300
C) $1,331
D) $1,500

17. A tank with a capacity of 2,400 liters is filled with water. If a valve is opened that drains 25 percent of the contents of the tank every minute, what is the volume of water (in liters) that remains in the tank after 3 minutes?

A) 1,800
B) 1,350
C) 1,012.5
D) 600

Solving Algebraic Equations or Inequalities with One Variable

Simple Equations Ⓐ Ⓢ

18. If $(2+3)(1+x)=25$, then $x=?$

A) $\frac{1}{5}$
B) $\frac{1}{4}$
C) 1
D) 4

Simple Inequalities Ⓐ Ⓢ

19. If $2x+3>9$, which of the following can be the value of x?

A) −3
B) 0
C) 3
D) 4

Equations Involving Rational Expressions Ⓐ Ⓢ

20. If $\frac{12}{x+1}-1=2$ and $x\neq -1$, then $x=?$

A) 1
B) 2
C) 3
D) 11

21. If $\frac{x}{x+2}=\frac{3}{4}$ and $x\neq -2$, then $x=?$

A) 6
B) 4
C) 3
D) 2

22. If $\frac{x}{x-2}-\frac{x+2}{2(x-2)}=8$ and $x\neq 2$, which of the following is the complete solution set for x?

A) {}
B) {−2}
C) {2}
D) {4}

Inequalities Involving Rational Expressions Ⓐ Ⓢ

23. If $\frac{3}{x-2} > \frac{1}{6}$, which of the following defines the possible values for *x*?

A) $x > 0$
B) $x > 2$
C) $0 < x < 20$
D) $2 < x < 20$

Equations Involving Radical Expressions Ⓐ Ⓢ

24. If $\sqrt{2x+1} - 1 = 4$, then $x = ?$

A) -5
B) -1
C) 1
D) 12

25. Which of the following is the complete solution set for $\sqrt{3x-2} - 3 = -4$?

A) {}
B) {−1}
C) {1}
D) {−1, 1}

26. If $\sqrt{2x-5} = 2\sqrt{5-2x}$, then $x = ?$

A) 1
B) 2
C) $\frac{5}{2}$
D) 10

27. Which of the following is the complete solution set for $\sqrt{x^2+9} = 5$?

A) {−4, 4}
B) {−4}
C) {0}
D) {4}

Equations Involving Exponents Ⓐ Ⓢ

28. If $4^{x+2} = 64$, then $x = ?$

A) 1
B) 2
C) 3
D) 4

29. If $8^x = 2^{x+3}$, then $x = ?$

A) 1
B) $\frac{2}{3}$
C) $\frac{3}{2}$
D) 3

30. If $3^{2x} = \frac{1}{81}$, then $x = ?$

A) -2
B) $-\frac{3}{2}$
C) $-\frac{2}{3}$
D) $\frac{2}{3}$

31. If $5^3 = \left(\sqrt{5}\right)^{-2x}$, then $5^x = ?$

A) $\frac{1}{125}$
B) $\frac{1}{25}$
C) $\frac{1}{5}$
D) 5

Equations Involving Logarithms Ⓐ

32. Which of the following is a value of x that satisfies the equation $\log_4 x = 4$?

A) 4
B) 16
C) 160
D) 256

33. Which of the following is a value of x that satisfies the equation $2\log_x 16 + \log_x 16 = 6$?

A) 2
B) 4
C) 16
D) 32

Equations Involving Absolute Value

ⒶⓈ

34. Which of the following is the complete solution set for $\left|\frac{2x+1}{3}\right| = 5$?

A) {–8,–7}
B) {–8, 7}
C) {–7, 8}
D) {7}

35. Which of the following is the complete solution set for $|x+6| = 3x$?

A) $\left\{-3, \frac{3}{2}\right\}$
B) $\left\{-\frac{3}{2}, 3\right\}$
C) $\left\{\frac{3}{2}, 3\right\}$
D) {3}

Inequalities Involving Absolute Value

ⒶⓈ

36. Which of the following is the complete solution set for $|2x-1| > 3$?

A) All real numbers
B) The null set
C) All real numbers less than –1 or greater than 2
D) All real numbers less than –2 or greater than 1

37. Which of the following identifies exactly those values of x that satisfy $|-2x+4| < 4$?

A) $x > -4$
B) $x < 4$
C) $x > 0$
D) $0 < x < 4$

38. If $|3x-6| > 9$, then which of the following must be true?

A) $-3 < x < 2$
B) $-2 < x < 3$
C) $x < -3$ or $x > 2$
D) $x < -1$ or $x > 5$

Creating, Expressing, and Evaluating Algebraic Equations and Functions

Creating Algebraic Equations ⒶⓈ

39. In a certain game, a player picks an integer between 1 and 10, adds 3 to it, multiplies the sum by 2, and subtracts 5. If x represents the number picked by a player and y represents the result of the manipulations, which of the following correctly expresses the final result of the game?

A) $y = x + (3)(2) - 5$
B) $y = 3x + 2 - 5$
C) $y = 2(x + 3 - 5)$
D) $y = 2(x+3) - 5$

40. At 9:00 a.m., when the heat is turned on, the temperature of a room is 55°F. If the room temperature increases by *n*°F each hour, which of the following can be used to determine the number of hours, *h*, needed to bring the temperature of the room to 70°F?

A) $h = (55+70)(n)$
B) $h = (55-70)(n)$
C) $h = \dfrac{70-55}{n}$
D) $h = \dfrac{n}{70-55}$

Function Notation Ⓐ Ⓢ

41. If $f(x)=x^2+x$, what is the value of $f(-2)$?

A) -8
B) -2
C) 2
D) 8

42. If $f(x)=\left(\dfrac{6x^2-2^{-x}}{|x|}\right)^{-\frac{1}{2}}$ for all integers and $x=-1$, what is the value of *y*?

A) 2
B) $\dfrac{1}{2}$
C) $\dfrac{1}{4}$
D) $-\dfrac{1}{2}$

43. If $f(x)=x+3$ and $g(x)=2x-5$, what is the value of $f(g(2))$?

A) -2
B) 0
C) 2
D) 4

44. If $f(x)=3x+2$ and $g(x)=x^2-x$, what is the value of $g(f(-2))$?

A) 20
B) 12
C) 6
D) -4

45. If $f(x)=2x^2+x$ and $g(x)=f(f(x))$, what is the value of $g(1)$?

A) 3
B) 18
C) 21
D) 39

46. If $f(x)=3x+4$ and $g(x)=2x-1$, for what value of *x* does $f(x)=g(x)$?

A) -5
B) -2
C) 0
D) 3

47. If $\boxed{x}=x^2-x$ for all integers, then $\boxed{-2}=$?

A) -2
B) 2
C) 4
D) 6

48. If $\boxed{x}=x^2-x$ for all integers, then $\boxed{\boxed{3}}=$?

A) 27
B) 30
C) 58
D) 72

Concepts of Domain and Range Ⓐ Ⓢ

49. If $f(x)=3x-2$ and $-5<x<5$, which of the following defines the range of $f(x)$?

A) $-17<f(x)<13$
B) $-13<f(x)<17$
C) $-5<f(x)<12$
D) $0<f(x)<17$

50. If $f(x)=\frac{x+2}{x-1}$, for which of the following values of x is $f(x)$ undefined?

A) -2
B) -1
C) $\frac{1}{2}$
D) 1

51. If $f(x)=\frac{2-2x}{x}$, which of the following defines the range of $f(x)$?

A) All real numbers
B) All real numbers except -2
C) All real numbers except 0
D) All real numbers except 2

52. Which of the following defines the domain of $|4x-8|<12$?

A) $-8<x<-4$
B) $-4<x<8$
C) $-1<x<5$
D) $1<x<5$

Functions as Models Ⓐ Ⓢ

53. The cost of making a call using a phone-card is a \$0.15 connection fee and \$0.04 per minute of connection time. Which of the following equations could be used to find the cost, y, of a call x minutes long?

A) $y=x(0.04+0.15)$
B) $y=0.04x+0.15$
C) $y=0.04+0.15x$
D) $y=0.15-0.04x$

Solving Algebraic Equations with Two Variables Ⓐ Ⓢ

54. If $x+y=3$, then $2x+2y=?$

A) $-\frac{2}{3}$
B) $\frac{1}{2}$
C) $\frac{2}{3}$
D) 6

Solving Simultaneous Equations Ⓐ Ⓢ

55. If $7x=2$ and $3y-7x=10$, then $y=?$

A) 2
B) 3
C) 4
D) 5

56. If $2x+y=8$ and $x-y=1$, what is the value of $x+y$?

A) 1
B) 2
C) 3
D) 5

57. If $4x+5y=12$ and $3x+4y=5$, what is the value of $7(x+y)$?

A) 7
B) 14
C) 49
D) 77

x	-2	-1	0	1	2
y	$\frac{10}{3}$	$\frac{8}{3}$	2	$\frac{4}{3}$	$\frac{2}{3}$

58. Which of the following equations correctly describes the relationship between the values shown for *x* and *y* in the table above?

A) $3x - 2y = 3$
B) $3x + 3y = 6$
C) $6x + 4y = 7$
D) $2x + 3y = 6$

Solving Quadratic Equations and Relations

Factoring Ⓐ Ⓢ

59. If $x^2 - 3x - 4 = 0$, then which of the following shows all possible values of *x*?

A) $\{1,4\}$
B) $\{-1,4\}$
C) $\{-4, 1\}$
D) $\{-4, -1\}$

60. If $x^2 + 30 = 11x$, then which of the following shows all possible values of *x*?

A) $\{-3, -10\}$
B) $\{-6, 5\}$
C) $\{-5, 6\}$
D) $\{5, 6\}$

61. Which of the following is the solution set for $2x^2 - 2x = 12$?

A) $\{-3, 2\}$
B) $\{-2, 3\}$
C) $\left\{\frac{2}{3}, 3\right\}$
D) $\left\{\frac{3}{2}, 2\right\}$

62. Which of the following is the solution set for $3x^2 + 3x = 6$?

A) $\{-2, 1\}$
B) $\{-1, 2\}$
C) $\left\{\frac{1}{3}, \frac{1}{2}\right\}$
D) $\left\{\frac{1}{2}, 1\right\}$

Difference of Two Squares Ⓐ Ⓢ

63. Which of the following is an equivalent form for the expression $x^2 - y^2$?

A) $2(x - y)$
B) $(x - y)(x + y)$
C) $(x + y)(x + y)$
D) $(x - y)(x - y)$

Trinomial Square Ⓐ Ⓢ

64. Which of the following is the solution set for $x^2 + 2x - 6 = -2$?

A) $\{-6,4\}$
B) $\{-1-\sqrt{5}, x = -1+\sqrt{5}\}$
C) $\{-1-\sqrt{5}, x = 1+\sqrt{5}\}$
D) $\{-1+\sqrt{5}, x = 1+\sqrt{5}\}$

65. Which of the following are the zero values of $2x^2 - 3x - 2 = 0$?

A) $-\frac{1}{2}$ and -2
B) $-\frac{1}{2}$ and 2
C) $\frac{1}{2}$ and -2
D) $\frac{1}{2}$ and 2

The Quadratic Formula Ⓐ Ⓢ

66. Which of the following is the solution set for $2x^2 - 3x = 2$?

A) $\left\{\frac{1}{2}, 2\right\}$
B) $\left\{-\frac{1}{2}, 2\right\}$
C) $\left\{-2, -\frac{1}{2}\right\}$
D) $\{-2, 2\}$

67. Which of the following is the solution set for $2x^2 - 5x + 2 = 0$?

A) $\left\{-2, -\frac{1}{2}\right\}$
B) $\left\{-2, \frac{1}{2}\right\}$
C) $\left\{-\frac{1}{2}, 2\right\}$
D) $\left\{\frac{1}{2}, 2\right\}$

Discriminants Ⓐ Ⓢ

68. Which of the following best describes the roots of $x^2 - 7x + 10 = 0$?

A) real, unequal, and irrational
B) real, unequal, and rational
C) real, equal, and rational
D) imaginary

Roots of Quadratic Equations Ⓐ Ⓢ

69. Which of the following are the sum and product, respectively, of the roots of $4x^2 - 3x - 9 = 0$?

A) $-\frac{3}{4}$ and $-\frac{9}{4}$
B) $-\frac{3}{4}$ and $\frac{9}{4}$
C) $\frac{3}{4}$ and $-\frac{9}{4}$
D) $\frac{3}{4}$ and $\frac{9}{4}$

70. Which of the following are the roots of $2x^2 - 5x + 2 = 0$?

A) -2 and 2
B) -2 and $\frac{1}{2}$
C) $-\frac{1}{2}$ and 2
D) $\frac{1}{2}$ and 2

71. Which of the following are the roots of $2x^2 - 8x + 7 = 0$?

A) $\frac{8+2\sqrt{2}}{4}$ and $\frac{8-2\sqrt{2}}{4}$
B) $\frac{8+\sqrt{2}}{4}$ and $\frac{8-\sqrt{2}}{4}$
C) $\frac{8+\sqrt{5}}{4}$ and $\frac{8-\sqrt{5}}{4}$
D) $128+\sqrt{2}$ and $128-\sqrt{2}$

72. If the roots of a quadratic equation are $\frac{3+\sqrt{11}}{2}$ and $\frac{3-\sqrt{11}}{2}$, which of the following is a form of the equation?

A) $2x^2 - 6x - 1 = 0$
B) $2x^2 + 6x - 2 = 0$
C) $x^2 + 3x + 2 = 0$
D) $x^2 - 3x - 2 = 0$

Binomial Expansion Ⓐ Ⓢ

73. The expansion of the binomial $(x+y)^7$ contains how many unique terms?

A) 3
B) 6
C) 7
D) 8

74. If the third term of the expansion of the binomial $(a+b)^n$, where n is a positive integer, is $10a^3b^2$, which of the following is equal to the fourth term of the expansion?

A) $30a^3b^2$
B) $10a^4b^3$
C) $10a^3b^4$
D) $10a^2b^3$

Algebra Alternative Strategies

"Test-the-Test" Ⓐ Ⓢ

75. In a certain game, a player had five successful turns in a row, and after each one, the number of points added to his total score was double what was added the preceding turn. If the player scored a total of 465 points, how many points did he score on the first play?

A) 15
B) 31
C) 93
D) 155

76. Harold is twice as old as Jack, who is three years older than Dan. If Harold's age is five times Dan's age, how old (in years) is Jack?

A) 2
B) 4
C) 5
D) 8

77. On a playground, there are 25 children, either riding on seesaws, two per seesaw, or swinging on tire swings, three per swing. If the total number of seesaws and swings combined is 9, what is the maximum number of swings on the playground?

A) 1
B) 2
C) 7
D) 8

78. $3x + 4y = 15$
$x - 3y = -8$

Given the system of equations above, what are the solutions for x and y?

A) $x = -3$ and $y = -1$
B) $x = -3$ and $y = 1$
C) $x = 1$ and $y = 3$
D) $x = 3$ and $y = 1$

79. Which of the following are the roots of $8 - 2x = x^2$?

A) −2 and −4
B) −2 and 4
C) 2 and −4
D) 2 and 4

80. Which of the following expressions is equivalent to $4a^2 + 2ab - 2b^2$?

A) $(4a - b)(a + b)$
B) $(2a + 2b)(2a + 2b)$
C) $(2a + b)(a - 2b)$
D) $(2a - b)(2a + 2b)$

"Plug-and-Chug" Ⓐⓢ

81. At a certain firm, d gallons of fuel are needed per day for each truck. At this rate, g gallons of fuel will supply t trucks for how many days?

A) $\frac{gt}{d}$
B) dgt
C) $\frac{t}{dg}$
D) $\frac{g}{dt}$

82. Paul was twice as old as Bob Y years ago. If Bob is now 18 years old, how old is Paul today in terms of Y?

A) $36+Y$
B) $18+Y$
C) $18-Y$
D) $36-Y$

83. If pencils cost x cents each, how many pencils can be purchased for y dollars?

A) $\frac{100}{xy}$
B) $\frac{xy}{100}$
C) $\frac{100y}{x}$
D) $\frac{y}{100x}$

84. A tank with capacity t gallons is empty. If water flows into the tank from Pipe X at the rate of x gallons per minute, and water is pumped out by Pipe Y at the rate of y gallons per minute, and x is greater than y, in how many <u>minutes</u> will the tank be filled?

A) $\frac{t}{y-x}$
B) $\frac{t}{x-y}$
C) $\frac{t-x}{y}$
D) $\frac{x-y}{60t}$

85. If a train travels m miles in h hours and 45 minutes, what is its average speed in miles per hour?

A) $\frac{m}{h+\frac{3}{4}}$
B) $\frac{m}{1\frac{3}{4}h}$
C) $m\left(h+\frac{3}{4}\right)$
D) $\frac{m+45}{h}$

86. A merchant increased the original price of an item by 10 percent. If she then reduces the new price by 10 percent, the final price, in terms of the original price, is equal to which of the following?

A) a decrease of 11 percent
B) a decrease of 1 percent
C) no net change
D) an increase of 1 percent

87. Machine *X* produces *w* widgets in five minutes. Machine *X* and Machine *Y*, working at the same time, produce *w* widgets in two minutes. How long will it take Machine *Y* working alone to produce *w* widgets?

A) 2 minutes, 30 seconds
B) 2 minutes, 40 seconds
C) 3 minutes, 20 seconds
D) 3 minutes, 30 seconds

Problem Solving with Algebraic Concepts Ⓐⓢ

88. An office supply store has two copy machines, B and C. Machine B operating independently produces *b* copies every *y* seconds, and Machine C operating independently produces *c* copies every *z* seconds. The following equation describes the operation of the copy machines when operating simultaneously but independently: $a = x\left(\frac{b}{y} + \frac{c}{z}\right)$.

In the equation above, what does *a* represent?

A) Number of copies produced by both machines operating simultaneously in *x* seconds
B) Number of seconds needed for both machines operating simultaneously to produce *x* copies
C) Difference in the number of copies produced by Machine B and Machine C in *y* seconds
D) Rate at which Machine B and Machine C operating simultaneously produce copies

89. When a wholesaler ships a certain type of fruit by rail from the West Coast to the East Coast, it expects that approximately 8 percent of the shipment, by weight, will be lost due to damage. Of the fruit that has not been damaged, approximately 12 percent, by weight, will be lost due to spoilage before it can be sold. If *w* represents the original weight, in pounds, of a shipment starting out on the West Coast and *n* represents the weight, in pounds, of the fruit finally sold, which of the following equations can be used to calculate the approximate weight, in pounds, of the fruit finally sold from a shipment of *w* pounds?

A) $n = w - 0.12(w - 0.08w)$
B) $n = w - 0.08w - 0.12w(w - 0.08w)$
C) $n = (0.92)(0.88)w$
D) $n = (0.08)(0.12)w$

90. Which of the following number lines represents the solution to the inequality $5x < 2(2x - 1)$?

A) 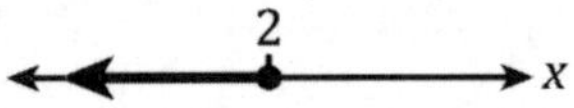

B) 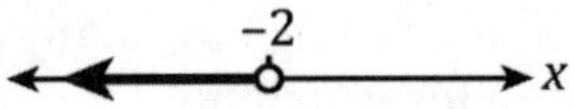

C) 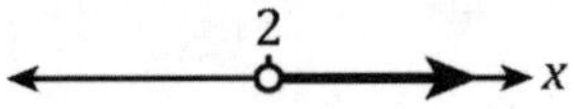

D) 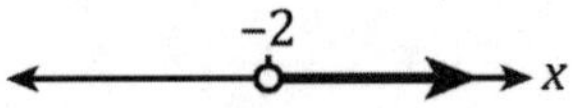

91. A college has at least \$5,000 in a scholarship fund that must be distributed. According to the terms of the fund, the aid must go to two candidates with one candidate receiving at least twice as much as the other candidate. Which of the following inequalities correctly describes the amount of the larger award, *m*?

A) $m \leq \$5{,}000$
B) $2m \geq \$5{,}000$
C) $m \geq \frac{\$5{,}000}{2}$
D) $m \geq \frac{2(\$5{,}000)}{3}$

92. A group of students rented some bowling lanes for an all-night bowling party with the cost of $120 to be shared equally. When another student joined the party and the cost per student was recalculated, the cost per student was $4 less than originally calculated. What was the original cost per student before the additional student joined the party?

A) $20
B) $24
C) $30
D) $48

93. Helga is ordering five pounds of mixed nuts for a graduation party. The party budget allows $12 for the nuts. If peanuts are $2.00 per pound, and cashews are $3.00 per pound, how much pounds of peanuts should Helga buy?

A) 2
B) 3
C) 4
D) 6

94. As a research project, a group of students interviewed 1,000 people and asked a series of questions, one of which was treated as a control question. Of the group, 25 percent of those under the age of 30 answered the control question in the negative and 60 percent of those 30 years or older answered the control question in the negative. If the students recorded 460 negative responses to the control question for the entire group, how many people in the survey group were under the age of 30?

A) 100
B) 240
C) 360
D) 400

LESSON 3 | COORDINATE GEOMETRY

ACT MATHEMATICS AND SAT MATH: MULTIPLE-CHOICE

The items in this section accompany the in-class review of the coordinate geometry skills and concepts tested by the ACT Mathematics and SAT Math: Multiple-Choice tests. You will work through the items with your instructor in class. Answers are on page 580.

The Coordinate System ⒶⓈ

1. Which of the following is a graph of the line that passes through the points $(-5,3)$, $(-1,1)$, and $(3,-1)$?

A)

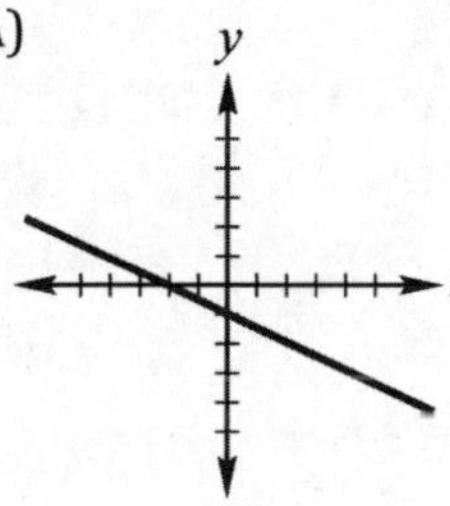

B)

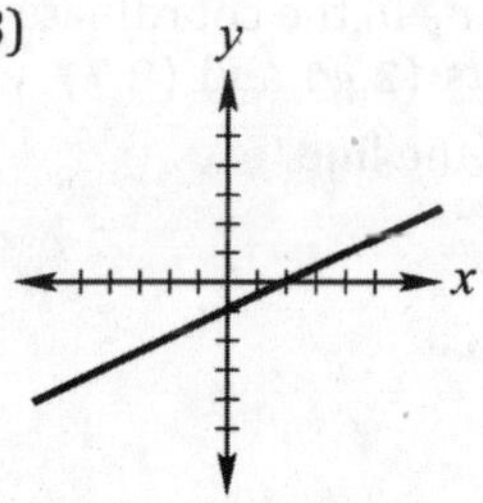

C)

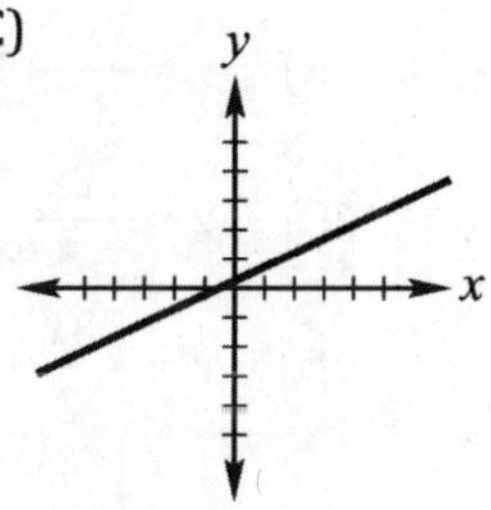

D)

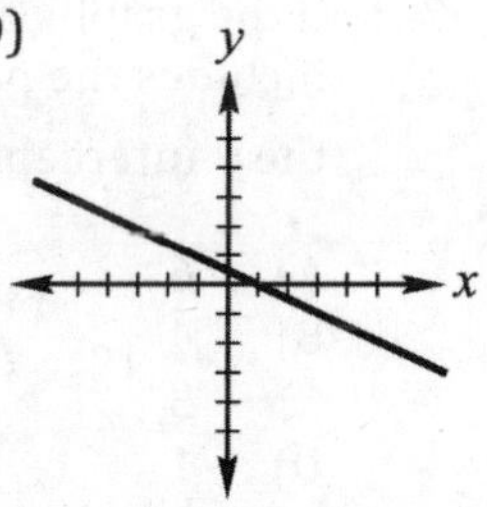

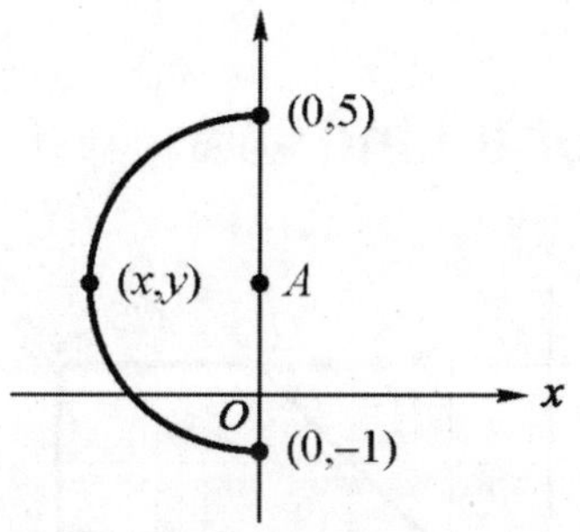

2. If point A is the center of the semicircle in the figure above, what are the coordinates, (x,y), of the point on the semicircle that is farthest from the y-axis?

A) $(-4,-4)$
B) $(-3,-3)$
C) $(-2,-3)$
D) $(-3,2)$

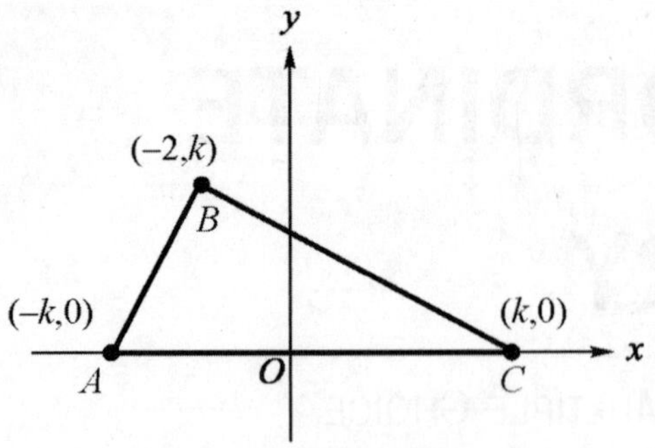

3. In the figure above, the area of ΔABC is 8. What is the value of k?

A) 2
B) $2\sqrt{2}$
C) 4
D) $4\sqrt{2}$

Slope of a Line Ⓐⓢ

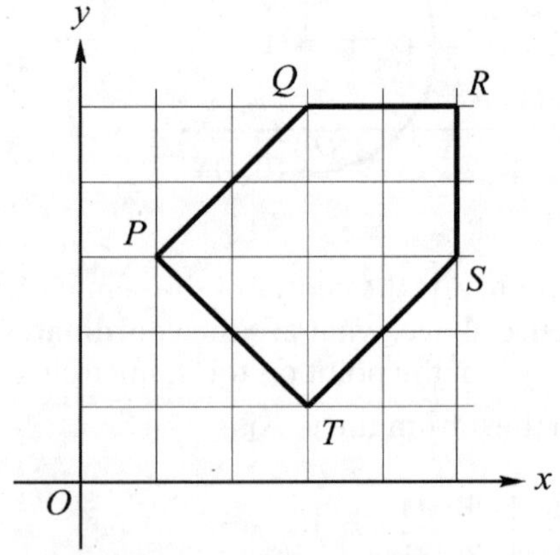

4. In the figure above, which two sides of polygon $PQRST$ have the same slope?

A) $\overline{PQ}$ and $\overline{QR}$
B) $\overline{PQ}$ and $\overline{RS}$
C) $\overline{PQ}$ and $\overline{ST}$
D) $\overline{QR}$ and $\overline{RS}$

5. If set $A = \{(-2,3), (-1,1), (-4,-5)\}$, and set $B = \{(3,4), (4,3), (2,-1)\}$, how many lines can be drawn with a positive slope that include exactly one point from set A and one point from set B?

A) 3
B) 4
C) 5
D) 6

Slope-Intercept Form of a Linear Equation Ⓐⓢ

6. Line l is the graph of the equation $y = \frac{3x}{2} + 2$. The graph of which of the following equations is perpendicular to line l at $(0,2)$?

A) $y = \frac{3x}{2} - 2$
B) $y = \frac{2x}{3} - 2$
C) $y = -\frac{2x}{3} + 2$
D) $y = -\frac{3x}{2} + 3$

7. If the graph of a line in the coordinate plane includes the points $(2,4)$ and $(8,7)$, what is the y-intercept of the line?

A) 6
B) 4
C) 3
D) −1

8. If the slope and y-intercept of a line are −2 and 3, respectively, then the line passes through which of the following points?

A) $(-5,10)$
B) $(-2,3)$
C) $(3,4)$
D) $(4,-5)$

Distance Formula Ⓐⓢ

9. What is the distance between the points (−3,−2) and (3,3)?

A) $2\sqrt{3}$
B) 5
C) $\sqrt{29}$
D) $\sqrt{61}$

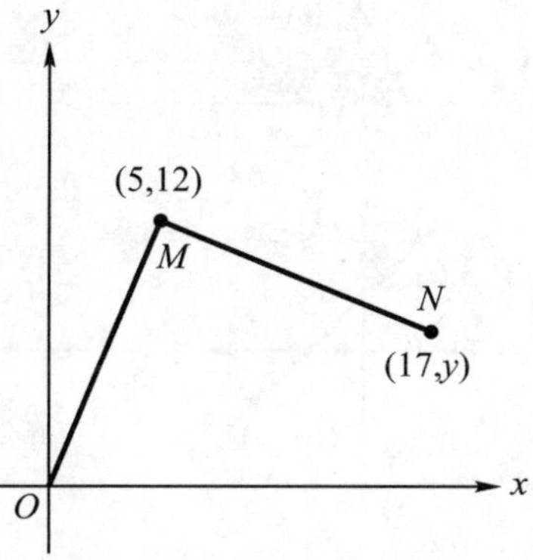

10. In the coordinate plane above, $\overline{MO} \cong \overline{MN}$ and $\overline{MO} \perp \overline{MN}$. What is the value of y?

A) 5
B) 7
C) 12
D) 13

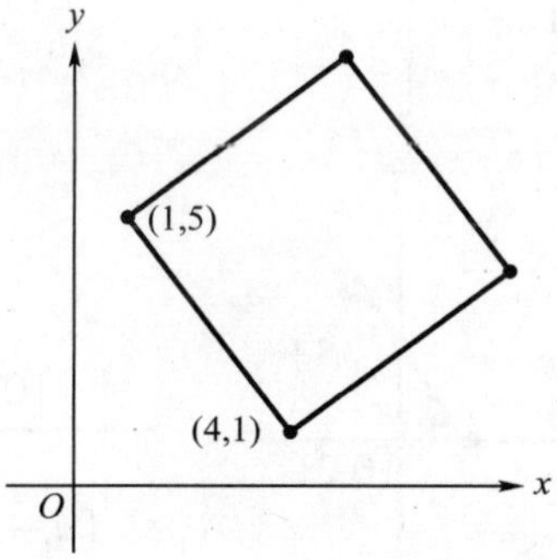

11. In the figure above, what is the area of the square region?

A) 8
B) $8\sqrt{2}$
C) 16
D) 25

Graphs of Linear Equations Ⓐⓢ

12. Which of the following is a graph of the equation $x = \dfrac{y+2}{3}$?

A)

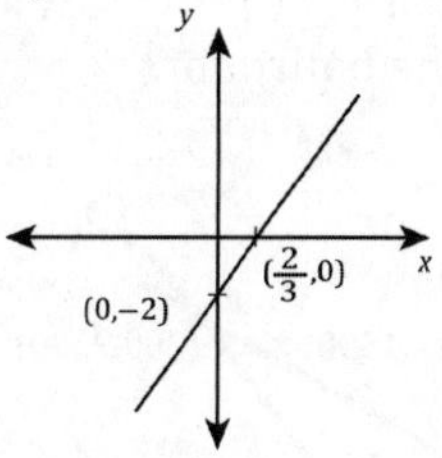

C)

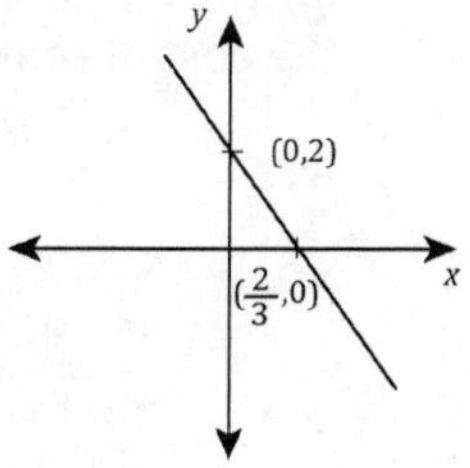

B)

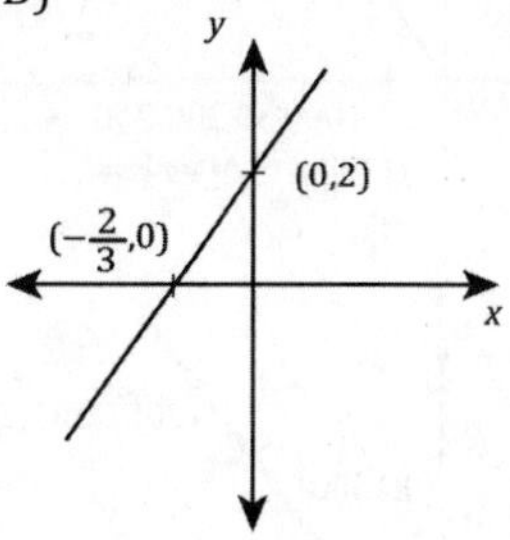

D)

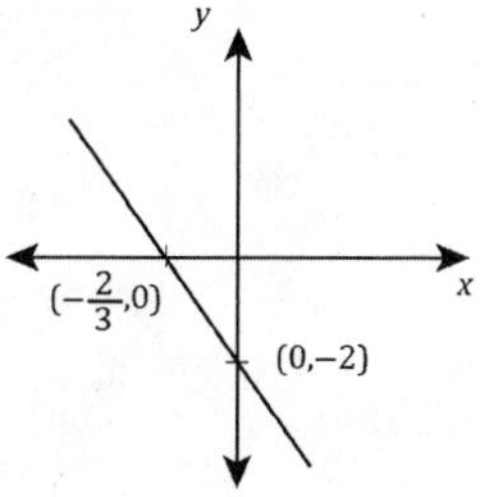

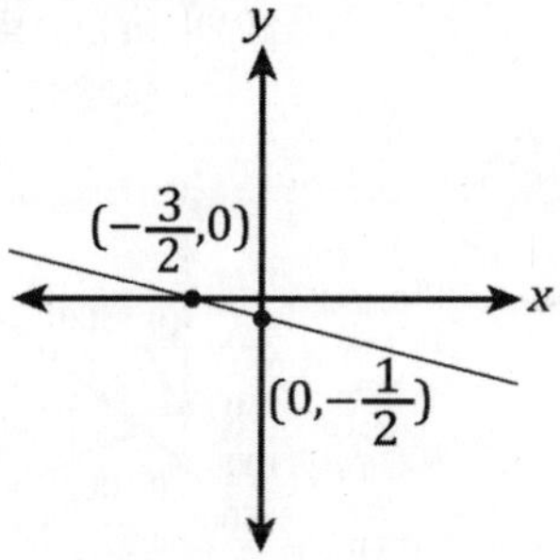

13. Which of the following is the equation for the graph of the line shown in the figure above?

A) $y = -3x - 2$
B) $y = -3x - \dfrac{1}{2}$
C) $y = -\dfrac{1}{3}x - \dfrac{1}{2}$
D) $y = \dfrac{1}{3}x + \dfrac{1}{2}$

14. A school rented a hotel ballroom for a dance. The cost of the rental is \$1500 plus \$5.00 per person who attends. Each person who attends will pay an admission charge of \$12.50. If x represents the number of people who attend, which of the graphs can be used to determine how many people must attend for the admission charges to cover exactly the cost of renting the ballroom?

A)

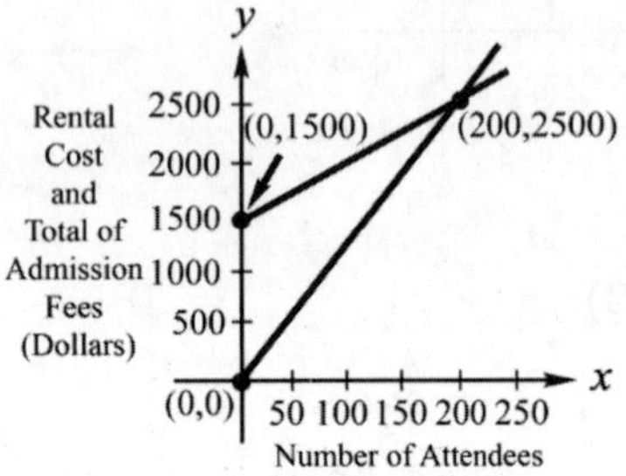

B)

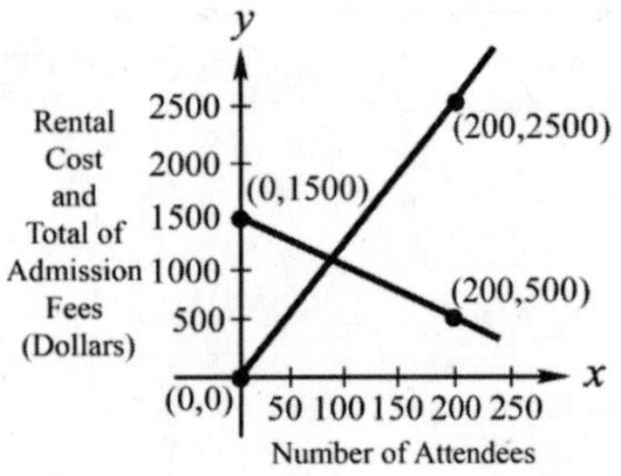

C)

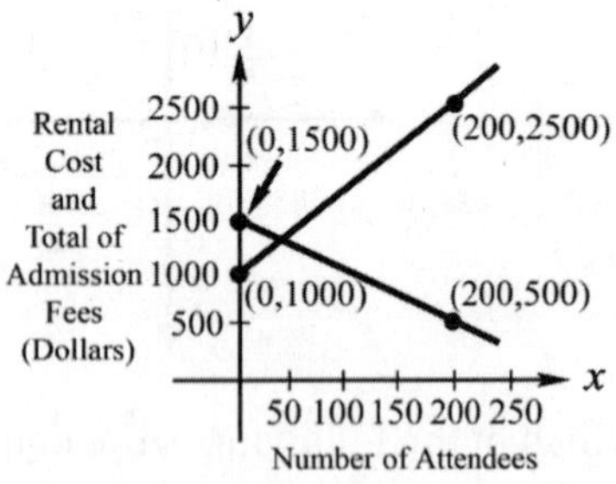

D)

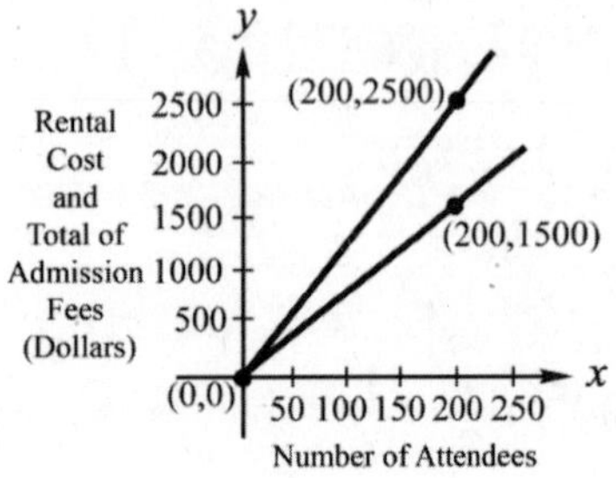

Graphs of First-Degree Inequalities Ⓐ Ⓢ

15. Which of the following is the graph of the inequality $y \geq 2x$?

A)

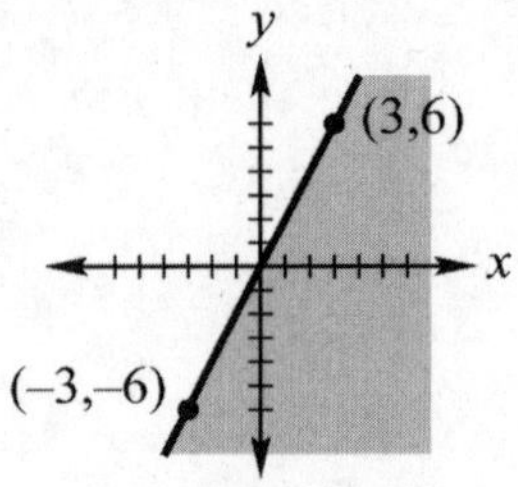

C)

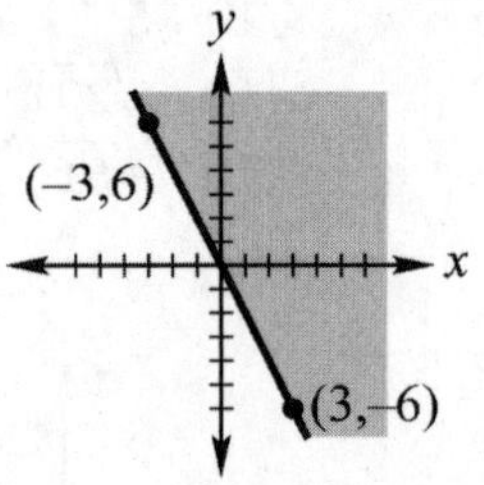

B)

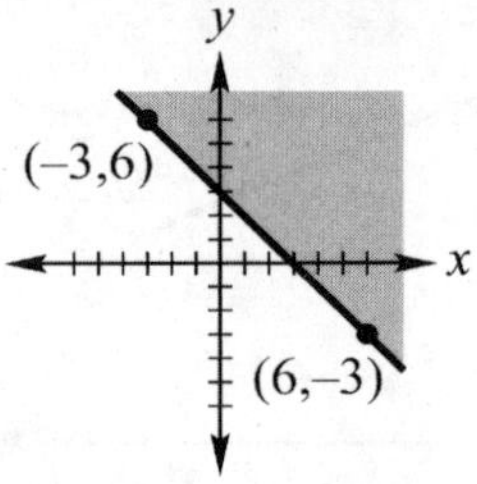

D)

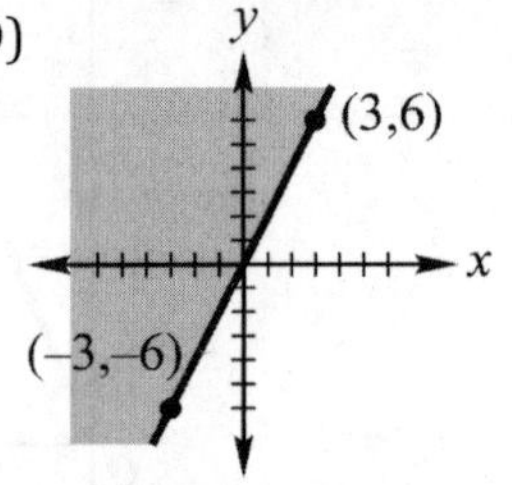

16. Which of the following could be the graph of the inequality $y < 2x + 1$?

A)

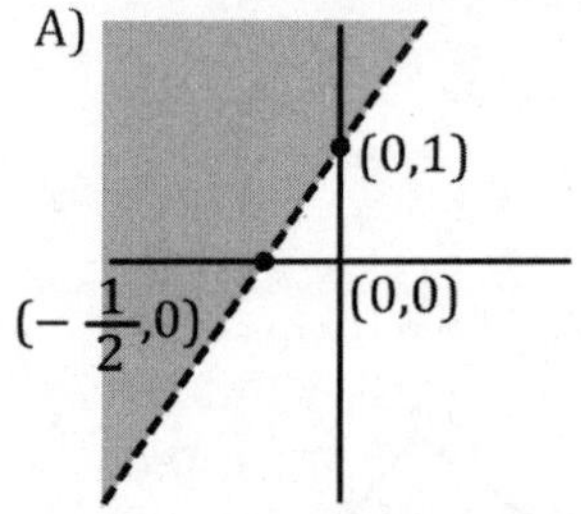

C)

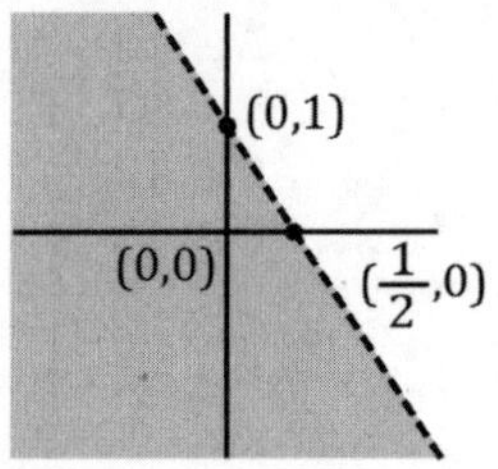

B)

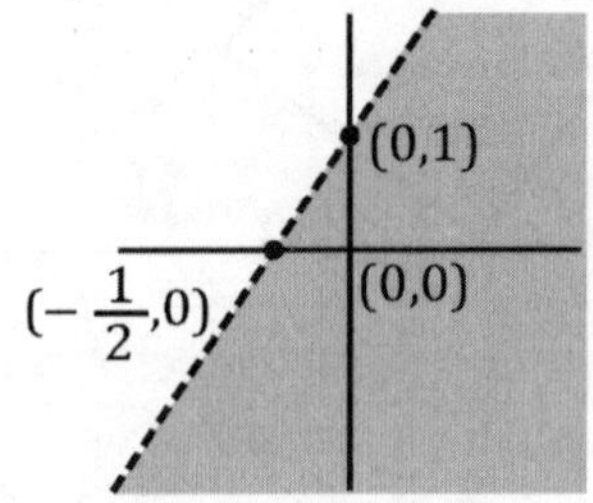

D)

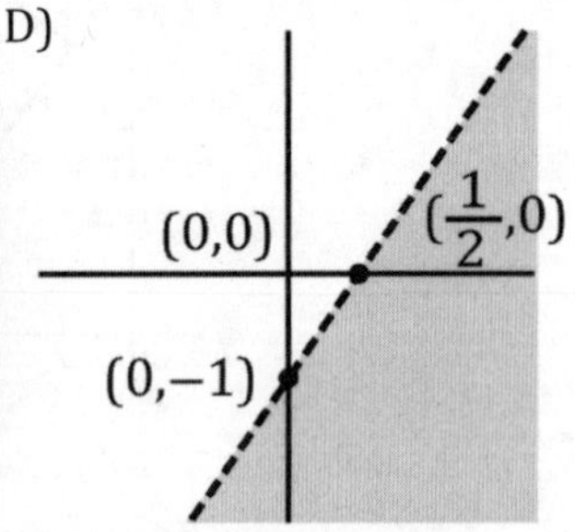

17. In which of the following graphs does the shaded area include all the coordinate (*x*,*y*) pairs that satisfy both of the inequalities below?

$y \geq -x$

$x \leq 5$

A)

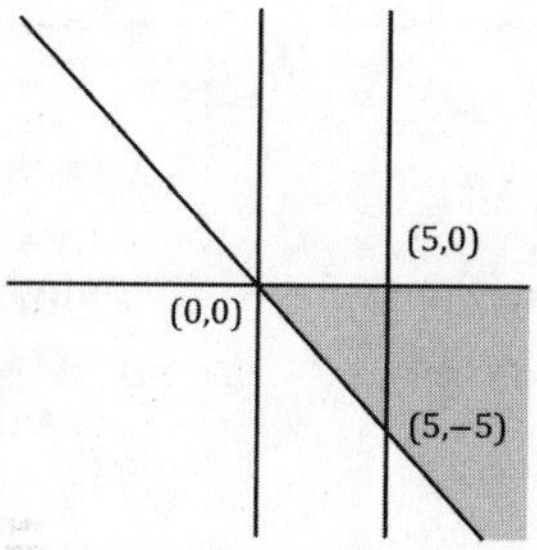

B)

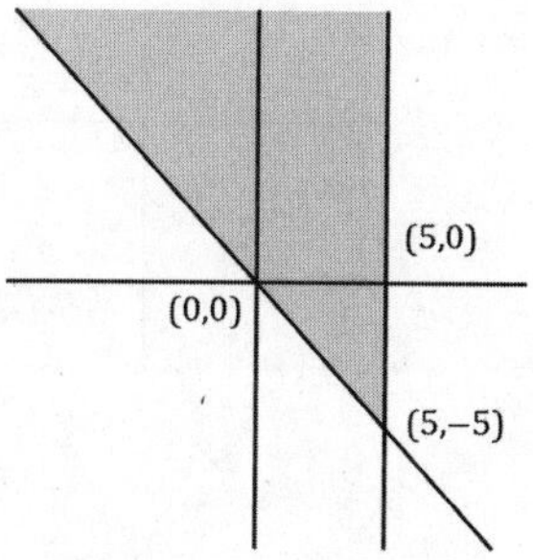

C)

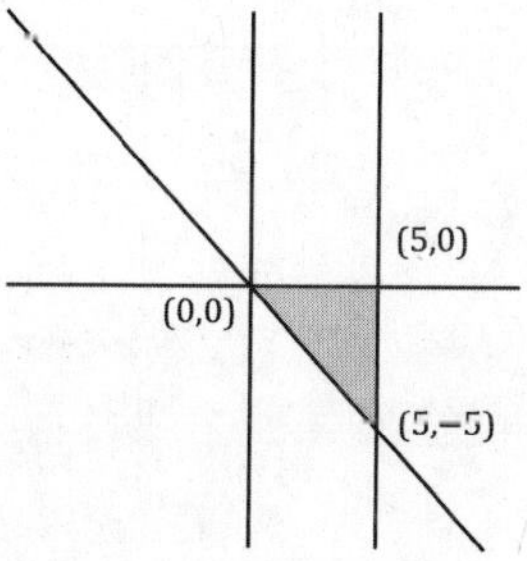

D)

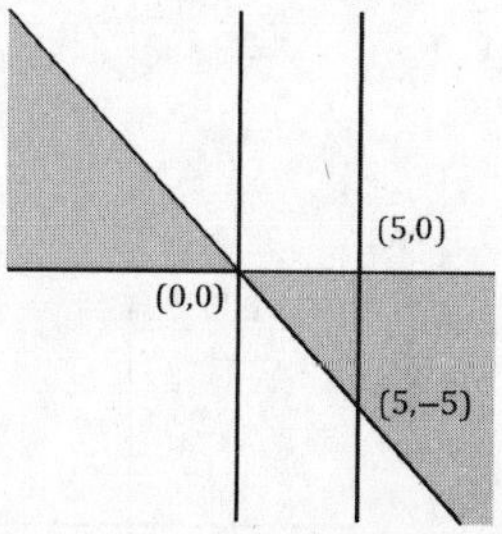

18. The parachute drop ride at an amusement park is intended for older children and adults. The ride is posted with the following notice:

To go on this ride, you must be (A) 60 inches or taller <u>or</u> (B) 12 years or older.

For which of the following graphs does the shaded area include all of the ordered pairs (height in inches, age in years) that are excluded from the ride?

A)

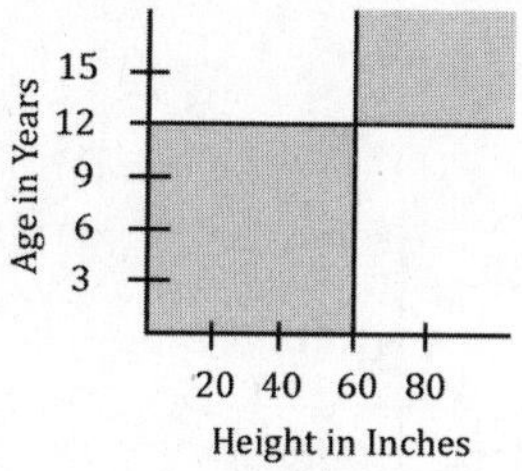

B)

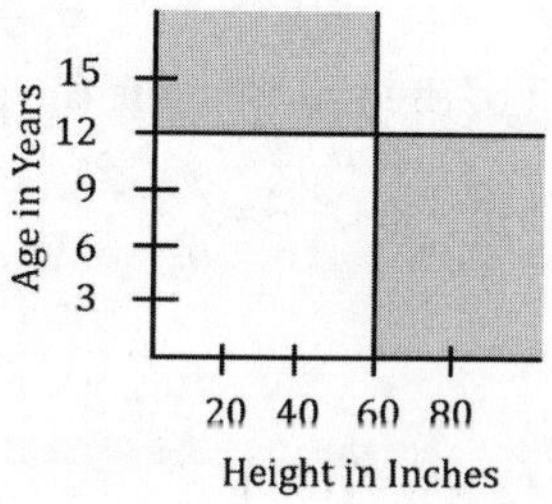

C)

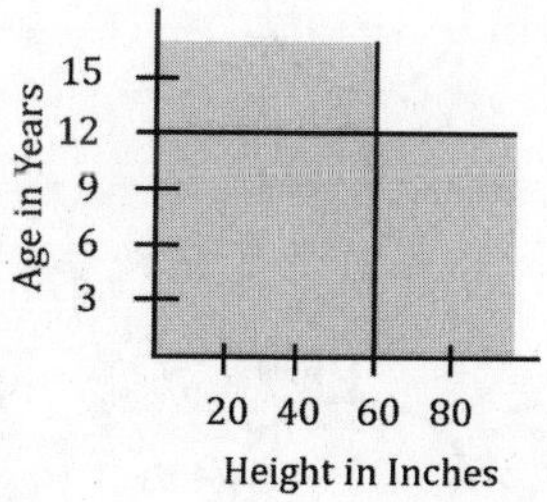

D)

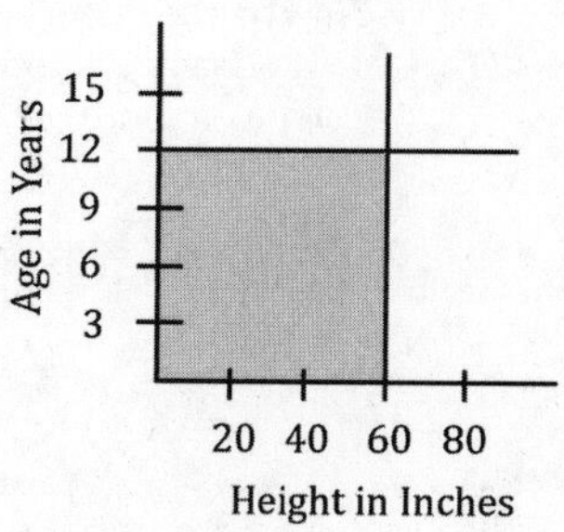

Graphs of Quadratic Equations and Relations Ⓐ Ⓢ

19. Which of the following is the graph of the equation $(x-1)^2+y^2=4$?

A)

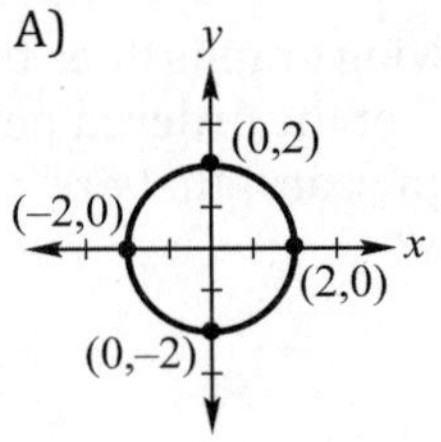

B)

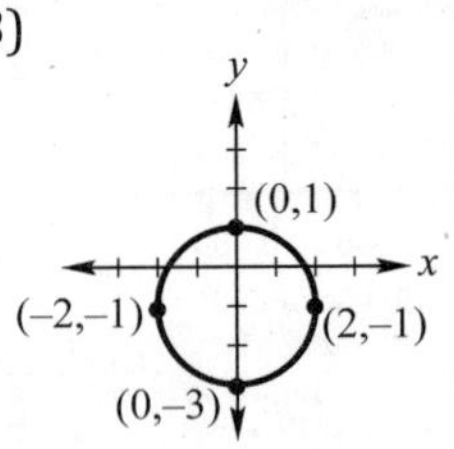

C)

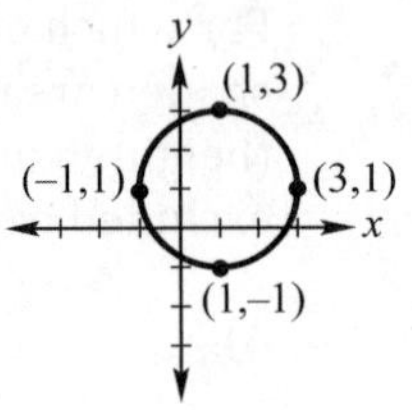

D)

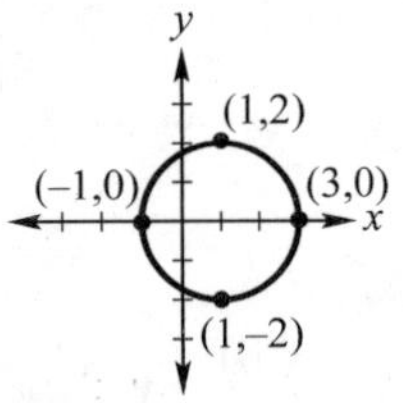

20. Which of the following is the graph of the equation $\dfrac{x^2}{9}+\dfrac{y^2}{16}=1$?

A)

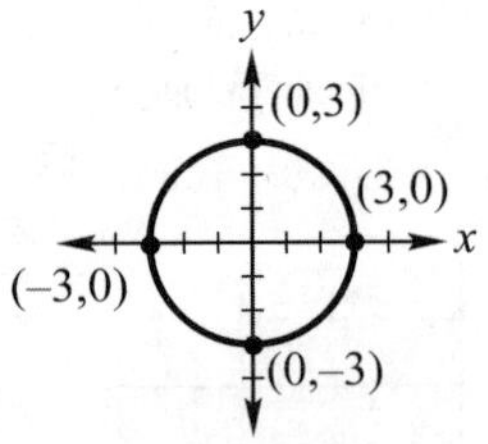

B)

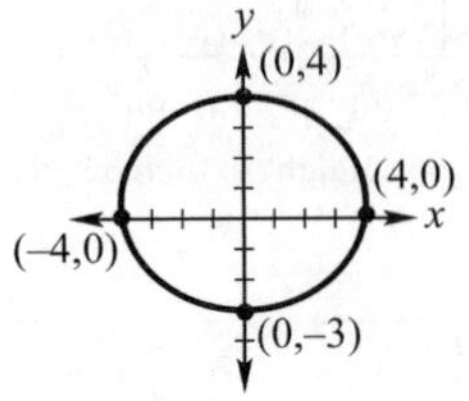

C)

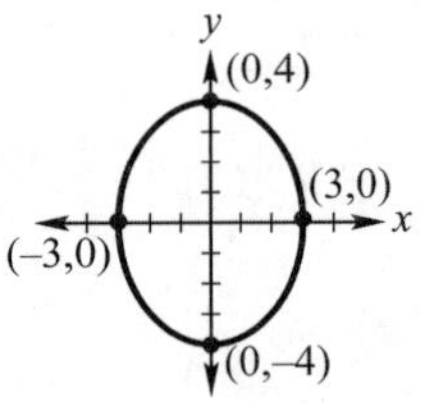

D)

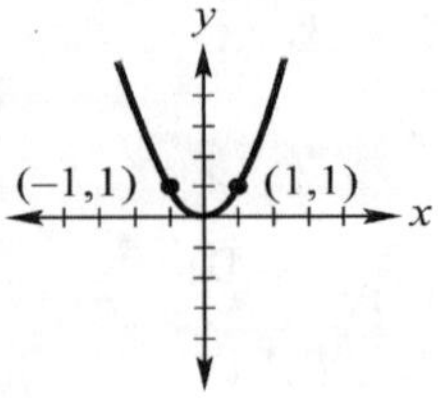

21. A circle in the standard (x,y) coordinate plane passes through the origin (0,0) and (4,0). Which of the following is an equation of the circle?

A) $x^2+y^2=2$

B) $x^2+y^2=4$

C) $\left(x^2-2\right)+y^2=4$

D) $(x-2)^2+y^2=4$

22. Which of the following could be a graph of the equation $y=ax^2+bx+c$, where $b^2-4ac=0$?

A)

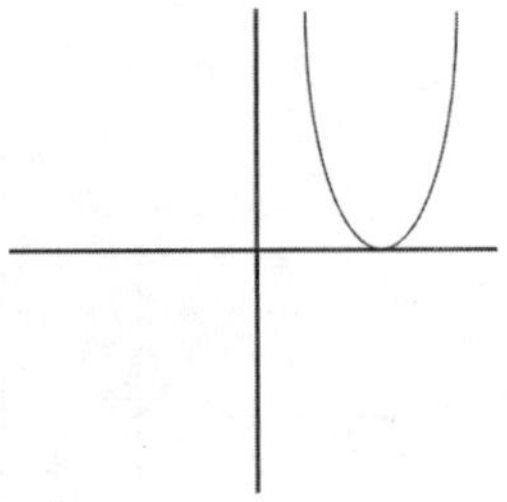

B)

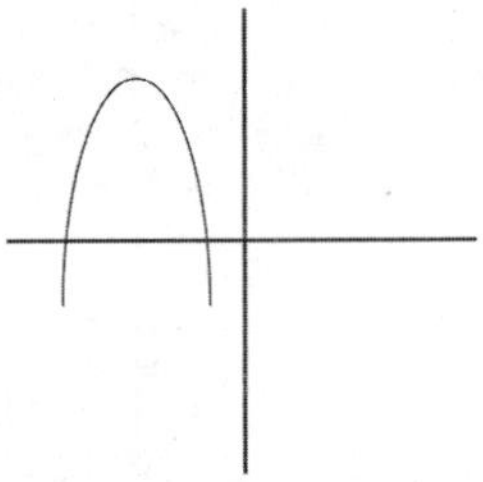

C)

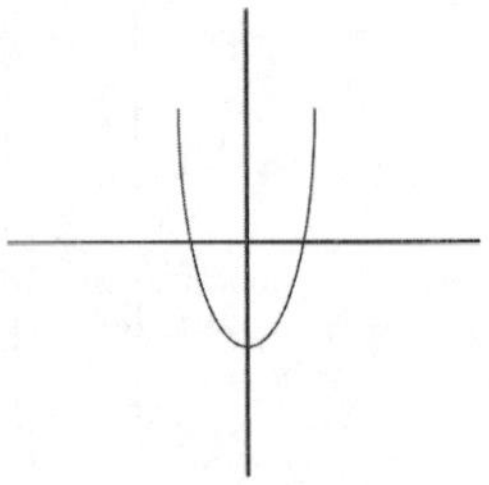

D)

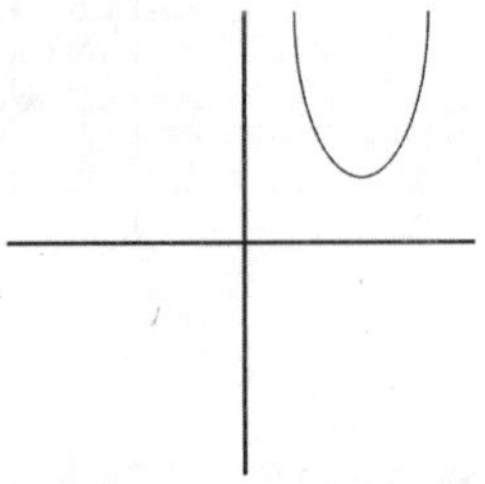

Qualitative Behavior of Graphs of Functions Ⓐ Ⓢ

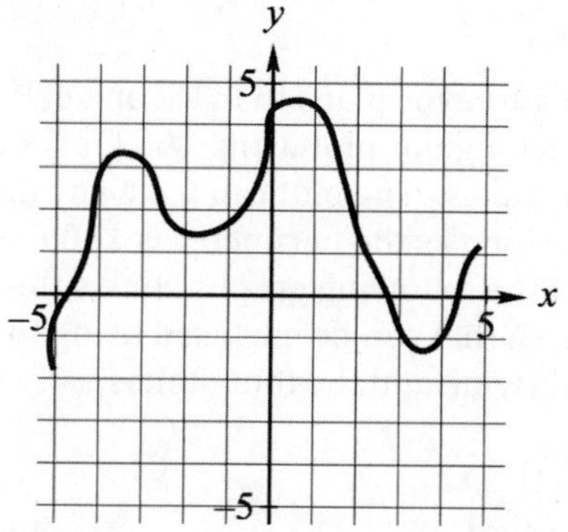

23. The figure above shows the graph of $f(x)$ in the coordinate plane. For the portion of the graph shown, for how many values of x is $f(x)=3$?

A) 1
B) 2
C) 3
D) 4

Transformations and Their Effects on Graphs of Functions

Ⓐ Ⓢ

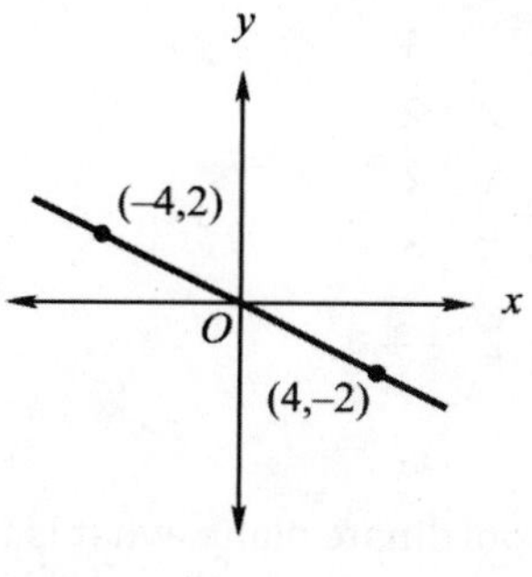

24. The figure above represents the graph of $y=f(x)$ in the coordinate plane. Which of the graphs that follow is the graph of $y=f(x-1)$?

A)

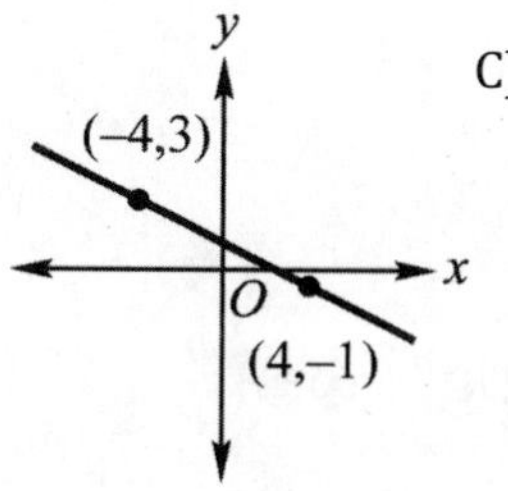

C)

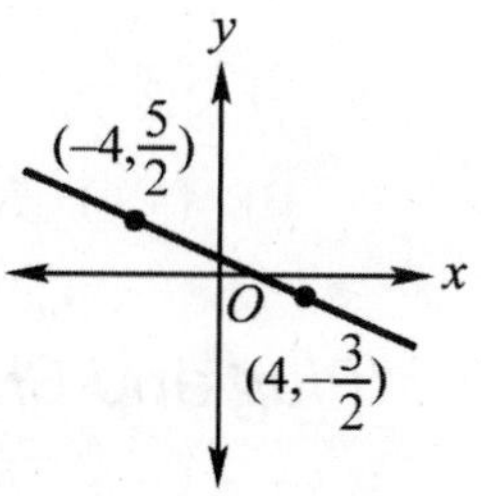

B)

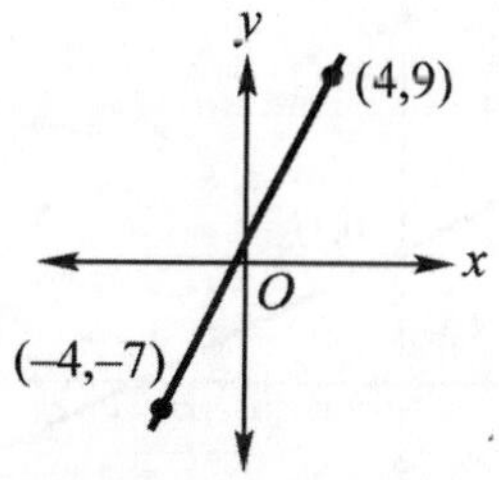

D)

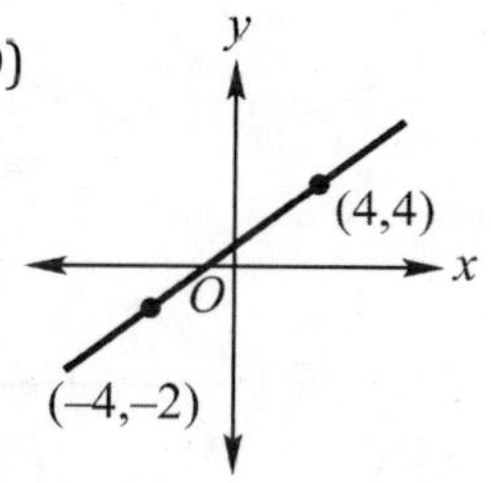

Coordinate Geometry Alternative Strategies

"Test-the-Test" Ⓐ Ⓢ

25. Which of the following is the equation for the line with slope of 2 that includes point $(0,2)$?

A) $y=x-1$
B) $y=2x-1$
C) $y=2x-2$
D) $y=2x+2$

26. Which of the following is the equation for the line that includes points $(-1,1)$ and $(7,5)$?

A) $y=\frac{x}{2}+2$

B) $y=\frac{x}{2}+\frac{3}{2}$

C) $y=\frac{x}{2}+\frac{2}{3}$

D) $y=2x+\frac{3}{2}$

27. In the coordinate plane, what is the midpoint of the line segment with endpoints $(-3,-5)$ and $(5,7)$?

A) $(1,1)$

B) $(1,6)$

C) $\left(3,\frac{7}{2}\right)$

D) $(4,6)$

"Plug-and-Chug" Ⓐ Ⓢ

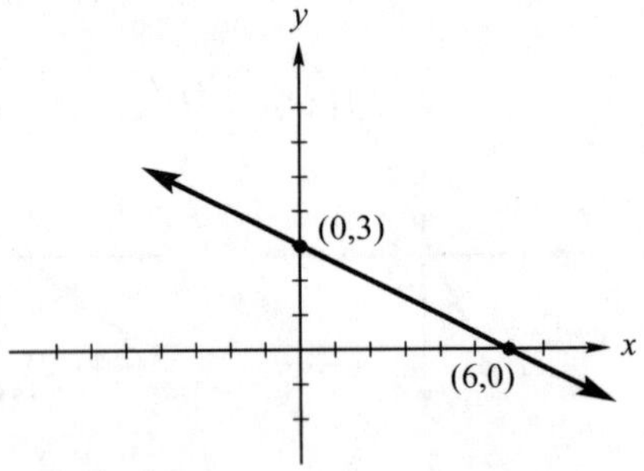

28. The figure above is the graph of which of the following equations?

A) $x+2y=6$

B) $2x+y=6$

C) $x+\frac{y}{2}=6$

D) $\frac{x}{2}+y=2$

Problem Solving with Coordinate Geometry Concepts

Ⓐ Ⓢ

29. A surveyor plans to mark an enclosed rectangular plot using 160 feet of twine and 4 stakes. The plot can have any dimensions so long as the perimeter is 160 feet. Which of the following graphs shows the maximum area that can be enclosed using the 160 feet of twine and the four stakes?

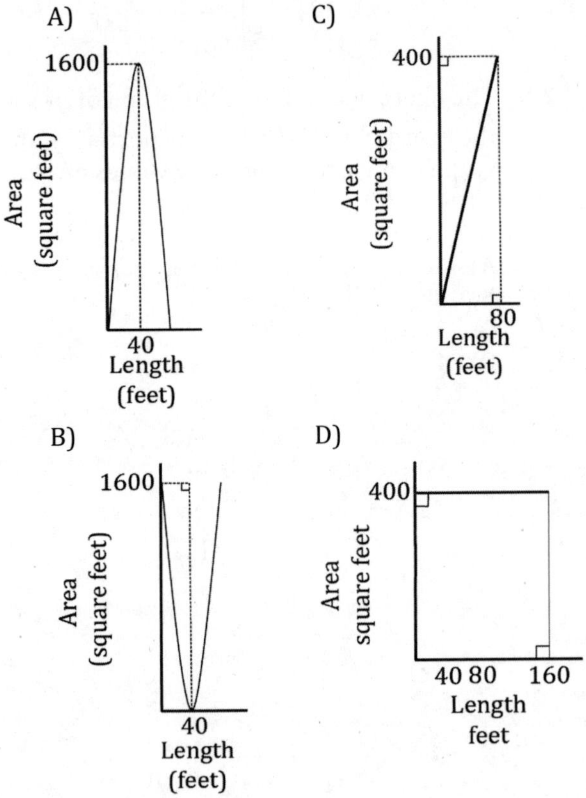

30. A group of students performed a physics experiment using two identical devices that produce sounds of variable frequency. A student began the experiment by setting the frequency emitted by the first device to 0, starting a timer, and uniformly increasing the frequency emitted by 100 hertz every 10 seconds. Thirty seconds later, another student set the second device to 0 and uniformly increased the frequency emitted by 160 hertz every 10 seconds. When the two devices reached the same frequency, the students stopped increasing the frequency. Which of the following graphs shows the result of the experiment?

A)

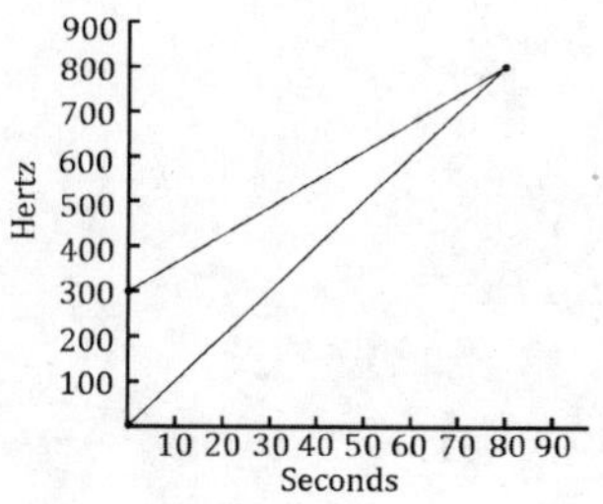

C)

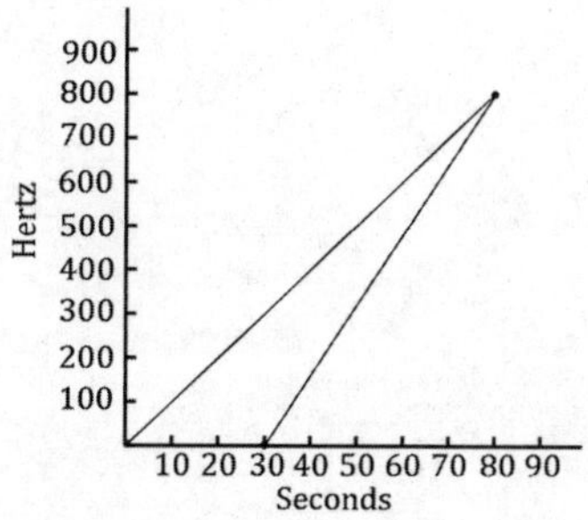

B)

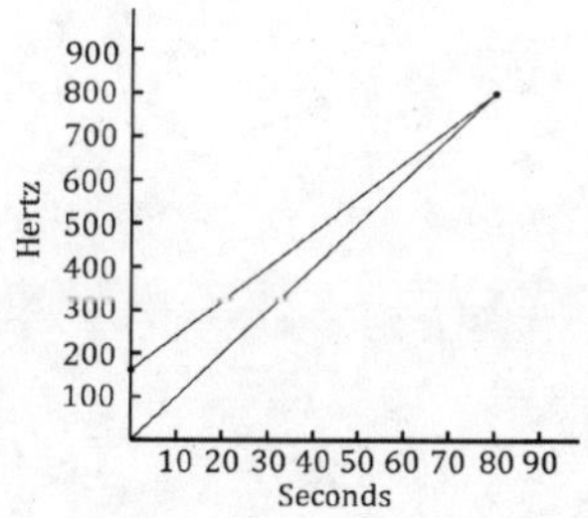

D)

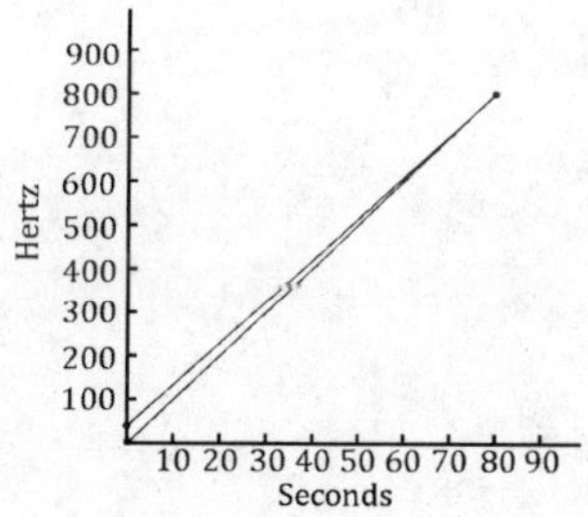

LESSON 4 | GEOMETRY

ACT MATHEMATICS AND SAT MATH: MULTIPLE-CHOICE

The items in this section accompany the in-class review of the geometry skills and concepts tested by the ACT Mathematics and SAT Math: Multiple-Choice tests. You will work through the items with your instructor in class. Answers are on page 580.

Lines and Angles Ⓐ Ⓢ

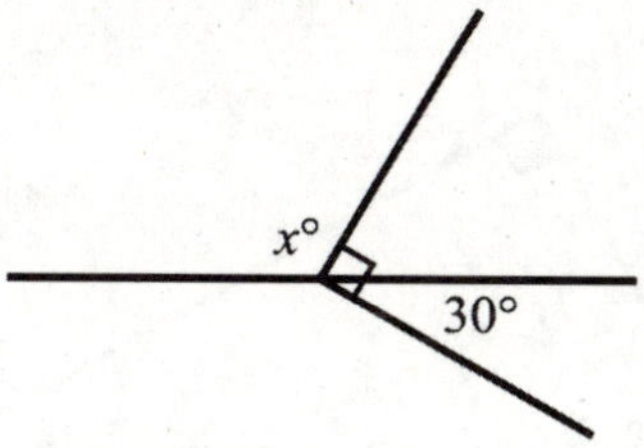

1. In the figure above, $x =$

A) 60
B) 90
C) 105
D) 120

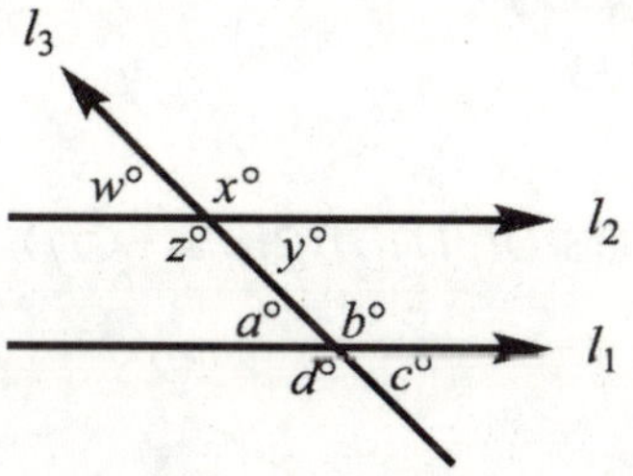

2. In the figure above, l_1 is parallel to l_2. Which of the following <u>must</u> be true?

I. $w = a$
II. $y + b = 180$
III. $x + d = 180$

A) I only
B) II only
C) I and II only
D) II and III only

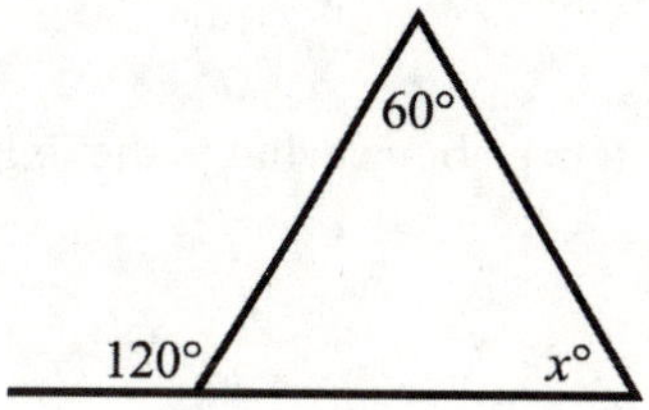

3. In the figure above, $x =$

A) 30
B) 45
C) 60
D) 75

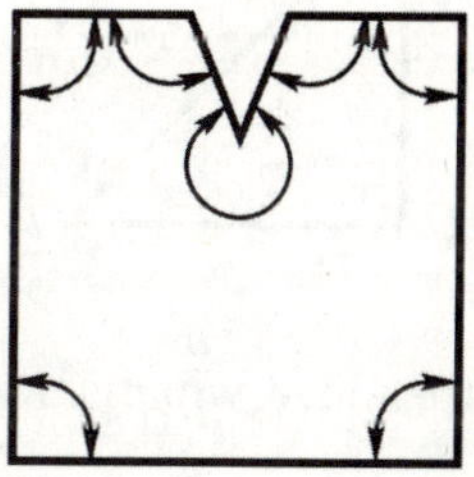

4. In the figure above, what is the sum of the indicated angles?

A) 540
B) 720
C) 900
D) 1,080

Triangles

Pythagorean Theorem ⒶⓈ

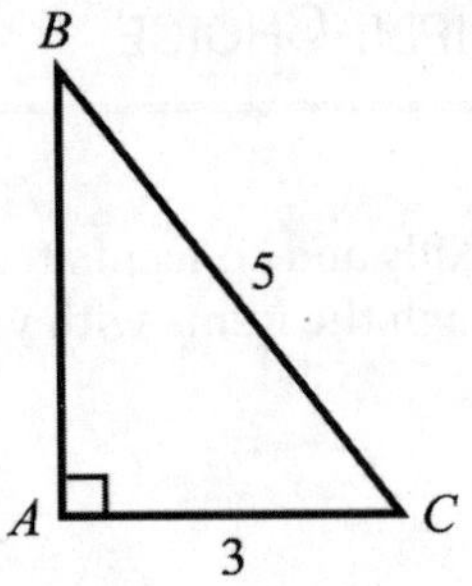

5. In the figure above, what is the length of $\overline{AB}$?

A) 2
B) $2\sqrt{3}$
C) 4
D) $4\sqrt{2}$

45°-45°-90° Triangles ⒶⓈ

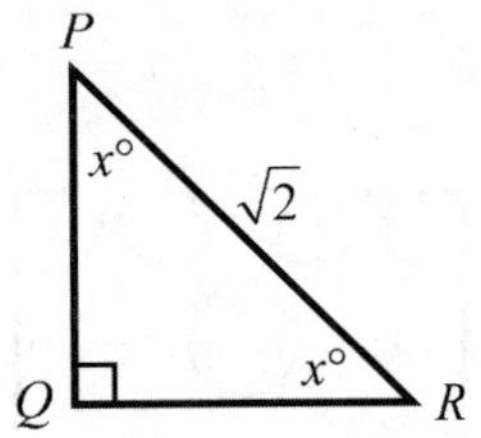

6. In the figure above, what is the length of $\overline{PQ}$?

A) 1
B) $\sqrt{2}$
C) $2\sqrt{2}$
D) 4

7. In a right isosceles triangle, the hypotenuse is equal to which of the following?

A) Half the length of either of the other sides
B) The length of either of the other sides multiplied by $\sqrt{2}$
C) Twice the length of either of the other sides
D) The sum of the lengths of the other two sides

30°-60°-90° Triangles ⒶⓈ

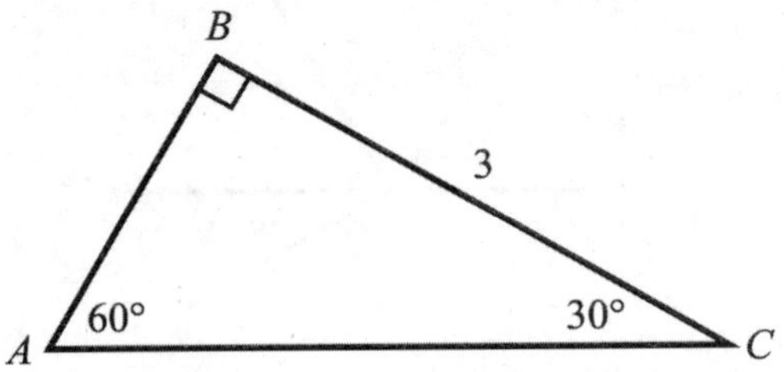

8. In the triangle above, what is the length of $\overline{AC}$?

A) 2
B) $\sqrt{3}$
C) $2\sqrt{3}$
D) $3\sqrt{3}$

Properties of Triangles ⒶⓈ

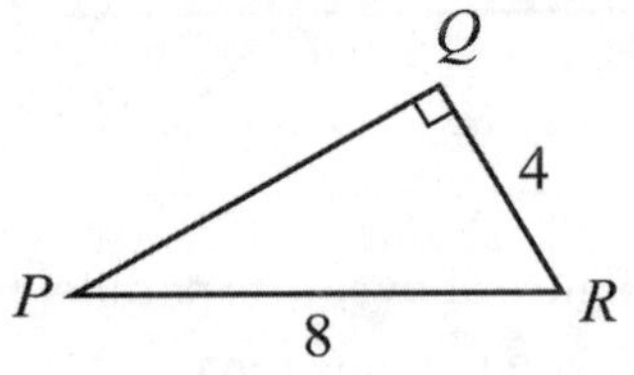

9. In the figure above, the perimeter of $\Delta PQR =$

A) $12+\sqrt{3}$
B) $12+2\sqrt{3}$
C) $12+4\sqrt{3}$
D) 28

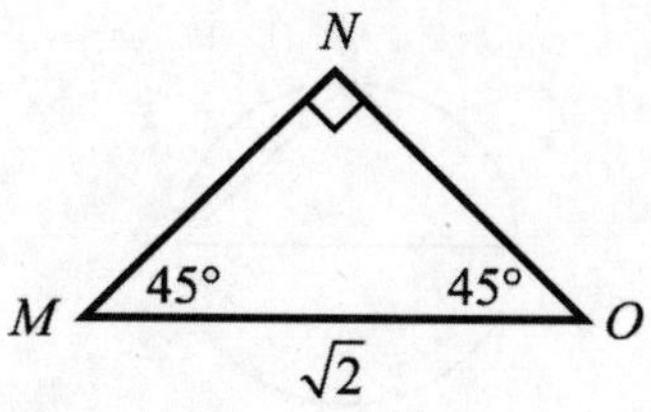

10. In the figure above, what is the area of ΔMNO?

A) $\frac{1}{2}$
B) $\frac{\sqrt{2}}{2}$
C) 1
D) $\sqrt{2}$

Rectangles and Squares Ⓐ Ⓢ

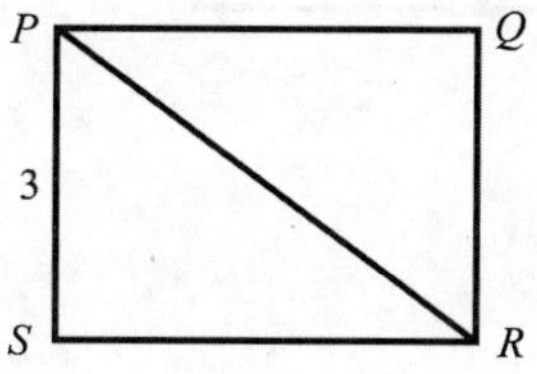

11. In the figure above, *PQRS* is a rectangle. If $PR = 5$ centimeters, what is the area, in square centimeters, of the rectangle?

A) 3
B) 4
C) 8
D) 12

Circles Ⓐ Ⓢ

12. If the area of a circle is equal to 9π, which of the following is (are) true?

I. The radius is 3.
II. The diameter is 6.
III. The circumference is 6π.

A) I only
B) III only
C) I and II only
D) I, II, and III

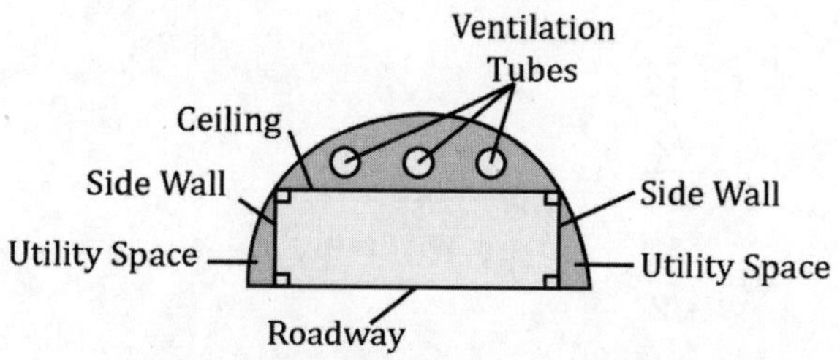

13. The figure above shows a cross-section of a tunnel used for motor vehicle traffic. If the width of the ceiling is $\frac{4}{5}$ of the diameter of the cylindrical tunnel, what is the height, in terms of radius *r*, of the ceiling above the roadway?

A) $\frac{2\sqrt{21}}{10}r$
B) $\frac{3}{5}r$
C) $\frac{3}{10}r$
D) $\frac{8r}{5}$

14. In the figure above, if the radius of the circle is r, then the ratio $\dfrac{\text{area of the larger square}}{\text{area of the smaller square}} =$

A) $\dfrac{2\sqrt{2}}{1}$

B) $\dfrac{2}{1}$

C) $\dfrac{\sqrt{2}}{1}$

D) $\dfrac{1}{\sqrt{2}}$

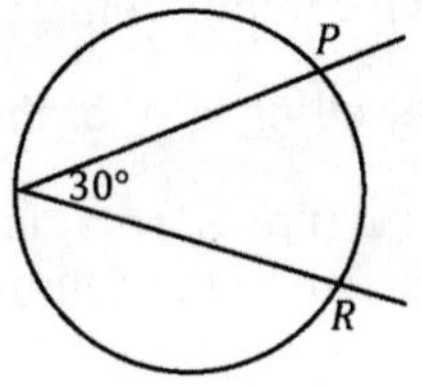

15. In the figure above, if the circle has a radius of 3, what is the length of minor arc PR?

A) $\dfrac{\pi}{6}$

B) $\dfrac{\pi}{3}$

C) π

D) $\dfrac{3\pi}{2}$

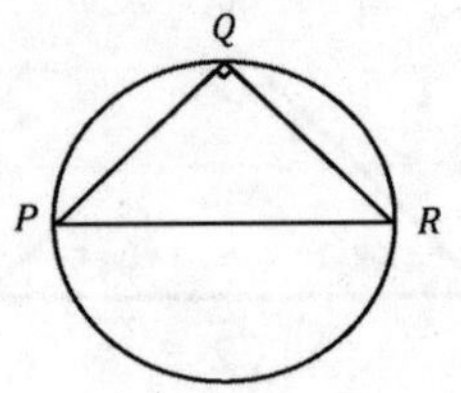

16. If the right isosceles triangle in the figure above has an area of 1, then the area of the circle is

A) π
B) 2π
C) $2\sqrt{3}\pi$
D) 4π

Properties of Tangent Lines

Ⓐ Ⓢ

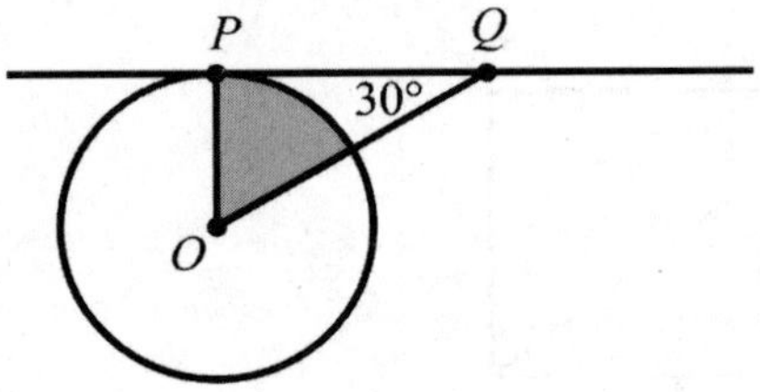

17. In the figure above, O is the center of the circle, and $\overline{PQ}$ is tangent to the circle at P. If the radius of circle O has a length of 6, what is the area of the shaded portion of the figure?

A) π
B) 3π
C) 6π
D) 9π

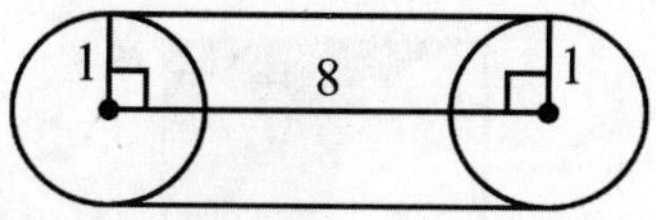

NOTE: Figure not drawn to scale.

18. The figure above shows two pulleys connected by a belt. If the centers of the pulleys are 8 feet apart and the pulleys each have a radius of 1 foot, what is the length, in feet, of the belt?

A) 8π
B) $8+\pi$
C) $16+\pi$
D) $16+2\pi$

19. In the figure above, a circle is inscribed in an equilateral triangle. If the radius of the circle is 1, what is the perimeter of the triangle?

A) $2\sqrt{3}$
B) $3\sqrt{3}$
C) 6
D) $6\sqrt{3}$

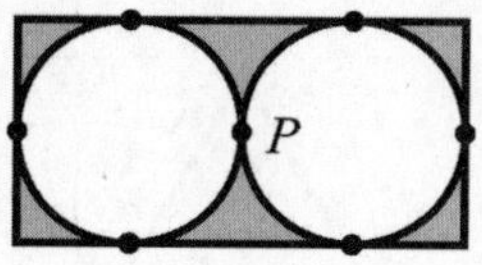

20. The figure above shows two circles of diameter 2 that are tangent to each other at point *P*. The line segments form a rectangle and are tangent to the circles at the points shown. What is the area of the shaded portion of the figure?

A) $8-2\pi$
B) $8-\pi$
C) $4-2\pi$
D) $4-\pi$

Complex Figures Ⓐ Ⓢ

21. An isosceles right triangle is inscribed in a circle with a radius of 1 inch such that all three vertices of the triangle touch the perimeter of the circle. What is the area, in square inches, of the triangle?

A) $\frac{\sqrt{2}}{3}$
B) $\frac{1}{2}$
C) 1
D) $\sqrt{2}$

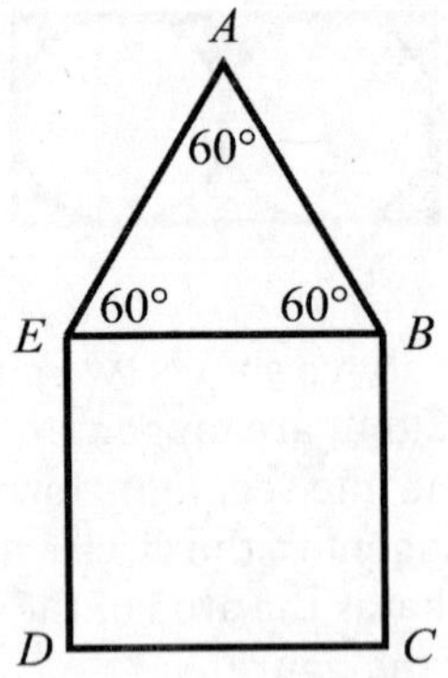

22. In the figure above, $BCDE$ is a square with an area of 4. What is the perimeter of ΔABE?

A) 3
B) 4
C) 6
D) 8

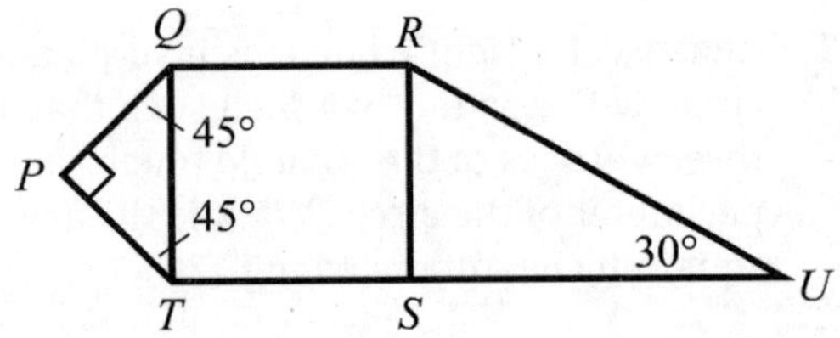

23. In the figure above, if $QRST$ is a square and the length of $\overline{PQ}$ is $\sqrt{2}$, what is the length of $\overline{RU}$?

A) $\sqrt{2}$
B) $2\sqrt{2}$
C) $\sqrt{6}$
D) 4

24. In the figure above, $PQRS$ is a square, and $\overline{PS}$ is the diameter of a semicircle. If the length of $\overline{PQ}$ is 2, what is the area of the shaded portion of the diagram?

A) $4-2\pi$
B) $4-\pi$
C) $4-\frac{\pi}{2}$
D) $8-\pi$

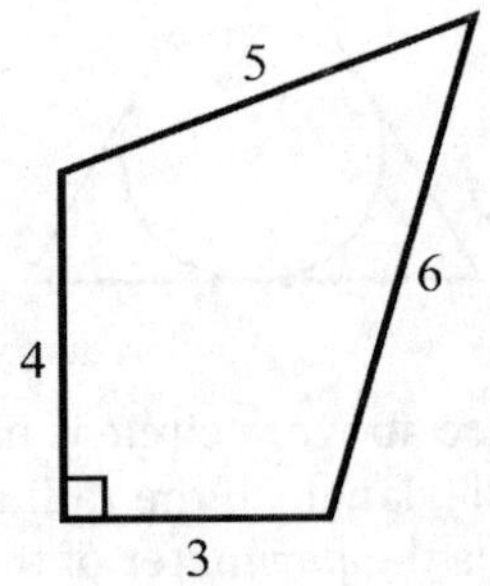

25. If the lengths of the sides, in inches, are as marked on the figure above, what is the area, in square inches, of the quadrilateral?

A) 6
B) $6+\sqrt{3}$
C) 12
D) 18

Solids

Surface Area Ⓐ

26. The prism below has bases with sides 12, 16, and 20. The distance between the bases is 30. What is the lateral surface area of the prism?

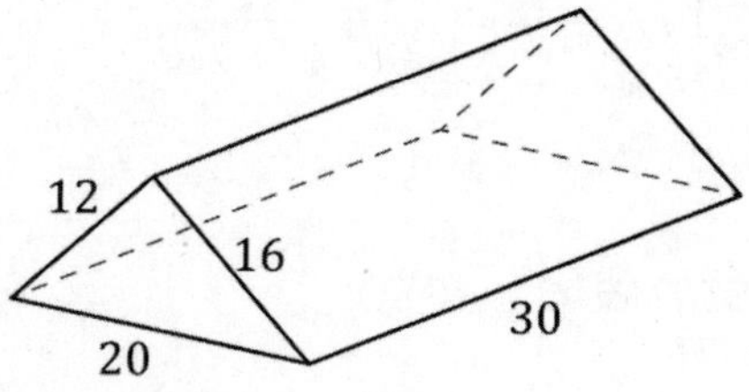

A) 1,632
B) 1,440
C) 600
D) 480

27. What is the approximate surface area, in square inches, of a ball of largest circumference 12π inches?
($SA_{\text{Sphere}} = 4\pi r^2$)

A) 12π
B) 36π
C) 144π
D) 576π

Volume ⒶⓈ

28. The volume of a cone can be found using the formula $V = \frac{1}{3}\pi r^2 h$. If a cone has a height of 10 cm and a volume of 120π cm^3, what is the diameter of its base, in centimeters?

A) 6
B) 12
C) 36
D) 72

29. A construction company is building a silo. The silo is a cylinder with a hemisphere on top. The diameter of the cylinder is 42 feet and the height of the cylinder is 40 feet. How much hay can you store in your silo, in cubic feet?

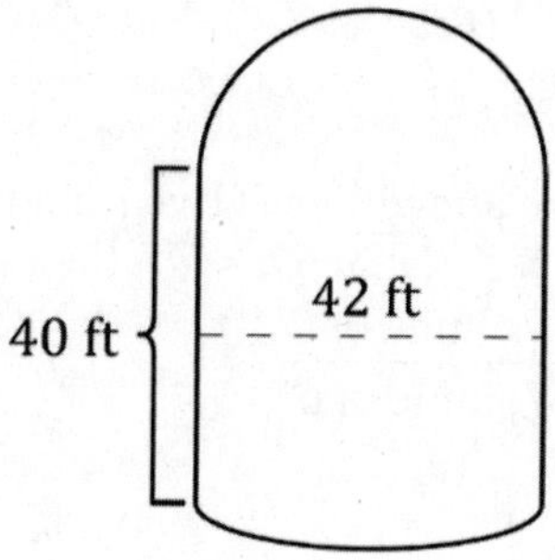

A) $23{,}814\pi$
B) $29{,}988\pi$
C) $711{,}774\pi$
D) $717{,}948\pi$

30. Each side of a cube is a square with an area of 81 square centimeters. What is the volume of the cube, in cubic centimeters?

A) 81
B) 9^3
C) 9^4
D) 81^9

31. The surface area of a sphere is given by $SA_{\text{sphere}} = 4\pi r^2$, where r is the radius of the sphere. If the surface area of the sphere is 324π, what is the sphere's volume?

A) 243π
B) 324π
C) 729π
D) 972π

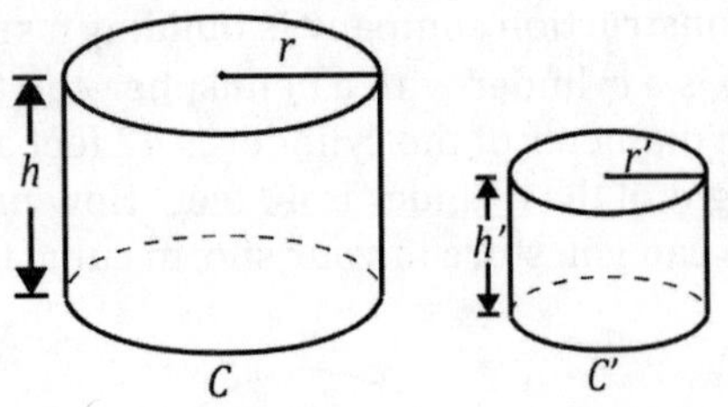

32. The figure above shows two right cylinders, C and C'. If $r = kr'$ and $h = kh'$, then what is the ratio of $\frac{\text{Volume of } C}{\text{Volume of } C'}$? ($V_{\text{cylinder}} = \pi r^2 h$)

A) π
B) $k\pi$
C) $\frac{1}{k^3}$
D) k^3

33. Cube Q has volume V. In terms of V, a cube with edges only one-fourth the length of those of Q will have a volume of

A) $\frac{V^3}{64}$
B) $\frac{V^3}{4}$
C) $\frac{V}{64}$
D) $\frac{V}{4}$

Geometry Alternative Strategies

"Test-the-Test" Ⓐ Ⓢ

34. What is the width of a rectangle with an area of $48x^2$ and a length of $24x$?

A) 2
B) $2x$
C) $24x$
D) $2x^2$

"Plug-and-Chug" Ⓐ Ⓢ

35. If the width of a rectangle is increased by 10 percent and the length of the rectangle is increased by 20 percent, by what percent does the area of the rectangle <u>increase</u>?

A) 2%
B) 10%
C) 15%
D) 32%

"Guesstimate" Ⓐ Ⓢ

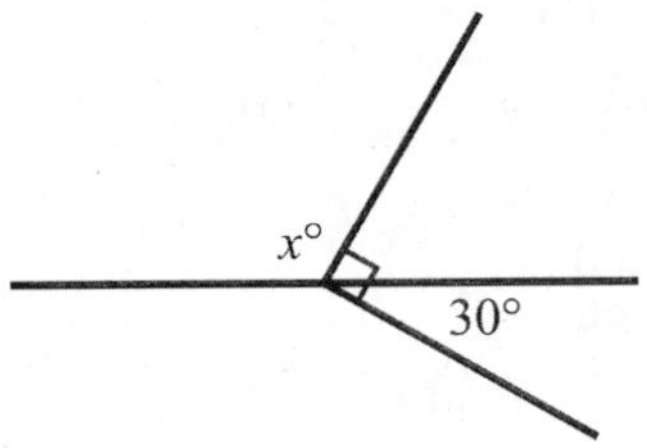

36. In the figure above, $x =$

A) 30
B) 65
C) 120
D) 150

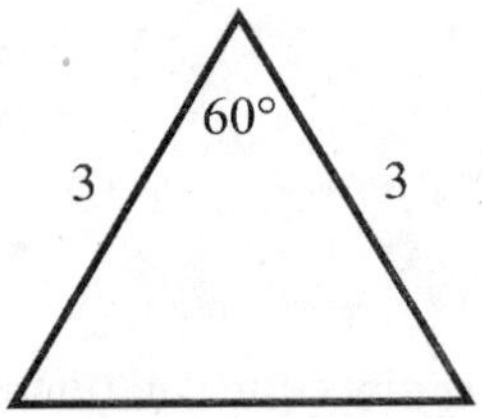

37. What is the perimeter of the triangle shown above?

A) $3\sqrt{2}$
B) 6
C) 7.5
D) 9

Measure Ⓐ Ⓢ

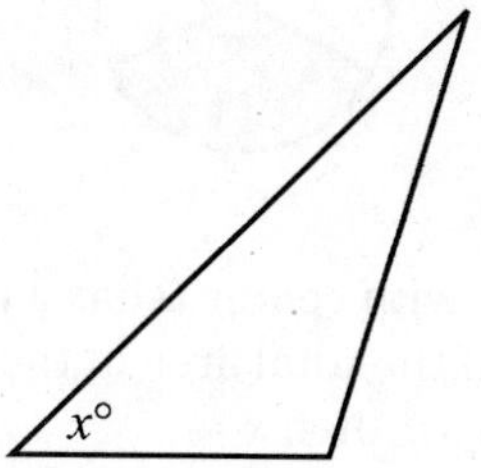

38. In the figure above, $x =$

A) 30
B) 45
C) 60
D) 75

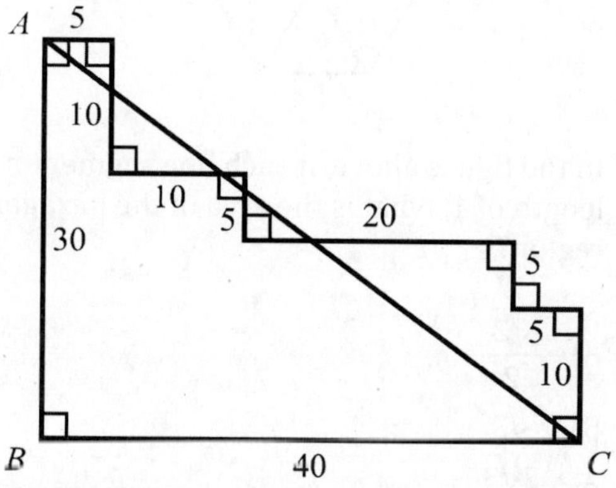

39. In the figure above, what is the length of $\overline{AC}$?

A) $30\sqrt{2}$
B) 50
C) 75
D) $60\sqrt{2}$

"Meastimate" Ⓐ Ⓢ

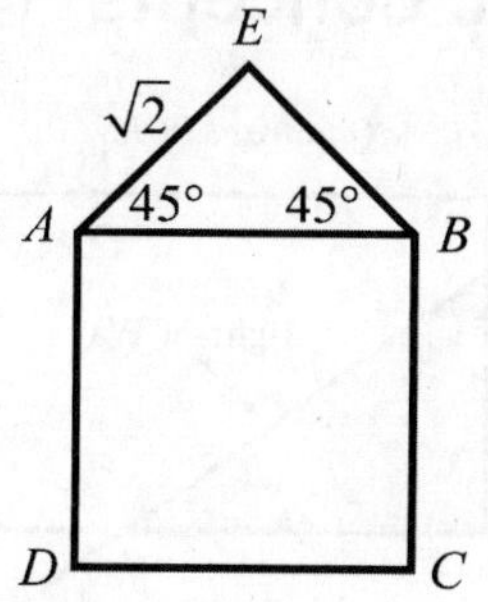

40. In the figure above, what is the area of square *ABCD*?

A) 2
B) $2\sqrt{2}$
C) 4
D) $4\sqrt{2}$

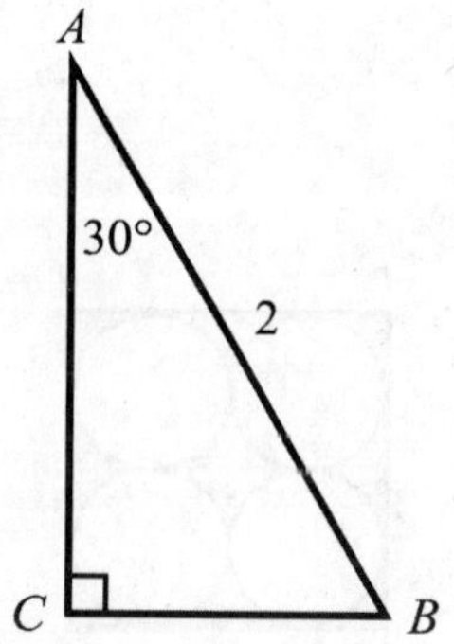

41. In the triangle above, the measure of $\angle BAC$ is 30° and the length of $\overline{AB}$ is 2. Which of the following best approximates the length of $\overline{AC}$?

A) 0.8
B) 1.0
C) 1.7
D) 1.9

Problem Solving with Geometric Concepts Ⓐ Ⓢ

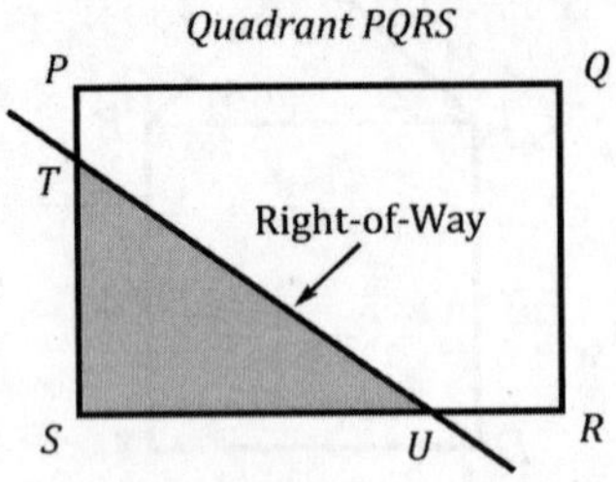

42. The figure above shows a utility right-of-way that will cut across a rectangular quadrant of land isolating a portion of the property as shown. If the area of the shaded portion is 54 square miles and $\overline{SU}$ is 3 miles longer than $\overline{ST}$, what is the length, in miles, of $\overline{TU}$?

A) 9
B) 12
C) 15
D) 17

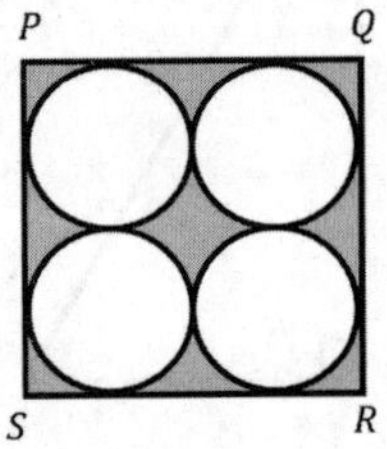

43. In the figure above, *PQRS* is a square and each of the four circles has a radius of *r*. What fractional part of the area of the square is shaded?

A) $\frac{\pi - 4}{2}$
B) $\frac{4 - \pi}{4}$
C) $\frac{\pi}{4}$
D) $\frac{4}{\pi}$

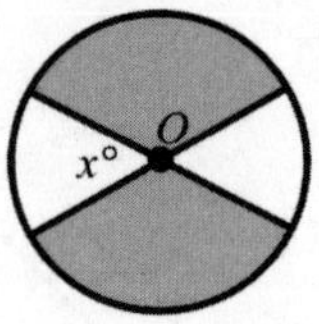

44. The circle with center *O* has a radius of length 2. If the total area of the shaded regions is 3π, then $x =$

A) 180
B) 120
C) 90
D) 45

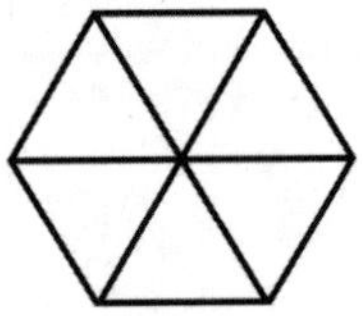

45. In the figure above, if each line segment has a length of 1, what is the area of the hexagonal region?

A) $\frac{\sqrt{3}}{2}$
B) $\sqrt{3}$
C) $\frac{3\sqrt{3}}{2}$
D) $2\sqrt{3}$

46. What is the ratio of the area of an equilateral triangle inscribed in a circle to the area of the circle?

A) $\frac{\pi\sqrt{3}}{2}$
B) $\frac{\sqrt{3}}{2}$
C) $\frac{\sqrt{3}}{4\pi}$
D) $\frac{3\sqrt{3}}{4\pi}$

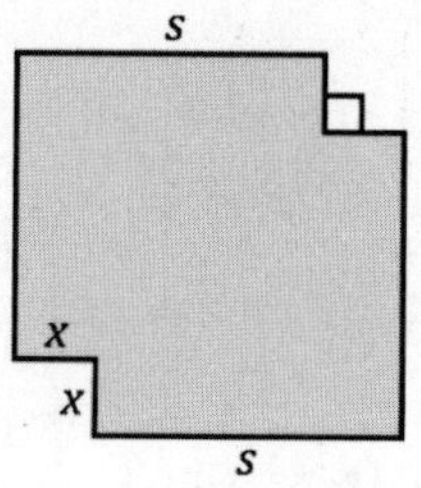

47. The figure above shows two overlapping and superimposed squares, both with side s. If $x = \frac{1}{4}s$, what is the area of the figure?

A) $\frac{23s^2}{16}$
B) s^2
C) $\frac{3s^2}{4}$
D) $\frac{5s^2}{8}$

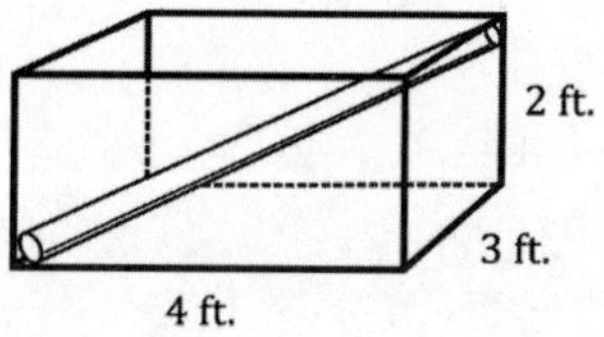

48. A glass tube used in scientific experiments is packed in a crate of dimensions shown. Which of the following measurements, in feet, most closely approximates the length of the tube?

A) $\sqrt{13}$
B) $\sqrt{29}$
C) $\sqrt{41}$
D) $2\sqrt{13}$

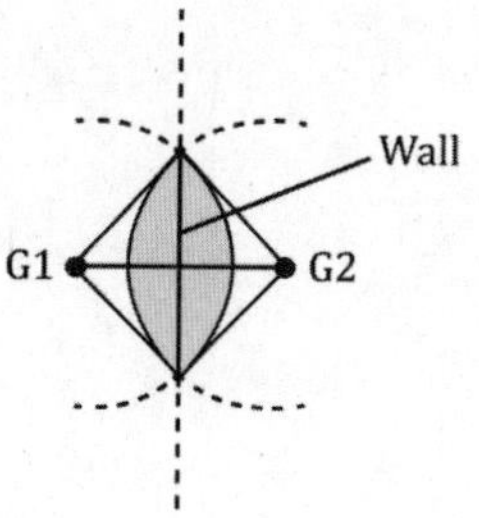

49. In the figure above, two guard stations, G1 and G2, are both 80 yards from the wall on either side, as shown. The line segment between the two guard stations is perpendicular to the wall. Each station has a spotlight projected onto the wall that illuminates a circular region with a radius of 100 yards. What is the length, in yards, of the portion of the wall that is illuminated by both security lights?

A) 120
B) 90
C) 75
D) 60

LESSON 5 | DATA INTERPRETATION, PROBABILITY, AND STATISTICS

ACT MATHEMATICS AND SAT MATH: MULTIPLE-CHOICE

The items in this section accompany the in-class review of the data analysis, probability, and statistics skills and concepts tested by the ACT Mathematics and SAT Math: Multiple-Choice tests. You will work through the items with your instructor in class. Answers are on page 580.

Data Interpretation

Bar, Cumulative, and Line Graphs Ⓐ Ⓢ

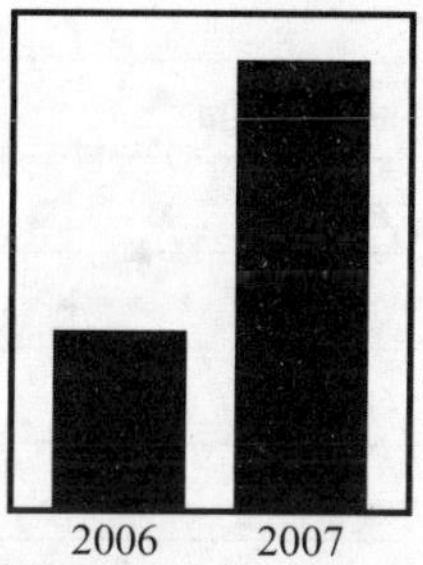

1. If the graph above represents expenditures by Corporation X in two different years, what was the approximate ratio of expenditures in 2006 to those in 2007?

A) $\frac{1}{5}$

B) $\frac{2}{5}$

C) $\frac{1}{2}$

D) $\frac{2}{3}$

Number of Corporation *X* Employees

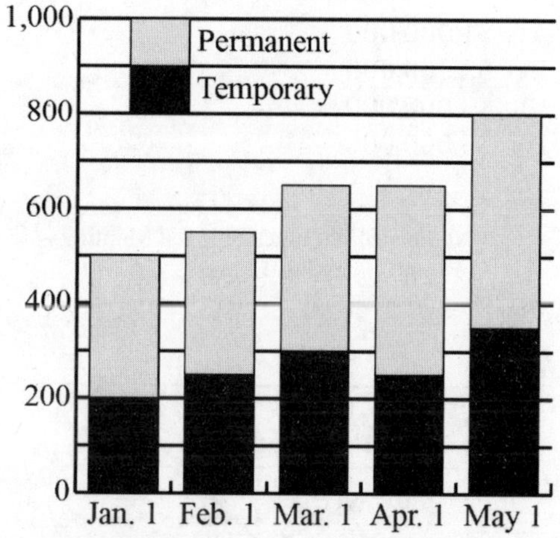

2. Based on the data presented above, what was the difference, if any, between the number of permanent workers employed by Corporation *X* on March 1st and the number of permanent workers employed by Corporation *X* on April 1st?

A) 0
B) 50
C) 100
D) 150

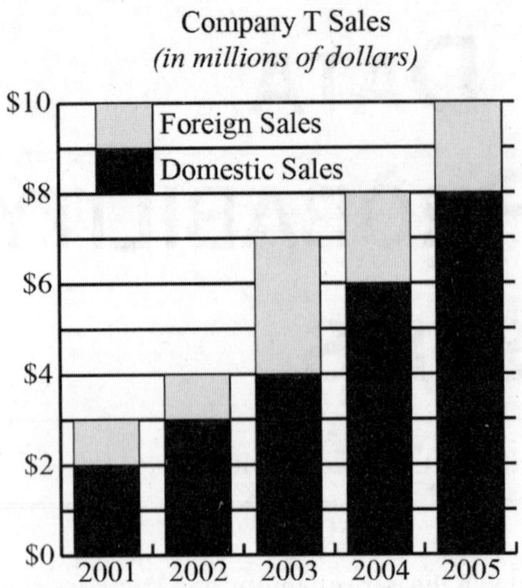

3. Based on the data presented above, what was the difference in the value of foreign sales by Company *T* between 2003 and 2005?

A) $1,000,000
B) $2,000,000
C) $3,000,000
D) $5,000,000

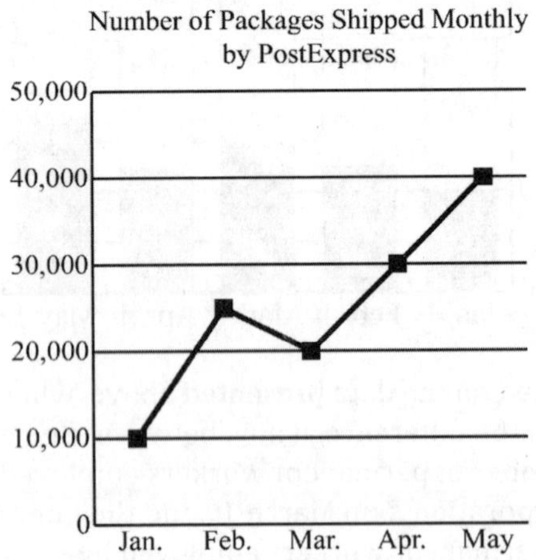

4. Based on the data presented above, what was the approximate total number of packages shipped by PostExpress for the months January, February, and March, inclusive?

A) 40,000
B) 55,000
C) 60,000
D) 70,000

Pie Charts Ⓐ Ⓢ

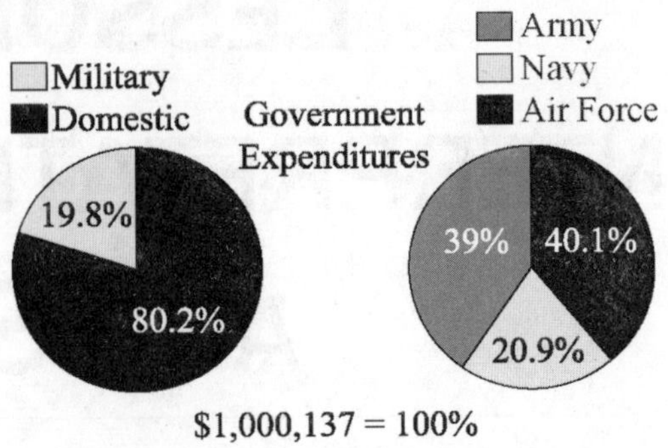

5. Based on the data presented above, approximately how much money was spent on the Air Force?

A) $39,704
B) $79,409
C) $96,123
D) $198,027

Scatterplots Ⓐ Ⓢ

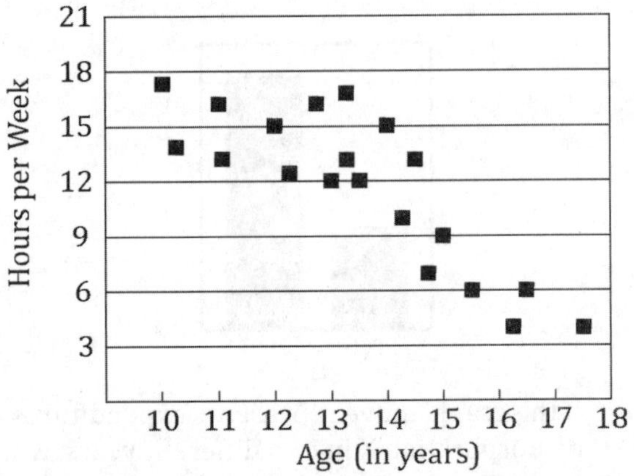

6. The above scatterplot shows the video-game playing habits of 20 students. The graph most strongly supports the conclusion that the number of hours per week spent playing video-games

A) is constant from age 10 to age 18
B) increases as age increases from 10 to 18
C) decreases as age increases from 10 to 15 and then increases
D) is constant for ages 10 through 14 and then decreases

Daily Temperature vs. Bird Feeder Visits in Winter (14 Days)

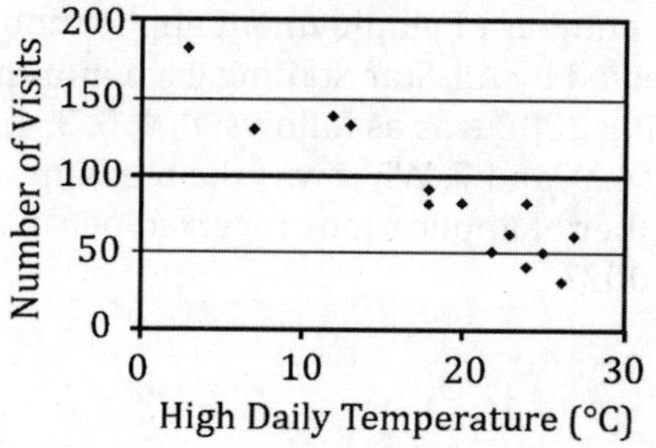

7. The scatterplot above shows the number of bird visits to a feeder for 14 consecutive days in winter versus the high temperature recorded for the day. Which of the following would be the line of best fit for the data?

A)

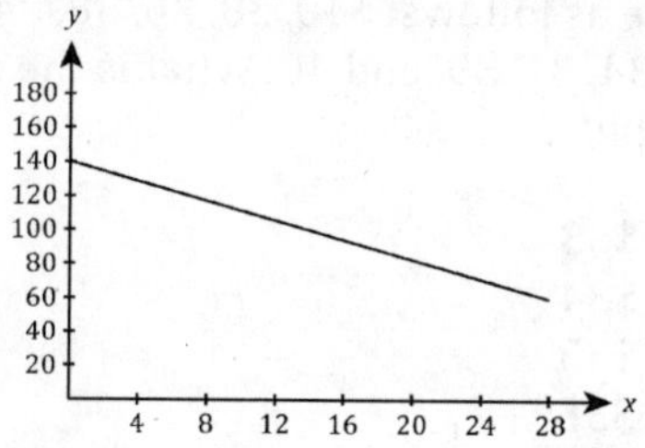

B)

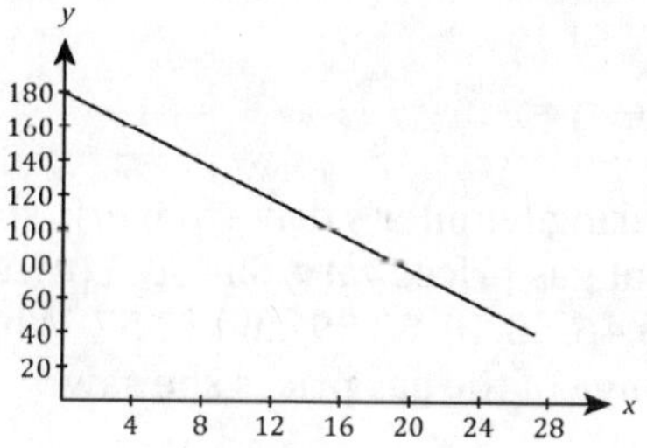

C)

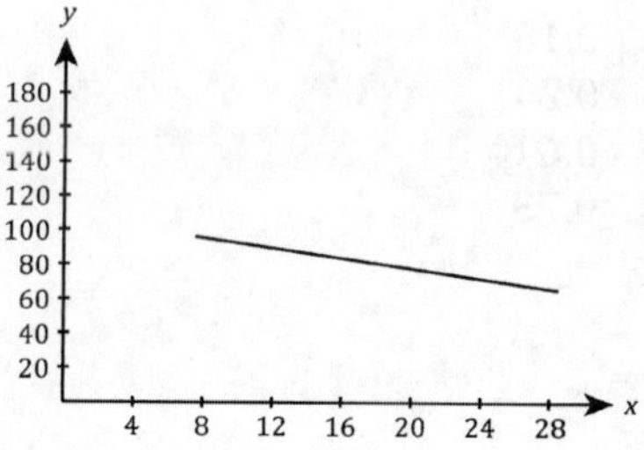

D)

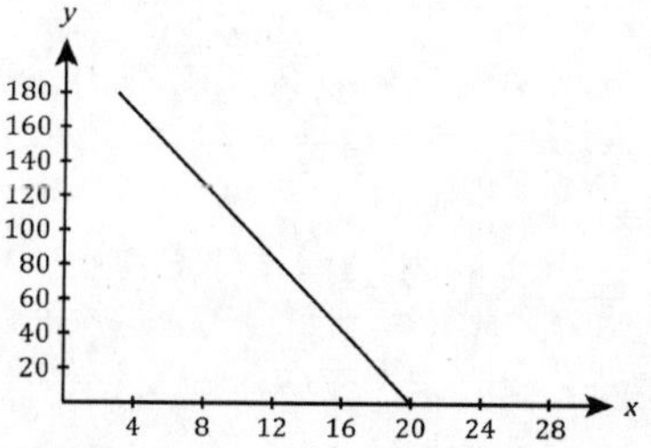

Manatee Deaths in Florida Waters versus Boat Registrations (x1,000)

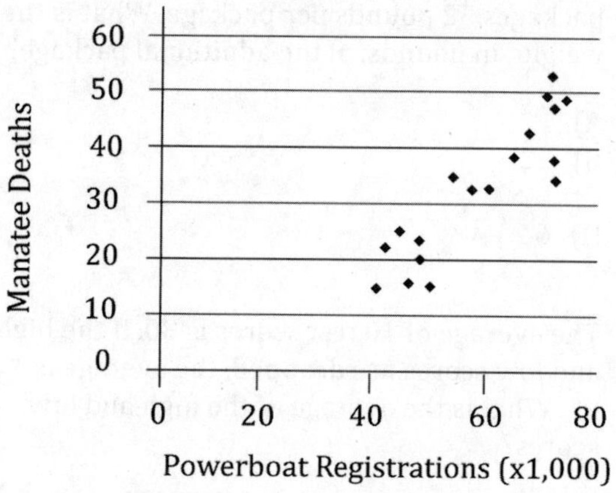

8. The graph shows the number of manatee deaths in Florida waters resulting from powerboat-manatee collisions versus the number of powerboat registrations. Based on the line of best fit to the data, every 10,000 powerboat registrations is associated with how many manatee deaths?

A) 10
B) 20
C) 50
D) 70

Statistics

Averages Ⓐ Ⓢ

9. If the average of 35, 38, 41, 43, and x is 37, what is x?

A) 28
B) 30
C) 31
D) 34

10. The average weight of 6 packages is 50 pounds per package. Another package is added, making the average weight of the 7 packages 52 pounds per package. What is the weight, in pounds, of the additional package?

A) 7
B) 52
C) 62
D) 64

11. The average of 10 test scores is 80. If the high and low scores are dropped, the average is 81. What is the average of the high and low scores?

A) 76
B) 78
C) 80
D) 81

12. In Latin 101, the final exam grade is weighted two times as heavily as the mid-term grade. If Leo received a score of 84 on his final exam and 90 on his mid-term, what was his course average?

A) 88
B) 87.5
C) 86.5
D) 86

13. In a group of children, three children are 10 years old and two children are 5 years old. What is the average age, in years, of the children in the group?

A) 6.5
B) 7
C) 7.5
D) 8

Median Ⓐ Ⓢ

14. The number of employment applications received by All-Star Staffing each month during 2002 was as follows: 8, 4, 5, 3, 4, 3, 1, 0, 3, 4, 0, and 7. What was the median number of applications received per month in 2002?

A) 2.5
B) 3
C) 3.5
D) 4

Mode Ⓐ Ⓢ

15. William's monthly electric bills for last year were as follows: \$40, 38, 36, 38, 34, 34, 30, 32, 34, 37, 39, and 40. What is the mode of the bills?

A) \$33
B) \$34
C) \$35
D) \$36

Range Ⓢ

16. During Jennifer's drive to work, she notices that gas prices vary. She sees prices of \$3.28, \$3.46, \$3.16, \$3.89, and \$3.57. What is the range of the gas prices she saw?

A) 0.18
B) 0.29
C) 0.61
D) 0.73

Standard Deviation Ⓢ

17. The salary scale for players in a certain sports league is determined statistically by reference to a curve with a normal distribution. In 1960, the mean salary for players in the league was $10,000 with a standard deviation of $1000. That year, rookie players were paid $8,000. In 2010, the mean salary for players in the league was $1,175,000 with a standard deviation of $300,000. Rookies in 2010 were paid salaries in a dollar amount equal to a position on the normal curve for 2010 that rookie players were paid in the year 1960. What was the salary for rookie players in 2010?

A) $1,475,000
B) $1,175,000
C) $875,000
D) $575,000

18. A set of test scores is listed below:
78, 80, 80, 83, 86, 90, 91, 100
What would happen to the standard deviation if the highest and the lowest test scores were removed?

A) It would decrease
B) It would remain the same
C) It would increase
D) There is not enough information to determine the answer

Quartiles and Interquartile Range Ⓢ

19. During the last two weeks of January, Billy recorded the following outside temperatures (in °F) for each day: 24, 22, 7, 6, 10, 9, 9, 5, 1, 8, 14, 16, 9, 14. Which of the following is the interquartile range of Billy's data?

A) 6
B) 7
C) 9
D) 14

Drawing Inferences Ⓢ

20. A random sample of 10,000 college freshmen across the country showed that 6,500 prefer E-Books to traditional paper books. Which of the following is a valid conclusion?

A) Exactly 65% of all college freshmen prefer E-Books to paper books.
B) Approximately 35% of all college freshmen think that technology is bad.
C) Exactly 35% of all college freshmen prefer paper books to E-books.
D) Approximately 65% of all college freshmen prefer E-Books to paper books.

21. In a study of 20 gray mice, the mice were put into a maze at the same starting point. Food was put at the same place every time. The mice were able to determine the correct route to the food, without making mistakes, after a mean(average) of 32 trials, with a margin of error of 13 trials and a 95% confidence level. What conclusion is the most reasonable about gray mice?

A) They should all be able to find the route to their food in this maze, without making mistakes, in 32 trials.
B) They will probably be able to find the food in this maze, without making mistakes, in 19 to 45 trials.
C) No mouse will need more than 45 trials to find the food.
D) They will probably be able to find the food in this maze, without making mistakes, in 32 to 45 trials.

22. A random sample of 200 voting residents in a town showed that 32 of these residents do not have a driver's license, with a margin of error of 6 residents and a confidence level of 98%. If the town has 50,000 voting residents, what is the probable approximate range of voting residents in this town who do not have their driver's license?

A) 8,000 to 9,500 residents
B) 6,500 to 8,000 residents
C) 6,500 to 9,500 residents
D) 5,000 to 11,000 residents

23. In a random sample of people traveling for the winter holidays, 63% of people said they would be traveling by car with a margin of error of 9% and a 98% confidence level. Which of the following is the best conclusion from this data?

A) It is likely that 63% of all people traveling for the holidays will travel by car.
B) It is likely that 54% of all people traveling for the holidays will travel by car.
C) It is likely that between 63% and 72% of all people traveling for the holidays will travel by car.
D) It is likely that between 54% and 72% of all people traveling for the holidays will travel by car.

Data Interpretation in Statistics Contexts Ⓢ

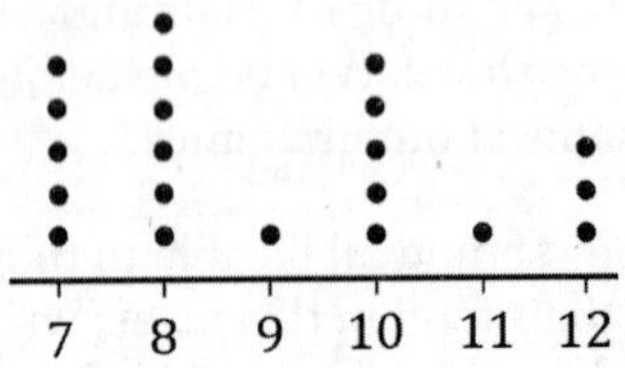

24. In the dot plot above, adding a dot to which column would NOT affect the median?

A) 8
B) 9
C) 10
D) 11

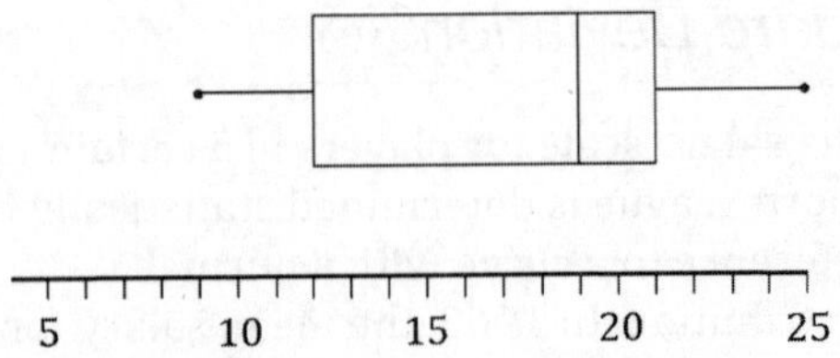

25. Which of the following statements is true about the box and whisker plot above?

A) The mean is 17.2 and the median is 19
B) The range is 16 and there is no mode
C) The median is 19 and the range is 16
D) The median is 19 and the range is 9

Set #1

Stem	Leaf
2	5 6 7 7 8
3	3 3 4
5	2 2 2 5 5

Set #2

Stem	Leaf
2	4 4 5 8 8
3	2 3 3
5	2 2 5 5 5

26. Which of the following statements is correct about the two stem and leaf plots above?

A) The mean of data set #1 is less than the mean of data set #2
B) The median of data set #1 is greater than the median of data set #2
C) The mode of data set #1 is greater than the mode of data set #2
D) The range of data set #1 is less than the range of data set #2

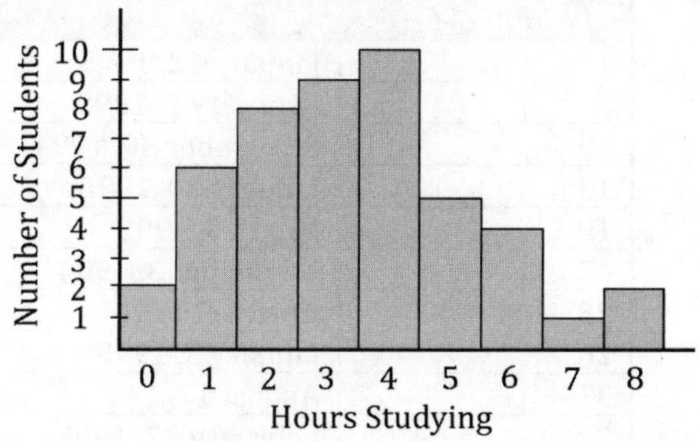

27. Which of the relationships is correct about the mean, median, and mode of the histogram above?

A) mean > median > mode
B) mode > median > mean
C) median > mean > mode
D) mode > mean > median

28. A teacher decides to raise his student's test scores by 3 points. Which of the following statements best describes what happens to the median score?

A) The median will increase by 3 points
B) The median will decrease by 3 points
C) The median will remain the same
D) There is not enough information to determine what will happen to the median

Data Collection Methods Ⓢ

29. A biologist wants to conduct an observational study of the effects of pollution on a specific type of bumblebee. Which of the following should NOT be a part of the study?

A) The biologist identifies a group of bumblebees to study
B) The biologist separates the bumblebees into a control group and an experimental group
C) The biologist collects data on the bumblebees
D) The biologist analyzes data on the bumblebees

30. A reporter wants to know public opinion about the candidates for Senate in Connecticut to try and predict who will win the next election. Which method should the reporter use to determine the sample population?

A) Assign random numbers to every person over the age of 18 in the state and use a random number generator to pick 50,000 to poll.
B) List every person in the state alphabetically and poll the first 50,000 people on the list.
C) Find a town in Connecticut with approximately 50,000 people in it and poll the residents.
D) Assign a random number to every person in the state between the ages of 18 and 21 and use a random number generator to pick the 50,000 people to poll.

	Percent of cell phone owners who have Smartphones for personal use			
Age	18–29	30–39	40–49	50–59
2006	20	15	13	10
2007	24	22	16	14
2008	35	31	23	24
2009	47	45	30	27
2010	61	56	39	37

31. The table above shows the results of an experiment done in Smart Town, USA to observe the cellular phone habits in different age groups between 2006 and 2010. Based on these results, which results are valid?

I. In each year of the study, cell phone owners between 18 and 29 years old were most likely to have Smartphones for personal use compared to the other age groups.

II. In a few years, there will be a larger percentage of Smartphone owners between 30 and 39 than between 18 and 29.

III. Every age group showed an increase in the percentage of cell phone owners who own Smartphones through the course of the study.

IV. The age group of 60+ does not own cell phones, so they are not in the study.

A) I, II, and III only
B) I only
C) I and III only
D) IV only

Player Number	Birthday
1	January 12, 1995
5	February 1, 1995
10	September 30, 1994
13	January 20, 1995
19	March 5, 1995
22	November 3, 1994
23	April 1, 1995
26	January 3, 1995
33	August 17, 1995
37	February 27, 1995
42	January 30, 1995

32. At a local high school, the soccer coach listed the birthdays of all of the starting players. Which of the following conclusions are valid based on the data shown above?

I. If you are born in January, you are more likely to be a starting player than any other month

II. There is a correlation between players being born between January and April and starting on the soccer team

III. There are more soccer players born in January than any other month

A) I only
B) II only
C) III only
D) I, II, and III

	Respond at School Only	Respond at Home Only	Respond at School and at Home
% of teachers	23%	22%	55%

33. The table above shows the responses of 5,000 teachers who respond to student emails to the question: "Do you respond to student emails while in school or while you are at home?" What conclusion is valid from this table?

A) If your school has 100 teachers who respond to student emails, exactly 23 of them will respond to student emails while in school only.
B) Exactly 55% of all teachers in the world respond to student emails both in school and at home.
C) Approximately 23% of all teachers respond to student emails while in school only.
D) Approximately 22% of all teachers who respond to student emails will respond only when they are home.

Probability

Arithmetic Probability Ⓐ Ⓢ

34. If set $A = \{1, 2, 3, 4, 5, 6\}$ and set $B = \{1, 2, 3, 4, 5, 6\}$, what is the probability that the sum of one number from set A and one number from set B will total 7?

A) $\frac{1}{12}$

B) $\frac{5}{36}$

C) $\frac{1}{6}$

D) $\frac{1}{5}$

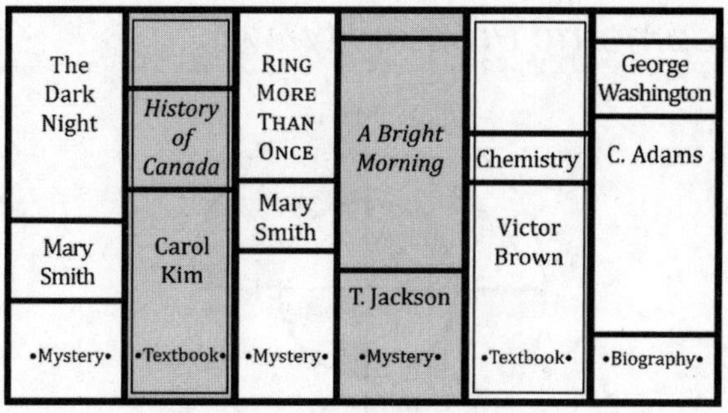

35. If a book is selected at random from the six-book collection shown above, which of the following has the greatest probability of being selected?

A) A book by Mary Smith
B) A textbook
C) A mystery
D) A book written by either Carol Kim or Victor Brown

36. If a jar contains r red marbles, b blue marbles, and g green marbles, which of the following expresses the probability that a marble drawn at random will NOT be red?

A) $\frac{r}{r+b+g}$

B) $\frac{b+g-r}{b+g+r}$

C) $\frac{r}{b+g}$

D) $\frac{b+g}{b+g+r}$

Geometric Probability Ⓐ Ⓢ

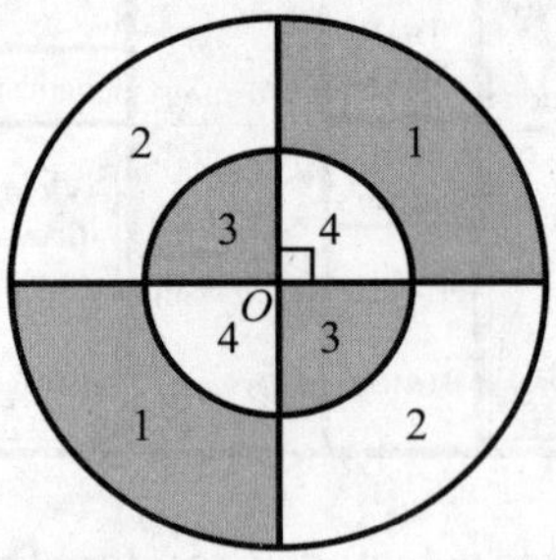

37. The figure above shows a dartboard consisting of two concentric circles with center O. The radius of the larger circle is equal to the diameter of the smaller circle. What is the probability that a randomly thrown dart striking the board will score a 3?

A) $\frac{1}{16}$

B) $\frac{1}{8}$

C) $\frac{1}{4}$

D) $\frac{1}{2}$

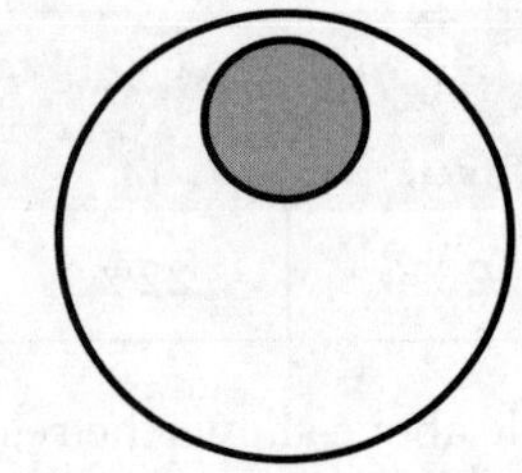

NOTE: Figure not drawn to scale.

38. An underwater salvage team is searching the ocean floor for a lost signal device using a large circular search pattern and a smaller circular search pattern with a radius equal to one-third that of the larger pattern. If the device is known to be inside the boundary of the larger search area, what is the probability that it is NOT located in the shaded portion of the figure?

A) $\frac{1}{9}$

B) $\frac{1}{6}$

C) $\frac{1}{3}$

D) $\frac{8}{9}$

LESSON 6 | TRIGONOMETRY

ACT MATHEMATICS AND SAT MATH: MULTIPLE-CHOICE

The items in this section accompany the in-class review of the trigonometry skills and concepts tested by the ACT Mathematics and SAT Math: Multiple-Choice tests. You will work through the items with your instructor in class. Answers are on page 581.

Definitions of the Six Trigonometric Functions and Other Relationships

Definitions of the Six Trigonometric Functions Ⓐ Ⓢ

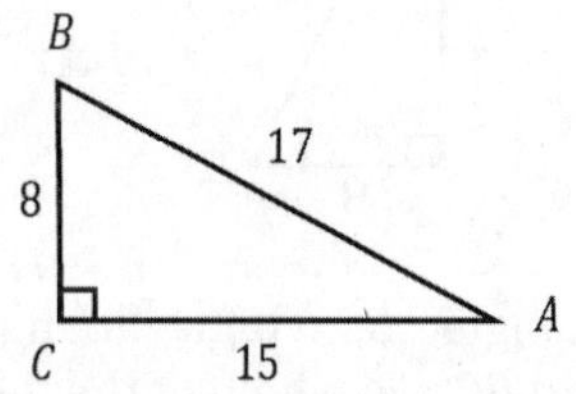

1. Given right triangle *ABC* above, what is the value of sin *A*?

A) $\frac{8}{17}$

B) $\frac{8}{15}$

C) $\frac{15}{17}$

D) $\frac{15}{8}$

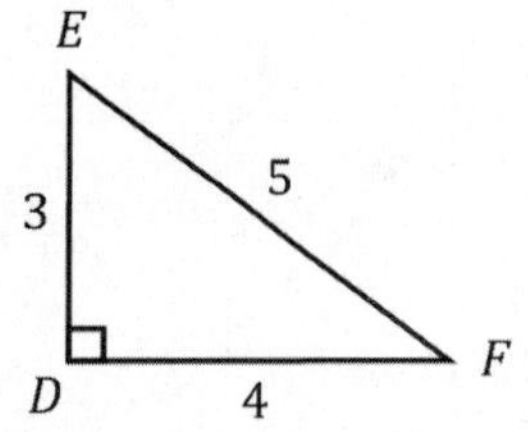

2. Given right triangle *DEF* above, which of the following is NOT true?

A) $\sec E = \frac{5}{3}$

B) $\cot F = \frac{4}{3}$

C) $\cos F = \frac{4}{5}$

D) $\tan E = \frac{3}{4}$

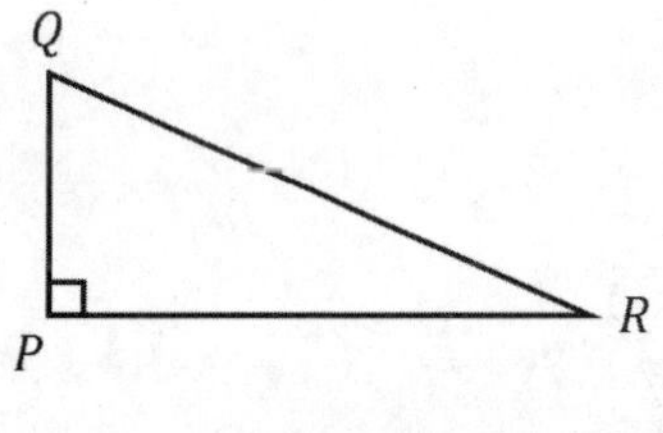

3. In right triangle *PQR* with right angle *P*, *PQ* = 5 cm and *QR* = 13 cm. What is cos *R*?

A) $\frac{5}{13}$

B) $\frac{8}{13}$

C) $\frac{12}{13}$

D) $\frac{12}{5}$

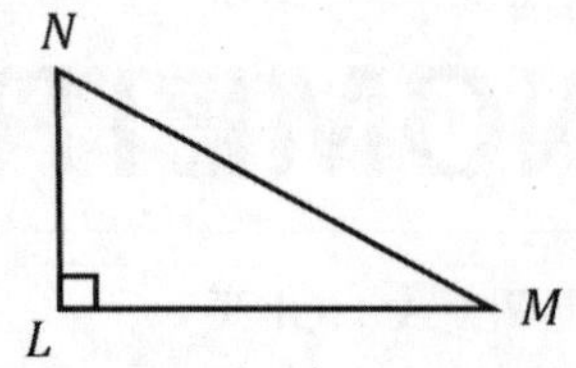

4. In right triangle LMN with right angle L, $\sec M = \frac{17}{15}$. What is $\cot M$?

A) $\frac{8}{15}$
B) $\frac{15}{17}$
C) $\frac{15}{8}$
D) $\frac{15}{2}$

Complementary Angles Ⓐ Ⓢ

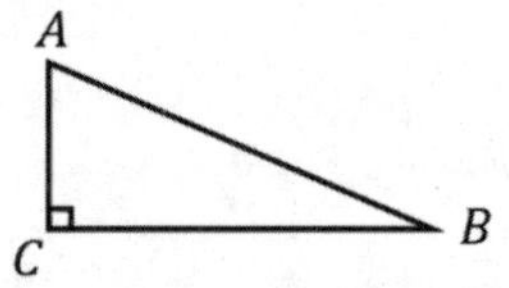

5. In right triangle ABC with right angle C, $\sin B = \frac{4}{7}$, what is $\cos A$?

A) $\frac{3}{7}$
B) $\frac{4}{7}$
C) $\frac{\sqrt{33}}{7}$
D) $\frac{\sqrt{33}}{4}$

Inverse Trigonometric Functions Ⓐ Ⓢ

6. In right triangle DEF with right angle D, $DE = 7$, and $DF = 24$. Which of the following is true?

A) $\sin^{-1}\left(\frac{7}{25}\right) = E$
B) $\cos^{-1}\left(\frac{7}{25}\right) = F$
C) $\tan^{-1}\left(\frac{7}{24}\right) = F$
D) $\sin^{-1}\left(\frac{7}{33}\right) = F$

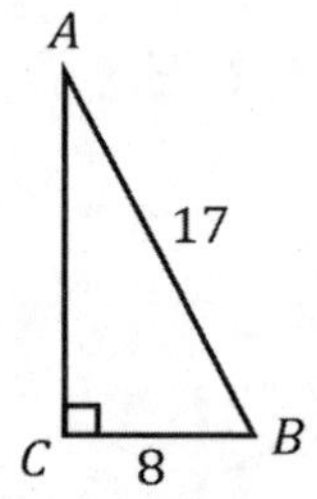

7. In right triangle ABC with right angle C, $AB = 17$ and $BC = 8$, which of the following equals $\angle A$?

A) $\sin^{-1}\left(\frac{15}{17}\right)$
B) $\tan^{-1}\left(\frac{15}{8}\right)$
C) $\tan^{-1}\left(\frac{8}{9}\right)$
D) $\sin^{-1}\left(\frac{8}{17}\right)$

8. In right triangle ABC, with right angle C, $AB \approx 50$ and $BC \approx 34$. If $\sin 20° \approx 0.34$ and $\sin 43° \approx 0.68$, which of the following is the best approximation for $\angle A$ in degrees?

A) 20
B) 40
C) 43
D) 86

The Pythagorean Identity Ⓐ Ⓢ

9. If $\sin D = \frac{\sqrt{3}}{2}$ and $\cos D = \frac{1}{2}$, what is the value of $\sin^2 D + \cos^2 D$?

A) $\frac{1}{2}$
B) 1
C) $\frac{\sqrt{3}+1}{2}$
D) 2

10. In right triangle ABC with right angle C, $AB = 10$ and $BC = 8$, what is the value of $\sin^2 A + \cos^2 A$?

A) 0
B) 1
C) $\frac{7}{5}$
D) 5

Special Right Triangles Ⓐ Ⓢ

11. In right triangle ABC, $\angle A = 60°$ and $\angle C = 90°$. What is $\cos B$?

A) 0
B) $\frac{1}{2}$
C) $\frac{\sqrt{2}}{2}$
D) $\frac{\sqrt{3}}{2}$

12. In right triangle LMN with right angle L, $\sin M = \frac{\sqrt{2}}{2}$. What is the measure of $\angle M$ in degrees?

A) 30
B) 45
C) 60
D) 90

13. In right triangle ABC with right angle C, $\tan A = \frac{\sqrt{3}}{3}$ and $AC = 12$. What is the area of triangle ABC?

A) $24\sqrt{3}$
B) 72
C) $48\sqrt{3}$
D) 144

Problem-Solving in Context

Finding Missing Angles and Sides Ⓐ Ⓢ

14. In right triangle DEF, $DE = 10$ cm, $\angle E = 20°$, and $\angle F$ is a right angle. What is the approximate length of DF in centimeters?

$\sin 20° \approx 0.34$
$\cos 20° \approx 0.94$
$\tan 20° \approx 0.36$

A) 3.4
B) 3.6
C) 5
D) 9.4

15. In right triangle ABC with right angle C, $BC = 12$ ft, and $\angle A = 30°$. What is the length of AC?

A) 6
B) $12\sqrt{3}$
C) 24
D) $24\sqrt{3}$

16. In isosceles right triangle LMN with right angle N, the hypotenuse is 18 cm. What is the length of MN in centimeters?

A) 9
B) $6\sqrt{3}$
C) $9\sqrt{2}$
D) $18\sqrt{2}$

17. In right triangle DEF with right angle F, $\angle D = 50°$ and $EF = 20$ ft, find the length of DF to the nearest tenth of a foot.

$\sin 40° \approx 0.64$
$\cos 40° \approx 0.77$
$\tan 40° \approx 0.84$

A) 16.8
B) 15.4
C) 12.8
D) 10

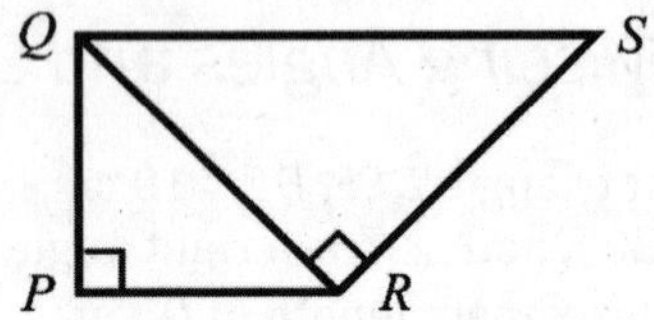

18. In the figure above, ΔPQR and ΔQRS are isosceles right triangles. If $QP = 3$, what is the length of QS? $\left(\sin 45° = \frac{\sqrt{2}}{2}\right)$

A) $\sqrt{2}$
B) $2\sqrt{2}$
C) 4
D) 6

Real World Scenarios Ⓐ Ⓢ

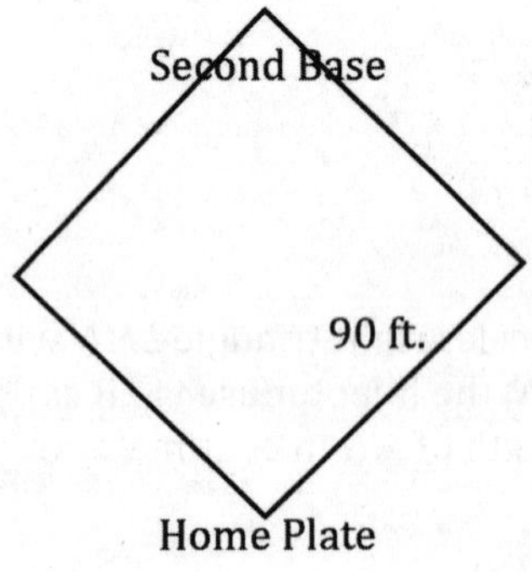

19. A baseball diamond is a square with 90 foot sides. Home plate and second base are on opposite vertices. How many feet is it from home plate to second base?

A) 90
B) $90\sqrt{2}$
C) $90\sqrt{3}$
D) 180

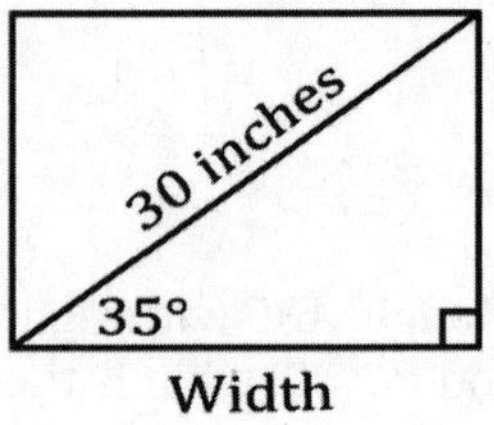

20. An advertisement lists televisions according to size and explains that a television is measured by the length of the diagonal of the screen. What is the width to the nearest tenth of an inch of the screen shown above?

$\sin 35° \approx 0.57$
$\cos 35° \approx 0.82$
$\tan 35° \approx 0.7$

A) 17.1
B) 18
C) 21
D) 24.6

21. Specifications for Highway Engineers require that a Yield sign be an equilateral triangle with a side of length 24 inches. What is the approximate area of the sign in square inches?

A) $144\sqrt{3}$
B) 288
C) $288\sqrt{3}$
D) 576

Altitude Ⓐ Ⓢ

22. Manufacturers recommend that the maximum angle a ladder makes with the ground be 65°. The ladder should be leaning against something perpendicular to the ground. If you need a ladder to reach a height of 36 feet up your house, what is the approximate length of the ladder you need in feet?

$\sin 65° \approx 0.9$
$\cos 65° \approx 0.4$
$\tan 65° \approx 2$

A) 18
B) 40
C) 74
D) 90

23. A surveyor stake is 40 feet from the base of a tree. The tree is perpendicular to the ground. The angle of elevation from the stake to the top of the tree is 55°. What is the approximate height of the tree in feet?

$\sin 55° \approx 0.82$
$\cos 55° \approx 0.57$
$\tan 55° \approx 1.43$

A) 22.8
B) 32.8
C) 57.2
D) 68

24. A man parachutes out of a plane. He pulls the chord so the parachute deploys at an altitude of 750 feet. At that moment, the angle of depression from the man to where he needs to land is 60°. What distance must the man travel, in feet, to get to the landing spot, assuming he goes in a straight line to the spot?

A) 500
B) $500\sqrt{3}$
C) 1,000
D) $1{,}000\sqrt{3}$

25. The Freedom Tower is approximately 1,776 feet tall. A six-foot-tall surveyor, Joe, is standing on the ground 207 feet from the base of the building. What expression gives the angle of elevation from the top of Joe's head to the top of the building?

A) $\sin^{-1}\left(\frac{207}{1{,}770}\right)$

B) $\tan^{-1}\left(\frac{1{,}770}{207}\right)$

C) $\tan^{-1}\left(\frac{207}{1{,}770}\right)$

D) $\cos^{-1}\left(\frac{207}{1{,}770}\right)$

Oblique Angles Ⓐ Ⓢ

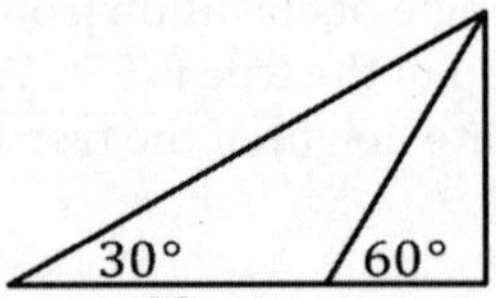

26. Christian is standing looking up at steeple at an angle of elevation from his line of sight of 30°. The steeple is perpendicular to the ground. Christian walks 40 feet closer and now the steeple is at an angle of elevation from his line of sight of 60°. What is the height of the steeple in feet if Christian's line of sight is 5 feet above the ground?

$(\tan 60 = \sqrt{3} \text{ and } \tan 30 = \frac{\sqrt{3}}{3})$

A) 25
B) $20\sqrt{3}+5$
C) 65
D) $60\sqrt{3}+5$

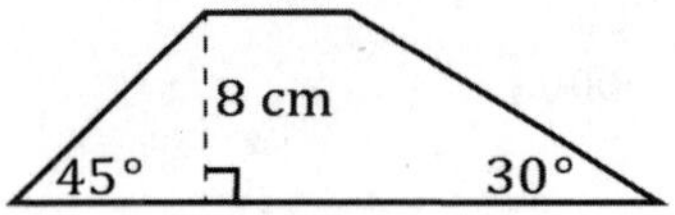

27. What is the area of the trapezoid above, in square centimeters?

A) $80+32\sqrt{3}$
B) 176
C) $160+64\sqrt{3}$
D) 352

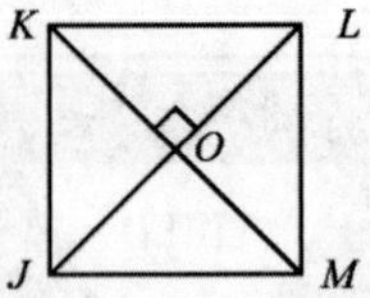

28. If the area of the square *JKLM* in the figure above is 4, what is the sum of the lengths of the diagonals *JL* and *KM*? $\left(\sin 45° = \frac{\sqrt{2}}{2}\right)$

A) $\frac{\sqrt{2}}{2}$
B) $2+\frac{\sqrt{2}}{2}$
C) $4\sqrt{2}$
D) $4+4\sqrt{2}$

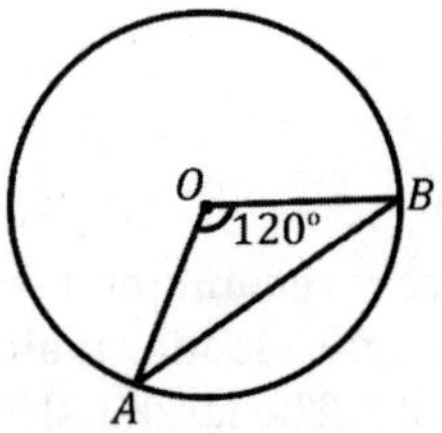

29. In the figure above, *O* is the center of the circle with radius 10. What is the area of ΔAOB ? $\left(\sin 30° = \frac{1}{2};\ \sin 60° = \frac{\sqrt{3}}{2}\right)$

A) 10
B) $10\sqrt{3}$
C) 25
D) $25\sqrt{3}$

Manipulating Trigonometric Functions

Basic Operations Ⓐ Ⓢ

30. $\sin x + \sin x$ is equivalent to which of the following?

A) $2\sin x$
B) $\sin(2x)$
C) $\sin(x^2)$
D) $\sin 2x$

31. $3\cos x + \sin x - (\cos x + 4\sin x)$ is equivalent to which of the following?

A) $2\cos x + 5\sin x$
B) $3 - 3\sin x$
C) $4\cos x - 3\sin x$
D) $2\cos x - 3\sin x$

32. Which of the following is NOT equivalent to $\dfrac{\sin^2 x + \sin x + \cos x}{\sin x}$?

A) $\sin x + 1 + \cot x$
B) $\tan x(\cos x + \cot x + 1)$
C) $\dfrac{1}{\csc x} + 1 + \dfrac{1}{\tan x}$
D) $\dfrac{\cos x + \cot x \sin^2 x}{\cos x} + \cot x$

Factoring Ⓐ Ⓢ

33. Which of the following is NOT equivalent to $\cos x(2\sin x + \cos x + \tan x)$?

A) $2\sin x \cos x + \cos^2 x + \sin x$
B) $\sin x(2\cos x + 1) + \cos^2 x$
C) $\cos x(2\sin x + \cos x) + \sin x$
D) $\cos x(2\sin x + \cos x + \sin x)$

34. Which of the following is equivalent to: $\sec x + \cot x + \cos x$?

A) $\cos x(\csc x + 1) + \csc x \tan x$
B) $\dfrac{1 + \cos^2 x + \cos x}{\cos x}$
C) $\sin x + \tan x + \csc x$
D) $\cos x(\tan x + 1) + \cot x$

Determining Values on the Unit Circle Ⓐ Ⓢ

35. What is the value of $\sin 225$?

A) -1
B) $-\dfrac{\sqrt{2}}{2}$
C) $\dfrac{\sqrt{2}}{2}$
D) 1

36. What is the value of $\cos 150$?

A) $-\dfrac{\sqrt{3}}{2}$
B) $-\dfrac{1}{2}$
C) $\dfrac{1}{2}$
D) $\dfrac{\sqrt{3}}{2}$

37. What is the value of $\tan 300$?

A) $-\sqrt{3}$
B) $-\dfrac{\sqrt{3}}{2}$
C) $\dfrac{\sqrt{3}}{2}$
D) $\sqrt{3}$

38. Which values of 280° are positive?

I. sin
II. cos
III. tan

A) I only
B) II only
C) II and III only
D) I, II, and III

39. An angle has a negative sine value and a positive tangent value. What quadrant must it lie in?

A) I
B) II
C) III
D) IV

Special Angles Ⓐ Ⓢ

40. Which of the following values equals sin75?

A) $\frac{\sqrt{2}-\sqrt{6}}{4}$
B) $\frac{\sqrt{2}}{2}$
C) $\frac{\sqrt{2}+\sqrt{6}}{4}$
D) $\frac{\sqrt{2}+\sqrt{6}}{2}$

41. Which of the following equals cos15?

A) $\frac{\sqrt{2}-\sqrt{6}}{4}$
B) $\frac{\sqrt{2}}{2}$
C) $\frac{\sqrt{2}+\sqrt{6}}{4}$
D) $\frac{\sqrt{2}+\sqrt{6}}{2}$

Restrictions Ⓢ

42. Which of the following could be true?

A) $\cos x = \frac{2}{15}$
B) $\cos x = \frac{15}{2}$
C) $\sin x = \frac{10}{9}$
D) $\sin x = 1.1$

43. Which of the following ratios of sine are undefined?

A) $-\frac{2}{3}$
B) 0
C) 1
D) $\frac{3}{2}$

Solving Equations Ⓐ Ⓢ

44. What is the solution set to $2\cos x + \sqrt{3} = 0$ if $0° \le x < 360°$?

A) 30° and 330°
B) 120° and 240°
C) 150° and 210°
D) 300° and 60°

45. What is the solution set to $2\sin x - \sqrt{2} = 0$ if $0° \le x < 360°$?

A) 45°
B) 135°
C) 45° and 135°
D) There is no solution

46. What is the solution set to $2\sin x - 5 = 4$ if $0° \le x < 360°$?

A) 30°
B) 150°
C) 30° and 150°
D) There is no solution

47. If $\tan^{-1}\left(\frac{4}{5}\right) \approx 39°$ and $\tan^{-1}(4) \approx 76°$, what is the approximate solution set to: $3\tan x = 4 - 2\tan x$?

A) 39°
B) 76°
C) 39° and 219°
D) 76° and 156°

Additional Topics in Trigonometry

Degrees and Radians Ⓢ

48. An angle that measures $\frac{11\pi}{6}$ radians has the same measure as an angle that measures how many degrees?

A) 180
B) 330
C) 660
D) 680

49. An angle that measures 300° has the same measure as an angle measuring how many radians?

A) $\frac{2\pi}{3}$
B) $\frac{5\pi}{6}$
C) $\frac{11\pi}{6}$
D) $\frac{5\pi}{3}$

50. An angle that measures $\frac{3\pi}{4}$ radians is the same as an angle that measures how many degrees?

A) 45
B) 135
C) 270
D) 315

51. In what quadrant does $\frac{9\pi}{4}$ terminate?

A) I
B) II
C) III
D) IV

52. What is the value of $\sin\left(\frac{7\pi}{6}\right)$?

A) $-\frac{\sqrt{3}}{2}$
B) $-\frac{1}{2}$
C) $\frac{1}{2}$
D) $\frac{\sqrt{3}}{2}$

53. What is the value of $\cos\left(\frac{5\pi}{4}\right)$?

A) -1
B) $-\frac{\sqrt{2}}{2}$
C) $\frac{\sqrt{2}}{2}$
D) 1

54. Which of the following trigonometric values of $\frac{35\pi}{18}$ are negative?

I. sin
II. cos
III. tan

A) I and II only
B) I and III only
C) II and III only
D) I only

Arc Length Ⓐⓢ

55. A circle has a radius of 6cm and an arc has a central angle of 40°. What is the arc length, in cm, created by this angle?

A) $\frac{4\pi}{3}$
B) 4π
C) 36π
D) 54π

56. An arc is created in a circle with a radius of 4 inches by a central angle of $\frac{5\pi}{8}$ radians. What is the arc length created by this angle?

A) $\frac{5}{2}\pi$
B) 5π
C) 8π
D) 16π

57. A central angle in a circle with a radius of 9 cm intercepts an arc of length 12π cm. What is the measure of the central angle in degrees?

A) 60
B) 120
C) 180
D) 240

58. A central angle of $\frac{5\pi}{6}$ intercepts an arc of length 15π m. What is the radius of this circle in meters?

A) 4
B) 6
C) 12
D) 18

Graphs of Trigonometric Functions Ⓐⓢ

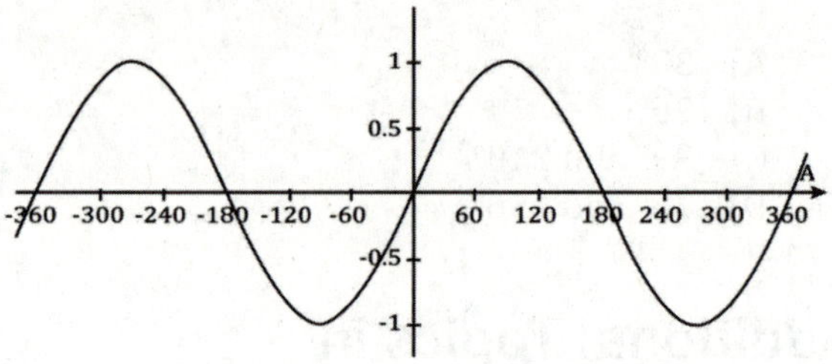

59. Which answer choice best describes the graph above?

A) $y = \cos x$
B) $y = \csc x$
C) $y = \tan x$
D) $y = \sin x$

60. Which of the following has a domain of x = ALL REALS?

A) $y = \csc x$
B) $y = \sec x$
C) $y = \tan x$
D) $y = \cos x$

TEST MECHANICS

ACT MATHEMATICS AND SAT MATH: MULTIPLE-CHOICE

ACT Mathematics Overview

The ACT Mathematics Test, according to the test-writers, presupposes a knowledge of pre-algebra and algebra, intermediate algebra and coordinate geometry, and geometry and trigonometry. The ACT Mathematics Test items are generally the same kind of questions you'd see on a classroom chapter test—except that they are multiple-choice questions.

In reality, however, you do not need to know all of those topics to do fairly well on the test. Intermediate algebra, coordinate geometry, and trigonometry combined account for less than 40 percent of the test. Here is the breakdown of items by topic on the ACT Mathematics Test:

ACT MATHEMATICS TEST TOPICS (60 items; 60 minutes)		
Content	**Approximate Number**	**Approximate Percent**
Pre-Algebra	14	23%
Elementary Algebra	10	17%
Intermediate Algebra	9	15%
Coordinate Geometry	9	15%
Plane Geometry	14	23%
Trigonometry	4	7%

This means that you could choose to skip all of the trigonometry items and the nine most difficult coordinate geometry and intermediate algebra items, miss another nine questions, and still get a 24 on the ACT Mathematics Test, which is a good score. For a very respectable score of 21 (above the national average), you need a raw score of about 33, which you can get if you choose to skip all the trigonometry, intermediate algebra, and coordinate geometry items and keep your wrong answers down to five.

This is not a recommended strategy; you should answer all the questions you know how to answer. These little "thought experiments" show that you can do quite well on the math even if you're not exactly a math whiz.

SAT Math: Multiple Choice Overview

The SAT Math test has 58 questions of two types, broken into two sections: calculator and no-calculator. Here is the distribution of items by type:

SAT MATHEMATICS TEST STRUCTURE
(58 items; 80 minutes)

Question Type	Number of Questions	Percent of Test Points
NO-CALCULATOR SECTION		
Multiple-Choice	15	25.9%
Student-Produced Response	5	8.6%
CALCULATOR SECTION		
Multiple-Choice	30	51.7%
Student-Produced Response	8	13.8%

The Math test sections presuppose knowledge of algebra, problem solving, data analysis, geometry, and trigonometry. These are the conceptual building blocks of the Math test sections. You do not have to know all of the tested topics to do well on the exam. For example, geometry and trigonometry combined account for 10.3 percent of the test. Here is the distribution of items by topic on the SAT Math Test:

SAT MATH TEST CONTENT
(58 items; 80 minutes)

Content	Number of Questions	Percent of Points
Heart of Algebra	19	32.8%
Problem Solving and Data Analysis	17	29.3%
Advanced Math	16	27.6%
Additional Topics (Geometry, Trigonometry)	6	10.3%

Additionally, 8 questions on the Math test will contribute to the Science cross-test score, meaning they will require you to apply math concepts in a science context such as a word problem with a graph from a scientific experiment. Likewise, 8 questions on the test will contribute to your History/Social Studies cross-test score.

ACT Mathematics Anatomy

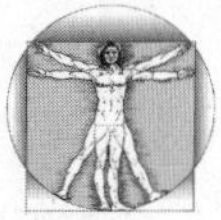

DIRECTIONS: Solve each item and choose the correct answer choice. Calculator use is permitted; however, some items are best solved without the use of a calculator.

NOTES: All of the following should be assumed, unless otherwise stated.

1. Illustrative figures are NOT necessarily drawn to scale.
2. The word *average* indicates arithmetic mean.
3. The word *line* indicates a straight line.
4. Geometric figures lie in a plane.

1. Paulo bicycled $6\frac{1}{3}$ miles on Wednesday and $8\frac{2}{5}$ miles on Thursday. How many miles did he bicycle during those two days?

A. $14\frac{2}{15}$

B. $14\frac{1}{4}$

C. $14\frac{3}{8}$

D. $14\frac{11}{15}$

E. $14\frac{13}{15}$

You really do not need the directions at all. You can use a calculator, and there will be further discussion of this in class.

Also, according to the directions, figures are not necessarily drawn to scale. However, the figures are almost always drawn to scale.

1. (D) *This item is solved by addition:*

$$\begin{aligned} 6\frac{1}{3}+8\frac{2}{5} &= \frac{19}{3}+\frac{42}{5} \\ &= \frac{95}{15}+\frac{126}{15} \\ &= \frac{221}{15} \\ &= 14\frac{11}{15} \end{aligned}$$

2. The average weight of 5 packages in a shipment is 8.7 pounds. The weights of 4 of the packages are 6.3 pounds, 7.5 pounds, 8.9 pounds, and 9.6 pounds. What is the weight of the fifth package?

F. 8.5
G. 8.8
H. 9.4
J. 11.2
K. 12.3

2. (J) *This item is a bit more difficult. First, set up an equation for the average:*

$$\frac{6.3+7.5+8.9+9.6+x}{5}=8.7$$

Then, solve for the missing weight:

$$(6.3+7.5+8.9+9.6)+x=(8.7)(5)$$
$$x=43.5-32.3=11.2$$

3. If $3x+4=7x-2$, $x=$?

A. $-\frac{1}{4}$
B. $\frac{1}{2}$
C. $\frac{3}{5}$
D. $\frac{2}{3}$
E. $1\frac{1}{2}$

3. (E) *For this item, solve for x:*

$$3x+4=7x-2$$
$$3x-7x=-2-4$$
$$-4x=-6$$
$$4x=6$$
$$x=\frac{6}{4}=\frac{3}{2}=1\frac{1}{2}$$

4. The ratio of the radii of two circles is $3:4$. What is the ratio of their areas?

F. $7:1$
G. $3:4$
H. $9:16$
J. $3:4\pi$
K. $9:16\pi$

4. (H) *With this item, since the ratio of the radii of the two circles is* $3:4$, *the ratio of their areas is:*

$$\frac{\pi(3)^2}{\pi(4)^2}=\frac{9\pi}{16\pi}=\frac{9}{16}=9:16.$$

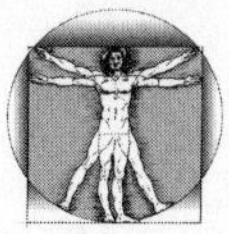

SAT Math: Multiple Choice Anatomy

DIRECTIONS: Solve each item and choose the correct answer choice. Use any available space for scratchwork.

Notes:
(1) All expressions and equations represent real numbers unless otherwise indicated.
(2) Figures that accompany problems in this test are intended to provide information useful in solving the problems. They are drawn as accurately as possible EXCEPT when it is stated in a specific problem that the figure is not drawn to scale. All figures lie in a plane unless otherwise indicated.
(3) The domain of a given function f is the set of all real numbers x for which $f(x)$ is a real number unless otherwise indicated.

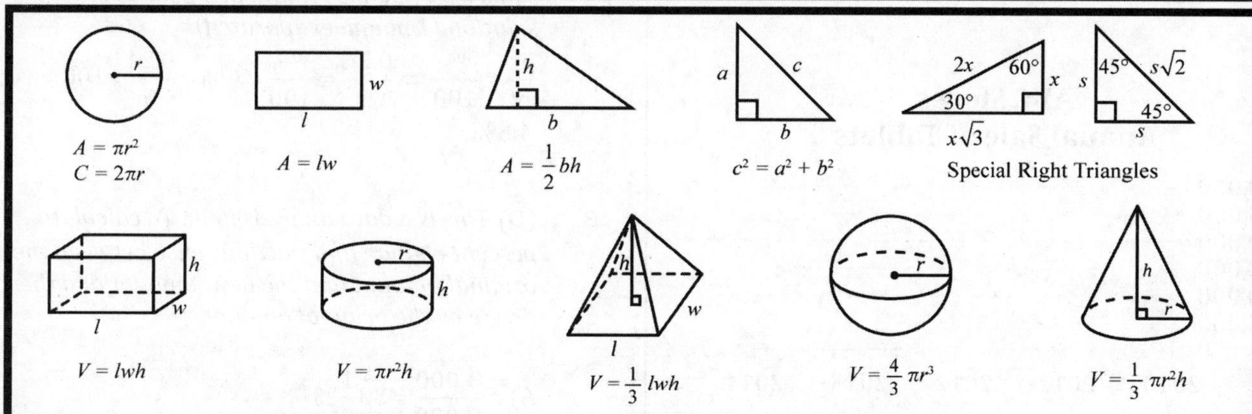

The number of degrees of arc in a circle is 360.
The sum of the measures in degrees of the angles of a triangle is 180.
The number of radians of arc in a circle is 2π.

You really do not need the directions at all. Problem-solving is your standard-issue Math: Multiple-Choice item. Expressions and equations represent real numbers and figures are not necessarily drawn to scale; these aspects of the test were addressed in greater detail in the ACT Mathematics and ACT Math: Multiple-Choice lessons.

1. If $x+5=8$, then $2x-1=$

A) 25
B) 12
C) 5
D) 4

2. A pound of water is evaporated from 6 pounds of seawater that is 4 percent salt. What is the percentage of salt in the remaining solution?

A) 3.6%
B) 4%
C) 4.8%
D) 5.2%

ABC Stores
Annual Sale of Tablets

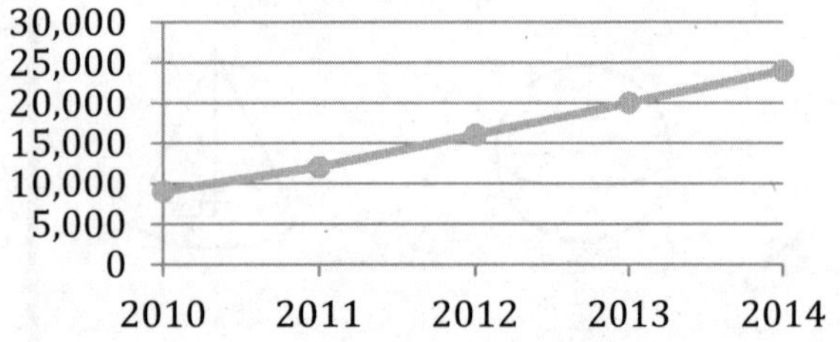

3. In the table above, which yearly period had the smallest percent increase in sales?

A) 2010–2011
B) 2011–2012
C) 2012–2013
D) 2013–2014

4. A cylindrical container has a diameter of 14 inches and a height of 6 inches. Since one gallon equals 231 cubic inches, what is the approximate capacity, in gallons, of the tank?

A) $1\frac{1}{7}$

B) $2\frac{2}{7}$

C) $2\frac{2}{3}$

D) 4

1. **(C)** *This is a manipulation item that tests algebra. The correct answer is (C). Since* $x+5=8$, $x=3$. *Then, substitute 3 for x in the expression:* $2x-1=2(3)-1=5$.

2. **(C)** *This is a story problem, and because of the topic, it would likely be considered a science analysis item (items dealing with science topics from all 3 tests are used to calculate the science cross-test score, as well as counting toward the test score). The original 6 pounds contained 0.24 pounds of salt* $(0.04 \bullet 6 = 0.24)$. *Now, the same 0.24 pounds remain in 5 pounds of solution (1 pound evaporated):*

$$\frac{\text{is}}{\text{of}} = \frac{\%}{100} \Rightarrow \frac{0.24}{5} = \frac{\%}{100} \Rightarrow \% = \frac{0.24}{5} \bullet 100 = 4.8\%.$$

3. **(D)** *This is a data analysis item. To calculate percent change find the difference between the original amount and the new amount and then divide by the original amount.*

A) $\frac{3{,}000}{9{,}000} = 33\frac{1}{3}\%$

B) $\frac{4{,}000}{12{,}000} = 33\frac{1}{3}\%$

C) $\frac{4{,}000}{16{,}000} = 25\%$

D) $\frac{4{,}000}{20{,}000} = 20\%$

4. **(D)** *This is a geometry problem. The volume of the container is the area of the cylinder at one end multiplied by its height. The area of the cylinder's end is:* $\text{area}_{\text{circle}} = \pi r^2 = \pi(7)^2 = 49\pi$. $\text{Volume}_{\text{cylinder}} = 49\pi h = 49\pi(6) \approx 924$ cubic inches. *Therefore, the capacity of the tank is:*

$$\left(924 \text{ in.}^3\right)\left(\frac{1 \text{ gallon}}{231 \text{ in.}^3}\right) = 4 \text{ gallons.}$$

There are three other features of both the ACT Mathematics and the SAT Math: Multiple-Choice items to note:

- ***Answer choices are arranged in order.*** For most ACT Mathematics and SAT Math: Multiple-Choice items, answer choices are arranged from least to greatest or vice versa. However, there are some exceptions. Choices that consist entirely of variables do not follow the rule, and items that ask "which of the following is the biggest?" obviously do not follow the rule. That the answer choices are usually arranged in order makes it easier for you to find your choice in the list. It also sets up an important test-taking strategy of starting with the middle choice when applying the "test-the-test" strategy, which you learned about in the ACT Mathematics and SAT Math: Multiple-Choice lessons.
- ***Answer choices are carefully constructed.*** The choices are not created so that you have to do repetitive calculations. Item #2 above nicely illustrates this point. The correct answer is 4.8%, but you are not given choices like 4.7% and 4.9%. Instead, the choices usually correspond to errors in thinking—not errors in arithmetic. This feature is important because it is the basis for a couple of time-saving strategies that you'll learn shortly.
- ***Items are arranged on a ladder of difficulty.*** Of course, you can't tell this from the four examples provided here, but the ladder is an important feature of the math test. Given that the problems become more difficult as you proceed, you're obviously going to have to make some important decisions about speed and skipping items.

ACT Mathematics Pacing

The ACT Mathematics Test consists of 60 items. The time limit is 60 minutes. The items are arranged on a ladder of difficulty, so you'll need a pacing plan that helps you move more quickly through the easier items at the beginning of the test and allows you to build up a time reserve for the harder items that are located toward the end. The following table summarizes an example of the timing for this approach:

ITEM NUMBERS	TIME TO SPEND PER ITEM	REMAINING TIME
#1–10	36 seconds	54 minutes
#11–20	42 seconds	47 minutes
#21–30	54 seconds	38 minutes
#31–40	66 seconds	27 minutes
#41–50	72 seconds	15 minutes
#51–60	90 seconds	0 minutes

This table is a schedule for the best of all possible math worlds. It's intended to be a guideline, not a rule. Try to stay on schedule, but be prepared to adjust your timing based on the number of items it is realistic to expect that you'll be able to do. Trying to stay on a schedule during the test will help you avoid the two biggest time wasters for timed tests.

First, staying on schedule will ensure that you are not plodding through the easy items at the beginning of the test. At first, with a 60-minute time limit, it will seem like you've got all the time in the world. But you don't. From the moment the test begins, you'll behind schedule and playing catch-up. So, keep a sense of urgency.

Second, the schedule will serve as a constant reminder that you cannot afford to spend too much time on any one problem. For example, if you make a mistake and spend three minutes on item #22, then you'll find that you've fallen behind schedule. The better choice is to leave that problem, hoping you'll have time at the end of the test to come back and finish it. Spending three minutes to get one question answered when three minutes could get you five questions answered is an inefficient use of time.

SAT Math: Multiple Choice Pacing

The items on the Math test sections are arranged on a ladder of difficulty, so you'll need a pacing plan that helps you move more quickly through the easier items at the beginning of the test and allows you to build up a time reserve for the harder items that are located toward the end.

MATH TEST NO-CALCULATOR SECTION
(20 items, 25 minutes)

Type of Item	Item Number	Time to Spend per Item	Remaining Time
Multiple-Choice	1–15	60 seconds	10 minutes
Student-Produced Responses	16–20	120 seconds	0 minutes

MATH TEST CALCULATOR SECTION
(38 items, 55 minutes)

Type of Item	Item Number	Time to Spend per Item	Remaining Time
Multiple-Choice	1–14	60 seconds	41 minutes
	15–26	90 seconds	23 minutes
	27–30	105 seconds	16 minutes
Student-Produced Responses	31–38	120 seconds	0 minutes

Notice that you'll devote more time to Student-Produced Responses items than to Multiple-Choice items. The reason for this is that you have to budget a little extra time for entering your answers on the Student-Produced Responses items. (You will learn more on this in the Math: Student-Produced Responses Lesson.)

ACT Mathematics and SAT Math: Multiple-Choice Time Trial

(4 Items—5 minutes)

DIRECTIONS: Solve each item and choose the correct answer choice. Use any available space for scratchwork.

Notes:

(1) All expressions and equations represent real numbers unless otherwise indicated.

(2) Figures that accompany problems in this test are intended to provide information useful in solving the problems. They are drawn as accurately as possible EXCEPT when it is stated in a specific problem that the figure is not drawn to scale. All figures lie in a plane unless otherwise indicated.

(3) The domain of a given function *f* is the set of all real numbers *x* for which *f*(*x*) is a real number unless otherwise indicated.

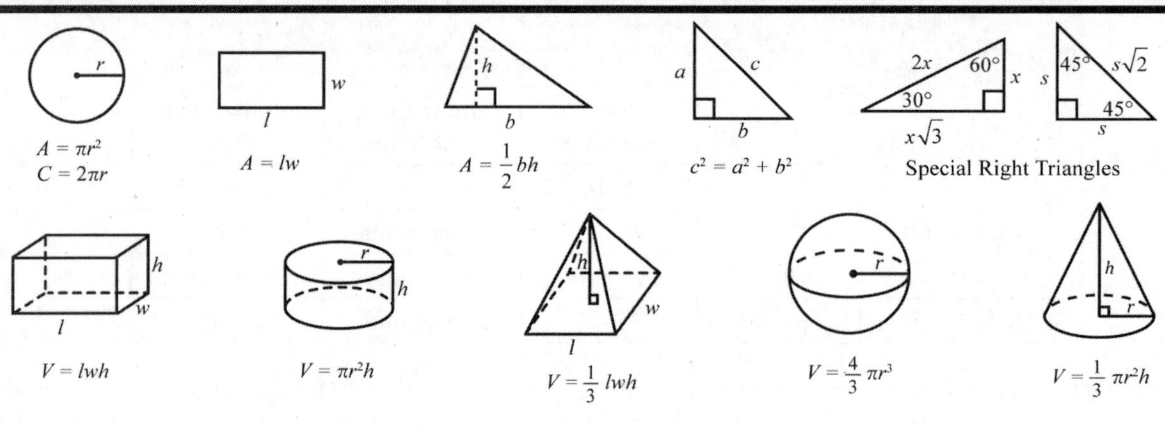

The number of degrees of arc in a circle is 360.
The sum of the measures in degrees of the angles of a triangle is 180.
The number of radians of arc in a circle is 2π.

1. $\frac{1}{10^{25}} - \frac{1}{10^{26}} =$

A) $\frac{9}{10^{25}}$

B) $\frac{1}{10^{25}}$

C) $\frac{9}{10^{26}}$

D) $-\frac{9}{10^{25}}$

Floor Readings for the Red River

Time (p.m.)	1:00	2:00	3:00	4:00
Inches above Normal	0.5	1.5	?	13.5

2. The table above shows readings of water levels for the Red River at various times. If readings of the rise of the water level followed a geometric progression, the water level at 3:00 p.m. was how many inches above normal?

A) 4
B) 4.5
C) 4.75
D) 5

3. If s, t, and u are different positive integers and $\frac{s}{t}$ and $\frac{t}{u}$ are positive integers, which of the following CANNOT be a positive integer?

A) $\frac{s}{u}$

B) $s \cdot t$

C) $\frac{u}{s}$

D) $(s+t)u$

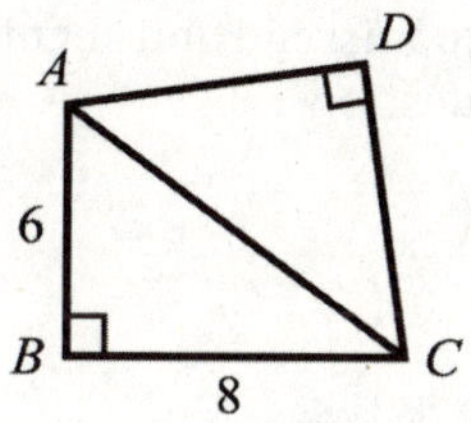

4. In the figure above, $\overline{AD} = \overline{DC}$. What is the value of $AD + DC$?

A) $18\sqrt{2}$
B) 18
C) $10\sqrt{2}$
D) 10

ACT Mathematics and SAT Math: Multiple-Choice Game Plan

Quickly Preview the Test Section, but Skip the Directions

As you get started, take a few seconds to preview the ACT Mathematics Test or the SAT Math: Multiple-Choice section. It's 99.99% certain that you're going to find everything in place and just as you expected. But a quick overview will guarantee against any unanticipated changes. Do NOT, however, read the directions. Remind yourself of your pacing plan and then get to work.

Answer the Question That Is Being Asked

Read the Question Carefully

Some problems are fairly simple, but others are more complex, particularly practical word problems and more difficult geometry problems. The more complex the question, the easier it is to misread and set off down the wrong track. If the question is very long, then underline the key part of the question.

Example:

If Mark traveled 20 miles in 3 hours and Lester traveled twice as far in half the time, what was Lester's average speed?

A) $6\frac{2}{3}$ miles per hour

B) 12 miles per hour

C) 26 miles per hour

D) $26\frac{2}{3}$ miles per hour

The stem states that Lester traveled twice as far as Mark in half the time, or 40 miles in 1.5 hours. Therefore, Lester's average speed was $\frac{40 \text{ miles}}{1.5 \text{ hours}} = 26.66\bar{6} = 26\frac{2}{3}$ miles per hour, (D).

Pay Attention to Units

Some items require you to convert units (e.g., feet to inches or hours to minutes). The item stem will tell you what units to use. When you see an item stem that includes units, circle the unit and put a star beside it.

Example:

A certain copy machine produces 13 copies every 10 seconds. If the machine operates without interruption, how many copies will it produce in an hour?

A) 780
B) 4,200
C) 4,680
D) 4,800

Create an expression that, after cancellation of like units, gives the number of copies produced in an hour:

$\frac{13 \text{ copies}}{10 \text{ seconds}} \bullet \frac{60 \text{ seconds}}{1 \text{ minute}} \bullet \frac{60 \text{ minutes}}{1 \text{ hour}} = 4{,}680 \text{ copies/hour}$. Therefore, the copy machine produces 4,680 copies in an hour, (C).

Pay Attention to Thought-Reversers

A thought-reverser is any word, such as "not," "except," or "but," that turns a question inside out. As shown below, make sure that you mark the thought-reverser so that it is staring you in the face as you work the problem.

Example:

How many integers in the set of integers from 1 to 144, inclusive, are NOT a square of an integer?

A) 0
B) 2
C) 12
D) 132

Since 1 is the square of 1, and 144 is the square of 12, there are a total of 12 integers in the set of integers from 1 to 144, inclusive, that are a square of an integer (1^2, 2^2, 3^2, 4^2, 5^2, 6^2, 7^2, 8^2, 9^2, 10^2, 11^2, 12^2). Therefore, there are a total of $144-12=132$ integers in the set that are NOT a square of an integer, (D).

Use the Answer Choices

In the ACT Mathematics and SAT Math: Multiple-Choice lessons, you learned some very powerful test-taking strategies that use the multiple-choice answers to test items to help solve items. Here are two simple suggestions to keep in mind.

Eliminate Answer Choices That Cannot Be Correct

Sometimes, the array of answers will include choices that, taken at face value, seem to be plausible, but when examined more carefully, must be incorrect.

Example:

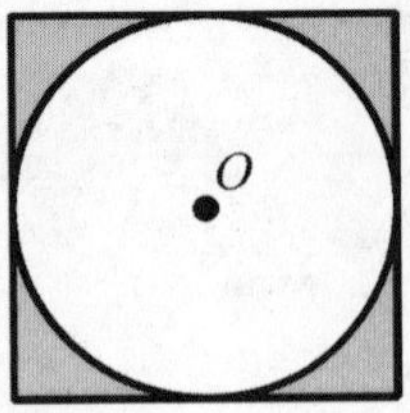

In the figure above, a circle with center O and a radius of 2 is inscribed in a square. What is the area of the shaded portion of the figure?

A) $2-\pi$
B) $4-2\pi$
C) $16-2\pi$
D) $16-4\pi$

The shaded area is equal to the area of the square minus the area of the circle. Since the radius of the circle is 2, the side of the square is 4 and its area is $4 \cdot 4 = 16$. The area of the circle is $\pi(2)^2 = 4\pi$. Therefore, the shaded area is $16-4\pi$, (D). Notice that without even solving the item, you can eliminate answer choices. Take a closer look at (A) and (B). Since π is approximately 3.14, (A) and (B) are negative. Area, however, cannot be a negative number, so (A) and (B) must be wrong, and you can eliminate them without doing any other work. Now, if you had to, you can make an educated guess from the remaining choices and the odds of guessing correctly are 50 percent.

Use the Answer Choices to Check Your Math

While the ACT and SAT tests do not test repetitive calculations, some items do require a calculation or two. One of the fundamental rules of math in school is "check your work." On the ACT and SAT tests, however, this is a real waste of time. Let's say that you do a calculation (with or without your calculator) and the result is $23.10. If one of the choices is $23.10, pick it, mark your answer sheet, and move on to the next item. Do NOT check your arithmetic. The possibility that you did the arithmetic, made a mistake, and still got a number like 23.10 is just too unlikely to consider. On the other hand, if you do not find a choice that matches your calculation, then you'd better check both your set-up of the problem and your arithmetic to find the error. In this way, the answer choices function as a feedback loop on the accuracy of your manipulations.

Don't Go Calculator Crazy

Just because you are allowed to use a calculator on one section of the test does not mean that you should try to solve every problem on that section with your calculator. In fact, for most problems, the calculator is the less efficient method of arriving at a solution. Assume, for example, that you have to do the following arithmetic to get your answer: $\left(\frac{2}{3}\right)\left(\frac{7}{4}\right)\left(\frac{1}{6}\right)$. Since this problem involves single digit multiplication, it's going to be easier to do the arithmetic with a pencil than with a calculator: $\left(\frac{2}{3}\right)\left(\frac{7}{4}\right)\left(\frac{1}{6}\right)=\frac{2 \cdot 7 \cdot 1}{3 \cdot 4 \cdot 6}=\frac{14}{72}=\frac{7}{36}$. By all means, use the calculator since it will be a definite advantage, but don't automatically assume that every problem is easier to solve with a calculator.

ACT Mathematics and SAT Math: Multiple Choice Calculator Exercise

This exercise is designed to illustrate when and when not to use your calculator. Make sure that the calculator you bring to the test is one with which you are thoroughly familiar. You may bring any of the following types of calculators: graphing, four-function, or scientific. (For more detailed information on calculator usage, including prohibited models, go to http://www.actstudent.org/faq/answers/calculator.html and http://sat.collegeboard.org/register/sat-test-day-checklist.) Although no item requires the use of a calculator, a calculator may be helpful at times. It may be useful for any item that involves complex arithmetic computations, but it cannot take the place of understanding how to set up a mathematical item. The degree to which you can use your calculator will depend on its features. Answers are on page 581.

DIRECTIONS: Label each of the items that follow according to one of the following categories.

Category 1: A calculator would be very useful (it would save valuable test time).
Category 2: A calculator might or might not be useful.
Category 3: A calculator would be counterproductive (it would waste valuable test time).

1. What is the average of 8.5, 7.8, and 7.7?

A) 8.3
B) 8.2
C) 8.1
D) 8.0

2. If $0 < x < 1$, which of the following is the largest?

A) $2x$
B) x^2
C) x^3
D) $x+1$

3. If 4.5 pounds of chocolate cost $10, how many pounds of chocolate can be purchased for $12?

A) $4\frac{3}{4}$
B) $5\frac{2}{5}$
C) $5\frac{1}{2}$
D) $5\frac{3}{4}$

4. What is the value of $\frac{8}{9}-\frac{7}{8}$?

A) $\frac{1}{72}$
B) $\frac{1}{8}$
C) $\frac{1}{7}$
D) $\frac{15}{72}$

5. Which of the following fractions is the largest?

A) $\frac{111}{221}$

B) $\frac{75}{151}$

C) $\frac{333}{998}$

D) $\frac{113}{225}$

QUIZ

ACT MATHEMATICS

This section contains an ACT Mathematics quiz. Complete the quiz under timed conditions. Use any available space in the section for scratch work. Answers are on page 581.

(20 items; 20 minutes)

DIRECTIONS: Solve each item and choose the correct answer choice. Calculator use is permitted; however, some items are best solved without the use of a calculator.

NOTES: All of the following should be assumed, unless otherwise stated.

1. Illustrative figures are NOT necessarily drawn to scale.
2. The word *average* indicates arithmetic mean.
3. The word *line* indicates a straight line.
4. Geometric figures lie in a plane.

1. In the triangle below, $x = ?$

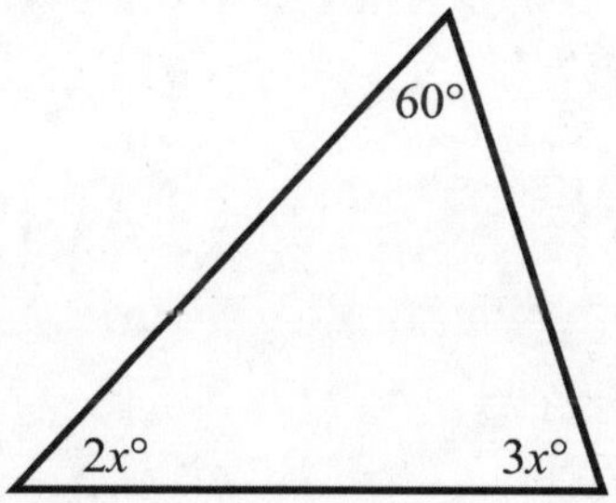

A. 24
B. 20
C. 16
D. 12
E. 10

2. A normal dozen contains 12 items, and a baker's dozen contains 13 items. If x is the number of items that could be measured either in a whole number of normal dozens or in a whole number of baker's dozens, what is the <u>minimum</u> value of x?

F. 1
G. 12
H. 13
J. 25
K. 156

3. In the figure below, what is the degree measure of the <u>smaller</u> of the two angles formed by the hour and minute hands of the clock?

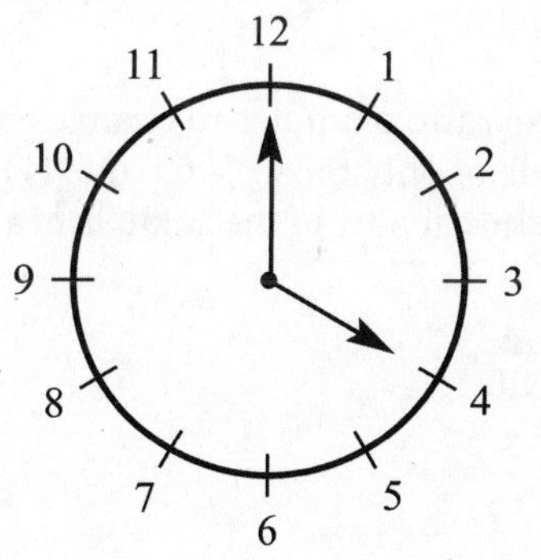

A. 45
B. 60
C. 90
D. 120
E. 240

4. Starting from points that are 200 kilometers apart, two trains travel toward each other along two parallel tracks. If one train travels at 70 kilometers per hour and the other travels at 80 kilometers per hour, how much time, in hours, will elapse before the trains pass each other?

F. $\frac{3}{4}$
G. 1
H. $\frac{4}{3}$
J. $\frac{3}{2}$
K. 2

5. A student begins heating a certain substance with a temperature of 50°C over a Bunsen burner. If the temperature of the substance will rise 20°C for every 24 minutes it remains over the burner, what will be the temperature, in degrees Celsius, of the substance after 18 minutes?

A. 52
B. 56
C. 60
D. 65
E. 72

6. If the ratio of apples to oranges in a fruit salad made of only those two fruits is 8 to 7, what fractional part of the salad is oranges?

F. $\frac{1}{56}$
G. $\frac{1}{15}$
H. $\frac{1}{7}$
J. $\frac{7}{15}$
K. $\frac{8}{7}$

7. The object of a popular board game is to use clues to identify a suspect and the weapon used to commit a crime. If there are 3 suspects and 6 weapons, how many different solutions to the game are possible?

A. 2
B. 3
C. 9
D. 12
E. 18

8. The average weight of three boxes is $25\frac{1}{3}$ pounds. If each box weighs at least 24 pounds, what is the greatest possible weight, in pounds, of any one of the boxes?

F. 25
G. 26
H. 27
J. 28
K. 29

9. If n subtracted from $\frac{13}{2}$ is equal to n divided by $\frac{2}{13}$, what is the value of n?

A. $\frac{2}{3}$
B. $\frac{13}{15}$
C. 1
D. $\frac{13}{11}$
E. 26

10. In the figure below, what is the area of the quadrilateral?

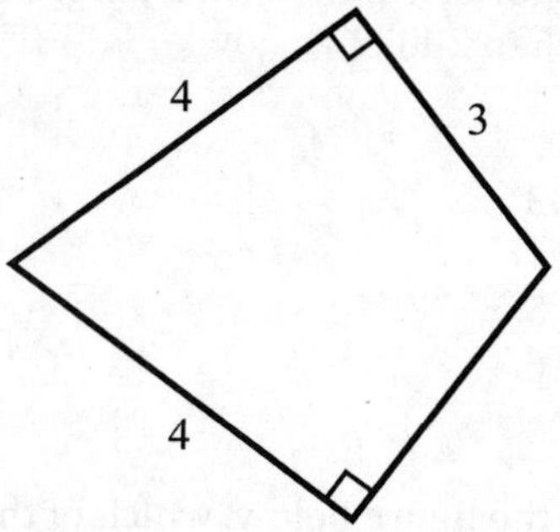

F. 18
G. 15
H. 12
J. 9
K. 8

11. In the figure below, what is the length of $\overline{BC}$? $\left(\sin 30° = \frac{1}{2}\right)$

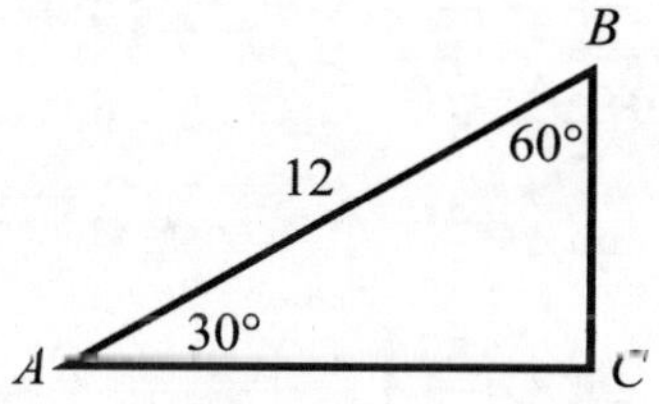

A. 2
B. 3
C. $3\sqrt{3}$
D. 6
E. $6\sqrt{3}$

12. After being dropped from a height of h meters, a ball bounces 3 meters high on the third bounce and $\frac{4}{3}$ meters high on the fifth bounce. The height of each bounce is lower by a constant factor. What is the value, in meters, of h?

F. $\frac{27}{8}$
G. $\frac{9}{2}$
H. $\frac{27}{4}$
J. $\frac{81}{8}$
K. $\frac{27}{2}$

13. Set $A = \{-2, -1, 0\}$, and set $B = \{-1, 0, 1\}$. If a is an element of set A and b is an element of set B, for how many pairs (a,b) is the product ab a member of both set A and set B?

A. 0
B. 2
C. 5
D. 6
E. 7

14. Which of the following is the complete solution set for $|2x+4| = 12$?

F. $\{-8, 4\}$
G. $\{-4, 8\}$
H. $\{0, 8\}$
J. $\{4, 8\}$
K. $\{6, 8\}$

15. If $f(x)=\frac{(x-1)^2}{(-2-x)}$, for what value of x is $f(x)$ undefined?

A. −2
B. −1
C. 0
D. 1
E. 2

Items #16–17 refer to the following table.

ANNUAL EXPENDITURES FOR THE JONES FAMILY (percent of annual expenditures)		
Category	**2006**	**2007**
Rent	23.0%	19.3%
Food	17.6%	18.2%
Clothing	14.2%	15.1%
Automobile	11.3%	12.3%
Utilities	10.9%	10.2%
Savings	6.2%	5.1%
Entertainment	5.2%	5.3%
Medical and Dental Care	4.0%	3.7%
Charitable Contributions	3.2%	3.9%
Household Furnishings	2.9%	3.1%
Other	1.5%	3.8%
Total	100.0%	100.0%
Total Expenditures	$34,987.00	$40,012.00

16. Approximately how much money did the Jones family spend on medical and dental care in 2006?

F. $1,200
G. $1,400
H. $1,520
J. $2,250
K. $4,000

17. If the categories in the table are rank ordered from one to eleven in each year, how many categories would have a different rank from 2006 to 2007?

A. 2
B. 3
C. 4
D. 5
E. 6

18. For the figure below, which of the following statements is INCORRECT?

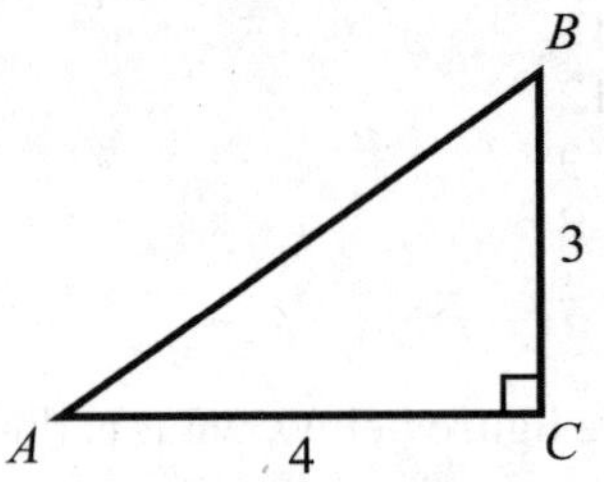

F. $\sin A=\frac{3}{5}$

G. $\cos A=\frac{4}{5}$

H. $\tan A=\frac{3}{4}$

J. $\cot A=\frac{5}{3}$

K. $\sec A=\frac{5}{4}$

19. When the 10-gallon tank of an emergency generator is filled to capacity, the generator operates without interruption for 20 hours, consuming fuel at a constant rate until all the fuel is consumed. Which of the graphs below represents the fuel consumption of the generator over time?

A.

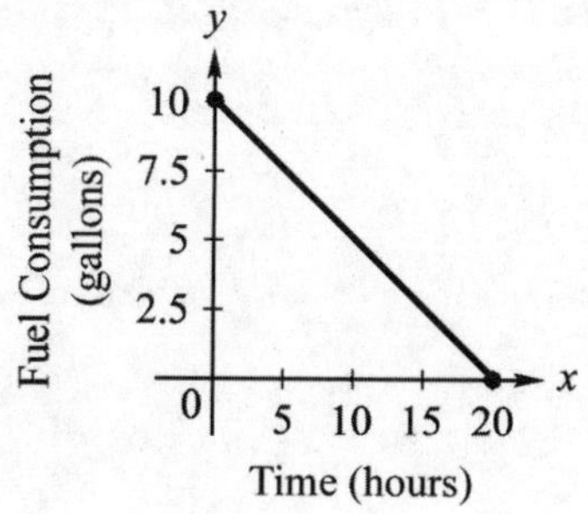

B.

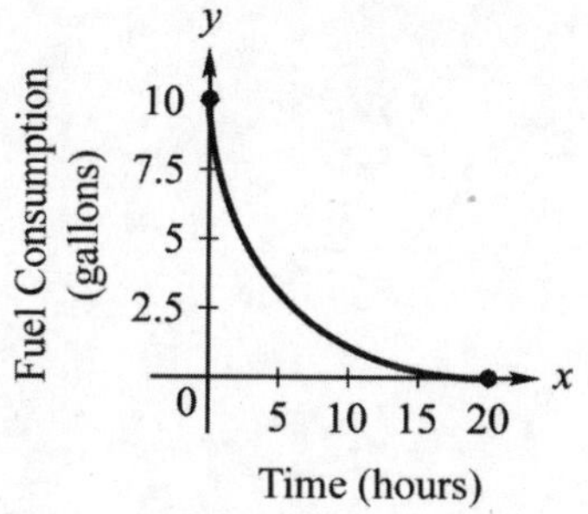

C.

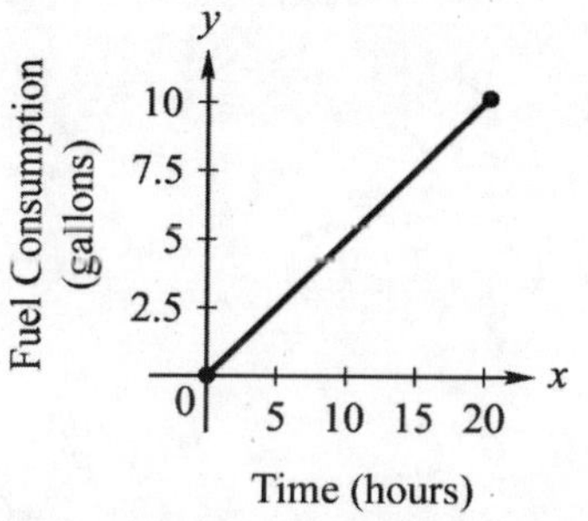

D.

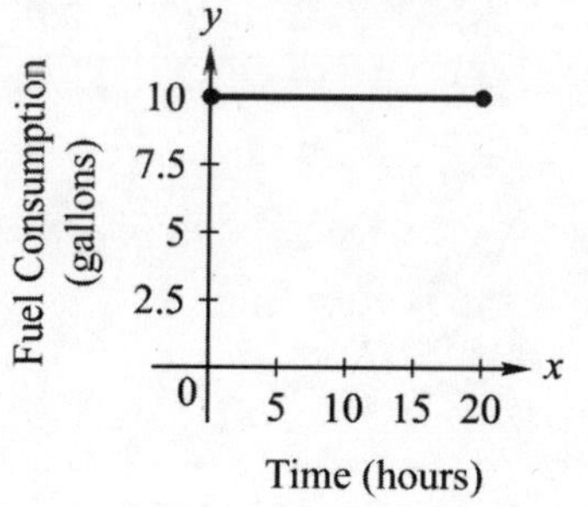

E.

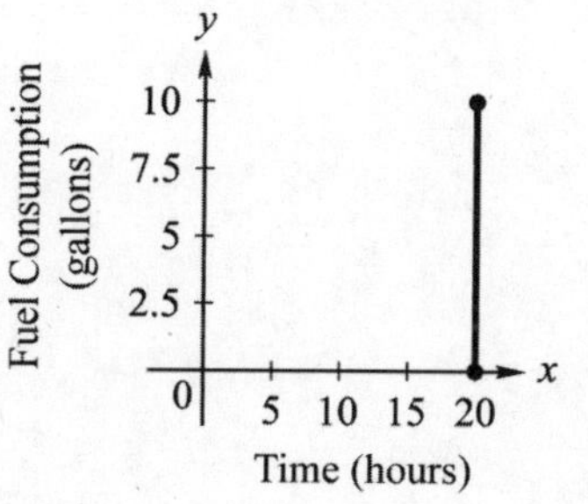

20. In the figure below, $\overline{PQ}$ is tangent to circle O at point S and $\overline{QR}$ is tangent to circle O at point T. If the radius of circle O is 2, what is the area of the shaded portion of the figure?

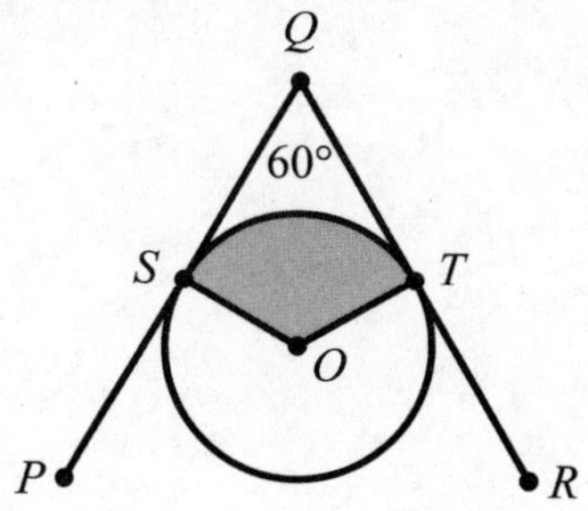

F. $\frac{\pi}{3}$

G. $\frac{2\pi}{3}$

H. π

J. $\frac{4\pi}{3}$

K. 2π

QUIZ

SAT MATH: MULTIPLE-CHOICE

This section contains a Math: Multiple-Choice quiz. Complete the quiz under timed conditions. Use any available space in the section for scratch work. Answers are on page 581.

(20 items; 25 minutes)

DIRECTIONS: Solve each item and choose the correct answer choice. Use any available space for scratchwork.

Notes:

(1) All expressions and equations represent real numbers unless otherwise indicated.

(2) Figures that accompany problems in this test are intended to provide information useful in solving the problems. They are drawn as accurately as possible EXCEPT when it is stated in a specific problem that the figure is not drawn to scale. All figures lie in a plane unless otherwise indicated.

(3) The domain of a given function f is the set of all real numbers x for which $f(x)$ is a real number unless otherwise indicated.

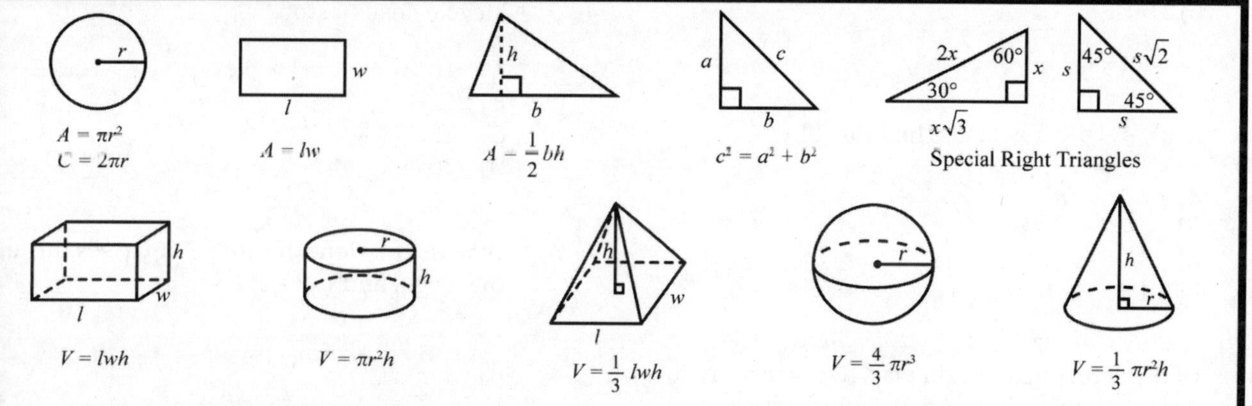

The number of degrees of arc in a circle is 360.
The sum of the measures in degrees of the angles of a triangle is 180.
The number of radians of arc in a circle is 2π.

1. Which of the following represents the solutions to the equation $3x^2-2x-10=0$?

A) $x=\frac{1}{3}$ and $x=10$
B) $x=-\frac{1}{3}$ and $x=10$
C) $x=\frac{1+\sqrt{31}}{3}$ and $x=\frac{1-\sqrt{31}}{3}$
D) $x=\frac{-1+\sqrt{31}}{3}$ and $x=\frac{-1-\sqrt{31}}{3}$

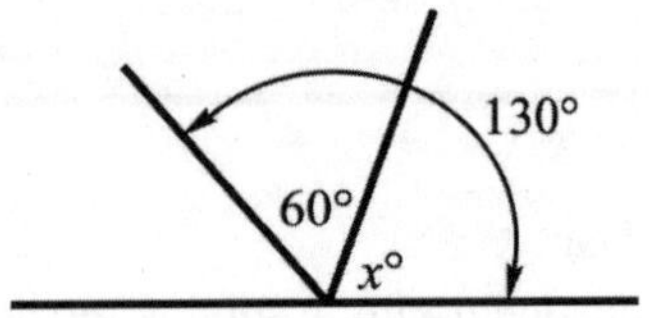

2. In the figure above, what is the value of x?

A) 70
B) 60
C) 50
D) 40

3. If $2^{x+1}=4^{x-1}$, what is the value of x?

A) 1
B) 2
C) 3
D) 4

4. Of the actors in a certain play, five actors are in Act I, 12 actors are in Act II, and 13 actors are in Act III. If 10 of the actors are in exactly two of the three acts and all of the other actors are in just one act, how many actors are in the play?

A) 17
B) 20
C) 24
D) 30

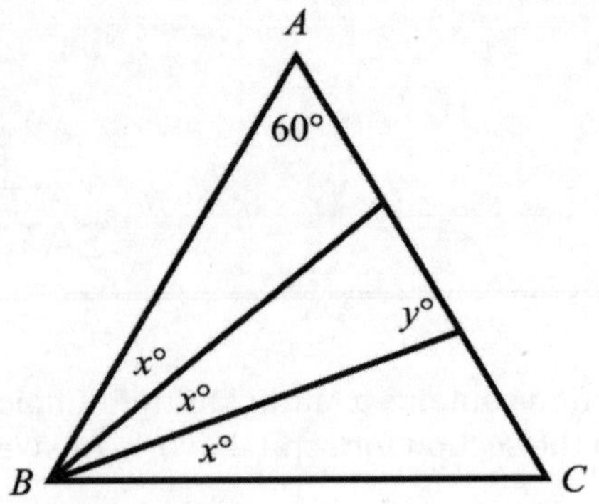

5. In the figure above, $\overline{AB}\cong\overline{BC}\cong\overline{CA}$. What is the value of y?

A) 20
B) 60
C) 80
D) 100

6. Under certain conditions, a bicycle traveling k meters per second requires $\frac{k^2}{20}+k$ meters to stop. If $k=10$, how many <u>meters</u> does the bicycle need to stop?

A) 10
B) 12
C) 15
D) 20

7. What is the slope of a line that passes through the origin and $(-3,-2)$?

A) $\frac{3}{2}$
B) $\frac{2}{3}$
C) 0
D) $-\frac{2}{3}$

8. An album contains x black-and-white photographs and y color photographs. If the album contains 24 photographs, then which of the following CANNOT be true?

A) $x=y$
B) $x=2y$
C) $x=3y$
D) $x=4y$

9. If $2a = 3b = 4c$, then what is the average (arithmetic mean) of a, b, and c, in terms of a?

A) $\frac{13a}{18}$
B) $\frac{13a}{9}$
C) $\frac{8a}{3}$
D) $\frac{4a}{3}$

10. If $x = 6 + y$ and $4x = 3 - 2y$, what is the value of x?

A) 4
B) $\frac{11}{3}$
C) $\frac{5}{2}$
D) $-\frac{2}{3}$

11. Johnny climbed to the top of a tree that is perpendicular to the ground. He looked down at his dog sitting on the ground. If the angle of depression from Johnny to his dog is 35° and the dog is sitting 25 feet from the base of the tree, approximately how tall, in feet, is the tree? ($\sin 35 \approx 0.57$, $\cos 35 \approx 0.82$, and $\tan 35 \approx 0.70$)

A) 14.25
B) 17.5
C) 20.5
D) 24.5

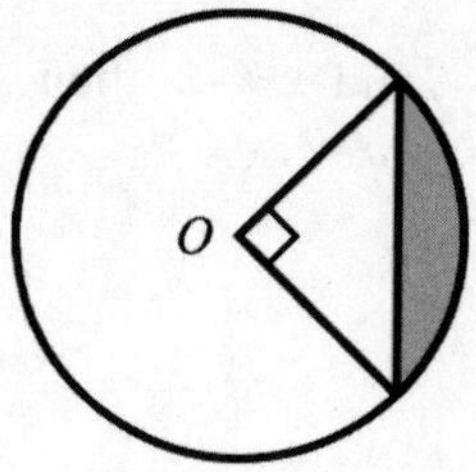

12. In the figure above, O is the center of the circle with radius 1. What is the area of the shaded region?

A) $\frac{3\pi}{4} + \frac{1}{2}$
B) $\frac{3\pi}{4} - \frac{1}{2}$
C) $\frac{\pi}{4} + \frac{1}{2}$
D) $\frac{\pi}{4} - \frac{1}{2}$

13. If $f(3) = 5$ and $f(7) = 7$, what is the slope of the graph of $f(x)$ in the coordinate plane?

A) -2
B) $-\frac{1}{2}$
C) 1
D) $\frac{1}{2}$

14. In right triangle ABC with right angle C, if $\overline{BA} = 17$ and $\overline{BC} = 8$, which of the following gives the measure of angle B?

A) $\sin^{-1}\left(\frac{8}{17}\right)$
B) $\sin^{-1}\left(\frac{17}{8}\right)$
C) $\sin^{-1}\left(\frac{15}{17}\right)$
D) $\sin^{-1}\left(\frac{17}{15}\right)$

15. If $\frac{x}{x+3}=\frac{3}{4}$, and $x \neq -3$, then $x=$

A) 3
B) 4
C) 5
D) 9

16. Which of the following is the complete solution set for $\sqrt{2x+3}+2=5$?

A) {}
B) {−1}
C) {3}
D) {−1, 3}

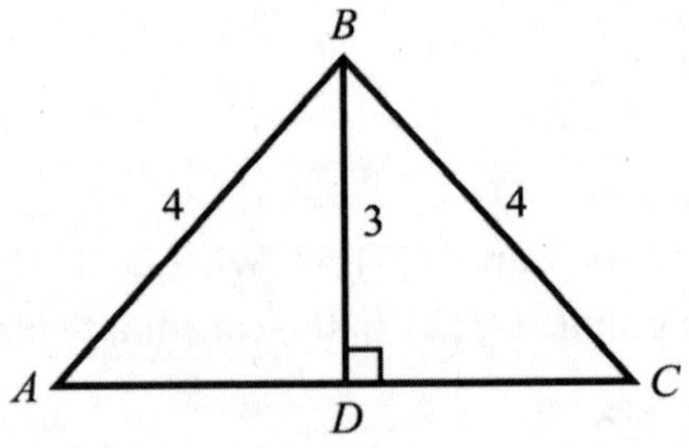

17. In the figure above, what is the length of $\overline{AC}$?

$\left(\sin\angle ABD=\frac{\sqrt{7}}{4}\right)$

A) 5
B) $2\sqrt{7}$
C) $4\sqrt{3}$
D) 7

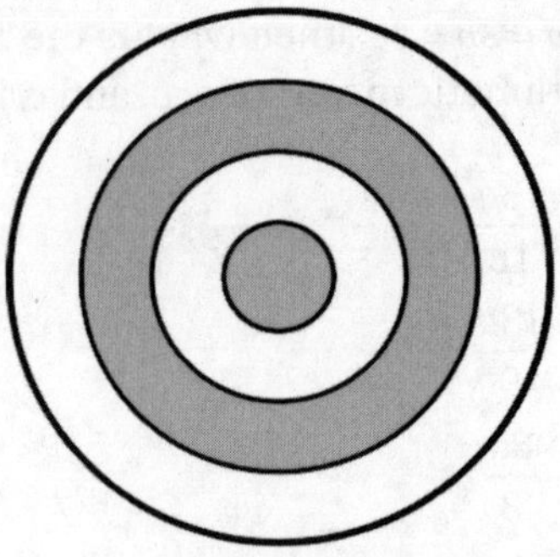

18. A dartboard has four concentric circles with the center as indicated in the figure above. If the diameter of each circle except for the smallest is twice that of the next smaller circle, what is the probability that a randomly thrown dart will strike the shaded portion of the figure?

A) $\frac{3}{16}$
B) $\frac{1}{4}$
C) $\frac{13}{64}$
D) $\frac{17}{64}$

19. If $f(3)=4$ and $f(-3)=1$, what is the y-intercept of the graph of $f(x)$ in the coordinate plane?

A) $-\frac{5}{2}$
B) $-\frac{2}{5}$
C) 0
D) $\frac{5}{2}$

Sales of Company *X* (in millions)

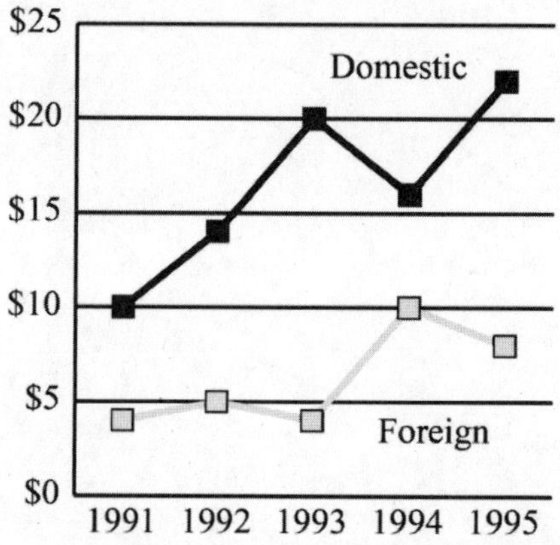

20. The above graph shows the data for domestic and foreign sales for Company *X* over five years. Which of the following pie graphs best represents the division of total sales between foreign and domestic sales for 2004?

A)

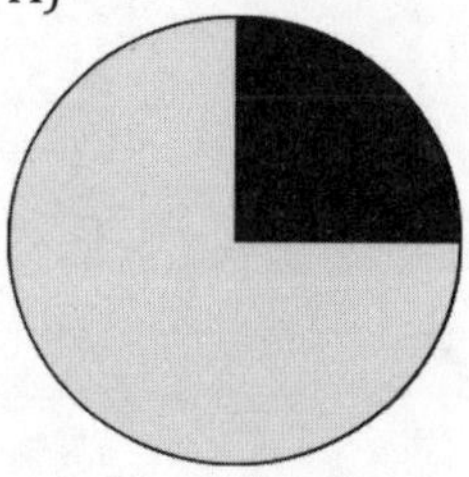

B)

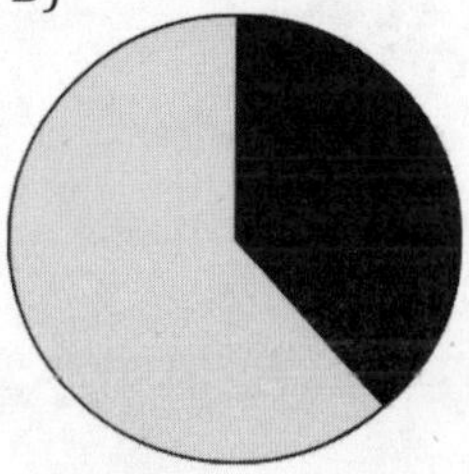

C)

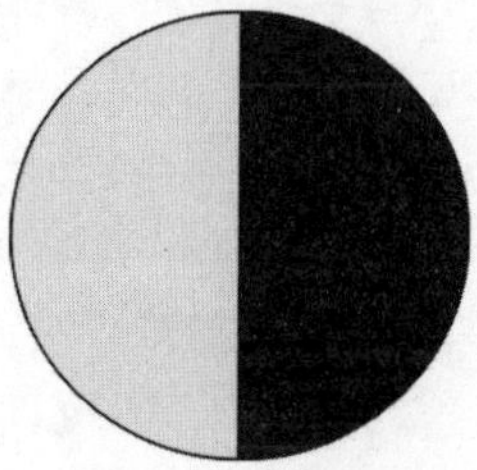

D)

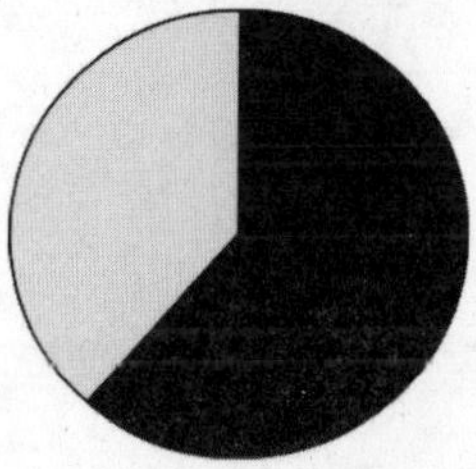

STRATEGY SUMMARY

ACT MATHEMATICS AND SAT MATH: MULTIPLE CHOICE

General Strategies

When approaching an ACT Mathematics or SAT Math: Multiple-Choice item, you should pay careful attention to several things:

Figures

Unless otherwise specifically noted, the figures included as illustrations are drawn to scale.

Answer Choices

Most answer choices are arranged in order of ascending or descending value and many incorrect answer choices correspond to conceptual errors.

"Signal" Words

"Signal" words such as thought-reversers (e.g., not, cannot, except) or specified units may be capitalized, underlined, or italicized. These words are critical to correctly understanding the item. Pay careful attention to thought-reversers, as they reverse the apparent meaning of an item.

Ladder of Difficulty

For each group of Multiple-Choice items in a Math test section, the difficulty level increases as the item number increases. Therefore, allot less time for earlier items. When solving items that are high on the ladder of difficulty, do NOT expect obvious answers or easy solutions. It is unlikely that answers corresponding to easy solutions or to numbers in the item stem will be the correct choice. Remember to pace yourself—difficult, time-consuming items have the same value as the easy items.

Preview Item Stems

Read the item stem first. Only then should you read the details of the item, keeping this item stem in mind.

Confirm Solutions

Double-check the solution by confirming that it answers the particular question that is being asked. When applicable, this confirmation includes verifying that the solution is given in the units specified by the item stem.

If you are unable to either find an elegant (quick) solution or solve the item directly based on subject knowledge, the following alternative solutions strategies can be extremely helpful:

1. **"Test-the-Test" Strategy:** The correct answer to any item is always one of five given choices. Sometimes, the easiest and quickest way to solve an item is to test each of the answer choices. The "test-the-test" strategy can mean plugging answer choices back into the item—starting with (C)—to test the validity of an expression, or it can mean checking each answer choice against any stated conditions. The "test-the-test" strategy is typically useful for items with numerical solutions or variables and values that meet stated conditions.

2. **"Plug-and-Chug" Strategy:** This strategy is similar to the "test-the-test" strategy because the item stem and answer choices (rather than direct mathematical solution strategies) are used to isolate the correct answer. The difference is that rather than testing the validity of each answer choice against the item stem conditions, the item stem and/or answer choices are evaluated by plugging in chosen numbers: "plug-and-chug." This strategy is especially helpful when solving Algebra items.

3. **"Eliminate-and-Guess" Strategy:** If unable to determine the correct answer directly by using mathematical methods or indirectly by using either the "test-the-test" or "plug-and-chug" strategy, eliminate as many answer choices as possible and then guess from the remaining answer choices. For difficult mathematics items, eliminate answer choices that can be reached either by a single step or by copying a number from the item.

Checklist of Skills and Concepts

Arithmetic

___ Simplifying: Fractions, Collecting Terms
___ Factoring
___ Approximation
___ The "Flying-X" Method
___ Decimal/Fraction Equivalents
___ Percents (Change, Original Amount, Price Increase)
___ Ratios (Two-Part, Three-Part, Weighted)
___ Proportions (Direct, Indirect)
___ Properties of Numbers (Odd, Even, Negative, Positive, Consecutive)
___ Scientific Notation
___ Sets (Union, Intersection, Elements)
___ Absolute Value
___ Matrices
___ Complex Numbers

Algebra

___ Basic Algebraic Manipulations
___ Evaluation of Expressions (Rational, Radical)
___ Exponents (Integer, Rational, Negative)
___ Factoring
___ Logarithmic Expressions and Equations
___ Sequences Involving Exponential Growth
___ Solving Single Variable Equations and Inequalities
___ Absolute Value
___ Function Math
___ Domain and Range
___ Solving Equations (Multi-Variable, Linear, Quadratic, Simultaneous, Rational, Radical)
___ Creating Algebraic Equations
___ Story Problems: Work (Joint Effort), Averages

Coordinate Geometry

___ Coordinate Plane
___ Slope of a Line
___ Slope-Intercept Form of a Linear Equation
___ Distance Formula
___ Graphing Linear Equations
___ Graphing First-Degree Inequalities
___ Graphing Quadratic Equations and Relations
___ Qualitative Behavior of Graphs of Functions
___ Transformations and Their Effects on Graphs of Functions

Geometry

__ Geometric Notation

__ Lines and Angles (Perpendicular, Parallel, Intersecting, Big Angle/Little Angle Theorem)

__ Triangles (Equilateral, Isosceles, Acute, Obtuse, Perimeter, Area, Altitudes, Angles, Bisectors, Pythagorean Theorem, 45°-45°-90° Triangles, 30°-60°-90° Triangles)

__ Quadrilaterals (Squares, Rectangles, Rhombuses, Parallelograms, Trapezoids, Perimeter, Area)

__ Polygons (Sum of Interior Angles)

__ Circles (Chords, Tangents, Radius, Diameter, Circumference, Area)

__ Properties of Tangent Lines

__ Solids (Cubes, Cylinders, Spheres, Volumes, Surface Areas)

__ Complex Figures

Data Interpretation

__ Graphs (Bar, Cumulative, Line)

__ Pie Charts

__ Tables

__ Scatterplots

Statistics

__ Averages (Simple, Weighted), Median, and Mode

__ Range

__ Standard Deviation

__ Quartiles and Interquartile Range

__ Drawing Inferences

__ Data Collection Methods

Probability

__ Arithmetic Probability

__ Geometric Probability

Trigonometry

__ Trigonometric Functions

__ Trigonometric Values

__ Trigonometric Relationships

__ Determining Values on the Unit Circle

__ Degrees and Radians

__ Arc Length

__ Graphs of Trigonometric Functions

SAT Math: Student-Produced Responses

Course Concept Outline

[1] Some concepts in this Course Concept Outline are not illustrated through examples in your student text but may be covered by your instructor in class. They are included here to provide a complete outline of your course.

LESSON | STUDENT-PRODUCED RESPONSES

SAT MATH: STUDENT-PRODUCED RESPONSES

The items in this section accompany the in-class review of the skills and concepts tested by the Student-Produced Responses part of the Math test sections. You will work through the items with your instructor in class. Answers are on page 582.

DIRECTIONS: Solve each item. Use any available space for scratchwork.

Notes:

(1) All expressions and equations represent real numbers unless otherwise indicated.

(2) Figures that accompany problems in this test are intended to provide information useful in solving the problems. They are drawn as accurately as possible EXCEPT when it is stated in a specific problem that the figure is not drawn to scale. All figures lie in a plane unless otherwise indicated.

(3) The domain of a given function f is the set of all real numbers x for which $f(x)$ is a real number unless otherwise indicated.

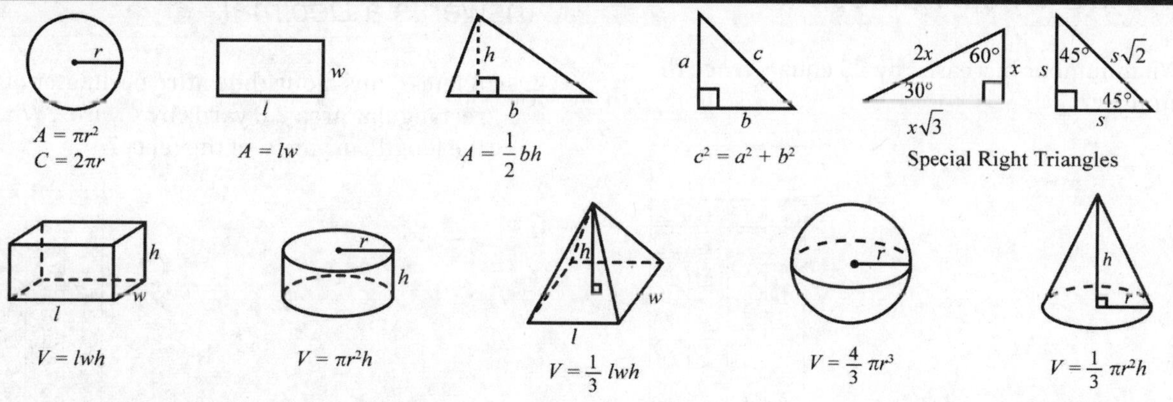

The number of degrees of arc in a circle is 360.
The sum of the measures in degrees of the angles of a triangle is 180.
The number of radians of arc in a circle is 2π.

Each item requires you to solve an item and mark your answer on a special answer grid. For each item, you should write your answer in the boxes at the top of each column and then fill in the ovals beneath each part of the answer you write. Here are some examples:

Answer: 7/2 or 3.5

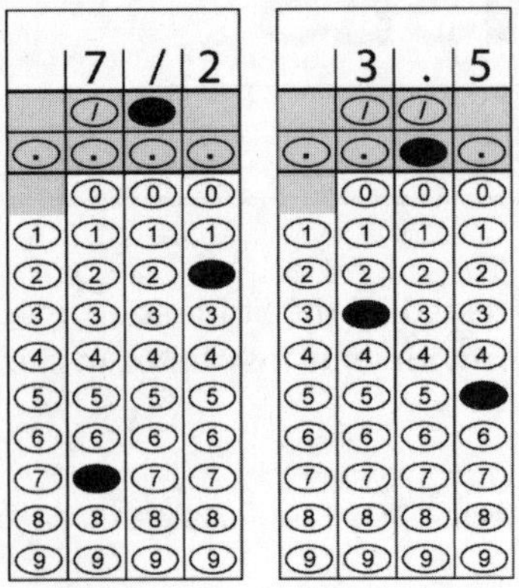

NOTE: A mixed number such as $3\frac{1}{2}$ must be gridded as 7/2 or as 3.5. If gridded as "31/2," it will be read as "thirty-one halves."

Answer: 325

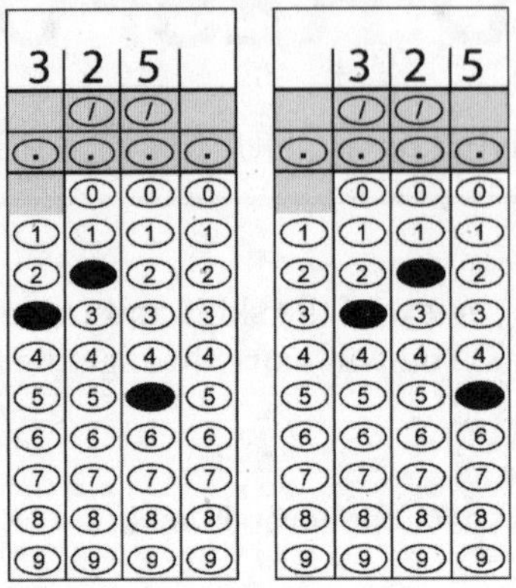

NOTE: Either position is correct.

Answer: 1/6, .166, or .167

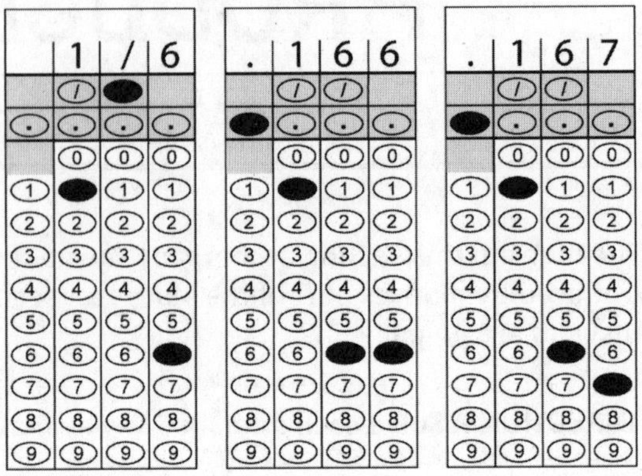

NOTE: A decimal answer with more digits than the grid can accommodate must be truncated. A decimal such as $0.16\overline{6}$ must be gridded as .166 or .167. A less accurate value such as .16 or .17 will be scored as incorrect.

Answer Is a Whole Number Ⓢ

1. What number increased by 25 equals twice the number?

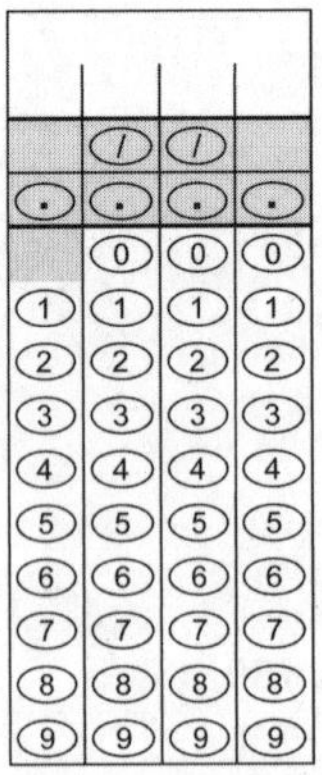

Answer Is a Decimal Ⓢ

2. A fence runs along the entire perimeter of a rectangular area 2.8 yards by 4 yards. What is the length, in yards, of the fence?

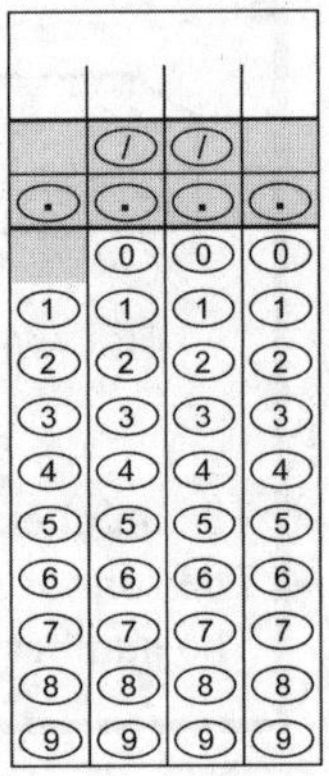

Answer Is a Fraction Ⓢ

3. At State College, one-fourth of the students are from abroad. Of those from abroad, one-eighth are from China. What fraction of the student body is from China?

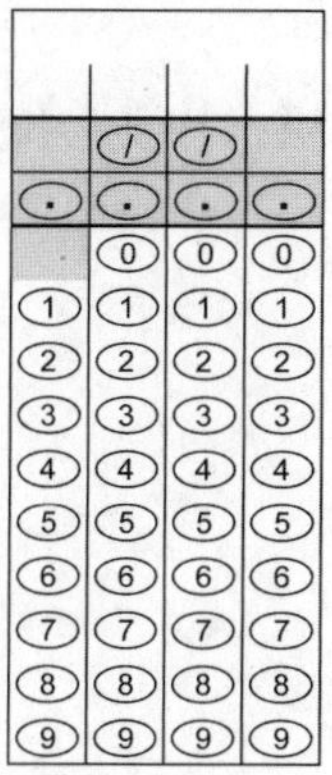

Math: Student-Produced Responses Items Illustrated Ⓢ

4. What is the value of $\frac{2}{3}-\frac{5}{8}$?

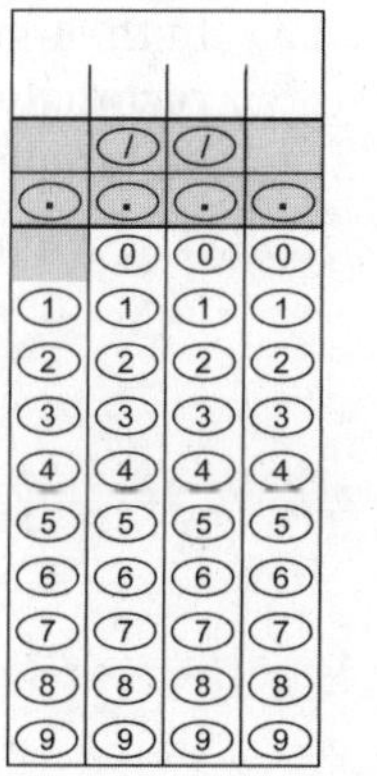

5. What is the value of $65(1)+65(2)+65(3)+65(4)$?

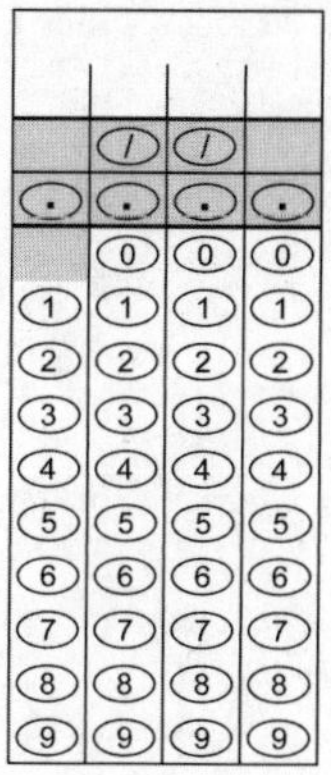

6. A jar contains 15 pennies and 25 nickels. Expressed in lowest terms, what fraction of the coins are pennies?

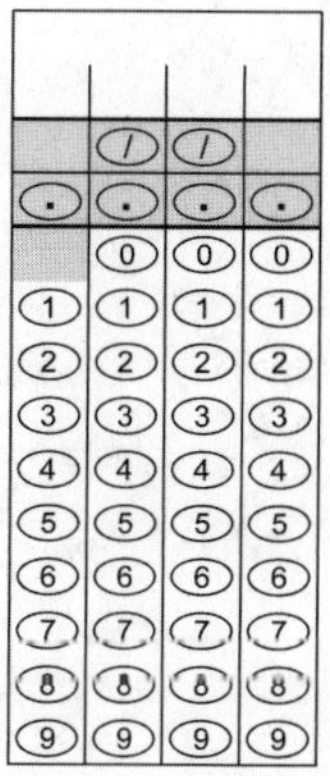

7. Matinee ticket prices are \$1.50 for children and \$3.50 for adults. Regular ticket prices are \$4.50 for children and \$6.50 for adults. If 3 adults and 1 child attend a matinee, what percentage of the regular price will they pay?

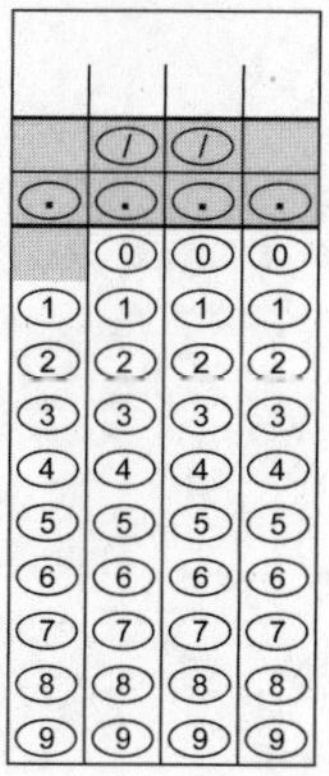

8. If the average of 8, 10, 15, 20, and x is 11, what is x?

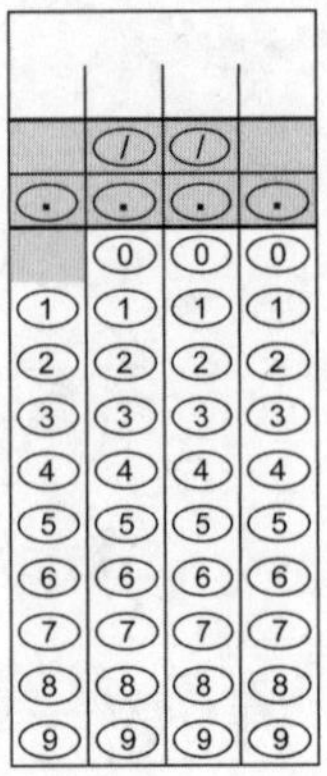

9. If $x = 14$, what is the value of $2x - (2 + x)$?

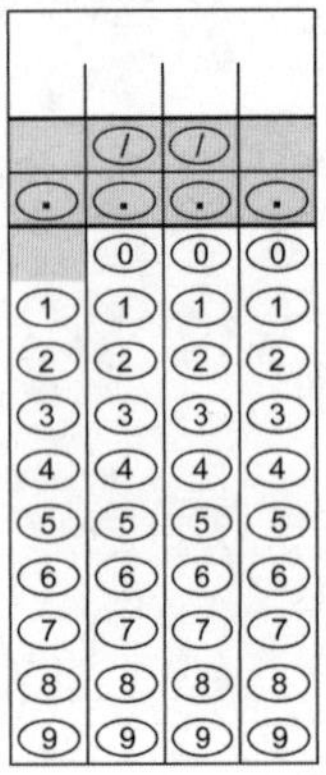

10. If $3x + y = 33$ and $x + y = 17$, then what is the value of x?

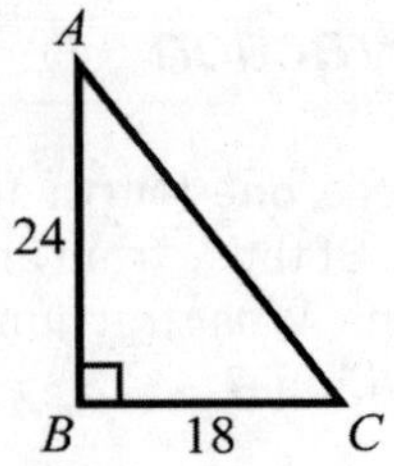

11. In the figure above, what is the length of $\overline{AC}$?

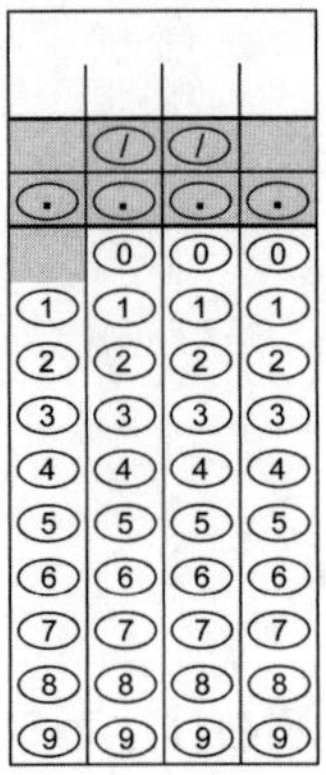

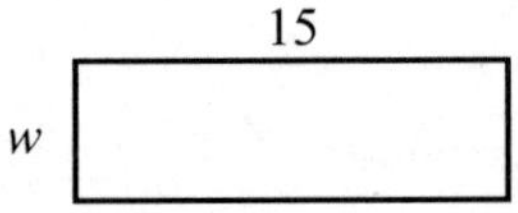

12. In the figure above, if the perimeter of the rectangle is 40, what is the area of the rectangle?

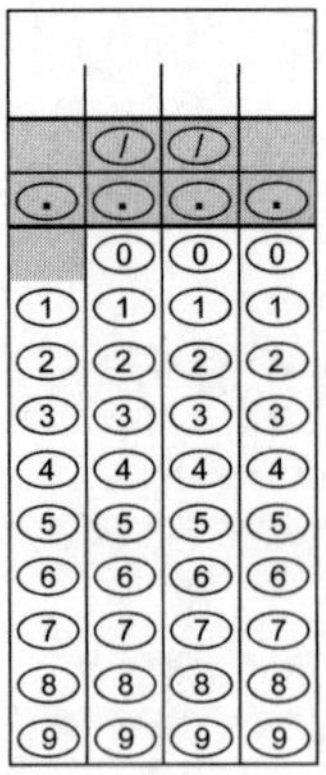

13. If a circle with radius 0.25 is inscribed in a square, what is the area of the square?

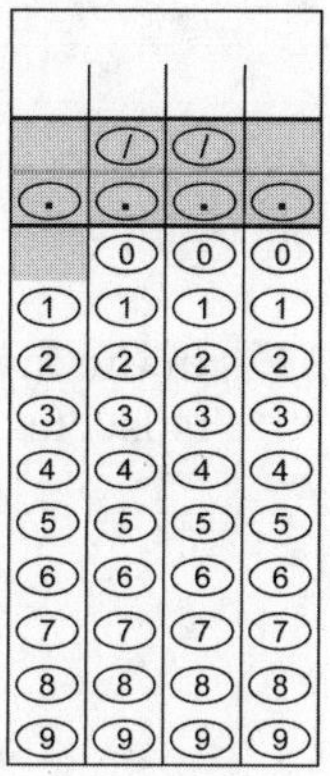

14. If the price of a book increases from \$10.00 to \$12.50, what is the percent increase in price?

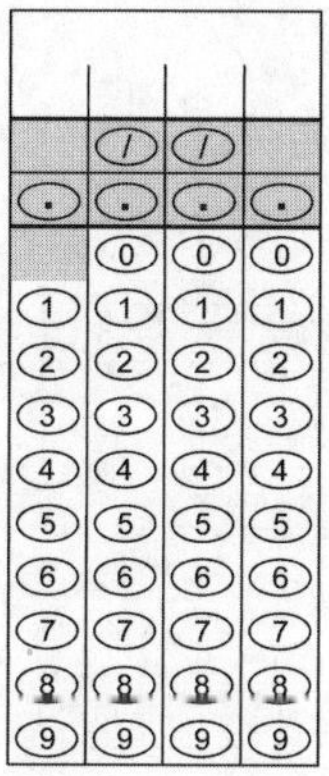

15. Boys and girls belong to the chess club. There are 36 people in the club, 15 of whom are girls. In lowest terms, what fraction of the club are boys?

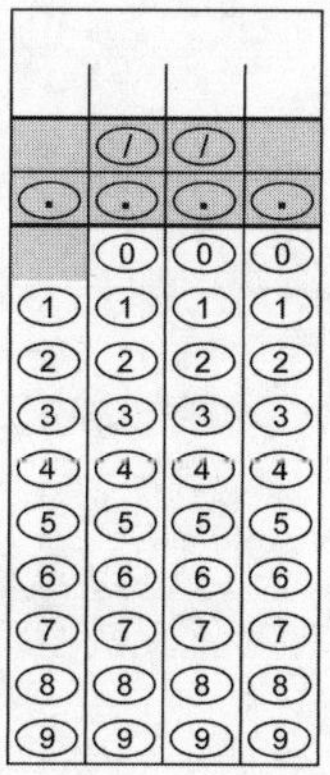

16. Jason built a fence around the perimeter of his rectangular garden. The width of the garden is 2.8 yards, and the length is twice the width. How many yards of fencing did Jason use?

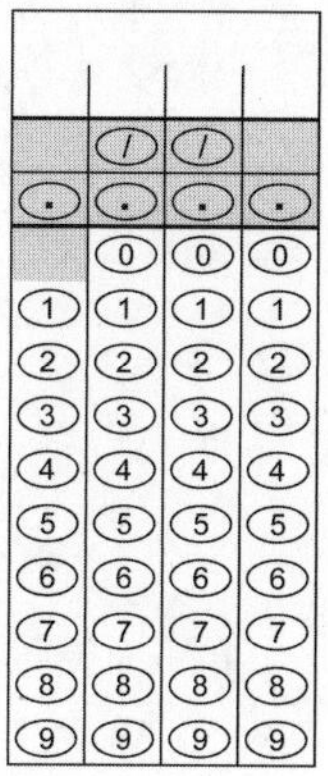

17. If $x = 9$, what is the value of $x^2 + 2x - 9$?

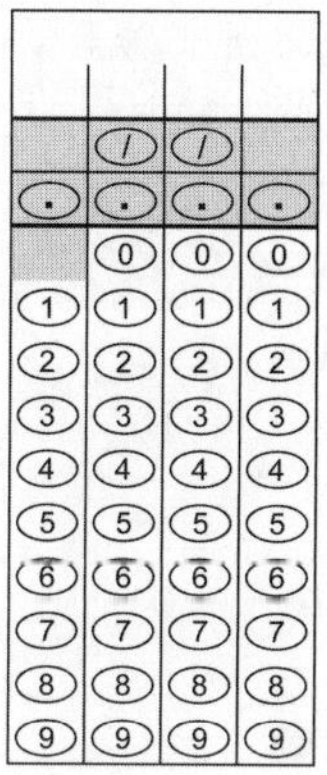

18. For all numbers, $x \blacktriangle y = 2xy$. What is $1.5 \blacktriangle 2.5$?

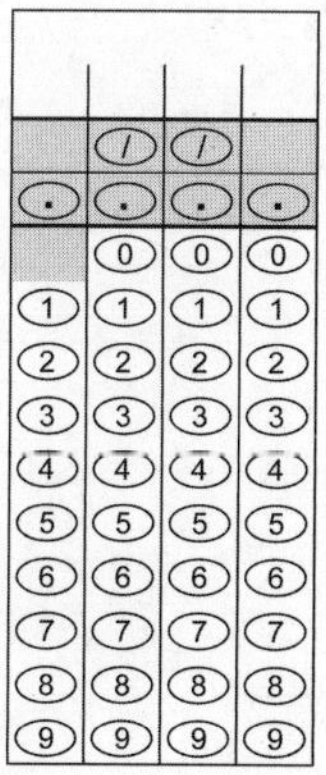

19. If $x = 3y - 1$ and $x + y = 15$, what is the value of x?

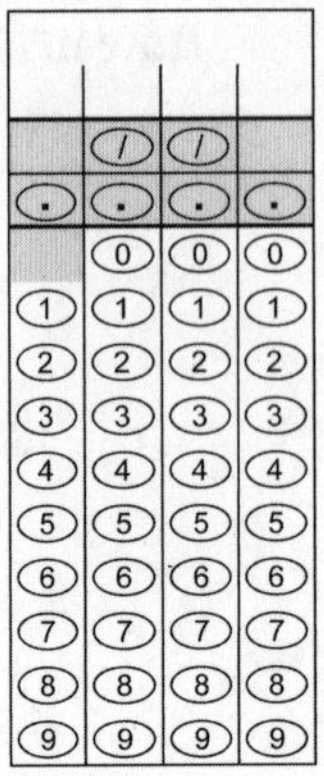

20. Jane and Hector have the same birthday. When Hector was 36, Jane was 30. How old was Jane when Hector was twice her age?

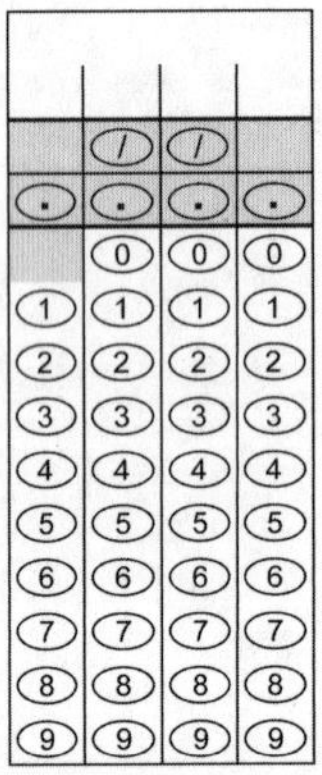

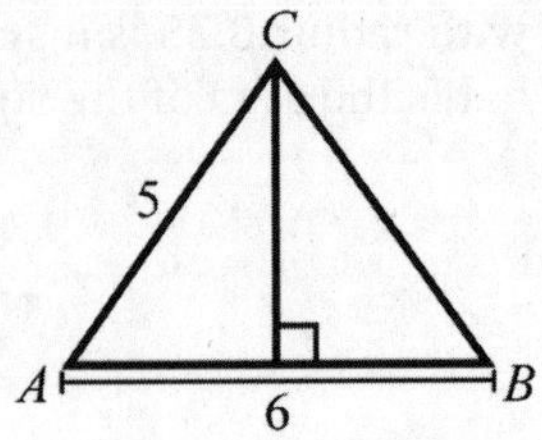

21. In the figure above, what is the area of isosceles ΔABC?

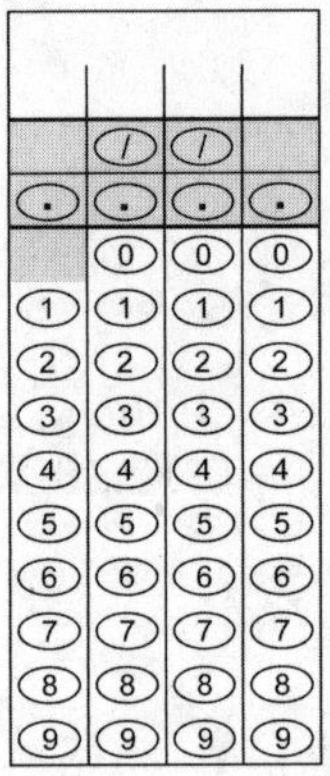

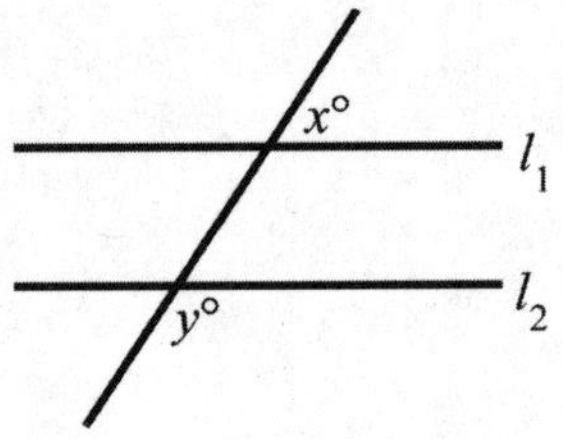

22. In the figure above, if l_1 and l_2 are parallel, what is $x + y$?

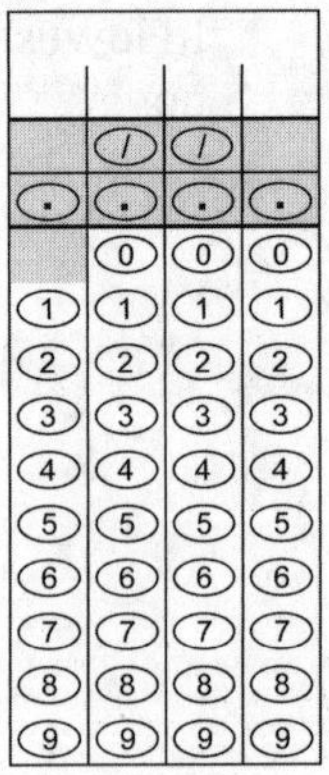

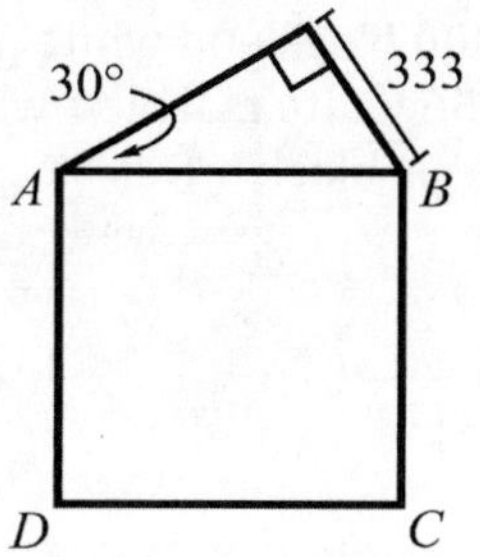

23. In the figure above, what is the perimeter of square *ABCD*?

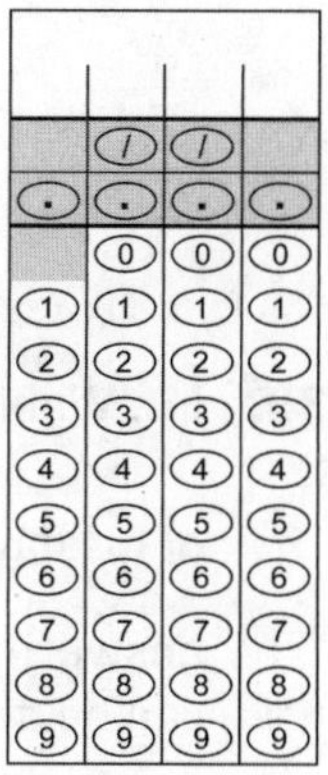

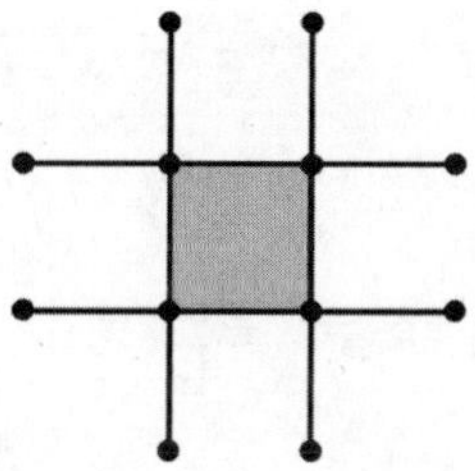

24. In the figure above, equally spaced points are joined by line segments that intersect each other at 90 degrees. If the total length of the four largest line segments in the figure is 24, what is the area of the shaded part?

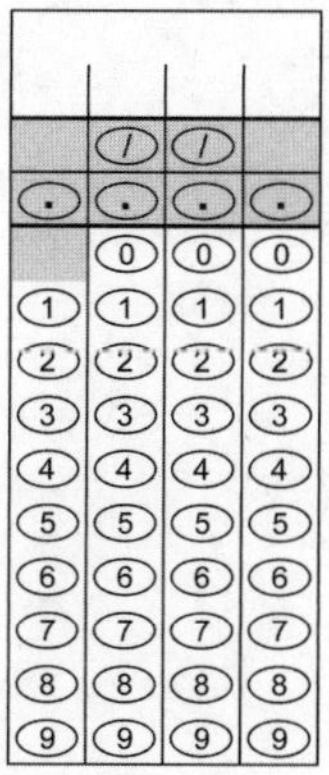

25. Su Li made \$45 working as a mother's helper. She spent $\frac{1}{5}$ of the money, deposited $\frac{1}{3}$ of the remainder in the bank, and kept the rest for expenses. What fraction of the original \$45 did she keep?

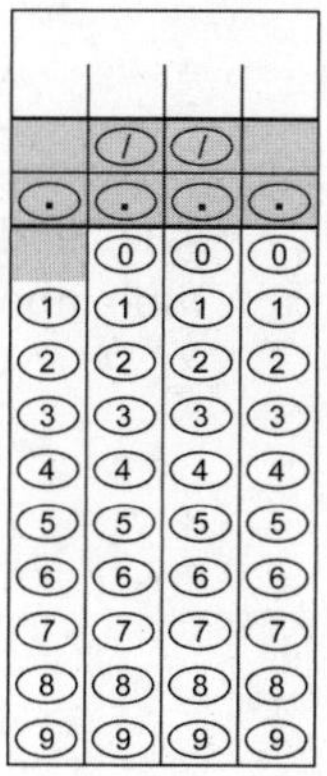

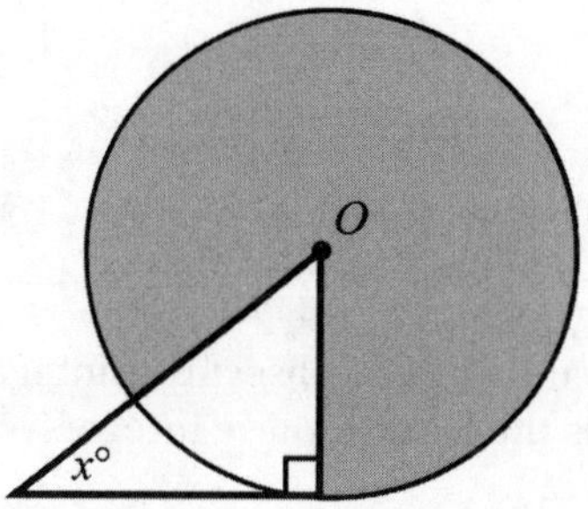

NOTE: Figure not drawn to scale.

26. In the figure above, the circle with center O has a radius of 6. If the area of the shaded region is 30π, what is the value of x?

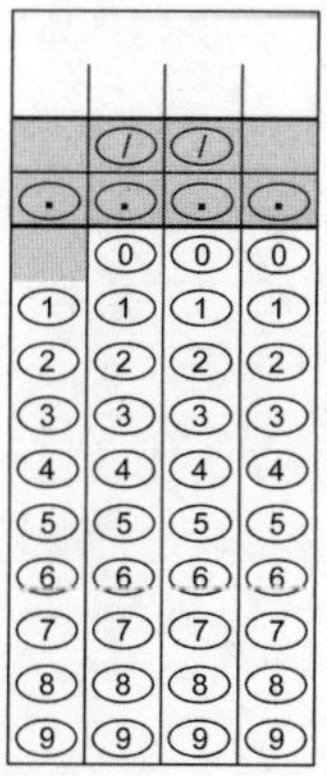

Day	Sales
Monday	$40
Tuesday	$60
Wednesday	$80
Thursday	$20
Friday	$50

27. What is the average (arithmetic mean) daily sales in dollars for the five days shown in the table above?

28. If the sum of two consecutive integers is 29, what is the least of these integers?

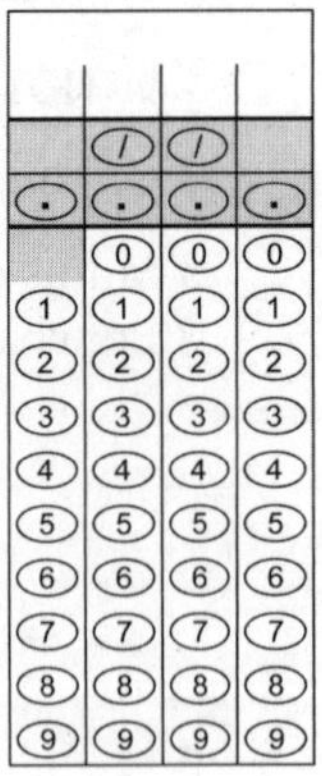

29. If a jar of 300 black and white marbles contains 156 white marbles, what percent of the marbles is black?

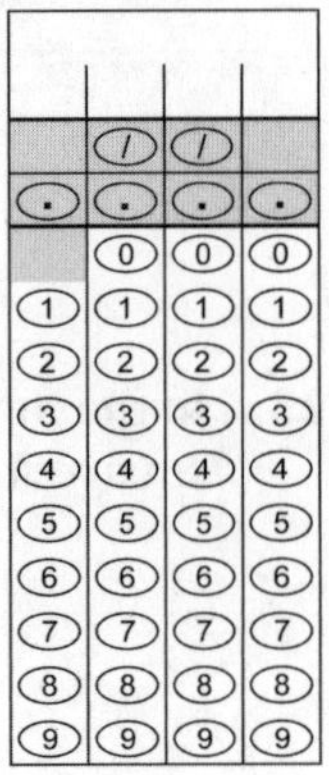

30. Mr. Wahl spends $\frac{1}{3}$ of his day in meetings, $\frac{1}{6}$ of his day on the phone, and $\frac{1}{8}$ of his day answering questions. What fraction of his day can be devoted to other things?

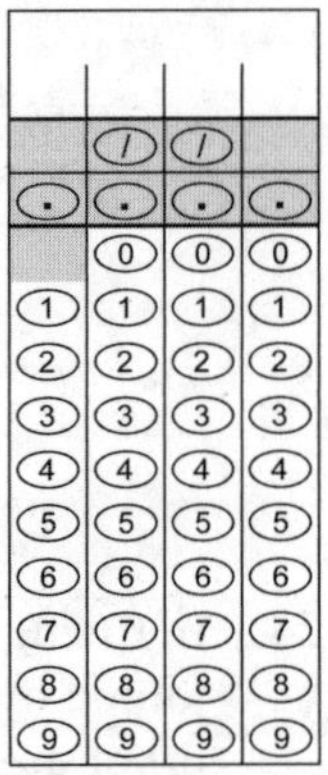

31. Line *l*, with a slope of $\frac{1}{2}$, passes through the points $\left(0, \frac{1}{4}\right)$ and $(2, y)$. What is the value of *y*?

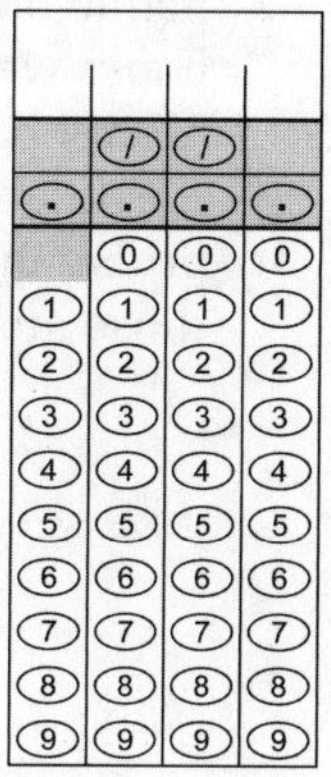

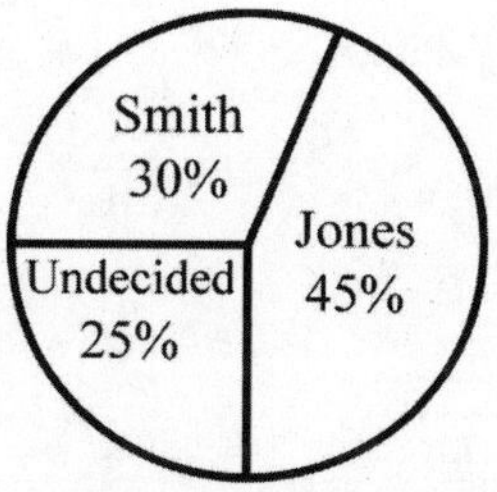

32. A total of 400 voters responded to the survey represented by the pie chart above. How many more respondents were in favor of Jones than Smith?

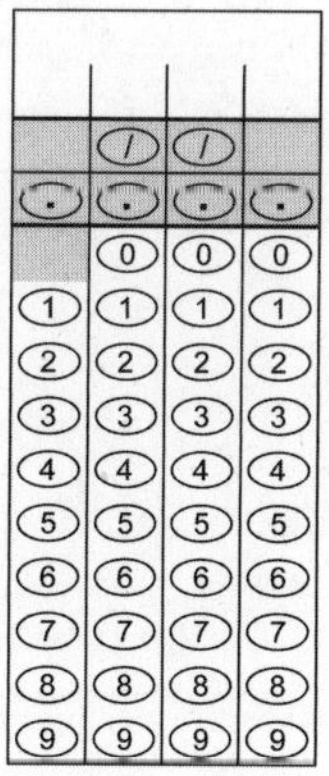

Paired Application Items Ⓢ

Questions #33–34 refer to the following information.

Travis is a part-time librarian at a branch of the public library. After a power surge damaged some of the library's computer files, Travis was given the task of recovering the data that survived. Surviving computer records show that the library has:

Paper-Bound Fiction	685 books
Cloth Bound Fiction	---
Total Fiction	930 books
Paper Bound Non-Fiction	---
Cloth Bound Non-Fiction	---
Total Non-Fiction	---
Paper Bound Other	---
Cloth Bound Other	250 books
Total Other	415 books
Total Paper Bound	1,987 books
Total Cloth Bound	---
Total All	3,220 books

33. Given this partial information, according to computer records, how many cloth-bound non-fiction books does the library have?

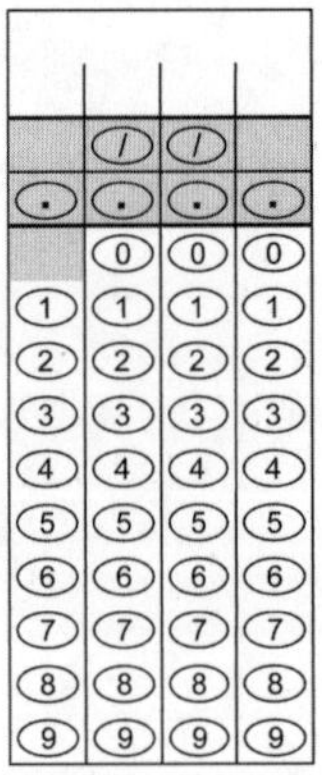

34. After reconstructing the computer records, Travis had a team of interns check the shelves and match each book listed in the database with the books physically in the library. When the survey was complete and books on loan were taken into account, 55 cloth-bound non-fiction books and 70 paper-bound non-fiction books were not in the library or on loan. If a library patron selects a non-fiction book from the database at random, what is the probability that the book chosen will be one of those missing books?

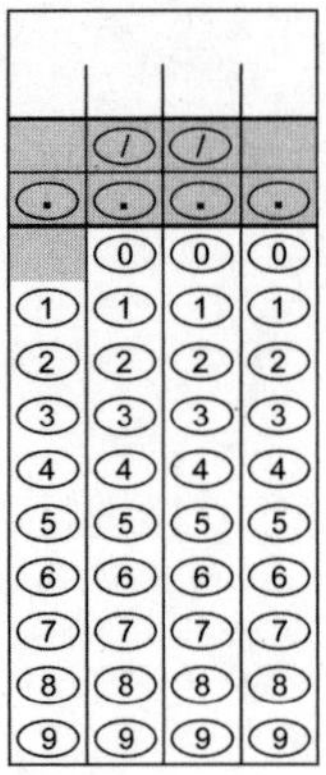

Questions #35–36 refer to the following information.

The 9th, 10th, and 11th graders at a high school took a survey that asked if they were involved in any afterschool clubs. The table below summarizes the data, but some of the cells are not filled in.

	Participate in an afterschool club	Do NOT participate in an afterschool club	TOTAL
9th Graders	785		1,030
10th Graders			
11th Graders		350	1,020
TOTAL	2,287		

35. According to this survey, 35% of the 10th graders do not participate in an afterschool club. How many 10th graders participated in the survey?

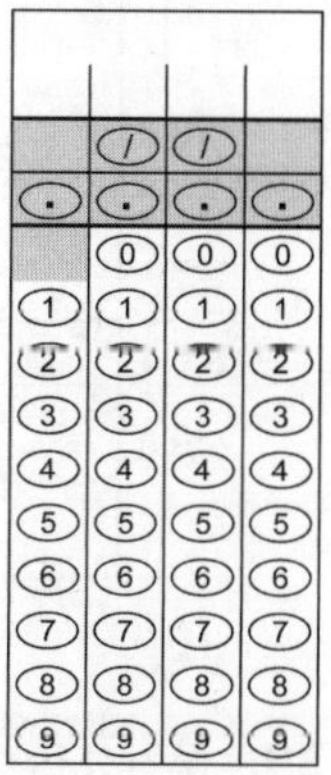

36. On the day of the survey, no 9th graders were absent. After the survey, a group of 240 transfer students enrolled in the school as 9th graders, due to a local private school closing. 85% of these students sign up for a club immediately. After this influx of students, what is the probability, represented as a decimal, that a 9th grader selected at random did not participate in any afterschool club, rounded to the nearest hundredth?

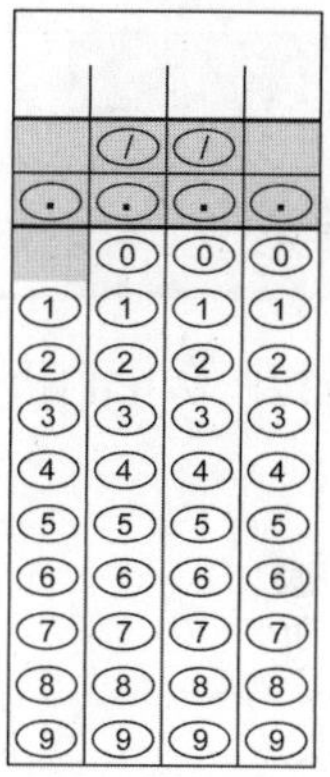

Questions #37–38 refer to the following information.

A statistics teacher gave his class a test that had a total of 20 points, with no partial credit. After the test, the teacher explained to the students that to calculate their percent score they need to divide the points they earned by 20 and then multiply the result by 100. He put a frequency table on the board to show the students how the class did:

Points Earned	7	14	15	16	17	18	19	20
# of Students	1	1	2	2	5	4	6	1

37. What is the median percent score on this test?

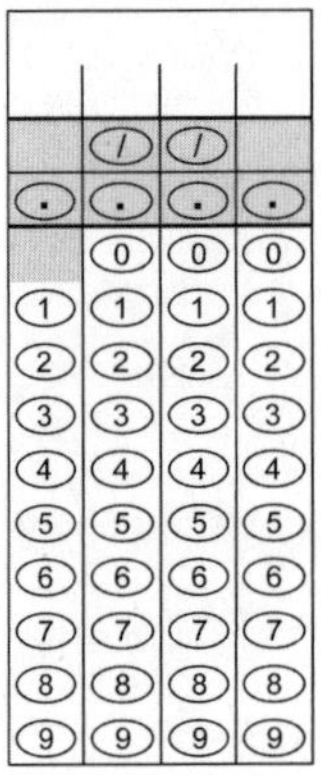

38. The teacher then explained how he curves a test grade. First, he finds the mean of the class grades. Then he finds the mean again after removing the highest and lowest grades. The difference between these means is added to every student's earned points (out of 20). What is the curved percent score for a student who originally earned 14 points, rounded to the nearest percent?

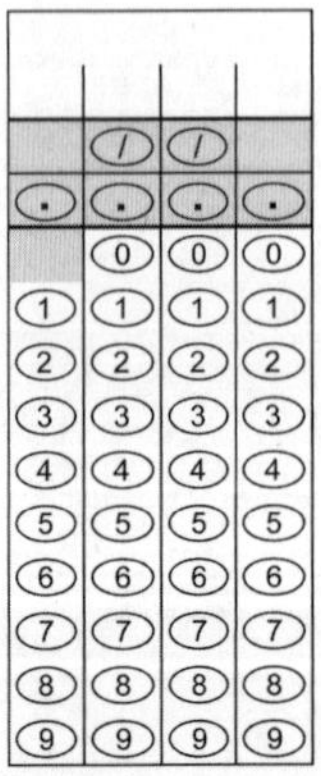

Questions #39–40 refer to the following information.

An architect is looking over the floor plans for a house she is designing. The diagram below shows a portion of the second floor. Bedroom 1 and Bedroom 2 are each to have an area that is $\frac{4}{5}$ the area of the master bedroom. All dimensions shown on the blueprint represent the actual dimensions to be built. The scale on the blueprint is $\frac{1}{4}$ inch = 1 foot.

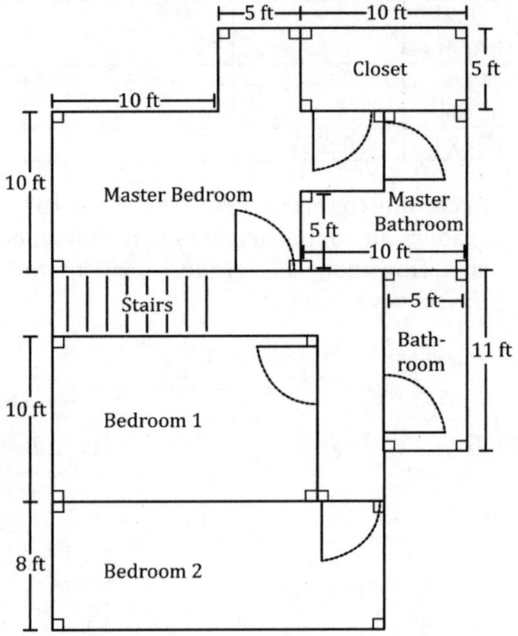

39. What is the perimeter of the master bedroom on the blueprint?

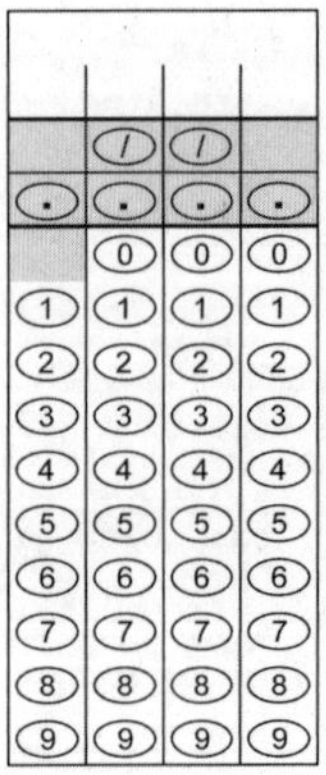

40. The family that is buying the house has one child who likes to hang up artwork in his room. He would like the bedroom with more wall space. What is the difference between the actual perimeters of Bedroom 1 and Bedroom 2, in feet?

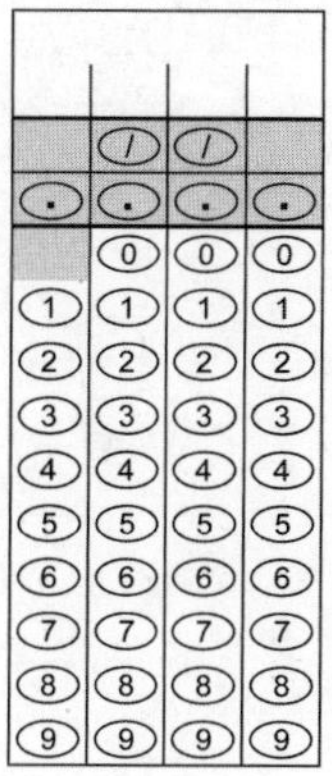

Questions #41–42 refer to the following information.

Paul and Linda are going shopping at a local department store during its annual 20% off sale. They each have a coupon for an additional 15% off one item. The state sales tax is 6%, which is added after discounts are taken off.

41. If Paul purchases a sweater that originally cost $56.99, what is the final amount he will have to pay, rounded to the nearest dollar, if he uses his coupon on the sweater?

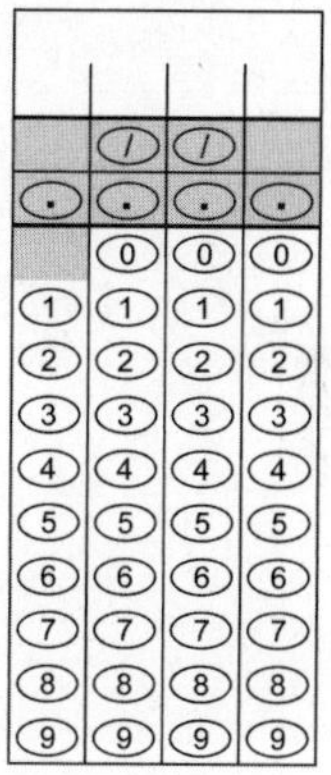

42. Linda purchases two pairs of jeans that originally cost the same amount of money per pair, and her final bill was $117.11. If she was allowed to use the coupon on one of the pairs of jeans, how much did each pair of jeans originally cost, rounded to the nearest dollar?

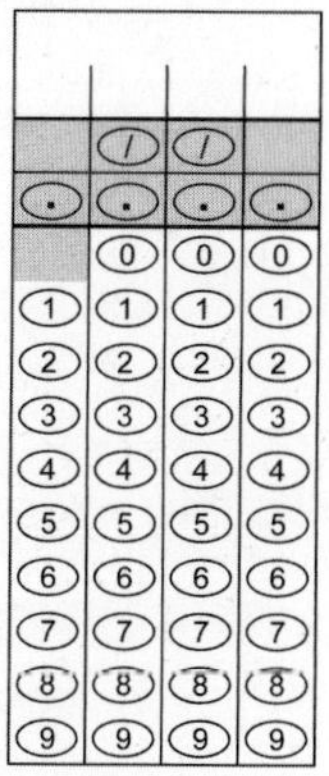

TEST MECHANICS

SAT MATH: STUDENT-PRODUCED RESPONSES

Overview

The SAT test includes two Math test sections that will be scored. One section does not allow calculator use and has 15 Multiple-Choice items and 5 Student-Produced Responses (SPR) items, with a time limit of 25 minutes. The other section allows calculator use and has 30 Multiple-Choice items and 8 SPR items, with a time limit of 55 minutes. The SPRs are NOT multiple-choice items. Instead, you need to arrive at a numerical solution to the problem and then enter your answer by coding it on the answer sheet. (This procedure will be described later in the Math: Student-Produced Responses Lesson.)

Like the Math: Multiple-Choice items, SPRs presuppose knowledge of algebra, problem solving, data analysis, geometry, and trigonometry. These are the conceptual building blocks of the Math test sections, whether the items are Math: Multiple-Choice items or SPRs. The multiple-choice items and SPRs fall into four categories: Heart of Algebra, Problem Solving and Data Analysis, Passport to Advanced Math, and Additional Topics.

In most ways, SPRs are really Multiple-Choice items that are simply stripped of the answer choices. The following example is the same item stem that appears in the Math: Multiple-Choice "Overview" feature, but as an SPR it lacks the four lettered answer choices.

Example:

How many integers in the set of integers from 1 to 144, inclusive, are NOT a square of an integer?

Of course, the numerical solution is the same as when the item is presented in multiple-choice format. Since 1 is the square of 1, and 144 is the square of 12, there are a total of 12 integers in the set of integers from 1 to 144, inclusive, that are a square of an integer (1^2, 2^2, 3^2, 4^2, 5^2, 6^2, 7^2, 8^2, 9^2, 10^2, 11^2, 12^2). Therefore, there are a total of $144-12=132$ integers in the set that are NOT a square of an integer. But in this case, you must code the number "132" on the answer grid according to procedures that will be discussed later in the Math: Student-Produced Responses lesson.

Anatomy

DIRECTIONS: Solve each item. Use any available space for scratchwork.

Notes:

(1) All expressions and equations represent real numbers unless otherwise indicated.

(2) Figures that accompany problems in this test are intended to provide information useful in solving the problems. They are drawn as accurately as possible EXCEPT when it is stated in a specific problem that the figure is not drawn to scale. All figures lie in a plane unless otherwise indicated.

(3) The domain of a given function f is the set of all real numbers x for which $f(x)$ is a real number unless otherwise indicated.

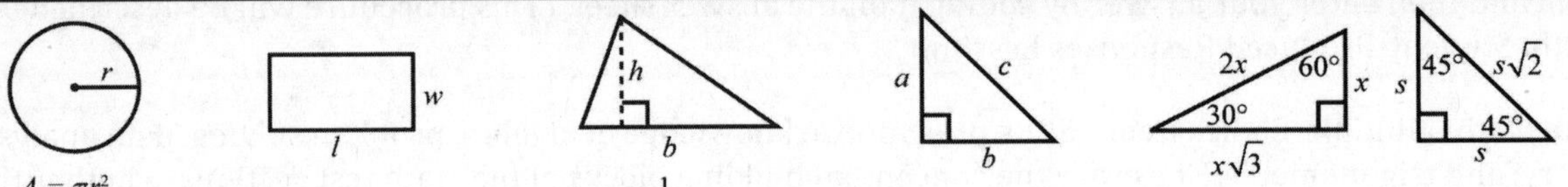

$A = \pi r^2$ $C = 2\pi r$ $A = lw$ $A = \frac{1}{2}bh$ $c^2 = a^2 + b^2$ Special Right Triangles

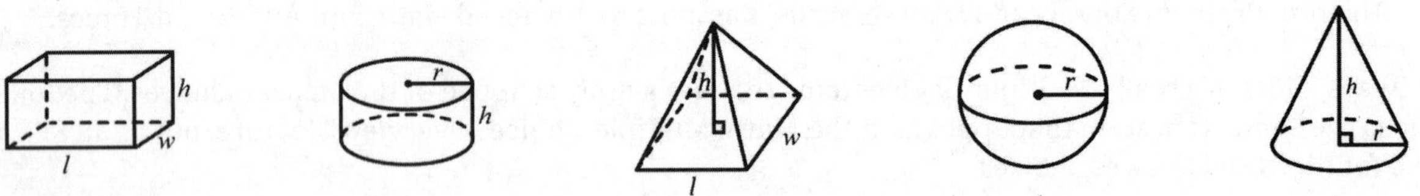

$V = lwh$ $V = \pi r^2 h$ $V = \frac{1}{3}lwh$ $V = \frac{4}{3}\pi r^3$ $V = \frac{1}{3}\pi r^2 h$

The number of degrees of arc in a circle is 360.

The sum of the measures in degrees of the angles of a triangle is 180.

The number of radians of arc in a circle is 2π.

Each item requires you to solve an item and mark your answer on a special answer grid. For each item, you should write your answer in the boxes at the top of each column and then fill in the ovals beneath each part of the answer you write. Here are some examples:

Answer: 7/2 or 3.5

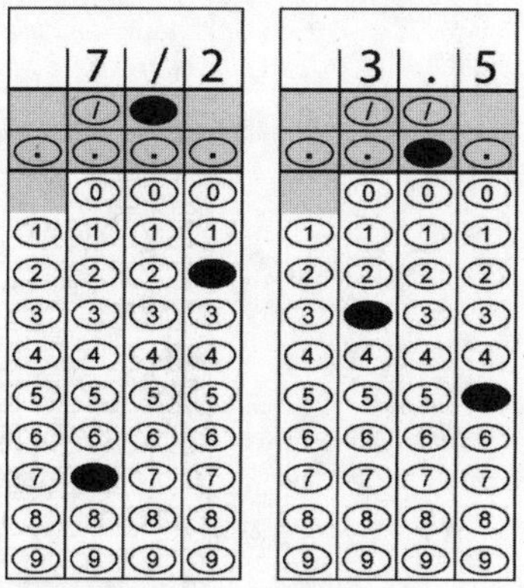

NOTE: A mixed number such as $3\frac{1}{2}$ must be gridded as 7/2 or as 3.5. If gridded as "31/2," it will be read as "thirty-one halves."

Answer: 325

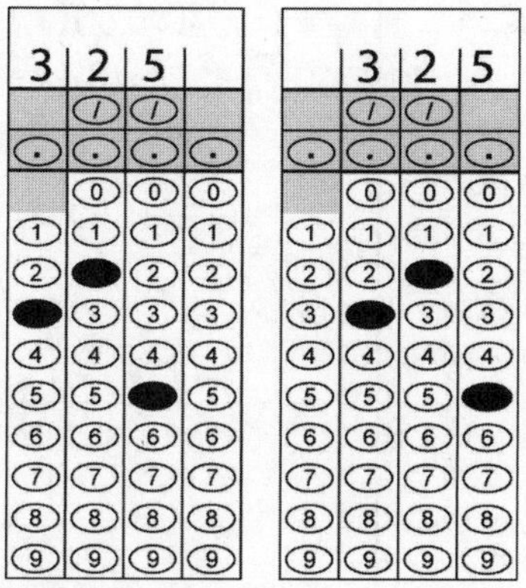

NOTE: Either position is correct.

Answer: 1/6, .166, or .167

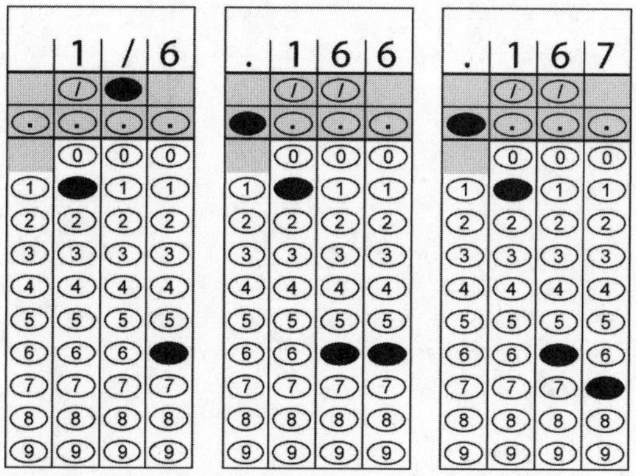

NOTE: A decimal answer with more digits than the grid can accommodate must be truncated. A decimal such as $0.16\overline{6}$ must be gridded as .166 or .167. A less accurate value such as .16 or .17 will be scored as incorrect.

1. An hour-long class included 40 minutes of instruction. What fraction of the hour-long class was NOT instructional?

1. *This is an arithmetic item with the thought-reverser "NOT." If 40 minutes of the 60 minutes were devoted to instruction, then 20 minutes were not instructional. Therefore, the fraction of the hour-long class that was NOT instructional is:* $\frac{20}{60}=\frac{1}{3}$.

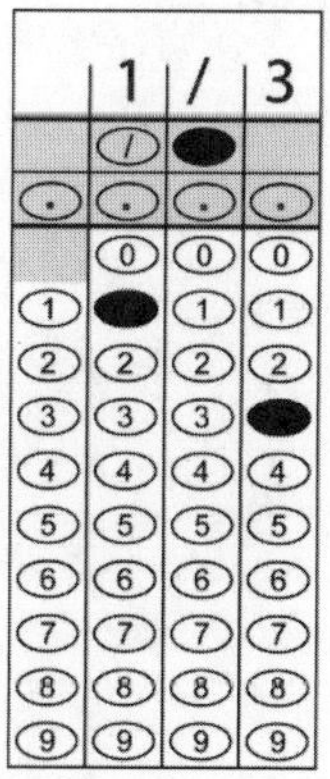

2. If $2(x-y)(x+y)=24$ and $x-y=3$, then what is the value of $x+y$?

2. *This is an algebra item with variables, but the answer will still be a number. Since* $x-y=3$, *substitute 3 for* $x-y$ *in the given expression and solve for* $x+y$:

$$2(x-y)(x+y)=24$$
$$2(3)(x+y)=24$$
$$x+y=4$$

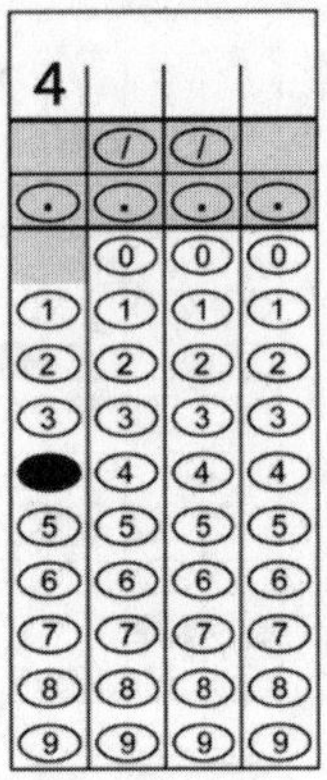

3. In a rectangular coordinate system, the center of a circle has coordinates $(3,4)$, and the circle touches the *x*-axis at only one point. What is the radius of the circle?

3. *This item tests coordinate geometry. Since the center has coordinates* $(3,4)$ *and rests on the x-axis, we have:*

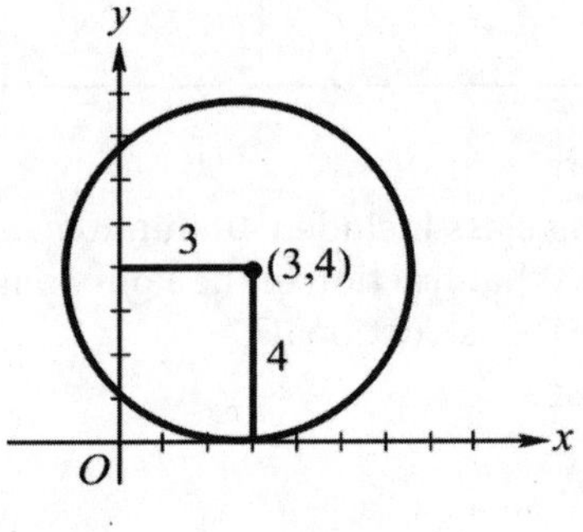

Therefore, $r=4$.

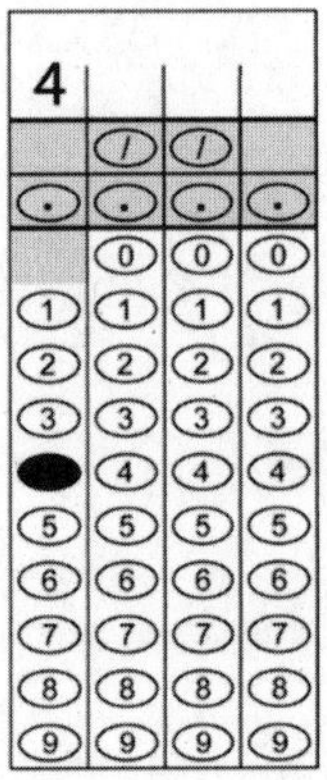

Questions #4–5 refer to the following information.

While traveling on business, Emeralda used the hotel business center's internet connection to stay in contact with her office. The hotel's fee for allowing guests to use the business center is determined by the amount of data used and an equipment usage fee. During her stay, the hotel charged her \$0.015 per megabyte used, rounded to the nearest whole number, and an equipment usage fee equal to 6% of the amount charged for data.

4. If the hotel posted a charge for business center use to Emeralda's room in the amount of \$19.08 for one 24-hour period, then the hotel billed her for how many megabytes of data?

5. The hotel gives guests the option of paying for business center use on the plan described above or of purchasing unlimited usage for a 24-hour period at a flat cost of \$25, which includes equipment usage. What is the least number of megabytes of data, rounded to the nearest whole number, a guest would need to use for the flat rate to be cheaper than paying for the data under the plan above?

4. *Set up an equation to represent the charges and solve:* $19.08 = 1.06(0.015x) \Rightarrow$ $18 = 0.015x \Rightarrow 1{,}200 = x$.

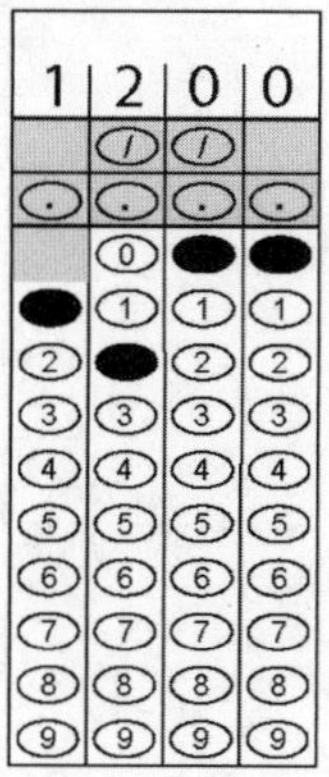

5. *Set up an inequality and solve:* $25 < 1.06(0.015x) \Rightarrow 1{,}572.3 < x$. *Since x must be greater than 1,572.3, the least number of megabytes a guest would need to use for the flat rate to be cheaper is 1,573.*

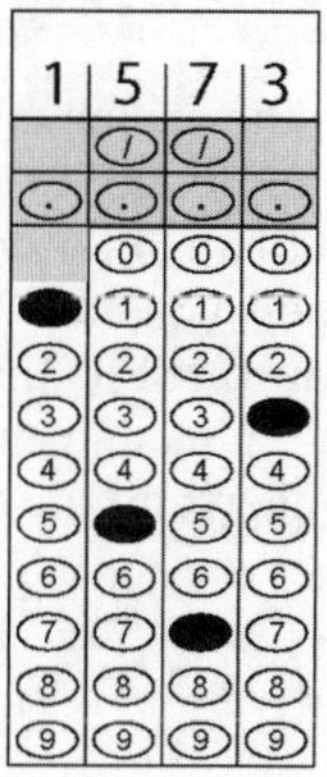

Pacing

When you think about pacing for the SPRs, you have to do so in the context of the Math test sections as a whole.

MATH TEST CALCULATOR SECTION (38 items, 55 minutes)			
Type of Item	**Item Number**	**Time to Spend per Item**	**Remaining Time**
Multiple-Choice	1–14	60 seconds	41 minutes
	15–26	90 seconds	23 minutes
	27–30	105 seconds	16 minutes
Student-Produced Responses	31–38	120 seconds	0 minutes

MATH TEST NO-CALCULATOR SECTION (20 items, 25 minutes)			
Type of Item	**Item Number**	**Time to Spend per Item**	**Remaining Time**
Multiple-Choice	1–15	60 seconds	10 minutes
Student-Produced Responses	16–20	120 seconds	0 minutes

As the pacing tables show, you'll spend more time on SPRs than on the Multiple-Choice items. This is because it takes longer to code in the answer to an SPR item than it does to code in the one circle for a Multiple-Choice item. With an SPR item, you need to write down your answer, making sure to include a decimal or a slash if required. Then, you have to code the whole sequence of numbers and symbols. A second reason that you will spend more time on SPRs than on Multiple-Choice items is that you will not be able to use some of the quicker strategies like the "plug and chug" method. You will have to work from the start instead of taking a shortcut. So, it takes a little longer, and the times suggested in the chart take that into account.

Time Trial

(6 Items; 7 minutes)

DIRECTIONS: Solve each item. Use any available space for scratchwork.

Notes:

(1) All expressions and equations represent real numbers unless otherwise indicated.

(2) Figures that accompany problems in this test are intended to provide information useful in solving the problems. They are drawn as accurately as possible EXCEPT when it is stated in a specific problem that the figure is not drawn to scale. All figures lie in a plane unless otherwise indicated.

(3) The domain of a given function f is the set of all real numbers x for which $f(x)$ is a real number unless otherwise indicated.

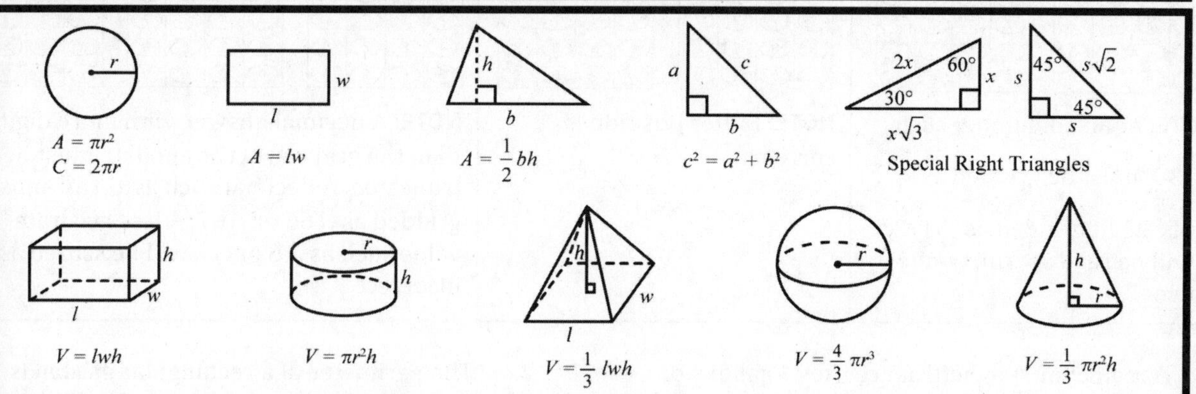

The number of degrees of arc in a circle is 360.
The sum of the measures in degrees of the angles of a triangle is 180.
The number of radians of arc in a circle is 2π.

Each item requires you to solve an item and mark your answer on a special answer grid. For each item, you should write your answer in the boxes at the top of each column and then fill in the ovals beneath each part of the answer you write. Here are some examples:

Answer: 7/2 or 3.5

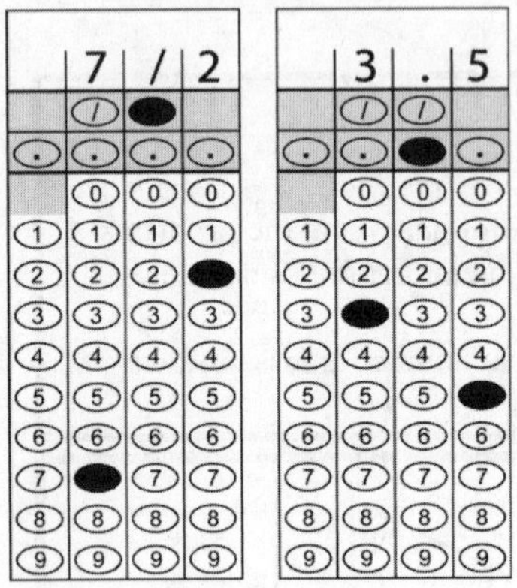

NOTE: A mixed number such as $3\frac{1}{2}$ must be gridded as 7/2 or as 3.5. If gridded as "31/2," it will be read as "thirty-one halves."

Answer: 325

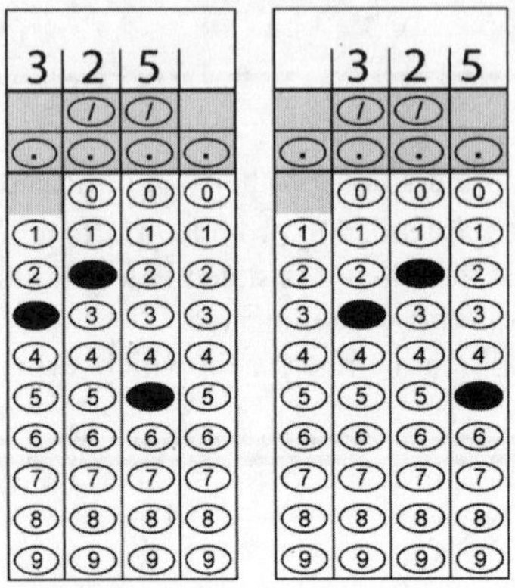

NOTE: Either position is correct.

Answer: 1/6, .166, or .167

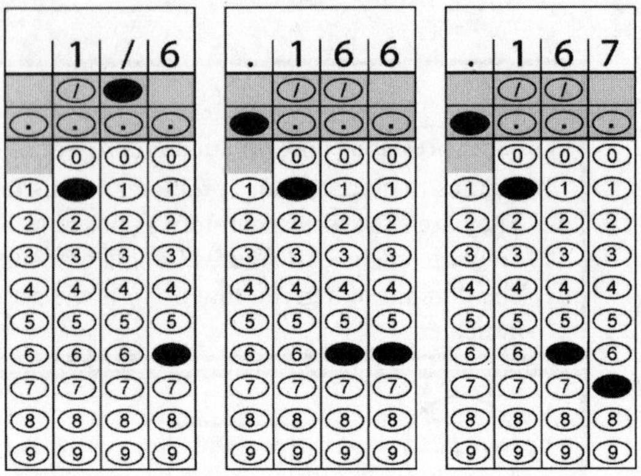

NOTE: A decimal answer with more digits than the grid can accommodate must be truncated. A decimal such as $0.16\overline{6}$ must be gridded as .166 or .167. A less accurate value such as .16 or .17 will be scored as incorrect.

1. A recipe for spaghetti sauce uses 4 gallons of tomatoes to make 32 servings. At this rate, how many gallons of tomatoes are needed to make 144 servings of spaghetti sauce?

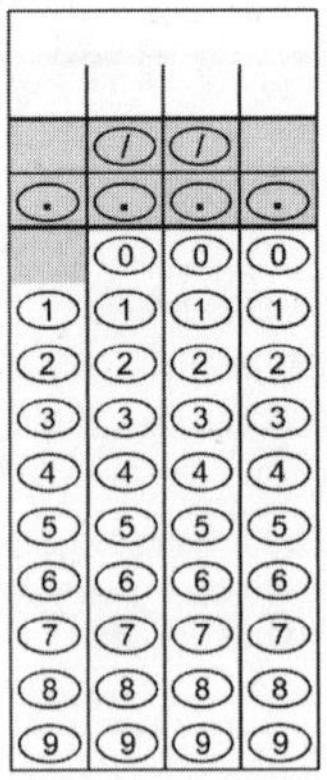

2. The perimeter of a rectangular garden is 280 feet. If the length of one side of the garden is 60 feet, what is the area of the garden, in square feet?

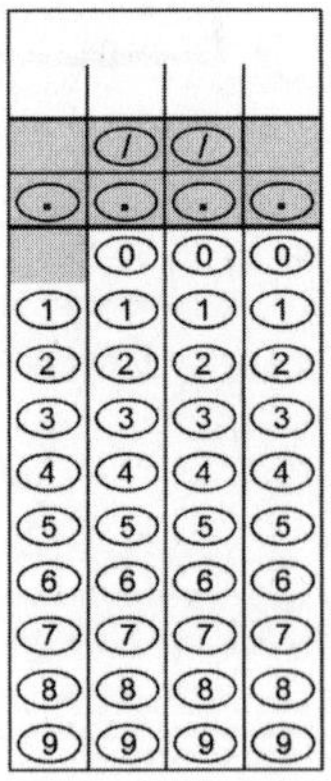

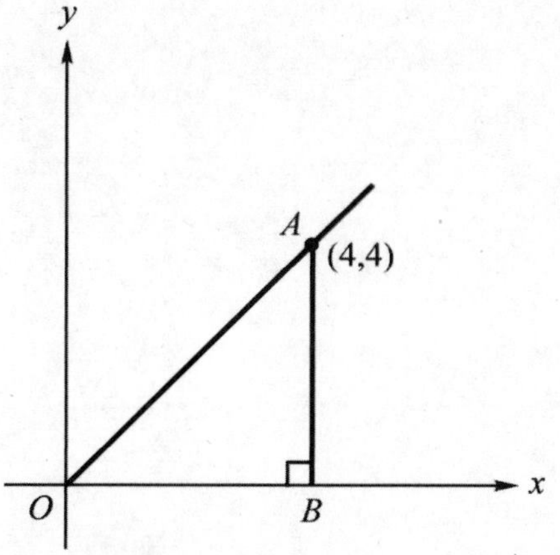

3. Line l (not shown) passes through O and intersects $\overline{AB}$ between A and B at point (x, y). If y is an integer, what is one possible value of the slope of line l?

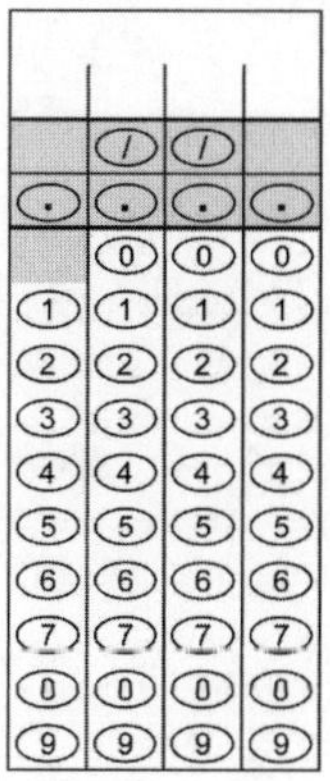

4. If $f(x) = x^2 + 32$, what is the positive number n such that $2[f(n)] = f(2n)$?

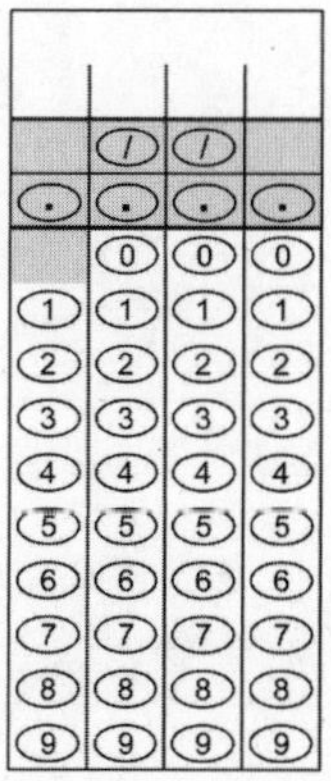

Questions #5–6 refer to the following information.

A gourmet sandwich company is interested in opening a store in City 1 or City 2. To understand the demand for sandwiches in City 1 and City 2, the company polled a sample of the population in these cities on the average number of sandwiches they purchased at similar, currently established restaurants per week. The table below summarizes the results from the survey.

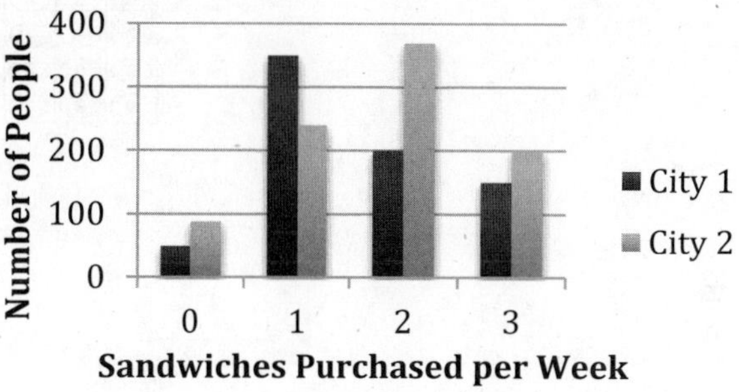

5. What is the median number of sandwiches purchased among the population sample in City 2? Round your answer to the nearest whole number.

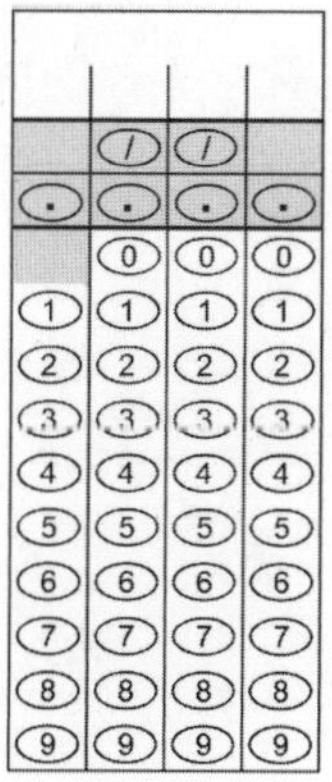

6. What is the average number of sandwiches a resident of City 1 who participated in the survey purchases per week?

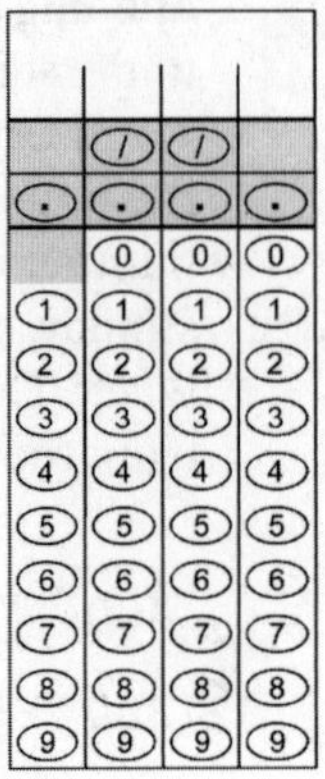

Game Plan

Quickly Preview the Test Section, but Skip the Directions

As you get started, take a few seconds to preview the Math test section. It's 99.99% certain that you're going to find everything in place and just as you expected. But a quick overview will guarantee against any unanticipated changes. Do NOT, however, read the directions. Remind yourself of your pacing plan and then get to work.

Answer the Question That Is Being Asked

Read the Question Carefully

Some problems are fairly simple, but others are more complex, particularly practical word problems and more difficult geometry problems. The more complex the question, the easier it is to misread and set off down the wrong track. If the question is very long, underline the key part of the question.

Pay Attention to Units

Some items require you to convert units (e.g., convert feet to inches or hours to minutes). The item stem will tell you what units to use, and if the test-writer senses any possible confusion, the units for the answer choices will be emphasized—underlined or in boldface or capitalized. When you see a word emphasized with any of those signals, circle it and put a star beside it. It is very important.

Pay Attention to Thought-Reversers

A thought-reverser is any word, such as "not," "except," or "but," that turns a question inside out. Make sure that you mark the thought-reverser so that it is staring you in the face as you work the problem.

Code Your Answers Carefully

With the Math: Multiple Choice items, coding choices is a fairly simple process: locate the circle and fill it in. Here, however, you must enter your answer in the answer grids provided, and then code each element—number and "slash" or decimal, if required—in the corresponding circles. Later in the Math: Student-Produced Responses Lesson, you'll review all of the detailed rules for entering the information. For now, just remember to obey those rules, or you won't receive credit for your response.

Guess If You Want To

As with other sections of the test, if you are unsure of an answer, you should make an educated guess and move on. When applying this strategy to SPRs, consider the following:

- First, there is no penalty for a wrong answer, so a wrong answer will not hurt your score.
- Second, if you have worked on a problem but are not sure of your method or your answer, it's still worth taking the time to make a guess.
- However, if you literally have no idea about the item, it's a waste of time to code in an answer when this time could be better spent working on another item.

Don't Go Calculator Crazy

Just because you are allowed to use a calculator on one section of the test does not mean that you should try to solve every problem with your calculator. In fact, for most problems, the calculator is the less efficient method of arriving at a solution. Assume, for example, that you are presented with an item that requires the following

manipulation: $\left(\frac{2}{3}\right)\left(\frac{7}{4}\right)\left(\frac{1}{6}\right)$. Since this problem involves single-digit multiplication, it's going to be easier to do the arithmetic with a pencil than with a calculator: $\left(\frac{2}{3}\right)\left(\frac{7}{4}\right)\left(\frac{1}{6}\right)=\frac{2\cdot 7\cdot 1}{3\cdot 4\cdot 6}=\frac{14}{72}=\frac{7}{36}$. By all means, use the calculator when necessary since it will be a definite advantage, but don't automatically assume that every problem requires its use.

Calculator Exercise

This exercise is designed to illustrate when and when not to use your calculator. Make sure that the calculator you bring to the test is one with which you are thoroughly familiar. You may bring any of the following types of calculators: graphing, four-function, or scientific. Although no item requires the use of a calculator, a calculator may be helpful to answer some items. The calculator may be useful for any item that involves complex arithmetic computations, but it cannot take the place of understanding how to set up a mathematical item. The degree to which you can use your calculator will depend on its features. Answers are on page 582.

DIRECTIONS: Label each of the items that follow according to one of the following categories.

Category 1: A calculator would be very useful (saves valuable test time).
Category 2: A calculator might or might not be useful.
Category 3: A calculator would be counterproductive (wastes valuable test time).

1. If $2m + 4n$ is equal to 175 percent of $4n$, what is the value of $\frac{m}{n}$?

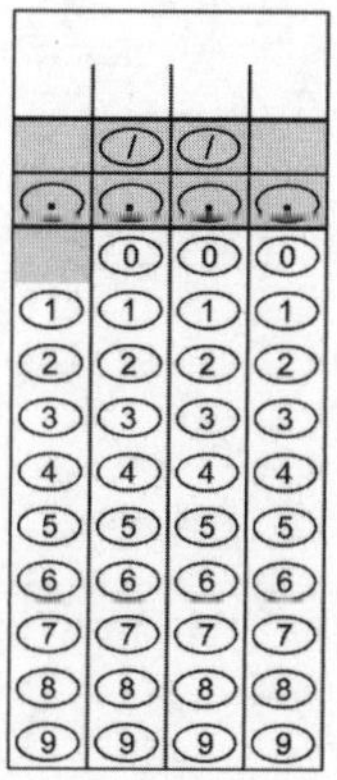

2. A company distributes samplers that include 1 jar of jam and 2 jars of jelly. If the company makes 4 different jams and 4 different jellies, how many different samplers are possible?

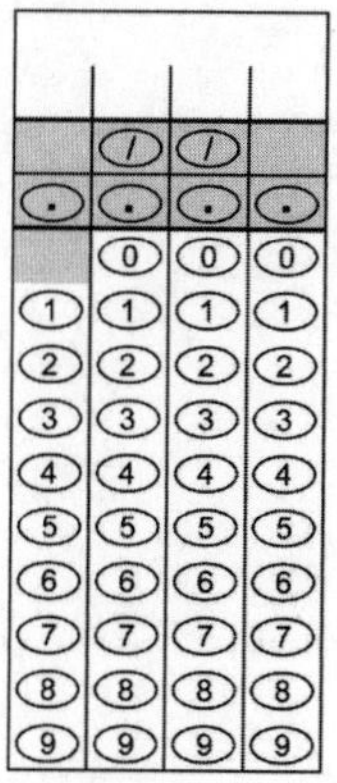

3. Lyle played in 5 basketball games and scored at least 1 point in each game. If Lyle scored an average of 8 points for the 5 games, what is the greatest possible number of points he could have scored in any one game?

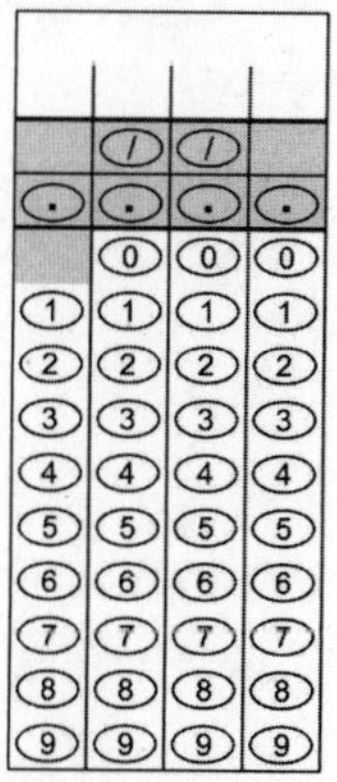

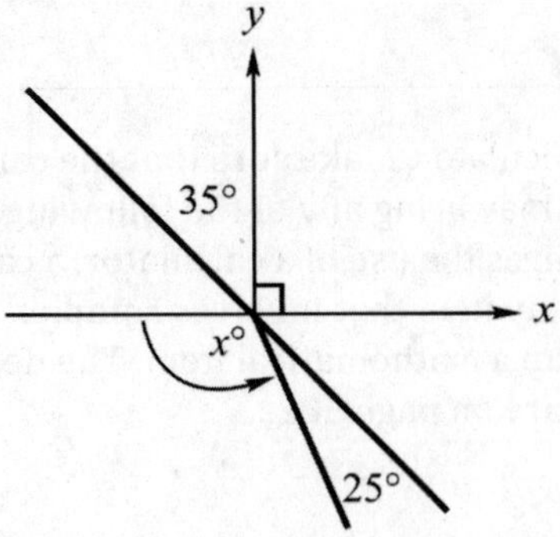

NOTE: Figure not drawn to scale.

4. In the figure above, what is the value of *x*?

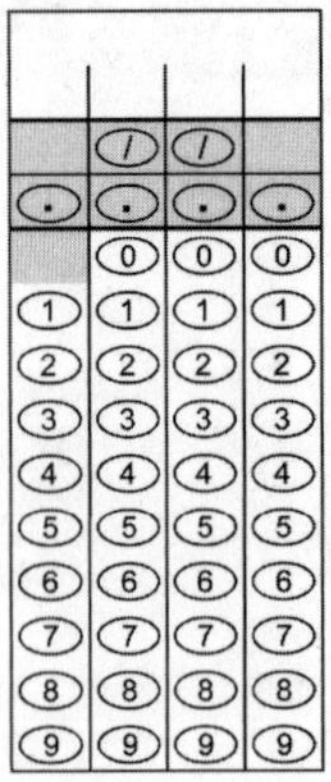

5. Let the function $g(x)$ be defined by $g(x)=12+\frac{x^2}{9}$. If $g(3n)=7n$, what is one possible value of *n*?

QUIZ

SAT MATH: STUDENT-PRODUCED RESPONSES

This section contains one SAT Math: Student-Produced Responses quiz. Complete the quiz under timed conditions. Use any available space in the section for scratch work. Answers are on page 595.

(12 items; 20 minutes)

DIRECTIONS: Solve each item. Use any available space for scratchwork.

Notes:

(1) All expressions and equations represent real numbers unless otherwise indicated.

(2) Figures that accompany problems in this test are intended to provide information useful in solving the problems. They are drawn as accurately as possible EXCEPT when it is stated in a specific problem that the figure is not drawn to scale. All figures lie in a plane unless otherwise indicated.

(3) The domain of a given function f is the set of all real numbers x for which $f(x)$ is a real number unless otherwise indicated.

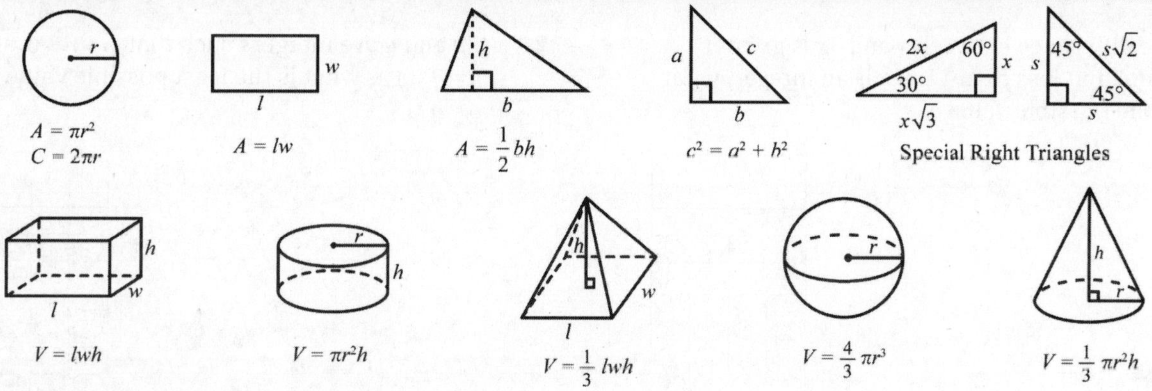

The number of degrees of arc in a circle is 360.

The sum of the measures in degrees of the angles of a triangle is 180.

The number of radians of arc in a circle is 2π.

Each item requires you to solve an item and mark your answer on a special answer grid. For each item, you should write your answer in the boxes at the top of each column and then fill in the ovals beneath each part of the answer you write. Here are some examples:

Answer: 7/2 or 3.5

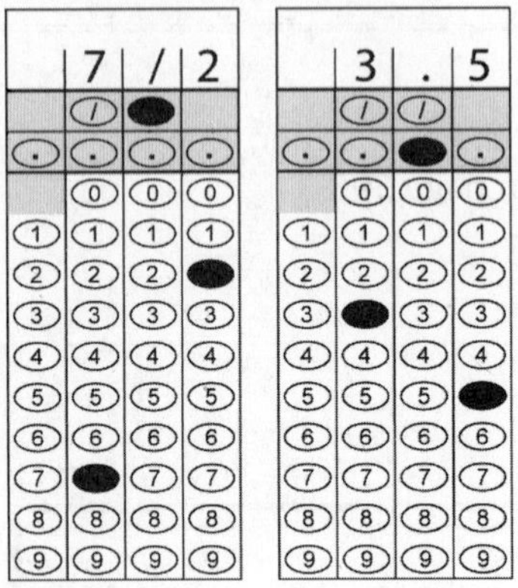

NOTE: A mixed number such as $3\frac{1}{2}$ must be gridded as 7/2 or as 3.5. If gridded as "31/2," it will be read as "thirty-one halves."

Answer: 325

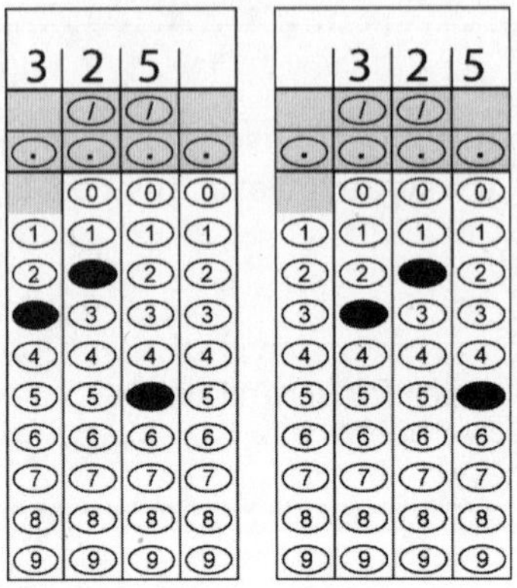

NOTE: Either position is correct.

Answer: 1/6, .166, or .167

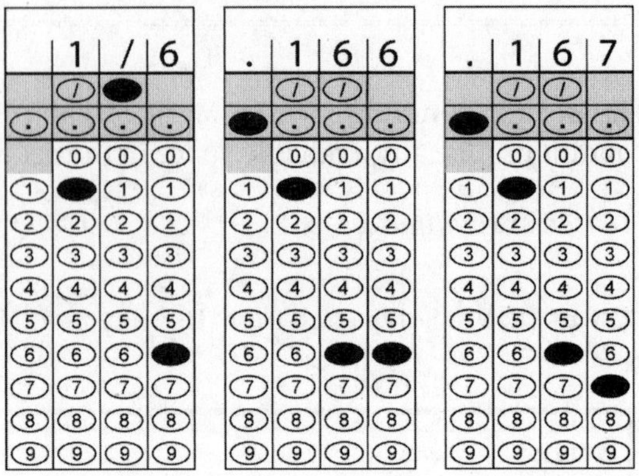

NOTE: A decimal answer with more digits than the grid can accommodate must be truncated. A decimal such as $0.16\overline{6}$ must be gridded as .166 or .167. A less accurate value such as .16 or .17 will be scored as incorrect.

1. The difference between x and $3x$ is greater than 7 but less than 11. If x is an integer, what is one possible value of x?

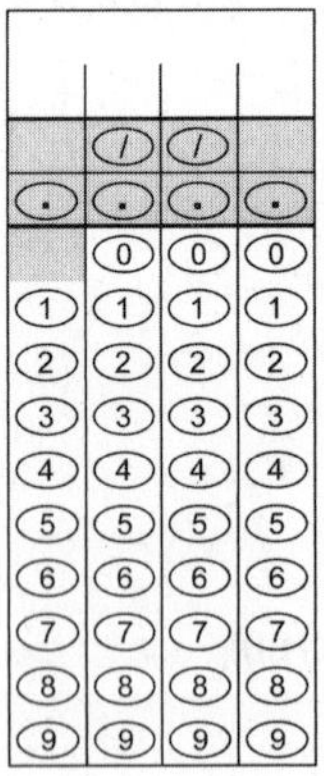

2. If p and q are integers such that $p > q > 0$ and $p + q = 12$, what is the least possible value of $p - q$?

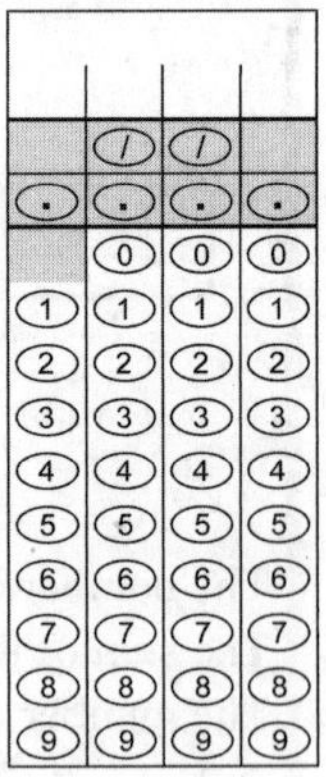

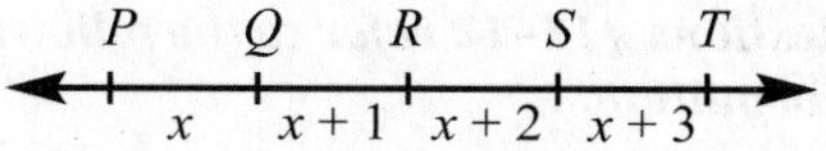

3. In the figure above, if $\overline{PT}$ has a length of 12, then what is the value of x?

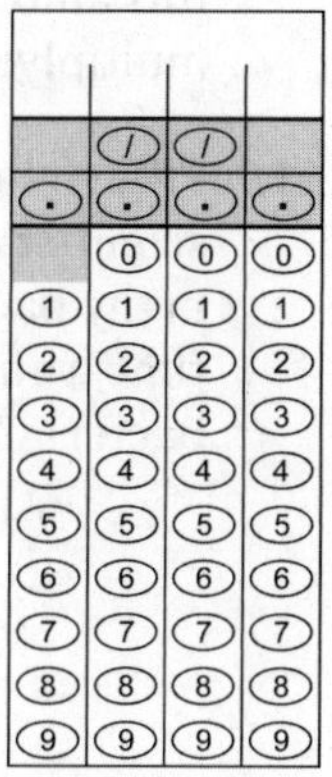

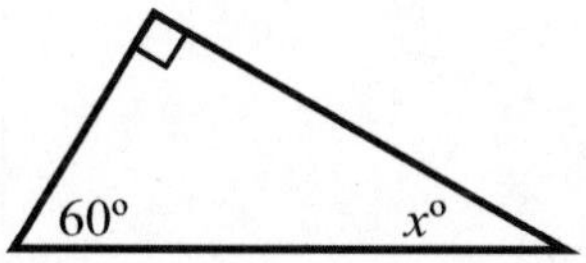

4. In the figure above, what is the value of x?

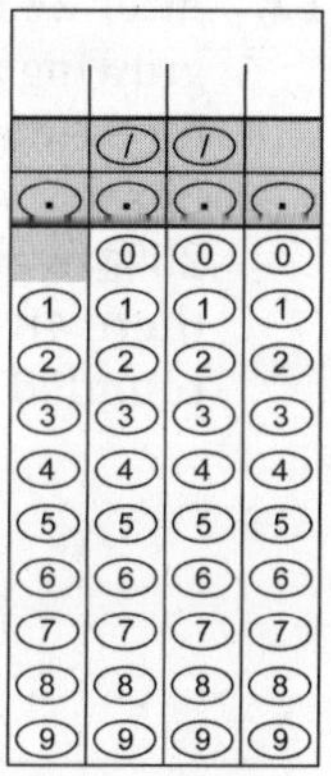

5. As part of an orienteering exercise, a hiker walks due north from point P for 3 miles to point Q and then due east for 4 miles to point R. What is the straight-line distance (in miles) from point R to point P?

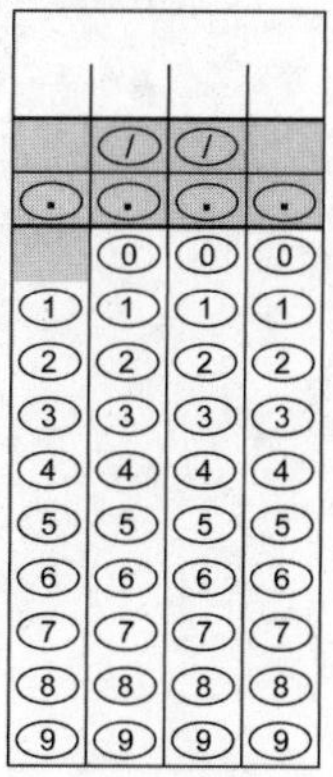

6. If 0.129914 is rounded off to the nearest hundredth, what is the value of the hundredths digit?

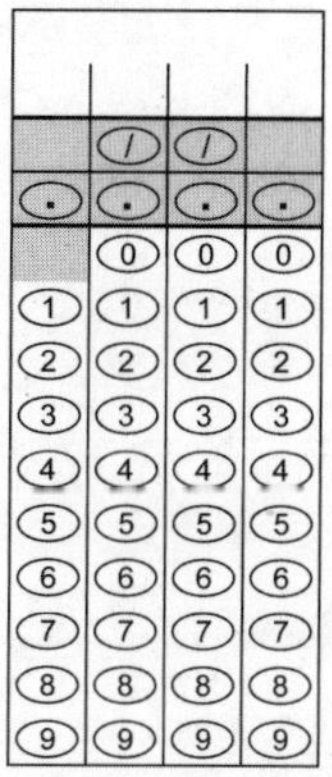

7. The average of 4, 5, x, and y is 6, and the average of x, z, 8, and 9 is 8. What is the value of $z - y$?

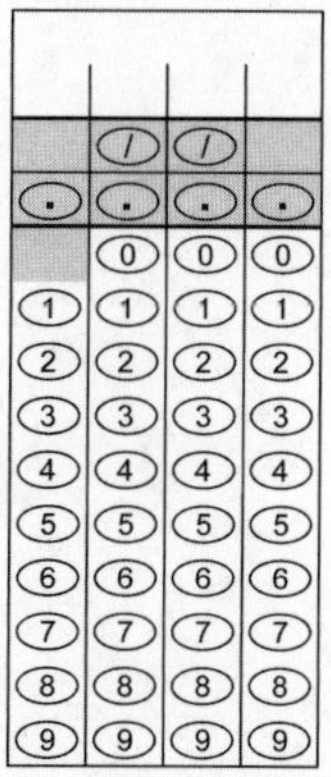

8. Copy Machine X produces 20 copies per minute, and Copy Machine Y produces 30 copies per minute. If Y is started 1 minute after X, how many minutes after X is started will Y have produced the same number of copies as X?

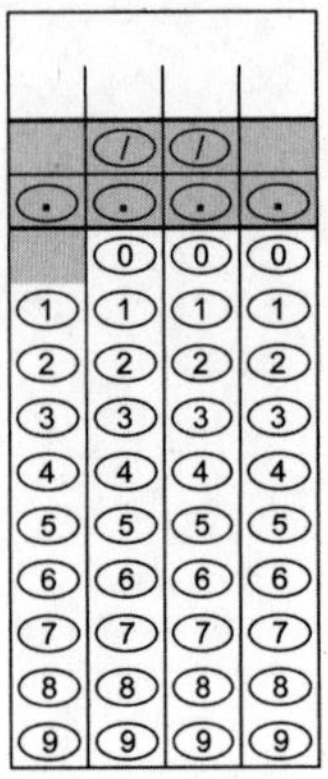

9. A triangle has sides of x, 4, and 5. If x is an integer, what is the maximum value of x?

10. Ray is now 10 years older than Cindy. In 8 years, Ray will be twice as old as Cindy is then. How old is Cindy now?

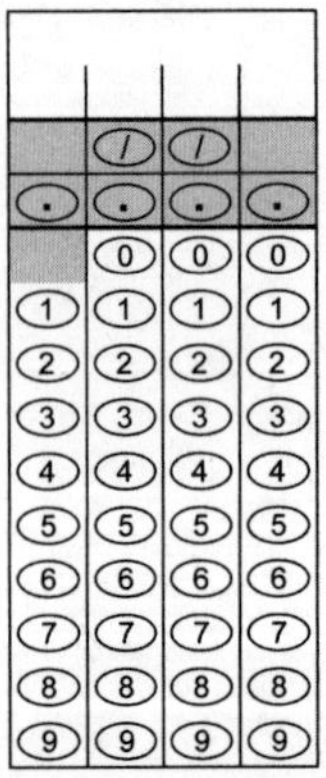

Questions #11–12 refer to the following information.

A scientist conducted an experiment that required bacteria cultures. The culture used in the experiment began with 12 bacteria and this amount doubled every 2 hours, multiplying at a constant rate.

11. Fifteen hours after the experiment began, the scientist checked the bacteria culture. How many bacteria are there in the culture at this time, rounded up to the nearest whole bacteria?

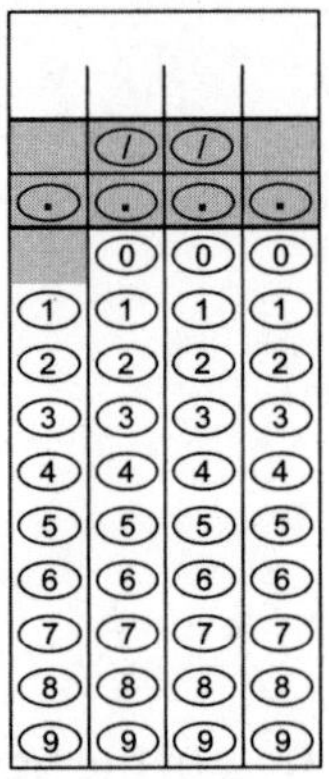

12. After 24 hours, the population stopped growing and entered into a "stationary phase" for 9 hours. Then the bacteria entered a "death phase" where the population decreased by 25% every hour. How many bacteria were there 48 hours after the experiment began, rounded up to the nearest whole bacteria?

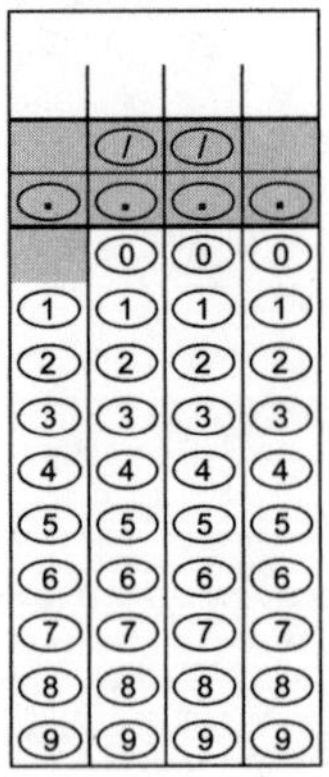

STRATEGY SUMMARY

SAT MATH: STUDENT-PRODUCED RESPONSES

General Strategies:

1. Remember the following details about the grid:
   - grid answers are no more than four digits in length;
   - grid answers, if decimals (non-zero digits to the right of the decimal point), are between .001 and 99.9;
   - grid answers, if fractions, are between 1/99 and 99/1; and
   - grid answers are always positive.
2. Write answers so that the final digit is on the right.
3. Make sure to fill in the circles corresponding to the answer.
4. A decimal point fills one whole space, and therefore it counts as one of the four digits.
5. A fraction bar fills one whole space, and therefore it counts as one of the four digits.
6. Reduce fractions to lowest terms when necessary.
7. Omit unnecessary zeros.
8. Watch the units of measure.

Pay attention to thought-reversers (in all capital letters) and underlined words. Items are arranged according to a ladder of difficulty. The material tested is the same as that for the Math: Multiple-Choice items—strategies and concepts are also the same.

ACT Science

Course Concept Outline

I. Lesson | Preliminaries[1]

A. Lesson Features

B. What Is Tested

C. Directions

D. Item Profiles

E. Facts about the Science Test

1. Three Types of Passages
   a) Data Representation
   b) Research Summary
   c) Conflicting Viewpoints
2. Science Items Test Reasoning, Not Knowledge

F. Item-Types

1. Comprehension
2. Analysis
3. Application

G. General Strategies

1. Plan Your Attack—Easiest Passages First
2. Do Not Preview Item Stems before Reading a Passage
3. Underline Key Words and Phrases
4. Pay Attention to What Is There, Not What Isn't There

---

[1] Some concepts in this Course Concept Outline are not illustrated through examples in your student text but may be covered by your instructor in class. They are included here to provide a complete outline of your course.

1. Quickly Preview the Test Section, but Skip the Directions
2. Personalize the Passage Order
3. Read the Passage
4. Answer the Items
5. Use the Answer Choices
6. Eliminate Choices, Guess (If Necessary), and Move On

VI. Quiz (Items 1–16, p. 431)

VII. Strategy Summary (p. 437)

LESSON 1 | DATA REPRESENTATION

ACT SCIENCE

The passages and items in this section accompany the in-class review of the skills and concepts tested by the ACT Science Test. You will work through the items with your instructor in class. Answers are on page 583.

DIRECTIONS: Each passage below is followed by several items. After reading a passage, choose the best answer to each item. You may refer to the passages as often as necessary. You are NOT permitted the use of a calculator.

Graphs

Graph Reading Strategy Ⓐ

Passage I

The kinetic energy of an object with mass m (measured in grams) after a fall from a height h (measured in centimeters) was recorded for different heights. A graph was made representing the kinetic energy versus height.

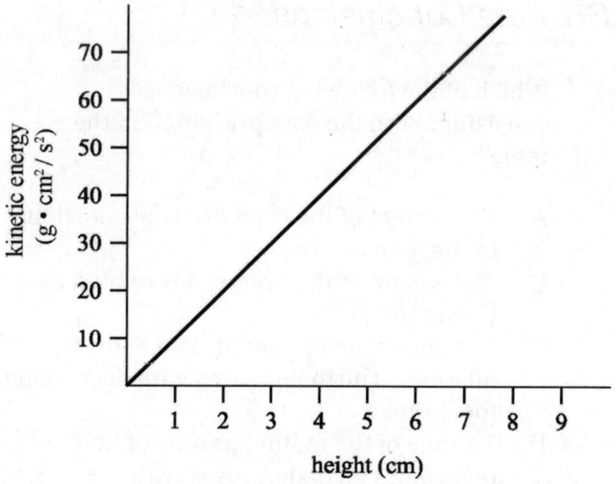

1. In the graph, if the kinetic energy is given in units of $g \cdot cm^2/s^2$, what units must the slope have?

   A. $g \cdot cm/s$
   B. $g \cdot cm/s^2$
   C. $s \cdot cm/g$
   D. $s^2/(g \cdot cm)$

2. It is discovered that if the experiment is repeated for an object with twice the mass, the kinetic energy obtained for every height is doubled. The slope of the new set of experiments can be obtained by doing what to the old slope?

   F. Multiplying by 2
   G. Dividing by 2
   H. Squaring
   J. Taking the square root

3. What would be the approximate kinetic energy (in $g \cdot cm^2/s^2$) of an object of mass m if it were dropped from a height of 4.5 cm?

   A. 4.5
   B. 9.0
   C. 45
   D. 90

Tables

Understanding the Nature of Data Ⓐ

Passage II

A scientist investigated the variables that affect the age at which a female of the animal species *Taedi periculum* first gives birth. Some of the results of this study are summarized in the table below.

EXPERIMENT	TEMPERATURE (°C)	AVERAGE FOOD INTAKE (grams)	AGE WHEN FIRST GAVE BIRTH (months)
1	25	15	7
2	25	30	6
3	25	45	4
4	35	15	5
5	35	30	3
6	35	45	3

4. Which of the following would be good animals to use for the experiment?

F. Adult females
G. Newborn females
H. Newborn males
J. Adult males

5. Which of the pairs of experiments listed below would be useful for studying the effect of temperature on the age of first birth?

A. 1 and 2
B. 1 and 5
C. 1 and 4
D. 2 and 6

Recognizing Trends Ⓐ

6. If all other variables are kept constant, which of the following will result in an increase in the age at which the animals give birth?

F. Increase in temperature from 25°C to 35°C
G. Increase in food from 15 grams to 45 grams
H. Decrease in food from 30 grams to 15 grams
J. Increase in temperature from 25°C to 30°C

7. Which of the following experiments was a control for temperature for Experiment 5?

A. Experiment 1
B. Experiment 2
C. Experiment 3
D. Experiment 6

8. If an experiment was set up with the temperature set at 30°C and the food intake at 30 grams, which of the following would be a reasonable prediction of the age in months of the animals when they first gave birth?

F. 7.5
G. 6.5
H. 4.5
J. 2.5

Drawing Conclusions Ⓐ

9. Which of the following conclusions is consistent with the data presented in the table?

A. The weight of the firstborn is proportional to the food intake.
B. The weight of the firstborn is related to the temperature.
C. The age of the mother at time of first offspring's birth increases with decreasing food intake.
D. The age of the mother at time of first offspring's birth decreases with decreasing food intake.

Typical Data Representation Items Ⓐ

Passage III

The chart below shows the average blood pressure and relative total surface area associated with the different types of human blood vessels.

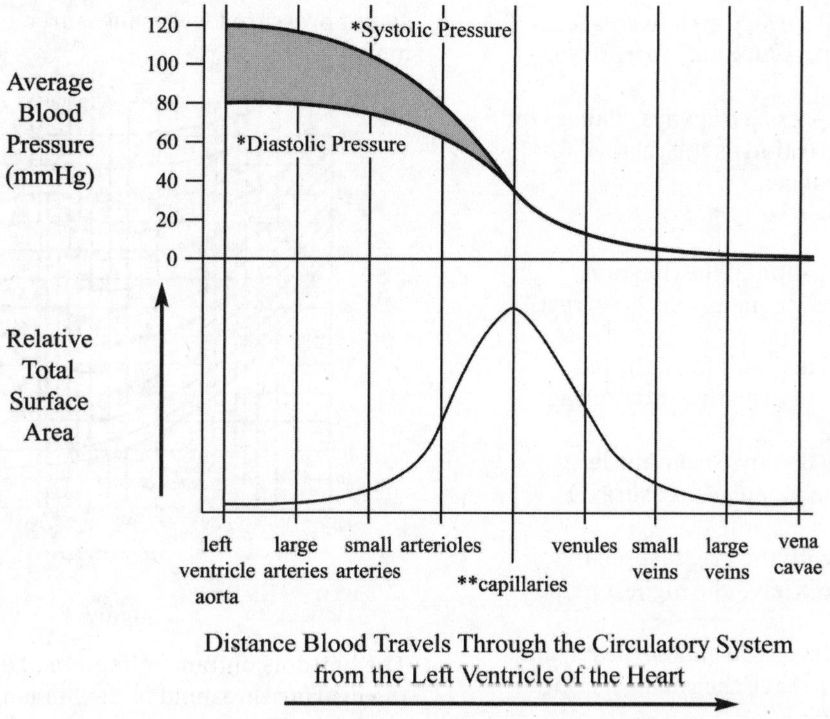

*Pulse pressure is the difference between systolic and diastolic pressure.
**Blood velocity is lowest in the capillaries (averaging 3 cm/sec).

10. According to the diagram, pulse pressure can be detected:

F. in large arteries only.
G. in large arteries as well as in large veins.
H. in blood vessels between the aorta and the capillaries.
J. primarily in the arterioles, capillaries, and venules.

11. Based on the information in the diagram, average blood pressure:

A. decreases with increasing blood vessel distance from the left ventricle.
B. remains approximately constant regardless of blood vessel distance from the left ventricle.
C. first increases, then decreases with increasing blood vessel distance from the left ventricle.
D. is highest in blood vessels with the greatest relative total surface area.

12. Which of the following correctly states the relationship between the relative total surface area of blood vessels and the average blood pressure?

F. As relative total surface area decreases, average blood pressure increases.
G. As relative total surface area decreases, average blood pressure decreases.
H. As relative total surface area decreases, average blood pressure may increase or decrease.
J. Average blood pressure always changes in the opposite direction as the relative total surface area changes.

13. Based on the information in the diagram, which of the following conclusions is correct?

A. As blood vessel distance from the left ventricle increases, relative total surface area decreases.
B. As blood vessel distance from the left ventricle increases, pulse pressure increases.
C. Blood vessels with the greatest relative total surface area have the highest pulse pressure.
D. Blood vessels closest to and farthest from the left ventricle have the smallest relative total surface area.

14. A physician examining a newly discovered tribe of people deep in the Amazon jungles found that the relative total surface area of their capillaries was greater than that previously reported for any other group of people. If the physician were to predict the average velocity of blood through the capillaries of these people, which of the following values would be most reasonable?

F. 2 cm/sec
G. 3 cm/sec
H. 4 cm/sec
J. 5 cm/sec

Passage IV

In 1933, Dr. Fletcher and Dr. Munson of Bell Labs discovered that the sensitivity of the human ear varies with frequency. The Fletcher-Munson equal-loudness contours (Figure 1) show how the human ear's sensitivity to sound pressure level (SPL) varies with frequency. Each contour represents the loudness level as perceived by the human ear. Loudness is subjective but related to sound pressure level as measured by a sound level meter.

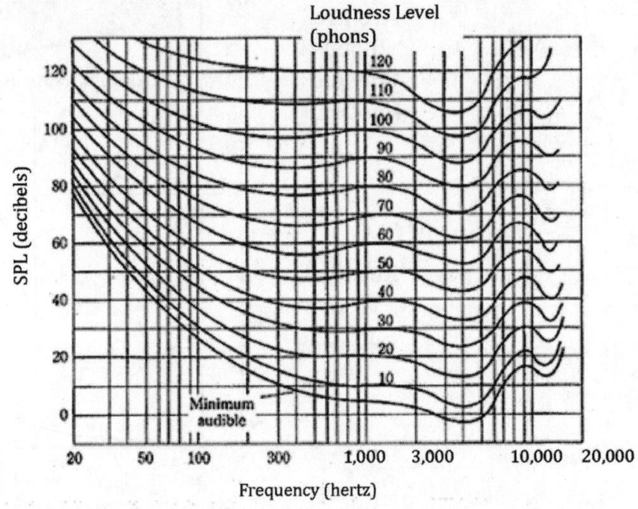

Figure 1

The bottom contour (minimum audible) represents the hearing threshold of the human ear, that is, the minimum SPL of a pure tone that the average human ear with normal hearing can hear with no other sound present. The top contour (120 phons) represents the pain threshold of the human ear, that is, the SPL beyond which sound becomes unbearable to the average listener. Prolonged exposure to sound pressure levels in excess of the pain threshold can cause physical damage, potentially leading to hearing loss.

15. The Fletcher-Munson contours indicate that the human ear is:

A. equally sensitive to all frequencies.
B. less sensitive to low and high frequencies and more sensitive to mid-range frequencies.
C. most sensitive to low and high frequencies and less sensitive to mid-range frequencies.
D. capable of hearing sounds below 20 hertz.

16. The threshold of human hearing:

F. does not depend on sound frequency.
G. is sometimes equal to the threshold of pain.
H. is based on an average ear with normal hearing.
J. is represented by the 10-phon Fletcher-Munson contour.

17. The range of maximum sensitivity for human hearing is approximately:

A. 50 to 100 hertz.
B. 100 to 500 hertz.
C. 500 to 5,000 hertz.
D. 3,000 to 6,000 hertz.

18. Which of the following is a true statement regarding loudness and SPL?

F. Loudness is measured in decibels; SPL is measured in phons.
G. SPL is a measure of subjective quantity; phons may be measured with a sound level meter.
H. Loudness is subjective, but related to SPL.
J. For any given SPL, loudness remains constant for all frequencies.

19. A 300-hertz sound with an SPL of 15 decibels has a loudness of:

A. 10 phons.
B. 20 phons.
C. 30 phons.
D. 40 phons.

20. For the human ear to hear a 20-hertz sound at a loudness of 70 phons, the SPL must be:

F. 50 decibels.
G. 75 decibels.
H. 100 decibels.
J. 110 decibels.

21. For the human ear to hear a minimum audible 30-hertz sound, the SPL must be:

A. 20 decibels.
B. 40 decibels.
C. 60 decibels.
D. 80 decibels.

22. The perceived loudness of a 300-hertz sound with an SPL of 15 decibels is the same as a 30-hertz sound with an SPL of:

F. 50 decibels.
G. 55 decibels.
H. 62 decibels.
J. 150 decibels.

Data Representation Strategies

Ⓐ

Passage V

Seawater contains dissolved salts. As a result, seawater freezes at a lower temperature than freshwater (Figure 1).

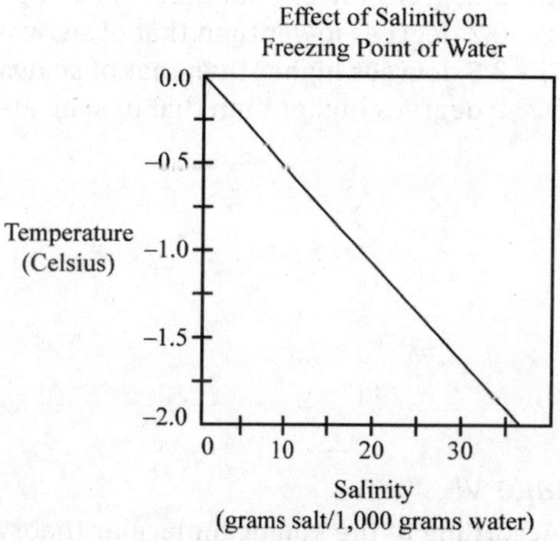

Figure 1

When seawater freezes, as the water molecules begin to form their characteristic ring-like structures, the salt ions, primarily sodium and chloride, are forced out of solution and form pockets of salt. The brine (salty water) leaches out of the bottom of the ice into the water below. Thus, sea ice, when melted, is generally considerably less saline than the original seawater. The solid-line graph below indicates the percentage of salt in a slab of ice that lies over seawater on a cold ocean surface (Figure 2).

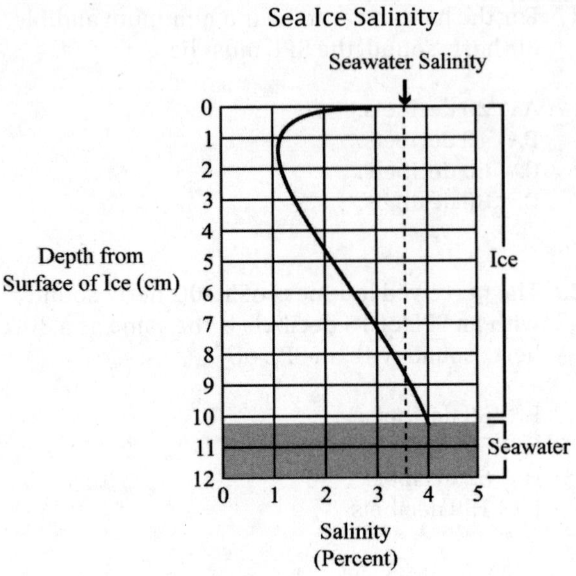

Figure 2

23. According to the information provided, the freezing temperature of pure water is approximately:

A. 2 degrees lower than that of seawater.
B. 0.2 degrees lower than that of seawater.
C. 3.5 degrees higher than that of seawater.
D. 2 degrees higher than that of seawater.

24. Compared to the ocean water below it, the salinity of sea ice in contact with seawater is:

F. higher than that of the seawater.
G. about the same as that of the seawater.
H. lower than that of the seawater.
J. sometimes lower and sometimes higher than that of the seawater.

25. The salinity of the ice at the surface of the slab is equal to the salinity of the:

A. sea ice at a depth of approximately 1.5 cm.
B. sea ice at a depth of approximately 7.0 cm.
C. sea ice at a depth of approximately 9.0 cm.
D. water beneath the sea ice.

26. According to Figure 2, the salt content of the sea ice:

F. equals 0.
G. is constant at all depths.
H. decreases, then increases with depth.
J. increases, then decreases with depth.

27. The researcher takes a 1 gram sample of ice from a depth of 10 cm, and wishes to take a sample of ice from a depth of 1.3 cm that will contain the same weight of total salts. Approximately how large a sample is needed?

A. 0.25 grams
B. 1.0 gram
C. 4.0 grams
D. 10.0 grams

Passage VI

According to the kinetic molecular theory of gases, all gases consist of particles (atoms or molecules) in continuous, random motion. In an ideal gas, particles move freely without interacting with one another except for brief elastic collisions. Particles of a gas at a particular temperature will have a range of different speeds. The distribution of particle speeds, that is, the number of particles moving with a certain speed, is given by the Maxwell-Boltzmann distribution curves. The most probable speed for the particles is represented by the peak of the curve. For a given distribution, the area under the curve corresponds to the total number of particles of a gas sample.

To illustrate how mass affects molecular speed, Figure 1 gives the Maxwell-Boltzmann distributions for the common gases in the table at a fixed temperature (300 K). To illustrate how temperature affects molecular speed, Figure 2 gives the Maxwell-Boltzmann distributions for nitrogen gas (N_2) at several temperatures.

Table 1: Molar Mass of Common Gases (grams/mole)	
H_2 (hydrogen)	2.02
He (helium)	4.00
N_2 (nitrogen)	28.01
O_2 (oxygen)	32.00
Cl_2 (chlorine)	70.91
Kr (krypton)	83.80

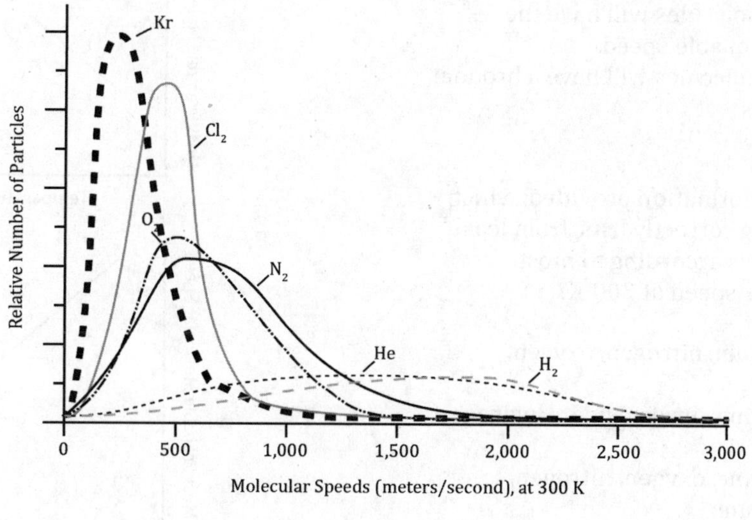

Figure 1

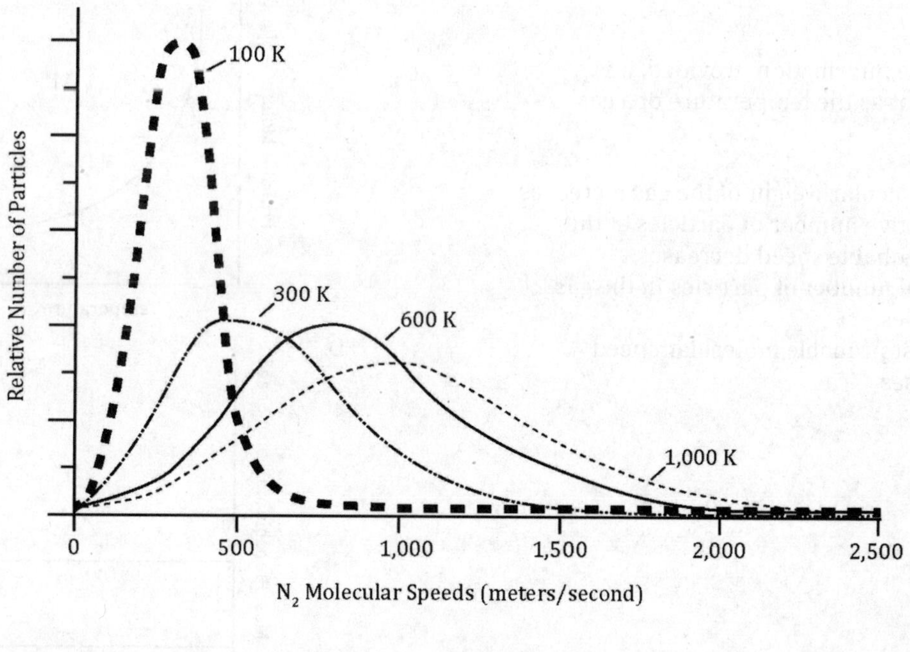

Figure 2

28. A scientist fills one metal cylinder with helium gas and a second metal cylinder with chlorine gas. After the scientist heats both gases to 300 K, which of the following will be true?

F. The molecules in both gases will have the same most probable speed.
G. The helium molecules will have the higher most probable speed.
H. The chlorine molecules will have the higher most probable speed.
J. The chlorine molecules will have a broader range of speeds.

29. According to the information provided, which one of the following correctly lists, from least to greatest, the gases according to most probable molecular speed at 300 K?

A. Hydrogen, helium, nitrogen, oxygen, chlorine, krypton
B. Krypton, chlorine, oxygen, neon, hydrogen, helium
C. Krypton, chlorine, oxygen, nitrogen, hydrogen, helium
D. Krypton, chlorine, oxygen, nitrogen, helium, hydrogen

30. Based on the information provided, it is inferable that as the temperature of a gas increases:

F. The molecular weight of the gas increases.
G. the relative number of particles at the most probable speed decreases.
H. the total number of particles in the gas decreases.
J. the most probable molecular speed decreases.

31. Based on the information provided, which of the following graphs best represents the most probable molecular speed for nitrogen as a function of gas temperature?

A.
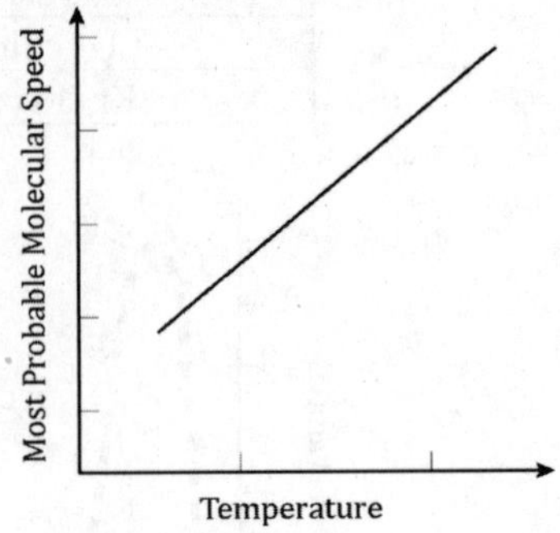

B.
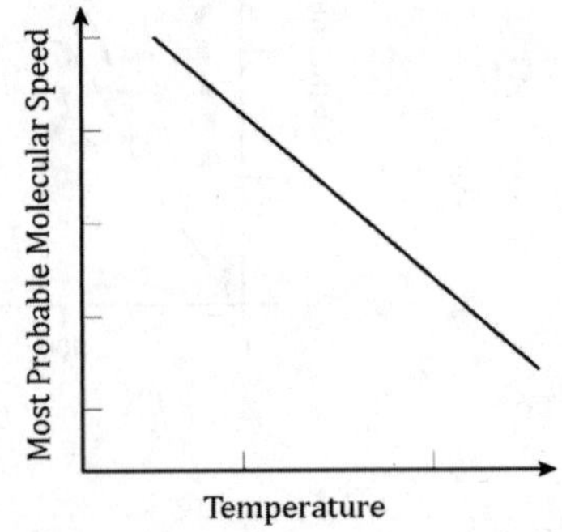

C.
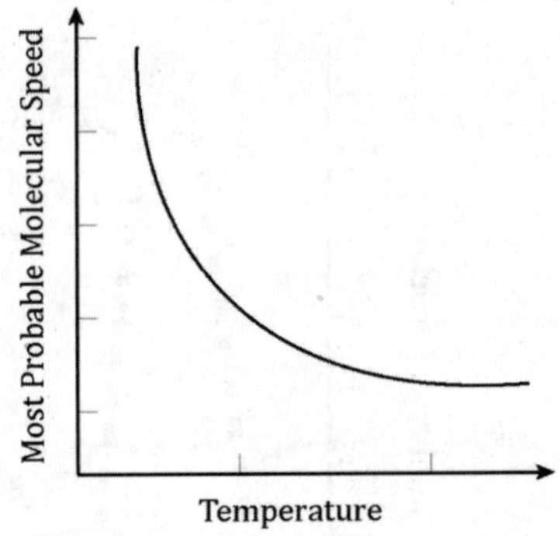

D.
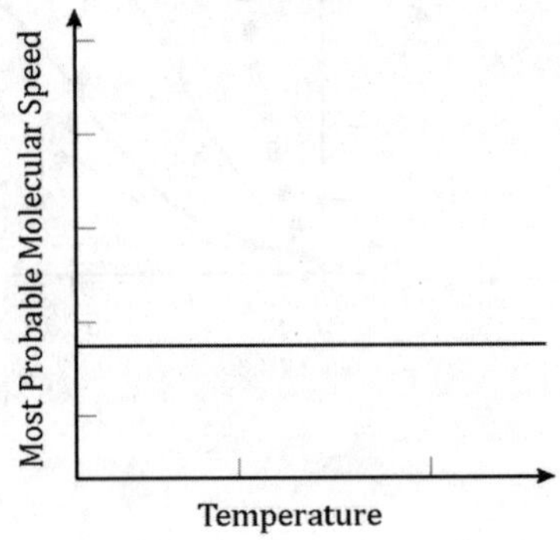

32. Which of the following statements best describes the relationship between nitrogen gas molecule speeds and the temperature of the gas?

F. As gas temperature increases, the range of molecular speeds increases and the most probable speed decreases.
G. As gas temperature decreases, the range of molecular speeds decreases and the most probable speed decreases.
H. As molar mass of gas increases, the range of molecular speeds decreases and the most probable speed decreases.
J. As molar mass of gas decreases, the range of molecular speeds increases and the most probable speed increases.

33. According to the information provided, as the molar mass of a gas increases:

A. the number of particles at greater speeds increases.
B. the number of particles in the gas increases.
C. the most probable molecular speed decreases.
D. the most probable molecular speed increases.

34. Argon is a gas with molar mass of 39.95 grams/mole. Based on the information provided, the most probable molecular speed of argon molecules at 100 K is:

F. less than 300 meters/second.
G. between 300 and 500 meters/second.
H. between 500 and 1,000 meters/second.
J. over 1,000 meters/second.

Passage VII

Phase diagrams illustrate the relationship between temperature, pressure, and the phases of matter. Each of the three phases—solid, liquid, and gas—is represented by a section of the phase diagram. The curves represent states of equilibrium between two phases—the substance is present in two phases at once as it passes from one phase to the next. All three phases are present at the triple point. For temperatures and pressures both below the triple point, matter passes directly between the solid and gas phases without passing through the liquid phase.

For pressures and temperatures beyond the critical point, the liquid and gas phases converge and become indistinguishable in what is known as a supercritical fluid. Supercritical fluids can dissolve materials like a liquid and effuse through solids like a gas. Beyond the critical point, no amount of pressure will restore a supercritical fluid to its liquid or solid phase without decreasing the temperature.

Figure 1 shows the phase diagram for water, a liquid at room temperature (21°C) and atmospheric pressure (1 atm). Figure 2 shows the phase diagram for carbon dioxide, a gas at room temperature and atmospheric pressure.

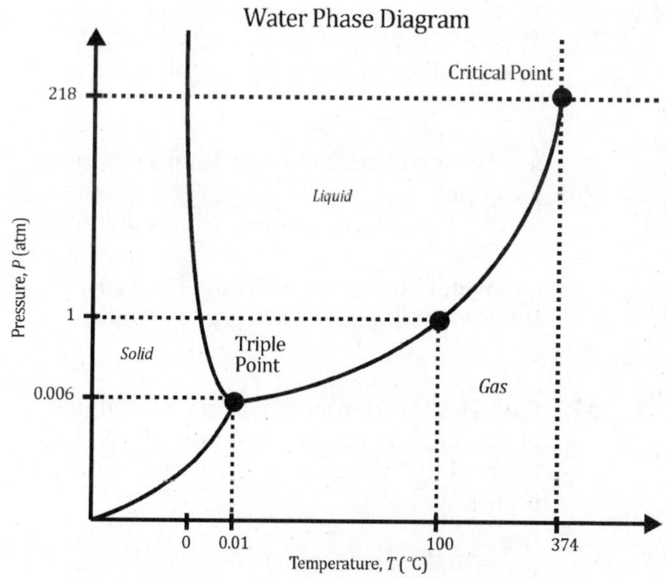

Figure 1

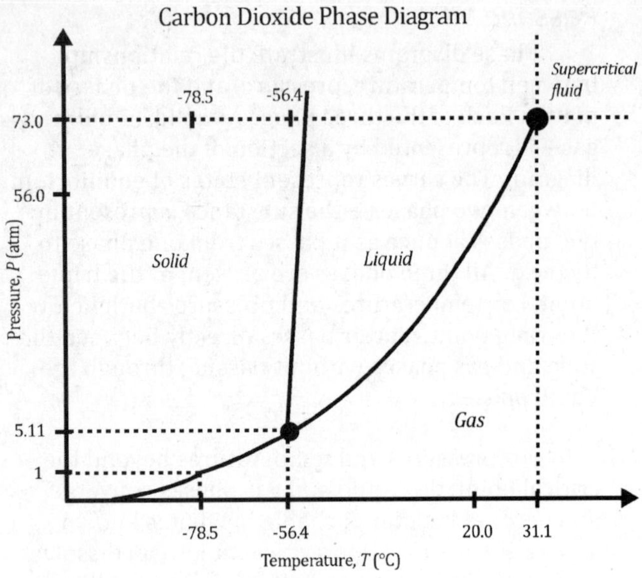

Figure 2

35. According to the information provided and Figure 1, water becomes a supercritical fluid when the temperature and pressure exceed:

F. 0.006°C and 0.01 atm.
G. 0.01°C and 0.006 atm.
H. 218°C and 374 atm.
J. 374°C and 218 atm.

36. At 100°C, as pressure is decreased from 1.5 atm to 0.006 atm, which of the following is true?

A. Carbon dioxide changes from a gas to a liquid.
B. Carbon dioxide changes from a liquid to a gas.
C. Water changes from a liquid to a gas.
D. Water changes from a gas to a liquid.

37. Based on the information provided and the phase diagram for carbon dioxide, it can be inferred that the triple point of carbon dioxide occurs at:

F. –78.5°C and 1 atm.
G. –56.4°C and 5.11 atm.
H. 0.01°C and 0.006 atm.
J. 31.1°C and 73 atm.

38. According to the information provided, both water and carbon dioxide exist solely as liquids at which of the following pressure and temperature combinations?

A. 10°C and 56 atm.
B. 0°C and 1 atm.
C. 30°C and 10 atm.
D. There is no point at which both water and carbon dioxide exist solely as liquids.

39. In Figure 1, the line indicating equilibrium between solid water (ice) and liquid water has a negative slope. This indicates that to maintain equilibrium between the two states:

A. as the temperature is decreased, the pressure must be decreased.
B. as the temperature is increased, the pressure must be decreased.
C. as the temperature is increased, the pressure must remain constant.
D. as the temperature is increased, the pressure must be increased, then decreased.

40. Sublimation occurs when a solid changes to a gas without going through a liquid phase. Under which of the following conditions can sublimation occur?

F. Water at 0°C and 0.80 atm.
G. Water at 80°C and 0.006 atm.
H. Carbon dioxide at –78.5°C and 1 atm.
J. Carbon dioxide at 0°C and 5.11 atm.

LESSON 2 | RESEARCH SUMMARY

ACT SCIENCE

The passages and items in this section accompany the in-class review of the skills and concepts tested by the ACT Science Test. You will work through the items with your instructor in class. Answers are on page 583.

DIRECTIONS: Each passage below is followed by several items. After reading a passage, choose the best answer to each item. You may refer to the passages as often as necessary. You are NOT permitted the use of a calculator.

Typical Research Summary Items Ⓐ

Passage I

To test the hypothesis that all antibiotics are equally effective in preventing bacterial growth, the following three experiments were carried out using clear plastic plates filled with nutrient agar (a mixture of ingredients that supports the growth of bacteria). When bacteria reproduce successfully, colonies form on the agar, giving it a cloudy appearance.

Experiment 1

Three plates (A, B, and C) of agar were set up, each with an equal amount of bacterial culture (Bacterium X) spread over the agar surface and with a paper disk placed in the center. Plate A's disk was soaked in Antibiotic I; Plate B's disk was soaked in Antibiotic II; Plate C's disk was soaked in plain water. After incubation overnight at 37°C (body temperature), Plates A and B had a clear area, 2" in diameter surrounding the paper disk, but beyond this 2" region, the plates were cloudy. Plate C was entirely cloudy, including the area adjacent to the paper disk.

Experiment 2

Identical procedures were followed except that Plates A, B, and C were incubated overnight at 22°C (room temperature). After incubation, Plate A had a clear area, 2" in diameter, surrounding the paper disk. Plates B and C were entirely cloudy.

Experiment 3

Identical procedures were followed except that the concentrations of Antibiotic I (Plate A) and Antibiotic II (Plate B) were made twice as strong. After incubation overnight at 22°C, Plates A and B both had clear, 2" areas around the paper disk, while Plate C remained entirely cloudy.

1. After incubation, a clear area around a previously soaked paper disk represents a region where:

A. agar had washed away.
B. decomposition had occurred due to high incubation temperatures.
C. bacterial growth did not occur.
D. bacteria grew best.

2. Which of the following results would indicate that the antibiotics being tested have nothing to do with the control of bacterial growth?

F. A clear, 2" region was always observed around the disks soaked in water.
G. All results remained the same at the two experimental temperatures and at the two antibiotic concentration levels.
H. Plates A and B always remained clear.
J. The disks soaked in water were not used in the experiments at all.

3. Which statement is supported by the results of Experiment 1 alone?

A. Antibiotic I, Antibiotic II, and water are equally effective as inhibitors (preventers) of bacterial growth at 37°C.
B. Dry paper disks can be effective in controlling bacterial growth at 37°C.
C. The concentration of an antibiotic may influence its effectiveness in controlling bacterial growth at 37°C.
D. Both Antibiotics I and II can inhibit bacterial growth at 37°C.

4. The results of both Experiment 2 and Experiment 3 lead to which of the following conclusions?

F. Antibiotics I and II have similar effects on bacterial growth, regardless of concentrations.
G. Antibiotic II and water have similar effects on bacterial growth, regardless of concentrations.
H. The effectiveness of Antibiotic I at 22°C depends on its concentration.
J. The effectiveness of Antibiotic II at 22°C depends on its concentration.

5. Which hypothesis best explains the observation that the agar plates never appear clear beyond a 2" area surrounding the soaked paper disks?

A. The bacteria cannot grow well within 2" of any moist paper disks.
B. The antibiotics cannot seep through the agar beyond a distance of 2".
C. At the experimental incubation temperatures used, the two antibiotics interfere with each other's effectiveness.
D. The paper disks can absorb nutrients out of the agar from the distance of 2".

6. If either Antibiotic I or II could be prescribed for internal use to prevent the spread of Bacterium X infections, which recommendation, based on the experimental results, is appropriate if the cost due to the amount of antibiotic used per dose is the most critical factor (the antibiotics are equal in cost for equal concentrations)?

F. Either Antibiotic I or II can be taken at equal cost.
G. Antibiotic I would be less expensive.
H. Antibiotic II would be less expensive.
J. Neither Antibiotic I nor II would be effective in preventing the spread of Bacterium X.

Passage II

To investigate the hypothesis that the quality of the detail of a fossil depends on the size of the particles that make up the rock surrounding it, three experiments were performed using a particular type of leaf with many fine veins.

Experiment 1

A leaf was placed on a flat bed made of paste from extrafine grade plaster and then completely covered with more of the same paste. A glass cover with a 5 pound weight was placed on top of the paste for one hour, until the plaster set. The plaster was then baked for 30 minutes at 225°C. When the cast was opened, the imprint of the leaf showed all of the veins, including the finest ones.

Experiment 2

A leaf was placed on a flat bed made of paste from fine grade plaster and then completely covered with more of the same paste. A glass cover with a 5 pound weight was placed on top of the plaster for one hour, until the plaster set. The plaster was then baked for 30 minutes at 225°C. When the casst was opened, all the main veins were visible, but only isolated traces of the finer veins were found.

Experiment 3

A leaf was placed on a flat bed made of paste from coarse grade plaster and then completely covered with more of the same paste. A glass cover with a 5 pound weight was placed on top of the plaster for one hour, until the plaster set. The plaster was then baked for 30 minutes at 225°C. When the cast was opened, only the thickest veins were visible, and some of the leaf edge was difficult to discern.

7. Should the investigator have used a different type of leaf in each experiment?

A. Yes: different types of structure could be studied.
B. Yes: in real life, many different types of fossils are found.
C. No: the type of leaf served as a controlled variable.
D. No: the nature of the leaf is not important.

8. When a fossil is formed, the sediment that surrounds it is normally compressed by the tons of earth deposited over it. What part of the model simulates this compressing element?

F. The 5 pound weight
G. The glass
H. The upper layer of paste
J. The baking oven

9. A fourth experiment was set up the same way as the previous three, except the paste was made by mixing equal amounts of very coarse sand with the extrafine grade plaster. The investigator is likely to discover:

A. no change from Experiment 1 because only the type of plaster is important.
B. no change because the same kind of leaf is used.
C. the imprint is better than Experiment 1 because the sand provides air pockets.
D. the imprint is worse than Experiment 1 because the average particle size is bigger.

10. Which of the following hypotheses is supported by the results of Experiment 1 alone?

F. The finer the sediment, the greater the detail of the resulting fossil.
G. Hardened sediment can preserve the imprint of a specimen.
H. All fossils must have been baked at high temperatures.
J. Only organic material can leave imprints in sediment.

11. Which of the following changes in the experiments would have permitted a test of the hypothesis that the quality of a fossil imprint depends on the pressure applied?

A. Repeat the experiments, except use a 10 pound weight in Experiment 2 and a 20 pound weight in Experiment 3.
B. Choose one of the plasters, and run experiments using the same plaster in all trials while varying the weights.
C. Rerun all the experiments without the glass.
D. Vary the depth of the leaf in each new trial, because, in nature, increased pressure means the fossil is at a greater depth.

Research Summary Strategies Ⓐ

Passage III

Erosion refers to processes that wear down rocks and soil, as well as processes that transport the worn-away materials to other locations. Although these processes usually cause effects gradually (over geologic time), laboratory models can be designed to investigate which environmental factors affect erosion rate.

Three experimental sandboxes were set up that were identical in size (10-by-10-foot), had identical types of soil and rocks, and were filled to equal depths (3 feet). The sandboxes were kept for two weeks in large environmental chambers, each maintained at a constant temperature, with a continuous wind flow of 5 mph.

Sandbox 1

One-half was kept bare (just soil and rocks), while the other half had a variety of grasses and weeds planted among the soil and rocks. After two weeks, the bare half had small channels (ruts) running along its length that averaged 1 inch in width. The planted half had few channels, and those that were found averaged less than 1 inch wide.

Sandbox 2

The conditions were identical to those of Sandbox 1, with the addition that both halves were subjected to light 15 minute showers of water every twelve hours. After two weeks, the bare half had channels averaging 4 inches wide, while the planted half had fewer channels averaging 2 inches wide.

Sandbox 3

The conditions were identical to those of Sandbox 2, but the entire box was mechanically raised to rest at an angle of 15° to simulate a steep slope. After two weeks, the bare half had channels averaging 7 inches wide, while channels in the planted half were less common and averaged 4 inches in width.

12. Results from all three sandboxes indicate that:

F. different types of soils and rocks are affected differently by environmental factors.
G. under all tested conditions, plants reduce erosion.
H. changing wind and temperature conditions can affect erosion patterns.
J. water from short periods of rain has little or no effect on erosion patterns.

13. The experimental design and results do NOT support which of the following claims?

A. Light winds have no erosive effect.
B. Slopes have more erosion than level surfaces.
C. Water has major erosive effects.
D. The effects of changing temperature remain unanswered.

14. Sudden cloudbursts are known to cause more erosion than longer periods of mild rains. How could the present experiments be changed to examine this idea?

F. Raise the angle in Sandbox 3 to produce a steeper slope.
G. Add the "rain conditions" from Sandbox 2 to the conditions in Sandbox 1.
H. Include light, 15 minute showers every six hours instead of every twelve hours.
J. Every twelve hours, allow the same total volume of water to fall in a 5 minute span rather than in a 15 minute span.

15. Should the investigator have used different soil types in each sandbox experiment?

A. Yes, because different soils may erode differently.
B. Yes, because a different group of plants could have been used in each sandbox as well.
C. No, because some soils can be washed completely away within the two week experiment.
D. No, because the soil type was a controlled variable in all three experiments.

16. Sandbox 3 specifically demonstrates the role of which particular variable in the set of experiments?

F. Rain
G. Wind
H. Gravity
J. Temperature

17. If another sandbox were set up, which of the following conditions would probably cause wider and deeper channels in the soil of the new sandbox than those in Sandbox 3?

I. Steeper angles for the sandbox
II. A greater volume of water during the 15 minute showers every twelve hours
III. Removal of plants from soil

A. I only
B. I and II only
C. II and III only
D. I, II, and III

Passage IV

Charles's law states that the volume, V, of a gas at constant pressure is proportional to its absolute temperature T (temperature in kelvins, K):

$$V \propto T \qquad \text{(Equation 1)}$$

Boyle's law states that the volume of a gas at constant temperature is inversely proportional to its pressure P (pressure in pascals, Pa):

$$V \propto 1/P \qquad \text{(Equation 2)}$$

Experiment 1

Students inserted a 30-mL syringe and a thermometer through holes in a rubber stopper. Then they placed the stopper into a flask that had been cooled in an ice bath to 273 K (Figure 1). They then removed the flask from the ice bath and placed it on a hot plate. The gas in the flask expanded as it warmed, slowly pushing the piston up the syringe. Students recorded the temperature and corresponding syringe volume readings as the gas expanded at a constant atmospheric pressure (100 kPa). To obtain the total volume of the gas in the system, they added the volume of the syringe to the volume of the flask. The students then created a graph of the experimental data.

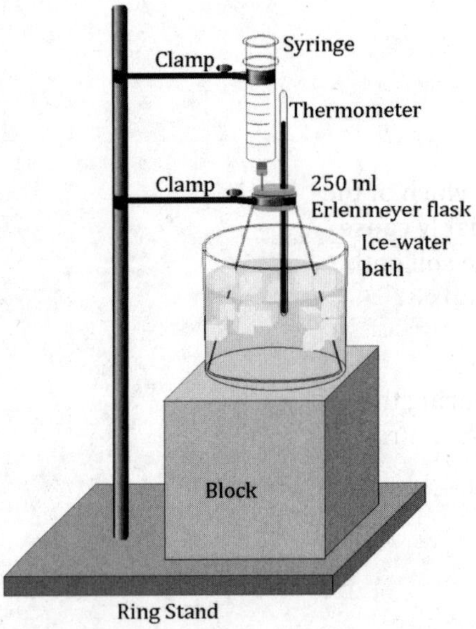

Figure 1

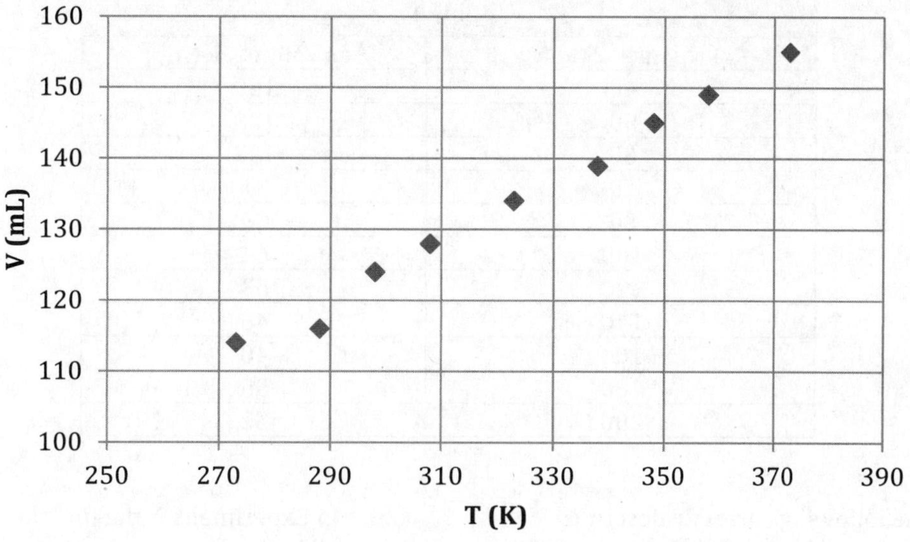

Figure 2

Experiment 2

The students investigated the change in the volume of a gas at room temperature (294 K) at different pressures using the apparatus shown in Figure 3. A glass tube contained a pure nitrogen gas sample (a), and its volume (in mL) was read from the scale. A column of oil (c) transmitted pressure from the reservoir (b), and the pressure value was read on the gauge (d). Table 1 summarizes the data.

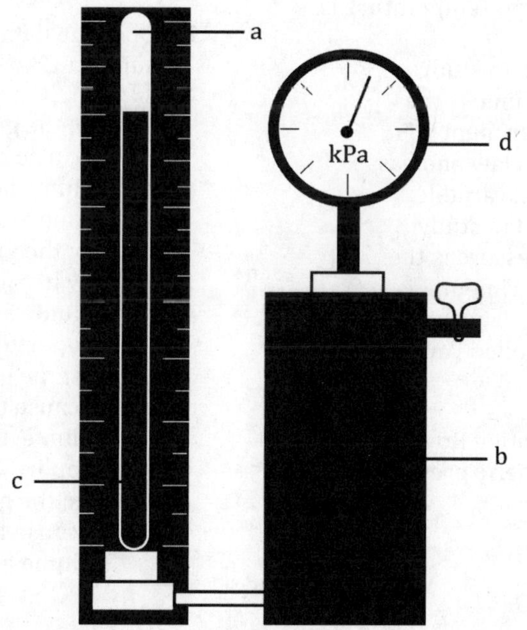

Figure 3

Table 1	
Pressure, P (kPa)	Gas Volume, V (mL)
40	160
50	128
60	107
70	91
80	80
100	64
120	53
140	46
160	40
180	35
200	32

18. Which of the following correctly describes Experiments 1 and 2?

F. Experiment 1 is designed to study Boyle's law and gas temperature is the controlled variable; Experiment 2 is designed to study Charles's law and gas pressure is the controlled variable.
G. Experiment 1 is designed to study Boyle's law and gas pressure is the controlled variable; Experiment 2 is designed to study Charles's law and gas temperature is the controlled variable.
H. Experiment 1 is designed to study Charles's law and gas volume is the controlled variable; Experiment 2 is designed to study Boyle's law and gas pressure is the controlled variable.
J. Experiment 1 is designed to study Charles's law and gas pressure is the controlled variable; Experiment 2 is designed to study Boyle's law and gas temperature is the controlled variable.

19. In the experiment demonstrating Boyle's law, the volume of gas at atmospheric pressure was:

A. 32 mL.
B. 64 mL.
C. 100 mL.
D. Cannot be determined from the given information.

20. In Experiment 2, the function of the column of oil in the experimental apparatus is to:

F. measure the pressure of the air in the glass tube as it expands or contracts.
G. measure the temperature of air in the glass tube as it expands or contracts.
H. transmit pressure from the reservoir to the gas in the glass tube.
J. transmit air to the gas in the glass tube.

21. Does the data graph from Experiment 1 support Charles's law?

A. No; the graph supports Boyle's law because the data demonstrates that volume and temperature are directly proportional.
B. No; the graph does not support Charles's law because the data demonstrates that volume and pressure are inversely proportional.
C. Yes; the graph supports Charles's law because the data demonstrates that volume and temperature are directly proportional.
D. Yes; the graph supports Charles's law because the data demonstrates that volume and temperature are equal.

22. To test the validity of Boyle's law, the students should graph gas volume as a function of:

F. temperature using the data from Experiment 1.
G. temperature using the data from Experiment 2.
H. pressure using the data from Experiment 1.
J. pressure using the data from Experiment 2.

23. Based on the information provided, which of the following is true for the pressure, *P*, temperature, *T*, and/or volume, *V*, of a sample of gas?

A. *PV* is constant for the same temperature.
B. *VT* is constant for the same pressure.
C. $\frac{V}{P}$ is constant for the same temperature.
D. *PVT* is constant for all pressures, volumes, and temperatures.

Passage V

Freezing point depression occurs when a non-volatile solute is added to a pure solvent, resulting in a solution with a lower freezing point than that of the pure solvent. The freezing point depression, ΔT, is roughly proportional to the concentration of the solute in the solution (as measured by molality):

$$\Delta T = -K_f \times m \times i$$

(Equation 1)

K_f is the freezing point depression constant for the solvent, *m* is the molality of the solution (moles of solute per kilogram of solvent), and *i* is the van't Hoff factor, which is equal to the number of particles produced by one molecule of solute.

A chemistry student uses the phenomenon of freezing point depression to determine the molar mass and identification of an unknown substance from Table 1.

Table 1

Chemical	Molar Mass (grams/mole)
Sodium iodide (NaI)	150
Calcium sulfate ($CaSO_4$)	136
Sodium nitrate ($NaNO_3$)	85
Sodium chloride (NaCl)	58
Sodium fluoride (NaF)	42

Part 1

A test tube filled with distilled water is placed in a salt/ice water bath at below −10°C and constantly stirred until crystals begin to form, at which point the distilled water temperature is recorded.

The procedure is repeated for a sugar-water solution of molality 1.0 *m* (1.0 mol sugar/1 kg water) and van't Hoff factor of 1. The student uses the freezing point depression for the sugar-water solution to calculate the freezing point depression constant for water (Table 2).

Table 2

1. Freezing point of distilled water	−0.04°C
2. Freezing point of 1.0 m sugar-water solution	−1.91°C
3. ΔT for sugar-water solution	−1.87°C
4. K_f value for distilled water	1.87°C/(mol/kg)

Part 2

A beaker is weighed before and after the addition of approximately 100 mL of distilled water. The beaker is weighed again after the addition of a sample of an unknown substance from Table 1 known to have a van't Hoff factor of 2. The student calculates the solution concentration (grams of solute per kilogram of water).

The freezing point depression of the unknown solution is determined as in Part 1, and the solution molality is calculated. Finally, the student calculates the molar mass of the unknown solute using Equation 2.

$$\text{molar mass (grams/mole)} = \frac{\text{concentration (grams/kilogram of water)}}{\text{molality (moles/kilogram of water)}}$$

(Equation 2)

The experimental data and calculation results are recorded in Table 3.

Table 3	
1. Mass of empty 250 mL beaker	125.45 g
2. Mass of beaker + water	225.86 g
3. Mass of water in beaker	100.41 g
4. Mass of beaker + water + unknown solute	239.11 g
5. Mass of unknown solute	13.25 g
6. Concentration of unknown solution	131.96 g solute/kg water
7. Freezing point of unknown solution	-8.49°C
8. ΔT for unknown solution	-8.45°C
9. Molality of unknown solution	2.26 mol/kg
10. Molar mass of the unknown solute	?

24. According to the information provided, the ultimate purpose of Part 1 was to experimentally determine:

F. the freezing point of distilled water.
G. the freezing point depression of distilled water.
H. the freezing point depression constant of sugar-water.
J. the freezing point depression constant for distilled water.

25. According to the information provided, which of the following entries in Table 3 were experimental observations?

A. 1, 2, and 7 only
B. 1, 2, and 4 only
C. 1, 2, 4, and 7 only
D. 1, 2, 3, 4, and 7 only

26. The student repeats Part 1 with a 2.0 *m* sugar-water solution. Based on the information provided, the student can expect that:

F. the freezing point depression for the 2.0 *m* sugar solution will be half that of the 1.0 *m* sugar solution.
G. the freezing point depression for the 2.0 *m* sugar solution will be twice that of the 1.0 *m* sugar solution.
H. the freezing point depression constant for distilled water will be twice that found using the 1.0 *m* sugar solution.
J. freezing point depression constant for distilled water will be half that found using the 1.0 *m* sugar solution.

27. Based on the information provided, it can be concluded that the unknown solute tested in Part 2 was most likely:

A. sugar.
B. calcium fluoride.
C. sodium chloride.
D. sodium fluoride.

28. Based on the information provided, decreasing the amount of salt in a salt-water solution will cause the freezing point of the solution to:

F. increase only.
G. decrease only.
H. decrease, then increase.
J. remain the same.

29. The student discovered that the scale was not calibrated properly (set to zero) before it was used in Part 2. Which of the following is the simplest way to correct this mistake?

A. Determine how much mass was added to the measurements from not zeroing the scale and subtract this value from entry 5 in Table 2.
B. Determine how much mass was added to the measurements from not zeroing the scale and subtract this value from entries 3 and 5 in Table 2.
C. Determine how much mass was added to the measurements from not zeroing the scale and subtract this value from entries 1, 2, and 5 and recalculate entries 3 and 5 in Table 2
D. No correction is necessary because any added mass from not zeroing the balance would cancel out in the calculations leading to entries 3 and 5.

Passage VI

A useful property of lenses is their ability to form images of objects due to the refraction of light as it passes from one medium to another. If the object and image sizes are h and h', respectively, the magnification of the lens is the ratio of the image size to object size, or:

$$\frac{h'}{h} = -\frac{i}{o} \qquad \text{(Equation 1)}$$

Where o represents the distance between the center of the lens and the object and i represents the distance between the center of the lens and the image. The magnification is represented as a negative number to indicate that an inverted image has a negative height and an upright image has a positive height.

Experiment 1

A student places an LED candle 100 centimeters from a thin converging lens. A paper screen on the other side of the lens is moved until a sharply focused image of the candle light appears on the screen (Figure 1). The image distance and height are measured. The candle is moved 20 centimeters closer to the lens and the experiment repeated until an object distance of 20 centimeters is reached. For each data set, the magnification is calculated (Table 1).

Table 1

Object Distance, o (cm)	Image Distance, i (cm)	Image Height, h' (cm)	Magnification
100.0	11.1	-0.55	-0.11
80.0	11.4	-0.71	-0.14
60.0	12.0	-1.00	-0.20
40.0	13.3	-1.66	-0.33
20.0	20.0	-5.00	-1.00

Experiment 2

The student repeats Experiment 1 after replacing the single lens with two identical lenses side-by-side and in contact with each other. Table 2 summarizes the results.

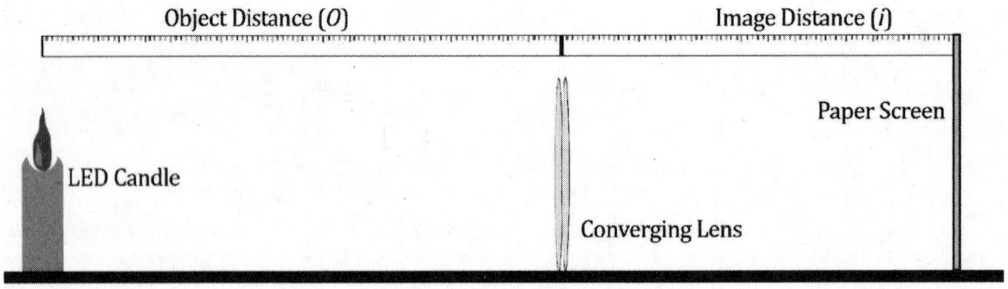

Figure 1

Table 2			
Object Distance, o (cm)	Image Distance, i (cm)	Image Height, h' (cm)	Magnification
100.0	5.3	−0.27	−0.05
80.0	5.3	−0.33	−0.07
60.0	5.5	−0.46	−0.09
40.0	5.7	−0.71	−0.14
20.0	6.7	−1.68	−0.34

Experiment 3

Using a similarly sized waterproofed LED candle and white plastic screen, the student repeats Experiment 1 in a water-filled tank until the length of the tank prevents further measurements. Table 3 summarizes the results.

Table 3			
Object Distance, o (cm)	Image Distance, i (cm)	Image Height, h' (cm)	Magnification
100.0	63.9	-3.20	-0.64
80.0	76.1	-4.76	-0.95
60.0	88.1	-7.34	-1.47

30. Which of the following best describes the purpose of Experiment 3?

F. To study how focal distance is affected by changing the medium surrounding a pair of converging lenses
G. To study how image formation is affected by combining converging lenses
H. To study how image formation is affected by changing the medium surrounding a converging lens
J. To study how image formation is affected by changing the position of an object relative to a converging lens

31. According to the experimental results, for the same object distance, the paired converging lenses in air produces a magnification:

A. less than that of a single converging lens in air.
B. greater than that of a single converging lens in air.
C. equal to that of a single converging lens in air.
D. greater than that of a single converging lens in water.

32. Which of the following graphs best represents the relationship between object distance and image distance for a thin converging lens in air?

F.

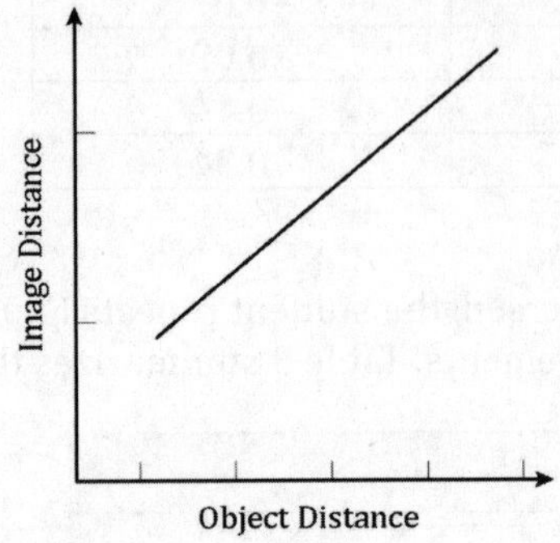

G.

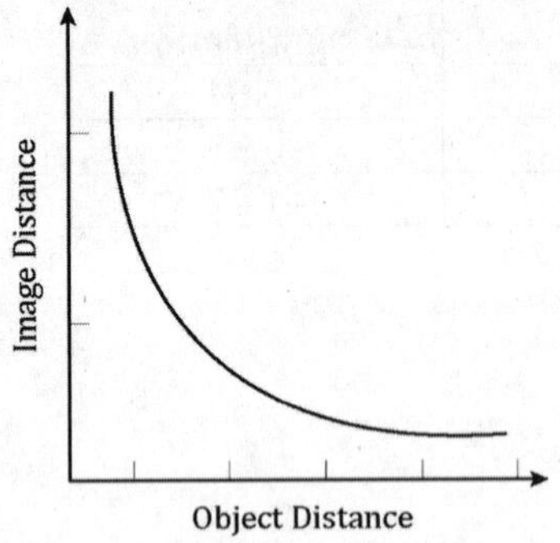

H.

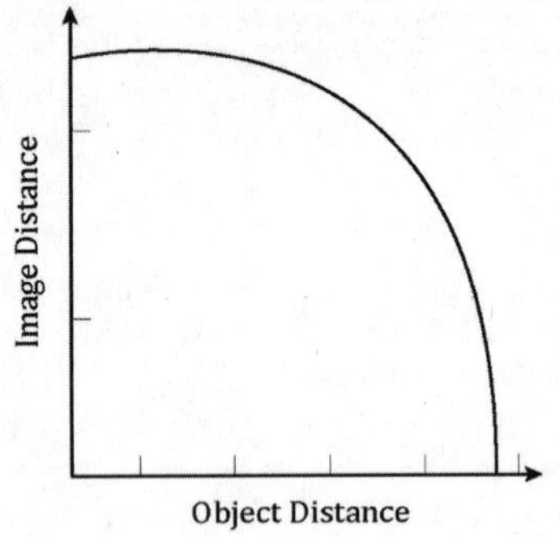

J.

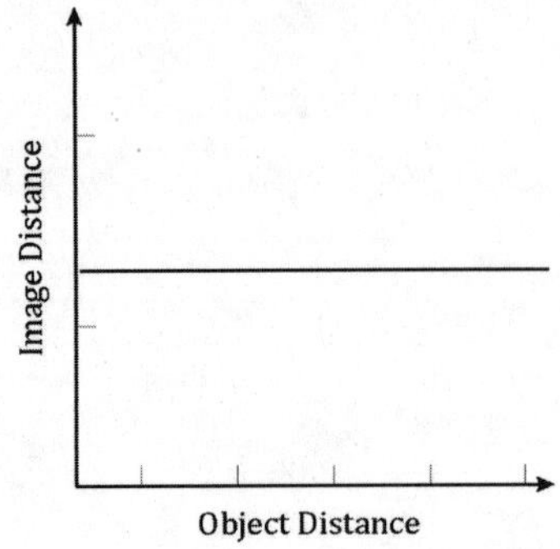

33. Based on the information provided, approximately how tall are the LED candles used in these experiments?

A. 5 cm
B. 10 cm
C. 20 cm
D. Cannot be determined from the given information

34. Focal length is the distance between the center of a lens and the point at which a clear image of a very distant object is formed. . For a thin converging lens in air, the lens formula relates focal length, *f*, to object distance, *o*, and image distance, *i*:

$$\frac{1}{f} = \frac{1}{i} + \frac{1}{o}$$

Using this information, what is the focal length of the lens used in Experiment 1?

F. 33.3
G. 40
H. 10
J. 5

LESSON 3 | CONFLICTING VIEWPOINTS

ACT SCIENCE

The passages and items in this section accompany the in-class review of the skills and concepts tested by the ACT Science Test. You will work through the items with your instructor in class. Answers are on page 583.

DIRECTIONS: Each passage below is followed by several items. After reading a passage, choose the best answer to each item. You may refer to the passages as often as necessary. You are NOT permitted the use of a calculator.

Typical Conflicting Viewpoints Items Ⓐ

Passage I

Theory 1

Early in the twentieth century, many chemists believed that the stability of the molecule methane, CH_4, could be explained by the "octet" rule, which states that stability occurs when the central atom, in this case carbon, is surrounded by eight "valence," or outer, electrons. Four of these originally came from the outer electrons of the carbon itself, and four came from the four surrounding hydrogen atoms (the hydrogen atom was considered an exception to the rule since it was known to favor a closed shell of two electrons as helium has). According to the octet rule, neither CH_3 nor CH_5 should exist as stable compounds, and this prediction has been borne out by experiment.

Theory 2

While the octet rule predicted many compounds accurately, it also had shortcomings. Ten electrons, for example, surround the compound PCl_5. The greatest shock to the octet rule concerned noble gases such as krypton and xenon, which have eight electrons surrounding them in their atomic states, and therefore should not form compounds since no more electrons would be needed to make an octet. The discovery in 1960 that xenon could form compounds such as XeF_4 forced consideration of a new theory, which held that (a) compounds formed when electrons were completely paired, either in bonds or in non-bonded pairs; (b) the total number of shared electrons around a central atom varied, and could be as high as twelve; (c) the shapes of compounds were such as to keep the pairs of electrons as far from each other as possible.

For example, since six electrons in the atomic state surround sulfur, in the compound SF_6 it acquired six additional shared electrons from the surrounding fluorines for a total of twelve electrons. The shape of the compound is "octahedral," as shown in Figure 1, since this conformation minimizes the overlap of bonding pairs of electrons.

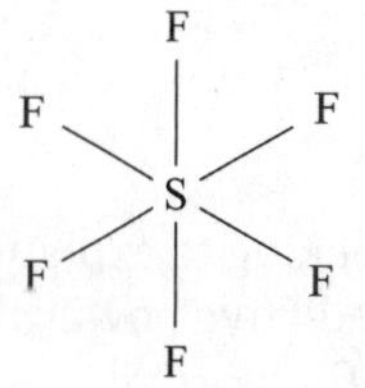

Figure 1

1. According to Theory 1, the compound CH_2Cl_2:

   A. should have eight electrons surrounding the carbon atom.
   B. cannot exist since the original carbon atom does not have eight electrons.
   C. should have eight electrons surrounding each hydrogen atom.
   D. requires more electrons for stability.

2. According to Theory 1, the compound XeF_4:

F. exists with an octet structure around the xenon.
G. should not exist since more than eight electrons surround the xenon.
H. will have similar chemical properties to CH_4.
J. exists with the xenon surrounded by twelve electrons.

3. The atom boron has three outer electrons, and in bonding to boron, a fluorine atom has a single, unpaired electron to bond with a boron atom. The BF_3 molecule is known to exist. Which of the following is true?

A. BF_3 obeys Theory 1.
B. The existence of BF_3 contradicts Theory 2.
C. According to Theory 2, the structure of BF_3 is a pyramid:

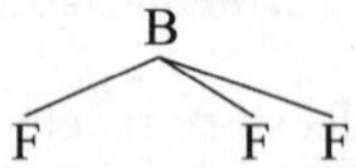

D. According to Theory 2, the structure of BF_3 is triangular and planar:

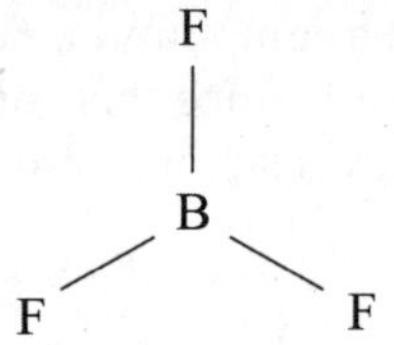

4. A scientist seeking to explain why Theory 2 has more predictive power than Theory 1 might argue that:

F. eight electrons shall represent a "closed shell."
G. while eight electrons represent a "closed shell" for some atoms, for others the closed shell may be six, ten, or twelve.
H. it is incorrect to assume that a given atom always has the same number of electrons around it.
J. CH_4 is not as important a compound as XeF_4.

5. Theory 2 could be threatened by evidence of:

A. the existence of SF_4.
B. the existence of XeF_5.
C. molecules with stable octets.
D. the existence of SF_6.

Passage II

Scientist 1

The atmosphere of Earth was at one time almost totally lacking in oxygen. One piece of evidence supporting this assertion is the very fact that life got started at all. The first chemical reactions that are necessary for the origin of life, the formation of amino acids, require ultraviolet light. Most of the ultraviolet light coming from the Sun is now absorbed by oxygen in the atmosphere. If there were as much oxygen in the atmosphere then as there is now, there would have been too little ultraviolet light available to enable life to begin. Also, the oldest bacteria, the ones that have the shortest DNA, are almost all anaerobes—they either do not need oxygen or die if exposed to oxygen. Most of the oxygen that exists now entered the atmosphere later from volcanic fumes.

Scientist 2

The prevailing opinion is that the atmosphere, though thicker now than it was in the past, is not essentially different in composition. The argument that Earth must originally have been deficient in oxygen is flawed. First of all, the presence of iron and other oxides in the rocks from this time indicates that there was oxygen available. Secondly, the requirement for a great deal of ultraviolet light holds only if there is a low concentration of the starting materials in the water. If the water in some prehistoric lake began to freeze, the starting materials would be concentrated in a small volume of unfrozen water. The high concentration of the starting materials would offset the so-called deficiency of ultraviolet light, and life could begin.

6. According to the hypothesis of Scientist 1, which of the following would have been among the last living things to evolve?

F. Anaerobes
G. Amino Acids
H. Insects
J. Viruses

7. According to the information presented by Scientist 1, if his theory of the origin of oxygen in the atmosphere is correct, the total amount of oxygen in the air over the next million years, on the average, should:

A. decrease, then increase.
B. increase, then decrease.
C. increase only.
D. decrease only.

8. Underlying the argument of Scientist 2 is the assumption that the oxygen in the oxides in the rocks was:

F. always tied up in the rocks.
G. involved in biological reactions.
H. completely gaseous during the early days of the atmosphere.
J. proportional to the oxygen in the atmosphere at the time.

9. Underlying Scientist 1's suggestion that the evolutionary record supports the idea of an oxygen deficiency on early Earth is the assumption that the oldest living things:

A. have the shortest DNA.
B. have the most fragmented DNA.
C. have changed radically.
D. must have died out.

10. Which of the following is the strongest argument Scientist 1 could use to counter Scientist 2's suggested mechanism for the origin of life?

F. There was not enough ultraviolet light available.
G. Chemical reactions occurred differently then.
H. The temperature at the surface of Earth at that time was always above 35°C because of geothermal heat release.
J. Most lakes would not have covered large enough areas to guarantee that all the essential building blocks were present.

11. To refute Scientist 1's hypothesis, Scientist 2 might best show that:

A. the amount of oxide in rocks has changed little over the past four billion years.
B. there are ways of making the biologically important molecules without ultraviolet light.
C. there are complex anaerobic bacteria.
D. the atmospheric pressure has not changed over Earth's history.

Conflicting Viewpoints Strategies Ⓐ

Passage III

In the 1940s, 1950s, and 1960s, the growing field of animal behavior maintained an ongoing debate about the origin of observed behavior in many different animal species. Two extreme viewpoints were at the center of this "Nature vs. Nurture" debate.

Viewpoint 1 (Nature)

Many behaviors or instincts are literally programmed by one or more genes. Genes serve as "blueprints" that enable an individual to carry out a particular stereotyped behavior (Fixed Action Pattern) as soon as the appropriate stimulus (releaser) is observed. Other individuals do not have to be observed performing the behavior. The releasing stimulus need never have been seen before. At first view of the releaser and every time thereafter, the Fixed Action Pattern will be carried out to completion in the exact same way—even if the releaser is removed before the Fixed Action

Pattern is finished! Examples include: a) the pecking of baby gulls at the red spot on their mother's bill (which causes the mother gull to regurgitate food), b) song birds producing their species song without ever having heard it before, and c) a male stickleback fish defending its territory by attacking anything red because other breeding males always have red underbellies.

Viewpoint 2 (Nurture)

Many behaviors are determined by experience and/or learning during an individual's lifetime. Genes provide the limits of the "blank slate" that each individual starts out as, but then various experiences will determine the actual behavior patterns within the individual genetic range of possibilities. In other words, behavior can be modified. Examples include: a) positive ("reward") reinforcement and punishment causing a behavior to increase and decrease (respectively), and b) songbirds producing their species song only after having heard it performed by other individuals of their species.

12. The red spot on a mother gull's bill is called a(n):

F. Fixed Action Pattern.
G. instinct.
H. releaser.
J. stereotyped response.

13. To refute the strict "genetic blueprint" ideas of Viewpoint 1, a scientist could show that:

A. baby gulls peck at a stick with a red spot.
B. baby gulls will peck at mother gulls' red spot as soon as they hatch out of their eggs.
C. baby gulls pecking at the red spot happens exactly the same way each time.
D. baby gulls' accuracy in pecking at mother gulls' red spot improves with practice.

14. A food-seeking blue jay captured a distinctively colored butterfly that had a bad-tasting substance in its tissues. After spitting out the butterfly, it never again tried to capture a similarly colored butterfly. This incident seems to support:

F. Viewpoint 1.
G. Viewpoint 2.
H. both viewpoints.
J. neither viewpoint (the incident is irrelevant).

15. Which of the following supports Viewpoint 1?

A. A rat reaches the end of a maze by the same route, but finishes faster after each trip.
B. A monkey watches other monkeys wash sweet potatoes before they eat them; then, he washes sweet potatoes before he eats them.
C. A male stickleback fish attacks a picture of a red mailbox held in front of his aquarium.
D. A bird performs its species song after hearing the song only once.

16. If a female goose uses a repeated beak and neck movement to return an egg to her nest, continuing the movement even when the egg slides off course or is removed, then this:

F. supports Viewpoint 1.
G. supports Viewpoint 2.
H. does not refer to behavior.
J. is irrelevant to the Nature vs. Nurture debate.

17. It is thought that some species of birds "learn" to fly. This belief is based on observations of young birds fluttering and flapping their wings at the nest until they reach the age when flight is possible. In Species X, nestlings were kept in harmless, but tight plastic tubes in which they could not carry out such "practice movements." They were released when they reached the age of flight. Viewpoint 1 predicts that the birds will fly:

A. after fluttering their wings for a time.
B. after watching other birds flutter their wings.
C. after watching other birds flutter and fly.
D. immediately.

18. A songbird can sing its species song after it hears other birds of its own species singing. Yet, if it hears the song from another species, the bird will not sing the "foreign" song. This suggests that:

F. genetic "programming" and experience play a role in this species' ability to sing its song.
G. this species' song is a Fixed Action Pattern.
H. song development in this species is strictly a learned behavior with no genetic component.
J. genes appear to be far more important than experience in this example.

Passage IV

The Sun's atmosphere is divided into three major regions: the photosphere, the chromosphere, and the corona. The photosphere is the visible region of the Sun. Just above the photosphere is the chromosphere which is far less dense, but hotter. Consisting of low-density plasma, the corona is the thin, outermost atmosphere of the sun that extends for millions of kilometers above the Sun's surface.

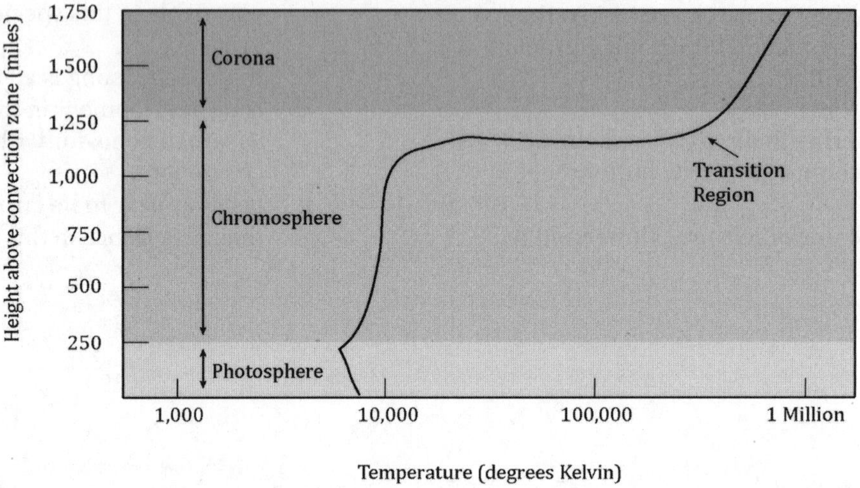

One would expect that the atmosphere of the Sun should become cooler with increasing distance from its surface. To the contrary, as the graph above shows, coronal temperatures increase with increasing distance from the sun's visible photosphere, rising to over a million degrees. The mechanism responsible for this heating remains a fundamental question of modern astrophysics.

Three scientists discuss the heating mechanism.

Scientist 1

Just above the surface of the sun, in the chromosphere, there are approximately 10,000 regions of violently rotating columns of air, or vortices. These vortices are likely produced by magnetic activity within the sun that exerts pressure on the plasma in the atmosphere. Computer simulations suggest that plasma particles trapped within the vortices are accelerated as they spiral toward the corona. The accelerated plasma particles greatly increase the average speed of the coronal particles, which translates into higher coronal temperatures.

Scientist 2

Solar telescopes have detected millions of magnetic patches on the sun's photosphere. The patches, between 50 and 1,000 kilometers wide, are constantly changing in size and shape due to the turbulent movement of the plasma in the chromosphere. The magnetic fields in the sun's corona constantly change as they respond to changes in the photosphere magnetic patches. As magnetic field lines in the corona interact, they undergo a process called reconnection: they snap apart and then reconnect. The reconnection releases a tremendous amount of heat and wave energy, causing the high coronal temperatures.

Scientist 3

Neutrons are produced in the sun's interior through thermonuclear reactions in the core and the stripping of complex particles at the surface. Due to solar flares and other magnetic phenomena, some of these neutrons reach the base of the sun's corona. Free neutrons last about 15 minutes before they undergo radioactive decay, creating electrons as energetic as 0.78 MeV. When these fast moving electrons collide with particles in the corona, they transfer some of their energy, causing the high coronal temperatures.

19. Which of the following best describes the question the three scientists attempt to answer?

A. What is the cause of vortices on the surface of the sun?
B. What is the cause of high coronal temperatures?
C. What are the physical characteristics of the sun's corona?
D. What is the temperature gradient of the sun's corona?

20. Based on the graph and the views of Scientist1, vortices may be found at heights:

F. less than 250 mi above the convection zone.
G. between 250 and 1,300 mi above the convection zone.
H. more than 1,300 mi above the convection zone.
J. more than 10,000 mi above the convection zone.

21. Scientist 2 states that the changing magnetic patches on the sun's photosphere are due to:

A. the radioactive decay of neutrons.
B. plasma particles trapped within vortices.
C. the movement of the plasma in the chromosphere.
D. fast moving electrons colliding with particles in the corona.

22. Magnetism plays a role in the explanation of the coronal heating in the views of:

F. only Scientist 1 and Scientist 2.
G. only Scientist 1 and Scientist 3.
H. only Scientist 2 and Scientist 3.
J. Scientist 1, Scientist 2 and Scientist 3.

23. All three scientists would likely agree with which of the following statements?

A. The energy source for high coronal temperatures in the corona originates near or in the Sun.
B. The coronal temperatures do not vary significantly from the average surface temperature of the Sun.
C. The decay of neutrons plays an important role in the creation of high coronal temperatures.
D. Magnetic-generated tornadoes produce neutrons that decay, creating energetic electrons.

Passage V

Space probes have imaged thousands of gullies on Mars—channels, or ravines, worn into the surface of the planet. On Earth, gullies form as running water erodes soil. Mars, however, is currently a frigid planet without rain or liquid water on the surface. Interestingly, some of the Martian gullies appear to have formed very recently. Three planetary scientists discuss the origins of gullies on Mars.

Scientist 1

Mars contains many deposits of solid carbon dioxide, or dry ice, buried under the dust and sand found on the slopes of hills and craters. When sunlight warms these deposits, the dry ice converts directly into a gas through the process of sublimation. As the carbon dioxide gas blows out of the ground, the surrounding dust and sand flow like a liquid in a process called fluidization.

An experiment conducted on Earth supports this mechanism for gully formation. A tub was filled with Mars-like dust and sand shaped into a small mound. An air pump buried beneath the mound forced air up toward the surface. The dust and sand flowed down the mound, creating gullies similar to those imaged on Mars.

Scientist 2

The gullies on Mars form when water from shallow aquifers seeps onto the surface and flows downslope. Although the surface of Mars is dry today, there is abundant evidence that at one time water flowed on its surface. Some of that water likely still exists in underground aquifers. Liquid water is unstable on the surface of Mars due to low temperatures and low atmospheric pressure.

However, computer models indicate that liquid water could be discharged onto the surface of Mars in two situations: the liquid in a shallow aquifer is water with a temperature of at least 350 K, or if the liquid is a water-based brine with a freezing point of no more than 250 K. In either scenario, the flow of water onto the surface is likely triggered by the melting of surface ice plugs, which otherwise act like caps for the water in the aquifers. Once the ice plugs melt, the sub-surface water gushes to the surface, forming gullies as the water flows downslope.

Scientist 3

The gullies on Mars form when snow packs melt. The melted snow (liquid water) at the bottom of snow packs does not undergo rapid evaporation due to the low atmospheric pressure on Mars. This water carves the gullies as it flows downslope. This theory is supported by the fact that most gullies found on Mars are on the cold, pole-facing slopes of hills and craters. These colder conditions allow for the accumulation of snow on these slopes, which with warmer temperatures, begin to melt, initiating the formation of gullies.

24. According to the information provided, which of the following accurately describes the current environmental conditions on Mars?

F. High temperatures and high atmospheric pressure
G. High temperatures and low atmospheric pressure
H. Low temperatures and high atmospheric pressure
J. Low temperatures and low atmospheric pressure

25. Which scientist's argument presents water as the primary agent in gully formation on Mars?

A. Scientist 1 only
B. Scientist 2 only
C. Scientists 1 and 3
D. Scientists 2 and 3

26. Which scientist's argument does NOT require the flow of a liquid to explain gully formation on Mars?

F. Scientist 1 only
G. Scientist 2 only
H. Scientist 3 only
J. None of the scientists

27. All three scientists agree that gully formation on Mars is triggered by:

A. the flow of a liquid on the surface.
B. surface warming.
C. sublimation of sub-surface ices.
D. a drop in atmospheric pressure.

28. Which scientist's argument is best supported by the fact that most gullies on Mars are found on cold, pole-facing slopes?

F. Scientist 1
G. Scientist 2
H. Scientist 3
J. All three scientists

29. The gamma ray spectrometer (GRS) on-board the space probe Mars Odyssey detects water on the surface of Mars down to a depth of several meters. A strong correlation is found between areas on Mars where the GRS detected high levels of water and where the majority of gullies are found. That most gullies are found in water-rich areas supports the position(s) of:

A. Scientist 1 only.
B. Scientist 3 only.
C. Scientists 1 and 3.
D. Scientists 2 and 3.

TEST MECHANICS

ACT SCIENCE

Overview

The Science Test consists of 40 multiple-choice items divided into six or seven groups. Each group of items is based on a report of data findings, a description of an experiment, or the presentation of a debate on different scientific theories. The time limit for the Science Test is 35 minutes. Calculators are NOT allowed on the ACT Science Test.

We'll call the initial presentation a "passage," whether it is a report of data (Data Representation), a description of an experiment (Research Summary), or a debate of a theory (Conflicting Viewpoints). So, just as the English and Reading Tests have passages with associated items, the Science Test has passages (of the three types) with associated items. We'll use this terminology even though "passage" doesn't quite fit here since the Science Test uses a lot of diagrams, pictures, tables, and graphs.

The Science Test roughly follows the content of science courses taught in grades 7 through 12. Passages use content from the following areas:

- **Biology:** botany, cellular biology, ecology, evolution, genetics, microbiology, zoology
- **Chemistry:** biochemistry, organic chemistry, nuclear chemistry, thermo-chemistry, acids and bases, kinetics and equilibria, properties of matter
- **Earth/Space Sciences:** astronomy, environmental science, geology, meteorology, oceanography
- **Physics:** mechanics, thermodynamics, fluids, solids, electromagnetism, optics

Although these are obviously "science" subjects, you don't really need to know any science—beyond some basic concepts—to do well on this part of the exam. In fact, the ACT Science Test would be more accurately labeled "Science Reasoning" Test because that phrase would emphasize that the items test reasoning ability and not the mastery of some specific body of scientific knowledge.

Anatomy

DIRECTIONS: The passage below is followed by several items. After reading the passage, choose the best answer to each item. You may refer to the passage as often as necessary. You are NOT permitted the use of a calculator.

Passage I

A student studied the process by which malodorzane is produced by heating protocrud in a closed system and then releasing it into the surrounding atmosphere.

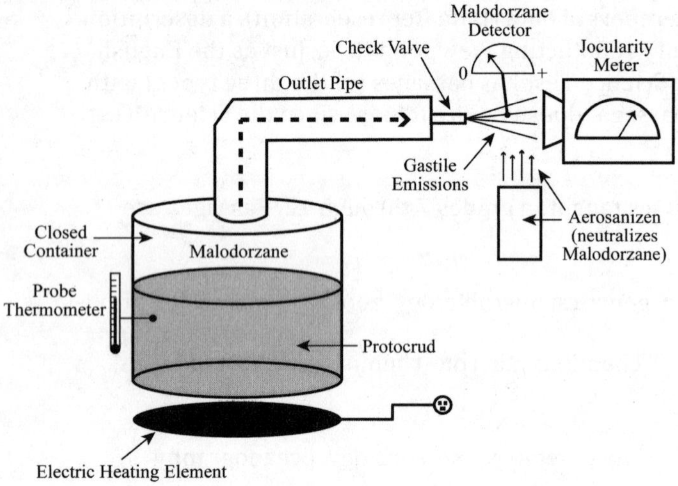

Experiment 1

The concentration of malodorzane produced by the protocrud at various temperatures was measured by determining how much aerosanizen was needed to neutralize the malodorzane (Table 1).

Now that you've read the directions, you don't need to read them again, especially not during the test. The only thing of real significance is that you CANNOT use your calculator on this part, even though you might think it would be nice. But you should be able to remember that one point without re-reading the directions.

In this Science passage, there is a single device and a series of tables that report data from the operation of the device. You'll see examples of other types of passages later in the Science Lessons.

TABLE 1	
Temperature of Protocrud	Aerosanizen (spritz/minute)
20°C	46–198
22.5°C	199–377
25°C	378–612

Experiment 2

The student observed that the release of gastiles, whether or not the malodorzane was counteracted by aerosanizen, produced primary and secondary jocularities. The intensity of the jocularities was measured and recorded for different durations of gastiles (Table 2).

TABLE 2		
	Intensity of Jocularities	
Gastiles (seconds)	Primary Jocularities (decibels)	Secondary Jocularities (decibels)
1.0	30 dB	—*
2.0	35 dB	—*
5.0	40 dB	30 dB
12.0	60 dB	40 dB
19.0	120 dB	60 dB

*Intensity was below measurable levels.

Experiment 3

The student measured and recorded the duration of the jocularities for different durations of gastiles (Table 3).

TABLE 3		
	Duration of Jocularities	
Gastiles (seconds)	Primary Jocularities (seconds)	Secondary Jocularities (seconds)
0.2	3	—*
1.0	7	—*
2.5	13	11
5.0	25	9
12.0	51	4

*Duration was below measurable levels.

1. Data from the passage indicate that duration was greatest for secondary jocularities produced by gastiles of what duration?

A. 1.0 seconds
B. 2.5 seconds
C. 5.0 seconds
D. 12.0 seconds

2. Gastiles with a duration of 13.0 seconds would probably produce primary jocularities of a duration:

F. between 3 and 7 seconds.
G. between 7 and 13 seconds.
H. between 13 and 25 seconds.
J. greater than 51 seconds.

3. A primary jocularity of 90 decibels would most likely be produced by a gastile of:

A. less than 1.0 seconds.
B. between 1.0 and 2.0 seconds.
C. between 12.0 and 19.0 seconds.
D. greater than 19.0 seconds.

4. The data in Table 1 would be most useful in determining whether:

F. the temperature of aerosanizen affects the chemical's ability to neutralize malodorzane.
G. the volume of malodorzane varies with the chemical composition of the protocrud.
H. the closed system produces a greater volume of malodorzane than aerosanizen.
J. the temperature of the protocrud affects the rate of malodorzane production.

1. **(B)** *Data for the duration of jocularities is given in Table 3, and the greatest entry, 11 seconds, corresponds to gastiles of duration 2.5 seconds.*

2. **(J)** *Again, the answer is in Table 3, but this time there is no entry for 13 seconds. The largest entry is 12.0 seconds. Because primary jocularity duration increases as gastile duration increases, the corresponding entry in the "Primary Jocularities" column, if one existed, would likely be greater than 51 seconds.*

3. **(C)** *The relevant information is located in Table 2, but there is no entry in the table for 90 dB. However, 90 dB is between 60 dB and 120 dB. The most likely conclusion, then, is that the corresponding entry in the first column, if one existed, would be between 12.0 and 19.0 seconds.*

4. **(J)** *Table 1 shows the amount of aerosanizen needed to neutralize the quantity of malodorzane at various temperatures. So, the data in that table would provide information about how the temperature of the protocrud affects the rate of malodorzane production.*

Pacing

The Science Test presents six or seven passages, with a total of 40 items, to be completed in 35 minutes. The table below establishes the time that you can afford to spend on various parts of the Science Test if your goal is to complete the entire test. For many people, completing the entire test may be an unrealistic goal, and a better goal for a test with seven passages is to complete six of the seven passages. Or perhaps even only five passages. If you choose to define your goal differently than completing the entire test, then you can adjust the timing for the remaining passages so that you'll have more time (e.g., four minutes for five items equals 48 seconds per item).

TESTS WITH SIX PASSAGES		
PASSAGE	TIME TO SPEND	REMAINING TIME
I	5 minutes	30 minutes
II	6 minutes	24 minutes
III	6 minutes	18 minutes
IV	6 minutes	12 minutes
V	6 minutes	6 minutes
VI	6 minutes	0 minutes

TESTS WITH SEVEN PASSAGES		
PASSAGE	TIME TO SPEND	REMAINING TIME
I	5 minutes	30 minutes
II	5 minutes	25 minutes
III	5 minutes	20 minutes
IV	5 minutes	15 minutes
V	5 minutes	10 minutes
VI	5 minutes	5 minutes
VII	5 minutes	0 minutes

You should begin work on each passage by reading the passage itself and familiarizing yourself with the main purpose of the data reports or experiments or the focus of the debate. This should be an overview of the information, not a detailed study. You are reading primarily to learn where information is located so that you can retrieve it—if an item asks about it.

Preview the number of questions associated with each passage. Allow yourself one minute to learn about the passage, then spend between 40 and 50 seconds answering each item. Thus, the time you spend on each passage will vary depending on the number of items associated with that passage. So, on the Science Test (perhaps more so than on any other test), time is of the essence.

Time Trial

(6 items; 5 minutes)

DIRECTIONS: The passage below is followed by several items. After reading the passage, choose the best answer to each item. You may refer to the passage as often as necessary. You are NOT permitted the use of a calculator.

Passage I

How old is the earth? Two opposing views are presented.

Scientist 1

The earth is approximately five billion years old. We know this to be true because of radioactive dating. Some chemical elements are unstable and will fall apart into smaller pieces over time. This disintegration occurs over a period of time that is very regular for the particular element. In general, we talk about the half-life of the element, which is the time necessary for one-half of the material to disintegrate. This time is constant whether we have an ounce or a ton of the material. So, by measuring the relative amounts of the material left and the disintegration products, we can form an accurate idea of how old the earth is by determining how many half-lives have occurred.

Scientist 2

The argument that supports the hypothesis that the earth is only five billion years old is seriously flawed. What the argument fails to take into account is that the earth is the constant recipient of a shower of cosmic debris in the form of meteorites. These meteorites replenish the stock of radioactive material on the surface of the earth, making it seem as though the earth has gone through fewer half-lives than it really has. Therefore, all estimates of the age of the earth based on radioactive dating are too low.

1. Which of the following is a major assumption of Scientist 1?

A. The earth has life that recycles carbon-14.
B. The half-life of all radioactive elements is five billion years.
C. The radioactive material was formed at the same time as the earth.
D. There is no longer any radioactivity on the earth.

2. Which of the following is a major assumption of Scientist 2?

F. The meteorites that land on the earth are radioactive.
G. Few meteorites have landed on the earth.
H. The earth is more than five billion years old.
J. The earth is highly radioactive.

3. Which of the following, if true, would best refute Scientist 2's argument?

A. Recent meteorites have been found to be radioactive.
B. The earth has a greater amount of radioactive material on the surface than in the mantle.
C. The earth's orbit intersects the orbits of a number of meteorites.
D. Few meteorites have been found to contain radioactive material.

4. Which of the following would be most likely if Scientist 2's hypothesis were correct?

F. The amount of radioactive material and its disintegration products on the earth has decreased over time.
G. The amount of radioactive material and its disintegration products has increased over time.
H. The amount of radioactive material and its disintegration products has stayed essentially the same over time.
J. The earth will reach a critical mass and explode.

5. Which of the following would be most likely if Scientist 1's hypothesis were correct?

A. The total amount of radioactive material and its disintegration products has decreased over time.
B. The total amount of radioactive material and its disintegration products has increased over time.
C. The total amount of radioactive material and its disintegration products has stayed essentially the same over time.
D. The earth will reach a critical mass and explode.

6. Which of the following conditions, if true, would prevent an estimation of the earth's age by Scientist 1's method?

F. No radioactive disintegration has occurred.
G. Only some of the radioactive material has disintegrated.
H. Eighty percent of the radioactive material has disintegrated.
J. All of the radioactive material has disintegrated.

Game Plan

Quickly Preview the Test Section, but Skip the Directions

Last-minute adjustments to the test format are theoretically (but not practically) possible, so check the subject test before you start to work, especially the number of passages, the number of items, and the time limit. And yes, the test-writers always tell you to "read the directions carefully." But they don't tell you that you have to read them during the test. Instead, become familiar with them <u>before</u> test day. That way, you won't waste 30 seconds or more (enough time to answer an item) re-reading directions you are already familiar with.

Personalize the Passage Order

You are not required to do the passages in the order in which they appear in the test booklet. You can do the first passage second, or fourth, or last; and you can do the last passage first or third. So, you have the flexibility of choosing which ones you will do before the others, and you'll want to do first those passages that seem <u>easier</u>. "Easier," in this context, is really a subjective matter; it means the ones with which you are most comfortable, either because of the type of presentation or the subject matter.

- First, do those passage formats that you find easiest to handle.
- Then, of the remaining passages, do the familiar ones.
- Finally, do the rest of the passages, from the simplest to the most complicated.

Put large numbers in the margins of the test booklet beside each passage to indicate where the passage comes in the order.

Read the Passage

For the Science Test, "reading the passage" means "reading through" the passage. You can't afford to study the passage, and don't forget that this is an "open-book" test. So, learn generally what is going on and where things are located. Then, let the items tell you where to look more carefully.

- Read any introductory paragraph(s). Not only does this material usually explain why an experiment is being conducted or data are being collected, but it often defines a key term that is essential to understanding the connections of the various parts of the passage.
- Examine any diagrams or schematics. The focus of a passage is often a device that includes beakers, tubing, switches, pulleys, test tubes, and other paraphernalia associated with science. Try to understand what the device is designed to accomplish and how the various parts work together.
- Look at the various subparts of the passage. The subparts are things such as experiments that change initial conditions, tables of data, and graphs. Do not try to fully understand these. Just get a general notion of what they do. For example, for a graph, read the title and the labels of the x- and y-axes. For tables, read the column heads and the titles of the rows. Do not, however, read specific values on a graph or in a table. There are too many of them, and only one or two are likely to be relevant to answering one of the few items based on that passage (compared to all the different questions that the test-writers could have chosen).

Answer the Items

Answer the question that is being asked. One of the most commonly made mistakes is to read the item stem carelessly and then answer the "wrong" question. It's just a matter of inattention, in which you respond to what you think you read rather than what is actually there on the page. Since wrong answers often correspond to wrong readings, if you make this mistake, you are probably going to find a pretty good answer—to the wrong question.

Pay attention to thought-reversers. "Thought-reversers" are words in the item stem like "NOT," "BUT," and "EXCEPT." These words turn the question upside-down. What is normally the right answer is now a wrong answer, and what is normally a wrong answer is the right answer. Circle these words or put stars beside them so that they get your attention again.

Locate the relevant information. The first and often last step in answering an item is to locate the information you need. Most item stems use a key word or phrase to tell you where to look. For example, "in Table 2" tells you that the information you need is located in Table 2; "the troposphere" tells you that you need the graph, table, or description that supplies information about the troposphere; and "lowering the temperature" indicates that the answer is in the subpart of the passage that provides information about temperature.

Use the Answer Choices

Study the answer choices for guidance. The answer choices, like an item stem, can direct you to the subpart of the passage that contains the information you need. Consider the following item, in which only the answer choices are visible:

Example:

A. Sodium
B. Potassium
C. Lithium
D. Oxygen

With this array, you know to look at that table or graph or paragraph that includes that list of terms. The choices will also give you guidance as to what degree of precision is required by the item.

Often, the choices are ranges of values, such as $0.015w$ to $0.018w$, rather than specific values, such as simply $0.018w$. Do not look for more precision than the choices allow.

Read the answer choices carefully. The test-writers love to put in wrong answers that look right. For example, if a particular value doubles with a decrease in temperature from 40°C to 20°C, a question might ask: "Assuming the temperature rises from 20°C to 40°C, what happens to the value?" The correct answer is, of course: "The value is reduced by half." But you can bet that the wrong answers will include ideas like "doubles," "increases by one-fourth," and "decreases by four"—or some other variation on those ideas.

Eliminate Choices, Guess (If Necessary), and Move On

Do NOT spend too much time on any one item. Remember that you get +1 for the hardest item and +1 for the easiest item. The items that correspond to a Science passage tend to be arranged from easiest to most difficult. (This is not an absolute rule; it is just a useful tool.) The first item may ask you to find a single number in a table. The second item may ask for a value that is the largest or smallest in a series. And the third item may require you

to interpolate a value. Then, the going might get considerably more difficult. So, try the next item, and if it is totally confusing, skip the rest of the questions and go to the next passage where the difficulty resets to the lowest setting. And don't forget: the ACT test has no penalty for guessing. If you find yourself stuck on a difficult item, eliminate as many choices as possible, guess, and move on!

QUIZ

ACT SCIENCE

This section contains an ACT Science quiz. Complete the quiz under timed conditions. Answers are on page 583. *(16 items; 15 minutes)*

DIRECTIONS: Each passage below is followed by several items. After reading a passage, choose the best answer to each item. You may refer to the passages as often as necessary. You are NOT permitted the use of a calculator.

Passage I

The ecological pyramid below shows the relative biomass* of organisms at each trophic feeding level of a marine food chain.

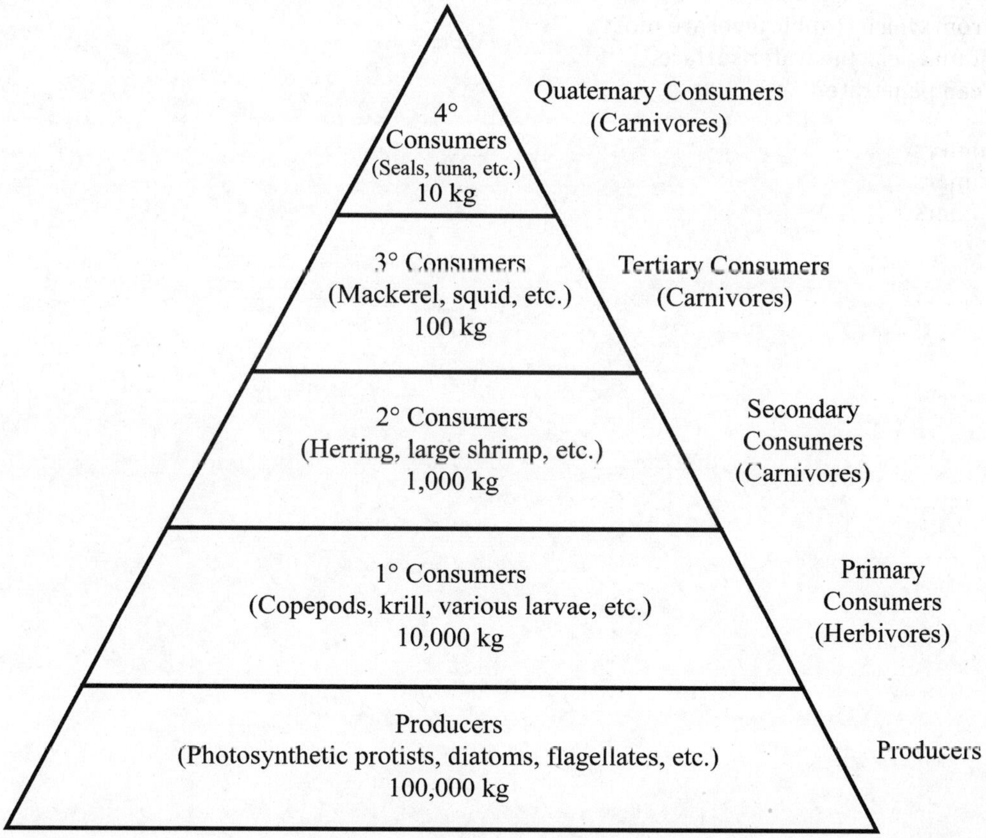

*Biomass is the total dry weight of organisms (useable chemical energy stored in organic matter) at each trophic level at any given time.

1. According to the diagram, the trophic level with the largest relative biomass is the:

A. 4° consumers.
B. 3° and 2° consumers.
C. 1° consumers.
D. producers.

2. From the information in the diagram, one can conclude that at any given time:

F. 10 seals may be found for every mackerel.
G. the relative dry weight of all carnivores combined is far greater than that of the herbivores alone.
H. only 1 percent of all producers live long enough to be eaten by a mackerel.
J. the relative dry weight of every consumer trophic level is usually less than that of the trophic level on which they feed.

3. Organisms from which trophic level are most likely to be found near the water surface where light can penetrate?

A. 4° consumers
B. 2° consumers
C. 3° consumers
D. producers

4. If there were an additional trophic level of carnivores (5° consumers), its relative biomass at any given time would be approximately:

F. 1 kg.
G. 11 kg.
H. 111 kg.
J. 1,000,000 kg.

5. The best explanation for biomass being measured as dry weight is:

A. if water weight were included, efficiency ratios at each trophic level would be unpredictable.
B. body fluids contribute little to the mass of marine organisms.
C. water molecules contain little or no usable chemical energy.
D. each trophic level contains a different amount of water.

Passage II

The table below shows various characteristics of different layers of the atmosphere.

APPROXIMATE ALTITUDE (KM)	LAYERS OF THE ATMOSPHERE	APPROXIMATE MEAN TEMPERATURE (° C)	CLOUDS
60,000			
6,000			
	THERMOSPHERE		
600		1200	
80		−90	
	MESOSPHERE		
50		−3	
	STRATOSPHERE		Cirrus
12		−50	
			Cirrostratus
	TROPOSPHERE		Altostratus
0		18	Nimbostratus

6. Which statement accurately describes the relationship between the approximate altitude and the approximate mean temperature of the layers of the atmosphere?

F. As altitude increases, temperature increases.
G. As altitude increases, temperature decreases.
H. As altitude increases, temperature first decreases then continuously increases.
J. As altitude increases, temperature first decreases, then increases, then decreases, and then increases.

7. Based on the information in the table, the atmospheric layer with the narrowest range of altitude is the:

A. thermosphere.
B. troposphere.
C. mesosphere.
D. stratosphere.

8. The type of cloud(s) most likely to consist of ice crystals is (are):

F. nimbostratus only.
G. nimbostratus and altostratus.
H. cirrus and cirrostratus.
J. cirrostratus only.

9. The absorption of solar heat energy increases as the gases of the atmosphere become less dense, or rarefied. The layer of the atmosphere that appears most rarefied is the:

A. thermosphere.
B. mesosphere.
C. stratosphere.
D. troposphere.

10. According to the table, which atmospheric layer shows a decrease in temperature of approximately 3°C for every 1 kilometer increase in altitude?

F. thermosphere
G. mesosphere
H. stratosphere
J. troposphere

Passage III

Using electrical circuits, three experiments were performed to investigate the relationship between voltage (volts), resistance (ohms) (total resistance equals the sum of individual resistances), and current (amperes). Each experiment was set up with the following circuit design:

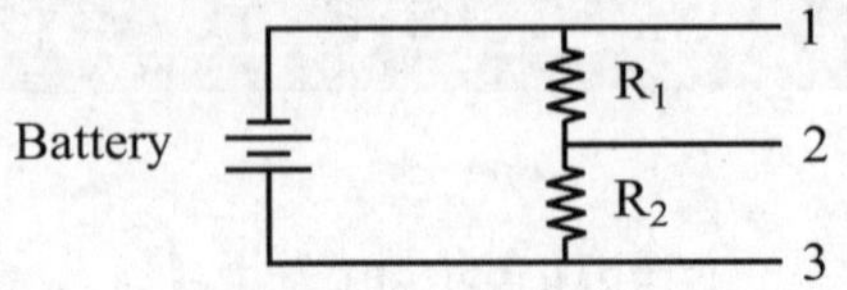

Experiment 1

Using a 6 volt battery (far left), and two 1,000 ohm resistors (R_1 and R_2), the measured voltages between points 1 and 2 and between points 2 and 3 were 3 volts each.

Experiment 2

When the battery voltage was increased to 12 volts, and the resistors were kept the same (1,000 ohms each), the measured voltages between points 1 and 2 and between points 2 and 3 were 6 volts each.

Experiment 3

Using the original 6 volt battery, R_1 was replaced with a 2,000 ohm resistor. The voltages measured between points 1 and 2 and between points 2 and 3 were 4 volts and 2 volts, respectively.

11. Judging from the results in Experiment 1 and Experiment 2, if the battery voltage were changed to 1.5 volts and both resistors were 1,000 volts, what voltage would be expected between point 1 and point 2?

A. 0.75 volts
B. 1.5 volts
C. 3.0 volts
D. 6.0 volts

12. After studying the measurement made in the previous question, as well as those made earlier in Experiments 1, 2, and 3, the experimenter could reasonably hypothesize that:

F. voltage measured across a resistor is inversely proportional to the value of that resistor.
G. voltage measured across a resistor is directly proportional to the value of that resistor.
H. voltage measured across a resistor is not related to the value of that resistor.
J. voltage measured across a resistor equals the battery voltage.

13. When the experimenter recorded the current in the circuit of Experiment 1, it measured 0.003 amperes. In Experiment 3, however, the current measured 0.002 amperes. These results show that current and total resistances are:

A. directly proportional.
B. inversely proportional.
C. equal.
D. unrelated.

14. Which of the following formulas for the current in the circuit best summarizes the above results? (The battery voltage is given by V_b and the total resistance is given by R.)

F. $V_b R$
G. $\frac{R}{V_b}$
H. $\frac{V_b}{R}$
J. $V_b + R$

15. A new circuit is set up, similar in design to those in the experiments. The battery voltage and the size of the resistors are unknown, but the current measures 0.001 amperes. If the battery voltage is doubled and one of the two resistors is replaced with one having a smaller value, which answer most accurately describes the new current?

A. It will be smaller than 0.001 amperes.
B. It will be unchanged.
C. It will be greater than 0.001 amperes.
D. Cannot be determined from the given information

16. Which of the following single changes to Experiment 2 would produce a current of 0.004 amperes?

F. Decrease the voltage to 8 volts.
G. Increase the resistance to 3,000 ohms.
H. Neither (F) nor (G) will create a current of 0.004 amperes.
J. Either (F) or (G) will create a current of 0.004 amperes.

STRATEGY SUMMARY

ACT SCIENCE

General Strategies

Science items test your reasoning skills, not your scientific knowledge. So, most of the passages have all of the information that you will need to answer the items. In some cases, background information at the level of your high school general science courses is required, but do not assume data that is not given. The following are general strategies for the Science Test:

1. Before reading any Science passage, *quickly glance over all of the passages and code them according to passage-type* in order to determine the order in which you will attack them. Identifying and coding the passages should take no more than five seconds each.

2. *Do NOT preview the item stems.* Since the Science item stems tend to be confusing without having first read the corresponding passage, previewing them will only confuse you and slow you down.

3. It is important to only *read the passage thoroughly once*, rather than to skim over it several times. The material can be difficult to understand; thus, it is important to read thoughtfully and carefully. *Be an active reader.* Use your pencil to underline key words and points of information. That way, you will be able to locate them easily when answering the items.

4. When a Science passage includes tables or graphs, make sure that you *read and understand the labels* on axes, columns, and rows. You need to know what information is being presented and what units of measure are being used.

5. Many passages will contain much more information than you need to answer a particular item. In your search for a logical conclusion, *do not be misled by data that does not relate to the item at hand.*

6. In Data Representation passages, tables and graphs present results, often of observations or experiments. Corresponding items will usually ask you to spot patterns in the data, so *look for trends*, such as upward movement, downward movement, inverse variation, etc.

7. The experiments described in Research Summary passages are based on scientific assumptions. However, if an assumption is faulty, the experiment may not prove what it claims, and conclusions drawn from it may therefore be invalid. So, for items that ask about the validity of a scientific conclusion, *consider the validity of any underlying assumptions.*

8. The arguments presented in Conflicting Viewpoints passages are also based on scientific assumptions. Again, *if the assumption is wrong, the entire argument is open to challenge.* Assumptions that are based on scientific fact add strength to an argument; faulty assumptions weaken an argument.

9. Offering the assumptions that you started with as proof of your argument is called circular reasoning, and this type of proof is not acceptable. For that reason, any conclusions discussed in Science passages or offered as answer choices must be based on additional evidence (e.g., experiments) to be valid. *Beware of any conclusions that are nothing more than a restatement of an underlying premise.*

10 All of the information that you need to answer the items is provided in the passage—do not infer any information that is not given or relate any previous experience to the passage. *Pay attention to material noted with an asterisk.*

11 *Transcribe your answers from the test booklet to the answer sheet in groups (by passage).* However, when you arrive at the last passage, transcribe each answer as it is determined.

Strategies for Each Passage-Type

- ***Data Representation Passages:*** When given data in the form of a graph or a chart, pay particular attention to the scale, units, legend, and other noted information.
- ***Research Summary Passages:*** When given multiple experiments, identify the controls and variables. Note that the controls must remain the same and that variables can only change one at a time in all experiments.
- ***Conflicting Viewpoints Passages:*** When given two points of view on a topic, identify the main points of difference and the logical value of each argument. After you understand the nature of the passage, attack the items.

Strategies for Each Item-Type

- ***Comprehension Items:*** Recognize basic concepts. Read carefully. Make sure that your answers consider appropriate scales and units. Also, note the difference between absolute and percentage changes.
- ***Analysis Items:*** Identify relationships and trends. Pay particular attention to direct and inverse relationships.
- ***Application Items:*** Draw conclusions, predict outcomes, and synthesize new information. In answering Application items, beware of the following terms: "all," "none," "always," and "never." Remember that a single case of contradictory evidence is all that is necessary to disprove an absolute theory.

Cambridge Practice Test Reinforcement

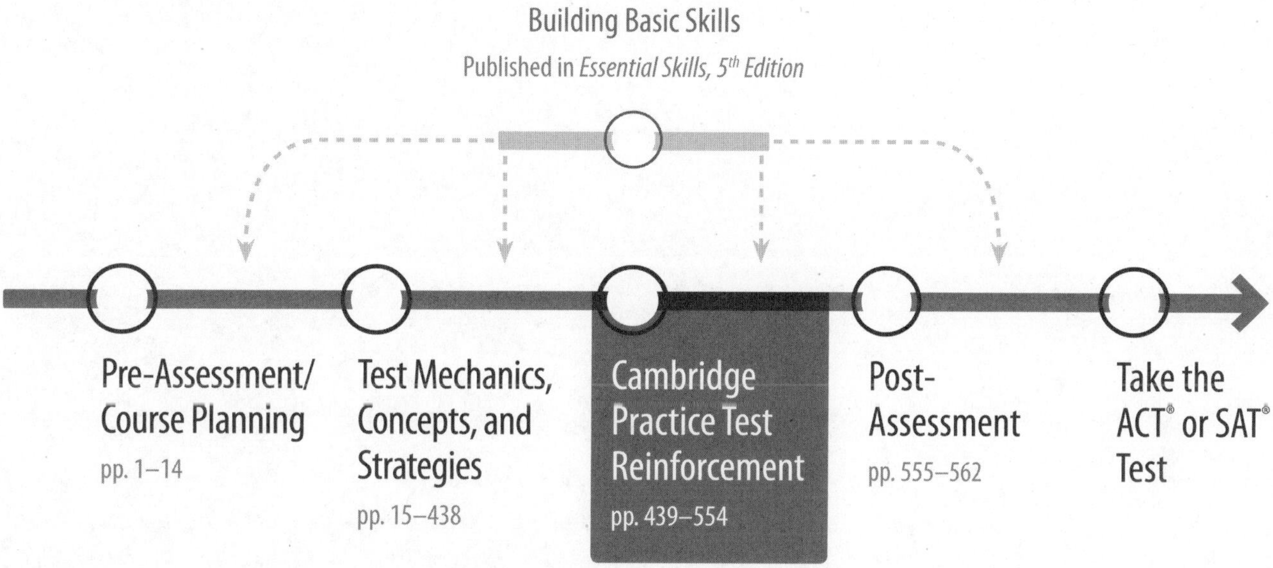

CAMBRIDGE
VICTORY FOR THE
ACT® AND SAT® TESTS

ACT Practice Test

Outline

DIRECTIONS

The ACT Practice Test includes five subject tests: English, Mathematics, Reading, Science, and Writing. Calculator use is permitted on the Mathematics Test only.

Cambridge offers several services for schools utilizing our practice tests. Ask your teacher whether your school has decided to send your answers to Cambridge for scoring or to score your answers at your school. If Cambridge is scoring your test, you will use a Scantron™ form provided by your teacher, or you will enter your answers online. If your school is scoring your test, you may use a Scantron form provided by your teacher, or you may write your answers on paper.

If you are entering your test answers on a Scantron form, please be sure to include the following information on the Scantron:

Book and edition	*Victory for the ACT® and SAT® Tests, 5th Edition*
Practice Test	**ACT Practice Test**

If you are only completing a single section of this practice test, make sure to also include the following information:

Subject	**English**, **Mathematics**, **Reading**, or **Science**
Section Number	**Section 1**, **2**, **3**, or **4**

The items in each multiple-choice test are numbered and the answer choices are lettered. The Scantron form has numbered rows that correspond to the items on the test. Each row contains lettered ovals to match the answer choices for each item on the test. Each numbered row has a corresponding item on the test.

For each item, first decide on the best answer choice. Then, locate the row number that corresponds to the item. Next, find the oval in that row that matches the letter of the chosen answer. Then, use a soft lead pencil to fill in the oval. DO NOT use a ballpoint pen.

Mark only one answer for each item. If you change your mind about an answer choice, thoroughly erase your first mark before marking your new answer.

Note that only responses marked on your Scantron form or written on your paper will be scored. Your score on each test will be based only on the number of items that are correctly answered during the time allowed for that test. You will not be penalized for guessing. Therefore, it is to your best advantage to answer every item on the test, even if you must guess.

On the Writing Test, write your response to the prompt using the essay response sheets or loose-leaf paper provided by your teacher. Your teacher might also direct you to enter your essay response online. (Note that the Writing Test is optional.)

You may work on each test only during the time allowed for that test. If you finish a test before time is called, use the time to review your answer choices or work on items about which you are uncertain. You may not return to a test on which time has already been called, and you may not preview another test. You must lay down your pencil immediately when time is called at the end of each test. You may not for any reason fill in or alter ovals for a test after time has expired for that test. Violation of these rules will result in immediate disqualification from the exam.

GO ON TO THE NEXT PAGE.

ACT Practice Test

SECTION 1: ENGLISH TEST

45 Minutes—75 Items

DIRECTIONS: In the passages below, certain parts of the sentences have been underlined and numbered. In the right-hand column, you will find different ways of writing each underlined part; the original version is indicated by the "NO CHANGE" option. For each item, select the choice that best expresses the intended idea, is most acceptable in standard written English, or is most consistent with the overall tone and style of the passage.

There are also items that ask about a section of the passage or the passage as a whole. These items do not refer to an underlined portion of the passage; these items are preceded by statements that are enclosed in boxes.

Read the passage through once before you begin to answer the accompanying items. Finding the answers to certain items may depend on looking at material that appears several sentences beyond the item. So, be sure that you have read far enough ahead before you select your answer choice. Answers are on page 585.

PASSAGE I

Trade in the Northwest Territory

[1]

In 1849, San Francisco became the first official port of entry on the Pacific Coast. In 1851, <u>on account of</u> [1] the rapid growth of the lumber industry and a corresponding expansion of population in the Northwest Territory, the government established the Puget Sound District of the Bureau of Customs. <u>Nonetheless,</u> [2] smuggling grew rapidly, fostered by the tempting proximity of British havens and the natural cover afforded by vast forested areas and by the coves and inlets of <u>countless heavy</u> [3] timbered islands.

1. A. NO CHANGE
   B. since
   C. because of
   D. for

2. F. NO CHANGE
   G. Therefore,
   H. Consequently,
   J. On the contrary,

3. A. NO CHANGE
   B. countless, heavy
   C. countless, heavily
   D. countlessly heavy

GO ON TO THE NEXT PAGE.

[2]

Such fears were well foundationed[4]. In 1851, US customs officers seize[5] the Hudson Bay Company's steamer *Beaver* for a technical violation of the revenue laws[6]. This incident signaled an end to the era of unrestricted trade in the Pacific Northwest and drove some traders on both sides of the international border into illicit commercial arrangements. British wool, blankets, and liquor were the principle articles[7] of this trade. In fact,[8] so much British wool was smuggled into the San Juan Islands selling[9] as domestic wool by American sheepmen one[10] naive textbook writer credited San Juan sheep with a world's record annual production of 150 pounds of wool per animal.

4. **F.** NO CHANGE
   G. well founded
   H. founded well
   J. well found

5. **A.** NO CHANGE
   B. seized
   C. were seizing
   D. have seized

6. **F.** NO CHANGE
   G. on account of violating the revenue laws
   H. for technically being in violation of the revenue laws
   J. in that they were in technical violation of the revenue laws

7. **A.** NO CHANGE
   B. was the principle article
   C. were the principal articles
   D. was the principal article

8. **F.** NO CHANGE
   G. Furthermore,
   H. Moreover,
   J. On the contrary,

9. **A.** NO CHANGE
   B. to sell
   C. and sold
   D. and would be sold

10. **F.** NO CHANGE
    G. sheepmen, one
    H. sheepmen that one
    J. sheepmen, and a

GO ON TO THE NEXT PAGE.

[3]

Although (11) American settlers in the Northwest Territory welcomed (12) the assertion of national control to the forty-ninth parallel, they were less amenable to restrictions on trade with Vancouver Island. They wanted the duty-free rum and woolens offered by the British but were fearing (13) that the imposition and enforcement of permanent tariffs on goods from British North America might be resulting in the losing (14) of British markets for American products.

11. A. NO CHANGE
    B. Since
    C. Therefore
    D. Thus

12. F. NO CHANGE
    G. welcoming
    H. would welcome
    J. were welcomed by

13. A. NO CHANGE
    B. and were fearing
    C. and was fearful
    D. but feared

14. F. NO CHANGE
    G. might result in the losing
    H. might result in the loss
    J. results in the loss

Items #15–16 ask about the preceding passage as a whole.

15. Which of the following represents the most logical order of the three paragraphs?

    A. 1, 2, 3
    B. 1, 3, 2
    C. 2, 3, 1
    D. 3, 1, 2

16. Which of the following does NOT represent a technique used in the development of the essay?

    F. Narrative
    G. Example
    H. Statistics
    J. Quotations

GO ON TO THE NEXT PAGE.

PASSAGE II

Mapping the Cosmos

One of the beauties of astronomy <u>is that one does not have to be an expert to enjoy it</u>. [17] Anyone can step outside on a clear, moonless night, gaze at thousands of stars shining across the vast interstellar <u>spaces, and then one can become</u> [18] intoxicated by a heady mix of grandeur and existential chill. The same questions come to mind time and <u>again, how</u> [19] far away are the stars? How many are there? Are they strewn endlessly through space, or are we a part of an island universe of suns <u>ending</u> [20] abruptly somewhere out there in the black ocean of space?

It has been the sometimes heroic and often frustrating task of astronomers since the dawn of science <u>to chart</u> [21] our position in the cosmic ocean. In the twentieth century, significant progress <u>had been made</u> [22] in constructing an accurate map of the cosmos. We know, for example, that our solar system is part of a much larger system of hundreds of billions of stars.

17. **A.** NO CHANGE
B. is the not having to be an expert to enjoy it
C. is that the enjoying of it does not have to be done by an expert
D. is that one doesn't necessarily have to be an expert in order to derive some enjoyment from it

18. **F.** NO CHANGE
G. spaces—and became
H. spaces, and become
J. spaces and becomes

19. **A.** NO CHANGE
B. again and how
C. again how
D. again. How

20. **F.** NO CHANGE
G. that end
H. that ends
J. ended

21. **A.** NO CHANGE
B. charting
C. having charted
D. who charted

22. **F.** NO CHANGE
G. was made
H. is made
J. will be made

GO ON TO THE NEXT PAGE.

As such, this [23] system is the Milky Way Galaxy, a huge disk of stars and gas. We also know that ours is not the only galaxy in the universe. As far as the largest telescopes in the world can see, there are galaxies in every direction. The [24] nearest galaxies to our own are the Magellanic Clouds; the "crown jewels" [25] of the southern skies.

Since they are so near, they offer a laboratory in which astronomers can study the evolution of stars and galaxies. The nearest large galaxy to the Milky Way is the Andromeda Galaxy, which is about two million light years away. It is a giant spiral galaxy, much like [26] our own in size, shape, and number and type of stars. This nearby sister galaxy provides to us [27] an opportunity to get a bird's eye view of a galaxy much like our own—in effect, to see ourselves as others do. [28]

23. A. NO CHANGE
B. Obviously, this
C. Doubtless, this
D. This

24. F. NO CHANGE
G. These
H. (Begin a new paragraph here rather than after "skies") The
J. (Begin a new paragraph here rather than after "skies") As the

25. A. NO CHANGE
B. Clouds, the crown jewels
C. Clouds which is the "crown jewels"
D. Clouds, the "crown jewels"

26. F. NO CHANGE
G. much as
H. like much
J. much the same like

27. A. NO CHANGE
B. provides us
C. provide us
D. providing to us

28. F. NO CHANGE
G. to see ourselves the way other people tend to see us
H. so that we would be seeing ourselves the way other people would be seeing us
J. so that in this way we would see ourselves as others do

GO ON TO THE NEXT PAGE.

Item #29 asks about the preceding passage as a whole.

29. Which of the following is NOT one of the reasons the author poses a series of questions in the first paragraph?

A. To give the reader a sense of the "grandeur and existential chill"
B. To stimulate the reader's interest in astronomy
C. To give specific examples of questions about the cosmos that are still unanswered
D. To alert the reader that answers to these questions will follow later in the passage

PASSAGE III

A Brief History of the Mercury Space Program

The first astronauts entered the Mercury program in April 1959. They were volunteer, military pilots, graduated (30) of test pilot schools. Each were required having (31) a bachelor's degree in engineering (or its equivalent) and at least 1,500 hours of jet time. Of the first group of sixty candidates called to Washington to hear about the program, more than 80 percent volunteered. Only seven got (32) chosen. (Officials assumed that no more than seven men would have the

30. **F.** NO CHANGE
G. pilots graduates
H. pilots; graduates
J. pilots, graduates

31. **A.** NO CHANGE
B. was required to have
C. required having
D. had been required to have

32. **F.** NO CHANGE
G. were
H. had been
J. has been

GO ON TO THE NEXT PAGE.

opportunity to fly.) [33] These men were true pioneers, they volunteered at a time when the plans for space travel were only on paper and no one knew what the chance of success was.
34

Scientists were able to learn from each failure.
35

Fortunately they had these failures early in the program. The astronauts and the animal passengers as well were flown without mishap when their time came for them.
36 37

33. Is the second use of parentheses in the first paragraph appropriate?

A. Yes, because the information contained in the parentheses is irrelevant to the passage.
B. Yes, because the information explains something the author said but is not vital to the understanding of the passage.
C. No, because the material is vital to the understanding of the author's main argument.
D. No, because an entire sentence should never be placed in parentheses.

34. F. NO CHANGE
G. pioneers but
H. pioneers yet
J. pioneers. They

35. Which of the following phrases would best replace the word *scientists* to provide a transition from the first to the second paragraph?

A. It was lucky that the men volunteered because scientists
B. There were failures as well as successes in the Mercury program, but scientists
C. Since the chances for success were unknown, scientists
D. Since the volunteers were also engineers, scientists

36. F. NO CHANGE
G. Fortunately, they had these failures occurring
H. These failures occurred fortunately
J. Fortunately, these failures occurred

37. A. NO CHANGE
B. the time for them finally came
C. their time finally came for them
D. their time came

GO ON TO THE NEXT PAGE.

astronauts <u>to have</u> 49 suitable methods of exercise and nutrition. [50]

49. A. NO CHANGE
B. have
C. had had
D. are sure to have

50. Which of the following might be an appropriate concluding sentence for the essay?
F. Although the Mercury program had some failures, it was on the whole a successful part of the space program.
G. Although the Mercury program had some successes, it was on the whole a failure.
H. Many people have objected to the use of animals in testing programs.
J. Science fiction writers have often written about space travel.

PASSAGE IV

Advances in Modern Medicine

It was not until the nineteenth century that medicine was able, in any broad and real <u>way, to help</u> 51 the suffering individual. During this century, technical advances aided the diagnostician <u>and also</u> 52 the surgeon, and the beginnings of an understanding of the fundamental mechanisms of disease <u>had been emerging</u> 53. All aspects of medicine—from the research laboratory to the operating table—<u>was enjoying</u> 54 the benefits of the rigorous application of the scientific method.

51. A. NO CHANGE
B. way of help
C. way to help
D. way, of helping

52. F. NO CHANGE
G. as well as
H. with
J. as opposed to

53. A. NO CHANGE
B. was emerging
C. were emerging
D. emerged

54. F. NO CHANGE
G. were enjoying
H. is enjoying
J. enjoys

By the end of the nineteenth century, a person's chances were fairly good that a doctor could not only give a name to his medical complaint yet probably had [55] an elementary understanding of what it was and how it progressed. With somewhat more luck, the doctor could select the proper treatment and he could also mitigate [56] the symptoms if not cure the disease altogether.

This transition to modern medicine depended on three important advances. First, it required an understanding of the true nature and origin of disease. Second, it required that an organized body of standard medical practice be available to [57] guide physicians in the diagnosis and treatment of disease. Last, it presupposes [58] a degree of medical technology never before available.

Among the more dramatic [59] nineteenth-century medical advances were those in the field of human

55. A. NO CHANGE
    B. but probably had
    C. consequently probably has
    D. but, probably would have

56. F. NO CHANGE
    G. but could mitigate
    H. and mitigate
    J. and can mitigate

57. A. NO CHANGE
    B. was available to
    C. is available for
    D. be available as

58. F. NO CHANGE
    G. it is presupposed
    H. it presupposed
    J. they presuppose

59. A. NO CHANGE
    B. (Do NOT begin a new paragraph) Among the more dramatic
    C. Since
    D. (Do NOT begin a new paragraph) Since

GO ON TO THE NEXT PAGE.

physiology. [60] In 1822, an obscure American army camp surgeon practicing medicine near where the Canadian frontier is (61) was transformed almost overnight into a specialist on the mechanism of human digestion. The physician, William Beaumont, was called to treat a young trapper who had been accidentally shot in the stomach. Beaumont's operating skill (62) saved the boy's life but the patient was left with an abnormal opening leading to the stomach. To Beaumont's credit, he recognized this unique opportunity to study the human digestive process, but (63) for the next 10 years he conducted hundreds of experiments with the reluctant cooperation of his not-so-willing patient.

From his experiments, Beaumont was able to describe the physiology of digestion, demonstrating

60. Which of the following correctly describes the function of the first sentence of this paragraph?

F. It introduces a topic that has nothing to do with the material discussed in the first three paragraphs.
G. It introduces material that will contradict what was discussed in the first three paragraphs.
H. It provides a transition that sets up a contrast to the material that came before.
J. It provides a transition that moves from a general discussion to a more specific yet related topic.

61. A. NO CHANGE
B. near where the Canadian frontier is,
C. near where the Canadian frontier was
D. near the Canadian frontier

62. F. NO CHANGE
G. (Begin a new paragraph) Beaumont's operating skill
H. The skill of Beaumont at operating
J. (Begin a new paragraph) The skill of Beaumont at operating

63. A. NO CHANGE
B. process, and
C. process,
D. process. But

GO ON TO THE NEXT PAGE.

the characteristics of gastric motility and describe[64] the properties of gastric juice. He determined that the stomach contained hydrochloric acid and that it broke down food by a chemical process and not by maceration or putrefaction. Beaumont's pioneering work made him a famous man. The young trapper did not fare as well; he was forced to tour medical schools as "the man with the window in his stomach."

64. **F.** NO CHANGE
G. to describe
H. that describe
J. and describing

PASSAGE V

All About Babies

Newborn babies are not the passive creatures most people assume him to be.[65] Recent research shows that the newborn comes well-endowed of[66] charm and full potential for social graces. His eyes are equipped with surprisingly good vision. Shortly after birth, he begins to watch his mother's face, which he soon comes to recognize. He also learns to know her voice and will turn toward her when he hears it. This[67] is about the time when affection begins. The infant's cry alerts the mother and causes a biological including[68] an emotional reaction. The infant's ability to cling and

65. **A.** NO CHANGE
B. he was
C. them to be
D. it is

66. **F.** NO CHANGE
G. for
H. with
J. by

67. **A.** NO CHANGE
B. it, this
C. it this
D. it

68. **F.** NO CHANGE
G. and
H. with
J. but

GO ON TO THE NEXT PAGE.

cuddle communicates a pleasurable warmth to the mother, and the infant's odor is pleasant and uniquely its own. The newborn also smiles. The human infant, <u>unfortunately,</u> [69] <u>is in possession of</u> [70] attributes that <u>are guaranteeing</u> [71] its attractiveness.

69. **A.** NO CHANGE
B. on the other hand
C. nevertheless
D. in fact

70. **F.** NO CHANGE
G. possessed
H. possesses
J. are in possession of

71. **A.** NO CHANGE
B. guaranteed
C. guarantee
D. guarantees

Although there is some argument about whether the child sparks the development of love <u>or whether or not</u> [72] a special physiological state of the mother prompts her to interact with the new <u>infant. But most</u> [73] researchers agree that the newborn does mold or trigger adult behavior. The neonate organizes the mother's behavior by crying and by eye-to-eye contact. The newborn is not a passive creature at all.

72. **F.** NO CHANGE
G. or whether
H. and whether if
J. or whether if

73. **A.** NO CHANGE
B. infant: but most
C. infant. Most
D. infant, most

GO ON TO THE NEXT PAGE.

Items #74–75 ask about the preceding passage as a whole.

74. Which of the following best describes the function of the last sentence of the essay?

F. It introduces a new topic for the reader to investigate.
G. It contradicts everything that was said before.
H. It reiterates the main theme of the passage.
J. It establishes the author as an authority.

75. Which of the following best describes the overall development of the essay?

A. A comparison and contrast using anecdotes
B. A narrative using examples
C. A description using statistics
D. An argument using examples

END OF TEST 1
STOP! DO NOT TURN THE PAGE UNTIL TOLD TO DO SO.

NO TEST MATERIAL ON THIS PAGE

GO ON TO THE NEXT PAGE.

ACT Practice Test

SECTION 2: MATHEMATICS TEST

60 Minutes—60 Items

DIRECTIONS: Solve each item and choose the correct answer choice. Then, fill in the corresponding oval on the bubble sheet.

Allocate time wisely. Try to solve as many items as possible, returning to skipped items if time permits.

Calculator use is permitted on this test; however, some items are best solved without the use of a calculator.

Note: All of the following should be assumed, unless otherwise stated.

1. Illustrative figures are NOT necessarily drawn to scale.
2. The word *average* indicates arithmetic mean.
3. The word *line* indicates a straight line.
4. Geometric figures lie in a plane.

Answers are on page 585.

DO YOUR FIGURING HERE.

1. Amanda has to arrange the five shapes below in a row. How many arrangements can Amanda make if the circle cannot be placed at the beginning or end of the row?

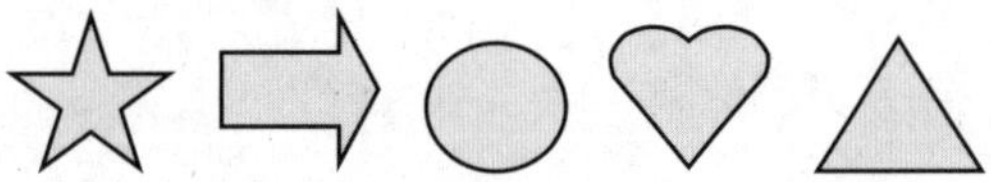

A. 5
B. 24
C. 36
D. 72
E. 120

2. John is now three times Pat's age. Four years from now, John will be x years old. In terms of x, how old is Pat now?

F. $\frac{x+4}{3}$
G. $3x$
H. $x+4$
J. $x-4$
K. $\frac{x-4}{3}$

DO YOUR FIGURING HERE.

3. If $\frac{3}{4}$ of x is 36, then $\frac{1}{3}$ of $x = ?$

A. 9
B. 12
C. 16
D. 24
E. 42

4. In the figure below, what is the value of $x + y$?

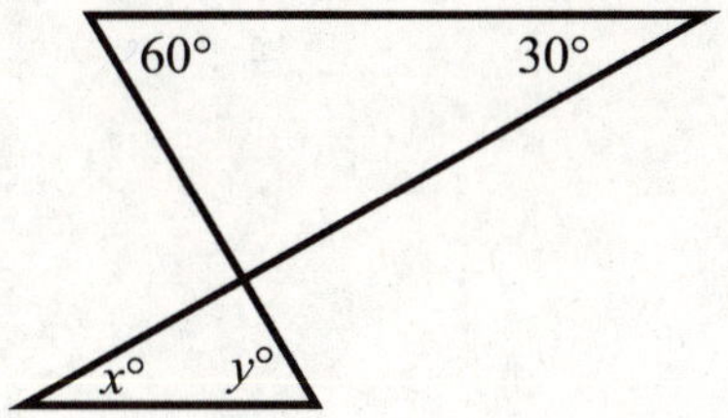

F. 45
G. 60
H. 75
J. 90
K. 120

5. If n is a multiple of 3, which of the following expressions is also a multiple of 3?

A. $2 + n$
B. $2 - n$
C. $2n - 1$
D. $2n + 1$
E. $2n + 3$

6. Which of the following is NOT equal to the ratio of 2 whole numbers?

F. $\left(\frac{1}{5}\right)^2$
G. 5%
H. $\frac{1}{5}$
J. 0.25
K. $\frac{\sqrt{5}}{1}$

GO ON TO THE NEXT PAGE.

DO YOUR FIGURING HERE.

7. Nine playing cards from the same deck are placed as shown in the figure below to form a large rectangle of area 180 sq. in. What is the perimeter, in inches, of this large rectangle?

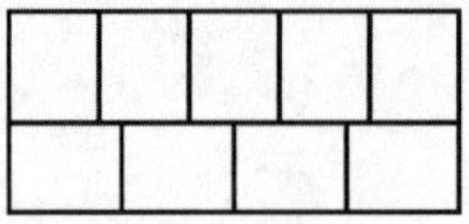

A. 29
B. 58
C. 64
D. 116
E. 210

8. A train running between two towns arrives at its destination 10 minutes late when it travels at a constant rate of 40 miles per hour and 16 minutes late when it travels at a constant rate of 30 miles per hour. What is the distance, in miles, between the two towns?

F. $8\frac{6}{7}$
G. 12
H. 192
J. 560
K. 720

9. What is the greatest factor of the expression $3x^2y^3z + 6x^3yz^3 + 2xy^2z^2$?

A. $3x^2y^2z^2$
B. $2x^2y^2z^2$
C. $x^3y^3z^3$
D. xyz
E. xz

10. Depending on the value of k, the expression $3k + 4k + 5k + 6k + 7k$ may or may not be divisible by 7. Which of the terms, when eliminated from the expression, guarantees that the resulting expression is divisible by 7 for every positive integer k?

F. $3k$
G. $4k$
H. $5k$
J. $6k$
K. $7k$

GO ON TO THE NEXT PAGE.

DO YOUR FIGURING HERE.

11. If $\frac{1}{3} < x < \frac{3}{8}$, which of the following is a possible value of x?

A. $\frac{3}{16}$
B. $\frac{17}{48}$
C. $\frac{9}{24}$
D. $\frac{5}{12}$
E. $\frac{1}{2}$

12. If $x^2 - y^2 = 3$ and $x - y = 3$, then $x + y = $?

F. 0
G. 1
H. 2
J. 3
K. 9

13. If n is a positive integer, which of the following *must* be an even integer?

A. $n+1$
B. $3n+1$
C. $3n+2$
D. n^2+1
E. n^2+n

14. If the area of a square inscribed in a circle is 16 square centimeters, what is the area of the circle, in square centimeters?

F. 2π
G. 4π
H. 8π
J. 16π
K. 32π

GO ON TO THE NEXT PAGE.

DO YOUR FIGURING HERE.

15. Ellen bought a CD player on sale for 25% off the usual price of $120. If the store also collected an 8% sales tax on the sale price of the CD player, how much did Ellen pay for the CD player, including sales tax?

A. $106.30
B. $101.40
C. $97.20
D. $95.10
E. $88.44

16. A certain mixture of gravel and sand consists of 2.5 kilograms of gravel and 12.5 kilograms of sand. What percentage of the mixture, by weight, is gravel?

F. 10%
G. $16\frac{2}{3}\%$
H. 20%
J. 25%
K. $33\frac{1}{3}\%$

17. The figure below is the top-view of a folding room divider, hinged at P and Q. If sections $\overline{PR}$ and $\overline{QS}$ are moved as shown until R and S meet, what will be the enclosed area, in square feet? (Ignore the thickness of the hinges and the screen's sections.)

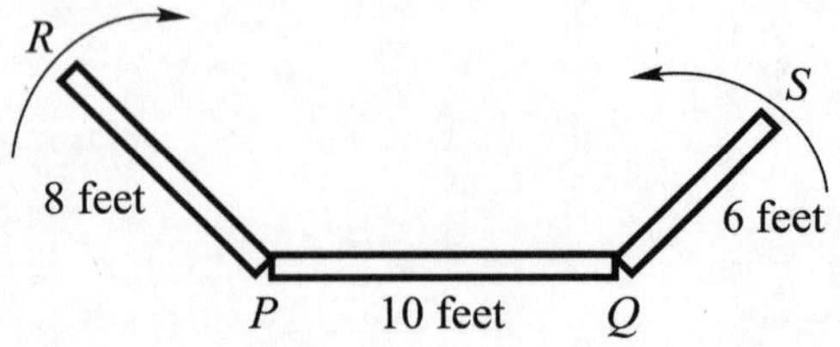

A. 6
B. 12
C. 6π
D. 24
E. 12π

GO ON TO THE NEXT PAGE.

DO YOUR FIGURING HERE.

18. Motorcycle A averages 40 kilometers per liter of gasoline while Motorcycle B averages 50 kilometers per liter. If the cost of gasoline is $2 per liter, what will be the difference in the cost of operating the two motorcycles for 300 kilometers?

F. $3
G. $6
H. $12
J. $15
K. $20

19. If $f(x) = x^2 - 2x + 1$, then what is $f(f(3))$?

A. 3
B. 9
C. 14
D. 27
E. 39

20. If $N! = N(N-1)(N-2) \ldots [N-(N-1)]$, what does $\frac{N!}{(N-2)!}$ equal?

F. $N^2 - N$
G. $N^5 + N^3 - N^2 + \frac{N}{N^2}$
H. $N + 1$
J. 1
K. 6

21. Mailing a letter costs x cents for the first ounce and y cents for every additional ounce or fraction of an ounce. What is the cost, in cents, to mail a letter weighing a whole number of ounces, w?

A. $w(x + y)$
B. $x(w - y)$
C. $x(x-1) + y(w-1)$
D. $x + wy$
E. $x + y(w-1)$

GO ON TO THE NEXT PAGE.

DO YOUR FIGURING HERE.

22. $|-3| \cdot |2| \cdot \left|-\frac{1}{2}\right| + (-4) = ?$

F. -1
G. 0
H. 1
J. $\frac{3}{2}$
K. 4

23. In the figure below, the area of the square *OPQR* is 2 square inches, what is the area of the circle with center *O* (in square inches)?

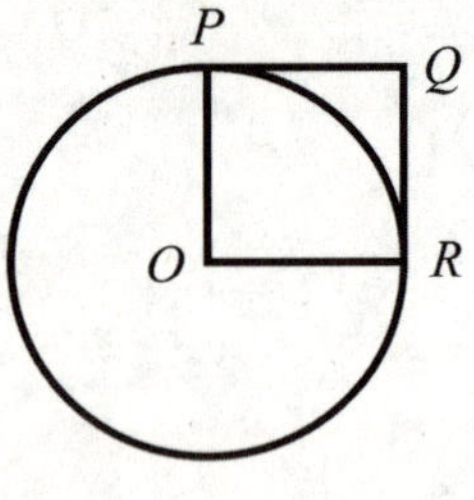

A. $\frac{\pi}{4}$
B. $\pi\sqrt{2}$
C. 2π
D. $2\pi\sqrt{2}$
E. 4π

24. Which of the following *must* be an odd number?

I. The product of a prime number and another prime number
II. The sum of a prime number and another prime number
III. The product of an odd number and another odd number

F. I only
G. III only
H. I and II only
J. II and III only
K. I, II, and III

GO ON TO THE NEXT PAGE.

25. What is the area of the shaded portion of the figure below, expressed in terms of a and b?

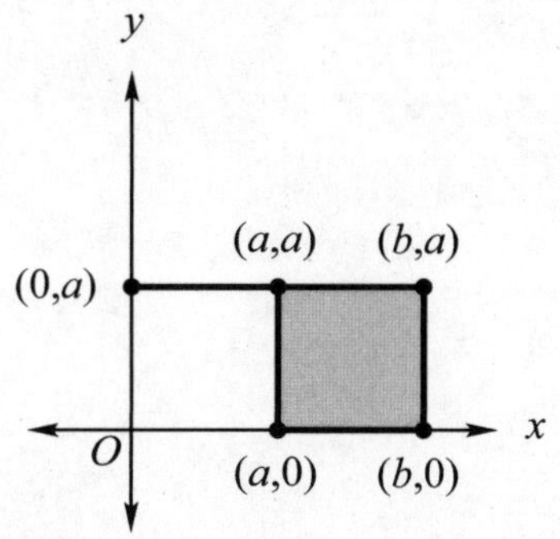

A. $a(b-a)$
B. $a(a-b)$
C. $b(a-b)$
D. $b(b-a)$
E. ab

26. $\sqrt{(43-7)(29+7)} = ?$

F. $3\sqrt{3}$
G. 6
H. 36
J. 42
K. 1,296

27. A concrete mixture contains 4 cubic yards of cement for every 20 cubic yards of grit. If a mason orders 50 cubic yards of cement, how much grit (in cubic yards) should he order if he is to use all of the cement?

A. 250
B. 200
C. 100
D. 80
E. 10

DO YOUR FIGURING HERE.

GO ON TO THE NEXT PAGE.

DO YOUR FIGURING HERE.

28. In the figure below, $\overline{QT} = \overline{QR}$. If $x = 150$, then $y = ?$

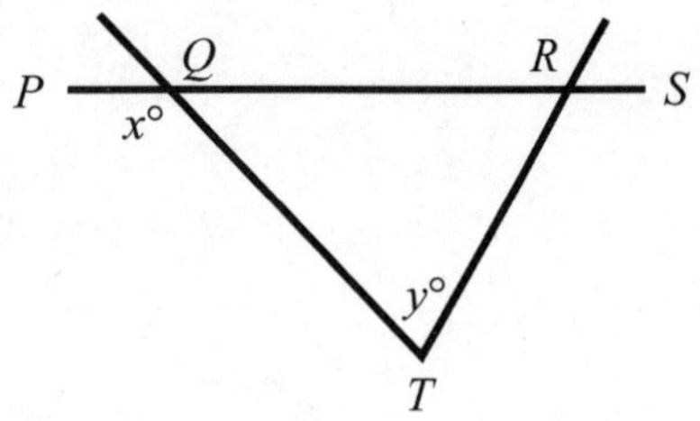

F. 30
G. 60
H. 75
J. 90
K. 120

29. If $\frac{x}{y} = -1$, then $x + y = ?$

A. 2
B. 1
C. 0
D. –1
E. –2

30. According to the table below, which fabric costs the LEAST per yard?

Fabric	Cost
F	3 yards for $8
G	2 yards for $6
H	4 yards for $9
J	5 yards for $7
K	8 yards for $10

F. F
G. G
H. H
J. J
K. K

GO ON TO THE NEXT PAGE.

31. In ΔPQR below, if $\overline{PQ} \parallel \overline{ST}$, then $y = ?$

DO YOUR FIGURING HERE.

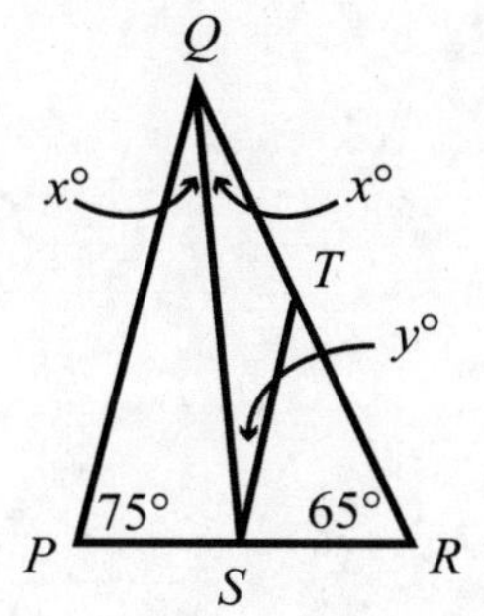

A. 20
B. 40
C. 45
D. 50
E. 55

32. $\dfrac{10^3\left(10^5+10^5\right)}{10^4} = ?$

F. $2\left(10^2\right)$
G. 10^4
H. $2\left(10^4\right)$
J. 10^6
K. $2\left(10^9\right)$

33. What is the solution set for the following equation: $x^2 - 5x + 4 = 0$?

A. $\{-4, -1\}$
B. $\{-3, -1\}$
C. $\{-1, 3\}$
D. $\{1, 4\}$
E. $\{2, 3\}$

GO ON TO THE NEXT PAGE.

DO YOUR FIGURING HERE.

34. The average of seven different positive integers is 12. What is the greatest that any one integer could be?

F. 19
G. 31
H. 47
J. 54
K. 63

35. If $x = b + 4$ and $y = b - 3$, then in terms of x and y, $b = ?$

A. $x + y - 1$
B. $x + y + 1$
C. $x - y - 1$
D. $\frac{x + y + 1}{2}$
E. $\frac{x + y - 1}{2}$

36. If $5x = 3y = z$, and x, y, and z are positive integers, all of the following must be an integer EXCEPT:

F. $\frac{z}{xy}$
G. $\frac{z}{5}$
H. $\frac{z}{3}$
J. $\frac{z}{15}$
K. $\frac{x}{3}$

37. What is the width of a rectangle with an area of $48x^2$ and a length of $24x$?

A. 2
B. $2x$
C. $24x$
D. $2x^2$
E. $3x^2$

GO ON TO THE NEXT PAGE.

38. If $x = \frac{1}{y+1}$ and $y \neq -1$, then $y =$?

DO YOUR FIGURING HERE.

F. $x+1$
G. x
H. $\frac{x+1}{x}$
J. $\frac{x-1}{x}$
K. $\frac{1-x}{x}$

39. In the figure below, if the area of the triangle is 54, then $x =$?

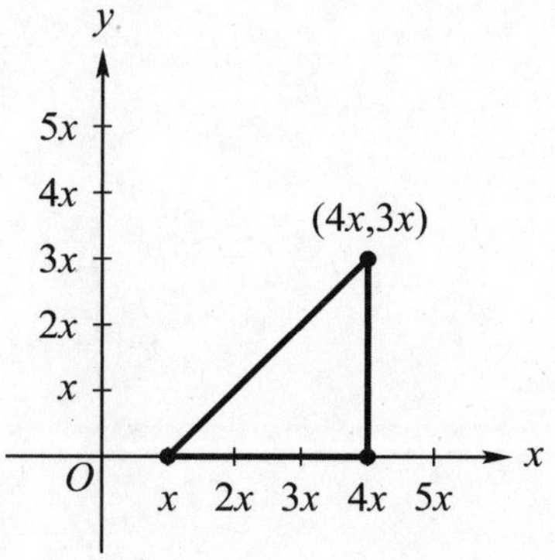

A. $3\sqrt{3}$
B. $2\sqrt{3}$
C. 3
D. 2
E. $\sqrt{2}$

40. A drawer contains 4 green socks, 6 blue socks, and 10 white socks. If socks are pulled out of the drawer at random and not replaced, what is the minimum number of socks that must be pulled out of the drawer to *guarantee* that 2 of every color have been pulled out of the drawer?

F. 6
G. 7
H. 11
J. 12
K. 18

GO ON TO THE NEXT PAGE.

41. In the figure below, the circle with center O has a radius that is 4 units long. If the area of the shaded region is 14π square units, what is the value of x?

DO YOUR FIGURING HERE.

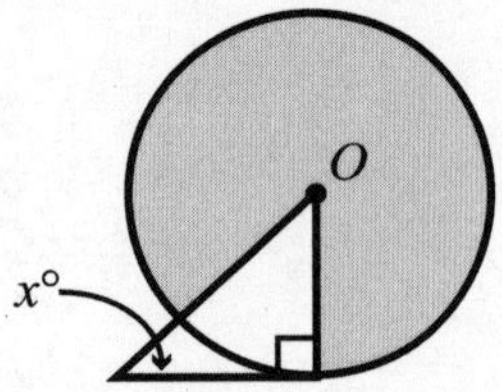

A. 55
B. 50
C. 45
D. 40
E. 35

42. In the figure below, a circle is inscribed in a square that is in turn inscribed in a larger circle. What is the ratio of the area of the larger circle to the area of the smaller circle?

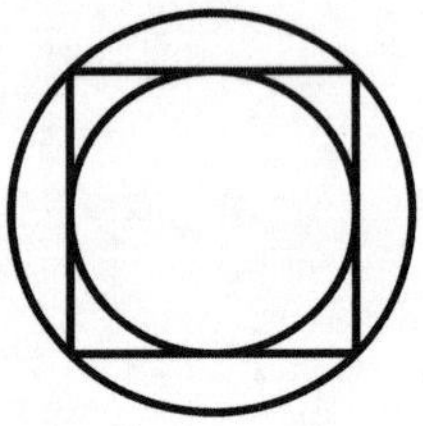

F. $8:1$
G. $4:1$
H. $2\sqrt{2}:1$
J. $2:1$
K. $\sqrt{2}:1$

43. $2^0 + 2^3 - 2^{-2} = ?$

A. 4
B. $6\frac{1}{4}$
C. 7
D. $8\frac{3}{4}$
E. $9\frac{3}{4}$

GO ON TO THE NEXT PAGE.

44. The graph of $y = x^2 - 3$ is a parabola with the axis of symmetry given by the equation $x = 0$. Which of the following are the (x, y) coordinates of the point on the parabola that is symmetric, with respect to the axis of symmetry, to the point with coordinates $(-1, -2)$?

F. $(-2, -1)$
G. $(-1, 2)$
H. $(0, -3)$
J. $(1, -2)$
K. $(1, 2)$

DO YOUR FIGURING HERE.

45. If two lines with equations $y = m_1 x + b_1$ and $y = m_2 x + b_2$ are perpendicular, which of the following *must* be true?

A. $m_1 = m_2$
B. $m_1 m_2 = 1$
C. $m_1 m_2 = -1$
D. $b_1 = b_2$
E. $b_1 b_2 = -1$

46. The figure below has lengths as marked, in units. What is the area, in square units, of the figure?

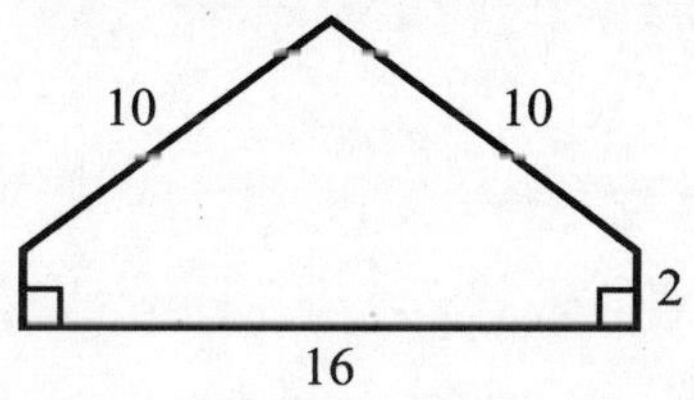

F. 36
G. 48
H. 56
J. 64
K. 80

GO ON TO THE NEXT PAGE.

DO YOUR FIGURING HERE.

47. For all $x > 0$ and $y > 0$, $\dfrac{\sqrt{x}}{2\sqrt{x}-\sqrt{y}}$ is equivalent to which of the following expressions?

A. $\dfrac{2x+\sqrt{xy}}{4x-y}$

B. $\dfrac{4x+\sqrt{xy}}{4x-y}$

C. $\dfrac{2\sqrt{x}+\sqrt{y}}{4xy}$

D. $\dfrac{2\sqrt{x}+\sqrt{xy}}{2x-y}$

E. $\dfrac{2\sqrt{x}-\sqrt{y}}{2}$

48. In the figure below, if $l_1 \parallel l_2$, then $x = ?$

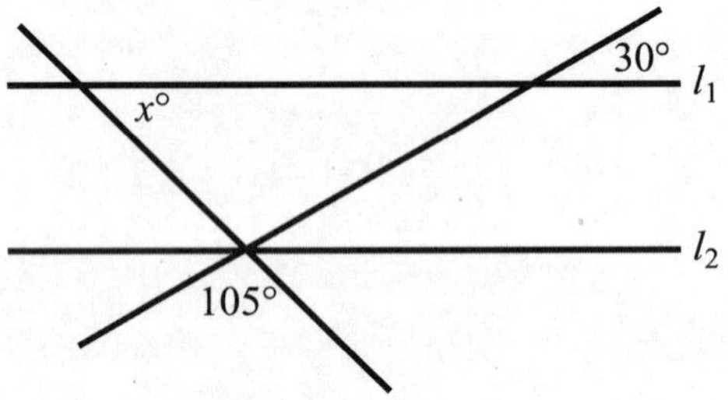

F. 20
G. 30
H. 45
J. 65
K. 130

49. The graph of $y = 2\cos(2x) + 2$ intersects the y-axis where $y = ?$

A. 0
B. 2
C. 3
D. 4
E. 5

GO ON TO THE NEXT PAGE.

50. In the figure below, *PQRS* is a square, and each of the 4 circles has a radius of *r*. What fractional part of the area of the square is shaded?

DO YOUR FIGURING HERE.

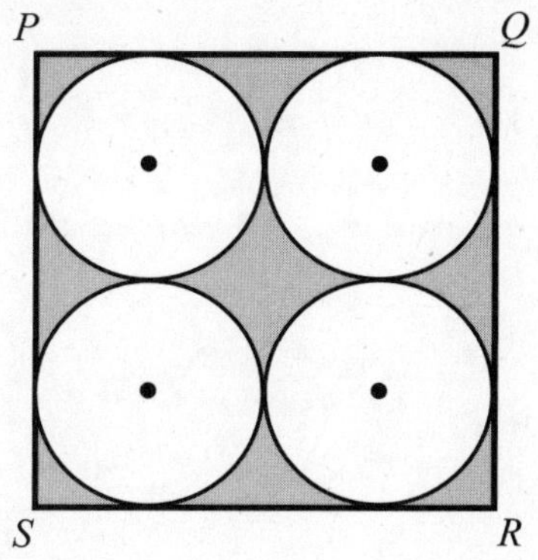

F. $\frac{\pi - 4}{2}$

G. $\frac{4 - \pi}{4}$

H. $\frac{\pi}{4}$

J. $\frac{4}{\pi}$

K. π

51. If $0° < \theta < 90°$, $\frac{\sin^2 \theta + \cos^2 \theta}{\sin \theta}$ is equivalent to:

A. $\sin \theta$
B. $\cos \theta$
C. $\csc \theta$
D. $\sec \theta$
E. $\cot \theta$

GO ON TO THE NEXT PAGE.

DO YOUR FIGURING HERE.

52. In the figure below, ABC is a right triangle. If $\sin 35° \approx 0.57$ and $\tan 55° \approx 1.4$, which of the following is the best approximation of the length of $\overline{AC}$?

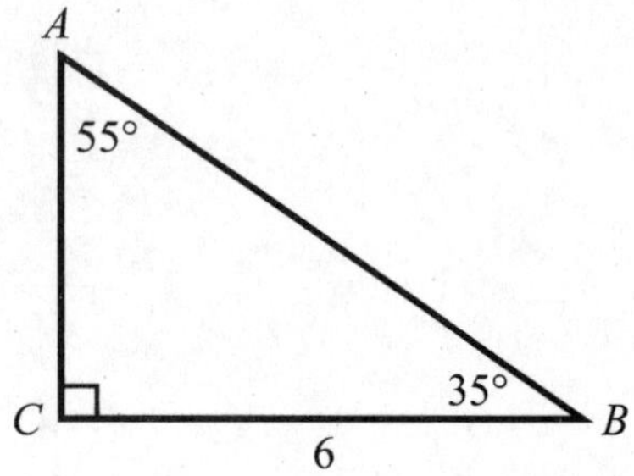

F. 3.42
G. 4.28
H. 8.57
J. 10.50
K. 12.25

53. For what value(s) of x is $\frac{x(x+3)}{(x-1)(x+2)}$ undefined?

A. {–3}
B. {–2}
C. {1}
D. {–2, 1}
E. {–3, –2, 1}

54. What is the maximum value of $3y$ for x and y satisfying the system of inequalities below?

$$x \geq 0$$
$$y \geq 0$$
$$x + y \leq 6$$

F. –3
G. 0
H. 6
J. 12
K. 18

GO ON TO THE NEXT PAGE.

55. Which of the following graphs correctly shows the points on the graph of $y(x) = \left|x^2 - 3\right|$ for $x = -1, 0,$ and 1?

DO YOUR FIGURING HERE.

A.

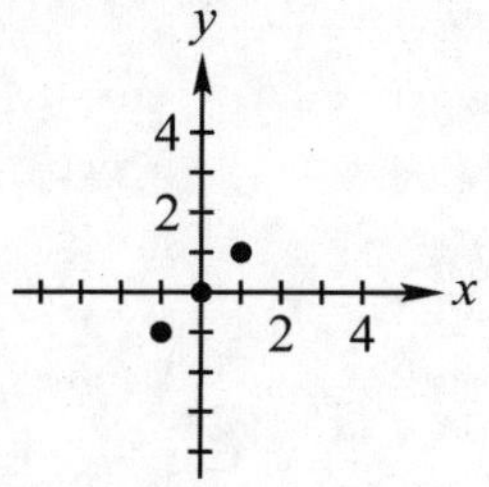

B.

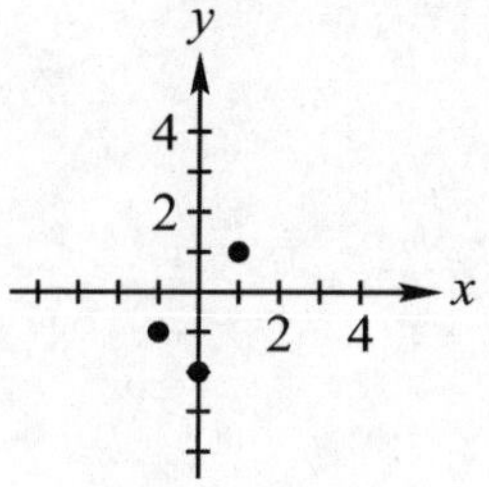

C.

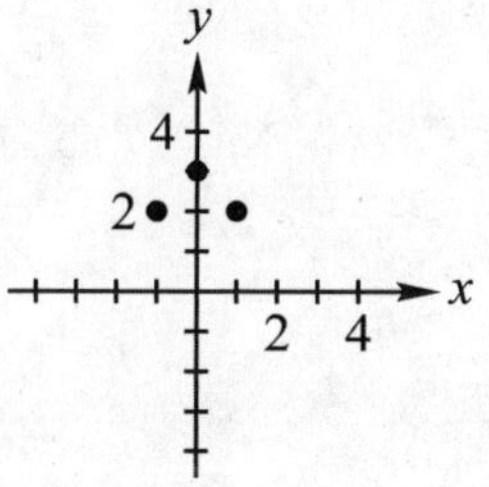

D.

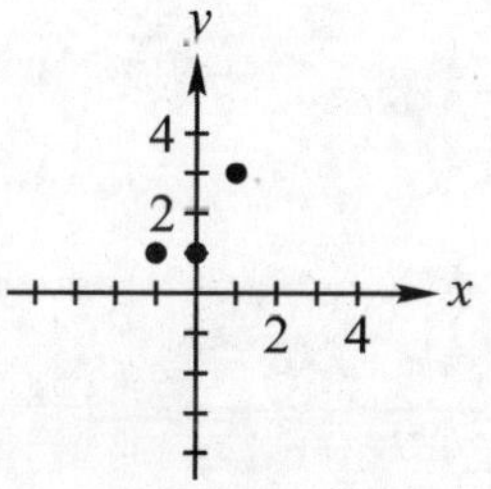

E.

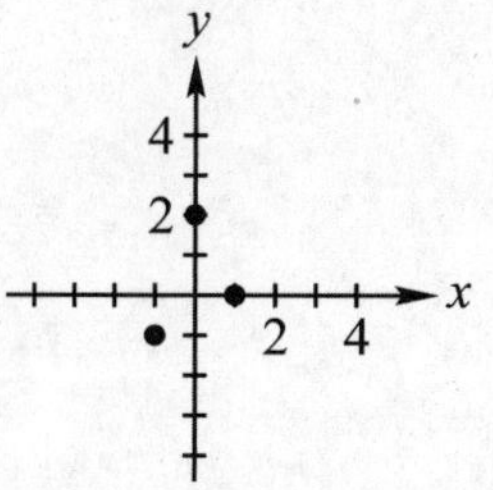

GO ON TO THE NEXT PAGE.

DO YOUR FIGURING HERE.

56. The figure below is a graph of which of the following equations?

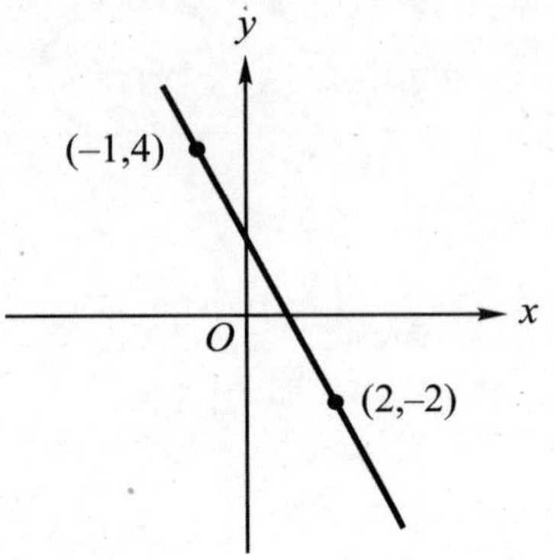

F. $y=-3x+5$
G. $y=-2x+2$
H. $y=-\frac{3}{2}x-2$
J. $y=\frac{2}{3}x+3$
K. $y=x+2$

57. The roots of equation $ax^2+bx+c=0$ are $\frac{-3+\sqrt{5}}{2}$ and $\frac{-3-\sqrt{5}}{2}$. Which of the following could be the equation?

A. $x^2+3x+1=0$
B. $x^2-3x+1=0$
C. $x^2+3x-1=0$
D. $x^2-3x-1=0$
E. $-x^2+3x+1=0$

58. The relation defined by the set of ordered pairs {(0,3), (2,1), (3,0), (−1,2), (0,5), (−2,5)} is NOT a function. Deleting which of the ordered pairs will make the resulting set a function?

F. (0,3)
G. (2,1)
H. (3,0)
J. (−1,2)
K. (−2,5)

GO ON TO THE NEXT PAGE.

59. Trapezoid *ABCD* has lengths, in units, and angle measures as marked in the figure below. What is the area of the trapezoid *ABCD*?

DO YOUR FIGURING HERE.

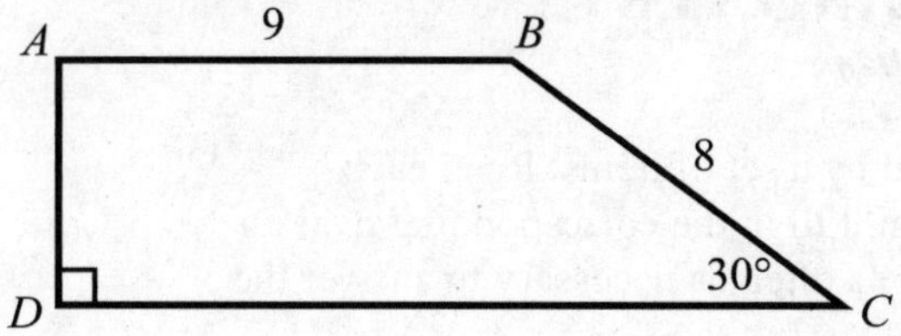

A. $18+8\sqrt{2}$
B. $18+8\sqrt{3}$
C. 42
D. $36+8\sqrt{2}$
E. $36+8\sqrt{3}$

60. What is $\tan\theta$ if $\sin\theta = \frac{3}{5}$ and $\cot\theta = \frac{4}{3}$?

F. $\frac{3}{4}$
G. $\frac{4}{5}$
H. $\frac{7}{8}$
J. $\frac{5}{3}$
K. $\frac{20}{9}$

END OF TEST 2
STOP! DO NOT TURN THE PAGE UNTIL TOLD TO DO SO.
DO NOT RETURN TO THE PREVIOUS TEST.

ACT Practice Test

SECTION 3: READING TEST

35 Minutes—40 Items

DIRECTIONS: Each passage below is followed by a set of items. Read each passage and choose the best answer for each item. Fill in the corresponding oval on your bubble sheet. You may refer to the passage as often as necessary to answer the items. Answers are on page 586.

Passage I

PROSE FICTION: Passage A is adapted from Henry David Thoreau's *Walden* (1854) in which the author discusses his life of solitude in the New England woods. Passage B is adapted from *Public Opinion*, published in 1922 by Walter Lippman, a noted journalist and commentator.

Passage A

I am sure that I never read any memorable news in a newspaper. If we read of one man robbed or murdered or killed by accident, or one steamboat blown up, or one mad dog killed, or one lot of grasshoppers in the winter—we never need read of another. One is enough. If you are acquainted with the principle, what do you care for a myriad instances and applications? All news, as it is called, is gossip, even though many people insist on hearing it. If I should pull the bell-rope of the local church to sound a fire alarm, almost everyone in the entire area would stop everything and come running, not mainly to save property from the flames but to see the blaze, especially if it were the parish church itself on fire.

After a night's sleep the news is as indispensable to most people as breakfast: "Pray tell me everything important that has happened anywhere on this globe." They read over coffee and rolls that a man has had his eyes gouged out the previous evening on the Wachito River. There was such a rush the other day at the railway office to learn the foreign news by the last arrival, that several large squares of plate glass were broken—news that I seriously think a ready wit might have written a year or twelve years earlier with surprising accuracy. As for Spain, for instance, if you know how to throw in Don Carlos and the Infanta or Don Pedro and Seville and Granada from time to time in the right proportions—they may have changed the names a little since I last saw the papers—and serve up a bull-fight when other entertainments fail, it will be true to the letter and give as good an idea of the exact state of ruin of things in Spain as the most succinct and lucid reports under this head in the newspapers. And as for England, almost the last significant scrap of news from that quarter was the revolution of 1649; and if you have learned the history of her crops for an average year, you never need attend to that thing again, unless your speculations are of a merely pecuniary character. If one may judge who rarely looks into the newspapers, nothing new does ever happen in foreign parts, a French revolution not excepted.

Passage B

There is an island in the ocean, where in 1914 a few Englishmen, Frenchmen, and Germans lived. The island was not served by telegraph, and the British mail steamer came once every sixty days. On a day in mid-September, they learned of the start of the war and that for over six weeks those of them who were English and those of them who were French had acted as if they were friends with those of them who were Germans, when in fact they were enemies.

Their plight was not so different from that of most of the population of Europe. They had been mistaken for six weeks. There was a moment when the picture of Europe on which business was conducted as usual, and it did not correspond in any way to the Europe that was about to make a jumble of so many lives. All over the world as late as July 25th people were making goods that they would not be able to ship, and buying goods that they would not be able to import. Then, over four years later, on a Thursday

GO ON TO THE NEXT PAGE.

morning, came the news of an armistice, and people gave vent to their unutterable relief that the slaughter was over. Yet, in the five days before the real armistice came, though the end of the war had been celebrated, several thousand young men died on the battlefields.

Looking back, we can see how indirectly we know the environment in which we live. We can see that the news of it comes to us sometimes quickly, sometimes slowly, but whatever we believe to be a true picture, we treat as if it were the environment itself. It is harder to remember that about the beliefs upon which we are now acting, but in respect to other peoples and other ages, we flatter ourselves that it is easy to see when they were in deadly earnest about ludicrous pictures of the world. We insist, because of our superior hindsight, that the world as they needed to know it and the world as they did know it were often two quite contradictory things. We can see, too, that while they governed and fought, traded and reformed in the world as they imagined it to be, they produced results, or failed to produce any, in the world as it was. They started for the Indies and found America.

1. The newspaper report that a man has had his eyes gouged out is included by the author of Passage A as an example of:

A. a local event that affects people's lives directly.
B. an insignificant incident that does not affect the reader.
C. an unusual occurrence that merits special coverage.
D. an international incident that warrants detailed description.

2. The author mentions Don Carlos and the Infanta in order to:

F. demonstrate a thorough familiarity with current events in Spain.
G. familiarize the reader with recent events that occurred in Spain.
H. explain how events in Europe affect people all over the world.
J. illustrate the point that news from Spain repeats itself.

3. The attitude of the author of Passage A towards the news is:

A. ridicule.
B. admiration.
C. indifference.
D. confidence.

4. As used in this context, "attend to" (line 37) means:

F. be present at.
G. be ignorant of.
H. be concerned with.
J. grow weary of.

5. The author adds "especially if it were the parish church" (line 14) in order to:

A. emphasize that people are fascinated by the bizarre.
B. prove that citizens do not care about public property.
C. show that residents take an interest in local events.
D. stress the importance of the church to community.

6. According to the author of Passage B, the people on the island "acted as if they were friends" (lines 48–49) because they:

F. originally came from European countries.
G. were isolated from the rest of the world.
H. disagreed over the outcome of the trial.
J. did not realize that war had started.

7. The "plight" to which the author refers in line 51 was:

A. incorrect reporting about the progress of the war.
B. lack of accurate information about current conditions.
C. an inability to obtain reports on a regular basis.
D. slanted war news from the European front.

GO ON TO THE NEXT PAGE.

8. In line 82, the author implies that people of another time:

F. accomplished something significant based upon wrong information.
G. failed to realize that the information available was wrong.
H. could have foreseen that America lay between Europe and India.
J. realized only in hindsight that they had landed in America.

9. Which of the following best summarizes the different points of view of the two passages?

A. The author of Passage B believes that news is important while the author of Passage A believes it is irrelevant.
B. The author of Passage A believes that news is unreliable while the author of Passage B believes that it is accurate.
C. The author of Passage A believes that newspapers provide critical information while the author of Passage B believes newspapers are too slow.
D. The author of Passage A believes that news coverage could be improved while the author of Passage B believes that it is already adequate.

10. If the two authors had been able to write about the internet, they likely would:

F. say that their points apply to the news content on the worldwide web.
G. acknowledge that the new media makes reporting more relevant and more reliable.
H. insist that newspapers remain a better source of information than electronic media.
J. conclude that global news coverage gives readers a more accurate view of the world.

GO ON TO THE NEXT PAGE.

Passage II

SOCIAL SCIENCE: This passage discusses the regulation of corporate takeovers.

American financial markets are regulated by the federal government through the Securities and Exchange Commission and by various state agencies. In recent years, there has been considerable discussion of the need for more regulation due to the increased number of corporate takeovers. Many argue that much of this activity has had harmful effects not only on stockholders but also on the economy as a whole.

Many corporate takeovers are hostile; that is, an outside group or company tries to seize control of an existing company whose management opposes the takeover. Most hostile takeovers begin with a tender offer in which the outside raiders offer to buy a sufficient amount of the company's outstanding stock at a stated price—usually well above the current market price. Another takeover strategy is to orchestrate a proxy battle in which a vote of shareholders of record on a specific date is taken to approve or reject a new slate of directors put forth by the raiders. The raiders generally argue that the new directors will make the company more profitable and thereby enhance the value of the stock for the existing stockholders.

Regardless of the takeover strategy employed, most raiders must purchase a significant portion of the company's stock at a price above its current market value. Outsiders usually finance such large purchases of stock through the sale of bonds that pay a very high rate of interest. The raiders argue that the debt to be incurred can easily be paid off by selling parts of the targeted company or by drawing on the additional profits that the new management insists it can make.

In 1986 and 1987, charges emerged that individuals within Wall Street firms specializing in raising capital for corporate takeovers were, in fact, selling inside information about future takeover attempts. Some of the individuals involved were sentenced to jail terms. In addition, such scandals have added to pressure on Congress and the Securities and Exchange Commission to provide more effective regulation of the financial aspects of attempted corporate takeovers.

Critics of hostile corporate takeovers believe that the managers of the company to be taken over usually engage in short-term activities that have very negative long-term effects. In order to avoid hostile takeovers, managers of companies generally take measures to make the takeovers less desirable. For instance, they may insert a *golden parachute clause* in employment contracts. This clause requires a company to pay very large bonuses to any management members who are fired after a takeover. Another tactic, the *poison pill,* restructures the financial base of the corporation so that a takeover would make the company less profitable. Yet another anti-raid tactic is to pay *greenmail* to the raiders; that is, the target of the takeover pays the raiders to sell their shares back to the targeted company at a much higher price. This prevents the takeover, but it usually adds a large sum to the company's debt.

Supporters of corporate raiders counter-argue that, in fact, it is the threat of a takeover that makes managers more efficient. For instance, it may cause managers to sell parts of the company that they are not managing well in order to raise the money to fend off the takeover. In addition, those who believe that takeovers are good argue that the existing shareholders always do better in a hostile takeover since they end up getting a higher price for each share of stock than the current market value.

11. Which statement expresses the main idea of this passage?

A. The government is regulating the financial aspects of corporate takeovers adequately.
B. There has been recent debate over the need for additional government regulation of corporate takeovers.
C. Hostile corporate takeovers are beneficial to the targeted corporation.
D. Trading insider secrets has become a common problem in hostile corporate takeovers.

GO ON TO THE NEXT PAGE.

12. A corporation's board of directors votes to approve a new company policy. According to the plan, each member of the board and of upper management would receive severance of two to five years' pay if the new owner fired the member after a corporate takeover. This action would be considered:

F. a poison pill.
G. a golden parachute.
H. greenmail.
J. a hostile takeover.

13. What is the most important difference between a hostile and a non-hostile takeover?

A. In a hostile takeover, stockholders must pay greenmail to the existing directors.
B. In a non-hostile takeover, raiders sell bonds with high interest rates.
C. In a hostile takeover, the existing management is opposed to the takeover.
D. In a non-hostile takeover, the existing management uses golden parachutes.

14. According to the passage, which of the following parties in a hostile takeover will likely incur new debt?

F. The raiders, because they need money to buy large blocks of stock
G. The Securities and Exchange Commission, because it must oversee the transactions more closely
H. The stockholders, because they must furnish additional funds
J. The critics of hostile takeovers, because they make less money in the stock market

15. According to the passage, a poison pill strategy involves:

A. paying the raiders high prices to buy back the company's stock from them.
B. paying high bonuses to the members of the old management who are fired by the new management.
C. more regulation by the Securities and Exchange Commission.
D. restructuring the financial base of the company so that it will be less profitable or valuable to the raiders.

16. According to the passage, supporters of corporate takeovers believe that:

F. the shareholders always lose money because a takeover profits only the raiders.
G. fear of being targeted for a takeover makes managers more efficient.
H. insider trading should be made legal.
J. a proxy fight is the best way to win control.

17. According to the passage, in a proxy fight:

A. the raiders sell bonds to buy the targeted company's stock.
B. the raiders offer to buy stock at a higher-than-market price.
C. insider information is traded illegally.
D. the shareholders vote for approval or rejection of a new board of directors put forth by the raiders.

18. The management of a business recently targeted for takeover decides to sell two of its unprofitable subsidiaries to raise cash and cut expenses. Supporters of corporate takeovers would say that this action:

F. is an example of how the greenmail strategy works.
G. is an example of how a golden parachute strategy works.
H. is an example of how the fear of a takeover makes managers more efficient.
J. is an example of how the poison pill strategy works.

GO ON TO THE NEXT PAGE.

19. The Securities and Exchange Commission is a:

A. state regulatory agency that polices financial markets.
B. federal regulatory agency that polices financial markets.
C. source of funding for hostile takeovers.
D. board of business executives who promote fair business practices.

20. Some individuals working on Wall Street have been sentenced to jail terms for:

F. attempting to greenmail other companies.
G. forcing companies to swallow a poison pill.
H. selling inside information about takeover attempts.
J. agreeing to pay greenmail to corporate raiders.

GO ON TO THE NEXT PAGE.

Passage III

HUMANITIES: This passage explores the contributions of Josquin des Prez to Western music.

Until Josquin des Prez (1440–1521), Western music was liturgical, designed as an accompaniment to worship. Like the intricate gargoyles perched atop medieval cathedrals beyond sight of any human, music was composed to please God before anyone else; its main theme was reverence. Emotion was there, but it was the grief of Mary standing at the foot of the Cross, the joy of the faithful hailing Christ's resurrection. Even the secular music of the Middle Ages was tied to predetermined patterns that sometimes seemed to stand in the way of individual expression.

While keeping one foot firmly planted in the divine world, Josquin stepped with the other into the human world. He scored magnificent masses, but also newly expressive motets such as the lament of David over his son Absalom or the *Deploration d'Ockeghem*, a dirge on the death of Ockeghem, the greatest master before Josquin. This motet was written all in black notes and was one of the most profoundly moving scores of the Renaissance. Josquin was the first composer to set psalms to music. But alongside *Benedicite omnia opera Domini Domino* ("Bless the Lord, all ye works of the Lord") he put *El Grillo* ("The cricket") and *Allegez moy* ("Solace me"). Martin Luther praised Josquin, for his music blends respect for tradition with a rebel's willingness to risk the horizon. What Galileo was to science, Josquin was to music. While preserving their allegiance to God, both asserted a new importance for man.

Why then should Josquin languish in obscurity? The answer has to do with the separation of concept from performance in music. In fine art, concept and performance are one; both the art lover and the art historian have thousands of years of paintings and sculptures to study and enjoy. Similarly with literature: poetry, fiction, and criticism survive on the printed page or in manuscript for judgment and admiration by future generations. But musical notation on a page is not art, no matter how lofty or excellent the composer's conception; it is, crudely put, a set of directions for making art.

Being highly symbolic, musical notation requires training before it can even be read, let alone performed. Moreover, because the musical conventions of other days are not ours, translation of a Renaissance score into modern notation brings difficulties of its own. For example, the Renaissance notation of Josquin's day did not provide the tempo at which the music should be played or sung. It did not indicate all flats or sharps; these were sounded in accordance with musician rules, which were capable of changing major to minor, minor to major, diatonic to chromatic sound, and thus affect melody, harmony, and musical expression. A Renaissance composition might include several parts—but it did not tell which were to be sung or played, or whether instruments were to be used at all.

Thus, Renaissance notation permits many interpretations. A creative musician may give an interpretation that is a revelation. But no matter how creative, few modern musicians can offer any interpretation of Renaissance music. The public need for it is small, limiting the number of musicians who can afford to learn, rehearse, and perform it. Most of those who attempt it at all are students organized in *collegia musica* whose memberships have a habit of changing every semester. This prevents directors from maintaining the year-in, year-out continuity required to achieve excellence of performance. Finally, the instruments used in Renaissance times—krummhorns, rauschpfeifen, shawms, sackbuts—must be specially procured.

21. The primary purpose of the passage is to:

- **A.** introduce the reader to Josquin and account for his relative obscurity.
- **B.** describe the main features of medieval music and show how Josquin changed them.
- **C.** place Josquin's music in an historical context and show its influence on later composers.
- **D.** enumerate the features of Josquin's music and supply critical commentary.

GO ON TO THE NEXT PAGE.

22. The passage contains information that would help answer all of the following items EXCEPT:

F. What are the titles of some of Josquin's secular compositions?
G. What are the names of some Renaissance musical instruments?
H. Who was the greatest composer before Josquin?
J. What are the names of some of Josquin's most famous students?

23. It can be inferred from the passage that modern musical notation has which of the following characteristics?

I. The tempo at which a composition is to be played is indicated in the notation.
II. Whether a note is a sharp or a flat is indicated in the notation.
III. The notation indicates which parts of the music are to be played by which instruments.

A. I only
B. II only
C. I and III only
D. I, II, and III

24. The author would most likely agree with which of the following statements?

F. Music is a better art form than painting or sculpture.
G. Music can be said to exist only when it is being performed.
H. Josquin was the greatest composer of the Middle Ages.
J. Renaissance music is superior to music produced in modern times.

25. The passage leads most logically to a proposal to:

A. establish more *collegia musica*.
B. study Josquin's compositional techniques in greater detail.
C. include Renaissance music in college studies.
D. provide funds for musicians to study and play Josquin.

26. The author cites all of the following as reasons for Josquin's relative obscurity EXCEPT:

F. the difficulty one encounters in attempting to read his musical notation.
G. the inability of modern musicians to play instruments of the Renaissance.
H. the difficulty of procuring the unusual instruments needed to play the music.
J. the lack of public interest in Renaissance music.

27. The author's attitude toward Galileo can best be described as:

A. admiring.
B. critical.
C. accepting.
D. analytical.

28. Which of the following statements about liturgical music is consistent with the selection?

F. It is lacking in any emotion.
G. It is written to entertain people.
H. It is intended to be reverential.
J. It treats primarily nonreligious themes.

29. Which of the following is NOT an example of fine art as that term is used in the passage?

A. A ballet
B. A novel
C. A poem
D. A mural

30. Josquin des Prez is important in the history of music because he:

F. wrote motets using only black notes.
G. wrote only nonliturgical music.
H. wrote both liturgical and nonliturgical music.
J. invented new musical instruments for his music.

GO ON TO THE NEXT PAGE.

Passage IV

NATURAL SCIENCE: This passage discusses supernova explosions and their effects.

About twice every century, the light reaches us from one of the massive stars in our galaxy that blew apart millions of years ago in a supernova explosion, a type of explosion that sends massive quantities of radiation and matter into space and generates shock waves that sweep through the arms of the galaxy. The shock waves heat the interstellar gas, evaporate small clouds, and compress larger ones to the point at which they collapse under their own gravity to form new stars. The general picture that has been developed for the supernova explosion and its aftermath goes something like this. Throughout its evolution, a star is much like a leaky balloon; it keeps its equilibrium figure through a balance of internal pressure against the tendency to collapse under its own weight. The pressure is generated by nuclear reactions in the core of the star that must continually supply energy to balance the energy that leaks out in the form of radiation. Eventually, the nuclear fuel is exhausted, and the pressure drops in the core. With nothing to hold it up, the matter in the center of the star collapses inward, creating higher and higher densities and temperatures, until the nuclei and electrons are fused into a super-dense lump of matter known as a neutron star.

As the overlying layers rain down on the surface of the neutron star, the temperature rises until, with a blinding flash of radiation, the collapse is reversed. A thermonuclear shock wave runs through the now expanding stellar envelope, fusing lighter elements into heavier ones and producing a brilliant visual outburst that can be as intense as the light of 10 billion suns. The shell of matter thrown off by the explosion plows through the surrounding gas, producing an expanding bubble of hot gas, with gas temperatures in the millions of degrees. This gas will emit most of its energy at X-ray wavelengths, so it is not surprising that X-ray observatories have provided some of the most useful insights into the nature of the supernova phenomenon. More than twenty supernova remnants have now been detected in X-ray studies.

Recent discoveries of meteorites with anomalous concentrations of certain isotopes indicate that a supernova might have precipitated the birth of our solar system more than four and a half billion years ago. Although the cloud that collapsed to form the Sun and the planets was composed primarily of hydrogen and helium, it also contained carbon, nitrogen, and oxygen, elements essential for life as we know it. Elements heavier than helium are manufactured deep in the interior of stars and would, for the most part, remain there if it were not for the cataclysmic supernova explosions that blow giant stars apart. Additionally, supernovas produce clouds of high-energy particles called cosmic rays. These high-energy particles continually bombard the Earth and are responsible for many of the genetic mutations that are the driving force of the evolution of species.

31. According to the passage, we can expect to observe a supernova in our galaxy about:

A. twice each year.
B. 100 times each century.
C. once every 50 years.
D. once every other century.

32. According to the passage, all of the following are true of supernovas EXCEPT:

F. they are extremely bright.
G. they are an explosion of some sort.
H. they are emitters of large quantities of X-rays.
J. they are caused by the collision of large galaxies.

33. The author employs which of the following to develop the first paragraph?

A. Analogy
B. Irony
C. Statistics
D. Example

GO ON TO THE NEXT PAGE.

34. It can be inferred from the passage that the meteorites mentioned by the author (line 41):

F. contain dangerous concentrations of radioactive materials.
G. give off large quantities of X-rays.
H. include material not created in the normal development of our solar system.
J. are larger than the meteorites normally found in a solar system like ours.

35. The author implies that:

A. it is sometimes easier to detect supernovas by observation of the X-ray spectrum than by observation of visible wavelengths of light.
B. life on Earth is endangered by its constant exposure to radiation forces that are released by a supernova.
C. recently discovered meteorites indicate that the Earth and other planets of our solar system survived the explosion of a supernova several billion years ago.
D. lighter elements are formed from heavier elements during a supernova as the heavier elements are torn apart.

36. According to the passage, what is the first event in the sequence that leads to the occurrence of a supernova?

F. An ordinary star begins to emit tremendous quantities of X-rays.
G. A superheated cloud of gas envelops a neutron star.
H. An imbalance between light and heavy elements causes an ordinary star to collapse.
J. An ordinary star exhausts its supply of nuclear fuel and begins to collapse.

37. According to the passage, a neutron star is:

A. a gaseous cloud containing heavy elements.
B. an intermediate stage between an ordinary star and a supernova.
C. the residue that is left by a supernova.
D. the core of an ordinary star that houses the thermonuclear reactions.

38. The author is primarily concerned with:

F. speculating about the origins of our solar system.
G. presenting evidence proving the existence of supernovas.
H. discussing the nuclear reaction that occurs in the core of a star.
J. describing a theory about the causes and effects of supernovas.

39. How long ago was our galaxy formed?

A. 100 million years
B. 1 billion years
C. 2 billion years
D. Over 4.5 billion years

40. What is the connection between supernovas and the evolution of species on Earth?

F. There is no connection.
G. Cosmic radiation from supernovas retards evolution.
H. Cosmic radiation from supernovas drives evolution.
J. Evolution makes future supernovas possible.

END OF TEST 3
STOP! DO NOT TURN THE PAGE UNTIL TOLD TO DO SO.
DO NOT RETURN TO THE PREVIOUS TEST.

ACT Practice Test

SECTION 4: SCIENCE TEST

35 Minutes—40 Items

DIRECTIONS: Each passage below is followed by several items. After reading a passage, choose the best answer for each item. Fill in the corresponding oval on your bubble sheet. You may refer to the passage as often as necessary. You are NOT permitted the use of a calculator on this test. Answers are on page 586.

Passage I

Before making their historic first powered flight, the Wright Brothers made extensive lift tests in 1901 using a glider. Their data differed from that obtained twelve years earlier by the German, Otto Lilienthal.

Results of both tests (Wright: thin line; Lilienthal: thick line) are shown below. "Lift" is the force that pulls the wing away from the earth, in a direction perpendicular to the flight path, and the "angle of incidence" is the angle that the flight path makes with the horizon.

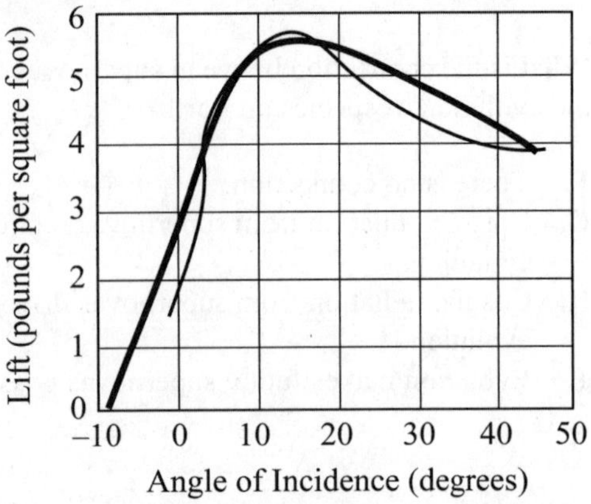

Modified from Culick, F.E.C, "The Wright 'Flyer' was the outcome of an intensive program of research." *Sci. Amer. 241* (1): 86–100, 1979.

1. The two curves differ chiefly in that:

   A. the Wrights' data were more accurate.
   B. lift was generally greater in Lilienthal's experiments.
   C. lift was generally greater in the Wrights' experiments.
   D. the peak value for lift was greater in Lilienthal's experiments.

2. In the Wrights' experiments, the greatest lift occurred at an angle of incidence of about:

   F. –5.5 degrees.
   G. 0 degrees.
   H. 14 degrees.
   J. 46 degrees.

3. At an angle of incidence of 50 degrees, by how much would you expect the two experiments to show a difference in lift?

   A. 0–1 pounds per square foot.
   B. 1–2 pounds per square foot.
   C. 2–3 pounds per square foot.
   D. 3–4 pounds per square foot.

4. The two sets of experiments differed most in lift at which of the following angles?

   F. 10 degrees
   G. 15 degrees
   H. 30 degrees
   J. 40 degrees

GO ON TO THE NEXT PAGE.

5. The widest range of angles, in degrees, over which the Lilienthal values for lift continuously exceeded the Wrights' values was:

A. 43.
B. 25.
C. 19.
D. 10.

GO ON TO THE NEXT PAGE.

Passage II

Two experiments were performed to determine the effects of temperature on the rate of cellular respiration* in germinating peas.

*Summary Equation:

$$\underbrace{\underset{\text{(glucose)}}{C_6H_{12}O_6} + \underset{\text{(oxygen)}}{6O_2}}_{\text{consumed}} \Rightarrow \underbrace{\underset{\text{(carbon dioxide)}}{6CO_2} + \underset{\text{(water)}}{6H_2O}}_{\text{produced}}$$

Experiment 1

A simple respirometer was used, primarily consisting of a large test tube partially filled with germinating peas. The peas were covered with a layer of cotton and a small amount of potassium hydroxide (KOH), a substance that can absorb and remove carbon dioxide from the tube. The remainder of the tube, with its starting volume of air sealed inside, was closed to the outside with a rubber stopper. Attached was a meter designed to detect and measure any changes in pressure in the tube during the experiment. The experiment was conducted at room temperature (22°C), and the respirometer was monitored for 15 minutes. At the end of 15 minutes, the pressure inside the tube had *decreased* from its starting pressure of 760 torr to 722 torr.

Experiment 2

An identical experiment was conducted at 30°C. At this temperature, the pressure inside the tube after 15 minutes had decreased from 786 torr (starting pressure) to 707 torr.

6. Separate control experiments were performed alongside Experiments 1 and 2. The control contained plastic beads (the same size as peas) instead of germinating peas. All other conditions were identical. Any decrease in pressure inside the control tube would suggest that:

   F. plastic beads utilize oxygen at approximately the same rate as germinating peas.
   G. plastic beads produce carbon dioxide at about the same rate as germinating peas.
   H. plastic beads carry out all aspects of cellular respiration at approximately the same rate as germinating peas.
   J. factors having nothing to do with cellular respiration must be responsible.

7. In both experiments, the decrease in pressure in the tube was mainly due to a change in the volume of what specific gas?

   A. Oxygen
   B. Carbon dioxide
   C. Potassium hydroxide
   D. All of the above

8. If potassium hydroxide (KOH) were not included in the tubes, what would happen to the pressure during each experiment?

   F. Final pressure would approximately be the same as starting pressure.
   G. Final pressure would be higher than starting pressure.
   H. Final pressure would decrease faster than what was observed in Experiments 1 and 2.
   J. Results would not be different from what was observed in Experiments 1 and 2.

9. Experiment 2 showed a greater decrease in pressure in the tube because:

   A. at higher temperatures, peas use oxygen slower.
   B. at higher temperatures, potassium hydroxide absorbs and removes carbon dioxide slower.
   C. at higher temperatures, peas use oxygen faster.
   D. at lower temperatures, peas use oxygen slower than they produce carbon dioxide.

GO ON TO THE NEXT PAGE.

10. An additional set of experiments with germinating peas is conducted in the dark at 22°C and 30°C. All other conditions are identical to those in Experiments 1 and 2. After 15 minutes, if the final pressure inside the tube at 22°C is 722 torr, and the final gas volume inside the tube at 30°C is 707 torr, which hypothesis best explains the results?

F. Darkness affects cellular respiration in germinating peas the same way that a rise in temperature affects cellular respiration in germinating peas.
G. Light/dark conditions have little or no effect on cellular respiration in germinating peas.
H. Cellular respiration in germinating peas occurs faster in the light than in the dark.
J. Cellular respiration in germinating peas occurs faster in the dark than in the light.

11. The summary equation in the passage shows that during cellular respiration, germinating peas must consume glucose. In Experiments 1 and 2, glucose molecules:

A. were in the peas.
B. were not available.
C. were consumed at equal rates.
D. were available but not consumed at all.

GO ON TO THE NEXT PAGE.

Passage III

Two different views of the earth's past are presented below.

Scientist 1

The history of our planet has been marked by sudden spectacular events that have no counterpart in the natural processes observed today (catastrophism). Today's valleys formed during periods of downward slippage by fragments of the earth's crust. Mountains rose due to gigantic upheavals of land during the earth's beginnings. The three major types of rock formed when one worldwide ocean precipitated out great masses of different materials during three sudden and separate events. Substances such as granite were precipitated first (today's igneous rocks), while materials in the flat upper layers precipitated last (today's sedimentary rocks). This was followed by the disappearance of much of this great ocean's water (perhaps by evaporation during years of intensive heat). Distinct assemblages of animal and plant fossils, found in successive rock layers of a region, can be explained by local catastrophic events, such as massive fires or floods. Old forms were wiped out, and eventually new forms replaced them as foreign species immigrated from other geographic areas.

Scientist 2

Processes now in operation are adequate to account for changes in the earth's past (principle of uniform change). Although today's processes seem to have negligible effects on the landscape, great changes can result from ongoing processes, if given long enough periods of time. Valleys form as flowing water cuts through the sides and bottom of the land and rock they pass across. Rocks and mountains can be formed, destroyed and reformed by processes still going on today. Volcanic activity, heat and pressure under the earth's surfaces, erosion, weathering, and even shifts and movements can lift massive areas below the land and ocean surfaces to high elevations. Different fossil types in successive layers of rocks represent the changes in form that can take place among related organisms as a result of evolutionary processes over vast periods of time.

12. One major difference between the views of Scientist 1 and Scientist 2 relates to:

F. where fossils are found.
G. when the processes that shaped the earth took place.
H. the size of mountain ranges.
J. whether water played a role in forming any of the earth's characteristics.

13. Which of the following provides the strongest evidence against Scientist 1's point about mountain formation?

A. The beginnings of the earth are not well documented.
B. Floods and fires have never been massive enough to eliminate fossils from all mountain areas.
C. Volcanic activity, weathering, and erosion are believed to be less common today than in years past.
D. Fossils of recent sea creatures can be found in rocks on mountain peaks.

GO ON TO THE NEXT PAGE.

14. Which of the following best characterizes the main difference between catastrophism and the principle of uniform change?

F. Catastrophism maintains that violent changes in the relatively recent past shaped the earth's landscape while the principle of uniform change holds that gradual changes over an enormous span are responsible.
G. Catastrophism predicts that sudden, violent events will soon reshape the earth's landscape while the principle of uniform change expects the landscape to remain mostly unchanged.
H. Catastrophism theorizes that the landscape was largely shaped by cataclysmic events in the distant past while the principle of uniform change holds that the landscape is the result of a steady transformation over a long time.
J. Catastrophism holds that relatively recent events of enormous magnitude created the landscape while the principle of uniform change holds that the landscape has remained relatively unchanged since the earth's formation.

15. According to Scientist 1, which of the major types of rocks should be found at the lowest levels?

A. Igneous (granite)
B. Metamorphic (marble)
C. Sedimentary (limestone)
D. Cannot be determined from the given information

16. According to the views of Scientist 1, the number of major rock types will most likely:

F. remain unchanged.
G. decrease.
H. increase.
J. Cannot be determined from the given information

17. To refute Scientist 2's point of view about strictly uniform processes of change, Scientist 1 could argue that:

A. the streams of today are not measurably effective in cutting through the sides and bottoms of rock they pass across.
B. fossils are not found everywhere today.
C. at some early point in time, the actual formation of the earth had to involve very different processes than those now in evidence.
D. no mountain ranges have formed in our lifetime.

18. Which argument does NOT support the views of Scientist 2?

F. There are many regions of lava where no volcanoes are present today.
G. There are three major types of rock that exist today.
H. Many rivers today are flowing far below their former channels.
J. Distinctive fossils in upper layers of rock show similarities to those in lower layers, yet they are never found in any other geographic areas.

GO ON TO THE NEXT PAGE.

Passage IV

Cold-blooded animals cannot regulate their body temperatures internally. Their body temperature varies as the environmental temperature varies. Consequently, the rates of many bodily processes also vary as outside temperatures change (as environmental temperatures increase, body temperature as well as the rates of bodily processes may also increase). Warm-blooded animals, on the other hand, can maintain their body temperatures internally. Therefore, the rates of their bodily processes can remain relatively stable when environmental temperatures change.

Experiments were set up to determine how heart rate, a bodily process, may be affected by different temperatures in two species of live laboratory animals.

Experiment 1

In this experiment, 10 individuals from Species A and 10 individuals from Species B were kept in 20 separate containers at room temperature (22°C) for 30 minutes. Their heart rates (heart beats/minute) were recorded every 10 minutes starting 10 minutes into the experiment. Average heart rates for the entire experiment were calculated for each species: Species A had an average heart rate of 150 beats/minute, while Species B averaged 100 beats/minute.

Experiment 2

Identical procedures were used to repeat the original experiment except that the containers holding the individuals of each species were placed in an incubator set at 35°C. At the end of 30 minutes, the average heart rate for both species was 148 beats/minute.

19. How many values were used to calculate the average heart beats for each species in each of these experiments?

A. 1
B. 10
C. 20
D. 30

20. Which of the following hypotheses is supported by the results of both experiments?

F. Species A is most likely cold-blooded.
G. Species B is most likely cold-blooded.
H. Both species are most likely cold-blooded.
J. Neither species is cold-blooded.

21. Which of the following statements best explains why 10 individuals of each species were used in each of the experiments?

A. In case a few died, there would still be others available for testing.
B. If only one individual was used, it would be lonely.
C. An average value for 10 individuals reduces the chance of getting an extreme value based on any one individual.
D. If only one individual was chosen from each species, it would be difficult to show differences.

22. If a third experiment were conducted at 6°C, which set of results for average heart rates (in beats/minute) is closest to what might be expected?

F. Species A: 146; Species B: 146
G. Species A: 50; Species B: 146
H. Species A: 50; Species B: 50
J. Species A: 146; Species B: 50

23. Which statement is accurate concerning Species A and Species B?

A. At 22°C, Species A has a higher average heart rate than Species B.
B. Species A has a larger average size than Species B.
C. As environmental temperature increases, average heart rate increases more for Species A than Species B.
D. As environmental temperature decreases, average heart rate increases more for Species A than Species B.

GO ON TO THE NEXT PAGE.

24. If the average body temperature for 10 individuals of each species were recorded during Experiments 1 and 2, which results would be expected?

F. Species A: Temperature stays the same in both experiments. Species B: Temperature increases in Experiment 2.
G. Species A: Temperature increases in Experiment 2. Species B: Temperature stays the same in both experiments.
H. Both Species: Temperature increases in Experiment 2.
J. Both Species: Temperature stays the same in both experiments.

GO ON TO THE NEXT PAGE.

Passage V

The chart below shows a set of "energy levels" that an electron in molecule X can occupy. The value of the energy in each level is shown to the right.

Energy Level	Energy Value
E_5	------2.07 eV
E_4	------1.75 eV
E_3	------1.52 eV
E_2	------1.20 eV
E_1	-------0.60 eV

An electron can move from one level to the next (transition) in two ways:

(1) The molecule can absorb a particle of light, called a "photon," of just the right energy to lift the electron to a higher level. For example, an electron in level 4 can be raised to level 5 if the molecule absorbs a photon whose energy is 0.32 eV.

(2) The molecule can emit, or give off, a photon of just the right energy necessary to lower an electron to another level. For example, an electron in level 4 can move to level 2 if the molecule emits a photon whose energy is 0.55 eV.

25. A sample containing many X molecules absorbs light, each photon of which carries 0.60 eV. As each photon is absorbed an electron moves from:

A. level 1 to level 2.
B. level 2 to level 4.
C. level 2 to level 1.
D. level 4 to level 2.

26. A sample containing many X molecules emits light, each photon of which carries 0.32 eV. As each photon is emitted, an electron moves from:

F. level 3 to level 2.
G. level 2 to level 3.
H. level 5 to level 4.
J. level 3 to level 2 or from level 5 to level 4.

27. A sample of molecule X emits light, each photon of which carries 0.92 eV. As each photon is emitted an electron moves from:

A. level 5 to level 2.
B. level 1 to level 5.
C. level 1 to level 3.
D. level 3 to level 1.

28. Suppose that in a sample containing many X molecules, all of the electrons are in level 5. Based on the information in the chart, the sample could emit photons of how many different energies, if each emission resulted in an electron transitioning to a new level?

F. One
G. Two
H. Three
J. Four

29. Assume that each of the molecules in a sample containing many X molecules has two electrons, and those two electrons are on the same level, but the level is not known. Light is passed through the sample, and photons, each of energy 0.23 eV, are absorbed. A very short time later, photons of the same energy are emitted. It is likely that:

A. electrons are moving from level 1 to level 2.
B. electrons are moving from level 4 to level 3, then back again to level 4.
C. electrons are moving from level 3 to level 4, then back again to level 3.
D. electrons are moving from level 5 to level 4.

30. If photons whose individual energies are each 2.07 eV encounter a sample containing many X molecules, then:

F. electrons will be promoted from level 1 to level 5.
G. electrons will be promoted from all levels to level 5.
H. electrons will drop from level 5 to level 1.
J. no electron transitions will occur between levels 1 and 5.

GO ON TO THE NEXT PAGE.

Passage VI

A student performs three experiments in which a light beam passes through water and air. The "refraction angles" are the angles that the light beam makes with a line perpendicular to the surface of the water or air. In the water, this angle is called θ_1. When the beam leaves the water and passes into air, a second angle, θ_2, can be measured. Figure 1 illustrates θ_1 and θ_2.

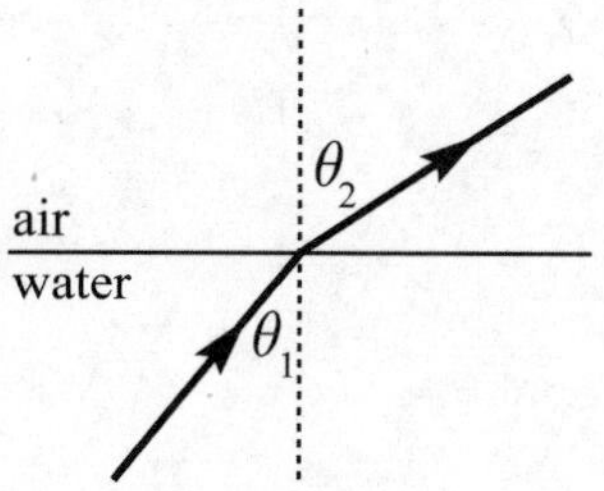

Figure 1

Experiment 1

The entry angle, θ_1, and the exit angle, θ_2, are both equal to zero.

Experiment 2

The angles observed are shown in Figure 2.

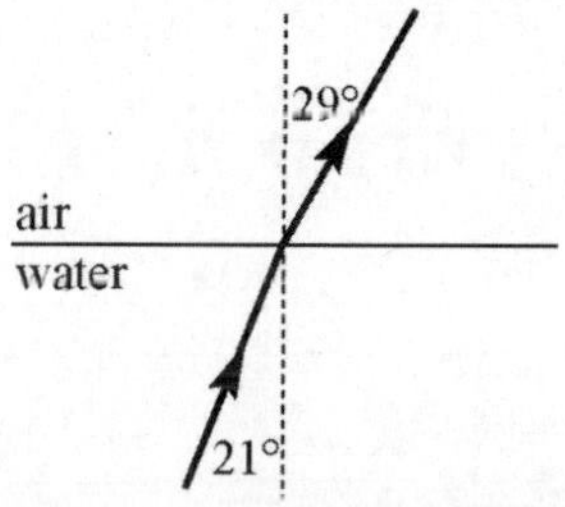

Figure 2

Experiment 3

The angles observed are shown in Figure 3.

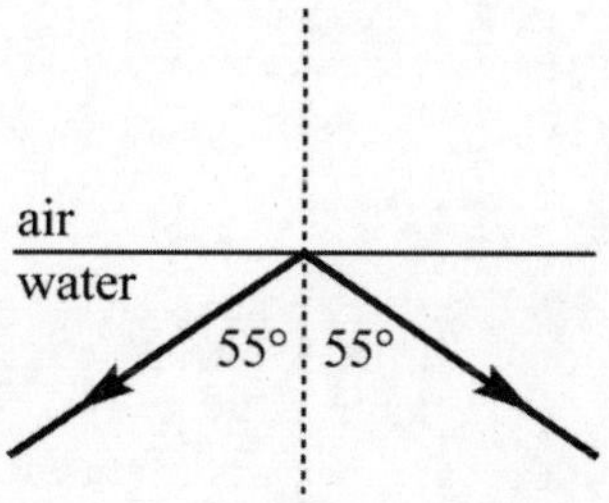

Figure 3

31. Which of the following diagrams could represent the observations of Experiment 1?

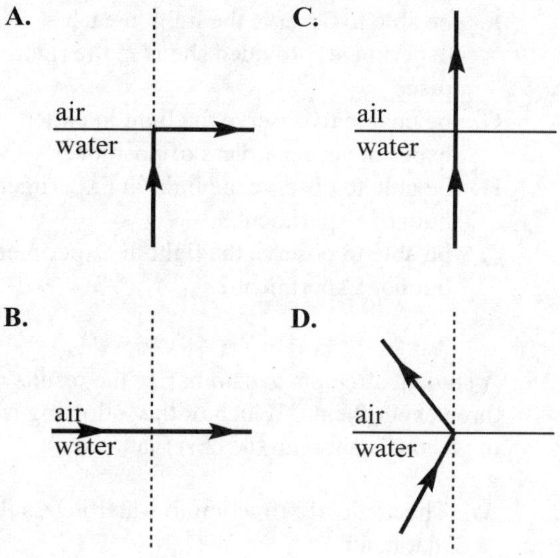

32. The student attempts to draw a conclusion from Experiments 1 and 2 that may apply to all other measurements as well. Which of the following is justified by the data?

F. Refraction angles in water are greater than those in air.
G. Refraction angles in water are less than those in air.
H. Refraction angles are equal in air and in water.
J. Refraction angles in water are equal to or less than those in air.

33. In Experiment 3, the beam travels through the water and:

A. is reflected back down from the surface of the water.
B. enters the air.
C. is absorbed completely.
D. is reflected back on itself.

34. An observer in the air attempts to see the beam of light in Experiments 2 and 3. She will:

F. be able to observe the light in each experiment, provided she is in the right place.
G. be unable to observe the light in either experiment, regardless of position.
H. be able to observe the light in Experiment 2 but not Experiment 3.
J. be able to observe the light in Experiment 3 but not Experiment 2.

35. A student attempts to summarize the results of all three experiments. Which of the following is most consistent with the observations?

A. The angle of refraction in water is less than that in air.
B. The angle of refraction in air is less than that in water.
C. The angle of refraction in water is less than or equal to that in air, but at high angles in the water, the light is reflected back into the water.
D. The angle of refraction in water is less than or equal to that in air.

GO ON TO THE NEXT PAGE.

Passage VII

The table below presents the results of a study in which butterflies of different size and color were captured in flight for marking with a chemical, and then recaptured in flight a few weeks later.

	White		Tan		Dark Brown	
Size	Marked	Recaptured	Marked	Recaptured	Marked	Recaptured
Small (less than 20 mm)	35	30	40	10	20	10
Medium (20–40 mm)	30	15	40	20	20	10
Large (greater than 40 mm)	50	25	60	30	30	10

36. For all sizes of butterflies, the color that seems most difficult to capture for marking is:

F. white.
G. tan.
H. dark brown.
J. Both tan and dark brown are almost equally difficult

37. The specific type of butterfly that is easiest to recapture after being marked is:

A. between 10–20 mm and tan.
B. greater than 40 mm and tan.
C. greater than 40 mm and dark brown.
D. less than 20 mm and white.

38. Based on the information in the table, which statement best represents the relationship between a butterfly's size and its tendency to be captured for marking?

F. The larger the butterfly, the harder it is to be captured for marking.
G. The larger the butterfly, the easier it is to be captured for marking.
H. Medium-sized butterflies are consistently the easiest to capture for marking.
J. The smaller the butterfly, the easier it is to be captured for marking.

39. The chemical used to mark all the butterflies was found to be poisonous to one specific type because it was being absorbed through the wings. Based on the data in the table, which type of butterfly appears most likely to have suffered from the effects of the marking chemical?

A. Greater than 40 mm and white
B. Less than 20 mm and tan
C. Greater than 40 mm and dark brown
D. Less than 20 mm and white

40. Which conclusion is correct concerning the information in the table?

F. For tan butterflies, the proportion of individuals that are recaptured always stays the same.
G. For medium-sized butterflies, the proportion of individuals that are recaptured always stays the same.
H. For small-sized butterflies, the proportion of individuals recaptured always stays the same.
J. For all sizes of butterflies, the darker the color the easier it is to recapture an individual.

END OF TEST 4
STOP! DO NOT TURN THE PAGE UNTIL TOLD TO DO SO.
DO NOT RETURN TO THE PREVIOUS TEST.

ACT Practice Test

SECTION 5: WRITING TEST (OPTIONAL)

30 Minutes—1 Essay Prompt

DIRECTIONS: You have 30 minutes to plan and write an essay. Read the prompt carefully and make sure you understand the instructions. A successful essay will have the following features: it will take a position on the issue presented in the writing prompt; it will maintain a consistent focus on the topic; it will use logical reasoning and provide supporting ideas; it will present ideas in an organized manner; and, finally, it will include clear and effective language in accordance with the conventions of standard written English. Sample essay responses begin on page616.

Online Voting Systems

Homes, schools, libraries, and churches all have Internet access. With the broad availability of Internet access, the problem of voter turnout can be addressed and effectively solved. In America's last national election, less than 40% of the eligible voters cast ballots. Internet access can be used to theoretically double voter turnout and maybe even increase it to 100%. The technology exists to allow each American to register and vote from a computer terminal of his or her choosing. Such a move would certainly increase democratic voice and popular participation in our elections, but would it lead to more voters who are uninformed about candidates and issues? It is important to address this controversy, as future generations of voters will be increasingly technology-oriented.

Perspective 1	Perspective 2	Perspective 3
Informed voters are the heart of democracy. Simply providing mechanical solutions that add quantity to the voter turnout would not necessarily lead to an educated electorate to shape our future.	This type of voting system is risky because it will be difficult to determine who will monitor the electronic machines that are used. We cannot trust the security systems to protect our most precious right when these very same systems regularly fail to protect our credit cards.	Voter turnout is supremely important to a democracy. A country needs the participation of its citizens to realize its fondest hopes and dreams. We need to get more people to vote to help America reach its potential.

Essay Task

Write a unified, coherent essay in which you evaluate multiple perspectives on the issue of online voting systems. In your essay be sure to:

- Analyze and evaluate perspectives given
- State and develop your own perspective
- Explain the relationship between your perspective and those given

Your perspective may be in full agreement with any of the others, in partial agreement, or wholly different. Whatever the case, support your ideas with logical reasoning and detailed, persuasive examples.

END OF TEST 5

STOP! DO NOT RETURN TO ANY OTHER TEST.

SAT Practice Test

Outline

DIRECTIONS

The SAT Practice Test includes five test sections: Reading, Writing and Language, Math, No Calculator, Math, Calculator, and the optional Essay.. Calculator use is permitted on the Math, Calculator section only.

Cambridge offers several services for schools utilizing our practice tests. Ask your teacher whether your school has decided to send your answers to Cambridge for scoring or to score your answers at your school. If Cambridge is scoring your test, you will use a Scantron™ form provided by your teacher, or you will enter your answers online. If your school is scoring your test, you may use a Scantron form provided by your teacher, or you may write your answers on paper.

If you are entering your test answers on a Scantron form, please be sure to include the following information on the Scantron:

Book and edition	*Victory for the ACT® and SAT® Tests, 5th Edition*
Practice Test	**SAT Practice Test**

If you are only completing a single section of this practice test, make sure to also include the following information:

Subject	**Reading, Writing and Language,** or **Math**
Section Number	**Section 1, 2, 3** or **4**

The items in each test section are numbered and the multiple-choice answers are lettered. The Scantron form has numbered rows that correspond to the items on the test. Each row contains lettered ovals to match the answer choices for each item on the test. Each numbered row has a corresponding item on the test.

For each multiple-choice item, first decide on the best answer choice. Then, locate the row number that corresponds to the item. Next, find the oval in that row that matches the letter of the chosen answer. Then, use a soft lead pencil to fill in the oval. DO NOT use a ballpoint pen. For each student-produced response item on the math test sections, decide on the correct answer. Then, locate the SPR grid that corresponds to the item. Write your answer in the top of the grid and use a soft lead pencil to fill in each corresponding oval. DO NOT use a ballpoint pen.

Mark only one answer for each item. If you change your mind about an answer choice, thoroughly erase your first mark before marking your new answer.

Note that only responses marked on your Scantron form or written on your paper will be scored. Your score on each test will be based only on the number of items that are correctly answered during the time allowed for that test. You will not be penalized for guessing. Therefore, it is in your best interest to answer every item on the test, even if you must guess.

On the Essay, write your response to the prompt using the essay response sheets or loose-leaf paper provided by your teacher. (Note that the Writing Test is optional.)

You may work on each test only during the time allowed for that test. If you finish a test before time is called, use the time to review your answer choices or work on items about which you are uncertain. You may not return to a test on which time has already been called, and you may not preview another test. You must lay down your pencil immediately when time is called at the end of each test. You may not for any reason fill in or alter ovals for a test after time has expired for that test. Violation of these rules will result in immediate disqualification from the exam.

SAT Practice Test

SECTION 1—READING

65 minutes—52 items

DIRECTIONS: Each passage or pair of passages is followed by a set of items. Choose the best answer to each question based on what is stated or implied in the passage or passages and in any accompanying graphics. Answers are on page 621.

Questions #1–11 are based on the following passage.

The following passage explores the results of various behavioral experiments exploring the causes and effects of helplessness.

Helplessness, the passivity that occurs when someone has faced problems that seemingly cannot be controlled, is a central theme in describing human depression. Laboratory experiments with animals have uncovered a phenomenon designated "learned helplessness." Researchers administered shocks to rats, accompanied by tones or lights, so that they would come to associate the tone or light stimuli with the shock's onset. The experimental set-up also included a lever. For part of the test population, the lever, when pressed, stopped the shock. For the other part, pressing the lever did nothing. So some of the rats learned to avoid the painful shocks by pressing the lever.

In the second stage of the experiment, each rat was set free inside a shuttle box, a two-compartment cage separated by a barrier of adjustable height. Each time the lights in the box went off, half of the floor would become electrified, but if the rat climbed over the barrier and into the next cage, the shock could be avoided. This time, every rat had the power to end its discomfort quite easily.

The rats exhibited a consistent pattern of behavior. The rats that had learned to avoid the shocks by pressing the lever were quick to climb over the barrier. Those in the other group, the ones that had been unable to escape the shocks, did not even try. They were free to move, explore, and escape—but they did not. The researchers called this "learned helplessness."

Is the helplessness caused by prior exposure to the inescapable electric shock really a form of learned behavior? Alternatively, is it simply a stress-induced behavior? Helplessness can be produced in rats by stress alone, for example, by brief submersion in cold water. But it seems that the behavior produced by exposure to extremely traumatic events must be produced by a very different mechanism than the changes from exposure to the less traumatic, uncontrollable aversive events in the learned-helplessness experiments. In fact, experiments using nonaversive stimulus, such as uncontrollable food delivery, also produces similar results.

Moreover, studies have shown the importance of prior experience in learned helplessness. Rats can be immunized against learned helplessness by prior experience with controllable electric shocks. Rats also show a "mastery effect" after extended experience with escapable shock. They work far longer trying to escape from inescapable shock than do rats lacking this prior mastery experience. Conversely, weanling rats given inescapable shock fail to escape shock as adults. These adult rats are also poor at nonaversive discrimination learning.

Similarities have been noted between conditions produced in animals by the learned-helplessness procedure and by the experimental neurosis paradigm. In the latter, animals are first trained on a discrimination task and are then tested with discriminative stimuli of increasing similarity. Eventually, as the discrimination becomes very difficult, animals fail to respond and begin displaying abnormal behaviors: first agitation, then lethargy. Inescapable noise or unsolvable problems have been shown to result in conditions in humans similar to those induced in laboratory animals, but an adequate model of

Continue

human depression must also be able to account for the cognitive complexity of human depression.

How analogous the model of learned helplessness and the paradigm of stress-induced neurosis are to human depression is not entirely clear.

1. The primary purpose of the passage is to

A) propose a cure for depression in human beings.
B) discuss research possibly relevant to depression in human beings.
C) criticize the result of experiments that induce depression in laboratory animals.
D) raise some questions about the use of laboratory animals for research.

2. The writer implies that the human reaction to uncontrollable events is

A) completely dissimilar to the behavior of laboratory animals.
B) like the stress experienced by rats when submerged in cold water.
C) similar to but much more complex than that of laboratory animals.
D) unpredictable because humans are more complex than laboratory animals.

3. Which choice provides the most support for the answer to the previous question?

A) Lines 36–38 ("Helplessness . . . cold water")
B) Lines 47–49 ("Moreover . . . learned helplessness")
C) Lines 59–62 ("Similarities . . . paradigm")
D) Lines 68–73 ("Inescapable . . . depression")

4. The author poses the two questions at the beginning of the fourth paragraph in order to

A) prove that learned helplessness is caused by neurochemical changes.
B) demonstrate that learned helplessness is also caused by nonaversive discrimination learning.
C) suggest that further research is not likely to produce a definitive answer to either question.
D) raise an alternative explanation of the cause of learned helplessness.

5. As used in line 58, the term "nonaversive" means

A) not painful.
B) beneficial.
C) unnoticeable.
D) traumatic.

6. The author implies that in the experimental neurosis paradigm abnormal behavior in laboratory animals is caused by

A) exposure to nonaversive stimuli such as irregular feedings.
B) inability to distinguish increasingly similar discriminative stimuli.
C) short-term stress associated with minimally aversive stimuli.
D) confusion as to whether the aversive stimuli are avoidable or unavoidable.

7. Which choice provides the most support for the answer to the previous question?

A) Lines 7–10 ("Researchers . . . onset")
B) Lines 26–30 ("The rats . . . even try")
C) Lines 55–58 ("Conversely . . . discrimination learning")
D) Lines 65–68 ("Eventually . . . lethargy")

Continue

8. The author cites the "mastery effect" (line 52) primarily in order to

A) prove the avoidance deficit caused by exposure to inescapable shock is not caused by shock per se but by the inescapability.
B) cast doubts on the validity of models of animal depression when applied to depression in human beings.
C) raise the possibility that changes in the brain cause learned helplessness.
D) suggest that the experimental-neurosis paradigm and the learned-helplessness procedure produce similar behavior in animals.

9. As used in line 49, "immunized against" most nearly means

A) trained to resist.
B) encouraged to imitate.
C) punished for.
D) rewarded for.

10. Which of the following would be the most logical continuation of the passage?

A) An explanation of the connection between the septum and the motivation centers of the brains of rats
B) An examination of techniques used to cure animals of learned helplessness
C) A review of experiments designed to create stress-induced noradrenergic deficiencies in humans
D) An elaboration of the differences between human depression and similar animal behavior

11. In the second stage of the experiment, described in paragraph two, the adjustable height of the barrier was most likely used to

A) separate two populations of laboratory subjects.
B) control the difficulty of escaping the shocks.
C) confine the laboratory rats to the first compartment.
D) permit the use of a variety of laboratory test animals.

Continue

Questions #12–21 are based on the following passage.

There has been considerable debate on the issue of violence in television and film. The following passage explores the question of whether violence in television commercials directed at children is a serious problem.

The violence employed in television directed specifically at children usually appears in the context of fantasy. The impact of the violent portrayals varies according to the number of fantasy cues present in the portrayal. Cartoon violence generally has three such cues (animation, humor, and a fictional setting); make-believe violence generally has two cues (humor and a fictional setting); and realistic, acted violence generally has only one cue (the viewer's knowledge that the portrayal is fictional).

Most children as young as four can distinguish these three contexts; however, about one-quarter of four- to eight-year-olds define cartoon violence as a depiction of violence *per se*, about half also perceive make-believe violence in this way, and over half see realistic (acted) violence as violence. Children appear to make these distinctions solely on the basis of the physical fantasy cues. There is no support for the idea that children, especially young children, can differentiate types of violence on a cognitive or rational basis—for example, by justification of the motives for the violent behavior or the goodness of its consequences.

Still, there is very little evidence of direct imitation of television violence by children, though there is evidence that fantasy violence, as well as portrayals of real-life violence, can energize previously learned aggressive responses such as a physical attack on another child during play. It is by no means clear, however, that the violence in a portrayal is solely responsible for this energizing effect. Rather, the evidence suggests that any exciting material triggers subsequent aggressive behavior and that it is the effect of violence that instigates or energizes any subsequent violent behavior.

Moreover, this type of "violent" behavior demonstrated in experiments with children is more likely to reflect either novel play activities or, more typically, a lowering of previously learned play inhibitions, than an increase in socially threatening aggression. In short, cold imitation of violence by children is extremely rare, and the very occasional evidence of direct, imitative associations between television violence and aggressive behavior has been limited to extremely novel and violent acts by teenagers or adults with already established patterns of deviant behavior.

The instigational effect means, in the short term, that exposure to violent portrayals could be dangerous to a child if shortly after the exposure (within 15 to 20 minutes and at most an hour) the child happens to be in a situation that calls for interpersonal aggression as an appropriate response, e.g., an argument between siblings or among peers. This same instigational effect, however, could be produced by other exciting but non-violent television content or by any other excitational source, including, ironically enough, television failure or a parent's turning off the set.

So, it seems unlikely that there are any cumulative instigational effects, such as more aggressive or violent dispositions in children. In fact, passivity is a more likely long-term result of heavy viewing of television violence. Any instigation of deviant behavior by children seems to be confined to short-term circumstantial effects.

All of this implies that an indictment of fantasy violence in children's programming must rest mainly on a very slight risk that the violent portrayal may be imitated and a somewhat greater risk that the violence may have a short-term instigational effect when circumstances suggest aggression as an appropriate response. The evidence does not warrant the strong conclusions advanced by many critics who tend to use television violence as a scapegoat to draw public attention away from the real causes of violence—causes like abusive spouses and parents and a culture that celebrates violence generally. The violent acts depicted in these television commercials can rarely be imitated and the duration of the violence is much too short to have an instigational effect.

Continue

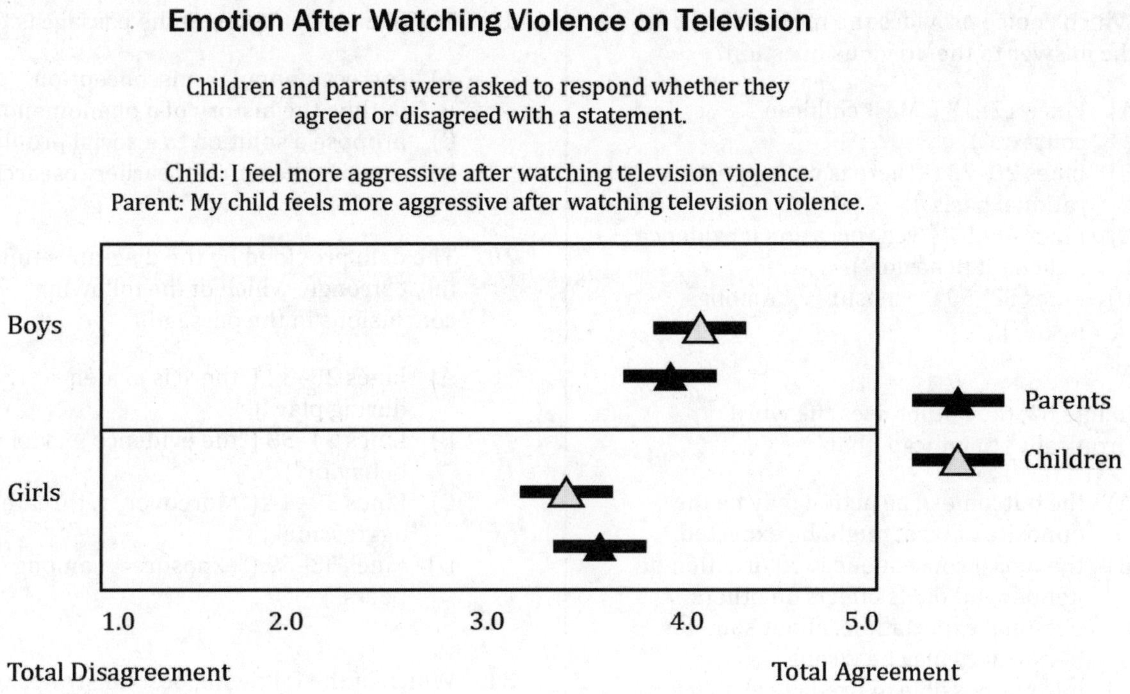

12. The author implies that

A) children most easily recognize cartoon violence as fantasy.
B) children most easily recognize make-believe violence as fantasy.
C) children most easily recognize realistic, acted violence as fantasy.
D) children are unable to recognize violence as fantasy in any form it is presented.

13. Which choice provides the most support for the answer to the previous question?

A) Lines 3–5 ("The impact . . . portrayal")
B) Lines 20–23 ("There is no support . . . rational basis")
C) Lines 28–32 ("there is evidence . . . during play")
D) Lines 46–51 ("very occasional evidence . . . deviant behavior")

14. In line 57, "appropriate" most nearly means

A) acceptable.
B) desirable.
C) normal.
D) learned.

15. The author implies that a child who has an argument with a sibling two to three hours after watching fantasy violence on television would

A) almost surely be more aggressive than usual.
B) tend to act out the fantasy violence on the sibling.
C) probably not be unusually violent or aggressive.
D) likely lapse into a state of total passivity.

Continue

16. Which choice provides the most support for the answer to the previous question?

A) Lines 12–13 ("Most children . . . contexts")
B) Lines 20–23 ("There is no support . . . rational basis")
C) Lines 46–51 ("very occasional evidence . . . deviant behavior")
D) Lines 53–59 ("exposure . . . among peers")

17. In line 62, the author uses the word "ironically" to indicate that

A) the outcome of an action may be the opposite of what might be expected.
B) the moral consequences of an action do not depend on its effects on others.
C) personal expectations about someone's personality may be wrong.
D) it is not possible to predict reliably how children will behave.

18. Which of the following best describes the author's attitude about critics who say that television is an important cause of violent behavior in children?

A) Qualified endorsement
B) Contemptuous dismissal
C) Enthusiastic acceptance
D) Moderate skepticism

19. The primary purpose of the passage is to

A) correct a popular misconception.
B) outline the history of a phenomenon.
C) propose a solution to a social problem.
D) criticize the work of earlier researchers.

20. The data provided by the diagram supports most strongly which of the following conclusions in the passage?

A) Lines 28–32 ("there is evidence . . . during play")
B) Lines 34–38 ("the evidence . . . violent behavior")
C) Lines 39–44 ("Moreover . . . threatening aggression")
D) Lines 53–59 ("exposure . . . among peers")

21. Which of the following best illustrates what the author means by "make-believe violence"?

A) cartoon characters performing amusing antics in an alien setting
B) cartoon characters in an alien setting acting in a serious manner
C) real people in a skit in a fictional setting who laugh at the outcome
D) real people acting in a skit who reach a moral conclusion about their behavior

Continue

Questions #22–31 are based on the following passage.

The following passage describes part of a journey taken by a man named Duane.

As swiftly as was consistent with a care for his steed, Duane put a distance of fifteen or eighteen miles behind him. With that he slowed up, and the matter of riding did not require all his faculties. He passed several ranches and was seen by men. This did not suit him, and he took an old trail across country. It was a flat region with a poor growth of mesquite and prickly-pear cactus. Occasionally he caught a glimpse of low hills in the distance. He had hunted often in that section and knew where to find grass and water. When he reached this higher ground he did not, however, halt at the first favorable camping spot, but went on and on. He came out upon the brow of a hill and saw a considerable stretch of country beneath him. It had the gray sameness characterizing all that he had traversed. He seemed to want to see wide spaces—to get a glimpse of the great wilderness lying somewhere beyond to the southwest. It was sunset when he decided to camp at a likely spot he came across. He led the horse to water, and then began searching through the shallow valley for a suitable place to camp. He passed by old campsites that he well remembered. These, however, did not strike his fancy this time, and the significance of the change in him did not occur at the moment. At last he found a secluded spot, under cover of thick mesquites and oaks, at a goodly distance from the old trail. He took the saddle and pack off the horse. He looked among his effects for a hobble, and, finding that his uncle had failed to put one in, he suddenly remembered that he seldom used a hobble, and never on this horse. He cut a few feet off the end of his lasso and used that. The horse, unused to such hampering of his free movements, had to be driven out upon the grass.

Duane made a small fire and prepared and ate his supper. This done, ending the work of that day, he sat down and filled his pipe. Twilight had waned into dusk. A few wan stars had just begun to show and brighten. Above the low, continuous hum of insects sounded the evening carol of robins. Presently the birds ceased their singing, and then the quiet was more noticeable. When night set in, the place seemed all the more isolated and lonely. For that, Duane had a sense of relief.

It dawned on him all at once that he was nervous, watchful, sleepless. The fact caused him surprise, and he began to think back, to take note of his late actions and their motives. The change one day had wrought amazed him. He who had always been free, easy, happy, especially when out alone in the open, had become in a few short hours bound, serious, preoccupied. The silence that had once been sweet now meant nothing to him except a medium whereby he might better hear the sounds of pursuit. The loneliness, the night, the wild, that had always been beautiful to him, now only conveyed a sense of safety for the present. He watched, he listened, he thought. He felt tired, yet had no inclination to rest. He intended to be off by dawn, heading toward the southwest. Had he a destination? It was as vague as his knowledge of that great waste of mesquite and rock bordering the Rio Grande. Somewhere out there was a refuge. This being an outlaw then meant eternal vigilance. No home, no rest, no sleep, no content, no life worth the living! He must be a lone wolf, or he must herd among men obnoxious to him. If he worked for an honest living, he still must hide his identity and take risks of detection. If he did not work on some distant outlying ranch, how was he to live? The idea of stealing was repugnant to him. The future seemed gray and somber enough. And he was twenty-three years old.

Why had this hard life been imposed upon him?

22. It can be inferred that Duane is a

A) hardened criminal who is a fugitive from the law.
B) good man who has done something terribly wrong.
C) reckless young teenager with no concern for the well-being of others.
D) long-term outlaw who has lived on the edge of society.

Continue

23. Which choice provides the most support for the answer to the previous question?

A) Lines 1–5 ("As swiftly . . . faculties")
B) Lines 44–47 ("Presently . . . relief")
C) Lines 48–51 ("It dawned . . . motives")
D) Lines 69–75 ("He must . . . repugnant to him")

24. It can be inferred that Duane chose the campsite for its

A) view.
B) isolation.
C) familiarity.
D) height.

25. Which choice provides the most support for the answer to the previous question?

A) Lines 5–8 ("He passed . . . cactus")
B) Lines 11–16 ("When . . . beneath him")
C) Lines 24–27 ("He passed . . . moment")
D) Lines 27–29 ("At last . . . trail")

26. At the beginning of paragraph three, Duane's mental state changes from a

A) concern for the future to a fear for the present.
B) sense of urgency to a mood of reflection.
C) worry about generalities to a focus on details.
D) fear for others to apprehension for himself.

27. As used in the context, a "hobble" (line 31) refers to a length of rope

A) looped about an animal's neck and secured to a stationary object such as a tree.
B) stretched between stationary objects to form a large animal enclosure.
C) tied around a horse's legs to prevent the animal from straying.
D) fitted over a horse's head to allow the horse to be ridden.

28. As used in the context of line 68, "vigilance" means

A) homelessness.
B) solitude.
C) wariness.
D) impoverishment.

29. According to the passage, Duane decided to camp in a

A) flat region with poor growth.
B) grouping of low hills.
C) stretch of gray country uniformly the same.
D) waste of mesquite and rock.

30. Which of the following best explains why Duane was surprised to learn that he was "nervous, watchful, sleepless" (line 49)?

A) He was exhausted from a long ride earlier in the day and from the chores of setting up a campsite.
B) He had not yet taken time to consider that he was now going to have to live life as an outlaw.
C) He was familiar with the general area in which he was camping but not with the specific spot.
D) The darkness, the sounds of the insects, and the singing of the birds all made him nervous.

31. It can be inferred that Duane feels a "sense of relief" (line 47) because

A) the solitude of the place assures him that he is not being pursued.
B) the surrounding quiet guarantees a night of restful sleep.
C) singing birds in the area will wake him early in the morning.
D) the remaining light would help him see anyone approach.

Continue

Questions #32–41 are based on the following passage.

The following is an excerpt from a report that was prepared by an engineering firm on the feasibility of electric cars. The excerpt focuses on the uses of electromechanical batteries as a power source.

Except that their output is alternating current rather than direct current, electromechanical batteries, or EMBs, would power an electric car in the same way as a bank of electrochemical batteries. The modular device contains a flywheel that is stabilized by nearly frictionless magnetic bearings integrated with a special, ironless generator motor and housed in a sealed vacuum enclosure. The EMB is "charged" by spinning its rotor to maximum speed with an integral generator/motor in its "motor mode." It is "discharged" by slowing the rotor of the same generator/motor to draw out the kinetically stored energy in its "generator mode." Initial research focused on the possibility of using one or two relatively large EMBs, but subsequent findings point in a different direction.

Compared to stationary EMB applications, such as with wind turbines, vehicular applications pose two special problems. Gyroscopic forces come into play whenever a vehicle departs from a straight-line course, as in turning. The effects can be minimized by vertically orienting the axis of rotation, and the designer can mount the module in limited-excursion gimbals to resist torque. By operating the EMB modules in pairs—one spinning clockwise and the other counterclockwise—the net gyroscopic effect on the car would be nearly zero.

The other problem associated with EMBs for vehicles is failure containment. Any spinning rotor has an upper speed limit that is determined by the tensile strength of the material from which it is made. On the other hand, at a given rotation speed, the amount of kinetic energy stored is determined by the mass of the flywheel. It was originally thought that high-density materials, such as metals, were optimal for flywheel rotors, and a metal flywheel does store more energy than an equivalent-size flywheel made of low-density material and rotating at the same speed. However, a low-density wheel can be spun up to a higher speed until it reaches the same internal tensile stresses as the metal one, where it stores the same amount of kinetic energy at a much lower weight. Lightweight graphite fiber, for example, is approximately 10 times more effective per unit mass for kinetic energy storage than steel. Plus, tests show that a well-designed rotor made of graphite fibers that fails turns into an amorphous mass of broken fibers. This failure is far more benign than that of metal flywheels, which typically break into shrapnel-like pieces that are difficult to contain.

Not only is the uncontrolled energy that can be released by each unit reduced, but the danger posed by a failed rotor is very small compared to that of rotors just two or three times larger. The strength of graphite fibers, now used in everything from tennis racquets to sailboat masts, has increased by a factor of 5 over the past couple of decades. Thus, an array of small EMB modules offers major advantages over one or two large units.

Continue

Density of Energy in Battery Materials

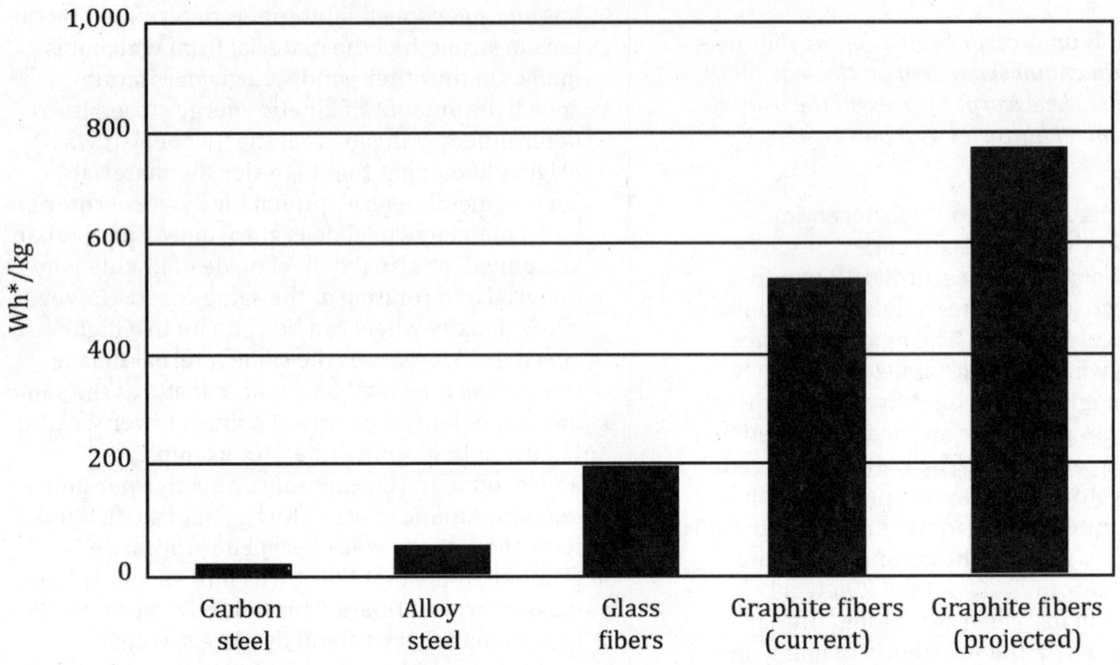

*The watt-hour (symbolized Wh) is a unit of energy equivalent to one watt (1 W) of power expended for one hour (1 h) of time.

32. The author's primary concern is to

A) describe technological advances that make possible containment of uncontrolled kinetic energy discharge due to cataclysmic rotor failure.
B) report on new technologies that will make electric cars competitive with vehicles employing conventional internal combustion engines.
C) argue that an array of small EMB modules mounted in an electric car is more energy efficient than a single large EMB.
D) demonstrate how a group of small EMB modules for use in an electric car can avoid technological problems that are associated with a single large EMB.

33. It can be inferred that a non-metallic, low-density flywheel that has stored kinetic energy equivalent to that of a metallic, high-density flywheel is

A) operating in its "motor mode" and discharging energy as it spins.
B) oriented vertically to the axis of rotation of the metallic flywheel.
C) spinning in the opposite direction of the metallic flywheel.
D) rotating at a higher speed than the metallic flywheel.

34. Which choice provides the most support for the answer to the previous question?

A) Lines 22–25 ("The effects . . . torque")
B) Lines 31–34 ("Any spinning . . . made")
C) Lines 41–45 ("However . . . lower weight")
D) Lines 55–58 ("Not only . . . three times larger")

Continue

35. In lines 51–52, the phrase "more benign" means

A) less dangerous.
B) more reliable.
C) equally stable.
D) less expensive.

36. The author suggests that the gyroscopic effect of EMB modules operating in pairs in a vehicle be minimized by

A) constructing the EMBs of high-density metal.
B) having them rotate in opposite directions.
C) operating them in their "motor" mode only.
D) stabilizing them using frictionless bearings.

37. Which choice provides the most support for the answer to the previous question?

A) Lines 9–14 ("The EMB . . . 'generator mode'")
B) Lines 25–29 ("By operating . . . nearly zero")
C) Lines 31–36 ("Any spinning . . . flywheel")
D) Lines 55–58 ("Not only . . . three times larger")

38. The phrase "net gyroscopic effect on the car" (lines 28–29) refers to the force exerted on the vehicle when it is

A) stationary.
B) accelerating.
C) turning.
D) slowing.

39. Which of the following best describes the logical development of the selection?

A) It mentions some technological challenges and describes some possible solutions.
B) It identifies some technological problems and dismisses attempts to solve them.
C) It outlines technological demands of an engineering application and minimizes their significance.
D) It presents a history of a technological question but offers no answers.

40. Which of the following statements in the text of the passage is directly supported by the data in the graph?

A) Lines 31–34 ("Any spinning . . . made")
B) Lines 34–36 ("On the other . . . flywheel")
C) Lines 41–45 ("However . . . lower weight")
D) Lines 46–48 ("Lightweight . . . steel")

41. The main purpose of the first paragraph is to

A) emphasize the dangers posed to occupants of an electric car by its electromechanical batteries.
B) contrast the effects of the failure of a graphite flywheel with the failure of one made of steel.
C) argue that electromechanical batteries utilizing metal flywheels are impractical in electric cars.
D) describe the functioning of the electromechanical battery in an electric vehicle.

Continue

Questions #42–52 are based on the following passage.

The following excerpts are from two different passages about the ideas of Frederick Jackson Turner.

Passage 1

In 1893, Frederick Jackson Turner presented a paper entitled "The Significance of the American Frontier in History." The paper drew little immediate reaction, yet no theory of history has had a greater influence on the direction and methodology of inquiry and the issues of debate in American history. Later, historians took issue with some of Turner's interpretations; even some of his own students were among those whose research proved some of his views to be wrong. However, these debates merely serve to illustrate the importance of Turner's hypothesis.

Turner's argument was a grand hypothesis about how the settlement of the frontier had shaped the American experience and character. Turner used statistical evidence from the 1880 census as the basis for a startling conclusion: Prior to 1880 there had been a frontier to be settled. By 1890, Turner pointed out, there was no longer any area of wilderness completely untouched by settlements. The frontier had disappeared.

Turner further claimed that the frontier experience had produced a distinctively American character, which was not as explainable as the predictable behavioral traits molded by English political institutions. Frontier settlers developed inquisitiveness, inventiveness, and a great passion for freedom. These attributes defined a new American character—one evidenced in nationalism, independence, and democracy. This new sense of national identity derived from the fact that people from every section of the country mixed at the Western frontier. Economic independence could be traced to the fact that the settlers no longer depended on England for goods but had become self-sufficient. In addition, the frontier settlers, whose basic social unit was the family, enjoyed freedom from direct governmental interference. Frontier life thus reinforced the fundamental ideals of populist democracy.

In addition, Turner argued that the frontier fostered democracy in the cities of the East. The availability of free land at the frontier provided a "safety-valve" against possible social unrest: those discontented with social inequities and economic injustice could strike out and settle the free land that was available in frontier territories.

Turner's thesis was thus original in both what it said and in the methodology used. Up to the time of Turner's essay, history had been essentially the history of politics. A Midwesterner, Turner challenged this traditional approach of Eastern historians by incorporating techniques of the social sciences, showing how factors of geography, economics, climate, and society influenced the development of the American West. Although now common among historians, at the time this interdisciplinary approach was novel.

Passage 2

Three years before Turner put forth the frontier thesis, the US Census Bureau announced the disappearance of a contiguous frontier line. For Turner, the significance of the frontier was its effect on the American character. According to Turner, uniquely American traits were developed by the frontier culture, including a can-do problem-solving attitude, a nervous energy, and rugged individualism.

Turner's thesis that the frontier is the key to American history as a whole has rightfully been abandoned. There is too much evidence for the critical influence of factors like slavery and the Civil War, immigration, and the development of industrial capitalism. But even as an account of the West and frontier, Turner's thesis was lacking.

Turner's formulation of "free land" ignored the presence of the numerous Indian peoples whose subjugation was required by the nation's westward march. The many Indian wars started by American expansion belie Turner's argument that the American frontier, in sharp contrast to European borders between nation-states, was "free land."

More fundamentally, the very concept of a frontier is dubious, because it applies to too many disparate places and times to be useful. How much do Puritan New England and the California of the transcontinental railroad really have in common? Many such critics have sought to replace the idea of a moving frontier with the idea of the West as a distinctive region, much like the American South.

Continue

Additionally, cooperation and communities of various sorts, not isolated individuals, made possible the absorption of the West into the United States. Most migrant wagon trains, for example, were composed of extended kinship networks. Moreover, the role of the federal government and large corporations grew increasingly important. Corporate investors built the railroads; government troops defeated Indian nations; even cowboys, enshrined in popular myth as rugged loners, were generally low-level employees of cattle corporations.

42. According to Passage 1, Turner's methodology was original in its

A) reliance on the history of politics to explain the American experience.
B) use of an interdisciplinary approach to study a historical question.
C) reliance on a presentation at a professional conference to announce a theory.
D) suggestion that key terms like "frontier" have to be more clearly defined.

43. The attitude of the author of Passage 1 toward Turner's work can best be described as

A) skeptical.
B) condescending.
C) noncommittal.
D) favorable.

44. In this context, "grand" (line 13) means

A) incorrect.
B) comprehensive.
C) lavish.
D) tentative.

45. The author of Passage 2 lists the "factors" in lines 71–73 in order to show that

A) Turner's thesis did not adequately explain the history of the frontier.
B) historians prior to Turner had tended to focus on only a single explanatory factor.
C) the frontier was only one of many important factors in American history.
D) different regions of America had different experiences of the frontier.

46. It can be inferred that the author of Passage 2 believes that Turner's thesis

A) is still generally valid.
B) had very limited usefulness.
C) was intellectually dishonest.
D) intentionally ignored evidence.

47. Which of the following textual excerpts provides the strongest support for the correct answer to the previous question?

A) Lines 63–67 ("According to . . . individualism")
B) Lines 68–70 ("Turner's . . . abandoned")
C) Lines 88–90 ("Many . . . South")
D) Lines 91–94 ("Additionally . . . United States")

48. In context, "belie" (line 79) means

A) tell an untruth about
B) conceal a flaw in
C) prove to be false
D) retract a point

49. Both passages mention all of the following as elements of Turner's view regarding the American character EXCEPT

A) practical inventiveness.
B) pro-democracy attitude.
C) skepticism toward authority.
D) nationalistic feelings.

Continue

50. The author of Passage 2 believes that Turner's contention that the frontier fostered "rugged individualism" was

A) accurate because life on the frontier required people to be self-reliant.
B) overstated because many elements of frontier life were produced by groups.
C) likely, but unproved, because records on the time period are incomplete.
D) descriptive of frontier life because the basic social unit was family.

51. Which of the following text excerpts most strongly supports the correct answer to the previous question?

A) Lines 68–70 ("Turner's . . . abandoned")
B) Lines 78–82 ("The many . . . 'free land'")
C) Lines 88–90 ("Many . . . South")
D) Lines 91–94 ("Additionally . . . the United States")

52. The evidence that frontier land was not free (lines 75–82) undermines which of the following principles of Turner's thesis, as explained in Passage 1?

A) safety-valve theory
B) census data of 1880
C) claim of self-sufficiency
D) mixing at the frontier

STOP

IF YOU FINISH BEFORE TIME IS CALLED, YOU MAY CHECK YOUR WORK ON THIS SECTION ONLY. DO NOT TURN TO ANY OTHER SECTION IN THE TEST.

SAT Practice Test

SECTION 2—WRITING AND LANGUAGE

35 minutes—44 items

DIRECTIONS: Each set of questions is based on a passage. For some questions, think about how the passage could be revised to improve the expression of ideas. For other questions, think about how to edit the passage to correct sentence structure, usage, or punctuation errors. Passages or questions may be accompanied by a graphic such as a table or graph that you will consider while you make revising and editing decisions.

Some questions reference an underlined word or phrase in the passage. Other questions refer to a location in the passage or to the passage as a whole.

After reading each passage, choose the answer that improves the expression of ideas in the passage or conforms to standard English conventions. Many questions include a "NO CHANGE" answer choice. Choose that answer if you think the best choice is to leave the passage as it is. Answers are on page 622.

Continue

Questions #1–11 are based on the following passage.

Art in the Middle Ages

In the art of the Middle Ages, we never encounter the artist as an individual; rather, the artist's personality is diffused through the artistic genius of centuries as incorporated in the rules of religious art. Art of the Middle Ages is first and foremost a sacred script, the symbols and meanings of which 1 are well settled. A circular halo placed vertically behind the head of a figure signifies 2 sainthood, meanwhile the halo impressed with a cross signifies divinity. By bare feet, we recognize God, the angels, Jesus Christ, and the apostles; but for an artist to have depicted the Virgin Mary with bare feet would have been tantamount to heresy. Saint Peter is always depicted with curly hair, a short beard, and a tonsure; Saint Paul always has a bald head and a long beard. Several concentric, wavy lines represent the sky, and parallel lines represent water or the sea. A tree, which is to say a single stalk with two or three stylized leaves, informs us that the scene is laid on earth. 3 4 A tower with a window indicates a village, and an angel watching from battlements identifies that city as Jerusalem.

Mathematics is also an important element of this iconography. "The Divine Wisdom," wrote Saint Augustine, "reveals itself everywhere in numbers," a doctrine derived from the 5 Neoplatonists had revived the teachings of Pythagoras. Twelve is the master number of the Church and is the product of three, the number of the Trinity, and four, the number of material elements. The number seven, the most mysterious of all numbers, is the sum of

1. A) NO CHANGE
B) is well settled
C) are settled well
D) would be settled

2. A) NO CHANGE
B) sainthood, because
C) sainthood because
D) sainthood, while

3. The writer is thinking of adding the following sentence at this point:

An open gate indicates heaven.

Should the writer make the addition?

A) Yes, because it preserves the parallelism of the pairs of examples in the paragraph.
B) Yes, because it restates the main point of the first paragraph of the essay.
C) No, because it introduces a topic that is not taken up until later in the passage.
D) No, because it adds too much detail to the first paragraph of the essay.

4. A) NO CHANGE
B) (Make the first sentence of next paragraph.) A tower
C) Towers
D) Having a tower

5. A) NO CHANGE
B) Neoplatonists, who
C) Neoplatonist's that
D) Neoplatonists' who

Continue

four and three. 6 <u>In the final analysis, the seven-tone scale of Gregorian music is the sensible embodiment of the order of the universe.</u> Furthermore, numbers require symmetry. At Chartres, a stained-glass window shows the four prophets Isaac, Ezekiel, Daniel, and Jeremiah carrying on their shoulders the four evangelists Matthew, Mark, Luke, and John.

A third characteristic of this art is to be a symbolic language, showing us one thing and inviting us to see another. In a painting of the final judgment, the foolish virgins can be seen 7 <u>by viewers</u> on the left of Jesus and the wise on the right, and we understand that this symbolizes 8 <u>who are lost and who have been saved</u>. In this respect, the artist was asked to imitate God, who had hidden a profound meaning behind the literal and who wished nature to be a moral lesson to man. 9 <u>Art, like, nature</u> was allegorical.

Within such a system, even the most mediocre talent was 10 <u>escalated</u> by the genius of centuries. The first artists of the Renaissance to break with tradition did so at great risk. Even when they are great, the artists of the Renaissance are no more than the equals of old masters of the Middle Ages who passively followed the sacred rules. 11

6. A) NO CHANGE
B) The order of the universe is ultimately embodied in the seven-tone scale of Gregorian music.
C) Finally, the seven-tone scale of Gregorian music is the sensible embodiment of the order of the universe.
D) DELETE

7. A) NO CHANGE
B) instead by us
C) by us, the viewers,
D) DELETE

8. A) NO CHANGE
B) those lost and saved
C) those who are lost and those who have been saved
D) those who are lost and those who are saved

9. A) NO CHANGE
B) Art like nature,
C) Art, like nature,
D) Art like nature

10. A) NO CHANGE
B) elicited
C) elevated
D) elongated

11. The author is considering adding the following sentence to the essay at the end:

When they are not great, their religious works are uninteresting and insignificant.

Should the author make the addition?

A) Yes, because the new sentence completes the comparison with artists who followed the rules for religious paintings.
B) Yes, because the new sentence presents an alternative interpretation of art to that given in the previous sentence.
C) No, because the new sentence raises a possible criticism of art of the Middle Ages not discussed in the passage.
D) No, because the new sentence expresses a conclusion that has already been stated in previous paragraphs.

Continue

Questions #12–22 are based on the following passage.

The Changing Science and Engineering Workforce

From time to time, various experts 12 raise a ruckus about a looming shortage of scientists and engineers in the United States. Have we really faced such shortages in the past? Do we face one now? As a starting point, consider different conditions that might be described as a shortage, such as lower production than that of some recent period, a lack of the product as signaled by rising prices, and lower production than business or government planners want.

While each of these different concepts of "shortage" is useful, 13 only the second is meaningful in an economic sense, for only it can be corrected by market forces.

To see this, consider the science and engineering workforce. If the number of scientists and engineers graduating from school is too small to fill all jobs offered by 14 academic, industrial, and government employers then the employers will bid up the price for graduates using higher salary offers. In other words, the price paid for scientists and engineers will increase. As a consequence, unemployment of the science and engineering workforce will decline. Then, as young people 15 observing this pattern and consider lifetime employment prospects, some will choose science and engineering rather than medicine, law, business, or another profession. As these people complete their education and join the science and engineering workforce, the shortage will 16 further intensify and prices will fall.

12. A) NO CHANGE
B) make a fuss
C) express concern
D) make a stink

13. A) NO CHANGE
B) only the first is meaningful in an economic sense, for only it
C) only the third is meaningful in an economic sense, for only it
D) all three can are also meaningful in an economic sense, for they

14. A) NO CHANGE
B) academic, industrial, and government employers;
C) academic, industrial, and government employers,
D) academic, industrial, and government employers—

15. A) NO CHANGE
B) observe this pattern and consider
C) observing this pattern and considering
D) observe this pattern and considering

16. A) NO CHANGE
B) further diminish and prices will stabilize
C) increase and prices will rise
D) remain steady but prices will stabilize

Continue

To the extent that production is "low" in either of the other two senses, policy actions to relieve a shortage will be artificial and effective only to the extent that they indirectly increase demand for the good or service or lower its cost of production. For example, government tax breaks to businesses that hire more science and engineering workers give those businesses an artificial incentive to raise wage rates. Or, government financial aid for science and engineering students 17 lower the cost of education and attract candidates who can then afford to work for a lower wage and still recoup their investment in training.

17. A) NO CHANGE
B) lower the cost of education and attract a candidate
C) lowering the cost of education and attracting candidates
D) lowers the cost of education and attracts candidates

Continue

Consider whether the United States is experiencing a shortage of science and engineering PhDs in the first sense. Figure 1 shows that the number of American PhDs awarded in each major area of science and engineering has been increasing. Hence, American PhD production has not been "low" in the sense that fewer are being produced.

Figure 1: Number of PhD Graduates USA, 2001–2011

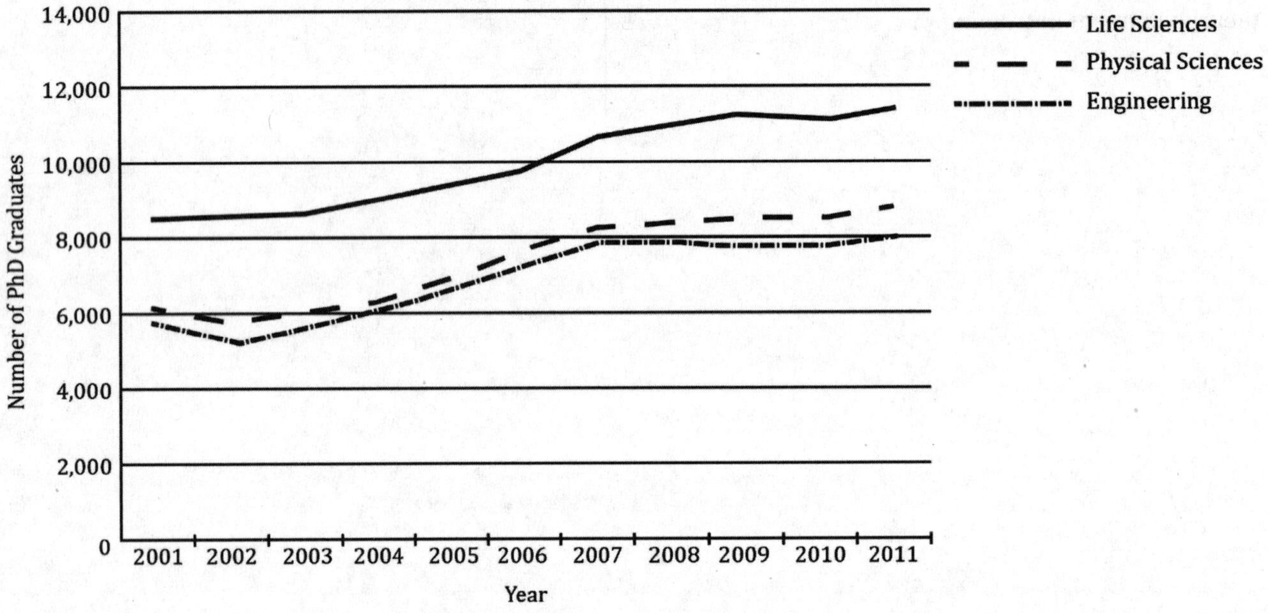

Continue

If such growth is insufficient, that is, if the numbers of American scientists and engineers are too small to fill the new jobs offered by academic, industrial, and government employers, then employers will be bidding to fill their empty positions. **18** Is growth of the science and engineering workforce insufficient to satisfy market demand? Job openings, lab facilities, salaries, advancement opportunities, and other components of career satisfaction will be on the rise, while unemployment and underemployment will be falling. Figure 2 compares annualized earnings for science and engineering PhDs with earnings of professional degree holders. Professional degree holders earn **19** less at nearly every age, indicating a relative shortage of those workers over scientists and engineers.

18. Where should the underlined sentence be placed in the paragraph?

A) WHERE IT IS NOW
B) As the first sentence of the paragraph.
C) As the third sentence of the paragraph.
D) As the last sentence of the paragraph.

19. Which choice offers an accurate interpretation of the data in the graph in Figure 2?

A) NO CHANGE
B) more at nearly every age, indicating a relative shortage
C) less at nearly every age, indicating a relative surplus
D) more at nearly every age, indicating a relative surplus

Figure 2: Annual Salary for Professional and Doctoral Degree Holders

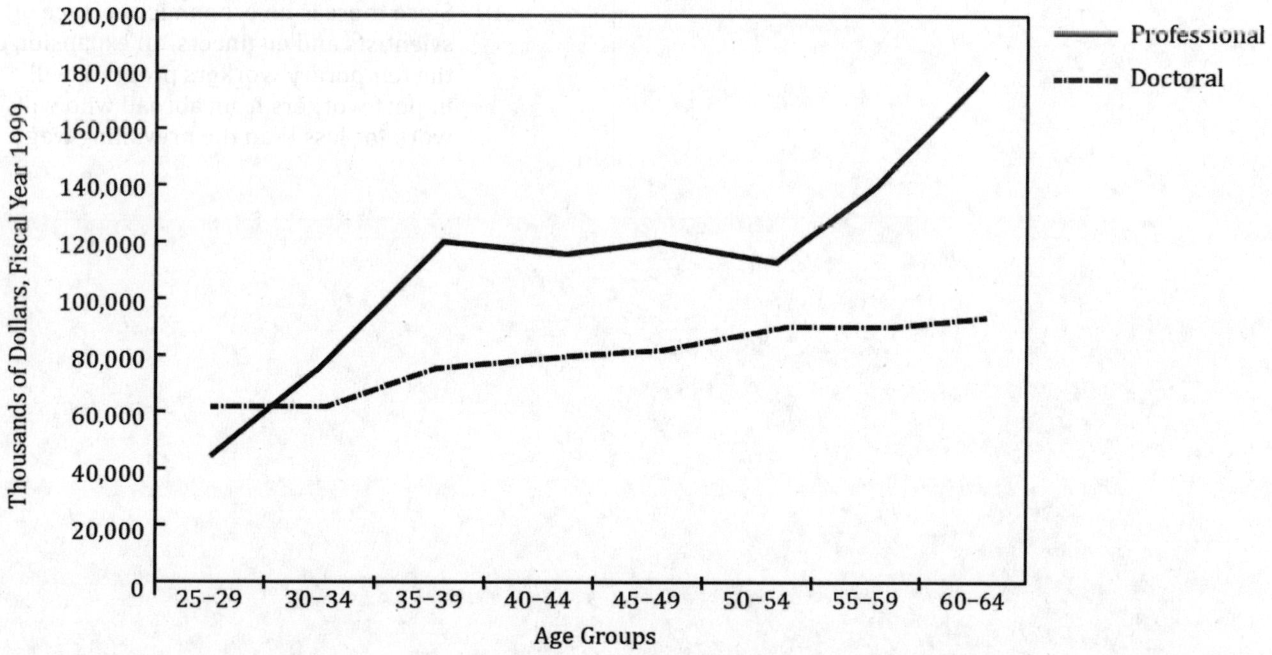

Continue

So in what sense is there a shortage?

The answer is found in the distinction between science and engineering workers and the temporary workers program that floods our labor markets with low-cost, high-tech, nonimmigrant 20 graduates, most work in computer-related industries. Business firms want to continue to staff operations with foreign expatriates who earn significantly less than 21 there American counterparts. The only way they can accomplish this objective is to cry "shortage" and encourage government planners to create more of the preferred scientific and engineering workers by loosening the restrictions on temporary workers from abroad. 22

20. A) NO CHANGE
B) graduates whom most work
C) graduates, mostly working
D) graduates, mostly work

21. A) NO CHANGE
B) they're
C) their
D) one's

22. Which of the following sentences, when placed at the end of the essay, would best summarize the writer's main point?

A) The current economic shortage of scientists and engineers can best be corrected by allowing prices for those workers to rise until the supply satisfies the demand.
B) There is no economic shortage of scientists and engineers, so expansion of the temporary workers program will not attract workers from other countries to fill such positions.
C) Expanding the temporary workers program will attract candidates from the professions such as law and medicine by depressing wages for those workers.
D) Since there is no economic shortage of scientists and engineers, an expansion of the temporary workers program will import workers from abroad who will work for less than the prevailing wage.

Continue

Questions #23–33 are based on the following passage.

The Introduction of Bitcoin

[1]

The digital currency called bitcoin first appeared in January 2009, the creation of a computer programmer using the 23 pseudonym Satoshi Nakamoto; and for most of that time, it remained little more than a technological curiosity of interest to a small segment of the population. Over the last year and a half, 24 however, Bitcoin use has grown substantially.

[2]

Bitcoin is an open-source, peer-to-peer, digital currency. Open source means that its controlling computer code is open to public 25 view, peer-to-peer means that transactions do not require a third-party intermediary such as PayPal or Visa. Like the US dollar, the bitcoin has no intrinsic value in that it is not redeemable for some amount of another commodity, such as an ounce of gold. Unlike a dollar, a bitcoin has no physical form, is not legal tender, is not backed by any government or any other legal entity, and its supply is not determined by a central bank. The bitcoin system is private, but with no traditional financial institutions involved in transactions. Unlike 26 the central controlling agency of earlier currencies, the bitcoin network is *completely decentralized*, with all parts of transactions performed by the users of the system.

[3]

Each bitcoin and each user address is encrypted with a unique identifier, and every transaction is recorded using the encrypted identifiers on a decentralized public ledger available to all computers on the network that does

23. A) NO CHANGE
B) nickname
C) pet name
D) stage name

24. A) NO CHANGE
B) instead
C) on the one hand
D) in the main

25. A) NO CHANGE
B) view; peer-to-peer
C) view, but peer-to-peer
D) view, so peer-to-peer

26. A) NO CHANGE
B) earlier currencies with central controlling agencies
C) currencies from earlier days with central controlling agencies
D) the central controlling agencies of earlier currencies

Continue

not reveal any personal information about the parties. Cryptographic techniques enable special users on the bitcoin **27** network, known as *miners*, to analyze blocks of new transactions and verify that the transactions are valid. This decentralized management of the public ledger is the distinguishing technological attribute of bitcoin. It solves the so-called "double spending" problem, i.e., forgery or counterfeiting, without the need for a trusted third party such as a bank or credit card company to verify the integrity of electronic transactions between a buyer and a seller.

[4]

To interact on the bitcoin network, users first download the free and open-source software. Once connected to the network, there are three ways to obtain bitcoins. First, a user can exchange conventional money (e.g., dollars, yen, and euros) for a fee on an online exchange (e.g., Okcoin, Coinbase, and Kraken). The exchange fee depends on the size of the transaction, ranging from 0.5% for small transactions down to 0.2% for large transactions.

[5]

[1] Second, a user can obtain bitcoins in exchange for the sale of goods or services, as when a merchant accepts bitcoin from a buyer for the sale of his product. [2] So a farmer who produces organic vegetables can sell them to a local restaurant and accept a transfer of bitcoins as payment. [3] **28** As discussed earlier, a user can serve as a miner and through their work can acquire new bitcoins by applying his or her computer's processing power to successfully verify the validity of new network transactions.

27. A) NO CHANGE
B) network known as *miners*
C) network, known as *miners*
D) network known, as *miners*,

28. A) NO CHANGE
B) (Begin new paragraph) Third, as
C) (Begin new paragraph) As
D) (Begin new paragraph) So

Continue

[4] 29 In order to *mine* and validate a new block of transactions, a difficult math problem must be solved by the miners. [5] The miner who solves the problem first validates the transactions in the block and broadcasts his or her proof-of-work to the bitcoin network. [6] Other miners in the network check the submission for accuracy. 30

[6]

[1] 31 Since its inception despite significant growth, bitcoin's scale of use remains that of a 32 notch currency with perhaps three to four million users worldwide. [2] As of mid-January 2015, the total number of bitcoins in circulation globally was about 13.7 million, up about 1 million coins from a year earlier. [3] With its recent market price of nearly $200, bitcoin's current market capitalization (price × number of coins in circulation) is about $2.7 billion. [4] In mid-January 2015, a single bitcoin was valued to be around $220. [5] However, the price of a bitcoin has been quite volatile, having been less than $20 in January 2013, above $1,100 in December 2013, and around $320 as recently as mid-December 2014 (representing more than a 30% fall in value in about one month). 33

29. A) NO CHANGE
B) In order to *mine,* validate a new block of transactions, and a difficult math problem must be solved by the miners.
C) In order to *mine* and validate a new block of transactions, miners must solve a difficult math problem.
D) In order to *mine* and validate, a new block of transactions, miners must solve a difficult math problem.

30. The author wishes to add the following sentence to the fifth paragraph:

If the miner's work is found to be correct, he or she is rewarded by the system with 25 new bitcoins.

Where should the sentence be placed?

A) As the first sentence of the paragraph.
B) As the second sentence of the paragraph.
C) As the third sentence of the paragraph.
D) As the last sentence of the paragraph.

31. A) NO CHANGE
B) Since its inception of significant growth
C) Despite significant growth since its inception
D) Despite significant growing after its inception

32. A) NO CHANGE
B) nook
C) nape
D) niche

33. The author wishes to add the following sentence to the last paragraph:

The price of bitcoin relative to other currencies is determined by supply and demand, and large swings in the price of bitcoin have caused that market capitalization to exhibit large changes during the year.

Where should the sentence be placed?

A) As the second sentence.
B) As the third sentence.
C) As the fourth sentence.
D) As the fifth sentence.

Questions #34–44 are based on the following passage.

The Meiji Restoration

The Meiji Restoration restored practical imperial rule to Japan under Emperor Meiji. Although there were emperors before the Meiji Restoration, the restoration re-established the powers of the office and re-consolidated the political system under the emperor rather than the shogunate. The period spanned the years 1868 to 1912 and was responsible for the emergence of Japan as a modernized nation in the early twentieth century. The leaders of the restoration, mostly young samurai from feudal domains historically hostile to shogun authority, 34 was motivated by growing domestic problems and the threat of foreign encroachment. Adopting the slogan "wealthy country and strong arms," they sought to create a nation-state capable of standing equal among Western powers.

Instead of casting aside traditional values, those leaders chose to preserve three traditions as the foundations on which they could build a modern Japan. The 35 older tradition and basis of the entire Japanese value system was 36 respect for and even worshipping the emperor. During the early centuries of Japanese history, the Shinto cult became the people's sustaining faith. Later, subordinated to imported Buddhism and Confucianism, Shintoism was 37 perpetuated in Ise and Izumo, the great shrines of the Imperial family, until the Meiji modernizers established it as a quasi-state religion to unify the people and restore the emperor as the symbol of national unity and the object of loyalty to the Japanese.

34. A) NO CHANGE
B) were motivated
C) was motivating
D) motivated

35. A) NO CHANGE
B) oldest
C) eldest
D) elder

36. A) NO CHANGE
B) respecting and even worshipping
C) respect and even worship of
D) respect for and even worship of

37. A) NO CHANGE
B) perpetrated
C) persisted
D) preserved

Continue

A second tradition was the hierarchical system of social relations based on feudalism and reinforced by 38 Neo-Confucianism, having been the official ideology of the pre-modern period. Confucianism prescribed the ethical obligations between groups of people within a fixed hierarchy.

A third tradition was respect for learning, 39 some basic idea of Confucius. In traditional Japan, study was the absolute duty of man. It was a religious mandate as well as a social duty and was a means of promoting a harmonious and stable society.

Though the first goal of the new government was the dismantling of the old feudal regime, it also carried out policies to unify the monetary and tax systems. Restoration leaders acting in the name of the emperor also directed the development of strategic industries such as transportation and communications. The first railroad was built in 1872, and by 1890 there 40 was more than 1,400 miles of rail. The telegraph linked all major cities by 1880. Private firms were also encouraged by government financial support and 41 got aided by the institution of a European-style banking system in 1882. These efforts at modernization required Western science and technology, and under the banner of "Civilization and Enlightenment," Western culture, from current intellectual trends to clothing and architecture, was widely promoted.

38. A) NO CHANGE
B) Neo-Confucianism, which has
C) Neo-Confucianism, which had
D) Neo-Confucianism had

39. A) NO CHANGE
B) one
C) another
D) a final

40. A) NO CHANGE
B) is
C) were
D) are

41. A) NO CHANGE
B) was aided
C) aided
D) being aided

Continue

42 Over-the-top Westernization was somewhat checked in the 1880s, however, when a renewed appreciation of traditional Japanese values emerged. Modern educational theory, though influenced by Western theory and practice, stressed the traditional values of samurai loyalty and social harmony. The same tendency prevailed in art and literature, where Western styles were first imitated, 43 and then eventually Western styles tastes fell into complete disfavor. Still, by the early twentieth century, the goals of the Meiji Restoration had been largely accomplished. 44

42. A) NO CHANGE
B) Hog-wild
C) Wholesale
D) Big-time

43. Which of the following versions of the underlined portion of the sentence is most consistent with the development of the passage?

A) NO CHANGE
B) but then Western and Japanese style eventually merged becoming virtually indistinguishable
C) until eventually Japanese styles were forgotten and Western form took over the arts
D) and then a more selective blending of Western and Japanese tastes was achieved

44. Which of the following additions to the final sentence of the passage as written would best serve to summarize the author's main point?

A) accomplished: Japan was well on its way to becoming a modern industrial nation.
B) accomplished, and Japan returned to its traditional pre-1868 lifestyle.
C) accomplished, and Japan discarded the historical baggage of the pre-Restoration period.
D) accomplished, though the country's political leaders could not hold on to their gains.

STOP

IF YOU FINISH BEFORE TIME IS CALLED, YOU MAY CHECK YOUR WORK ON THIS SECTION ONLY. DO NOT TURN TO ANY OTHER SECTION IN THE TEST.

SAT Practice Test

SECTION 3—MATH, NO CALCULATOR

25 minutes—20 items

DIRECTIONS: For #1–15, solve each item and choose the correct answer choice. Then fill in the corresponding bubble on your answer sheet. For #16–20, solve each item and enter your answer in the grid on the answer sheet. Refer to the directions before #16 on how to enter your answers for these items. Use any available space for scratchwork. Answers are on page 622.

Notes:

(1) All expressions and equations represent real numbers unless otherwise indicated.

(2) Figures that accompany problems in this test are intended to provide information useful in solving the problems. They are drawn as accurately as possible EXCEPT when it is stated in a specific problem that the figure is not drawn to scale. All figures lie in a plane unless otherwise indicated.

(3) The domain of a given function f is the set of all real numbers x for which $f(x)$ is a real number unless otherwise indicated.

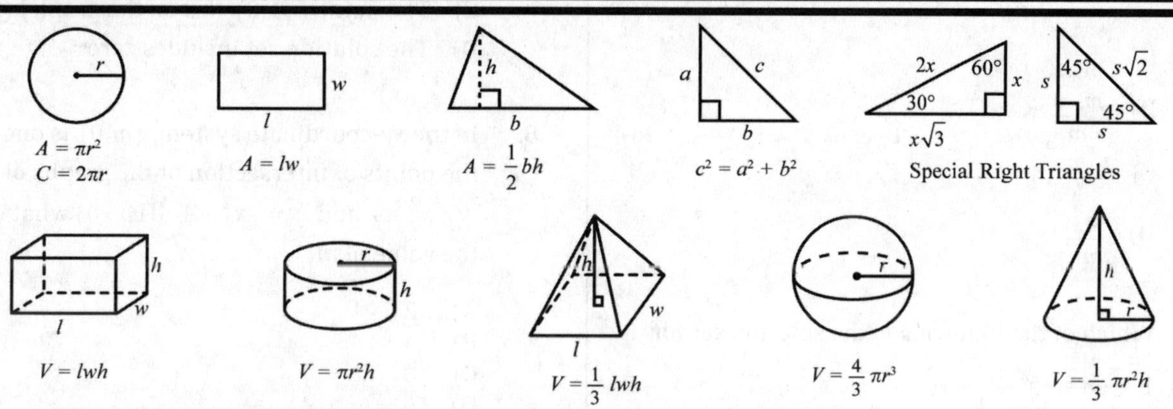

The number of degrees of arc in a circle is 360.
The sum of the measures in degrees of the angles of a triangle is 180.
The number of radians of arc in a circle is 2π.

Continue

1. For all numbers, $(a-b)(b-c)-(b-a)(c-b)=?$

A) -1
B) 0
C) $ab-ac-bc$
D) $2ab-2ac-2bc$

2. If $f(x)=x^2-x$, what is the value of $f(f(3))$?

A) 6
B) 30
C) 36
D) 42

3. Which of the following is equivalent to $\frac{m^2+mn}{m^2-n^2}$?

A) $\frac{m}{m-n}$
B) $\frac{m-n}{m}$
C) $\frac{m}{m+n}$
D) $\frac{1}{m-n}$

4. Which of the following is the solution set for $\left|\frac{x-2}{3}\right|=4$?

A) $\{10,-14\}$
B) $\{10,10\}$
C) $\{14,-10\}$
D) $\{14,10\}$

5. If the quadratic equation $y=ax^2+bx+c$, where *a*, *b*, and *c* are constants, has the solution set $\{-2, 4\}$, which of the following is NOT true?

A) $a+b+c=-9$
B) $a=8c$
C) $b=-2a$
D) $c=4b$

6. If $f(-1)=1$ and $f(2)=7$, what is the slope of the graph of $f(x)$ in the coordinate system?

A) $-\frac{1}{2}$
B) $\frac{1}{2}$
C) 2
D) $\frac{5}{2}$

7. Consider the polynomial $p(x)=x(x^2+x-4)-4$. Which of the following is true?

A) The polynomial $p(x)$ has no more than two unique factors.
B) A zero of the polynomial $p(x)$ is 1.
C) The point $(-1,0)$ lies on the graph $p(x)$.
D) The solution set includes zero.

8. In the *xy*-coordinate system, $(m,0)$ is one of the points of intersection of the graphs of $y=x^2-4$ and $y=-x^2+4$. If $m>0$, what is the value of *m*?

A) 2
B) 4
C) 8
D) 16

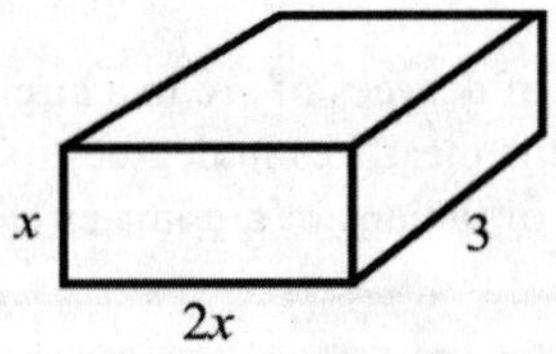

Note: Figure not drawn to scale.

9. In the figure above, the rectangular solid has a volume of 54. What is the value of *x*?

A) 2
B) 3
C) 6
D) 9

Continue

10. The equation $s = c + \frac{1}{2}ry$ is used to model the relationship between an employee's current yearly salary, *c*, and her yearly salary, *s*, *y* years from now. What is the meaning of the $\frac{r}{2}$ in the equation?

A) Every year, the employee receives a raise, *r*.
B) Every year, the employee's salary increases by fifty percent.
C) Every two years, the employee receives a raise, *r*.
D) Every two years, the employee receives a raise, *r*, equal to one-half the amount of the previous raise.

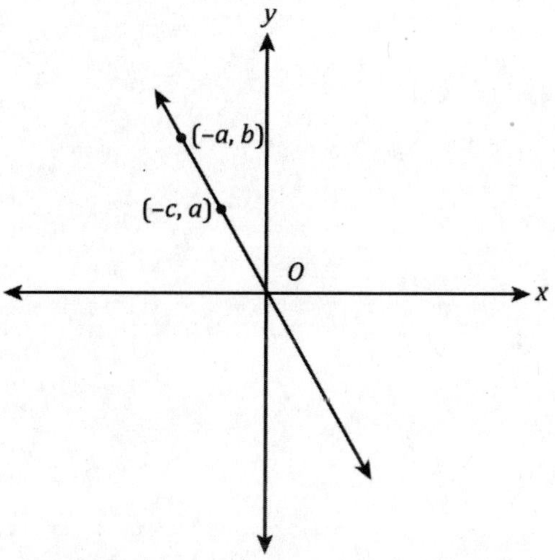

11. In the coordinate graph shown above, the line with equation $y = mx + n$, where *m* and *n* are constants, passes through the points $(-a,b)$ and $(-c,a)$. Which of the following must be true?

A) $b - a = c - a$
B) $b - a < c - a$
C) $c - a > b - a$
D) $a - c > 0$

12. In an organic chemistry lab, students grow bacteria in petri dishes. The experimental instructions state that the time for incubation at 25°C should be at least 24 hours but no more than 36 hours. If *t* is the number of hours a petri dish is incubated within the recommended time, which of the following represents all possible values of *t*?

A) $|t - 30| < 6$
B) $|t + 30| > 6$
C) $|t - 30| \leq 6$
D) $|t + 30| \leq 6$

13. A middle school social studies class is making a rectangular quilt for the state's bicentennial celebration. The quilt is 5 feet by 4 feet. The students plan to use the remaining 10 square feet of fabric to add a border of uniform width to the quilt. What should be the width of the quilt's border, in feet?

A) $\frac{1}{2}$
B) 1
C) 2
D) 5

14. If $0° \leq x \leq 90°$ and $\tan x - 1 = 0$, what is *x*?

A) 0°
B) 45°
C) 60°
D) 90°

Continue

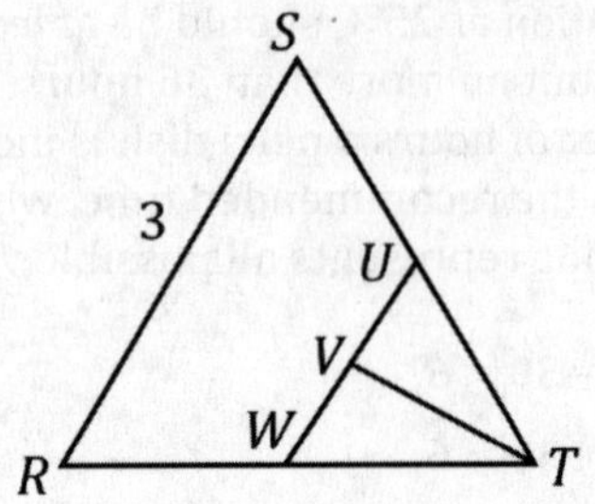

15. In the figure above, ΔRST is an equilateral triangle, U is the midpoint of $\overline{ST}$, V is the midpoint of $\overline{UW}$, and W is the midpoint of $\overline{RT}$. What is the length of $\overline{UV}$?

A) $\frac{3}{2}$

B) $\frac{4}{3}$

C) 1

D) $\frac{3}{4}$

Continue

DIRECTIONS: For #16–20, solve each item and mark your answer on a special answer grid.

1. For each item, you should write your answer in the boxes at the top of each column and then fill in the ovals beneath each part of the answer you write.
2. Mark no more than one oval in any column.
3. Questions do not have negative answers.
4. Some problems have more than one possible answer. Grid only one answer.
5. See the first example below to grid mixed numbers.
6. See the last example below to grid decimal answers with more digits than the grid can accommodate.

Here are some examples:

Answer: 7/2 or 3.5

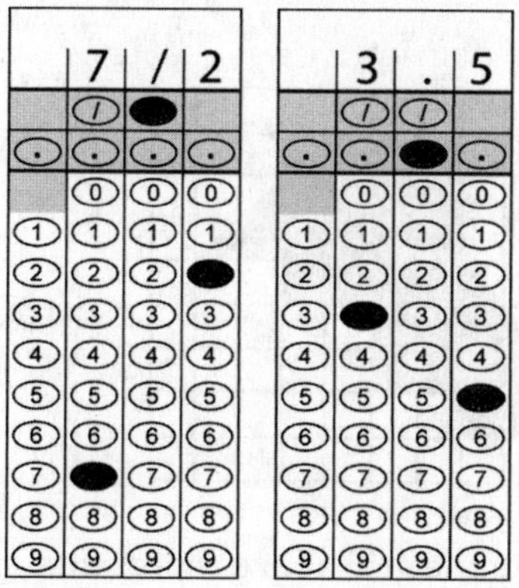

NOTE: A mixed number such as $3\frac{1}{2}$ must be gridded as 7/2 or as 3.5. If gridded as "31/2," it will be read as "thirty-one halves."

Answer: 325

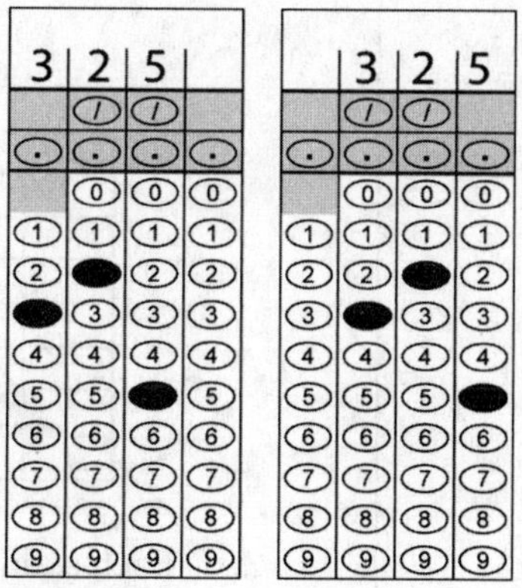

NOTE: Either position is correct.

Answer: 1/6, .166, or .167

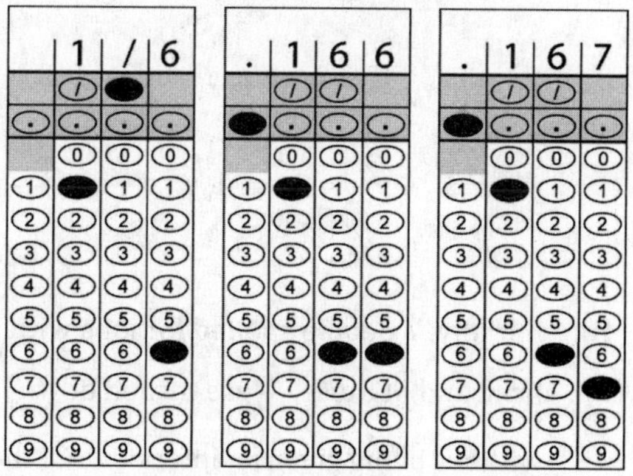

NOTE: A decimal answer with more digits than the grid can accommodate must be truncated. A decimal such as $0.16\overline{6}$ must be gridded as .166 or .167. A less accurate value such as .16 or .17 will be scored as incorrect.

Continue

16. $\frac{1}{2^{-3}} \bullet \frac{1}{3^{-2}} = ?$

17. If $\frac{64}{x^y} - 6 = 2$, $x < y$, and x and y are integers, what is a possible value for y?

18. Initially, T people applied for jobs with a firm, and of those, $\frac{1}{3}$ are turned down without being given an interview. Of the remaining applicants, $\frac{1}{4}$ are hired to fill four positions. How many people applied for jobs?

19. In a science class, 45 students are divided into 12 laboratory groups. Each group must have either three or four students. How many groups will have three students?

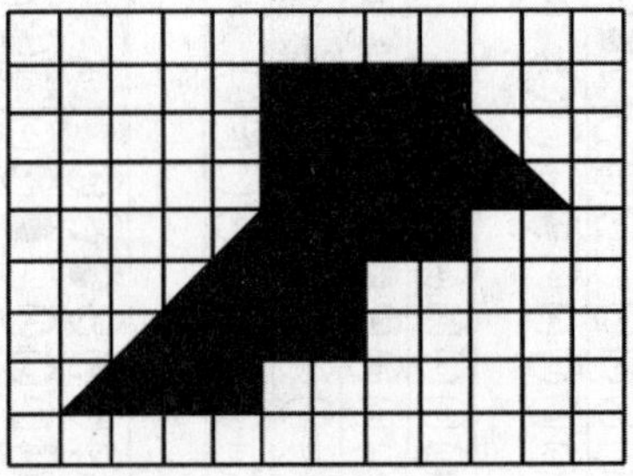

20. Each square in the grid above represents an acre in a farmer's field. A stand of trees occupies the shaded region of the field. How much of the farmer's field, in acres, is not occupied by trees?

STOP

IF YOU FINISH BEFORE TIME IS CALLED, YOU MAY CHECK YOUR WORK ON THIS SECTION ONLY. DO NOT TURN TO ANY OTHER SECTION IN THE TEST.

SAT Practice Test

SECTION 4—MATH, CALCULATOR

55 minutes—38 items

DIRECTIONS: For #1–30, solve each item and choose the correct answer choice. Then fill in the corresponding bubble on your answer sheet. For #31–38, solve each item and enter your answer in the grid on the answer sheet. Refer to the directions before #31 on how to enter your answers for these items. Use any available space for scratchwork. Answers are on page 623.

Notes:

(1) All expressions and equations represent real numbers unless otherwise indicated.

(2) Figures that accompany problems in this test are intended to provide information useful in solving the problems. They are drawn as accurately as possible EXCEPT when it is stated in a specific problem that the figure is not drawn to scale. All figures lie in a plane unless otherwise indicated.

(3) The domain of a given function f is the set of all real numbers x for which $f(x)$ is a real number unless otherwise indicated.

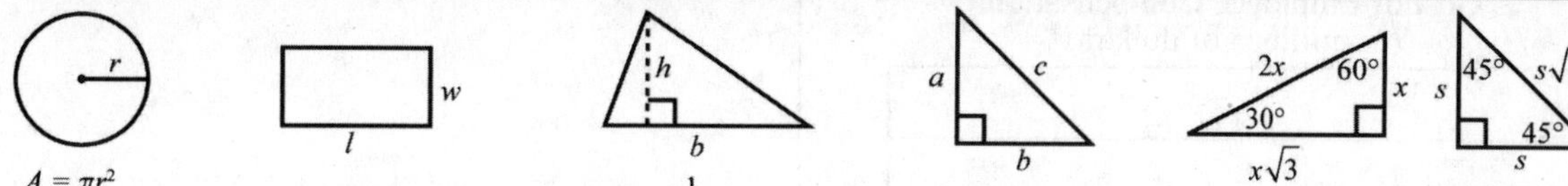

$A = \pi r^2$, $C = 2\pi r$

$A = lw$

$A = \frac{1}{2}bh$

$c^2 = a^2 + b^2$

Special Right Triangles

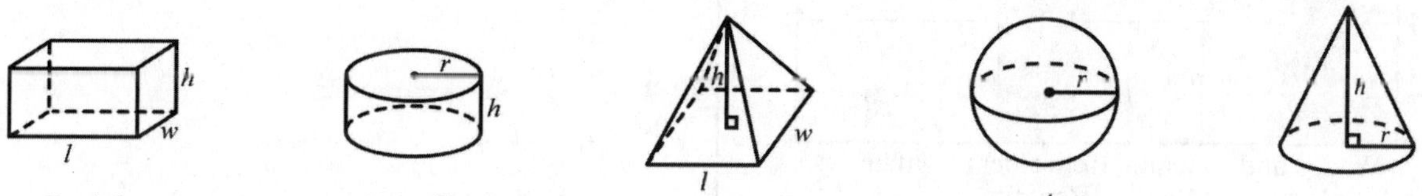

$V = lwh$

$V = \pi r^2 h$

$V = \frac{1}{3}lwh$

$V = \frac{4}{3}\pi r^3$

$V = \frac{1}{3}\pi r^2 h$

The number of degrees of arc in a circle is 360.
The sum of the measures in degrees of the angles of a triangle is 180.
The number of radians of arc in a circle is 2π.

Continue

1. The price of 5 boxes of pens is d dollars. If each box contains 30 pens, what is the price, in *cents*, of 12 pens?

A) $8d$
B) $12d$
C) $\frac{25d}{2}$
D) $50d$

2. A certain concrete mixture uses 4 cubic yards of cement for every 20 cubic yards of grit. If a contractor orders 50 cubic yards of cement, how much grit (in cubic yards) should he order if he plans to use all of the cement?

A) 1.6
B) 10
C) 25
D) 250

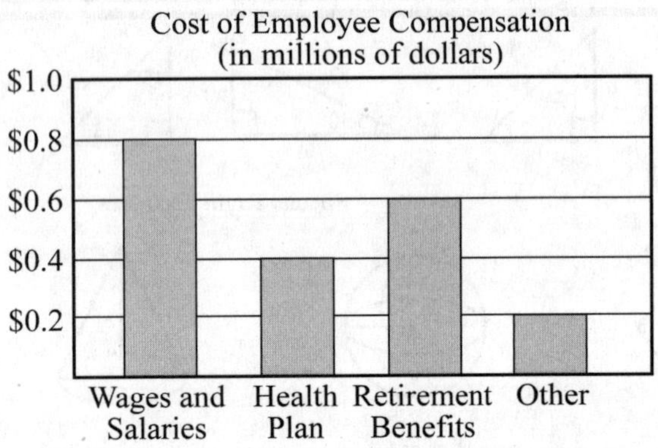

3. The graph above shows the cost of employee compensation for Corporation X. Based on the information provided, what percentage of employee compensation is spent on wages and salaries?

A) 8%
B) 10%
C) 25%
D) 40%

4. In a certain game, a person's age is multiplied by 2 and then the product is divided by 3. If the result of performing the operations on John's age is 12, what is John's age?

A) 8
B) 12
C) 18
D) 36

5. The cost of a taxi ride is $1.50 for hiring the cab and $0.40 per mile or any part of a mile of distance traveled. Which of the following equations can be used to find the cost, y, of a ride of exactly x miles, in which x is an integer?

A) $y = x(0.4 + 1.5)$
B) $y = 0.4 - 1.5x$
C) $y = 0.4 + 1.5x$
D) $y = 0.4x + 1.5$

Continue

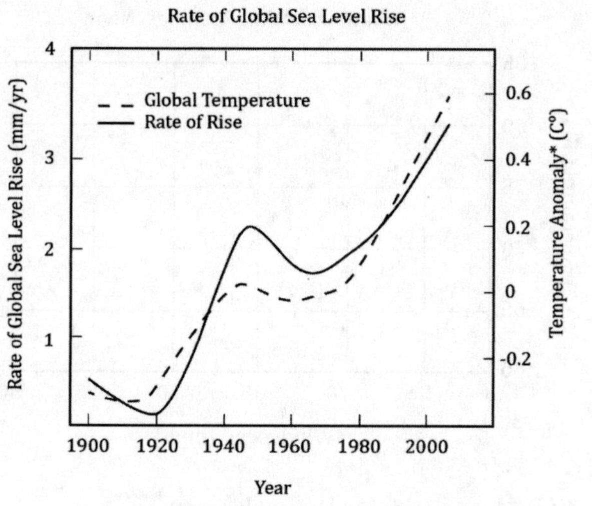

* Temperature anomaly refers to the difference between temperature for a given year and the long-term average.

6. The graph above shows the rate of rising global sea levels and temperature anomalies for 100 years. Based on the information provided, what is the increase in the rate of global sea-level rise from 1980 to 2000?

A) 5%
B) 50%
C) 100%
D) 150%

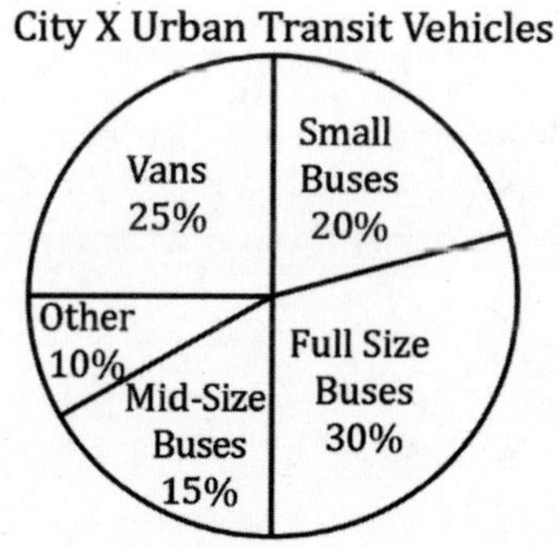

7. The graph above shows all of the urban transit vehicles in City X, categorized by type. If the city has 75 midsize busses, how many transit vehicles does it have?

A) 250
B) 300
C) 450
D) 500

8. If x and y are different positive integers and $\frac{x}{y}$ is an integer, then which of the following must be true?

I. $x > y$
II. $xy > 0$
III. $y - x < 0$

A) I only
B) III only
C) I and II only
D) I, II, and III

Questions #9–11 refer to the following information.

The histogram below shows the distribution of the number of children per home in a neighborhood of a medium sized Midwestern city.

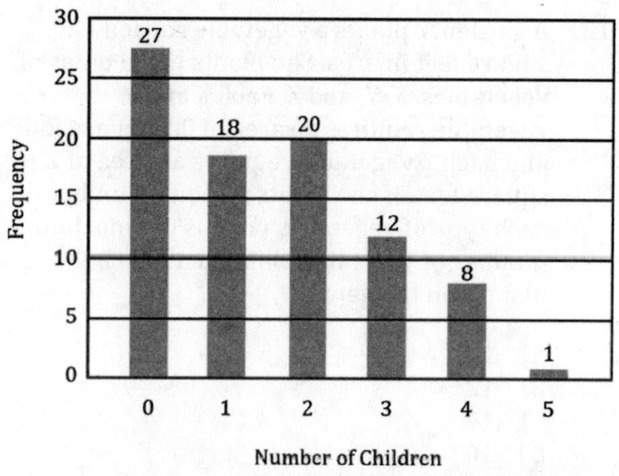

9. Which of the following is the median number of children per home in the neighborhood represented by data in the histogram?

A) 0
B) 1
C) 2
D) 3

Continue

10. What is the average (arithmetic mean) number of children per home, rounded to the nearest tenth, in the neighborhood represented by the data in the graph?

A) 0.5
B) 1.0
C) 1.5
D) 2.0

11. If the distribution of the number of children per residence in the neighborhood is representative of the entire Midwestern city, which includes 3.5×10^5 residences, approximately how many residences in the entire city are childless?

A) 1,100
B) 11,000
C) 110,000
D) 1,110,000

12. A gardener plants a vegetable garden 12 square feet in area. She plants three types of vegetables, X, Y, and Z. Each X and Y vegetable requires an area of 0.5 square foot, and each Z vegetable requires an area of 2 square feet. If she plants an equal number of each type of vegetable, what is the maximum number of vegetable plants that can be planted in the garden?

A) 10
B) 12
C) 14
D) 16

13. On a trip, a motorist drove 10 miles at 20 miles per hour, 10 miles at 30 miles per hour, and 10 miles at 60 miles per hour. What fraction of her total driving time was spent driving 60 miles per hour?

A) $\frac{1}{6}$
B) $\frac{1}{3}$
C) $\frac{5}{6}$
D) 1

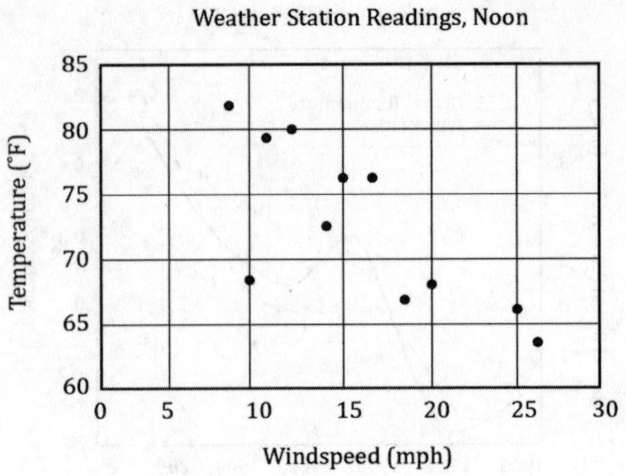

14. The scatterplot above shows the temperatures and windspeeds at eleven weather stations at noon on the day of the readings. What was the approximate windspeed, in miles per hour, at the weather station represented by the data point farthest from the line of best fit (not shown)?

A) 10
B) 20
C) 26
D) 68

Continue

15. Two students investigate the acceleration of a ball as it rolls down a ramp. The equation $\frac{x}{y} = 3$ can be used to model the speed of the ball, *y* in meters per second, as a function of time, *x* in seconds, after the ball begins to roll down the ramp. What does it mean that $(5, 1\frac{2}{3})$ is a solution to this equation?

A) It takes the ball $1\frac{2}{3}$ second to reach an acceleration of 5 meters per second-squared.
B) The acceleration of the ball 5 seconds following its release, is $1\frac{2}{3}$ meters per second-squared.
C) Five seconds after the ball is released, its speed measures $1\frac{2}{3}$ meters per second.
D) The acceleration of the ball at any time after its release is equal to 3 meters per second-squared.

16. The pressure, *p*, volume, *V*, and temperature, *T*, of a gas are related by the ideal gas equation: $pV = nRT$, where *n* is the number of moles of a gas (the amount of gas) and *R* is the gas constant. The gas in a balloon inflated to a volume of 1 liter is under 3 atmospheres of pressure. Assuming the temperature and amount of substance of gas do not change, what is the pressure, in atmospheres, of the gas in the balloon if it is compressed to one-third of its original volume?

A) 1
B) 3
C) 6
D) 9

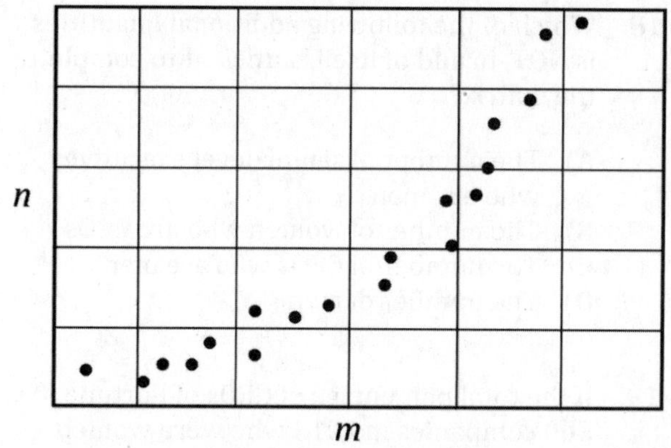

17. The scatterplot above depicts the relationship between the variable *m* and the variable *n*. Which of the following best describes the relationship depicted in the graph?

A) The two variables are not correlated.
B) As the value of *m* increases, the value of *n* increases.
C) There is a strong positive linear correlation between the two variables.
D) There is a strong positive non-linear correlation between the two variables.

Questions #18–20 refer to the following information.

A survey of the Fortune 500 companies was conducted to investigate gender inequalities in positions of leadership at U.S. corporations. The table below shows the number of women and men holding senior-level executive and chief executive officer positions at the Fortune 500 companies.

Fortune 500 Companies, 2013			
	Senior Level Executives	CEOs	Total
Women	8,785		
Men			
Total		500	35,500

Continue

18. Which of the following additional quantities is NOT, in and of itself, sufficient to complete the matrix?

A) The number of senior-level executives who are men
B) The number of women who are CEOs
C) The number of CEOs who are men
D) The number of men

19. If the total percentage of CEOs of Fortune 500 companies in 2013 who were women was 4.8%, approximately what percentage of CEOs and senior-level executives combined in Fortune 500 companies were men?

A) 2%
B) 25%
C) 75%
D) 95%

20. The total percentage of CEOs of Fortune 500 companies in 2013 who were women was 4.8% and the total number of companies in the United States was approximately 35 million. If the Fortune 500 survey results are used to estimate information about gender inequalities in leadership positions at companies across the country, which of the following is the best estimate of the total number of female CEOs in the U.S. in 2013?

A) 16,800
B) 68,000
C) 0.168 million
D) 1.68 million

$$2y \le 1 + 3x$$
$$y > -x + 2$$

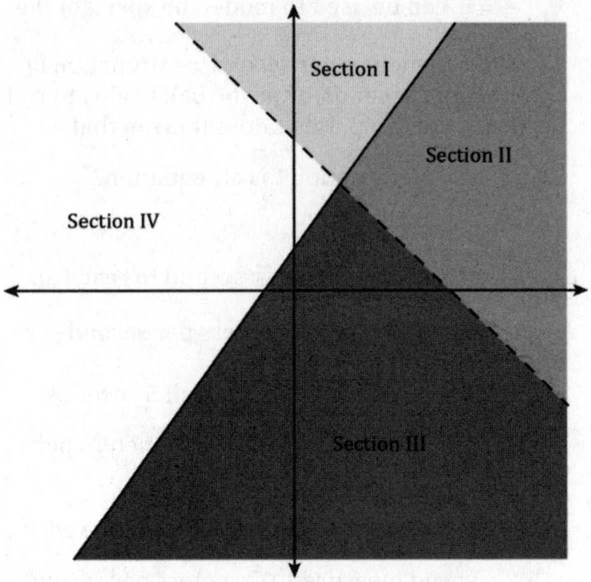

21. A system of inequalities and a graph are shown above. Which section or sections of the graph could represents the solution to the given system of inequalities?

A) Section II
B) Section III
C) Sections II and III
D) Sections III and IV

22. Which of the following graphs intersects the graph of $y = x^2$?

I. The graph of $y = x$
II. The graph of $y = |2x + 2|$
III. The graph of $y = x - 2$

A) I only
B) I and II only
C) III only
D) I, II, and III

Continue

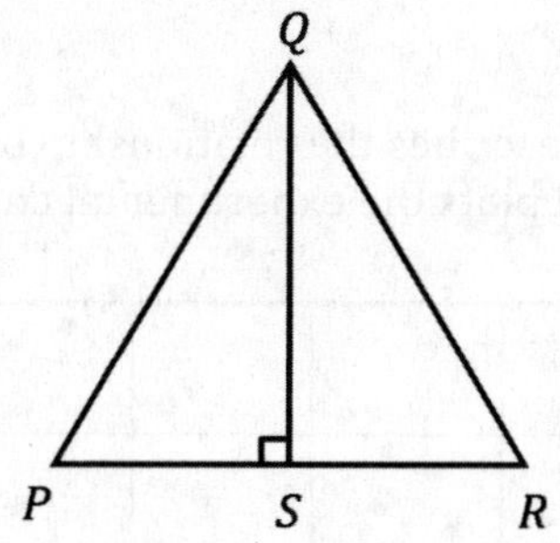

23. In the figure above, $\overline{PQ} = \overline{QR} = \overline{PR}$. If $\overline{PS} = 3$, what is the area of ΔPQR? ($\cos 30° = \frac{\sqrt{3}}{2}$)

A) $3\sqrt{3}$ (approximately 5.2)
B 6
C) $6\sqrt{3}$ (approximately 10.39)
D) $9\sqrt{3}$ (approximately 15.59)

24. After the first term of a series, each term in the sequence is $\frac{1}{2}$ the sum of the preceding term and 4. If n is the first term of the sequence and $n \neq 0$, what is the ratio of the first term to the second term?

A) $\frac{2}{n+4}$

B) $\frac{2n}{n+4}$

C) $\frac{2n}{n+2}$

D) $\frac{2n}{4-n}$

Continue

Questions #25–27 refer to the following information

A student performs an experiment demonstrating Hooke's law, which describes the relationship between the distance a spring is stretched and the force required to do so. The graph plots the experimental data.

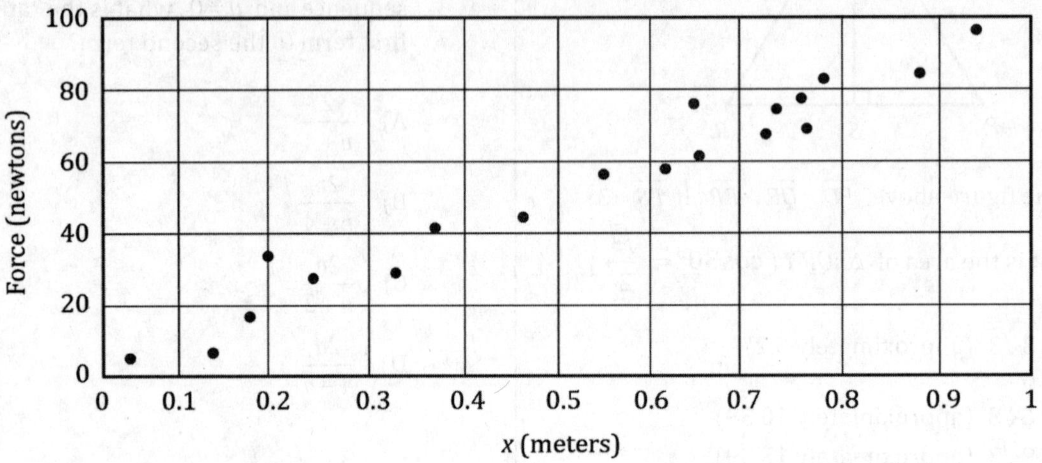

The experimental data can be modeled by the equation $F = kx$, where F is the force, in newtons, required to stretch the spring a distance x, in meters. The spring constant, k, is a measure of the spring's "springiness."

25. According to the experimental data, approximately how much force, in newtons, was required to stretch the spring a distance of 0.5 meters?

A) 20
B) 40
C) 50
D) 60

26. The student repeats the entire experiment for a different spring with a spring constant of 50 newtons per meter. Based on the model, what is the expected force, in newtons, required to stretch the new spring a distance of 0.25 meters?

A) 2.5
B) 12.5
C) 125
D) 200

27. The dyne is the unit of force in the CGS (centimeter-gram-second) system of units. A dyne equals 10 micronewtons. (1 newton equals 10^6 micronewtons). Based on the experimental data, which of the following could be the spring constant, k, of the spring used in the experiment, in dynes per centimeter?

A) 100
B) 10^3
C) 10^5
D) 10^6

Continue

28. Basket A contains 6 eggs and Basket B contains 24 eggs. Which of the following sets of equations can be used to solve for the number of eggs, *n*, that could be transferred from Basket B to Basket A such that the final number of eggs in Basket B, *b*, is at least twice the final number of eggs in Basket A, *a*?

A) $a=6-n;\ b=n+24;\ a \le 2b$
B) $a=n+6;\ b=24-n;\ 2a=b$
C) $a=n+6;\ b=24-n;\ 2a \le b$
D) $a=n+6;\ b=n+24;\ 2a \ge b$

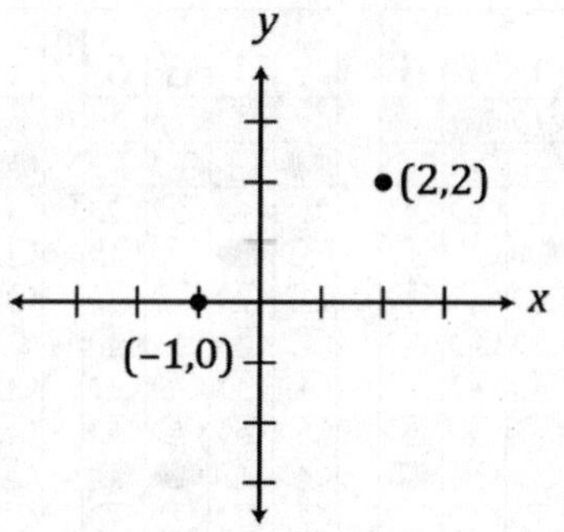

29. What is the linear equation for the line through ordered pairs (−1,0) and (2,2) in the coordinate graph above?

A) $y=\frac{2x}{3}-\frac{2}{3}$

B) $y=\frac{2x}{3}-3$

C) $y=\frac{2x}{3}+\frac{2}{3}$

D) $y=x+\frac{2}{3}$

30. Consider the graph of $y-2x^2+3x \le 2$. How many of the following ordered pairs are NOT part of the solution?

$$(-1,2),\ (1,2),\ (\tfrac{3}{2},2),\ (3,4)$$

A) Zero
B) One
C) Two
D) Three

Continue

For #31–38, solve each item and mark your answer on a special answer grid.

1. For each item, you should write your answer in the boxes at the top of each column and then fill in the ovals beneath each part of the answer you write.
2. Mark no more than one oval in any column.
3. Questions do not have negative answers.
4. Some problems have more than one possible answer. Grid only one answer.
5. See the first example below to grid mixed numbers.
6. See the last example below to grid decimal answers with more digits than the grid can accommodate.

Here are some examples:

Answer: 7/2 or 3.5

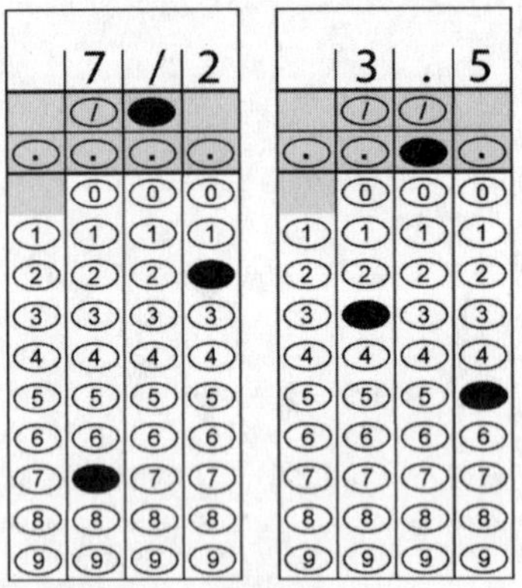

NOTE: A mixed number such as $3\frac{1}{2}$ must be gridded as 7/2 or as 3.5. If gridded as "31/2," it will be read as "thirty-one halves."

Answer: 325

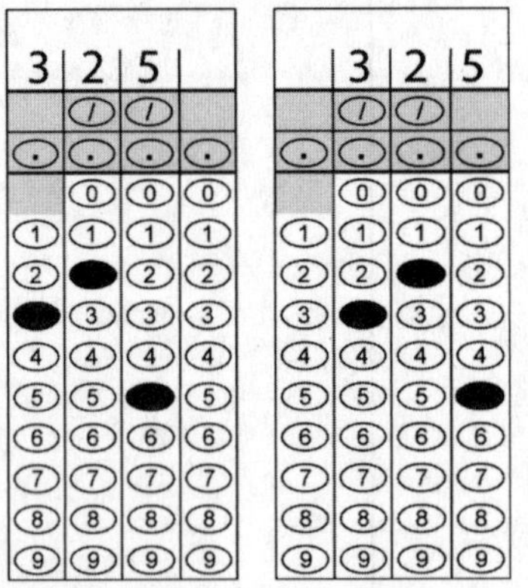

NOTE: Either position is correct.

Answer: 1/6, .166, or .167

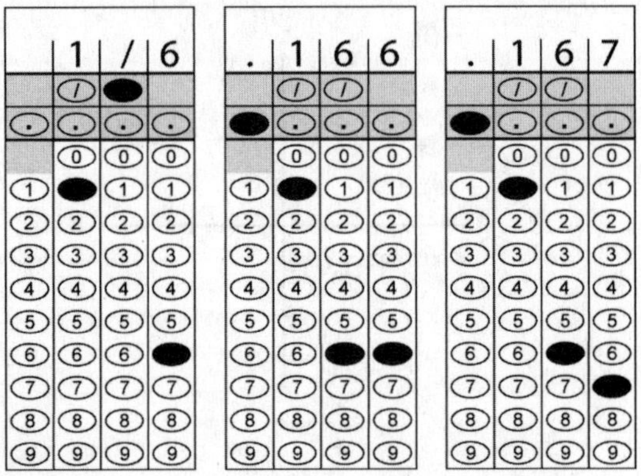

NOTE: A decimal answer with more digits than the grid can accommodate must be truncated. A decimal such as $0.16\overline{6}$ must be gridded as .166 or .167. A less accurate value such as .16 or .17 will be scored as incorrect.

Continue

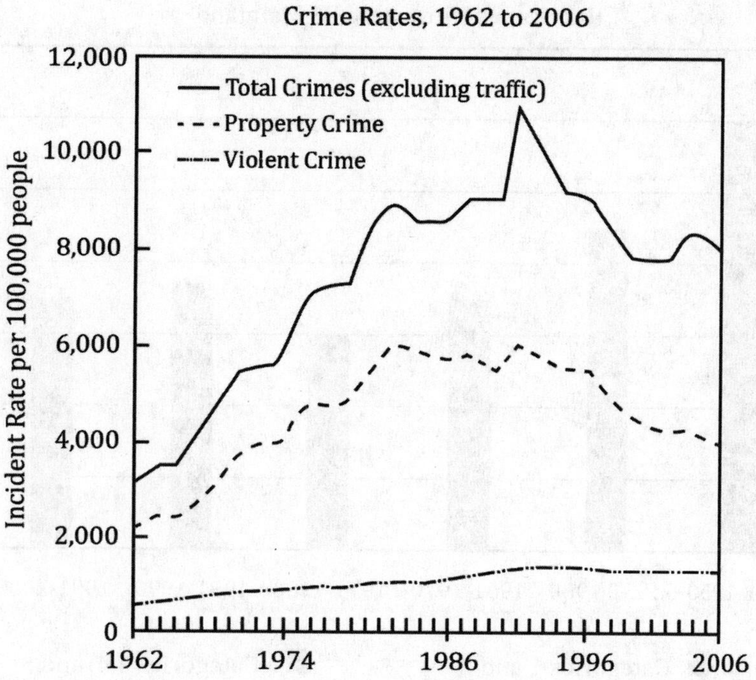

31. The graph above represents the crime rates from 1962 to 2006. Total crime, excluding traffic, includes violent, nonviolent, and property crimes. Based on the graph, by approximately what fraction of total crime did property crime decrease from its peak in 1991 to 2006?

Continue

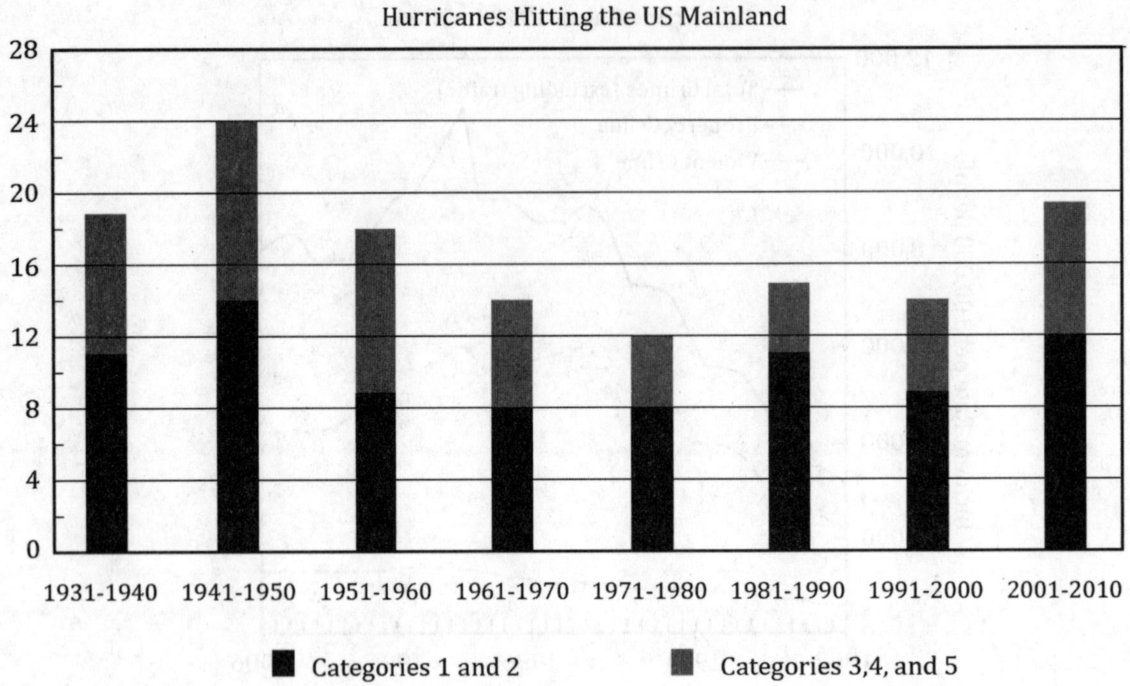

32. The graph above shows the number of hurricanes that hit the US mainland during the last eight decades. What is the mean number of hurricanes in categories 3, 4, and 5 that hit the US mainland per decade for the years shown, rounded to the nearest whole number?

Continue

33. The quadratic equation $3x^2 - 2x = 16$ has roots *r* and *s*. What is the value of $r + s$?

34. A marine biology research institute is replacing a cylindrical aquarium tank 36 feet in height and 24 feet in diameter. If the new tank diameter is 50% larger than the old tank diameter and an overall volume increase of at least 25% is desired, what is the minimum height of the new tank, in feet?

35. If $3^{n-4} = 27$, what is the value of *n*?

36. A pie chart is drawn to represent an employee's 8-hour workday. The size of each sector corresponding to an activity is proportional to the amount of time spent on that activity. If an employee has two 20-minute breaks and an hour for lunch each day, what is measure, in degrees, of the central angle of the sector that represents the total time allotted for breaks and lunch each day?

37. If $\frac{4+2i}{3-i} = a + bi$, where *a* and *b* are real numbers and $i = \sqrt{-1}$, what is the value of *a*?

38. Dream Lanes Bowling Alley has two specials on Sunday: 1) \$5 per bowler per game, which includes shoes and a \$20 group discount for more than 3 games per bowler, or 2) \$3 per bowler for shoes and \$3 per bowler per game. For four players on Sunday, how many complete games per bowler must be played for the two specials to cost the same?

STOP

IF YOU FINISH BEFORE TIME IS CALLED, YOU MAY CHECK YOUR WORK ON THIS SECTION ONLY. DO NOT TURN TO ANY OTHER SECTION IN THE TEST.

SAT Practice Test

SECTION 5—ESSAY (OPTIONAL)

50 minutes—1 essay prompt

DIRECTIONS: The essay measures your ability to read and understand a passage and write an essay that analyzes the passage. In your essay, demonstrate that you have carefully read the passage, write a clear and logical analysis, and use language precisely.

You have 50 minutes to read the passage and write an essay in response to the provided prompt. Sample essays are on page 649.

Read the passage below and think about how Arne Duncan uses

- evidence (facts, examples, etc.) to support claims.
- reasoning to develop the passage and to connect claims and evidence.
- rhetorical or persuasive elements, such as language choices or emotional appeals, to increase the impact of the ideas expressed.

Adapted from "Sixty Years After Brown: Where is the Outrage?," a speech given by Secretary of Education Arne Duncan on May 20, 2014.

1 Today I want to take a few minutes to talk about a landmark moment that transformed our nation's schools, the moment the Supreme Court issued the Brown v. Board of Education decision, striking down Jim Crow school segregation.

2 I believe in my heart that education is the civil rights issue of our generation.

3 In Brown, the Supreme Court struck down the "separate but equal" doctrine, affirming the value of integration. But a Supreme Court opinion can't fully make equal opportunity a reality on the ground—in schools, in classrooms, or in hearts and minds. So, Brown is not just part of our history. It is part of our future.

4 Sixty years after Brown, education remains an urgent civil rights issue for four reasons.

5 First, while Brown struck down de jure segregation as unconstitutional, de facto school segregation has worsened in many respects in the last two decades. Since 1991, all regions of the nation have experienced an increase in the percentage of black students who attend highly-segregated schools, where 90 percent or more of students are students of color.

6 Here in the South, more than a third of black students attend such racially-isolated schools; in the Northeast, more than 50 percent do.

7 Second, education remains a civil rights issue because the Brown ruling sparked a sweeping expansion of the entire concept of educational opportunity.

8 This sweeping expansion of equal educational opportunity to protect disadvantaged students, girls and women, students with disabilities, LGBT students, and English-language learners means that education remains an urgent civil rights issue in ways that would have been unimaginable 60 years ago.

9 Today, we also have a much more sophisticated understanding that ensuring equal opportunity means more than just striking down Jim Crow laws.

10 That's a third reason why education remains the civil rights issue of our generation.

Today, we worry about both achievement gaps and opportunity gaps. Because we haven't provided access to high-quality early learning to all families, millions of children enter kindergarten already behind their peers at the starting line of school.

11 Our expectations of what constitutes a world-class education have risen dramatically since Brown. That's why, in a knowledge-based, globally-competitive economy, access to STEM courses and AP classes is also a civil rights issue.

12 And just 68 percent of black students—only two-thirds—attend a high school that actually offers calculus. By comparison, 81 percent of white high school students have the option of taking calculus, as do 87 percent of Asian-American students.

13 Without accountability, there's no expectation that all children will learn. Without accountability, there's no urgency. Without accountability, without meaningful assessments of student learning, parents don't have an objective way to know whether their children are getting the education they need and deserve.

14 Without accountability—without a straightforward system of knowing which students are learning—we cannot fulfill the promise of Brown.

15 The progress since Brown has been nothing short of phenomenal—and it's obviously not just limited to the fact America has its first black president. During the same time-span, the percentage of young black adults who earned a bachelor's degree or higher increased seven-fold, from about 3 percent to 21 percent. But the catch is that for all our progress, it's not nearly enough to fulfill the promise of Brown.

16 The fourth and final reason that education is the civil rights issue of our generation is that sadly, discrimination continues to exist in too many places. Our department's Office for Civil Rights receives roughly 10,000 complaints every year.

17 OCR's job is to enforce the law. It means telling schools in a New York county that they cannot systematically reduce the grades of students with disabilities by a multiple of 0.69.

18 And it means telling a principal in rural Alabama that he cannot justify disparities in offering AP courses at predominantly-minority high schools because he feels black students can't succeed in advanced courses.

19 So for these four reasons, education is very much the leading civil rights issue of our generation: School re-segregation; the expanded reach of laws regulating equal opportunity; the elevated importance of education and opportunity gaps; and the continued persistence of discrimination. All combine to make closing opportunity gaps an educational, economic, and moral imperative.

Write an essay explaining how Arne Duncan develops his argument that education is one of the biggest civil rights issues facing this generation. In your essay, analyze how Duncan uses one or more of the elements listed above (or other elements) to make his argument more logical and persuasive. Be sure to focus on the most relevant aspects of the passage.

Your essay should not discuss whether you agree with Duncan's claims, but rather discuss how Duncan develops his argument.

Post-Assessment

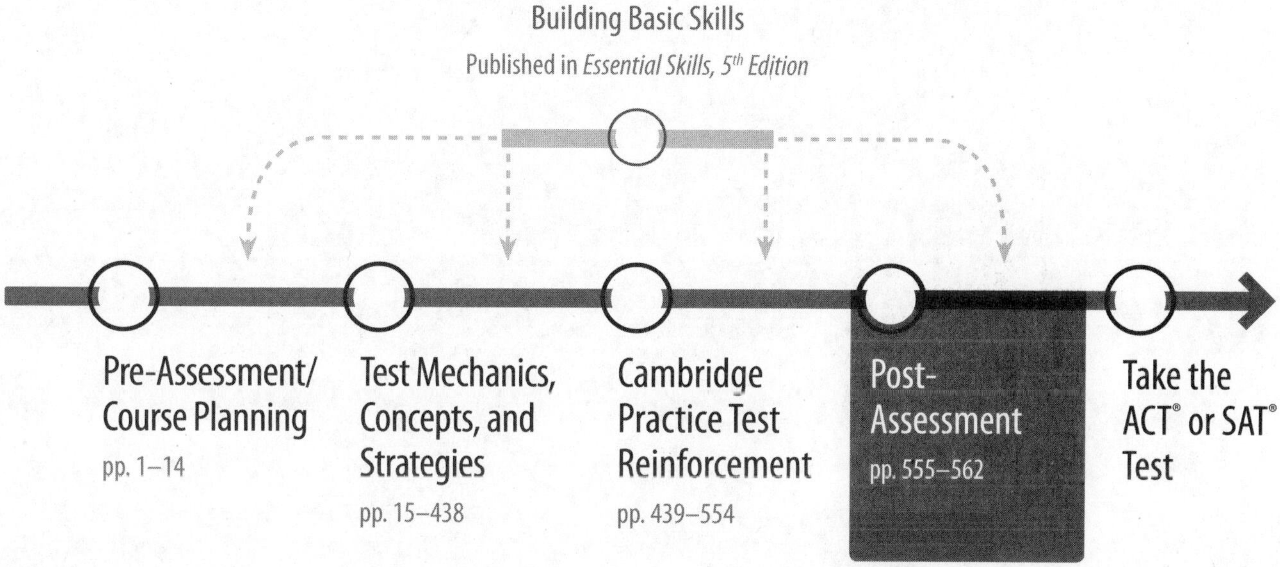

CAMBRIDGE
VICTORY FOR THE
ACT® AND SAT® TESTS

POST-ASSESSMENT ADMINISTRATION

At the end of the course, you will take a post-assessment. This post-assessment consists of a previously administered ACT or SAT test. When you take the post-assessment, you should bring the following items to the classroom in addition to anything else your teacher instructs you to bring:

1. Sharpened, soft-lead, No. 2 pencils
2. A calculator that is approved for use on the test. Most graphing calculators and all scientific and four-function calculators are permitted, but four-function calculators are not recommended. The following are not permitted:
    - Handheld or laptop computers, tablets, cell phones, or smart phones
    - Electronic writing pad or pen-input devices
    - Models that can access the internet, have wireless, Bluetooth, cellular, audio/video recording or playing, camera, or any other smart phone-type feature
    - Models with a QWERTY (typewriter) keypad
    - Models with paper tape
    - Models that make noise or "talk"
    - Models that must be plugged into an outlet
3. A watch (to pace yourself as you work through each test section)

How to Use the Post-Assessment Reports

You will receive the results of your post-assessment in the form of Student Summary and Student Item Analysis reports approximately six days after taking the test. These reports provide details about your performance and will help you determine where to focus your efforts from now until your test date, which you'll do by targeting the skills, concepts, and strategies that will help you improve in your areas of weakness. Just as you did with the pre-assessment, review the details of the sample reports on pages 6–9 of this book so that you are familiar with their contents.

Once you have received your post-assessment reports, you can develop a Personal Action Plan. Make connections between the reports and the specific skills, concepts, and strategies that you need to study, then complete the "to do" list on the following page.

TOPIC	START DATE	DATE TO BE COMPLETED	DATE COMPLETED

PLANNING FOR FURTHER STUDY

You have received the results of your post-assessment. You have finished the Cambridge *Victory for the ACT® and SAT® Tests* program. Now what?

In most cases you will have some spare time before the test day. Planning a study schedule for the time between the post-assessment and the real test is critical to reinforce and maintain the skills, concepts, and strategies you have learned throughout the course. Below are three steps that will help you make the most of your time.

Take the Practice Tests

Most students grasp knowledge of the subjects, but many struggle with time management. If you have not yet done so, take the Cambridge ACT and/or SAT practice exam (pp. 441–553) included in the Cambridge Practice Test Reinforcement part of this book. These practice tests reinforce skills and strategies, simulate the experience of the real test by using time restrictions to emphasize time management, and are an excellent guide to targeting your study plan.

Create a Written Study Plan

Use the results of your post-assessment and the practice tests to determine a day-by-day schedule that will give you a clear and dependable guide for study. Create this plan based on the amount of time you have before the test day.

Several weeks before test day:

- Plan to review all material equally
- Pick a few subjects to focus on each week will help you manage your time between now and the test

A few days before test day:

- Focus on core subjects that are giving you difficulty or areas in which you would like to improve
- Divide your time proportionally among these subjects based on your assessment of their difficulty

Determine the topics you will study each day and allot the proper amount of time to study those sections of the book and complete relevant exercises.

Stick to the Plan

Once you have determined your rubric for study, stick to it without fail. Such discipline will surely reward you on the day of the test. Follow these helpful hints:

- Ask your teacher for insight. He or she can help you set goals for each core subject and may be able to suggest further strategies or a re-allotment of your time.

- Don't study too much – an hour or two of studying each day will be more productive than a severe study schedule.
- Practice every day.

Appendix A: Answers and Explanations

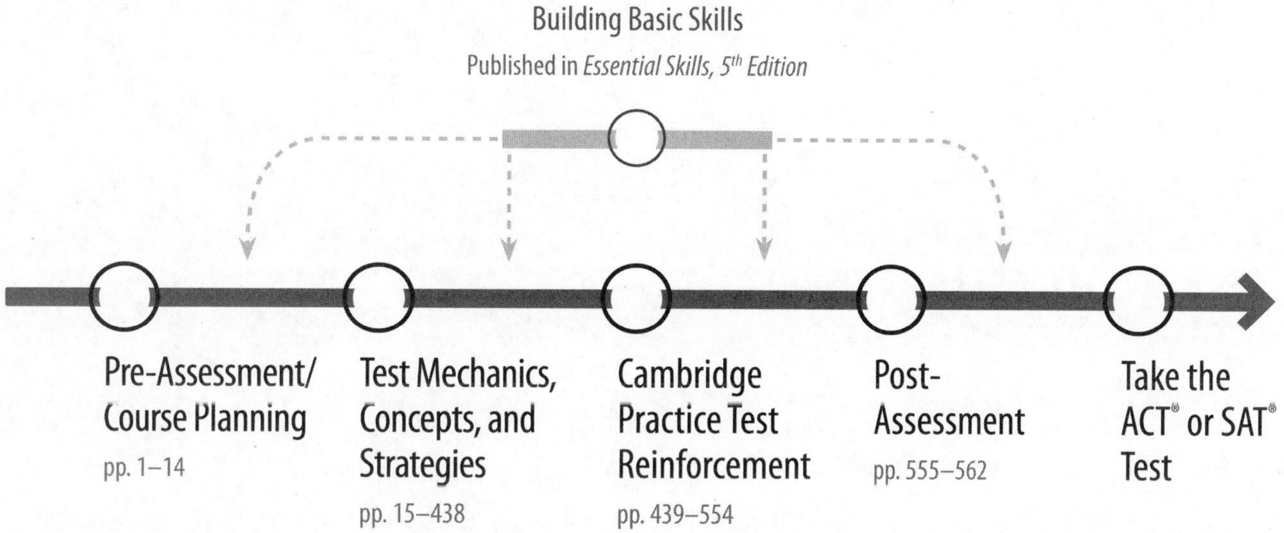

ACT READING AND SAT READING

Lesson 1 | Information and Ideas (p. 21)

1. C	**6.** D	**11.** A	**16.** D	**21.** C	**26.** C
2. A	**7.** D	**12.** A	**17.** C	**22.** B	**27.** A
3. A	**8.** A	**13.** C	**18.** B	**23.** D	**28.** C
4. D	**9.** B	**14.** D	**19.** A	**24.** C	**29.** C
5. B	**10.** D	**15.** C	**20.** A	**25.** C	**30.** B

Lesson 2 | Passage Development (p. 31)

1. B	**6.** A	**11.** B	**16.** C	**21.** D	**26.** A
2. B	**7.** B	**12.** D	**17.** A	**22.** D	**27.** A
3. A	**8.** D	**13.** A	**18.** A	**23.** B	**28.** C
4. A	**9.** B	**14.** B	**19.** C	**24.** A	**29.** B
5. A	**10.** A	**15.** A	**20.** B	**25.** D	**30.** B

Lesson 3 | Vocabulary (p. 39)

1. D	**14.** A	**27.** A	**41.** A	**55.** B	**69.** C
2. C	**15.** B	**28.** D	**42.** C	**56.** C	**70.** B
3. D	**16.** D	**29.** B	**43.** B	**57.** D	**71.** B
4. B	**17.** C	**30.** C	**44.** A	**58.** C	**72.** D
5. B	**18.** A	**31.** B	**45.** D	**59.** A	**73.** D
6. B	**19.** B	**32.** C	**46.** B	**60.** C	**74.** A
7. D	**20.** C	**33.** A	**47.** B	**61.** A	**75.** B
8. B	**21.** A	**34.** D	**48.** C	**62.** C	**76.** C
9. B	**22.** D	**35.** D	**49.** B	**63.** B	**77.** C
10. D	**23.** A	**36.** B	**50.** D	**64.** C	**78.** D
11. D	**24.** D	**37.** C	**51.** A	**65.** C	**79.** B
12. B	**25.** B	**38.** B	**52.** C	**66.** D	**80.** B
13. C	**26.** C	**39.** A	**53.** D	**67.** B	
		40. D	**54.** B	**68.** A	

Lesson 4 | Data Presentations (p. 55)

1. A
2. C
3. A
4. A
5. C
6. B
7. A
8. C
9. B
10. A
11. B
12. A
13. C
14. D
15. C
16. B
17. D
18. A
19. C
20. D
21. B
22. D
23. B
24. C
25. A
26. B
27. A
28. C
29. A
30. D
31. A
32. A
33. B
34. C
35. A
36. D
37. B
38. B
39. D
40. C
41. D
42. C
43. C
44. A

Lesson 5 | Paired Passages (p. 73)

1. A
2. B
3. A
4. D
5. D
6. C
7. D
8. B
9. D
10. D
11. A
12. C
13. C
14. A
15. D
16. A
17. B
18. D
19. B
20. B
21. D
22. D
23. A
24. B
25. D
26. A
27. C
28. A
29. D
30. B
31. A
32. A
33. A

Lesson 6 | Additional Practice (p. 83)

1. C
2. A
3. A
4. D
5. D
6. D
7. B
8. C
9. B
10. D
11. A
12. C
13. D
14. A
15. D
16. D
17. B
18. D
19. C
20. A
21. C
22. C
23. D
24. A
25. D
26. C
27. D
28. C
29. A
30. B
31. D
32. D
33. C
34. D
35. B

Quizzes (p. 105)

ACT Quiz	SAT Quiz
1. A	**1.** B
2. H	**2.** B
3. A	**3.** B
4. G	**4.** A
5. A	**5.** D
6. H	**6.** C
7. D	**7.** A
8. J	**8.** A
9. B	**9.** C
10. J	**10.** B
11. D	**11.** D
12. F	**12.** B
13. D	**13.** B
14. H	**14.** C
15. D	**15.** A
16. H	**16.** D
17. C	**17.** C
18. G	

ACT ENGLISH AND SAT WRITING AND LANGUAGE

Lesson 1 | Standard English Conventions (p. 123)

1. B
2. B
3. C
4. B
5. D
6. B
7. C
8. C
9. D
10. B
11. D
12. A
13. D
14. C
15. D
16. C
17. B
18. D
19. C
20. D
21. C
22. A
23. D
24. C
25. D
26. B
27. C
28. B
29. C
30. D
31. C
32. D
33. C
34. B
35. C
36. B
37. D
38. B
39. B
40. A
41. B
42. B
43. A
44. D
45. D
46. C
47. C
48. B
49. D
50. D
51. C
52. B
53. D
54. C
55. C
56. B
57. C
58. B
59. C
60. C
61. B
62. D
63. B
64. D
65. A
66. C
67. B
68. C
69. D
70. C
71. B
72. B
73. D
74. C
75. C
76. C
77. C
78. D
79. B
80. C
81. B
82. A
83. A
84. A
85. A
86. A
87. B
88. C
89. A
90. C
91. B
92. C
93. A
94. A
95. B
96. C
97. D
98. D
99. D
100. B
101. A
102. A
103. B
104. D
105. C
106. B
107. B
108. D
109. B
110. D
111. A
112. C
113. A
114. D
115. On Monday, Mark received a letter of acceptance from State College. He immediately called his mother—herself a graduate of State College—to tell her about his acceptance. When he told her he had also been awarded a scholarship, she was very excited. After hanging up, Mark's mother decided to throw a surprise party for Mark. She telephoned his brother, his sister, and several of his friends. Because the party was supposed to be a surprise, she made them all promise not to say anything to Mark. Mark, however, had a similar idea: a party for his mother to celebrate his acceptance at her alma mater. He telephoned his brother, his sister, and several of his parents' friends to invite them to a party at his house on Saturday night, and he made them all promise to say nothing to his mother. On Saturday night, both Mark and his mother were surprised.

Lesson 2 | Expression of Ideas (p. 139)

1. D	11. B	21. C	31. B	42. A	53. D
2. D	12. B	22. A	32. B	43. C	54. C
3. D	13. C	23. C	33. D	44. C	55. C
4. B	14. B	24. B	34. D	45. C	56. D
5. B	15. D	25. A	35. D	46. A	57. C
6. A	16. D	26. A	36. C	47. B	58. C
7. B	17. B	27. D	37. A	48. C	59. D
8. A	18. D	28. C	38. A	49. A	60. B
9. C	19. B	29. C	39. D	50. B	
10. A	20. B	30. A	40. B	51. A	
			41. A	52. C	

Lesson 3 | Words in Context (p. 157)

1. B	8. A	15. A	22. B	29. D	36. D
2. A	9. A	16. B	23. B	30. A	37. C
3. A	10. D	17. D	24. D	31. B	38. C
4. D	11. C	18. D	25. C	32. B	39. A
5. B	12. B	19. C	26. D	33. B	40. B
6. D	13. D	20. B	27. C	34. D	
7. B	14. D	21. A	28. D	35. D	

Lesson 4 | Data Presentations (p. 163)

1. D	10. D	19. D	28. B	37. B	46. D
2. B	11. C	20. C	29. A	38. B	47. B
3. C	12. B	21. A	30. C	39. C	48. C
4. A	13. A	22. A	31. C	40. D	
5. C	14. D	23. D	32. C	41. B	
6. D	15. C	24. C	33. D	42. C	
7. C	16. C	25. B	34. C	43. B	
8. A	17. B	26. B	35. A	44. C	
9. B	18. A	27. D	36. A	45. B	

Lesson 5 | Strategies (p. 181)

1. A
2. D
3. D
4. C
5. A
6. B
7. C
8. D
9. A
10. A
11. A

Quizzes (p. 197)

ACT Quiz

1. D
2. F
3. D
4. J
5. C
6. F
7. B
8. G
9. A
10. F
11. B
12. F
13. B
14. G
15. D
16. F
17. D
18. F
19. C
20. G
21. A
22. J
23. B
24. H
25. D
26. H
27. D
28. F
29. B

SAT Quiz

1. B
2. C
3. B
4. A
5. C
6. A
7. C
8. C
9. D
10. D
11. C
12. B
13. A
14. D
15. D
16. A
17. A
18. C
19. D
20. C
21. D
22. C
23. A
24. A
25. B
26. A
27. B
28. A
29. C
30. C
31. D
32. A
33. B
34. B

ACT ESSAY

Lesson (p. 217)

Sample Essay Outline

I. Introduction

A. My three supporting arguments relate to technology making it easier and faster to communicate, lack of meaningful content in quick, impersonal communication, and the need to use technology with care.

B. Thesis statement: Technological advances have opened many possibilities for communication and are professionally and socially indispensable in today's world; however, one must use this technology wisely in order to build meaningful relationships.

II. Online communication has revolutionized professional and personal interactions, and it is essential for maintaining relationships in today's globalized society.

A. Ease of communication for personal and business purposes

B. You can keep in contact with people if you have to move

C. You can learn about a greater diversity of people and places

III. There are some potential drawbacks of online communication.

A. Since information is shared so quickly, there is a greater chance that it might not be accurate or express complex viewpoints

B. In the workplace, close relationships are important for some tasks

IV. One can benefit the most from online communication by using it cautiously.

A. Verify online information with other sources

B. Use forms of technology that require closer communication, such as video chatting

V. Conclusion

A. Restatement of thesis: To avoid the risks of online communication, one must assess the value of the information received and use technologies that allow for more personal interaction.

Sample Essay—Above Average Response

Thanks to online communication, you can share news, conduct meetings, or make friends across the globe. Technologies such as email and video chats allow you to contact others instantaneously and cheaply. However, some argue that the low cost of online communication isn't the only thing that's "cheapened" by the use of these technologies. When online interactions are quick and easy, they can lack deep and meaningful information and be insufficient to build relationships. Technological advances have opened many possibilities for communication and are professionally and socially indispensable in today's world; however, one must use this technology wisely in order to build meaningful relationships.

Online communication has revolutionized professional and personal interactions in the twenty-first century, and in today's increasingly globalized society, it is essential for maintaining relationships. As Perspective 3 states, communication has become instantaneous. Instead of waiting days or paying expensive phone bills to reach colleagues and friends abroad, businesses can hold online meetings between London and New York, and you can chat with a friend on another continent. Moving to another country or even another state used to isolate you from the people you had met, but now, it is possible to stay in close contact with people you cannot see on a regular basis. Furthermore, even if you never leave your hometown, you can be exposed to a diverse array of cultures and opinions across the globe.

Although technology has had a positive impact on the ease of communication, it comes with some potential dangers. For example, when information or opinions can be shared instantaneously, there is a temptation to post information without thoroughly checking for accuracy or developing a nuanced viewpoint. This leads to what Perspective 1 calls "fast food" information that is "empty of real depth." Additionally, it is harder to build significant, lasting relationships with people you only meet online. In a professional context, weak relationships could cause problems when one needs to negotiate with colleagues abroad. And while social networking allows one to have a wide range of personal contacts, commenting on someone's post or browsing through a friend's online photos does not require direct contact.

One can optimize the benefits of online communication by using it cautiously. For example, instead of reading news updates on social media and believing them at face value, one should verify the information with other sources. Furthermore, the type of technology that one uses can make a huge difference in the quality of communication. As Perspective 2 argues, "We have a need for closer contact with the people we know." Some technologies, such as video chats, facilitate closer communication. While talking to someone important, such as a colleague or a close friend, it is better to use this type of technology, rather than relying on instant messaging or social media.

Technology has made it easier to maintain communication that is crucial for conducting business and establishing relationships. However, reliance on these instantaneous interactions can compromise the accuracy of information shared, as well as the depth of one's relationships. To avoid these risks, one must assess the value of the information received and use technologies that allow for more personal interaction. And if it is possible, one should make an effort to see friends in person from time to time.

Sample Essay—Below Average Response

I agree with the third perspective that online communication is a positive change. You can read information from all over the world and keep in touch with family and friends who live far away. Some people argue that online communication is not real communication, I disagree.

When my family and I moved to another state, I was afraid that I would lose touch with all of my friends from home. However, thanks to email, and Facebook, we have stayed in contact. I think the smartphone is the most important piece of technology for staying connected with other people because you can take it with you everywhere. No matter where I am. I can text my friends, send them photos through Instagram, or see what their up to on social media. I know that commenting one someone's Twitter post isn't enough to stay friends with them, but for people who I really care about, I can always message them directly or video chat with them. The video chat makes it very easy to have a conversation.

Online communication also makes it easier to get information from all over the world. For example, if you need to do business with people from another country, you can contact them right away instead of waiting several days for a response. It's also easier to learn about global topics because there's so much information on the internet.

It's true that I would feel lonely, as perspective 2 says, if I only talked to people online. However, online communication makes it easier to talk to people who I can't see face to face.

Quiz (p. 225)

Sample Essay—Above Average Response

With fuel to heat our homes and run our cars, our need for fossil fuels will not disappear any time soon. However, because of the environmental risks involved, fracking should be undertaken with caution, and the long-term focus should be on renewable energy sources. The methods used through fracking to extract natural gas could cause environmental problems, such as pollution or even earthquakes. Companies, therefore, should be required to follow strict environmental and safety regulations and to cooperate with nearby communities. Furthermore, fracking should not detract from long-term goals of developing renewable energy sources.

Although the debate is controversial, critics of fracking argue that it causes serious environmental problems, such as air and water pollution and instability of the earth's crust. The process of fracking involves drilling at least a few thousand feet below the earth's surface, as well as drilling horizontally. A combination of water and chemicals is poured down the drill at an extremely high pressure, which fractures shale rocks and releases natural gas. Studies in communities near fracking sites reported higher amounts of methane in well water, which could endanger the local population. Critics also argue that because fracking wells run thousands of feet deeper than wells for more traditional methods of natural gas extraction, fracking could destabilize the earth's crust and cause earthquakes.

However, because renewable energy sources are not sufficiently developed to replace fossil fuel consumption, it is important to find additional sources of fossil fuels. Fracking, therefore, should be undertaken with caution. Governmental agencies should regulate which chemicals can be used during fracking and should require companies to construct wells in ways that would minimize the risk of natural gas leakage. Additionally, companies should be required to drill at a safe distance from surrounding communities, to eliminate health risks involved with fracking. Although fracking could bring many economic benefits, especially greater energy independence for the US, the process should not jeopardize local ecosystems and the health of surrounding communities.

Furthermore, fracking is not a permanent solution because it extracts a nonrenewable resource. It should not compromise efforts to develop renewable sources of energy. Although developing equipment and researching safe methods for fracking will be an extremely expensive endeavor, it should not cripple government and private funding for development of other sources of energy, such as wind or solar energy. Renewable energy sources will have a greater long-term impact on energy independence and will be safer for the environment than fracking.

Despite the environmental problems that it can cause, fracking is currently a necessary risk, until renewable energy resources are more developed and widely available. However, companies should be required to follow strict regulations to minimize risks for the surrounding communities. Economic gains from fracking should not come at the expense of environmental and health disasters.

Sample Essay—Below Average Response

Fracking can be a dangerous process, causing pollution and other environmental problems. It can even cause health issues for people who live nearby. However, we use fossil fuels for so many things, like heating and driving, so we have no choice but to do it.

People who argue against fracking argue that it causes environmental problems. For example, if the well used for drilling isn't built correctly, gas and chemicals could leak out and pollute the surrounding community. I even heard that it could cause earthquakes because you have to dig so deeply underground.

These environmental problems can be harmful for the surrounding communities. Water pollution can kill animals that live nearby and can also cause health problems for humans. Wouldn't want to live in a community that was harmed by fracking. Just look at past oil spills to see how much damage drilling can do. For example, the Gulf of Mexico oil spill in 2010 killed workers, destroyed local ecosystems, and is still contaminating the water.

However, the reality is that we still need fossil fuels, so fracking might be a good thing. Communities might need to move away from fracking cites if they're unsafe, and unfortunately, our energy needs make us cause environmental problems.

SAT ESSAY

Lesson (p. 231)

Sample Essay—Above Average Response

Over the years, women have struggled and fought for many rights. In modern times, women have the same rights as men, but there are still areas in which women are not equal or are underrepresented. Some of these areas are seats in parliaments, councils, and negotiating tables. In her speech Melanne Verveer effectively articulates the noticeable absence of women in the political arena as well as the importance of the presence of women in politics. However, her argument could be strengthened with an example of a successful woman or group of women participating in conflict resolution.

One of the things that makes Verveer's argument that women are underrepresented in the political arena so compelling is her use of statistics. Toward the beginning of her speech, she explains the disparity in the number of females involved in politics when compared to the female population worldwide. She says, "Let me state this another way, women are half of the population yet hold one-fifth of the positions in national governments." Verveer also provides the ratio of female parliamentarians to male parliamentarians in Papua New Guinea: 1 to 109. These numbers provide her audience with a real idea of just how absent females are from worldwide politics.

Verveer also clearly articulates the importance of female political participation. Verveer discusses the impact that females make when involved in government, which provides a more positive outlook on her topic of discussion. She uses India as an example, where 40% of elected officials in village and municipal councils, or Panchayats, are females. These councils have been very successful, and Verveer says they have been described as a "silent revolution" in India. According to research studies, these councils are better able to deliver public services and are responsible for making sure public resources benefit their local communities. It has also been shown that women play a key role in conflict resolution and peacemaking. By discussing these documented gains from women-led governments, Verveer is able to demonstrate to her audience the very real impact that women in government can have.

Verveer argues that women should also participate in conflict resolution and peacemaking, citing a UN resolution that recognized the importance of female participation in these activities. She states that women are victims of violence in times of conflict and can be part of the resolution of this violence. She includes a moving quote from a woman in Kabul. However, her argument on this point would be stronger if she provided an example of a situation where women participated in conflict resolution and saw a positive outcome, as she did in her point about the impact of growing female political participation.

Verveer's argument for more female participation in politics is made powerful by her use of emotional appeal. She discusses statistics that call attention to the disparity of female participation in the political arena, she provides encouraging evidence for the benefits of women in government, and she shows that women's involvement in politics can help improve something as huge as the worldwide economy. Her speech could be even further strengthened with an example of successful conflict resolution involving women in key roles. Verveer's speech provides information about a topic that is probably largely overlooked by the general population, but it also, and perhaps more importantly, effectively makes a successful argument for female participation in politics.

Assessment of the Essay: The writer effectively selects specific parts of the passage to discuss how the speaker makes her argument more powerful and identifies an area where the author could further strengthen the speech. The inclusion of textual evidence (both direct quotes and paraphrasing) makes the writer's response flow logically and shows comprehension of the passage. The response is well organized and includes a wide variety of vocabulary and sentence structure.

Sample Essay—Below Average Response

Most people know that women are still not really considered equals, not even in the United States which is the most likely place to see equality. For example we have never had a female president and it doesn't seem like we will have one anytime soon. Melanne Verveer in her speech talks about how women are not very involved in politics and this is a problem. It's not because they are not allowed, but maybe because they're not as interested as men in politics or because they feel intimidated by government. It doesn't matter what the reason is it just matters that there aren't enough women in politics and that is a problem. It is bad because women do not have equal rights, the economy is bad and there is less peace because women are not involved in politics.

First, women do not have all equal rights and it is because they are not involved in the government that makes decisions about women's rights. For example women still do not get paid as much as men. Women need to be involved in the decisions to make sure that they are getting the same amount of pay as men are. There are also countries where women are not even close to being equal to men not like in the US where they are pretty much equal. If women were involved in politics in those countries it might be a different story.

Second of all, the economy is bad. Pretty much every newspaper you see or every news show you watch will talk about the economy. People are always worried about the economy. Melanne Verveer says that women in politics can help to make the economy better. Maybe one of the ways to help the economy is to get women involved in the government and politics and things might turn around.

Thirdly, everyone knows that there are always wars going on. Not necessarily in our country but in other countries of the world. Its possible that by having women be in politics and making decisions there might be more peace in the word. Melanne Verveer talks about women and peacemaking and peace negotiations. If they are more involved there might be more peace and less wars so that is another reason why women should get involved in government.

In conclusion it is important for women to be in government because they can have equal rights, the economy is better, and it would make the world much more peacefull. If you don't think that women need to be involved in politics than you should read Melanne Verveer's speech because after that you will reconsider your thoughts about women in politics.

Assessment of the Essay: The writer makes some claims that are not supported by the passage and do not make sense in the response. Many sentences are either grammatically incorrect or awkwardly constructed such that comprehension becomes difficult. The writer does not make an effective case for how the speaker makes her argument persuasive, but rather discusses problems and possible solutions to the topic presented in the passage.

Quiz (p. 241)

Sample Essay—Above Average Response

In recent times, the heavy focus on "tested" academic subjects (reading, writing, mathematics, and science) has caused arts education to be pushed to the side. Because subjects like art and music do not usually show up on ACT or SAT tests, the opportunities to study them become fewer and fewer as math and science curricula become the priority. In her essay, "Does in-school arts education matter?" Mariale Hardiman discusses how a push to incorporate arts education resulted in more engaged learners than a "narrowed curriculum" including mostly only tested subjects. Hardiman is able to argue this point through the use of evidence from her own experiences in the academic world. Results from studies conducted on arts-integration programs further solidify her argument that a well-rounded education requires the addition of arts education to the curricula of typical "tested" subjects. However, Hardiman's argument would be stronger if she described in greater detail the problems with her school before the implementation of the arts program.

Hardiman noticed that, despite award-winning academic achievement at her large Baltimore school, students were seeming to lack something in their educational experience. She determined the missing factor to be an education in the arts, and she predicted that incorporating an education in the arts would make for a more "robust" educational experience for the students. Hardiman's argument for the inclusion of arts education is made credible by her first-hand experience as a principal. It was obvious to her that, even though her school was consistently recognized for academic performance, there was still something to be desired in the students' overall educational experience.

The idea of an arts-integrated education was put to the test in Hardiman's K-8 school after she trained teachers to use art as a teaching tool and expanded visual and performing arts positions. It was clear that students were more engaged and creative after the addition of arts education. In a study conducted at Johns Hopkins School of Education, Hardiman led teams in the development of a curriculum that included arts education that would be compared to a curriculum that did not include an integration of arts. For the 16 classrooms in which the study was conducted, students who received an education with the arts-integrated curriculum showed a higher level of retention than the students who did not receive an art-integrated curriculum. By conducting this study, Hardiman further solidified her argument for the inclusion of the arts, despite a push toward a "narrowed curriculum." She expressed the desire and need for further studies to determine if there is evidence for improved critical thinking and problem solving with an arts-integrated education.

Hardiman's blog post clearly demonstrates the positive effects of an arts education in her own school and in the schools studied by Johns Hopkins, but the essay would be stronger if she explained why her own school was providing students with an inadequate education before the arts program was implemented. In the third paragraph, she said that "something was amiss" in her school's academic climate after it increased focus on testing, and she concluded that her school's academic vitality "could only be accomplished through robust arts programs." However, she does not say how, exactly, she reached this conclusion. "Something was amiss" is a vague statement that could be clarified with specific examples. Were students unenthusiastic in class? Did their assignments lack original thinking? Were students unable to perform well academically outside the subjects that were tested? Answering specific questions such as these would make a stronger case for the need of an arts education program at Hardiman's school.

Although the blog post would be stronger if Hardiman contrasted the conditions at her school before and after the implementation of the arts program, her argument that an education in the arts makes for a better overall academic experience is made credible by her first-hand academic experience and the results of studies she conducted alongside research and curriculum-writing teams. Her position as a principal in a large metropolitan school allows her to speak with authority on the type and quality of the students' education. The evidence produced by her push to include arts in her high-performing school and the controlled trial study she conducted at Johns Hopkins add even more credibility to her claim that arts education is essential to a well-rounded academic experience.

Assessment of the Essay: This response does a thorough job of both providing an overview of the author's main point and analysis of the author's argument. The writer accurately discusses the author's observations and the steps taken to test and prove the author's theory regarding an education in the arts. The essay also explains how one of the author's arguments could benefit from more specific examples. The essay response includes varied sentence structure and an appropriate level of vocabulary. The writer clearly understood both the article and the author's method for creating a sound argument.

Sample Essay—Below Average Response

In the article, Mariale Hardiman talks about how schools should stop focusing so much on tested subjects and should make sure to include art in the education experience. I think that this is a good idea because its important to make sure that students get an education in all subjects and not just the ones that will show up on a test. Plus, some students are really interested in art, so if they don't have the opportunity to study that, they probably will not preform as well in school.

The first reason why schools should include art as a subject is because the students will be able to remember more of that they are being taught. The author talks about how students were able to remember more when they were studying art, so that is pretty good evidence right there for including art in school. If schools are so worried about how students will do on tests, and art will help students to remember what they learn better, it should be obvious that schools should educate students in art because they will only be able to remember even more information to preform on the state tests.

The second reason why school should include art as a subject is because it will make the students more creative. Art is all about being creative so if teachers are teaching students about creativity, the students should definitely end up being more creative as a result. It will help their brains to think differently about the things that they see every day, and this will make them better students.

The third reason why schools should include art as a subject is because they will not be as cultured. Art is apart of culture. If students aren't learning about art, they are not understanding their culture and the culture of the world. This makes them disadvantaged, especially to the rest of the world which is much more cultured than the United States. It is important to teach students about important works of art, music and sculpture so they can keep up with the rest of society.

In conclusion, I agree that art should be apart of every students education for many reasons. Because they will remember more information, they will be more creative, and they will know more about culture. If they don't have art education, they will not have these things and they will probably not do as well on the state tests that are really important to the schools.

Assessment of the Essay: This response does not follow the instructions provided in the prompt; the essay takes a stance on the issue offered by the author of the passage and does not discuss how the author presents her argument. The response contains grammatical errors such as run-on sentences, fragments, and misspellings. The writer discusses observations and subjects that are not supported by the author's passage.

ACT MATHEMATICS AND SAT MATH: MULTIPLE-CHOICE

Lesson 1 | Problem Solving and Advanced Arithmetic (p. 251)

1. A
2. C
3. B
4. C
5. D
6. A
7. A
8. D
9. D
10. C
11. D
12. B
13. D
14. C
15. C
16. A
17. A
18. C
19. D
20. B
21. D
22. B
23. B
24. D
25. A
26. C
27. D
28. B
29. D
30. C
31. B
32. D
33. C
34. A
35. D
36. D
37. D
38. D
39. C
40. D
41. D
42. D
43. D
44. C
45. D
46. A
47. D
48. D
49. D
50. C
51. D
52. D
53. D
54. D
55. D
56. C
57. D
58. D

Lesson 2 | Algebra (p.261)

1. C
2. D
3. D
4. B
5. D
6. D
7. A
8. D
9. C
10. B
11. A
12. D
13. A
14. B
15. D
16. C
17. C
18. D
19. D
20. C
21. A
22. A
23. D
24. D
25. A
26. C
27. A
28. A
29. C
30. A
31. A
32. D
33. B
34. B
35. D
36. C
37. D
38. D
39. D
40. C
41. C
42. B
43. C
44. A
45. C
46. A
47. D
48. B
49. A
50. D
51. B
52. C
53. B
54. D
55. C
56. D
57. C
58. D
59. B
60. D
61. B
62. A
63. B
64. B
65. B
66. B
67. D
68. B
69. C
70. D
71. A
72. A
73. D
74. D
75. A
76. C
77. C
78. C
79. C
80. D
81. D
82. D
83. C
84. B
85. A
86. B
87. C
88. A
89. C
90. B
91. D
92. B
93. B
94. D

Lesson 3 | Coordinate Geometry (p. 275)

1. D
2. D
3. B
4. C
5. D
6. C
7. C
8. D
9. D
10. B
11. D
12. A
13. C
14. A
15. D
16. B
17. B
18. D
19. D
20. C
21. D
22. A
23. D
24. C
25. D
26. B
27. A
28. A
29. A
30. C

Lesson 4 | Geometry (p. 285)

1. D
2. C
3. C
4. C
5. C
6. A
7. B
8. C
9. C
10. A
11. D
12. D
13. B
14. B
15. C
16. A
17. C
18. D
19. D
20. A
21. C
22. C
23. D
24. C
25. D
26. B
27. C
28. B
29. A
30. B
31. D
32. D
33. C
34. B
35. D
36. C
37. D
38. B
39. B
40. C
41. C
42. C
43. B
44. D
45. C
46. D
47. A
48. B
49. A

Lesson 5 | Data Interpretation, Statistics, and Probability (p. 297)

1. B
2. B
3. A
4. B
5. B
6. D
7. B
8. A
9. A
10. D
11. A
12. D
13. D
14. C
15. B
16. D
17. D
18. A
19. B
20. D
21. B
22. C
23. D
24. A
25. C
26. D
27. D
28. A
29. B
30. A
31. C
32. B
33. D
34. C
35. C
36. D
37. B
38. D

Lesson 6 | Trigonometry (p. 307)

1. A
2. D
3. C
4. C
5. B
6. C
7. D
8. C
9. B
10. B
11. D
12. B
13. A
14. A
15. B
16. C
17. A
18. D
19. B
20. D
21. A
22. B
23. C
24. B
25. B
26. B
27. A
28. C
29. D
30. A
31. D
32. B
33. D
34. A
35. B
36. A
37. A
38. B
39. C
40. C
41. C
42. A
43. D
44. C
45. C
46. D
47. C
48. B
49. D
50. B
51. A
52. B
53. B
54. B
55. A
56. A
57. D
58. D
59. D
60. D

Test Mechanics Calculator Exercise (p. 331)

1. D; 1
2. D; 2
3. B; 2
4. A; 3
5. A; 2

Quizzes (p. 333)

ACT Quiz

1. A
2. K
3. D
4. H
5. D
6. J
7. E
8. J
9. B
10. H
11. D
12. J
13. D
14. F
15. A
16. G
17. E
18. J
19. C
20. J

SAT Quiz

1. C
2. A
3. C
4. B
5. C
6. C
7. B
8. D
9. A
10. C
11. B
12. D
13. D
14. C
15. D
16. C
17. B
18. C
19. D
20. D

SAT MATH: STUDENT-PRODUCED RESPONSES

Lesson | Student-Produced Responses (p. 351)

1. 25
2. 13.6 or 68/5
3. 1/32 or .031
4. 1/24, .041, or .042
5. 650
6. 3/8
7. 50
8. 2
9. 12
10. 8
11. 30
12. 75
13. .25 or 1/4
14. 25
15. 7/12 or .583
16. 16.8 or 84/5
17. 90
18. 7.5 or 15/2
19. 11
20. 6
21. 12
22. 180
23. 2664
24. 4
25. 8/15 or .533
26. 30
27. 50
28. 14
29. 48
30. 3/8 or .375
31. 5/4 or 1.25
32. 60
33. 738
34. 1/15
35. 1280
36. .22
37. 87.5
38. 72
39. 17.5
40. 4
41. 41
42. 75

Test Mechanics Calculator Exercise (p. 337)

1. 3/2 or 1.5; 3
2. 24; 3
3. 36; 3
4. 100; 2
5. 3 or 4; 3

Quiz (p. 379)

1. 4 or 5
2. 2
3. 3/2 or 1.5
4. 30
5. 5
6. 3
7. 0
8. 3
9. 8
10. 2
11. 2173
12. 657

ACT SCIENCE

Lesson 1 | Data Representation (p. 389)

1. B	**8.** H	**15.** B	**22.** H	**29.** D	**36.** C
2. F	**9.** C	**16.** H	**23.** D	**30.** G	**37.** G
3. C	**10.** H	**17.** D	**24.** F	**31.** A	**38.** A
4. G	**11.** A	**18.** H	**25.** B	**32.** G	**39.** B
5. C	**12.** H	**19.** A	**26.** H	**33.** C	**40.** H
6. H	**13.** D	**20.** J	**27.** C	**34.** F	
7. D	**14.** F	**21.** C	**28.** G	**35.** J	

Lesson 2 | Research Summary (p. 399)

1. C	**7.** C	**13.** A	**19.** B	**25.** C	**31.** A
2. F	**8.** F	**14.** J	**20.** H	**26.** G	**32.** G
3. D	**9.** D	**15.** D	**21.** C	**27.** C	**33.** A
4. J	**10.** G	**16.** H	**22.** J	**28.** F	**34.** H
5. B	**11.** B	**17.** D	**23.** A	**29.** D	
6. F	**12.** G	**18.** J	**24.** J	**30.** H	

Lesson 3 | Conflicting Viewpoints (p. 413)

1. A	**6.** H	**11.** B	**16.** F	**21.** C	**26.** F
2. G	**7.** C	**12.** H	**17.** D	**22.** J	**27.** B
3. D	**8.** J	**13.** D	**18.** F	**23.** A	**28.** H
4. G	**9.** A	**14.** G	**19.** B	**24.** J	**29.** D
5. B	**10.** H	**15.** C	**20.** G	**25.** D	

Quiz (p. 431)

1. D	**6.** J	**11.** A	**16.** J
2. J	**7.** B	**12.** G	
3. D	**8.** H	**13.** B	
4. F	**9.** A	**14.** H	
5. C	**10.** G	**15.** C	

ACT PRACTICE TEST

Multiple-Choice Answer Keys

DIRECTIONS: For the correct answer, check the corresponding unshaded box. Then, total the number of checkmarks for each of the content areas, and add these totals to determine the raw score for that test.

Section 1: English (Student Text, p. 444)

#	UM	RH	#	UM	RH	#	UM	RH	#	UM	RH	#	UM	RH
1. C			16. J			31. B			46. H			61. D		
2. F			17. A			32. G			47. D			62. F		
3. C			18. H			33. B			48. G			63. B		
4. G			19. D			34. J			49. B			64. J		
5. B			20. H			35. B			50. F			65. C		
6. F			21. A			36. J			51. A			66. H		
7. C			22. G			37. D			52. G			67. A		
8. F			23. D			38. G			53. D			68. G		
9. C			24. H			39. A			54. G			69. D		
10. H			25. D			40. J			55. B			70. H		
11. A			26. F			41. B			56. H			71. C		
12. F			27. B			42. F			57. A			72. G		
13. D			28. F			43. A			58. H			73. D		
14. H			29. D			44. G			59. A			74. H		
15. B			30. J			45. A			60. J			75. D		

Usage and Mechanics (UM): ______/46 Rhetorical Skills (RH): ______/29 Raw Score (UM + RH): ______/75

Section 2: Mathematics (Student Text, p. 460)

#	EA	AG	GT	#	EA	AG	GT	#	EA	AG	GT	#	EA	AG	GT
1. D				16. G				31. A				46. K			
2. K				17. D				32. H				47. A			
3. C				18. F				33. D				48. H			
4. J				19. B				34. K				49. D			
5. E				20. F				35. E				50. G			
6. K				21. E				36. F				51. C			
7. B				22. F				37. B				52. G			
8. G				23. C				38. K				53. D			
9. D				24. G				39. B				54. K			
10. G				25. A				40. K				55. C			
11. B				26. H				41. C				56. G			
12. G				27. A				42. J				57. A			
13. E				28. H				43. D				58. F			
14. H				29. C				44. J				59. E			
15. C				30. K				45. C				60. F			

Pre-Algebra/Elementary Algebra (EA): ______/26 Plane Geometry/Trigonometry (GT): ______/18

Int. Algebra/Coordinate Geometry (AG): ______/16 Raw Score (EA + AG + GT): ______/60

Section 3: Reading (Student Text, p. 480)

		SS	AL
1.	B		
2.	J		
3.	A		
4.	H		
5.	A		
6.	J		
7.	B		
8.	F		
9.	A		
10.	F		

		SS	AL
11.	B		
12.	G		
13.	C		
14.	F		
15.	D		
16.	G		
17.	D		
18.	H		
19.	B		
20.	H		

		SS	AL
21.	A		
22.	J		
23.	D		
24.	G		
25.	D		
26.	G		
27.	A		
28.	H		
29.	A		
30.	H		

		SS	AL
31.	C		
32.	J		
33.	A		
34.	H		
35.	A		
36.	J		
37.	B		
38.	J		
39.	D		
40.	H		

Social Studies/Sciences (SS): _____/20 Arts/Literature (AL): _____/20 Raw Score (SS + AL): _____/40

Section 4: Science (Student Text, p. 490)

		B	C	P	ES
1.	B				
2.	H				
3.	A				
4.	H				
5.	B				
6.	J				
7.	A				
8.	F				
9.	C				
10.	G				
11.	A				

		B	C	P	ES
12.	G				
13.	D				
14.	H				
15.	A				
16.	F				
17.	C				
18.	G				
19.	D				
20.	G				
21.	C				
22.	J				
23.	A				
24.	F				

		B	C	P	ES
25.	A				
26.	J				
27.	D				
28.	J				
29.	C				
30.	J				
31.	C				
32.	J				
33.	A				
34.	H				
35.	C				
36.	H				
37.	D				
38.	G				
39.	B				
40.	G				

Biology (B): _____/17 Physics (P): _____/10 Raw Score (B + C + P + ES): _____/40

Chemistry (C): _____/6 Earth/Space Sciences (ES): _____/7

Multiple-Choice Explanations

Section 1: *English*

1. **(C)** (p. 444) ***English/Usage and Mechanics/Grammar and Usage/Diction.*** The original sentence is not idiomatic. "On account of" cannot be used as a substitute for "because of." (C) is the correct answer because it makes the needed correction. As for the other answer choices, (B) is wrong because "since" is a conjunction that can only be used to introduce a dependent clause; however, the material that follows is not a clause since it does not include a verb. As for (D), "for" can be a preposition; however, its meaning is not appropriate in this context.

2. **(F)** (p. 444) ***English/Rhetorical Skills/No Change.*** The original sentence is correct. "Nonetheless" provides the meaning required in this context since it means "in spite of this." As for the other answer choices, (G) and (H) are wrong because the author means to say that smuggling grew in spite of government efforts (not because of government efforts). As for (J), "on the contrary" generally means "in opposition to what has been stated"; however, it does not provide the precise meaning ("in spite of this") that is required here.

3. **(C)** (p.444) ***English/Usage and Mechanics/Grammar and Usage/Adjectives versus Adverbs*** and ***Punctuation/Commas.*** The original sentence contains two errors. First, an adjective cannot modify an adjective ("heavy timbered islands"). Only an adverb can modify an adjective ("heavily timbered islands"). Second, a comma is needed after "countless" ("countless, heavily timbered islands") to make it clear that "countless" modifies "islands" (and not "heavily timbered"). (C) is the correct answer choice because it makes both of these corrections.

4. **(G)** (p. 445) ***English/Usage and Mechanics/Grammar and Usage/Diction.*** The original sentence, (H), and (J) are all incorrect because they are not idiomatic. The correct idiomatic phrase is "well founded."

5. **(B)** (p. 445) ***English/Usage and Mechanics/Grammar and Usage/Sequence and Verb Tense.*** The original sentence is incorrect because "seize" (a present tense verb) is inconsistent with the past tense verbs used throughout the rest of the paragraph. Past events are being described here, so "seized" (a past tense verb) is the correct answer choice. As for the other answer choices, (C) and (D) refer to past events; however, they provide meanings that are inappropriate in this context. First, "were seizing" (a progressive past tense verb) implies an action that occurred over and over again in the past (e.g., "during this period, customs officials were seizing tons of wool each month"). Second, "have seized" (a present perfect tense verb) implies an action that began in the past but that also continues into the present (e.g., "the British have repeatedly seized our ships and continue to do so"). Neither of these meanings is appropriate here, so both (C) and (D) are incorrect.

6. **(F)** (p. 445) ***English/Rhetorical Skills/No Change.*** The original sentence is correct. As for the other answer choices, both (G) and (J) are awkward and needlessly wordy compared to the original sentence. (H) is incorrect because it misconstrues the meaning of the original sentence. Specifically, the original states that the *Beaver* was seized because of a "technical violation"; in contrast, (H) says the *Beaver* was seized "for technically being in violation" of the law, which incorrectly suggests that the author believes the violation was minor or perhaps even non-existent.

7. **(C)** (p. 445) ***English/Usage and Mechanics/Grammar and Usage/Diction.*** The original sentence is incorrect because it includes an incorrect word choice. "Principle" is a noun which means "rule" or "belief," and it cannot modify the plural noun "articles." The word required here is the adjective "principal," which means "main" or "important." Therefore, (C) is the correct answer choice. As for the other answer choices, (B) is wrong for two reasons. First, it does not fix the original, incorrect word choice. Second, it introduces a singular verb ("was"), which does not agree with the plural subject

("British wool, blankets, and liquor") of the sentence. (D) is also incorrect because it introduces a singular verb, "was," which does not agree with the plural subject of the sentence.

8. **(F)** (p. 445) ***English/Rhetorical Skills/No Change.*** The original sentence is correct. "In fact" is used to introduce a sentence that illustrates or emphasizes a point made in the previous sentence. In this paragraph, the sentence about British wool being smuggled into the San Juan Islands illustrates the point made in the previous sentence—namely, that British wool was a principal article of illicit trade. So, "in fact" is correctly used here. As for the other answer choices, (G) and (H) are wrong for the same reason. "Furthermore" and "moreover" are used to introduce a sentence that includes an idea similar to (but that is not an illustration of) an idea from the previous sentence. In this paragraph, though, the sentence about British wool being smuggled into the San Juan Islands is an illustration of an idea in the previous sentence; so, both "furthermore" and "moreover" are incorrect answer choices. Finally, (J) is incorrect because "on the contrary" is used to signal that a contrasting idea will be introduced; however, the author does not introduce a contrasting idea.

9. **(C)** (p. 445) ***English/Usage and Mechanics/Grammar and Usage/Verb Tense.*** The original sentence is incorrect because it includes an incorrect verb form. A passive past tense verb ("was smuggled") is used earlier in the sentence, and another passive past tense verb ("and sold") is needed to agree with it. So, (C) is the correct answer choice. As for the other answer choices, they are all incorrect because they do not provide the required passive past tense verb.

10. **(H)** (p. 445) ***English/Usage and Mechanics/Grammar and Usage/Diction.*** The original sentence is incorrect because it sets up an idiom ("so much...that") but does not successfully complete it. (H) is the correct answer choice because it successfully completes the idiomatic phrase. As for the other answer choices, they are all incorrect because they do not complete the idiomatic phrase.

11. **(A)** (p. 446) ***English/Rhetorical Skills/No Change.*** The original sentence is correct. In the sentence, there is a contrast between how settlers welcomed national control and how they resented the accompanying restrictions on trade. "Although" is the right word for introducing this type of contrast. As for the other answer choices, none of them would be appropriate for introducing the type of contrast discussed in this sentence.

12. **(F)** (p. 446) ***English/Usage and Mechanics/No Change.*** The original sentence is correct. The simple past tense verb ("welcomed") is consistent with the other verb in this sentence ("they <u>were</u> less amenable") as well as the other past tense verbs in the passage. As for the other answer choices, (G) is incorrect because it eliminates the only conjugated verb ("welcomed") in the clause; as a result, the sentence becomes a sentence fragment. (H) is wrong because "would welcome" is inconsistent with the past tense verbs in the paragraph. (J) is incorrect because it creates a completely illogical sentence; in short, an "assertion of national control" cannot welcome people.

13. **(D)** (p. 446) ***English/Usage and Mechanics/Grammar and Usage/Diction.*** The original sentence is incorrect because it includes an incorrect verb form. An active past tense verb ("They wanted") is used earlier in the sentence, and another active past tense verb ("but feared") is needed here to agree with it. So, (D) is the correct answer choice. As for the other answer choices, (A) and (B) are incorrect because "were fearing" is not an idiomatic expression; the correct idiomatic expression is "were fearful." (C) is incorrect because, although it uses the correct idiomatic phrase ("was fearful"), the singular verb ("was") does not agree with the plural subject ("they") of the sentence.

14. **(H)** (p. 446) ***English/Usage and Mechanics/Grammar and Usage/Sequence and Verb Tense*** **and** ***Diction.*** The original sentence includes two errors. First, the underlined portion includes a verb phrase ("might be resulting") that is awkward and needlessly wordy; it should be replaced by the more accurate and succinct verb phrase "might result." Second, the underlined portion includes a prepositional phrase ("in the losing of") that is non-idiomatic; the correct idiomatic phrase is "in the loss of." (H) is the correct

answer choice because it makes both of these corrections. As for the other answer choices, (G) is incorrect because it only makes one of these corrections. (J) is incorrect because a present tense verb ("results") does not suggest the element of uncertainty or contingency required here. Verb phrases such as "might result" or "would result" accomplish this task. However, a present tense verb ("results") does not.

15. (B) (p. 446) ***English/Rhetorical Skills/Organization/Passage-Level Structure.*** The paragraphs need to be in chronological order. Therefore, (B) is the correct answer choice here. Paragraph 1 is first because it describes the earliest event (the opening of the customs office). Paragraph 3 is next because it describes events that followed (the settlers' concerns about the new office). Paragraph 2 is last because it describes events that occurred last (the Americans' concerns turned out to be true).

16. (J) (p. 446) ***English/Rhetorical Skills/Organization/Passage-Level Structure.*** The author does not provide any quotations in the essay. So, (J) is correct. (F) is incorrect because the author describes or provides a narrative of several events. (G) is incorrect because the author gives specific examples in the essay. (H) is incorrect because the author provides statistics related to the production of wool.

17. (A) (p. 447) ***English/Rhetorical Skills/No Change.*** The original sentence is the best choice. In comparison, the other answer choices are awkward and needlessly wordy.

18. (H) (p. 447) ***English/Usage and Mechanics/Sentence Structure/Faulty Parallelism.*** The original sentence is incorrect due to a lack of parallelism. All three verbs in the sentence ("step," "gaze," and "become") are governed by the first instance of "can," which establishes the present tense. It is unnecessary for another instance of "can" to appear in the sentence. However, the original sentence has an instance of "can" before "become." As a result, a series is created in which the elements are not parallel or do not have exactly the same form. (H) is the correct answer choice because it eliminates the problem and brings the third verb into line with the other two. As for the other answer choices, (G) is incorrect because a past tense verb ("became") destroys the parallelism needed here. (J) is incorrect because the verb ("becomes") does not agree in number with the subject ("anyone") of the sentence.

19. (D) (p. 447) ***English/Usage and Mechanics/Sentence Structure/Comma Splices.*** The original sentence is incorrect because it is a run-on sentence. A run-on sentence is two or more complete sentences joined together without the necessary punctuation or conjunctions. For example, the first clause in the sentence ("The same questions come to mind time and again") is a complete sentence by itself. For the sake of correctness and clarity, it would be best to put a piece of end-stop punctuation at the end of this clause and then start an entirely new sentence. (D) is the correct answer choice because it accomplishes this task. As for the other answer choices, (B) and (C) are incorrect because they also result in run-on sentences.

20. (H) (p. 447) ***English/Usage and Mechanics/Sentence Structure/Misplaced Modifiers.*** The original sentence is incorrect because it is too ambiguous. Specifically, "ending" seems to modify "suns"; however, the author intends for it to modify "island universe." The ambiguity is eliminated by replacing the ambiguous "ending" with the relative clause "that ends...." It is now clear that the relative clause modifies "island universe." So, (H) is correct. (G) creates the appropriate relative clause to modify "island universe"; however, the plural verb "end" does not agree in number with the singular noun antecedent of the relative clause ("island universe"). Finally, (J) is incorrect because it suffers from the same defect as the original; "ended" seems to modify "suns" rather than "island universe."

21. (A) (p. 447) ***English/Usage and Mechanics/No Change.*** The original sentence is correct. Standard written English requires the infinitive "to chart" in this context. (B) and (C) are incorrect because standard written English does not allow for participles ("charting" or "having charted") in this context. (D) is incorrect because it creates a sentence that is illogical and impossible to understand.

22. **(G)** (p. 447) ***English/Usage and Mechanics/Grammar and Usage/Verb Tense.*** The original sentence is incorrect because it includes an incorrect verb tense. The past perfect tense ("progress had been made") implies that progress was actually made *before* the twentieth century. Of course, the author intends to say that progress was made "in the twentieth century," so a simple past tense verb ("was made") is needed. Therefore, (G) is the correct answer choice. (H) is incorrect because a present tense verb form ("is made") fails to communicate that progress has already been made during the twentieth century. (J) is incorrect because a future tense verb form ("will be made") incorrectly suggests that progress has not yet been made at all.

23. **(D)** (p. 448) ***English/Rhetorical Skills/Strategy/Effective Transitional Sentence.*** The original sentence is incorrect because it begins with a misleading introductory phrase. "As such" is a phrase which suggests a connection between two events or ideas. For example, "He is the head of security. As such, he helped develop the emergency response procedures." So, because he is head of security he helped develop the procedures. As for this particular sentence, though, it is certainly not the case that the Milky Way was so named because our solar system was discovered to be part of it. In fact, there is not a cause-and-effect relationship between the name of the Milky Way and our solar system's relationship to it. (D) is the correct answer choice here because it eliminates any suggestion that there is any relationship of this type. As for the other answer choices, (B) and (C) are both incorrect because it is not clear why the statement made is obvious or beyond doubt.

24. **(H)** (p. 448) ***English/Rhetorical Skills/Organization/Paragraph-Level Structure.*** The original sentence is incorrect because the material in it belongs in the next paragraph. Therefore, the original sentence should actually be the first sentence of the following paragraph. It should then be immediately followed (i.e., without a break for a new paragraph) by the sentence that used to begin that paragraph ("Since they are so near..."). Both (H) and (J) make the required changes. However, (J) is incorrect because "As" would turn the sentence into a dependent clause that did not have a supporting independent clause. (H) does not introduce this error. So, (H) is the correct answer choice.

25. **(D)** (p. 448) ***English/Usage and Mechanics/Punctuation/Commas.*** The original sentence is incorrect because only a comma or a dash (and not a semicolon) should be used to separate an appositive phrase ("the 'crown jewels' of the southern skies") from the main part of the sentence. (D) is the correct answer choice because it provides the appropriate punctuation. As for the other answer choices, (B) also provides the appropriate punctuation. However, it improperly removes the quotation marks from "crown jewels." The phrase is an example of words that are used in an uncommon, unusual, or unfamiliar way (i.e., the galaxies are not literally jewels); as a result, the phrase needs to appear inside quotation marks. (C) is incorrect because a singular verb ("is") does not agree with a plural noun ("Magellanic Clouds").

26. **(F)** (p. 448) ***English/Usage and Mechanics/No Change.*** The original sentence is correct. As for the other answer choices, they are either not idiomatic or not grammatically correct.

27. **(B)** (p. 448) ***English/Rhetorical Skills/Style/Conciseness.*** The original sentence is incorrect because the "to" in the underlined portion is unnecessary and makes the phrasing stilted. Both (B) and (C) make the needed correction. However, (C) is incorrect because a plural verb ("provide") does not agree with the singular subject ("galaxy") of the sentence.

28. **(F)** (p. 448) ***English/Rhetorical Skills/No Change.*** The original sentence is the best choice. In comparison, the other answer choices are awkward and needlessly wordy.

29. **(D)** (p. 449) ***English/Rhetorical Skills/Organization/Paragraph-Level Structure.*** (A), (B), and (C) are incorrect because the author does pose questions for these very reasons in the essay. (D) is the correct answer choice because the author does not promise that answers will be provided later in the essay to

what are, simply, many unanswerable questions (i.e., How many stars are there? Where and how does the universe end?).

30. **(J)** (p. 449) ***English/Usage and Mechanics/Grammar and Usage/Diction.*** The original sentence is incorrect because it includes an improperly formed appositive. The final phrase in the sentence ("graduated of test pilot schools") is meant to be an appositive for "volunteer, military pilots." To properly form the appositive, simply rewrite the final phrase as "graduates of test pilot schools." (J) is the correct answer choice because it makes this revision. As for the other answer choices, both (G) and (H) are wrong because an appositive can be set off only by a comma or a dash.

31. **(B)** (p. 449) ***English/Usage and Mechanics/Grammar and Usage/Subject-Verb Agreement* and *Diction.*** The original sentence is incorrect for two reasons. First, a plural verb ("were") does not agree with the singular subject ("each") of the sentence. Second, the use of a present participle ("having") here is not idiomatic. (B) is the correct answer choice because it corrects both of these errors. As for the other answer choices, (C) does not correct the second error. (D) corrects both errors, but the past perfect "had been required" is inconsistent with the past tense verbs in the rest of the paragraph.

32. **(G)** (p. 449) ***English/Rhetorical Skills/Style/Idiomatic Expression.*** The original sentence is incorrect because it includes informal usage. Specifically, it is not acceptable standard written English to use "got" when forming a passive verb form. Instead, use a form of the verb "to be" (e.g., "was," "were," etc.). (G) is the correct answer choice because it makes the needed correction. As for the other answer choices, (H) is a form of the passive voice; however, the past perfect "had been chosen" is inconsistent with the past tense verbs in the rest of the paragraph. (J) is incorrect for two reasons. First, the present perfect "has been" is not consistent with the past tense verbs in the rest of the paragraph. Second, a singular verb ("has") does not agree with the plural subject ("seven") of the sentence.

33. **(B)** (p. 450) ***English/Rhetorical Skills/Strategy/Appropriate Supporting Material.*** The information contained in the parentheses explains why only seven astronauts were chosen. However, this information is not vital to the development of the passage. By placing the explanation in parentheses, the author signals to the reader that the information is not vital.

34. **(J)** (p. 450) ***English/Usage and Mechanics/Sentence Structure/Comma Splices.*** The original sentence is incorrect because it is a run-on sentence. A run-on sentence is two or more complete sentences joined together without the necessary punctuation or conjunctions. For example, the first clause in the sentence ("These men were true pioneers") is a complete sentence by itself. For the sake of correctness and clarity, it would be best to put a piece of end-stop punctuation at the end of this clause and then start an entirely new sentence. (J) is the correct answer choice because it accomplishes this task. As for the other answer choices, (G) and (H) are incorrect because they also result in run-on sentences.

35. **(B)** (p. 450) ***English/Rhetorical Skills/Strategy/Effective Transitional Sentence.*** The topic of the second paragraph is the failures experienced during the early days of the Mercury space program. (B) is the correct answer choice because it provides the best signal to the reader that this will be the topic of the paragraph.

36. **(J)** (p. 450) ***English/Usage and Mechanics/Grammar and Usage/Pronoun Usage.*** The original sentence is incorrect for two reasons. First, the subject ("they") of the original sentence is too ambiguous. Who were "they"? The scientists? The pilots? The full scientific staff? It is not clear. Second, "fortunately" should be set off from the rest of the sentence by a comma. (J) is the correct answer choice because it eliminates both of these errors. As for the other answer choices, (G) is incorrect because it does not correct the first error. (H) is incorrect because "fortunately" is improperly placed in the sentence; as a result, it almost sounds as if "fortunately" were intended to modify "early."

37. **(D)** (p. 450) ***English/Rhetorical Skills/Style/Conciseness.*** (A), (B), and (C) are all incorrect because they are needlessly wordy. (D) is the correct answer choice because it is succinct and to the point.

38. **(G)** (p. 451) ***English/Rhetorical Skills/Strategy/Appropriate Supporting Material.*** When the author uses the word "spectacular" to describe a failure during a rocket flight, the reader is led to expect sensational, extraordinary, and quite likely terrifying details. However, as the author quickly points out, the details of this "spectacular" failure were instead quite mundane and pathetic. In short, after all the preparation leading up to the launch, the rocket only traveled two inches due to a circuit error. This is a classic case of irony, where there is a great incongruity or difference between anticipated and actual results.

39. **(A)** (p. 451) ***English/Usage and Mechanics/No Change.*** The original sentence is correct. Only an adverb ("relatively") can modify an adjective ("simple"). As for the other answer choices, (B) is incorrect because "relative" is intended to modify "simple" in this context; and, as stated above, only an adverb can modify an adjective. (D) is incorrect because an adjective cannot modify an adverb.

40. **(J)** (p. 451) ***English/Usage and Mechanics/Sentence Structure/Faulty Parallelism.*** The original sentence is incorrect because the underlined verb ("shutting") is not parallel with the other verb ("to ignite") in the sentence. (J) is the correct answer choice because it makes the needed correction ("to ignite and then to shut down"). As for the other answer choices, neither (G) nor (H) solves the original problem. In addition, (H) suffers from the further defect that "they" does not have a referent; in other words, it is not at all clear who or what "they" are.

41. **(B)** (p. 451) ***English/Usage and Mechanics/Punctuation/Quotation Marks.*** This is another example of irony. The rocket never really launched, and it never achieved true flight. In fact, as the passage tells us, the rocket only moved two inches. So, the quotation marks signal that the word "flight" is being used in a non-standard way.

42. **(F)** (p. 451) ***English/Rhetorical Skills/No Change.*** The original sentence is correct. A new topic is being introduced (i.e., the role of animals in the Mercury space program), so a new paragraph should be started. As for the other answer choices, they are all incorrect because they do not introduce a change in paragraphs to signal the change in topics.

43. **(A)** (p. 452) ***English/Rhetorical Skills/No Change.*** The original sentence is correct. In comparison with the other answer choices, it is the most concise and least awkward.

44. **(G)** (p. 452) ***English/Usage and Mechanics/Grammar and Usage/Sequence and Verb Tense.*** The original sentence is incorrect because it includes a verb tense error. The "delay" in picking up the spacecraft and the "leak" of water into the capsule belong to the same time frame. So, they should be expressed in the same verb tense. The "delay" is expressed in the past tense ("The pickup...was delayed"), so the "leak" should also be expressed in the past tense ("water leaked into the capsule"). For this reason, (G) is the correct answer choice.

45. **(A)** (p. 452) ***English/Usage and Mechanics/No Change.*** The original sentence is correct. As for the other answer choices, none of the other suggested positions for "unharmed" are idiomatic.

46. **(H)** (p. 452) ***English/Usage and Mechanics/Sentence Structure/Fragments.*** The original sentence is incorrect because "returning" is not a conjugated verb and, thus, cannot be the main verb of a sentence. (H) is the correct answer choice because it provides a conjugated verb that is consistent with the other past tense verbs in the paragraph. As for the other answer choices, (G) and (J) are incorrect because neither a present tense verb ("return") nor a future tense verb ("will return") are consistent with the past tense verbs in the paragraph.

47. (D) (p. 452) ***English/Usage and Mechanics/Grammar and Usage/Sequence and Verb Tense.*** The original sentence is incorrect because it includes a verb tense error. The question of how long an astronaut could tolerate weightlessness was unanswered at the time. So, a verb is required here that reflects that uncertainty. (D) is the correct answer choice because it provides the appropriate verb ("could tolerate"). As for the other answer choices, they are all incorrect because they do not supply a verb which suggests the degree of uncertainty required here.

48. (G) (p. 452) ***English/Usage and Mechanics/Grammar and Usage/Diction.*** The original sentence is incorrect because it includes language that is both superfluous and not idiomatic. Specifically, in the underlined portion, "like" is not grammatically required and also makes the sentence sound stilted. (G) is the correct answer choice because it eliminates this unnecessary word. As for the other answer choices, (H) and (J) are both incorrect because they introduce new language that is similarly superfluous and not idiomatic.

49. (B) (p. 453) ***English/Usage and Mechanics/Grammar and Usage/Verb Tense.*** The original sentence is incorrect because it includes a grammar error. Specifically, the underlined portion is an infinitive verb ("to have"). However, an infinitive verb cannot serve as the main verb for a clause. (B) is the correct answer choice because it supplies a main verb for the clause ("astronauts have...methods...") that is consistent with the verb tenses in the rest of the paragraph. As for the other answer choices, (C) is incorrect because the past perfect tense ("had had") suggests a sequence of events not supported by the meaning of the sentence. (D) is incorrect because the phrase "are sure to" is unnecessary before "have," and it creates a sentence that is not idiomatic.

50. (F) (p. 453) ***English/Rhetorical Skills/Strategy/Effective Concluding Sentence.*** Over the course of the passage, the author emphasizes the successes of the Mercury space program and downplays its failures. (F) is the correct answer choice because it best reflects the general theme and argument of the essay.

51. (A) (p. 453) ***English/Usage and Mechanics/No Change.*** The original sentence is correct. As for the other answer choices, (B) is incorrect for two reasons. First, it omits a required comma; specifically, both the beginning and the end of an aside ("in any broad and real way") must be marked with a comma. Second, the phrase "of help" is simply not idiomatic or grammatically correct. (C) is incorrect because it too omits the required comma that is mentioned above. Finally, (D) is incorrect because the phrase "of helping" is not idiomatic or grammatically correct.

52. (G) (p. 453) ***English/Rhetorical Skills/Style/Conciseness.*** The original sentence is incorrect because it is needlessly wordy. "And" and "also" mean the same thing, so it is redundant to include both. (G) is the correct answer choice because it replaces the redundant phrase ("and also") with "as well as," a phrase which means "and." As for the other answer choices, (H) is incorrect because "with" does not provide the meaning required in this context. (J) is incorrect because "as opposed to" signals a contrast between two ideas; however, the author does not intend to contrast two ideas.

53. (D) (p. 453) ***English/Usage and Mechanics/Grammar and Usage/Sequence and Verb Tense.*** The original sentence is incorrect because it includes a verb tense error. Earlier in the sentence, a simple past tense verb ("aided") is used. For the sake of consistency, another simple past tense verb ("emerged") should be used here. (D) is the correct answer choice because it is the only option that provides the appropriate verb form.

54. (G) (p. 453) ***English/Usage and Mechanics/Grammar and Usage/Subject-Verb Agreement.*** The original sentence is incorrect because it includes an error of subject-verb agreement. The plural subject of the sentence ("All aspects of medicine") requires a plural verb ("were enjoying"). (G) is the correct answer choice because it supplies the appropriate verb form. As for the other answer choices, (H) and (J) are incorrect because they do not supply plural verbs.

55. (B) (p. 454) ***English/Usage and Mechanics/Grammar and Usage/Diction.*** The original sentence is incorrect because it includes an expression that is not idiomatic. The correct idiom is "not only this but that." (B) is the correct answer choice because it provides the language needed to complete the idiom correctly. As for the other answer choices, (C) is incorrect because "not only this consequently that" is not a correct idiom. (D) supplies the correct idiom ("not only this but that"), but it includes a new error. Specifically, the comma after "but" is illogical and grammatically incorrect.

56. (H) (p. 454) ***English/Usage and Mechanics/Sentence Structure/Run-On Sentences.*** The original sentence is incorrect because it is a run-on sentence. A run-on sentence is two or more complete sentences joined together without the necessary punctuation or conjunctions. For example, the first clause ("With somewhat more luck, the doctor could select the proper treatment") is a complete sentence by itself. Similarly, the following clause ("he could also mitigate the symptoms...") is also a complete sentence by itself. Usually, there are two ways to fix a run-on sentence. First, it could be divided into two separate and correctly punctuated sentences. Second, it could be fixed by supplying the punctuation and conjunction needed between the two clauses. Since neither option is offered here, review the answer choices for the best solution possible. (H) is the correct answer choice because it rewrites the underlined portion so there is only one subject in the sentence ("the doctor"); as a result, the sentence is no longer a run-on sentence. As for the other answer choices, (G) is incorrect because "but" signals a contrast; however, a contrast is not then introduced. (J) is incorrect because it creates a sentence where the verbs are not parallel ("the doctor could select...and can mitigate...").

57. (A) (p. 454) ***English/Usage and Mechanics/No Change.*** The original sentence is correct. The subjunctive verb form ("be available") is the appropriate verb form in this context. As for the other answer choices, (B) is incorrect because the past tense ("was available") is not required here. (C) is incorrect for two reasons. First, a present tense verb ("is available") is inconsistent with the past tense verbs in the rest of the paragraph. Second, "for" does not have the same meaning as "to"; as a result, the sentence becomes grammatically incorrect. Finally, (D) is wrong because "as" does not have the same meaning as "to"; as a result, the sentence again becomes grammatically incorrect.

58. (H) (p. 454) ***English/Usage and Mechanics/Grammar and Usage/Sequence and Verb Tense.*** The original sentence is incorrect because a present tense verb ("presupposes") is not consistent with the past tense verbs in the rest of the paragraph. (H) is the correct answer choice because it provides the past tense verb required here. As for the other answer choices, (G) is incorrect because the passive verb form ("it is presupposed") is inconsistent with the past tense verbs in the rest of the paragraph and also creates a sentence that is grammatically incorrect. (J) is incorrect for two reasons. First, a present tense verb ("presuppose") is not consistent with the past tense verbs in the rest of the paragraph. Second, a plural subject ("they") is not consistent with the singular subject ("it") used in the rest of the paragraph.

59. (A) (p. 454) ***English/Rhetorical Skills/No Change.*** The original sentence is correct. A new topic is being introduced, so a new paragraph should be started. As for the other answer choices, (B) and (D) are incorrect because they do not introduce a change in paragraphs to signal the change in topics. (C) is incorrect because it results in a subordinate or dependent clause that does not have a supporting independent clause.

60. (J) (p. 455) ***English/Rhetorical Skills/Organization/Sentence-Level Structure.*** The first three paragraphs are a general discussion of medical advances during the nineteenth century. The last two paragraphs are about a specific example of this progress. As for the first sentence of the fourth paragraph, it serves as a transition from the general discussion to a more detailed look at the specific example. So, (J) is the correct answer choice.

61. (D) (p. 455) ***English/Rhetorical Skills/Style/Conciseness.*** The original sentence, (B), and (C) are all awkward and needlessly wordy. (B) and (C) also introduce grammatical errors into the sentence. (D) is the correct answer choice here because it concisely and clearly conveys the idea; in addition, it also does not introduce any new errors.

62. (F) (p. 455) ***English/Rhetorical Skills/No Change.*** The original sentence is correct. The underlined portion is clear, concise, and contains no errors. As for the other answer choices, (H) is incorrect because it is awkward and needlessly wordy. (G) and (J) are both wrong because they incorrectly start a new paragraph—a new paragraph should not be started because this portion of the essay continues to be about Dr. Beaumont. (J) is also incorrect for the same reason as (H).

63. (B) (p. 455) ***English/Usage and Mechanics/Sentence Structure/Problems of Coordination and Subordination.*** The original sentence is incorrect because it includes a logical error. The conjunction "but" should only be used to introduce an idea that modifies or contrasts with another idea. For example, "It was sunny, but clouds were approaching." In this sentence, though, "but" introduces a clause ("for the next 10 years he conducted hundreds of experiments…") that in no way modifies or contrasts with the earlier part of the sentence. So, it is a logical error to use "but" here. (B) is the correct answer because "and" correctly signals that the following clause continues and elaborates upon information from the earlier part of the sentence. As for the other answer choices, (C) is incorrect because it creates a run-on sentence. (D) is incorrect for the same reason as (A).

64. (J) (p. 456) ***English/Usage and Mechanics/Sentence Structure/Faulty Parallelism.*** The original sentence is incorrect because it includes an example of faulty parallelism. The forms of "demonstrate" and "describe" have the same function in this sentence, and they should be expressed in the same or parallel verb forms. "Demonstrating" is a present participle, so the present participle of "describe" must also be used. Therefore, (J) is the correct answer choice. As for the other answer choices, (G) and (H) are both wrong because they do not create the required parallelism.

65. (C) (p. 456) ***English/Usage and Mechanics/Grammar and Usage/Pronoun Usage.*** The original sentence is incorrect because it includes an error of pronoun usage. The subject of the sentence ("Newborn babies") is a plural noun. So, any pronoun used in its place must also be plural. (C) is the correct answer choice because it provides the appropriate plural pronoun. As for the other answer choices, (B) and (D) are incorrect for the same reason as the original. (B) and (D) are also incorrect because they introduce singular verbs ("was" and "is") that do not agree with the plural subject of the sentence.

66. (H) (p. 456) ***English/Usage and Mechanics/Grammar and Usage/Diction.*** The original sentence is incorrect because it is not idiomatic. The correct idiom is "endowed with." As for the other answer choices, (G) is incorrect because it is not idiomatic in any context. (J) is incorrect because, although the phrase "endowed by" is idiomatic, it is not appropriate in this context. It would be appropriate in other contexts (i.e., "…endowed by their Creator with certain inalienable rights"), but it is not correct here.

67. (A) (p.456) ***English/Usage and Mechanics/No Change.*** The original sentence is correct. As for the other answer choices, (B) and (C) both create run-on sentences. (D) is incorrect because it removes the subject ("This") of the second clause; as a result, the reader is left with a hybrid of the two sentences that is illogical, grammatically incorrect, and nearly impossible to understand.

68. (G) (p. 456) ***English/Usage and Mechanics/Sentence Structure/Problems of Coordination and Subordination.*** The original sentence is incorrect because it includes an error related to word choice. The author intends to say that an infant's cry causes two parallel reactions—a biological reaction as well as an emotional reaction. As the sentence is currently written, though, "including" illogically implies that the emotional reaction is a part or a component of the biological reaction. (G) is the correct answer choice because "and" is a conjunction that allows the reader to understand that the author is talking about two distinct and parallel reactions. Neither (H) nor (J) accomplishes the same task.

69. (D) (p. 457) ***English/Rhetorical Skills/Strategy/Effective Transitional Sentence.*** The original sentence is incorrect because "unfortunately" has a meaning that is not appropriate here. In the last sentence of this paragraph, the author intends to make a statement that summarizes the details provided earlier in the paragraph. The word "unfortunately" is only used when introducing information that contradicts or contrasts with earlier information. For example, "He is very handsome; unfortunately, he is also unfriendly." (D) is the correct answer choice here because the phrase "in fact" can be used to introduce an idea that complements or is related to earlier ideas. As for the other answer choices, (B) and (C) are incorrect for the same reason as the original.

70. (H) (p. 457) ***English/Rhetorical Skills/Style/Conciseness.*** The original sentence is incorrect because the underlined portion is needlessly wordy. (H) is the correct answer choice because it clearly and concisely summarizes the underlined portion in one word. As for the other answer choices, (G) is incorrect because a past tense verb ("possessed") is inconsistent with the present tense verbs in the paragraph. (J) is incorrect for the same reason as the original; in addition, a plural verb ("are") does not agree with the singular subject ("the human infant") of the sentence.

71. (C) (p. 457) ***English/Usage and Mechanics/Grammar and Usage/Verb Tense.*** The original sentence is incorrect because it includes a verb tense error. A present progressive verb ("are guaranteeing") is used to describe and emphasize activity happening at this very moment. However, the author is speaking in broad terms about babies in general; the author is not talking about a specific baby and what that particular baby is doing at this very moment. (C) is the correct answer choice here because a simple present tense verb ("guarantee") is consistent with the other simple present tense verbs in the rest of the paragraph. As for the other answer choices, (B) is incorrect because a past tense verb is not consistent with the present tense verbs in the rest of the paragraph. (D) is incorrect because a singular verb ("guarantees") does not agree with its plural subject ("attributes").

72. (G) (p. 457) ***English/Usage and Mechanics/Grammar and Usage/Diction.*** The original sentence is incorrect because it is not idiomatic. The correct idiom required here is "whether *this*... or whether *that*..." The phrase "whether or not" is another English idiom, but its use here is not appropriate. As for the other answer choices, (H) and (J) are both incorrect because "whether if" is not idiomatic in any context.

73. (D) (p. 457) ***English/Usage and Mechanics/Sentence Structure/Fragments.*** The original sentence is incorrect because the period after "infant" turns the first clause into a dependent clause without a supporting independent clause; in other words, it turns the dependent clause into a sentence fragment. (D) is the correct answer choice because it connects the initial dependent clause to a supporting independent clause, combines them in one sentence, and does so without introducing any grammatical or punctuation errors. As for the other answer choices, (B) and (C) are incorrect for the same reason as the original.

74. (H) (p. 458) ***English/Rhetorical Skills/Organization/Sentence-Level Structure.*** The final sentence summarizes the author's main point in an emphatic way. So, (H) is the correct answer choice. As for the other answer choices, they are all incorrect because they are simply not true.

75. (D) (p. 458) ***English/Rhetorical Skills/Organization/Passage-Level Structure.*** The passage is an argument. The author makes a claim (i.e., newborn infants are not passive creatures) and then supports the claim with several examples of how newborn infants actively engage with their worlds and their caregivers. So, (D) is the correct answer choice. As for the other answer choices, (A) is incorrect for two reasons: first, the author does not provide contrasting information in an attempt to disprove the main argument; second, the author does not supply any anecdotes or specific stories. (B) is incorrect because this essay is not a narrative or story filled with examples or anecdotes about specific newborn infants. Finally, (C) is incorrect because the author never uses statistics.

Section 2: Mathematics

1. **(D)** (p. 460) ***Mathematics/Arithmetic/Simple Manipulations.*** Since there is a restriction on the placement of the circle, the counting principal must be modified. Four shapes can be placed as normal, so the total number of arrangements including only these four shapes is $4! = 4 \cdot 3 \cdot 2 \cdot 1 = 24$. The restriction on the circle limits it to the 3 center places, so there are a total of $24 \cdot 3 = 72$ different arrangements of the five shapes that meet the stated condition.

2. **(K)** (p. 460) ***Mathematics/Algebra/Creating, Expressing, and Evaluating Algebraic Expressions and Functions.*** Let *J* be John's age and *P* be Pat's age. John is 3 times as old as Pat: $J = 3P$. In four years, John's age will be: $x = J + 4$. Substitute 3*P* for *J*: $x = 3P + 4 \Rightarrow x - 4 = 3P \Rightarrow \frac{x-4}{3} = P$.

   Alternatively, plug in numbers: if Pat is 9 years old, then John is 27 years old; in 4 years, John will be 31. "Test-the-test" by plugging 31 into the given formulas to produce an answer of 9, (K).

3. **(C)** (p. 461) ***Mathematics/Algebra/Manipulating Algebraic Expressions/Evaluating Expressions.*** This question really just tests fractions. If $\frac{3}{4}$ of *x* equals 36, then: $\frac{3}{4}x = 36 \Rightarrow x = 36 \cdot \frac{4}{3} = 48$ and $\frac{1}{3}x = \frac{1}{3}(48) = 16$.

4. **(J)** (p. 461) ***Mathematics/Geometry/Lines and Angles.*** The measure of the unlabeled angle in the top triangle is 90°. The angle vertically opposite it in the bottom triangle is also equal to 90°. Therefore, $x + y + 90° = 180°$ and $x + y = 90°$.

5. **(E)** (p. 461) ***Mathematics/Problem Solving and Advanced Arithmetic/Common Advanced Arithmetic Items/Properties of Numbers.*** There are two ways to attack this question. One is to reason as follows:

   A. $2+n$ cannot be a multiple of 3: since *n* is a multiple of 3, when $2+n$ is divided by 3 there will be a remainder of 2.
   B. $2-n$ cannot be a multiple of 3: since *n* is a multiple of 3, when $2-n$ is divided by 3 there will be a remainder of 1.
   C. $2n-1$ cannot be a multiple of 3: since *n* is a multiple of 3, 2*n* will also be a multiple of 3, and $2n-1$ cannot be a multiple of 3.
   D. $2n+1$ cannot be a multiple for the same reason that $2n-1$ cannot be a multiple of 3.
   E. $2n+3$ is a multiple of 3: 2*n* is a multiple of 3; 3 is a multiple of 3; thus, $2n+3$ is a multiple of 3.

   Alternatively, substitute an assumed value into the choices. For example, let $n = 3$:

   A. $2+n = 2+3 = 5$ ✗ (Not a multiple of 3)
   B. $2-n = 2-3 = -1$ ✗ (Not a multiple of 3)
   C. $2n-1 = 2(3)-1 = 6-1 = 5$ ✗ (Not a multiple of 3)
   D. $2n+1 = 2(3)+1 = 6+1 = 7$ ✗ (Not a multiple of 3)
   E. $2n+3 = 2(3)+3 = 6+3 = 9$ ✓ (A multiple of 3)

6. **(K)** (p. 461) ***Mathematics/Problem Solving and Advanced Arithmetic/Common Problem Solving Items/Ratios.*** A ratio is just another way of writing a fraction. Simply inspect each of the answer choices. As for (F), $\left(\frac{1}{5}\right)^2$ is equal to $\frac{1}{25}$, and both 1 and 25 are whole numbers. Choice (G) is not the

correct because 5% can be written as $\frac{5}{100}$, or $\frac{1}{20}$, which is a ratio of two whole numbers. As for (J), 0.25 is equal to $\frac{1}{4}$, the ratio of two whole numbers. As for (H), $\frac{1}{5}$ is the ratio of 1 to 5, so (H) is a ratio of two whole numbers. Only (K) is not a ratio of two whole numbers.

7. **(B)** (p. 462) ***Mathematics/Geometry/Rectangles and Squares.*** Let L equal the length and W equal the width of each playing card. The area of the large rectangle is equal to the sum of the areas of the nine playing cards: $\text{area}_{\text{rectangle}} = 9(\text{area}_{\text{card}}) \Rightarrow 180 = 9(LW) \Rightarrow LW = 20$. Both $5W$ and $4L$ are equal to the length of the large rectangle, and $L+W$ is equal to its width: $\text{area}_{\text{rectangle}} = (\text{length}_{\text{rectangle}})(\text{width}_{\text{rectangle}}) \Rightarrow 180 = (5W)(L+W) = 5LW + 5W^2 \Rightarrow LW + W^2 = 36 \Rightarrow W^2 = 36 - 20 \Rightarrow W = \sqrt{16} \Rightarrow W = 4$. Since $5W = 4L$, $L = 5$. Therefore, the perimeter of the large rectangle is: $2[5W + (L+W)] = 2(20+9) = 58$.

8. **(G)** (p. 462) ***Mathematics/Algebra/Solving Algebraic Equations or Inequalities with One Variable.*** Let t be the train's scheduled arrival time. If the train travels at 40 mph, the journey takes $t + \frac{10}{60} = t + \frac{1}{6}$ hours; if it travels at 30 mph, the journey takes $t + \frac{16}{60} = t + \frac{4}{15}$ hours. Since the distance traveled is the same in each case, write an equation equating the two distances, where the distances are written in terms of the travel time and the train speed. When formulating the equation, make sure that the units on each side of the equality are equivalent and that the final answer will be in miles. $\left(\frac{40 \text{ miles}}{\text{hour}}\right)\left(t + \frac{1}{6} \text{ hour}\right) = \left(\frac{30 \text{ miles}}{\text{hour}}\right)\left(t + \frac{4}{15} \text{ hour}\right) \Rightarrow 40t + \frac{40}{6} = 30t + \frac{30 \cdot 4}{15} \Rightarrow$ $10t = \frac{120}{15} - \frac{40}{6} = 1\frac{1}{3} \text{ hours} = 80 \text{ minutes} \Rightarrow t = 8 \text{ minutes}$. Therefore, the distance between the two towns is: $d = \left(\frac{40 \text{ miles}}{\text{hour}}\right)\left(\frac{8}{60} \text{ hour} + \frac{10}{60} \text{ hour}\right) = (40 \text{ miles})\left(\frac{18}{60}\right) = 12 \text{ miles}$.

9. **(D)** (p. 462) ***Mathematics/Algebra/Manipulating Algebraic Expressions/Factoring Expressions.*** The coefficients are 3, 6, and 2: 1 is the only common factor of those numbers. The smallest term containing the variable *x* is simply *x*. The same is true for the terms containing *y* and *z*. Therefore, the greatest common factor is *xyz*.

10. **(G)** (p. 462) ***Mathematics/Problem Solving and Advanced Arithmetic/Common Advanced Arithmetic Items/Properties of Numbers.*** The sum of $3k$, $4k$, $5k$, $6k$, and $7k$ is $25k$, which is divisible by 7 if the value of k is divisible by 7. If, however, the coefficient of k were divisible by 7, then that number would be divisible by 7 regardless of the value of k. Dropping the term $4k$ from the group, the sum of the remaining terms is $21k$. Since 21 is divisible by 7, $21k$ will be divisible by 7, regardless of the value of k.

11. **(B)** (p. 463) ***Mathematics/Arithmetic/Complicated Manipulations/Decimal-Fraction Equivalents.*** Use a benchmark or approximate to eliminate the wrong answer choices. First, eliminate (E): $\frac{1}{2}$ is more than $\frac{3}{8}$. Next, eliminate (A): $\frac{3}{15}$ is equal to $\frac{1}{3}$, so $\frac{3}{16}$ is smaller than $\frac{1}{3}$. As for (C), $\frac{9}{24}$ is equal to $\frac{3}{8}$,

not less than $\frac{3}{8}$. As for (D), $\frac{5}{12}$ is equal to $\frac{10}{24}$, and $\frac{3}{8}$ is equal to $\frac{9}{24}$. Only (B) is a possible value for *x*: $\frac{17}{48}$ is close to and slightly less than $\frac{18}{48}=\frac{3}{8}$.

Alternatively, express each fraction as a decimal and compare the answer choices to find a value between $\frac{1}{3}\approx 0.333$ and $\frac{3}{8}=0.375$:

A. $\frac{3}{16}=0.1875$

B. $\frac{17}{48}\approx 0.3542$

C. $\frac{9}{24}=0.375$

D. $\frac{5}{12}\approx 0.4167$

E. $\frac{1}{2}=0.5$

Only (B) is between $\frac{1}{3}$ (approximately 0.333) and $\frac{3}{8}$ (0.375).

12. (G) (p. 463) ***Mathematics/Algebra/Manipulating Algebraic Expressions/Factoring Expressions.*** Simply factor the expression as the difference of two squares: $x^2 - y^2 = (x+y)(x-y) = 3$. Since $x - y = 3$, then $(x+y)(3) = 3 \Rightarrow x+y=1$.

13. (E) (p. 463) ***Mathematics/Problem Solving and Advanced Arithmetic/Common Advanced Arithmetic Items/Properties of Numbers.*** As for (A), whether $n+1$ is odd or even will depend on whether *n* is odd or even. The same is true for (B) and (C) since whether 3*n* is odd or even will depend on whether *n* is odd or even. As for (D), n^2 will be odd or even depending on whether *n* is odd or even. However, (E) is even regardless of whether *n* is odd or even: n^2+n can be factored as $n(n+1)$, and since either *n* or $n+1$ is even, the product must be even.

14. (H) (p. 463) ***Mathematics/Geometry/Complex Figures* and *Rectangles and Squares* and *Circles.*** For any square with a side of *x*, the diagonal of that square is equal to $x\sqrt{2}$. Since the square has an area of 16, it has a side of 4 and a diagonal of $4\sqrt{2}$. The diagonal of the square is also the diameter of the circle. Therefore, the circle has a diameter of $4\sqrt{2}$ and a radius of $2\sqrt{2}$. Finally, a circle with a radius of length $2\sqrt{2}$ has an area of $\pi r^2 = \pi\left(2\sqrt{2}\right)^2 = 8\pi$.

15. (C) (p. 464) ***Mathematics/Problem Solving and Advanced Arithmetic/Common Problem Solving Items/Percents.*** First, calculate the sale price of the CD player that Ellen bought: $\$120-(25\%\text{ of }\$120) = \$120-(0.25\bullet\$120)=\$120-\$30=\$90$. Next, calculate the sales tax: $\text{tax}=8\%\text{ of }\$90=0.08\bullet\$90=\$7.20$. Therefore, the total price was $\$90+\$7.20=\$97.20$.

16. (G) (p. 464) ***Mathematics/Problem Solving and Advanced Arithmetic/Complicated Problem Solving Items* and *Common Problem Solving Items/Percents.*** Use the "is-over-of" equation. The "of," which is the denominator of the fraction, is the mixture. There is a total of $2.5+12.5=15$ kilograms of mixture.

The word "is," which is the numerator of the fraction, is the 2.5 kilograms of gravel. Thus:
$\frac{\text{is}}{\text{of}}=\frac{\%}{100}\Rightarrow\frac{2.5}{15}=\frac{\%}{100}\Rightarrow\frac{250}{15}=16\frac{2}{3}\%$.

17. **(D)** (p. 464) ***Mathematics/Geometry/Triangles/Properties of Triangles.*** The triangle has sides of 6, 8, and 10 (multiples of 3, 4, and 5). Therefore, the triangle is a right triangle. The sides of 6 and 8 form the right angle, so they can be used as altitude and base for finding the area:

$\text{area}_{\text{triangle}}=\frac{1}{2}\bullet\text{altitude}\bullet\text{base}=\frac{1}{2}\bullet 6\bullet 8=24$.

18. **(F)** (p. 465) ***Mathematics/Problem Solving and Advanced Arithmetic/Common Problem Solving Items/Proportions and Direct-Inverse Variation.*** First, determine the amount of fuel used by Motorcycle A using a direct proportion:
$\frac{\text{Fuel Used } X}{\text{Fuel Used } Y}=\frac{\text{Kilometers Driven } X}{\text{Kilometers Driven } Y}\Rightarrow\frac{1}{x}=\frac{40}{300}\Rightarrow 40x=300\Rightarrow x=7.5$. Thus, Motorcycle A uses 7.5 liters of fuel for the 300-kilometer trip. Now, do the same for Motorcycle B:
$\frac{1}{x}=\frac{50}{300}\Rightarrow 50x=300\Rightarrow x=6$. Therefore, Motorcycle B uses 6 liters. Since Motorcycle A uses

$7.5-6=1.5$ liters more than Motorcycle B, the fuel for Motorcycle A costs $1.5 \text{ liters}\bullet\frac{\$2}{\text{liter}}=\$3$ more.

19. **(B)** (p. 465) ***Mathematics/Algebra/Creating, Expressing, and Evaluating Algebraic Expressions and Functions/Function Notation.*** First, substitute 3 for x in $f(x)$: $f(3)=3^2-2(3)+1=9-6+1=4$. Now, substitute 4 for x in $f(x)$: $f(4)=4^2-2(4)+1=16-8+1=9$. Therefore, $f(f(3))=9$.

20. **(F)** (p. 465) ***Mathematics/Algebra/Manipulating Algebraic Expressions/Factoring Expressions.***
$\frac{N!}{(N-2)!}=\frac{N(N-1)(N-2)(N-3)(N-4)...[N-(N-1)]}{(N-2)(N-3)(N-4)...[N-(N-1)]}$. Canceling like factors in the numerator and the denominator leaves only $\frac{N(N-1)}{1}=N(N-1)=N^2-N$.

21. **(E)** (p. 465) ***Mathematics/Algebra/Creating, Expressing, and Evaluating Algebraic Expressions and Functions.*** The formula will be x, the cost for the first ounce, plus some expression to represent the additional postage for each additional ounce over the first ounce. The postage for the additional weight is y cents per ounce, and the additional weight is w minus the first ounce, or $w-1$. Therefore, the additional postage is $y(w-1)$, and the total postage is $x+y(w-1)$.

Alternatively, assume some numbers. For ease of calculations, assume that the first ounce costs 1 cent and every additional ounce is 2 cents. If $x=1$ and $y=2$, then a letter of, for example, 3 ounces ($w=3$) will cost $1+2(2)=5$ cents. Substitute these values for x, y, and w into the answer choices and the correct choice will return the value 5:

A. $w(x+y)=3(1+2)=3(3)=9$ ✗
B. $x(w-y)=1(3-2)=1(1)=1$ ✗
C. $x(x-1)+y(w-1)=1(1-1)+2(3-1)=1(0)+2(2)=4$ ✗
D. $x+wy=1+3(2)=7$ ✗
E. $x+y(w-1)=1+2(3-1)=1+2(2)=5$ ✓

22. **(F)** (p. 466) ***Mathematics/Problem Solving and Advanced Arithmetic/Common Advanced Arithmetic Items/Absolute Value.*** Apply the absolute value function: $|-3|=3$, $|2|=2$, and $\left|-\frac{1}{2}\right|=\frac{1}{2}$.

Therefore, $|-3|\bullet|2|\bullet\left|-\frac{1}{2}\right|+(-4)=3\bullet2\bullet\frac{1}{2}-4=3-4=-1$.

23. **(C)** (p. 466) ***Mathematics/Geometry/Complex Figures*** and ***Rectangles and Squares*** and ***Circles.*** The side of the square is also the radius of the circle. Since the square has an area of 2, $s\bullet s=2\Rightarrow s^2=2\Rightarrow s=\sqrt{2}$, and $\sqrt{2}$ is the radius of the circle. Therefore, the area of the circle is $\pi r^2=\pi\left(\sqrt{2}\right)^2=2\pi$.

24. **(G)** (p. 466) ***Mathematics/Problem Solving and Advanced Arithmetic/Common Advanced Arithmetic Items/Properties of Numbers.*** Test each statement. As for statement (I), the product of 2 (the first prime number) and any other number must be even. Thus, (I) is not part of the correct answer. As for (II), the sum of two prime numbers might be odd, (e.g., $2+3=5$), but the sum of two prime numbers might also be even, (e.g., $3+5=8$). As for (III), however, the product of two odd numbers is necessarily odd.

25. **(A)** (p. 467) ***Mathematics/Coordinate Geometry/The Coordinate System.*** The coordinates establish that this figure is a rectangle. The width of the rectangle is *a*, and the length is $b-a$. Therefore, the area is $a(b-a)$.

Alternatively, "test-the-test," assuming that $a=2$ and $b=4$. The rectangle has a width of 2, a length of $4-2=2$, and an area of $2\bullet2=4$. Substitute 2 for *a* and 4 for *b* into the answer choices and the correct formula will yield 4.

26. **(H)** (p. 467) ***Mathematics/Arithmetic/Simple Manipulations.*** Perform the indicated operations: $\sqrt{(43-7)(29+7)}-\sqrt{(36)(36)}-36$.

27. **(A)** (p. 467) ***Mathematics/Problem Solving and Advanced Arithmetic/Common Problem Solving Items/Proportions and Direct-Inverse Variation.*** Set up a direct proportion and solve for the unknown value: $\frac{\text{Cement } X}{\text{Cement } Y}=\frac{\text{Grit } X}{\text{Grit } Y}\Rightarrow\frac{4}{50}=\frac{20}{x}\Rightarrow 4x=(20)(50)\Rightarrow x=\frac{(20)(50)}{4}=250$.

28. **(H)** (p. 468) ***Mathematics/Geometry/Lines and Angles.*** Label the other two angles in the triangle:

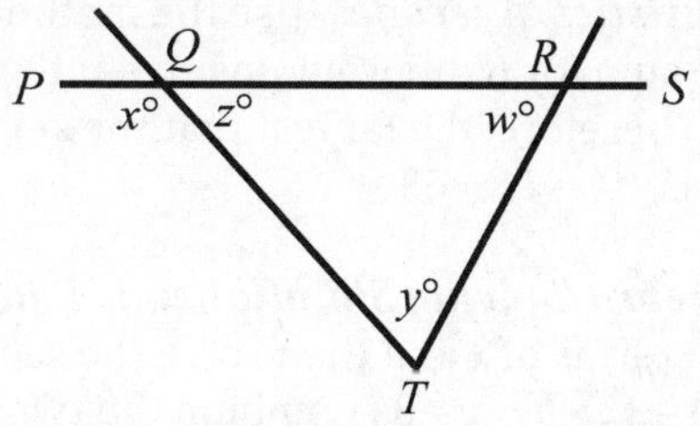

Therefore, $x+z=180\Rightarrow150+z=180\Rightarrow z=30$. Furthermore, since $\overline{QT}=\overline{QR}$, $y=w$, and $x+y+z=180\Rightarrow30+y+y=180\Rightarrow2y=150\Rightarrow y=75$.

29. (C) (p. 468) ***Mathematics/Algebra/Solving Algebraic Equations with Two Variables.*** There is only one equation but two variables, so *x* and *y* cannot be solved for individually. Instead, look for a way to rewrite the first equation to give the information needed: $\frac{x}{y}=-1 \Rightarrow x=-y \Rightarrow x+y=0$.

30. (K) (p. 468) ***Mathematics/Data Interpretation/Tables*** **and** ***Problem Solving and Advanced Arithmetic/Common Advanced Arithmetic Items/Decimal-Fraction Equivalents.*** Set up the cost per yard of each fabric as a decimal and compare the decimals directly:

F. $\frac{\$8}{3\text{ yd.}} \approx \$2.67/\text{yd.}$

G. $\frac{\$6}{2\text{ yd.}} = \$3/\text{yd.}$

H. $\frac{\$9}{4\text{ yd.}} = \$2.25/\text{yd.}$

J. $\frac{\$7}{5\text{ yd.}} = \$1.4/\text{yd.}$

K. $\frac{\$10}{8\text{ yd.}} = \$1.25/\text{yd.}$

Therefore, the (K) fabric costs the least per yard.

31. (A) (p. 469) ***Mathematics/Geometry/Lines and Angles.*** Since $\overline{PQ} \parallel \overline{ST}$, we know $x=y$ because the alternate interior angles of parallel lines are equal. Furthermore, since the sum of angles in ΔPRQ is 180°, $75+65+x+x=180 \Rightarrow 2x+140=180 \Rightarrow 2x=40 \Rightarrow x=20$. Therefore, $y=20$.

32. (H) (p. 469) ***Mathematics/Arithmetic/Complicated Manipulations/Simplifying.*** Perform the indicated operations: $\frac{10^3(10^5+10^5)}{10^4}=\frac{10^5+10^5}{10}=10^4+10^4=2(10^4)$.

33. (D) (p. 469) ***Mathematics/Algebra/Solving Quadratic Equations and Relations.*** Factor and solve for *x*: $x^2-5x+4=0 \Rightarrow (x-4)(x-1)=0$. So, either $x-4=0$ and $x=4$, or $x-1=0$ and $x=1$.

Alternatively, substitute the values in the choices back into the equation to find the set that works.

34. (K) (p. 470) ***Mathematics/Statistics/Averages.*** Use the method for finding the missing elements of an average. The smallest possible sum for 6 different positive integers is $1+2+3+4+5+6=21$. The sum of all 7 integers is $7 \cdot 12=84$. Therefore, the largest that the seventh number could be (with the average of the seven numbers still 12) is $84-21=63$.

35. (E) (p.470) ***Mathematics/Algebra/Solving Simultaneous Equations.*** To find *b* in terms of *x* and *y*, solve the first equation for *b* in terms of *x* and then solve the second equation for *b* in terms of *y*: $x=b+4 \Rightarrow b=x-4$ and $y=b-3 \Rightarrow b=y+3$. Combine the two equations by adding:

$$\begin{array}{l} b=x-4 \\ +\ b=y+3 \\ \hline 2b=x+y-1 \Rightarrow b=\frac{x+y-1}{2} \end{array}$$

Alternatively, substitute some numbers. Let $b=1$. Therefore, $x=1+4=5$, and $y=1-3=-2$. Substitute 5 for *x* and -2 for *y* in the answer choices. The correct choice will yield the value 1.

36. **(F)** (p. 470) ***Mathematics/Problem Solving and Advanced Arithmetic/Common Advanced Arithmetic Items/Properties of Numbers.*** Since $z=5x=3y$, and *x*, *y*, and *z* are integers, *z* is a multiple of both 3 and 5, so *z* is evenly divisible by 5, (G), 3, (H), and 15, (J). And since $5x=3y$, and *x* and *y* are integers, *x* is a multiple of 3 (and evenly divisible by 3), (K). However, while *z* is divisible by both *x* and *y* individually, *z* is not necessarily divisible by the product of *x* and *y*.

Alternatively, substitute some numbers. The most natural assumption is to let *z* equal 15, so $x=3$ and $y=5$. However, on that assumption, every answer choice is an integer. Try the next multiple of 15. Let *z* equal 30, so $x=6$ and $y = 10$. Only (F) is no longer an integer: $30 \div (6 \bullet 10)=\frac{1}{2}$.

37. **(B)** (p. 470) ***Mathematics/Geometry/Rectangles and Squares.*** Use the equation for the area of a rectangle: $\text{area}_{\text{rectangle}}=\text{width} \bullet \text{length} \Rightarrow 48x^2=w(24x) \Rightarrow w=\frac{48x^2}{24x}=2x$.

Alternatively, substitute some numbers, such as $x=2$. The area of the rectangle is $48(2^2)=48(4)=192$, and the length is 48. And 48 times the width is equal to 192, so the width is $192 \div 48=4$. Therefore, if $x=2$, the correct choice yields the value 4. Only (B) works.

38. **(K)** (p. 471) ***Mathematics/Algebra/Manipulating Algebraic Expressions/Basic Algebraic Manipulations.*** Rewrite the equation: $x=\frac{1}{y+1} \Rightarrow x(y+1)=1 \Rightarrow y+1=\frac{1}{x} \Rightarrow y=\frac{1}{x}-1 \Rightarrow y=\frac{1-x}{x}$.

39. **(B)** (p. 471) ***Mathematics/Coordinate Geometry/The Coordinate System.*** The length of the base of the triangle is $4x-x=3x$, and the length of the altitude is $3x-0=3x$. Use the formula for finding the area of a triangle to determine *x*: $\frac{1}{2}(3x)(3x)=54 \Rightarrow (3x)(3x)=108 \Rightarrow 9x^2=108 \Rightarrow x^2=12 \Rightarrow x=\sqrt{12}=2\sqrt{3}$.

40. **(K)** (p. 471) ***Mathematics/Probability.*** This question is a little tricky, but it does not require advanced mathematics. If the room were completely dark, what is the worst thing that might happen? You might happen to pull all the blue and white socks first (the two colors with the largest number of socks). So you might have pulled 16 socks. Now, the only color left is the color (green) with the smallest number of socks. Then you would need to pull 2 of the only 4 socks left. So, on the worst assumption, $16+2=18$ picks will *guarantee* you a pair of each color.

41. **(C)** (p. 472) ***Mathematics/Geometry/Complex Figures*** **and** ***Circles*** **and** ***Lines and Angles.*** The question supplies the area of the shaded part of the figure, which is a portion of the circle. First, find what fraction of the circle is shaded. Then, use that value in order to determine the value of the unshaded angle at the center of the circle. The area of the entire circle is $\pi r^2=\pi(4^2)=16\pi$. $\frac{14\pi}{16\pi}=\frac{7}{8}$ of the circle is shaded, so $\frac{1}{8}$ of the circle is unshaded. Therefore, the unshaded angle at the center of the circle is $\frac{1}{8}$ of $360°=45°$. Now, find *x*: $x+45+90=180 \Rightarrow x+135=180 \Rightarrow x=45$.

42. **(J)** (p. 472) ***Mathematics/Geometry/Circles*** **and** ***Triangles/45°-45°-90° Triangles.*** This is a composite figure, so redefine one figure in terms of another. The diameter of the smaller circle is equal to the side of the square. The diagonal of the square is the diameter of the larger circle. First, let *r* be the radius of the smaller circle, so the smaller circle has an area of πr^2. The diameter of the smaller circle is $2r$, which is also the side of the square:

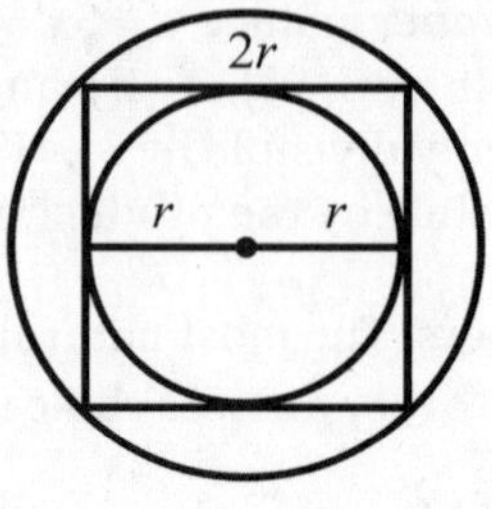

The diagonal of the square creates a 45°-45°-90° triangle with the sides of the square, so the hypotenuse of that triangle is equal to $2r \cdot \sqrt{2} = 2\sqrt{2}r$. Thus, the larger circle has a radius of $2\sqrt{2}r \div 2 = \sqrt{2}r$, and an area of $\pi\left(\sqrt{2}r\right)^2 = 2\pi r^2$. Therefore, the ratio of the area of the larger circle to the area of the smaller circle is $2\pi r^2 : \pi r^2 = 2:1$.

43. (D) (p. 472) ***Mathematics/Arithmetic/Simple Manipulations.*** Just perform the indicated operations:

$2^0 = 1$

$2^3 = 8$

$2^{-2} = \frac{1}{2^2} = \frac{1}{4}$

$1 + 8 - \frac{1}{4} = 8\frac{3}{4}$

44. (J) (p. 473) ***Mathematics/Coordinate Geometry/Graphs of Quadratic Equations and Relations.*** Since the axis of symmetry of the parabola is given by the equation $x = 0$, the parabola is symmetric about the *y*-axis. The point symmetric to the point with coordinates (–1,–2) will have the same *y*-coordinate, and the *x*-coordinate of the point will be the same distance from the *y*-axis but in a positive direction: $(1,-2)$. It might be easier to find the solution with a sketched graph of the equation:

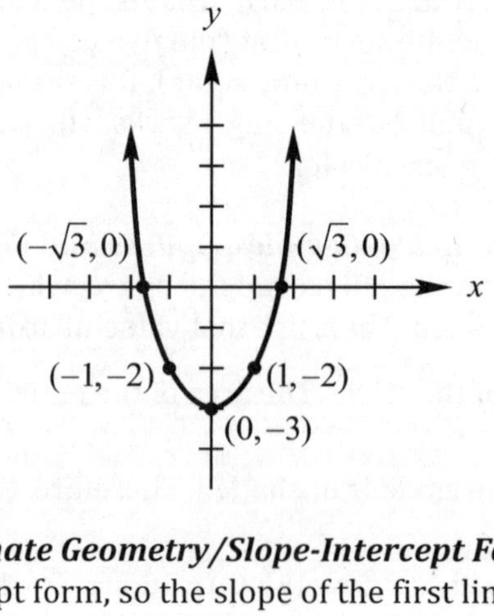

45. (C) (p. 473) ***Mathematics/Coordinate Geometry/Slope-Intercept Form of a Linear Equation.*** Each equation is written in slope-intercept form, so the slope of the first line is m_1, and the slope of the second line is m_2. If two lines in the coordinate plane are perpendicular to each other, then the product of their slopes is -1. Thus, $m_1 m_2 = -1$.

46. (K) (p. 473) ***Mathematics/Geometry/Complex Figures*** **and** ***Triangles/Properties of Triangles*** **and** ***Rectangles and Squares.*** Draw some additional lines to carve the figure into more familiar shapes, and use the Pythagorean theorem to determine the length of the shared third side of the two small triangles: $a^2+8^2=10^2 \Rightarrow a^2+64=100 \Rightarrow a^2=36 \Rightarrow a=6$. Note that this can also be immediately deduced by recognizing the triangles as Pythagorean triangles.

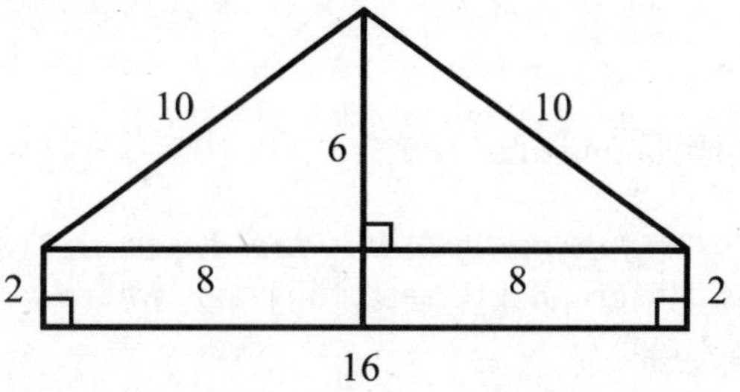

The area of the large rectangle is $16 \bullet 2 = 32$. The total area of the large triangle is $\frac{1}{2} \bullet 6 \bullet 16 = 48$. Therefore, the area of the composite figure is $32 + 48 = 80$.

47. (A) (p. 474) ***Mathematics/Algebra/Manipulating Algebraic Expressions/Evaluating Expressions.*** Rationalize the denominator: $\frac{\sqrt{x}}{2\sqrt{x}-\sqrt{y}} \bullet \frac{2\sqrt{x}+\sqrt{y}}{2\sqrt{x}+\sqrt{y}} = \frac{2x+\sqrt{xy}}{4x+2\sqrt{xy}-2\sqrt{xy}-y} = \frac{2x+\sqrt{xy}}{4x-y}$.

Alternatively, assume some values for *x* and *y*. Since the problem involves square roots, pick a couple of perfect squares, e.g., $x=9$ and $y=4$. The expression in the question stem becomes: $\frac{\sqrt{9}}{2\sqrt{9}-\sqrt{4}} = \frac{3}{2(3)-2} = \frac{3}{4}$. Now, substitute 9 for *x* and 4 for *y* into the answer choices. The correct choice will generate the value $\frac{3}{4}$:

A. $\frac{2x+\sqrt{xy}}{4x-y} = \frac{2(9)+\sqrt{(9)(4)}}{4(9)-4} = \frac{18+6}{32} = \frac{24}{32} = \frac{3}{4}$ ✓

B. $\frac{4x+\sqrt{xy}}{4x-y} = \frac{4(9)+\sqrt{(9)(4)}}{4(9)-4} = \frac{36+6}{36-4} = \frac{42}{32}$ ✗

C. $\frac{2\sqrt{x}+\sqrt{y}}{4xy} = \frac{2\sqrt{9}+\sqrt{4}}{4(9)(4)} = \frac{2(3)+2}{144} = \frac{8}{144}$ ✗

D. $\frac{2\sqrt{x}+\sqrt{xy}}{2x-y} = \frac{2\sqrt{9}+\sqrt{(9)(4)}}{2(9)-4} = \frac{6+6}{14} = \frac{12}{14}$ ✗

E. $\frac{2\sqrt{x}-\sqrt{y}}{2} = \frac{2\sqrt{9}-\sqrt{4}}{2} = \frac{2(3)-2}{2} = \frac{4}{2} = 2$ ✗

48. (H) (p. 474) ***Mathematics/Geometry/Lines and Angles.*** Since vertical angles are equal, the figure becomes:

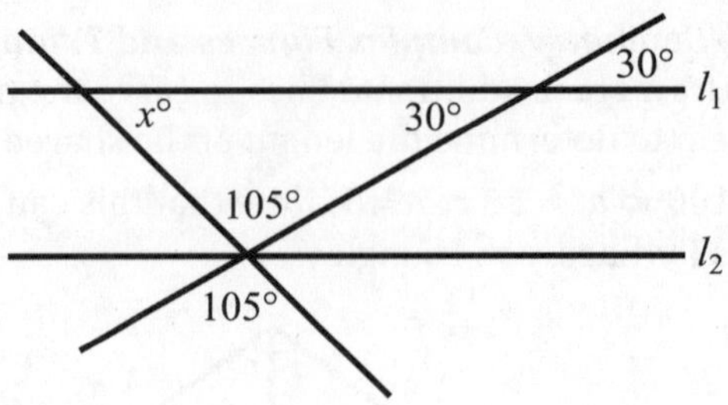

And the interior angles of a triangle total 180°, so $30+105+x=180 \Rightarrow x=45$.

49. (D) (p. 474) ***Mathematics/Trigonometry/Additional Topics in Trigonometry/Graphs of Trigonometric Functions.*** The graph intersects the *y*-axis where $x=0$: $y=2\cos(2 \cdot 0)+2=2\cos 0+2$. Since $\cos 0=1$, $y=2(1)+2=4$.

50. (G) (p. 475) ***Mathematics/Geometry/Complex Figures* and *Rectangles and Squares* and *Circles.*** The shaded area is equal to the whole square minus the four circles. On the assumption that each circle has a radius of *r*, the side of the square must be 4*r*, and the area of the square is $4r \cdot 4r=16r^2$. Furthermore, each circle with radius *r* has an area of πr^2, so the shaded area is $16r^2-4\pi r^2$. And the ratio of the shaded area to the area of the square is $\frac{16r^2-4\pi r^2}{16r^2}=\frac{4r^2(4-\pi)}{16r^2}=\frac{4-\pi}{4}$.

Note that a little common sense goes a long way when applied to the answer choices. Since π is less than 4, (F) is a negative number and is therefore impossible. Both (J) and (K) are greater than 1, asserting that the shaded area is larger than the square, an equally absurd conclusion. Now, there are only two answer choices remaining: (G) asserts that the shaded area is a little less than one-quarter of the square, and (H) asserts that the shaded area is about three-quarters of the square. After careful inspection of the figure, it is safe to assume that (G) is correct.

51. (C) (p.475) ***Mathematics/Trigonometry/Manipulating Trigonometric Functions/Basic Operations.*** The Pythagorean trigonometric identity is $\sin^2\theta+\cos^2\theta=1$. Therefore, $\frac{\sin^2\theta+\cos^2\theta}{\sin\theta}=\frac{1}{\sin\theta}$. And the reciprocal identity for the sine function is the cosecant function: $\frac{1}{\sin\theta}=\csc\theta$.

52. (G) (p. 476) ***Mathematics/Trigonometry/Definitions of the Six Trigonometric Functions.*** Since $\tan\theta=\frac{\text{side opposite }\theta}{\text{side adjacent to }\theta}$, $\tan 55°=\frac{6}{AC} \Rightarrow 1.4 \approx \frac{6}{AC} \Rightarrow \overline{AC} \approx \frac{6}{1.4} \approx 4.28$.

53. (D) (p. 476) ***Mathematics/Algebra/Manipulating Algebraic Expressions/Evaluating Expressions.*** The expression is undefined for every value of *x* that makes the denominator equal to zero. The denominator is zero if either $x-1$ or $x+2$ equals zero. Therefore, the expression is undefined for $x=1$ or $x=-2$.

54. (K) (p. 476) ***Mathematics/Algebra/Solving Simultaneous Equations.*** Since $x+y \le 6$, *y* will have its maximum value when *x* has its minimum value. The minimum value of *x* is 0; the maximum value of *y* is 6. Therefore, the minimum value for 3*y* is $3(6)=18$.

Alternatively, test the answer choices. Since the question asks for the maximum value of y, start with the largest choice: 18. If $3y = 18$, then $y = 6$. And $x + y \le 6 \Rightarrow x + 6 \le 6 \Rightarrow x \le 0$. Since x can be 0, $y = 6$ satisfies the system of inequalities.

55. (C) (p. 477) ***Mathematics/Coordinate Geometry/The Coordinate System.*** Find the corresponding values for y when $x = -1$, 0, and 1:

$$y(-1) = \left|(-1)^2 - 3\right| = |1 - 3| = |-2| = 2$$

$$y(0) = \left|(0)^2 - 3\right| = |-3| = 3$$

$$y(1) = \left|(1)^2 - 3\right| = |1 - 3| = |-2| = 2$$

Only (C) shows the correct plotting of the points (–1,2), (0,3), and (1,2).

56. (G) (p. 478) ***Mathematics/Coordinate Geometry/Graphs of Linear Equations.*** Each answer choice is an equation of a line in slope-intercept form ($y = mx + b$), and each has a different slope. Calculate the slope of the line shown in the graph: $m = \frac{(-2)-(4)}{(2)-(-1)} = \frac{-6}{3} = -2$. Only (G) has the correct slope.

57. (A) (p. 478) ***Mathematics/Algebra/Solving Quadratic Equations and Relations.*** The best approach to solving this item is to see that the roots are expressed in a form suggestive of the quadratic formula, the solution to the quadratic equation $ax^2 + bx + c$: $x = \frac{-b \pm \sqrt{b^2 - 4ac}}{2a}$. Thus, $-b = -3$, so $b = 3$, which eliminates (B) and (D). Next, $2a = 2$, so $a = 1$, which eliminates (E). Finally, $b^2 - 4ac = 5$. Since $b = 3$ and $a = 1$, $b^2 - 4ac = 5 \Rightarrow (3)^2 - 4(1)(c) = 5 \Rightarrow 9 - 4c = 5 \Rightarrow 4c = 4 \Rightarrow c = 1$. Thus, the equation is $x^2 + 3x + 1 = 0$.

58. (F) (p. 478) ***Mathematics/Algebra/Creating, Expressing, and Evaluating Algebraic Expressions and Functions/Concepts of Domain and Range.*** A function is a relationship such that each element of the domain is paired with one and only one element in the range. The domain is the set of all possibilities for the first coordinate. In the relationship given in the question stem, two pairs—(0,3) and (0,5)—have the same first coordinate. So, one element of the domain, 0, is paired with two different elements in the range: 3 and 5. We need to eliminate either (0,3) or (0,5). By dropping (0,3), the element, 0, is paired only with 5, and the set becomes a function.

59. (E) (p. 479) ***Mathematics/Geometry/Complex Figures* and *30°-60°-90° Triangles* and *Rectangles and Squares.*** Consider the trapezoid as a composite figure. Draw a line from point B perpendicular to $\overline{CD}$: the trapezoid is a combination of a right triangle and a rectangle. Since the triangle has degree measures of 30, 60, and 90, the side opposite the 30° angle has a length half that of the hypotenuse, or a length of 4. Thus, the rectangle has sides of 4 and 9 and an area of 36. Then, the side of the triangle opposite the 60° angle has a length equal to $\frac{\sqrt{3}}{2}$ times the hypotenuse, or $4\sqrt{3}$. The area of the triangle is $\frac{ab}{2} = \frac{(4)(4\sqrt{3})}{2} = 8\sqrt{3}$. So, the area of the trapezoid is $36 + 8\sqrt{3}$.

60. **(F)** (p. 479) ***Mathematics/Trigonometry/Definitions of the Six Trigonometric Functions/ Complimentary Angles.*** The cotangent and tangent are reciprocal functions, so if $\cot\theta = \frac{4}{3}$, then $\tan\theta = \frac{3}{4}$.

Section 3: *Reading*

1. **(B)** (p. 481) ***Reading/Literary Fiction/Development.*** The author is arguing that most of the stories in the newspaper are not really worth reading. He includes this report as an example to show how silly some news coverage is. It is an odd occurrence that does not really affect the person who reads about it—except as idle gossip. The other choices must be wrong because the event is not significant.

2. **(J)** (p. 481) ***Reading/Literary Fiction/Development.*** In the second paragraph, the author of Passage A is making the point that the foreign news is not really news and mentions the examples of Spain, England, and France. He writes that it is possible just to toss in some generic information about Spain, and the resulting report will be accurate. (J) best summarizes how the author uses this example. The other choices are wrong because the author is not offering real news, only a parody of the news.

3. **(A)** (p. 481) ***Reading/Literary Fiction/Voice.*** The point of Passage A is that the reports contained in the newspaper are really worthless, covering all kinds of events that ultimately have no significance. At key points in the passage, the author pokes fun at the news: people would come running in response to a fire alarm in the hope of seeing a good fire, even if it were the church that was burning. Since the author's attitude is negative, you can eliminate (B), (C), and (D).

4. **(H)** (p. 481) ***Reading/Literary Fiction/Vocabulary.*** Because this is a Vocabulary item, you can be pretty sure that the correct answer is not going to be the most common meaning of "attend." As a result, (F) is wrong. In this context, "attend" means to "pay attention to," and (H) is a good match. The other choices do not fit the meaning of the sentence; in fact, (G) and (J) are never synonymous with "attend."

5. **(A)** (p. 481) ***Reading/Literary Fiction/Development.*** The author says that people would respond to the fire alarm not because they want to help save property from destruction but because they want to watch a fire. The author adds that this is particularly true if the church itself is on fire. The author is adding emphasis to the point by saying that people would show up to watch their own church burn. As for (B), while it seems that these people might not care enough about property to put out the fire, this is not the point that the author wants to prove. He wants to prove that they would enjoy watching the church burn. (C) is wrong because the point is not that people are legitimately interested in local affairs but that in this case they are fascinated by something unusual. (D) has to be wrong because the point is that people are less interested in the church than in watching a fire.

6. **(J)** (p. 481) ***Reading/Literary Fiction/Explicit Detail.*** The author states that the people on the island had continued to act as friends even though they were enemies (meaning that the countries from which they originally came were at war). (F) and (G) are ideas mentioned in the selection but do not respond to the question asked. (H) is not discussed in that paragraph.

7. **(B)** (p. 481) ***Reading/Literary Fiction/Explicit Detail.*** The "plight" that both the islanders and the residents of Europe shared was the delay in the news reporting. Though the delay may have been longer (in the case of the islanders) or shorter (in the case of Europeans nearer to the events), there was still a delay during which people were in the position of acting on outdated and wrong information. As for (A), the reporting was not wrong; it was merely delayed. As for (C), even regular reports can be outdated. As for (D), the problem was not biased news but late news.

8. **(F)** (p. 482) ***Reading/Literary Fiction/Implied Idea.*** In the final paragraph, the author states that from our perspective we can see that results were achieved even though people were working with outdated or wrong information. The author offers overseas exploration as an example; with the backing of the Spanish government, Columbus set sail for India only to land in what is now the Americas, and was credited with a significant achievement. As for (G), while the Spanish government and Columbus worked with wrong information, this is not the author's point—the results are what matters. As for (H), the author talks about hindsight and does not fault those who made errors because their information was limited. (J) represents a misunderstanding of the final paragraph.

9. **(A)** (p. 482) ***Reading/Literary Fiction/Application.*** The author of Passage A thinks that the news is only gossip. The author of Passage B thinks that news is important, even if it arrives a little late. As for (B), the author of Passage A does not really care whether news is accurate or not; it's just gossip. As for (C), again, the author of Passage A insists that the news has no value at all. As for (D), the author of Passage B really does not hold out much hope for the news, though he or she might allow that faster reporting is better than slower reporting. As for (E), while it is true that Passage A mentions some local events, the author does not say that one type of event is more suitable for coverage than the other. Similarly, while the second author talks about international events, he does not say that reporting on international events is particularly suited to all newspapers.

10. **(F)** (p. 482) ***Reading/Literary Fiction/Implied Idea.*** We do not know what the authors would have said about the web because they obviously died before it was invented, but we can make a good guess. The author of Passage A would probably say, "See I told you so, more and faster junk." Figuring out author two is a little harder. The point of the second passage is that no matter how fast the news comes, there is always some delay between the event and the report, and during that time, we are operating on wrong information. That point is nicely summarized by the first sentence of the third paragraph: how indirectly we know the environment. Thus, the second author would probably say that while the web closes the gap somewhat, it does not eliminate it. As for (G), there is no way that author one is going to buy into this point. As for (H), surely author two would allow that the web is faster and therefore at least a little better. In any event, author one is going to say that both sources are terrible. The same reasoning applies to (J).

11. **(B)** (p. 483) ***Reading/Social Studies/Main Idea.*** (B) is the correct answer choice. It accurately summarizes the main idea developed in the passage; in addition, it is the only statement general enough to cover the full range of information discussed in the passage. As for the other answer choices, (A) is incorrect because it is contradicted by the passage; as the author says, the current lack of regulation may have led to events that have "had harmful effects not only on stockholders but also on the economy as a whole" (lines 6–8). (C) and (D) are incorrect because they are only two points or opinions presented during the passage; in other words, neither is a statement broad enough to encompass the main idea of the passage. In addition, it is hardly clear that the author shares or would endorse either of these opinions.

12. **(G)** (p. 484) ***Reading/Social Studies/Application.*** (G) is the correct answer choice. In lines 47–51, the author outlines the basic details of how a "golden parachute clause" works. The description in this item stem matches what is described in the passage.

13. **(C)** (p. 484) ***Reading/Social Studies/Implied Idea.*** (C) is the correct answer choice. In lines 9–12, the author gives the defining characteristic of a hostile takeover; specifically, the current management is opposed to it.

14. **(F)** (p. 484) ***Reading/Social Studies/Explicit Detail.*** (F) is the correct answer choice. In the third paragraph, the author explains how raiders must raise substantial capital to buy large quantities of a targeted company's stock (usually at above market price). According to the author, the raiders acquire "debt" (line 29) that they then attempt to liquidate by selling parts of the targeted company or by running the targeted company more efficiently.

15. **(D)** (p. 484) ***Reading/Social Studies/Explicit Detail.*** (D) is the correct answer choice. In lines 51–53, the author outlines the basic details of a "poison pill" strategy. The description in (D) matches what is outlined. As for the other answer choices, (A) is incorrect because it describes the "greenmail" strategy (lines 54–58). (B) is incorrect because it describes the "golden parachute" strategy (lines 47–51). Finally, (C) is incorrect because it is not supported by any material in the passage.

16. **(G)** (p. 484) ***Reading/Social Studies/Explicit Detail.*** (G) is the correct answer choice. In the final paragraph, the author explicitly says that supporters of corporate takeovers believe "the threat of a takeover...makes managers more efficient" (lines 60–61). As for the other answer choices, they are all incorrect because there is no evidence in the passage to suggest that supporters of corporate takeovers would hold these beliefs.

17. **(D)** (p. 484) ***Reading/Social Studies/Explicit Detail.*** (D) is the correct answer choice. A proxy fight is defined in lines 16–20. The description in (D) matches what is outlined in lines 16–20. As for the other answer choices, they are all incorrect because they are unrelated to proxy fights.

18. **(H)** (p. 484) ***Reading/Social Studies/Application.*** (H) is the correct answer choice. In the final paragraph, the author says that supporters of corporate takeovers believe "the threat of a takeover...makes managers more efficient" (lines 60–61). Selling unprofitable subsidiaries to raise cash and cut expenses is an example of being more efficient. As for the other answer choices, see the second to last paragraph of this passage for correct definitions of these terms.

19. **(B)** (p. 485) ***Reading/Social Studies/Explicit Detail.*** (B) is the correct answer choice. In the first sentence of the passage, the author explains that the Securities and Exchange Commission is a federal agency that regulates American financial markets.

20. **(H)** (p. 485) ***Reading/Social Studies/Explicit Detail.*** (H) is the correct answer choice. In the fourth paragraph, the author explains that people have been sent to jail for "selling inside information about future takeover attempts" (lines 35–36).

21. **(A)** (p. 486) ***Reading/Humanities/Main Idea.*** Although the passage includes an abundance of detail, nearly all of these details can be grouped into two main categories: first, a general introduction to Josquin des Prez; and second, an explanation as to why he is relatively unknown. (A) is the correct answer choice because it mentions both of these main points.

22. **(J)** (p. 487) ***Reading/Humanities/Explicit Detail.*** (J) is the correct answer choice because the author never mentions any of Josquin's students. As for the other answer choices, (F) is answered in the second paragraph (*El Grillo, Allegez moy*, etc.). (G) is answered in the final paragraph (sackbuts, krummhorns, etc.). (H) is answered in the second paragraph (Ockeghem).

23. **(D)** (p. 487) ***Reading/Humanities/Implied Idea.*** In the fourth paragraph, the author lists several difficulties associated with reading a musical score from the Renaissance. The author specifically mentions that no tempos are given, flats and sharps are not specified, and no instructions are provided as to which instruments are to play each part. It is logical to assume that, since these are mentioned as difficulties associated with musical scores from the Renaissance, modern musical notation must contain all of these features.

24. **(G)** (p. 487) ***Reading/Humanities/Implied Idea.*** In the third paragraph, the author discusses a distinction between concept and performance. The author states that music does not exist in notes printed on a page; instead, the author argues, a musical score is merely a set of instructions for producing music. Therefore, the author would agree with (G).

25. **(D)** (p. 487) ***Reading/Humanities/Application.*** Each answer choice provided here has a certain amount of merit. On the one hand, (A) seems like a good choice because the author mentions that members of *collegia musica* are generally the only ones who attempt to perform Renaissance music; however, the author also lists several shortcomings associated with these organizations. (B) seems like a good choice because study in general is an excellent method for producing positive results; however, the author mentions several deficiencies associated with musical scores from the Renaissance that even a lifetime of dedicated study could never overcome. (C) might seem like a good choice for the same reason as (B) since additional study or attention normally leads to positive results; however, the essay gives no specific evidence that merely adding Renaissance music to a college curriculum would increase public appreciation of this remote and esoteric art form. In the end, (D) is the best answer choice because it is actually supported by evidence from the essay. In lines 62–63, the author explicitly mentions that musicians cannot afford to study the type of music written by Josquin des Prez due to lack of financial support from an audience. If financial support were available from another source, though, musicians could afford to study and promote the music of Renaissance composers like Josquin des Prez.

26. **(G)** (p. 487) ***Reading/Humanities/Explicit Detail.*** (G) is the correct answer choice because, although the author says that musicians who read modern musical notation have difficulty reading Renaissance notation, the author never says that these musicians cannot play Renaissance instruments. As for the other answer choices, (F) is mentioned in the fourth paragraph. (H) and (J) are mentioned in the final paragraph.

27. **(A)** (p. 487) ***Reading/Humanities/Implied Idea.*** (A) is the correct answer choice because there are at least two reasons to believe that the author admires Galileo. First, in lines 28–29, the author says that both Josquin and Galileo "asserted a new importance for man." The author does not qualify or give any reason to doubt the goodness of this accomplishment. Second, the author has only praise and admiration for Josquin. If the author then says that Josquin and Galileo were comparable figures in their respective fields, we can assume that the author would have similar praise and admiration for Galileo.

28. **(H)** (p. 487) ***Reading/Humanities/Implied Idea.*** In line 6, the author states that the dominant theme of liturgical music "was reverence." So, (H) is the correct answer choice.

29. **(A)** (p. 487) ***Reading/Humanities/Implied Idea.*** (A) is the correct answer choice. In lines 32–33, the author says that "in fine art, concept and performance are one." Specifically, in arts such as painting and poetry, there is a permanent and physical artifact (i.e., a mural or a book of poems) that does not change. In contrast, the author says there is a "separation of concept from performance in music" (lines 31–32). Specifically, a composer writes a musical score that consists of notes on a page. However, the music itself does not exist until musicians perform it; the music then varies from performance to performance based on the quality and the interpretation of the musicians. Similarly, a choreographer creates a ballet and leaves instructions as to its performance. However, the ballet itself does not exist until dancers perform it; and, again, the ballet varies from performance to performance based on the same factors mentioned above.

30. **(H)** (p. 487) ***Reading/Humanities/Implied Idea.*** (H) is the correct answer choice. In lines 1–2, the author says that Western music was only liturgical up until the time of Josquin des Prez. The author then says that, while Josquin des Prez wrote liturgical music, he also "stepped with the other [foot] into the human world" (lines 12–14). In other words, Josquin des Prez also wrote nonreligious music. For example, the author cites the *Deploration d'Ockeghem*, a musical piece written in tribute to a fellow composer, as well as *Allegez moy*, a musical piece about a beautiful woman.

31. **(C)** (p. 488) ***Reading/Natural Sciences/Explicit Detail.*** (C) is the correct answer choice. In the first sentence of the passage, the author says that a supernova occurs about "twice every century" (line 1) or about once every fifty years.

32. **(J)** (p. 488) ***Reading/Natural Sciences/Explicit Detail.*** (J) is the correct answer choice. The passage never mentions or implies that supernovas are caused by the collision of large galaxies. As for the other answer choices, (F) is incorrect because supernovas are described as extremely bright (lines 30–31). (G) is incorrect because supernovas are described as a type of explosion (lines 2–4). Finally, (H) is incorrect because supernovas are said to emit large quantities of X-rays (lines 35–36).

33. (A) (p. 488) ***Reading/Natural Sciences/Development.*** (A) is the correct answer choice. Starting at line 12, the author compares a star to a leaky balloon. An analogy is a comparison.

34. (H) (p. 489) ***Reading/Natural Sciences/Implied Idea.*** (H) is the correct answer choice. The key word used to describe these meteorites is "anomalous," which means "uncharacteristic." These meteorites are uncharacteristic because they contain "certain isotopes" (line 42) not found in our solar system. If these isotopes are not found in our solar system, it can be inferred that they came from a supernova that gave birth to our solar system. As the author notes, elements such as these isotopes "are manufactured deep in the interior of stars and would...remain there if it were not for the cataclysmic supernova explosions that blow giant stars apart" (lines 49–52).

35. (A) (p. 489) ***Reading/Natural Sciences/Implied Idea.*** (A) is the correct answer choice. In the second paragraph, the author explains that the hot gas from a supernova "will emit most of its energy at X-ray wavelengths, so it is not surprising that X-ray observatories have provided some of the most useful insights into the nature of the supernova phenomenon" (lines 35–38). The author also notes that X-ray studies have detected "more than twenty supernova remnants" (line 39). In short, the author implies it is easiest to find evidence of a supernova using equipment that detects X-rays (rather than equipment that views visible light).

36. (J) (p. 489) ***Reading/Natural Sciences/Explicit Detail.*** (J) is the correct answer choice. In the first paragraph, the author describes how a star becomes a supernova. The sequence of events begins when, within the star, "the nuclear fuel is exhausted...[and] the matter in the center of the star collapses inward" (lines 19–21).

37. (B) (p. 489) ***Reading/Natural Sciences/Explicit Detail.*** (B) is the correct answer choice. In the first paragraph, the author begins the process of describing how a star becomes a supernova. According to the author, once a star completes its initial collapse, its "nuclei and electrons are fused into a super-dense lump of matter known as a neutron star" (lines 23–24). In the second paragraph, the author explains what follows this stage—namely, a supernova. Therefore, a neutron star is an intermediate stage between an ordinary star and a supernova.

38. (J) (p. 489) ***Reading/Natural Sciences/Main Idea.*** (J) is the correct answer choice for two reasons. First, it accurately summarizes the author's main purpose, which is to describe the sequence of events that precedes and follows a supernova. Second, it is the only statement general enough to cover the full range of information discussed in the passage. As for the other answer choices, they are all incorrect because they focus on only one element of the passage; in other words, (F), (G), and (H) are all too narrow to describe fully the author's main purpose in writing this passage.

39. (D) (p. 489) ***Reading/Natural Sciences/Explicit Detail.*** (D) is the correct answer choice. In line 44, the author says our galaxy was formed "more than four and a half billion years ago."

40. (H) (p. 489) ***Reading/Natural Sciences/Implied Idea.*** (H) is the correct answer choice. In the last paragraph, the author says "supernovas produce clouds of high-energy particles...[which] are responsible for many of the genetic mutations that are the driving force of the evolution of species" (lines 53–57).

Section 4: Science

1. **(B)** (p. 490) ***Science/Data Representation/Analysis.*** Generally, the Wright data show lower lift at a given angle than the Lilienthal data.

2. **(H)** (p. 490) ***Science/Data Representation/Comprehension.*** The highest point on the graph is at 14 degrees (approximately 5.7 pounds/sq. ft.).

3. **(A)** (p. 490) ***Science/Data Representation/Comprehension.*** By extending both lines to the 50° mark, the difference between them is clearly less than 1 pound/sq. ft.

4. **(H)** (p. 490) ***Science/Data Representation/Comprehension.*** According to the graph, the greatest difference in lift for the two experiments (corresponding to the greatest distance between the two curves for a given angle of incidence) occurs at approximately 30 degrees.

5. **(B)** (p. 491) ***Science/Data Representation/Comprehension.*** The widest region is between 18 and 43 degrees: $43-18=25$ degrees.

6. **(J)** (p. 492) ***Science/Research Summary/Analysis.*** Since plastic beads are not alive, they cannot possibly carry out cellular respiration. This control is designed to detect any atmospheric changes (in the laboratory) that may cause a change in pressure inside the tubes.

7. **(A)** (p. 492) ***Science/Research Summary/Comprehension.*** Oxygen in the air of the tube is consumed by the peas during cellular respiration (see summary equation).

8. **(F)** (p. 492) ***Science/Research Summary/Analysis.*** Without KOH to remove the carbon dioxide produced during cellular respiration, the same number of gas molecules ($6CO_2$) would always be added to the tube as gas molecules were being consumed in the tube ($6O_2$) and the pressure would remain constant.

9. **(C)** (p. 492) ***Science/Research Summary/Analysis.*** Experiment 2 was conducted at a higher temperature than Experiment 1. The greater decrease in pressure in the same time period demonstrates a faster consumption of oxygen.

10. **(G)** (p. 493) ***Science/Research Summary/Analysis.*** If results are identical in light and dark, then light/dark conditions are irrelevant to cellular respiration rates in the experiment; only temperature conditions are important.

11. **(A)** (p. 493) ***Science/Research Summary/Comprehension.*** Glucose must be consumed in order for cellular respiration to occur, eliminating (B) and (D). Cellular respiration did not occur at equal rates in Experiments 1 and 2, eliminating (C), so (A) is the only possible answer: peas are seeds containing a supply of glucose.

12. **(G)** (p. 494) ***Science/Conflicting Viewpoints/Analysis.*** Scientist 1 believes that processes associated with sudden events in the past shaped the earth, whereas Scientist 2 believes that the processes are continuing in the present.

13. **(D)** (p. 494) ***Science/Conflicting Viewpoints/Analysis.*** Mountains could not have formed only when land masses were raised at the beginnings of the earth if recent fossils of sea creatures are found at mountain tops. This evidence suggests that the rocks were underwater relatively recently.

14. **(H)** (p. 495) ***Science/Conflicting Viewpoints/Analysis.*** The two scientists agree that the changes that have shaped the landscape have operated over a long time span, but they disagree as to whether those

changes were sudden and violent (catastrophism) or constant and gradual (principle of uniform change). Furthermore, catastrophism holds that the cataclysmic events happened in the distant past, not recently, eliminating (F).

15. **(A)** (p. 495) ***Science/Conflicting Viewpoints/Comprehension.*** According to Scientist 1, the worldwide ocean precipitated granite first, so it must be the lowest layer, with other precipitated materials covering it later.

16. **(F)** (p. 495) ***Science/Conflicting Viewpoints/Comprehension.*** According to Scientist 1, the three major rock types formed when the worldwide ocean precipitated different materials on three occasions, so no further types can be expected since this ocean no longer exists (possibly due to evaporation).

17. **(C)** (p. 495) ***Science/Conflicting Viewpoints/Analysis.*** By arguing that processes that formed the earth at its origin differed from those that maintain and mold the earth as an existing planet, Scientist 1 would be refuting Scientist 2's view that processes are uniform from the beginning.

18. **(G)** (p. 495) ***Science/Conflicting Viewpoints/Analysis.*** Scientist 1 refers to three rock types forming during three separate precipitations. Regions of lava (with no present volcanoes), rivers presently continuing to cut their channels, and "related" fossils that could not have immigrated from other geographic areas are factors that support the views of Scientist 2.

19. **(D)** (p. 496) ***Science/Research Summary/Comprehension.*** Ten individuals had their heart rates recorded every 10 minutes during a 30-minute experiment (three times each). Therefore, 10(3) = 30 values were used to calculate the average heart rate for each of the experiments.

20. **(G)** (p. 496) ***Science/Research Summary/Analysis.*** Since Species B had an increase in heart rate when environmental temperature increased, it is the likely species to be cold-blooded (Species A's heart rate stayed about the same).

21. **(C)** (p. 496) ***Science/Research Summary/Analysis.*** Just by chance alone, any one individual might have an extremely high or extremely low heart rate. The larger the sample of individuals tested, the lower the chances of getting extreme average values.

22. **(J)** (p. 496) ***Science/Research Summary/Analysis.*** Since Species B (cold-blooded) had an increase in average heart rate when environmental temperature increased, a decrease in average heart rate is likely when temperatures drop. Species A should have approximately the same average heart rate at all three temperatures.

23. **(A)** (p. 496) ***Science/Research Summary/Analysis.*** At 22°C, Species A had an average heart rate of 150 beats/minute, while Species B averaged 100 beats/minute.

24. **(F)** (p. 497) ***Science/Research Summary/Analysis.*** The cold-blooded Species B should have an increase in body temperature in Experiment 2 (35°C conditions in the incubator compared to 22°C in Experiment 1). The warm-blooded Species A should have no significant change in body temperature during the experiments.

25. **(A)** (p. 498) ***Science/Data Representation/Comprehension.*** Each photon can promote an electron from level 1 to level 2 since the difference in energies is 0.60 eV. (Note that the actual value of level 1 alone, which happens to be 0.60 eV also, does not determine the answer. Differences in energy are what matter.)

26. **(J)** (p. 498) ***Science/Data Representation/Comprehension.*** There is no way to distinguish between the emission from level 3 to level 4 or from level 5 to level 4 since each releases a photon of 0.32 eV.

27. **(D)** (p. 498) ***Science/Data Representation/Comprehension.*** Only the level 3 to level 1 emission has an energy difference of 0.92 eV.

28. **(J)** (p. 498) ***Science/Data Representation/Comprehension.*** Each electron can go from level 5 to any other level, with each of the four transitions requiring the emission of a photon of a different energy.

29. **(C)** (p. 498) ***Science/Data Representation/Analysis.*** Since absorption of photons occurs first, then emission, electrons must be promoted (gaining the necessary energy from the absorbed photons), then emitted. Transitions between levels 3 and 4 have the necessary energy: 0.23 eV.

30. **(J)** (p. 498) ***Science/Data Representation/Comprehension.*** Although 2.07 eV is the absolute energy of level 5, there is no difference of energy levels anywhere on the diagram that equals 2.07 eV; hence, the photons will not be absorbed: no electron transitions will occur between levels 1 and 5.

31. **(C)** (p. 499) ***Science/Research Summary/Comprehension.*** Note how θ_1 and θ_2 are defined on the original drawing, then imagine how the diagram will change as the angles become smaller approaching zero: they would align along the vertical axis. Note that (B) would be correct if the angles were defined as those between the ray and the horizontal, not vertical, axis.

32. **(J)** (p. 499) ***Science/Research Summary/Analysis.*** In Experiment 1 the angle in water is equal to the angle in air. In Experiment 2 the angle in water is less than the angle in air. So, only the last choice fits both experiments.

33. **(A)** (p. 499) ***Science/Research Summary/Comprehension.*** This question simply requires interpretation of the meaning of the diagram: in Experiment 3, the beam is shown hitting the water surface and reflecting back, but not back on the beam itself.

34. **(H)** (p. 500) ***Science/Research Summary/Comprehension.*** The beam of light only passes into the air for observation in Experiment 2.

35. **(C)** (p. 500) ***Science/Research Summary/Analysis.*** Only this response covers all elements of the three diagrams.

36. **(H)** (p. 501) ***Science/Data Representation/Comprehension.*** The number of butterflies captured for marking is found under the heading "Marked." Reading across the table for each size group, the "dark brown" category always has the fewest butterflies marked.

37. **(D)** (p. 501) ***Science/Data Representation/Comprehension.*** Compare the number of butterflies recaptured to the number marked to derive a proportion that represents how easy it is to recapture each type of butterfly. The proportion for small, white butterflies (30/35) is much higher than that for any of the other choices.

38. **(G)** (p. 501) ***Science/Data Representation/Analysis.*** An examination of the table shows that for all colors, as size increases, the number of butterflies marked increases.

39. **(B)** (p. 501) ***Science/Data Representation/Application.*** A poisonous chemical will have adverse effects on the butterfly after marking (perhaps by killing or by preventing flight). The group with the lowest number (and proportion) of individuals recaptured in flight ($10/40=1/4$ recaptured) is the group consisting of small, tan butterflies.

40. **(G)** (p. 501) ***Science/Data Representation/Analysis.*** For medium-sized butterflies, the proportion of individuals recaptured in each color is as follows: white ($15/30=1/2$), tan ($20/40=1/2$), and dark brown ($10/20=1/2$).

Sample Essay Responses and Analyses

Section 5: Writing *(p. 502)*

Above Average Response

With online systems, Americans could easily register and vote without leaving their homes. While this method is a practical solution to increase voter registration, it should not be used for voting on Election Day because of the potential for technical problems and voter fraud. Online voter registration would make the process more convenient and would not necessarily result in less informed voters. However, since errors due to technical problems could skew election results, this system should not be used for voting itself.

Online systems could make voter registration a faster, easier process and, therefore, accessible to more people. As Perspective 3 states, a high voter turnout is crucial for a healthy democracy. The ability to register online would especially encourage younger voters who are used to the convenience of online services and may not take time out of their schedule to travel to a designated place to register. States that have implemented online registration have recorded an increase in youth voter turnout. Moreover, this option would also help people who cannot leave their homes due to illness or disability, and it would make it easier to register for an absentee ballot if you are living out of state. With one obstacle to registration removed, voter turnout could increase.

Online voter registration or voting would not necessarily lead to less informed voters. While the task of going to a designated place to register or to vote demands more effort from voters, this does not prevent people who are uninformed about the candidates from traveling to a polling station. One can accomplish many important tasks online, such as financial or legal transactions, and the online convenience does not make these actions any less important. Onsite registration and voting does, however, stop citizens who do not have the ability to reach a polling place, such as people with illnesses or inflexible work or childcare schedules. Although employers in some states are legally required to give employees time off for voting, employees may not be aware of this right, and in many states, they would lose pay while leaving work to vote.

While the convenience of online voting and registration would make voting accessible to more people, technological problems might lead to unfair elections. For example, an unreliable Internet connection might prevent one's vote from being counted, or it may be possible to tamper with an online system to skew election results. Voting remotely might also allow someone to vote multiple times. It is true that more traditional voting methods are not foolproof; for example, during the Presidential Election of 2000, problems with punch cards called into question the election results in Florida. However, a new method of voting could introduce even more technological problems. Voter registration could be moved online, since one can always verify whether the registration worked. However, voting itself is a time-sensitive issue, and accidental or intentional errors in an online system may go unnoticed until the election is over.

Online registration could make voter registration more accessible and therefore increase voter turnout. However, while the convenience of online voting may also increase turnout, there are too many technological risks involved to rely on it.

Ideas and Analysis: The writer clearly states his or her thesis in the introduction: an online system should be used for voter registration, but realistically, not for voting itself. The body paragraphs consider arguments for and against online registration and/or voting. The first paragraph addresses the accessibility of online voting (Perspective 3), and the second paragraph argues against the correlation between online voters and uninformed voters (Perspective 1). The third paragraph acknowledges the technical problems that could occur (Perspective 2).

Development and Support:

- The introduction states the thesis in its second sentence and previews the arguments that will support it.

- The body paragraphs begin with topic sentences that clearly state the main point or argument to be made in the paragraph.
- The body paragraphs include a mix of arguments and examples to support the author's opinion.
- The writer develops a "compromise" position on the subject by arguing for online registration but recognizing that online voting could cause too many technological problems. The writer is able to acknowledge both sides without contradicting his or her own arguments.

Organization:

- The writer introduces each paragraph with a topic sentence.
- The writer uses transitions to connect ideas between and within paragraphs. For example, the third body paragraph begins with the clause "While the convenience of online voting and registration would make voting accessible to more people" because the paragraph introduces an opposing argument to online voting.
- The second body paragraph could be stronger without the last sentence (about leaving work to vote). The argument of the paragraph is that online voting would not lead to uninformed voters, so this sentence might be seen as off-topic.
- The essay could also be improved with a longer and slightly more developed conclusion.

Language Use and Conventions:

The essay contains at least three principal strengths in this area:

- The essay does not have any mechanics/usage errors. As a result, the reader's attention is not distracted from the substance of the essay.
- The writer does not use any informal language.
- Stylistically, the writer varies sentence structures.
- The writer uses vivid verbs and avoids vague language. The verb choice shows a sophisticated vocabulary.

Summary and Conclusions: This essay demonstrates writing skills that are very well developed and analyzes multiple viewpoints of the issue. The writer incorporates all three perspectives in his or her argument. This essay would likely receive a score of 10.

Below Average Response

Online voting and registration is a great idea because it would allow more people to vote and would make our democracy stronger. It is elitist to assume that more people voting would lead to less informed voters. I also don't think that we should be afraid of using this technology we do so much online and it works really well, so why not vote online?

Online voting is a good idea because it is more convenient than going to a polling place or a government building and waiting in line to vote or to register. Our lives are much busier now since we work so much, so why not make voting easier to do? Young people are also used to doing everything online, and as these people make up more and more of the voting population, it makes sense to adapt to their ways and vote online.

I don't think that online voting would necessarily lead to less informed voters. The purpose of a democracy is to have citizens elect their leaders, not to only allow an elite group to vote. Also, so many people keep up with current events by reading online news. The internet has made people more informed, not less.

Some might worry about the technological problems involved with online voting and what would happen if the system didn't work. However, we do so many important things online, like transfer money and enter important information onto websites. If we can do this, why can't we vote?

Online voting seems like a logical, practical solution that will make voting more accessible to more people.

Ideas and Analysis: The writer clearly expresses his or her point of view in favor of online voting. However, the arguments are superficial because the writer offers little concrete evidence in favor of his or her argument and does not give enough consideration to opposing viewpoints.

Development and Support:

- The introduction clearly states the writer's opinion, but the writer should use more specific language rather than saying that online voting "is a great idea."
- The writer attempts to support the arguments with generalizations, rather than using concrete examples or clear logic.
    - In the first body paragraph, the writer has one relevant argument (that online voting would engage younger, technology-oriented voters). However, the statement that "our lives are much busier" is too general to be used as an argument.
    - In the second body paragraph, the writer claims to argue that online voting will not lead to uninformed voters. However, the writer attempts to support the argument with a generalization: "The purpose of a democracy is to have citizens elect their leaders, not to only allow an elite group to vote." This generalization does not answer the question that the writer needs to address: *Why* wouldn't online voting lead to uninformed voters?
    - In the third body paragraph, the writer acknowledges that there might be technological problems involved with online voting. However, the writer simply dismisses this argument without thoroughly engaging with it. He or she does not reflect on how technological problems could influence elections.
- The conclusion should be more developed and should revisit the writer's three main arguments.

Organization:

- The introduction has three separate sentences that show that the writer agrees with Perspective 3 and argues against Perspectives 1 and 2. However, the introduction would be stronger if the writer combined these opinions into a coherent thesis.
- The topic sentences should have transitions to introduce new ideas in the following paragraph.
- The last two sentences of the second paragraph do not support its main topic. ("Also, so many people keep up with current events by reading online news. The internet has made people more informed, not less.") The prompt does not ask whether the Internet makes people better informed about the news in general; it asks whether online voting could lead to less informed voters.

Language Use and Conventions:

The essay contains several weaknesses in this area:

- The essay contains some usage and mechanics errors.
  - Introduction: "I also don't think that we should be afraid of using this technology we do so much online and it works really well, so why not vote online?" is a run-on sentence. The first sentence should end after "technology."
- The writer uses informal language, such as "so many important things" (Body paragraph 3).
- The writer uses vague language. In the first body paragraph, when the writer says "**Our** lives are much busier now since **we** work so much" it is unclear what "our" and "we" are referring to.

***Summary and Conclusions*:** The writer's opinion is clear, but the essay relies too much on generalizations and does not give enough consideration to opposing arguments. The body paragraphs do not have enough evidence to support their arguments. This essay would likely receive a score of 5.

SAT PRACTICE TEST

Answer Key

DIRECTIONS: For the correct answer, circle the answer, then check any corresponding shaded box(es). Then, total the number of circled answers to determine the raw score for the test section. Total the number of checkmarks for each of the subscores and cross-test scores to determine each raw subscore and cross-test score.

Section 1: Reading (p. 505)

	Subscores		Cross-Test Scores	
	WC	**CE**	**S**	**H/S**
1. B			■	
2. C			■	
3. D		■	■	
4. D			■	
5. A	■		■	
6. B			■	
7. D		■	■	
8. A			■	
9. A	■		■	
10. D			■	
11. B			■	
12. A				■
13. A		■		■
14. C	■			■
15. C				■
16. D		■		■
17. A				■
18. B	■			■
19. A				■
20. D				■
21. C				■
22. B				
23. D		■		
24. B				
25. D		■		
26. B				
27. C	■			
28. C	■			
29. B				
30. B				
31. A				
32. D			■	
33. D			■	
34. C		■	■	
35. A	■		■	
36. B			■	
37. B		■	■	
38. C	■		■	
39. A			■	
40. D			■	
41. D			■	
42. B				■
43. D				■
44. B	■			■
45. C				■
46. B				■
47. B		■		■
48. C	■			■
49. D				■
50. B				■
51. D		■		■
52. A				■

Raw Score: _____/52

Section 2: Writing and Language (p. 519)

	Subscores		Cross-Test Scores	
	WC	CE	S	H/S
1. A				
2. D				
3. A				
4. A				
5. B				
6. D				
7. D				
8. D				
9. C				
10. C				
11. A				
12. C				
13. A				
14. C				
15. B				
16. B				
17. D				
18. B				
19. B				
20. C				
21. C				
22. D				
23. A				
24. A				
25. B				
26. B				
27. A				
28. B				
29. C				
30. D				
31. C				
32. D				
33. C				
34. B				
35. B				
36. D				
37. D				
38. C				
39. C				
40. C				
41. C				
42. C				
43. D				
44. A				

Raw Score: ______/44

Evidence-Based Reading and Writing Subscores

Words in Context (WC): ______/18 Command of Evidence (CE): ______/18

Section 3: Math, No Calculator (p. 533)

	Cross-Test Scores	
	S	H/S
1. B		
2. B		
3. A		
4. C		
5. B		
6. C		
7. C		
8. A		
9. B		
10. C		
11. D		
12. C		
13. A		
14. B		
15. D		
16. 72		
17. 3		
18. 24		
19. 3		
20. 78		

Section 4: Math, Calculator (p. 539)

	Cross-Test Scores S	Cross-Test Scores H/S		Cross-Test Scores S	Cross-Test Scores H/S		Cross-Test Scores S	Cross-Test Scores H/S
1. A			14. A			27. C		
2. D			15. C			28. C		
3. D			16. D			29. C		
4. C			17. D			30. B		
5. D			18. A			31. 1/20, 0.05		
6. B			19. C			32. 7		
7. D			20. D			33. 2/3, 4/6, 0.66		
8. D			21. A			34. 20		
9. B			22. B			35. 7		
10. C			23. D			36. 75		
11. C			24. B			37. 1		
12. B			25. C			38. 4		
13. A			26. B					

Math Raw Score (total of calculator and no-calculator sections): ______/58

Cross-Test Scores (All four test sections)

Science (S): ______/35 History/Social Studies (H/S): ______/35

Explanations

Section 1: Reading

Questions #1–11

1. (B) (p. 506) ***Reading/Natural Science/Main Idea.*** The main purpose of the passage is to review the findings of some research on animal behavior and suggest that this may have implications for the study of depression in humans. (B) neatly restates this. (A) can be overruled since the author proposes no cure and even notes that there are complex issues remaining to be solved. (C) is incorrect since the author does not criticize any experiments. It is important to recognize that in the fourth paragraph, the author is not being critical of any study in which rats were immersed in cold water but rather is anticipating a possible interpretation of those results and moving to block it. So, the author's criticism is of a possible interpretation of the experiment, not of the experiment itself or of the results. In any event, that can in no way be interpreted as the main theme of the passage. (D) is way off the mark. Though one might object to the use of animals for experimentation, that is not a burden the author has elected to carry.

2. (C) (p. 506) ***Reading/Natural Science/Implied Idea.*** In the final paragraph, the writer notes that inescapable noise or unsolvable problems produce human behavior similar to that induced in the lab subjects but adds that humans are much more complex.

3. (D) (p. 506) ***Reading/Natural Science/Textual Evidence.*** As noted in the explanation to the previous question, the explanation is found in the final paragraph, and (D) contains the relevant text excerpt.

4. (D) (p. 506) ***Reading/Natural Science/Development.*** The author introduces the questions in the fourth paragraph to anticipate a possible objection: perhaps the animal's inability to act was caused by the trauma of the shock rather than the fact that it could not escape the shock. The author then lists some experiments whose conclusions refute this alternative explanation. (A) is incorrect since the question represents an interruption of the flow of argument, not a continuation of the first paragraph. (B) represents a misreading of the passage. (C) can be eliminated since the author seems to think that the various questions asked do have an answer.

5. (A) (p. 506) ***Reading/Natural Science/Vocabulary.*** The author contrasts "nonaversive stimulus" with "uncontrollable aversive events" used in the experiments, namely, electric shocks. So the critical difference must be the pain—it is present in the shock experiments and not in the nonaversive parallels. This is further supported by the example of a nonaversive parallel, the uncontrollable delivery of food. So the relevant difference is articulated by (A). (B) is incorrect since none of the stimuli, even though they may not permanently injure, are enjoyable for the laboratory animals. (C) is incorrect because the events are all significant. (D) is incorrect since the author contrasts the nonaversive stimuli with the traumatic stimuli.

6. (B) (p. 506) ***Reading/Natural Science/Explicit Detail.*** According to the explanation of the experimental neurosis paradigm set out in paragraph six, as animals are presented with increasingly similar choices, they exhibit abnormal behavior such as agitation and then lethargy.

7. (D) (p. 506) ***Reading/Natural Science/Textual Evidence.*** The experimental neurosis paradigm is explained in paragraph six and is the basis for the correct answer to the preceding question.

8. (A) (p. 507) ***Reading/Natural Science/Development.*** The author raises a question in paragraph four in order to anticipate a possible objection; namely, that the shock, not the unavoidability of it, caused inaction. The author then offers a refutation of this position by arguing that we get the same results using similar experiments with nonaversive stimuli. Moreover, if trauma of shock caused the inaction, then we would expect to find learned helplessness induced in rats by the shock, regardless of prior experience with shock. The "mastery effect," however, contradicts this expectation. This is essentially the explanation provided in (A). (B) is incorrect since the author does not mention this until the end of the passage. (C) can be eliminated since the "mastery effect" reference is not included to support the conclusion that neurochemical changes cause the learned helplessness. (D) is incorrect, for though the author makes such an assertion, the "mastery effect" data is not adduced to support that particular assertion.

9. (A) (p. 507) ***Reading/Natural Science/Vocabulary.*** In the relevant paragraph, the author explains that prior experience can be used to immunize against learned helpless. The "immunization" manifests itself as a "mastery effect," that is, the rats work longer and harder to avoid the shock.

10. (D) (p. 507) ***Reading/Natural Science/Application.*** The author closes with a disclaimer that the human cognitive makeup is more complex than that of laboratory animals, and that for this reason, the findings regarding learned helplessness and induced neurosis may or may not be applicable to humans. The author does not, however, explain what the differences are between the experimental subjects and humans. A logical continuation would be to supply the reader with this elaboration. By comparison, the other answer choices are less likely. (B) is unlikely since the author begins and ends with references to

human depression, and that is evidently the motivation for writing the article. (C) is not supported by the text since it is nowhere indicated that any such experiments have been undertaken. Finally, (A) is perhaps the second-best answer; its value is that it suggests the mechanism should be studied further. But the most important question is not how the mechanism works in rats but whether that mechanism also works in humans.

11. (B) (p. 507) ***Reading/Natural Science/Implied Idea.*** The experimenters were interested in whether or not the test subjects would make the effort to escape the shocks or simply endure them. Adjusting the height of the barrier would make escape more or less difficult, helping to determine whether those that escaped did so at random or because they had learned to find an avoidance mechanism.

Questions #12–21

12. (A) (p. 509) ***Reading/Social Studies/Implied Idea.*** In paragraph one, the author states that cartoon violence has three cues, make-believe violence two cues, and an acted violence only one cue. Presumably, the easiest to distinguish is the one with the most cues.

13. (A) (p. 509) ***Reading/Social Studies/Textual Evidence.*** As noted in the explanation to the previous question, presumably the form with the greatest cues is the most readily identifiable. And (A) here provides the explicit statement of that presupposition.

14. (C) (p. 509) ***Reading/Social Studies/Vocabulary.*** This item tests a common word, so look for the meaning appropriate to the context. The author means to say that an aggressive action might happen only when it would otherwise be expected or normal.

15. (C) (p. 509) ***Reading/Social Studies/Implied Idea.*** In the fifth paragraph, the passage states that depiction of violence might have a short-term effect on a child, perhaps for 15 or 20 minutes after a child has viewed the violence. If, in that time frame, the child is then put in a situation that calls for aggressive behavior, he or she might act out aggressively. However, the author also points out that this effect tends not to last longer than an hour. Therefore, the author would conclude the child's behavior after a couple of hours is not likely to be affected by the earlier viewing of violence.

16. (D) (p. 510) ***Reading/Social Studies/Textual Evidence.*** As the excerpt makes clear, the author believes that any instigational effect would be short-term, less than 20 minutes.

17. (A) (p. 510) ***Reading/Social Studies/Implied Idea.*** The author theorizes that the behavior of children may be changed by watching violence on television, but not for the reason that most people think. According to the author, it is not the violence itself that gets kids worked up but the energy level in the depiction. The author goes on to explain that anything that gets a kid excited may have the same effect, even agitating the child by turning off the TV set.

18. (B) (p. 510) ***Reading/Social Studies/Voice.*** In this case, the author is clearly an opponent of the view that fantasy violence on television adversely affects children. (Though the author does say that violence may inspire teenagers or adults to commit violent acts.) In the last paragraph, the author takes on those who hold to the commonly accepted view and accuses them of using television as a scapegoat when the real causes of violence in our society are cultural. The use of the word "scapegoat" is strong and indicates that the author objects to that view.

19. (A) (p. 510) ***Reading/Social Studies/Main Idea.*** First, look at the first word of each answer choice and then look at the rest of each choice. The best first word to describe the purpose of the passage is probably "correct" since the author challenges a commonly accepted position. Looking at the rest of (A), it is clear that (A) is the correct answer: the author rejects the common notion that television violence affects the behavior of children.

20. (D) (p. 510) ***Reading/Social Studies/Data Presentations.*** The graph indicates that both parents and children agree that the child feels more violent immediately after viewing TV violence. This provides some support to statement (D): violent portrayals could be dangerous in the short run. Granted the data do not prove the point, but at least the data seem relevant to this claim. The data do not seem to support the other statements at all.

21. (C) (p. 510) ***Reading/Social Studies/Application.*** According to paragraph one, the distinguishing features of make-believe are humor and a fictional setting, those described by (C).

Questions #22–31

22. (B) (p. 512) ***Reading/Literary Fiction/Implied Idea.*** The first half of the passage tells us that Duane is fleeing from something but provides no details. Paragraph three, however, makes it clear that the event had taken place earlier in the day, so it was a single incident that had wrought this change in Duane, not a lifetime of crime. Duane's reflection in paragraph three presents him as an ordinary person whose life has suddenly changed and who feels that he must now live like an outlaw.

23. (D) (p. 512) ***Reading/Literary Fiction/Textual Evidence.*** (D) summarizes the dilemma that Duane finds himself in. He is not basically a bad person—he loathes bad people—but he will be forced to live either alone or among men he finds obnoxious. Or, if he chooses an honest living, he must be careful to protect his identity.

24. (B) (p. 512) ***Reading/Literary Fiction/Implied Idea.*** Everything in the first paragraph makes it clear that Duane is looking for a safe place to camp. He avoids the sites he is familiar with; he moves far off the trail; he finds a secluded valley that is undercover.

25. (D) (p. 512) ***Reading/Literary Fiction/Textual Evidence.*** The text states that Duane passed by campsites that were already familiar to him, looking for something more secluded, and chose a site far from the trail under cover.

26. (B) (p. 512) ***Reading/Literary Fiction/Implied Idea.*** The first paragraph says that Duane rode his horse a considerable distance and made a change of direction to avoid encountering other people. Everything in this part of the selection conveys a sense of urgency to put distance between himself and the place where an event occurred. After Duane sets up a camp, he then begins to think on the significant event of that day and its implications for his life.

27. (C) (p. 512) ***Reading/Literary Fiction/Vocabulary.*** At the end of the first paragraph, Duane makes a substitute hobble using a length of rope. It hampers the horse's movement but doesn't confine it to one spot, and it only requires a few feet of rope, so (C) must be correct.

28. (C) (p. 512) ***Reading/Literary Fiction/Vocabulary.*** "Vigilant" means "alert," "cautious," or "wary." In this context, Duane is obliged to be vigilant always against the possibility that someone will find him and hold him responsible for whatever he did earlier in the day.

29. (B) (p. 512) ***Reading/Literary Fiction/Explicit Detail.*** All four of the choices are types of terrain mentioned in the passage, but the first paragraph states that Duane chose the low hills that he had earlier seen from the distance.

30. (B) (p. 512) ***Reading/Literary Fiction/Implied Idea.*** The fact that he was nervous surprised Duane because he was already starting to develop new habits, the habits of someone perhaps pursued and concealing his identity, but not yet aware of that fact.

31. (A) (p. 512) ***Reading/Literary Fiction/Implied Idea.*** Duane selected the campsite for its solitude. He is hiding there from any pursuers. As darkness falls and the birds and insects become quiet, the place seems even more remote than during the day. This gives Duane a feeling of even greater safety.

Questions #32–41

32. (D) (p. 514) ***Reading/Natural Science/Main Idea.*** The first and last sentences of the selection effectively provide the answer. (A) is too narrowly drafted because the author does not only discuss the containment issue (the second issue). (B) goes beyond the explicit scope of the selection because competitiveness is not mentioned. (C) likewise is wide of the mark. The author focuses on physical forces, not energy efficiency.

33. (D) (p. 514) ***Reading/Natural Science/Implied Idea.*** In the third paragraph, the author explains that the energy stored by a flywheel is a function of its mass and speed, and that a lightweight flywheel would have to spin faster in order to store the same energy as a heavier one. So, you can infer that if the masses are different but the stored energy is the same, the lighter wheel is spinning faster—and that's (D). (A) is a confused reading of the first paragraph, and that information doesn't help answer the question that is asked. Similarly, (B) and (C) come out of the second paragraph and aren't relevant here.

34. (C) (p. 514) ***Reading/Natural Science/Textual Evidence.*** (B) provides explicit textual support for the explanation given to #33: lightweight rotating at higher speed = heavyweight rotating at lower speed.

35. (A) (p. 515) ***Reading/Natural Science/Vocabulary.*** If you know in advance that the meaning of "benign" is "nonthreatening" or "not dangerous," (A) is the obvious choice. The correct answer can also be found within the context of the third paragraph. The author is discussing what happens when one of these rapidly spinning wheels breaks up. If it's made of heavy metal, the result is a lot of shrapnel flying everywhere. But if it's made of graphite fiber, then the result is a tangled bunch of threads—much less dangerous than the alternative.

36. (B) (p. 515) ***Reading/Natural Science/Explicit Detail.*** The answer to this item is contained in the second paragraph: the net effect of the two modules on the car is nearly zero when they are spinning in opposite directions, (B).

37. (B) (p. 515) ***Reading/Natural Science/Textual Evidence.*** As noted in the explanation to the previous question, the answer is contained in the second paragraph.

38. **(C)** (p. 515) ***Reading/Natural Science/Vocabulary.*** The second sentence of paragraph two refers to gyroscopic forces that come into play when the vehicle is turning. The author discusses this issue and concludes in the final sentence of the paragraph that the net effect would be zero if the pairs are spun in opposite directions. So the net effect discussed is the effect when the car is turning.

39. **(A)** (p. 515) ***Reading/Natural Sciences/Development.*** The author introduces the idea of EMBs for use in cars and describes generally how they would work. Then, in the second paragraph, the author states that they pose "two special problems." The author describes those problems and explains how they are minimized by using different technological solutions, (A). The other choices simply do not fit the logical development of the passage.

40. **(D)** (p. 515) ***Reading/Natural Science/Data Presentation.*** The data in the graph show that that alloy steel flywheels are good for only 50 Wh/kg or so, while graphite fiber flywheels may generate up to 500+ Wh/kg, or nearly ten times more Wh/kg than the alloy steel flywheels.

41. **(D)** (p. 515) ***Reading/Natural Science/Main Idea.*** In the first paragraph, the author is primarily explaining how the EMB works in an electric car. To the extent that the ideas mentioned by the other choices are found in the passage, they are discussed in other paragraphs.

Questions #42–52

42. **(B)** (p. 517) ***Reading/Social Studies/Explicit Detail.*** In the last paragraph, and the last sentence in particular, the author of the first passage states that the interdisciplinary approach used by Turner was a new technique. (B) best captures this idea. As for (A), the same paragraph states specifically that the reliance on political history was characteristic of history prior to Turner. As for (C), although Turner made the original presentation at a conference, the passage does not say that presenting was a technique of study. While Turner used the opportunity to present his new theory, he could equally well have published an article or made an informal presentation to colleagues. As for (D), the first passage doesn't enter into such a debate, though you will find some mention of this in the second passage. But because the information appears in the second passage, it cannot be an answer to this Explicit Detail item about the first passage.

43. **(D)** (p. 517) ***Reading/Social Studies/Voice.*** The author of Passage 1 evidently approves of Turner's work. The passage says that it had great influence, that it was original, and that it used a novel approach. That's a pretty good review. As for (A), while the author allows that Turner's thesis was not immune to debate or even criticism, this does not mean that the author was "skeptical" of the work itself. After all, it could turn out to be that Turner's conclusions are ultimately false; but the groundbreaking approach and radical theory would still have value. As for (B), the thesis is not treated negatively, so "condescending" cannot be used to express the author's attitude. Finally, as for (C), the author takes a pretty strong position, so "noncommital" is not a good description.

44. **(B)** (p. 517) ***Reading/Social Studies/Vocabulary.*** Because "grand" is a word with some common meanings, you can pretty much discount any choices that use these more common synonyms. That would certainly eliminate (C). Instead, the author is using the word "grand" in a derivative sense to mean large or great or overall. Turner's thesis did try to be comprehensive, accounting for the uniquely American character. As for (A), though the author allows that Turner's thesis was not perfect, line 13 is not where that discussion occurs. And (D) must be wrong since Turner's thesis was not tentative.

45. **(C)** (p. 517) ***Reading/Social Studies/Development.*** The author of Passage 2 discusses the limitations of Turner's theory, and one of the most important of these is its attempt to explain everything American in terms of the frontier. At the referenced lines, the author lists some other very important historical factors in order to show that the frontier could not have been the entire story. As for (A), this is the topic introduced at the end of that paragraph and developed in the following paragraphs, but it is not an answer to this question. As for (B), even granting that this statement is correct, it is not an answer to this question. For example, the author mentions the Civil War in order to show that Turner's thesis was too limited, not that traditional histories were too limited. As for (D), this is a point that is raised in the fourth paragraph, so it is not an answer to the question asked about the second paragraph.

46. **(B)** (p. 517) ***Reading/Social Studies/Voice.*** The author of Passage 2 is critical of the frontier thesis, but you'll notice that the criticisms all deal with Turner's ideas. For example, Turner thought that the frontier offered free land, but the author of Passage 2 argues that he was wrong because the land was already used by indigenous people. So, while the passage criticizes Turner's idea, it doesn't criticize Turner himself. Thus, (C) and (D) are wrong, and (B) is correct. As for (A), the author says that the thesis has "rightfully" been abandoned because of its weaknesses.

47. **(B)** (p. 517) ***Reading/Social Studies/Textual Evidence.*** Perhaps the best summary statement of the second author's thesis is that the frontier thesis has been "rightfully abandoned." The author goes on to provide a refutation in detail, but as evidence of the writer's general attitude toward Turner's thesis, "rightfully abandoned" is a pretty good summary.

48. **(C)** (p. 517) ***Reading/Social Studies/Vocabulary.*** You get the information you need to answer the question from the discussion about the significance of the Indian Wars. Turner claimed that the land was free, but in reality, it was necessary to pursue a policy of military aggression to secure the land. So, when the author writes that the wars "belie" the free land theory, the author means "prove false." (A) is a distracting choice, but don't be misled by the superficial connection between "lie" and "untruth." In this context, the phrase is "prove to be false," not "lie about." As for (B) and (D), while these are phrases that relate generally to the idea of debating the merits of a theory, they don't focus on the connection between the wars and the free land thesis.

49. **(D)** (p. 517) ***Reading/Social Studies/Explicit Detail.*** The key word other than "EXCEPT" in this item is "both"; therefore, the correct answer choice is the only one that is *not* mentioned in *both* passages. Both authors mention (A), (B), and (C). However, "nationalism" is only mentioned in the first passage.

50. **(B)** (p. 518) ***Reading/Social Studies/Implied Idea.*** In the final paragraph, the author argues that group activity—migration of extended family groups, corporate undertakings such as the railroads, government military intervention—and not individual action settled the frontier.

51. **(D)** (p. 518) ***Reading/Social Studies/Textual Evidence.*** The final paragraph of Passage 2 contains a fairly thorough refutation of Turner's thesis that rugged individuals "tamed the frontier." And the first sentence of that paragraph provides a pretty good summary of its development.

52. **(A)** (p. 518) ***Reading/Social Studies/Application.*** To a certain extent, any weakening of Turner's theory would have implications for all aspects of the theory. So, you might argue that the referenced evidence, in some way, tends to show that people from different regions did not mix at the frontier because the frontier was not quite as well-defined as Turner thought. But that's a pretty feeble point, so (D) is wrong. You can apply similar reasoning to (B) and (C). The best answer here is (A). The "safety valve" point, as explained in Passage 1, maintained that people who were dissatisfied with life in the urban areas could simply pack up and move to the country because there was land for the claiming. If the "free land" thesis is false, then the "safety valve" thesis must also be false.

Section 2: Writing and Language

Passage 1

1. **(A)** (p. 520) ***Writing and Language/Standard English Conventions/No Change.*** SThe original sentence is correct. The subject of "are" is "symbols and meanings," and a plural subject requires a plural verb. On first reading, it might be unclear whether the use of the present tense is correct, but after reading the next few sentences, it is clear the author intends to write in the present tense, so the original sentence is correct.

2. **(D)** (p. 520) ***Writing and Language/Standard English Conventions/Sentence Structure/Problems of Coordination and Subordination.*** The underlined portion contains a transitional word that does not correctly express the relationship between the elements of the sentence. "Meanwhile" is used to imply events that occur simultaneously. For example, "Meanwhile, back at the ranch house, the cook was making dinner, unaware that the bandits were ready to strike." "While" is used to create a contrast; (D) creates this necessary contrast. As for (B) and (C), "because" is incorrect; the author does not intend to imply a causal connection between the two ideas.

3. **(A)** (p. 520) ***Writing and Language/Expression of Ideas/Organization/Paragraph-Level Structure***. The defining characteristic of the first paragraph is the series of parallel characteristics: circular halo vs. halo with cross; bare feet vs. Virgin Mary; Saint Peter vs. Saint Paul; etc. The addition completes the pair: earth vs. heaven.

4. **(A)** (p. 520) ***Writing and Language/Expression of Ideas/No Change.*** The main idea of the first paragraph is that art of the Middle Ages is a sacred script. The sentence that begins with the underlined portion should be part of the first paragraph because it is an example of the symbols and meanings that characterize this art as a sacred script. In other words, the example provides proof for the position the author develops in the first paragraph. As for the other choices, (C) introduces a problem of logical expression—several "towers" would not have a single window, and in (D), the expression "having a tower" seems to be an adjective phrase, but there is nothing for it to modify.

5. **(B)** (p. 520) ***Writing and Language/Standard English Conventions/Grammar and Usage/Nouns and Noun Clauses.*** The logic of the original sentence is distorted. Specifically, something is missing, and (B) supplies the missing element: the relative pronoun "who" to function as the subject of the verb "had revived." (C) uses the wrong relative pronoun ("who" is preferred for referring to people) and introduces an incorrect apostrophe. (D) also incorrectly uses the possessive.

6. **(D)** (p. 521) ***Writing and Language/Expression of Ideas/Strategy/Appropriate Supporting Material.*** The second paragraph discusses numbers in the art of the Middle Ages. The author gives several examples to prove the point that mathematics was an important element. The underlined sentence, however, talks about music. As used, the sentence doesn't support the author's point, isn't parallel to the other example, and doesn't belong in the paragraph.

7. **(D)** (p. 521) ***Writing and Language/Expression of Ideas/Style/Conciseness***. The original underlined version is needlessly wordy. "Can be seen" already includes the notion of "viewers," so the phrase can be deleted without losing any meaning.

8. **(D)** (p. 521) ***Writing and Language/Standard English Conventions/Grammar and Usage/Pronoun Usage.*** The original contains two errors. First, the relative clause introduced by "who" cannot serve as the object of the verb "symbolizes" because "who" introduces an adjective and we need some sort of noun. So a good alternative is to use the demonstrative pronoun "those" to function as the object, which is then modified by the relative clause introduced by "who." Second, the verb tenses are not parallel: . . . are lost and . . . have been saved. The first is present, the second imperfect. (D) corrects both errors.

9. **(C)** (p. 521) ***Writing and Language/Standard English Conventions/Punctuation/Commas.*** Remember that commas are needed to show interruptions in the flow of a sentence, interruptions such as introductory phrases and asides:

Introductory phrase: Hoping to impress the job interviewer, Shareen wore her brand-new Gucci suit.

Aside: Xavier, like his sister Maya, looks very much like their father.

In the item, the aside "like nature" must be set off by a pair of commas, one showing the start of the aside and the other showing its end.

10. **(C)** (p. 521) ***Writing and Language/Expression of Ideas/Style/Precision.*** The passage means to say that the works of artists who followed the rules were almost automatically good or even better, despite the skill of the artists, and the best choice to express that thought is "elevated."

11. **(A)** (p. 521) ***Writing and Language/Expression of Ideas/Strategy/Effective Concluding Sentence.*** Adding the suggested sentence to the passage serves two useful purposes. First, at that point, the writer distinguishes the Renaissance artists who break with tradition as either great or not so great. The great ones, according to the writer, produce paintings that are equal to those of the masters of the Middle Ages, but the works, for all the risk, aren't really better. Adding the sentence completes the comparison by discussing the Renaissance artists who break with tradition but aren't really all that talented: their works are just mediocre. That is sufficient reason to add the sentence. Now, once the sentence is added, the two-part comparison really wraps up the passage: the conventions were so powerful that later artists, whether great or ordinary, who broke with tradition did not at first make a lot of progress.

Passage 2

12. **(C)** (p. 522) ***Writing and Language/Expression of Ideas/Style/Tone.*** The original, (B), and (D) use expressions that are informal usage. The more neutral and detached "express concern" is more consistent with the academic tone of the rest of the passage.

13. **(A)** (p. 522) ***Writing and Language/Expression of Ideas/Strategy/Appropriate Supporting Material.*** This item requires you to show that you understand the writer's argument and its structure. The writer distinguishes three senses of "shortage," and in the next paragraph talks about shortages that can be corrected by rising prices. This is the second type of shortage listed.

14. **(C)** (p. 522) ***Writing and Language/Standard English Conventions/Punctuation/Commas.*** This item tests the use of commas, and the underlined portion includes two different usages. First, the series "academic, industrial, and government employees" is correctly punctuated. Remember that each element of a series with three or more elements is followed by a comma to set it off from the following element—except the last, of course. The serial comma or Oxford comma is optional; "academic, industrial and government employees" is also acceptable. So the original is correct so far as this practice is concerned. But it is also required that the end of an introductory dependent clause be marked with a comma, and the original is incorrect on this score. You need a comma following "employers," not because "employers" is an element of the series but because "employers" is the last word in the dependent clause.

15. (B) (p. 522) ***Writing and Language/Standard English Conventions/Sentence Structure/Faulty Parallelism.*** The two verbs here must both be conjugated forms and in the present tense. This is required by the sense of the sentence (they "observe," and they "consider") and not some requirement of parallelism. Thus, (C) is wrong because it imposes an unneeded parallelism that distorts the logic of the sentence.

16. (B) (p. 522) ***Writing and Language/Expression of Ideas/Strategy/Appropriate Supporting Material.*** This item asks for the correct conclusion to be drawn from the paragraph. The writer argues that a shortage will drive prices up. In the case of a particular kind of worker, a shortage will cause wages to rise as employers try to fill their empty positions. Then, when those in the education pipeline see that wages are rising, some will choose that area for a career, and more workers will be available, reducing the shortage. As the shortage is eliminated, prices will no longer rise.

17. (D) (p. 523) ***Writing and Language/Standard English Conventions/Grammar and Usage/Subject-Verb Agreement.*** The sentence needs a conjugated (main) verb that agrees with the singular subject "aid." The underlined portion has two verbs, and they should be "lowers" and "attracts."

18. (B) (p. 525) ***Writing and Language/Expression of Ideas/Organization/Paragraph-Level Structure.*** The underlined sentence poses a question that is answered by the rest of the paragraph. Therefore, it should be the first sentence.

19. (B) (p. 525) ***Writing and Language/Expression of Ideas/Strategy/Data Presentations.*** The graph shows that professions such as doctors and lawyers earn more than their counterparts in science and engineering. This suggests that there are fewer professionals for the jobs available than there are scientists and engineers for those jobs.

20. (C) (p. 526) ***Writing and Language/Standard English Conventions/Sentence Structure/Comma Splices.*** As written, the sentence seems to be a comma splice. Ordinarily, you might correct a comma splice by adding a conjunction:

... graduates, and most work ...

But that raises a problem of coordination because the two resulting clauses are not making statements of equal significance. So, perhaps the sentence intends a relative clause:

... graduates, most of whom work ...

That would solve the problem of the original while properly expressing the dependence of the relative clause, but it is not a possible choice. And (B) isn't equivalent. The remaining possibility seems to be that the writer intends an adjective phrase:

... graduates, mostly working ...

And that is answer (C).

21. (C) (p. 526) ***Writing and Language/Standard English Conventions/Grammar and Usage/Pronoun Usage.*** What is intended by the writer is a possessive pronoun that refers to "expatriates." The correct form is "their."

22. (D) (p. 526) ***Writing and Language/Expression of Ideas/Strategy/Main Idea.*** This is a main idea question. The writer has argued that there is no real shortage of scientists and engineers using data that shows that such workers are paid less than their professional counterparts. Lower compensation means that firms are able to find all the workers they need and so don't have to pay higher compensation. If the temporary workers program is expanded, then more foreign workers will apply for the jobs and are willing to work for less since "less" here is "more" than they would earn at home.

Passage 3

23. (A) (p. 527) ***Writing and Language/Expression of Ideas/No Change.*** "Pseudonym" or assumed name is what the writer intends here.

24. (A) (p. 527) ***Writing and Language/Expression of Ideas/No Change.*** "However" is a good conjunctive adverb for showing a contrast between two ideas. Here, the contrast is between the early days of bitcoin and its more recent history.

25. (B) (p. 527) ***Writing and Language/Standard English Conventions/Sentence Structure/Comma Splices.*** The original sentence contains a comma splice—two independent clauses jammed together using just a comma. There are at least three ways of correcting this error:

view; peer-to-peer

view. Peer-to-peer

view, and peer-to-peer

(B) joins the two clauses using a semicolon to mark the end of one clause and the beginning of the other. (C), while grammatically correct, would create a contrast that would change the meaning of the sentence.

26. (B) (p. 527) ***Writing and Language/Standard English Conventions/Grammar and Usage/Faulty or Illogical Comparisons.*** The problem with the original is an illogical comparison. The original attempts to compare the controlling agencies of earlier currencies with the bitcoin network: agency vs. network. But as the passage makes clear, those are two distinct ideas.

27. (A) (p. 528) ***Writing and Language/Standard English Conventions/No Change.*** This is a fairly standard item involving punctuation. Asides such as definitions and appositives need to be separated from the main body of the sentence using commas, one to mark the beginning and one to mark the end of the phrase.

28. (B) (p. 528) ***Writing and Language/Expression of Ideas/Strategy/Effective Transitional Sentence.*** This can be a fairly tricky item. The author announces in the fourth paragraph that there are <u>three</u> ways to obtain bitcoins. The first is explained in that same paragraph and is flagged "first" for the reader. The second is also flagged ("second"), and a new paragraph signals the start of the discussion of the second. Where is the third? Mining is the third, and it should be signaled for the reader.

29. (C) (p. 529) ***Writing and Language/Standard English Conventions/Sentence Structure/Misplaced Modifiers.*** The problem with the original is that the introductory modifier seems to apply to "math problem" when the writer intends for it to apply to "miners." (C) corrects this problem by repositioning "miners" to make it clear that it is the miners who must solve the problem. Another way of looking at the sentence is to say that it awkwardly uses the passive voice.

30. (D) (p. 529) ***Writing and Language/Expression of Ideas/Organization/Paragraph-Level Structure.*** This item tests whether or not the reader understands the sequence of steps that make up the paragraph. The certification of the correctness of the work is the final step in the mining process. At that point the miner is awarded the 25 bitcoins for having done the work correctly.

31. (C) (p. 529) ***Writing and Language/Standard English Conventions/Sentence Structure/Misplaced Modifiers.*** The problem with the underlined part of the original is that the modifiers are not presented in a logical order. The author means to say that bitcoin remains a niche currency despite its growth. In the original, we actually have two independent modifiers: "since its inception" and "despite significant growth." (C) solves the problem by making "since its inception" modify "growth."

32. (D) (p. 529) ***Writing and Language/Expression of Ideas/Style/Precision.*** A niche is a shallow cavity in a wall that is often used to display a figurine or other ornament. Because such an object fits nicely in the cavity, *niche* is also used to refer to a comfortable resting place or particularly appropriate place for an object. A niche market is a small part of the market that is served by a company that provides goods or services that satisfy the peculiar demands of that small area.

33. (C) (p. 529) ***Writing and Language/Expression of Ideas/Organization/Paragraph-Level Structure.*** The sentence explains why bitcoins are subject to extreme swings in value. This general explanation should come before the author's specific examples of the bitcoin's volatility. So it should be placed fourth, before the sentence that begins "In mid-January 2015."

Passage 4

34. (B) (p. 530) ***Writing and Language/Standard English Conventions/Grammar and Usage/Subject-Verb Agreement.*** The underlined part of the original sentence contains an error of subject-verb agreement. The subject of the sentence is "leaders," a plural noun. So the verb must also be plural: were.

35. (B) (p. 530) ***Writing and Language/Standard English Conventions/Grammar and Usage/Adjectives versus Adverbs.*** The problem with the original is the use of the comparative *–er* form. The comparative form of adjectives is used to compare two ideas; the superlative or *–est* is needed for three or more. In this case, the passage announces that there were three foundational elements to the Meiji Restoration, so "oldest" is required.

36. (D) (p. 530) ***Writing and Language/Standard English Conventions/Sentence Structure/Faulty Parallelism.*** The problem with the original is a failure of parallelism: respect (noun) and worshipping (verb form). (D) corrects the problem by using parallel forms: respect for and worship of. Both are noun forms. (C) is close but fails because "respect" is forced to use the preposition "of," but "respect of" is not idiomatic.

37. **(D)** (p. 530) ***Writing and Language/Expression of Ideas/Style/Precision.*** This item pretty much reduces to a choice between (A) and (D). The weakness in (A) is that "perpetuated" is usually used to refer to a state of affairs that is undesirable, but there is no element of that here. Better would be "preserved."

38. **(C)** (p. 531) ***Writing and Language/Standard English Conventions/Grammar and Usage/Nouns and Noun Clauses.*** The problem with the original is that the participle form "having been" functions as an adjective. But the intention of the author is not to say that Neo-Confucianism would reinforce feudalism *because* it was once an official ideology. Rather, Neo-Confucianism had that effect because of the tenets of the religious-philosophical thought that it adopted. So what is required here is a relative clause: "Neo-Confucianism, which had been the official . . . ."

39. **(C)** (p. 531) ***Writing and Language/Expression of Ideas/Strategy/Effective Transitional Sentence.*** "Some" is either non-idiomatic or informal usage (depending on how you read it), so the resulting phrasing is not very precise. Substituting "another" makes the connection between the second tradition and the third tradition clear. The second tradition was a basic tenet of Confucianism, and the third tradition is yet another basic tenet of Confucianism.

40. **(C)** (p. 531) ***Writing and Language/Standard English Conventions/Grammar and Usage/Subject-Verb Agreement.*** The underlined portion of the sentence occurs in a clause with an inverted subject and verb. That is, the subject comes after the verb. The subject is "miles," so the plural "were" is needed.

41. **(C)** (p. 531) ***Writing and Language/Expression of Ideas/Style/Idiomatic Expression.*** The original is not only clumsy and informal usage ("got aided"), but there is a lack of parallelism of form between "got aided" and "encouraged." Both problems are eliminated by (C).

42. **(C)** (p. 532) ***Writing and Language/Expression of Ideas/Style/Tone.*** (A), (B), and (D) are all inconsistent with the formal tone of the passage. "Wholesale" expresses the idea of "widespread" or "unchecked."

43. **(D)** (p. 532) ***Writing and Language/Expression of Ideas/Strategy/Main Idea.*** This item asks what conclusion can be drawn from the information provided earlier in the paragraph. Earlier in the paragraph, the author states that Westernization eventually slowed, and the passage describes educational theory: initially influenced by the West but also stressing traditional values. The passage implies that art and literature were subject to similar forces: initially influenced by the West but traditional styles reasserted.

44. **(A)** (p. 532) ***Writing and Language/Expression of Ideas/Strategy/Main Idea.*** This question really is about the main point of the passage and asks you to say what sort of conclusion the evidence presented will support. The passage explains that the organizers of the Restoration were primarily interested in moving Japan into the twentieth century while still preserving stability in the country, so they mixed traditions with policies of modernization. The passage lists the various accomplishments such as building a transportation and communication infrastructure that moved Japan into the modern century. One paragraph states that tradition remained strong in a couple of areas. But the last sentence of the passage, as originally written, states unequivocally that Japan has moved into the twentieth century. (A) best expresses this balance.

Section 3: Math, No Calculator

1. **(B) (p. 534) *Math: Multiple-Choice/Algebra/Manipulating Algebraic Expressions/Basic Algebraic Manipulations.*** Note that $(b-a)=-(a-b)$ and $(c-b)=-(b-c)$. Thus, $(b-a)(c-b)=(-1)^2(a-b)(b-c)$, and so $(a-b)(b-c)-(b-a)(c-b)=0$.

   This item can also be solved by evaluating the given expression. Use the FOIL (First, Outer, Inner, Last) method for multiplying polynomials: $(a-b)(b-c)= ab-ac-b^2+bc$; $(b-a)(c-b)=bc-b^2-ac+ab$. Subtract the second expression from the first expression: $\left(ab-ac-b^2+bc\right)-\left(bc-b^2-ac+ab\right)=0$.

2. **(B) (p. 534) *Math: Multiple-Choice/Algebra/Expressing and Evaluating Algebraic Functions/Function Notation.*** Substitute 3 for x in the given function and evaluate: $f(3)=3^2-3=6$. Repeat the procedure: $f(f(3))=f(6)=6^2-6=30$.

3. **(A) (p. 534) *Math: Multiple-Choice/Algebra/Manipulating Algebraic Expressions/Factoring Expressions*** Factor the top and bottom expressions, and simplify: $\frac{m^2+mn}{m^2-n^2}=\frac{m(m+n)}{(m+n)(m-n)}=\frac{m}{m-n}$.

4. **(C) (p. 534) *Math: Multiple-Choice/Algebra/Solving Algebraic Equations or Inequalities with One Variable/Equations Involving Absolute Value.*** First, set up the derivative equations: $\frac{x-2}{3}=4$ or $\frac{x-2}{3}=-4$. And solve for x: $x-2=12 \Rightarrow x=14$ or $x-2=-12 \Rightarrow x=-10$. Then, check both solutions to eliminate any extraneous solutions: $\left|\frac{x-2}{3}\right|=4 \Rightarrow \left|\frac{14-2}{3}\right|=4 \Rightarrow |4|=4$ and $\left|\frac{x-2}{3}\right|=4 \Rightarrow \left|\frac{-10-2}{3}\right|=4 \Rightarrow |-4|=4$.

   Alternatively, this problem is a good opportunity to use the "test-the-test" strategy—it may be a faster solution than the algebra approach in this case.

5. **(B) (p. 534) *Math: Multiple-Choice/Algebra/Solving Quadratic Equations and Relations*** The stem specifies that the solution set to the equation is $\{-2, 4\}$, so when $x = -2$ or $x = 4$, the equation is equal to zero: the factors are $x + 2$ and $x - 4$. Multiply the factors to determine a, b, and c: $(x+2)(x-4)=x^2-4x+2x-8=x^2-2x-8$, so $a = 1$, $b = -2$, and $c = -8$. Of the choices, only (B) is not true.

6. **(C)** (p. 534) ***Math: Multiple-Choice/Coordinate Geometry/Slope of a Line.*** The given functions $f(-1)=1$ and $f(2)=7$ define two coordinate points included in the graph of $f(x)$: $(-1,1)$ and $(2,7)$. Therefore, the slope of the line is $m=\frac{7-1}{2-(-1)}=\frac{6}{3}=2$.

7. **(C)** (p. 534) ***Math: Multiple-Choice/Algebra/Manipulating Algebraic Expressions/Factoring Expressions.*** As for (A), $p(x)=x^3+x^2-4x-4$, so it is a polynomial of the third degree and has three unique factors. As for (B), the zeroes of a polynomial are the values of *x* for which the expression equals zero, so test $x=1$: $1(1+1-4)-4=-2-4=-6$, which isn't zero, so (B) is false. As for (C), plug -1 for *x* in *p*(*x*) to determine if it equals 0: $(-1)[(-1)^2+(-1)-4]-4=(-1)(-4)-4=0$, so (C) is true. Note that (D) is false because substituting 0 for *x* in *p*(*x*) returns a value of -4, not 0.

8. **(A)** (p. 534) ***Math: Multiple-Choice/Coordinate Geometry/The Coordinate System.*** A point where two lines on a graph cross is called a point of intersection. Two graphs cross when their *y*-values, at a single value of *x*, are equal. To find the points of intersection for two equations, simply set the two equations equal and solve for *x*. In this instance, $x=m$. So, $x^2-4=-x^2+4 \Rightarrow 2x^2-8=0 \Rightarrow x^2-4=0 \Rightarrow x^2=4 \Rightarrow x=\pm 2$. If $m>0$, then $m = 2$.

Another way to solve the problem is to set one of the equations equal to zero: $(m,0) \Rightarrow 0=m^2-4 \Rightarrow m^2=4 \Rightarrow m=\pm 2$. Again, since $m>0$, $m=2$. Check that with the other equation: $y=-(2)^2+4=0$.

A third way to solve the problem would be to substitute each of the answer choices for *x* to find the value for which each equation equals zero. For example, starting with (A): $0=x^2-4 \Rightarrow 0=(2)^2-4 \Rightarrow 0=0$ and $0=-x^2+4 \Rightarrow 0=-(2)^2+4 \Rightarrow 0=0$.

9. **(B)** (p. 534) ***Math: Multiple-Choice/Geometry/Solids/Volume.*** The volume of a rectangular solid is equal to the area of one face multiplied by the remaining dimension. In this case, the volume is 54, so $(x)(2x)(3)=54 \Rightarrow x^2=\frac{54}{6}=9 \Rightarrow x=\sqrt{9}=3$.

10. **(C)** (p. 535) ***Math: Multiple-Choice/Algebra/Creating, Expressing, and Evaluating Algebraic Equations and Functions.*** The difference between the current salary, *c*, and the salary in *y* years, *s*, is $\frac{r}{2}(y)$. So, $\frac{r}{2}(y)$ has the same units as salary (say, dollars). Since *y* has units of years, *r* must have units of dollars per year, so the term in question is *r* dollars per year divided by 2, or *r* dollars per 2 years. Therefore, the $\frac{r}{2}$ term means that the employee receives a raise of *r* dollars every two years.

11. **(D)** (p. 535) ***Math: Multiple-Choice/Coordinate Geometry/The Coordinate System.*** Solve this item by inferring that $b>a$, so $b-a>0$. Similarly, $-c>-a$, so $c<a \Rightarrow a-c>0$. Therefore, (D) must be true.

12. **(C)** (p. 535) ***Math: Multiple-Choice/Algebra/Creating, Expressing, and Evaluating Algebraic Equations and Functions.*** According to the given information, $t \geq 24$ hours and $t \leq 36$ hours, so $24 \leq t \leq 36$. Based on

the answer choices, try subtracting 30 from all parts of the inequality: $24-30 \le t-30 \le 36-30$. Thus, $-6 \le t-30 \le 6$, which is the same as the resulting equations from $|t-30| \le 6$ ($t-30 \le 6$ and $t-30 \ge 6$).

13. (A) (p. 535) ***Math: Multiple-Choice/Algebra/Solving Quadratic Equations and Relations* and *Geometry/Rectangles and Squares and Complex Figures.*** The area of the border is equal to the area of the quilt with the border minus the area of the quilt without the border:

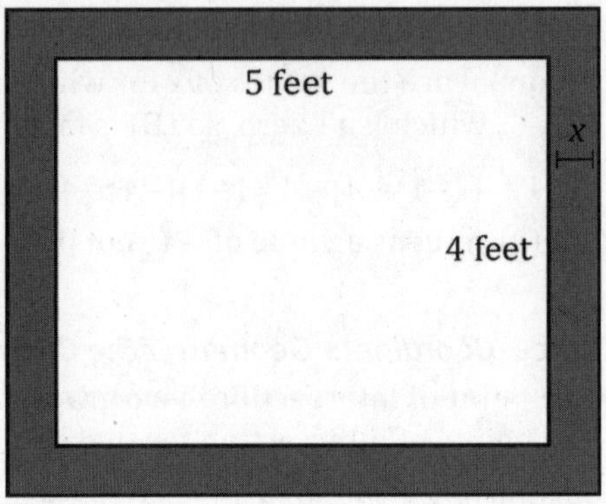

Therefore, $A_{\text{border}} = A_{\text{quilt with border}} - A_{\text{quilt}} \Rightarrow 10 = (2x+5)(2x+4)-(5)(4) \Rightarrow$ $10 = 4x^2 + 8x + 10x + 20 - 20 \Rightarrow 4x^2 + 18x - 10 = 0 \Rightarrow 2x^2 + 9x - 5 = 0 \Rightarrow (2x-1)(x+5) = 0$. Since distances can't be negative, x must be equal to $\frac{1}{2}$ foot.

14. (B) (p. 535) ***Math: Multiple-Choice/Trigonometry/Definitions of the Six Trigonometric Functions* and *Determining Values on the Unit Circle.*** Since $\tan x - 1 = 0$, $\tan x = 1$. And $\tan x = \frac{\sin x}{\cos x} \Rightarrow 1 = \frac{\sin x}{\cos x}$, so $\sin x = \cos x$. The item stem tells us that we are dealing with the first quadrant ($0° \le x \le 90°$). In the first quadrant, $\sin 45° = \frac{\sqrt{2}}{2}$ and $\cos 45° = \frac{\sqrt{2}}{2}$, thus $\sin x$ and $\cos x$ are equal when $x = 45°$.

15. (D) (p. 536) ***Math: Multiple-Choice/Geometry/Triangles/Properties of Triangles* and *30°-60°-90° Triangles.*** Complete the figure with the given information. The triangle is equilateral, so the angles are each equal to 60°. Since U and W are both midpoints, $\overline{UW}$ is parallel to $\overline{SR}$. ΔRST is similar to ΔWUT because the ratio of their sides is the same, and the angle between those sides has the same measurement. $UT{:}ST{::}WT{:}RT{::}1{:}2$ and $\angle STR = \angle UTW = 60°$. Therefore, $\angle VUT$ equals $\angle RST$: 60°. Since V is the midpoint of $\overline{UW}$ and because ΔTWU is an equilateral triangle, $\overline{VT}$ meets $\overline{UW}$ at a right angle, and ΔVUT is a 30°-60°-90° triangle.

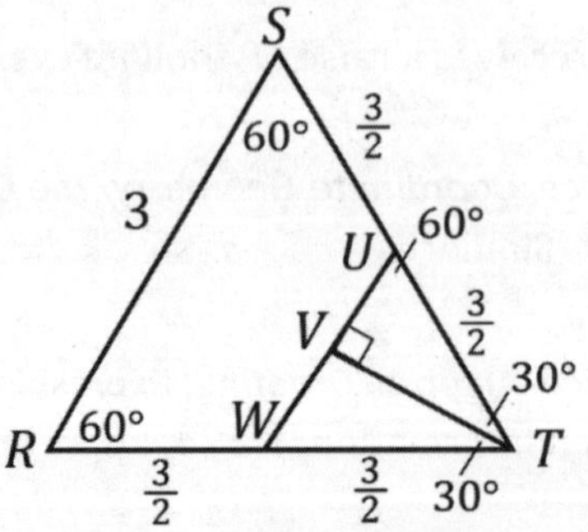

Note that each of the angles in ΔWUT is also 60°, so ΔWUT is an equilateral triangle. Thus, $\overline{UW} = \overline{UT} = \overline{WT} = \frac{3}{2}$ and $\overline{UV}$ is half of $\overline{UW}$, or $\frac{3}{4}$.

Alternatively, the length of $\overline{UV}$ can also be determined from the relationships between the sides and angles of a 30°-60°-90° triangle:

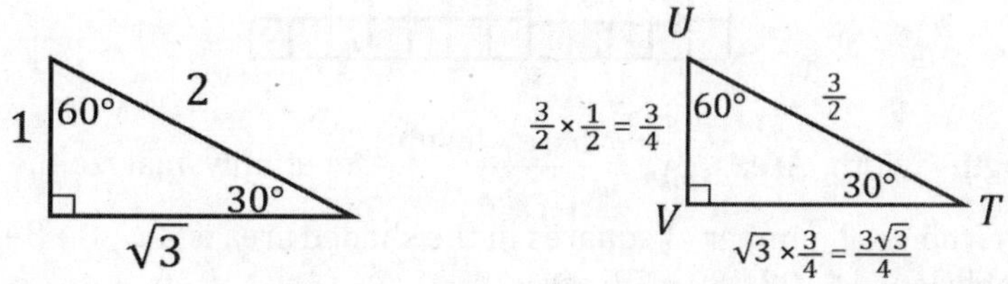

16. (72) (p. 538) ***Math: Student-Produced Responses/Problem Solving and Advanced Arithmetic/Complicated Manipulations.*** Perform the indicated operations: $\frac{1}{2^{-3}} \bullet \frac{1}{3^{-2}} = 2^3 \bullet 3^2 = 8 \bullet 9 = 72$.

17. (3) (p. 538) ***Math: Student-Produced Responses/Algebra/Solving Algebraic Equations or Inequalities with One Variable/Equations Involving Rational Expressions.*** Solve for x^y:
$\frac{64}{x^y} - 6 = 2 \Rightarrow \frac{64}{x^y} = 8 \Rightarrow x^y = \frac{64}{8} = 8$. Since $8 = 2^3$, $x^y = 2^3$. Therefore, $y = 3$.

18. (24) (p. 538) ***Math: Student-Produced Responses/Problem Solving and Advanced Arithmetic/Complicated Arithmetic Application Items.*** Work backward through the problem to arrive at *T*: one-fourth of 16 is 4, so after one-third were turned down, 16 remained. And 16 is two-thirds of 24, so 24 people applied for jobs.

Alternatively, set up an equation: $\left(\frac{1}{4}\right)\left(\frac{2}{3}\right)T = 4 \Rightarrow \frac{2}{12}T = 4 \Rightarrow 2T = 48 \Rightarrow T = 24$.

19. (3) (p. 538) ***Math: Student-Produced Responses/Algebra/Solving Simultaneous Equations.*** Translate the given information into a system of simultaneous equations. Let *x* equal the number of groups with 3 students and *y* equal the number of groups with 4 students: $x + y = 12$. And since there are 45 students, $45 = 3x + 4y$. Substitute $y = 12 - x$ for *y* in the second equation and solve for *x*:
$3x + 4y = 45 \Rightarrow 3x + 4(12 - x) = 45 \Rightarrow 3x + 48 - 4x = 45 \Rightarrow x = 3$.

20. (78) (p. 538) ***Math: Student-Produced Responses/Geometry/Complex Figures*** and ***Triangles/Properties of Triangles*** and ***Rectangles and Squares.*** Since each square is an acre, determine how many squares there are in total and how many are shaded. The entire figure is 12 squares by 9 squares, or 108 squares, and each is equal to an acre, so the entire piece of land is 108 acres. The shaded area is equal to the sum of the areas of two rectangles and two triangles:

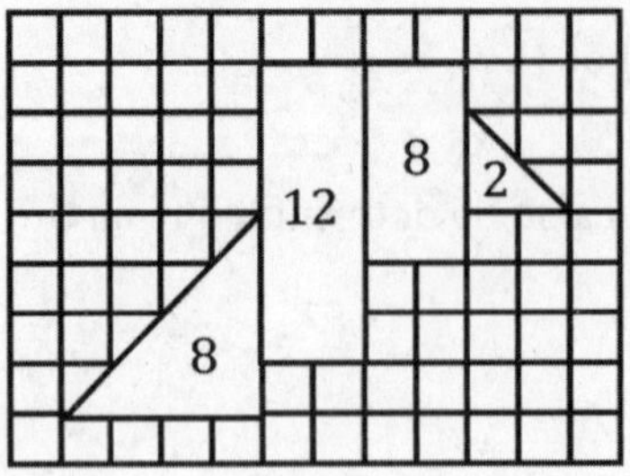

$\text{Area}_{\text{rectangle}} = \text{length} \bullet \text{width}$. $\text{Area}_{\text{triangle}} = \frac{\text{base} \bullet \text{height}}{2}$, or simply analyze the triangles as half-squares. Therefore, the total number of squares in the shaded area is $12+8+8+2=30$ acres. Therefore, the amount of tillable land is $108-30=78$ acres.

Section 4: Math, Calculator

1. **(A)** (p. 540) ***Math: Multiple-Choice/Algebra/Manipulating Algebraic Expressions/Evaluating Expressions.*** If the price of 5 boxes of pens is *d* dollars, then the price of 5 boxes of pens is 100*d* cents. Since each box contains 30 pens, the price is 100*d* cents per $5 \bullet 30 = 150$ pens, or $\frac{100d}{150}$. The cost of 12 pens is 12 times that, or $\frac{100d(12)}{150} = 8d$.

   Alternatively, assume some numbers and "test-the-test" by plugging the values into the answer choices.

2. **(D)** (p. 540) ***Math: Multiple-Choice/Problem-Solving and Advanced Arithmetic/Common Problem Solving Items/Proportions and Direct-Inverse Variation.*** Set up a direct proportion and solve for the missing value: $\frac{\text{Cement X}}{\text{Cement Y}} = \frac{\text{Grit X}}{\text{Grit Y}} \Rightarrow \frac{4}{50} = \frac{20}{x} \Rightarrow 4x = (20)(50) \Rightarrow x = \frac{(20)(50)}{4} = 250$ cubic yards of grit.

3. **(D)** (p. 540) ***Math: Multiple-Choice/Data Interpretation/Bar, Cumulative, and Line Graphs*** and ***Problems Solving and Advanced Arithmetic/Common Advanced Arithmetic Items/Percents.*** Add up the categories to find the total compensation: $0.8+0.4+0.6+0.2=2$ million dollars. Since wages and salaries account for 0.8 million dollars, the percentage is $\frac{0.8}{2} \times 100\% = 40\%$.

4. **(C)** (p. 540) ***Math: Multiple-Choice/Problem Solving and Advanced Arithmetic/Complicated Arithmetic Application Items.*** Set up an equation and solve for *J*, John's age: $\frac{2J}{3} = 12 \Rightarrow 2J = 36 \Rightarrow J = 18$.

   Alternatively, test the answer choices to find the one that works. Only (C) works: (18)(2) = 36, and $36 \div 3 = 12$.

5. **(D)** (p. 540) ***Math: Multiple-Choice/Algebra/Creating, Solving, and Interpreting Algebraic Equations and Functions.*** Since *y* is the cost of getting in the car plus *x* miles at $0.4 per mile, $y = 0.4x + 1.5$.

6. (B) (p. 541) ***Math: Multiple-Choice/Data Interpretation/Bar, Cumulative, and Line Graphs*** and ***Problem Solving and Advanced Arithmetic/Common Problem Solving Items/Percents.*** According to the graph, the rate of rise in 1980 was 2 mm/year. In 2000, the rate of rise was 3 mm/year. Therefore, the change in rate is an increase of $\frac{3-2}{2}=\frac{1}{2}=0.5\times 100\%=50\%$.

7. (D) (p. 541) ***Math: Multiple-Choice/Data Interpretation/Pie Charts*** and ***Problem Solving and Advanced Arithmetic/Common Arithmetic Items/Proportions and Direct-Inverse Variation.*** Begin by writing a simple sentence describing the situation: "75 is equal to 15% of the total." Set up a direct proportion or a percent problem: $\frac{75}{T}=\frac{15}{100}$, where T is the total number of transit vehicles. Solve for T:

$T=\frac{75\times 100}{15}=5\times 100=500$.

8. (D) (p. 541) ***Math: Multiple-Choice/Problem Solving and Advanced Arithmetic/Common Advanced Arithmetic Items/Properties of Numbers.*** Since $\frac{x}{y}$ is an integer, and x and y are different integers they cannot both be 1, so x must be greater than y. Otherwise, x would not be evenly divisible by y. Thus, (I) is part of the correct answer. As for (II), x and y are positive integers, so $xy > 0$. Finally, $y - x < 0$ is equivalent to $y < x$, which is the same as (I). Therefore, (D) is the correct choice.

9. (B) (p. 541) ***Math: Multiple-Choice/Statistics/Median.*** Median refers to the middle-most value when the numbers in a set are arranged in order. A histogram, by definition, shows the data arranged in order. Add the values and divide by two to find the median: 27 + 18 + 20 + 12 + 8 + 1 = 86 homes included, and $86 \div 2 = 43$, so the 43rd home is the median. Now count from the left to find the 43rd home. The 43rd home has one child.

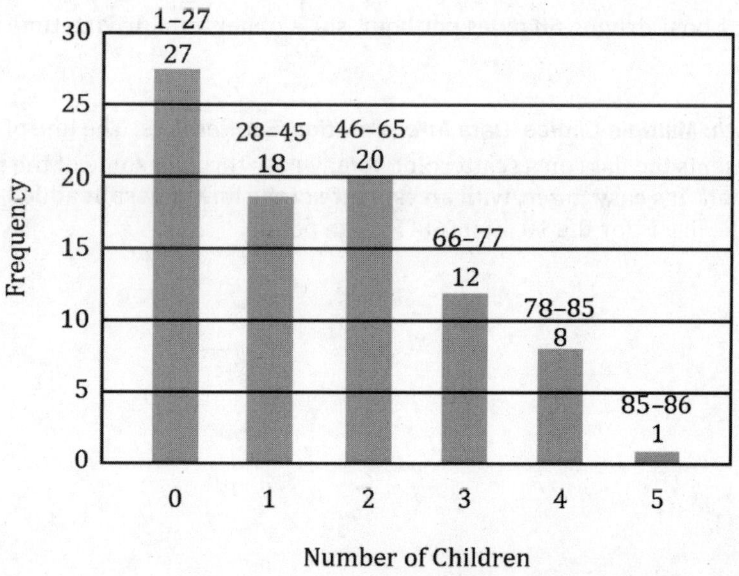

10. (C) (p. 542) ***Math: Multiple-Choice/Statistics/Averages.*** Create an expression for a weighted average: $\frac{\text{total \# of children}}{\text{total \# of households}} = \frac{27(0)+18(1)+20(2)+12(3)+8(4)+1(5)}{27+18+20+12+8+1} = \frac{131}{86} \approx 1.5$.

11. (C) (p. 542) ***Math: Multiple-Choice/Statistics/Data Interpretation in Statistics and Problem Solving and Advanced Arithmetic/Common Problem Solving Items/Proportions and Direct-Inverse Variation.*** The total number of residences in the represented neighborhood is $27+18+20+12+8+1=86$, 27 of which are childless. The item stem states that this proportion is true for the entire city, so $\frac{27}{86} = \frac{x}{3.5 \times 10^5}$. Solve for x: $x = \frac{27 \times 3.5}{86} \times 10^5 \approx 1.1 \times 10^5 = 110{,}000$ residences in the entire city are childless.

12. (B) (p. 542) ***Math: Multiple-Choice/Algebra/Solving Simultaneous Equations.*** Let x, y, and z represent the number of each type of vegetable. The total garden area is 12 square feet, so $x \text{ plants} \times \frac{0.5 \text{ square foot}}{\text{X plant}} + y \text{ plants} \times \frac{0.5 \text{ square foot}}{\text{Y plant}} + z \text{ plants} \times \frac{2 \text{ square feet}}{\text{Z plant}} = 12$ square feet: $\frac{1}{2}(x+y)+2z=12$. Since $x=y=z$, $\frac{1}{2}(2x)+2x=12 \Rightarrow 3x=12 \Rightarrow x=4$. Therefore, there are four of each type of vegetable, for a total of 12 plants.

13. (A) (p. 542) ***Math: Multiple-Choice/Problem-Solving and Advanced Arithmetic/Complicated Advanced Arithmetic Items.*** The time spent traveling is equal to the distance divided by the rate. In this case, the total time spent traveling is $\frac{10 \text{ miles}}{20 \text{ miles/hour}} + \frac{10 \text{ miles}}{30 \text{ miles/hour}} + \frac{10 \text{ miles}}{60 \text{ miles/hour}}$. Give the fractions a common denominator, so the total time is $\frac{3}{6}+\frac{2}{6}+\frac{1}{6}=\frac{6}{6}=1$ hour. The motorist spent $\frac{1}{6}$ hour of the total driving time of 1 hour driving 60 miles per hour, so $\frac{1}{6}$ of her total driving time was at that rate.

14. (A) (p. 542) ***Math: Multiple-Choice/Data Interpretation/Scatterplots.*** The line of best fit is a straight line that best represents the data on a scatterplot; it may pass through some of the points, none of the points, or all of the points. It's easy to see, with an estimate of the line of best fit added, that the data point farthest from the line is for the 10 mph (68°F) data point:

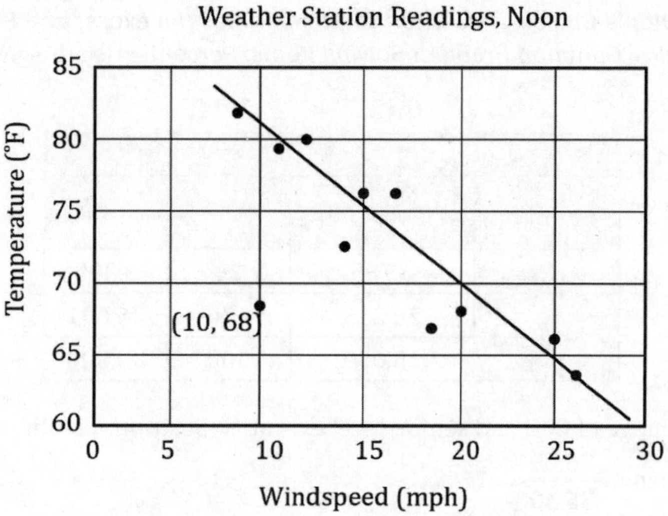

15. (C) (p. 543) ***Math: Multiple-Choice/Algebra/Creating, Expressing, and Evaluating Algebraic Equations and Functions.*** The given equation in slope-intercept form is $y=\frac{1}{3}x$. The solution notation, $(5,1\frac{2}{3})$, refers to (x,y). Therefore, when $x=5$ seconds, the speed of the ball is $1\frac{2}{3}$ meters per second.

16. (D) (p. 543) ***Math: Multiple-Choice/Problem Solving and Advanced Arithmetic/Common Problem Solving Items/Proportions and Direct-Inverse Variation.*** Using the ideal gas law $pV = nRT$, since n, R, and T are all constant, $p_1V_1 = p_2V_2$. Fill in the supplied values:

$$p_1V_1 = p_2V_2 \Rightarrow (3\text{ atm})(1\text{ L}) = p_2\left(\frac{1}{3}\text{ L}\right) \Rightarrow p_2 = \frac{(3\text{ atm})(1\cancel{\text{L}})}{\frac{1}{3}\cancel{\text{L}}} = 9\text{ atm}.$$

17. (D) (p. 543) ***Math: Multiple-Choice/Data Interpretation/Scatterplots.*** The scatterplot shows a positive association between x and y. The association is a non-linear correlation. Note that the nature of the scattered data means that the value of n does not necessarily increase with every increase in m.

18. (A) (p. 544) ***Math: Multiple-Choice/Data Interpretation/Tables (Matrices).*** The following information is implicit in the table:

Fortune 500 Companies, 2013			
	Senior Level Executives	CEOs	Total
Women	8,785		
Men	26,215		
Total	35,000	500	35,500

So, (A) is already known. Any of the other four numbers would allow for the completion of the table.

19. (C) (p. 544) ***Math: Multiple-Choice/Data Interpretation/Tables (Matrices)*** and ***Problem Solving and Advanced Mathematics/Common Problem Solving Items/Percents.*** Use the given information to fill in the table: $0.048 \times 500 = 24$.

Fortune 500 Companies, 2013			
	Senior Level Executives	CEOs	Total
Women	8,785	24	8,809
Men	26,215	476	26,691
Total	35,000	500	35,500

Therefore, the percentage of CEO and senior-level executive positions combined at Fortune 500 companies held by men is $\frac{26{,}691}{35{,}500} \approx 75\%$.

20. (D) (p. 544) ***Math: Multiple-Choice/Data Interpretation/Tables (Matrices)*** and ***Problem Solving and Advanced Arithmetic/Common Problem Solving Items/Proportions and Direct-Inverse Variation.*** Based on the given information, approximately $\frac{24}{500} = \frac{x}{35 \text{ million}} \Rightarrow x = \frac{24(35 \text{ million})}{500} = 1.68$ million.

21. (A) (p. 544) ***Math: Multiple-Choice/Algebra/Solving Simultaneous Equations.*** The possible values for y in each inequality are shown below:

$y \leq \frac{1}{2} + \frac{3}{2}x$

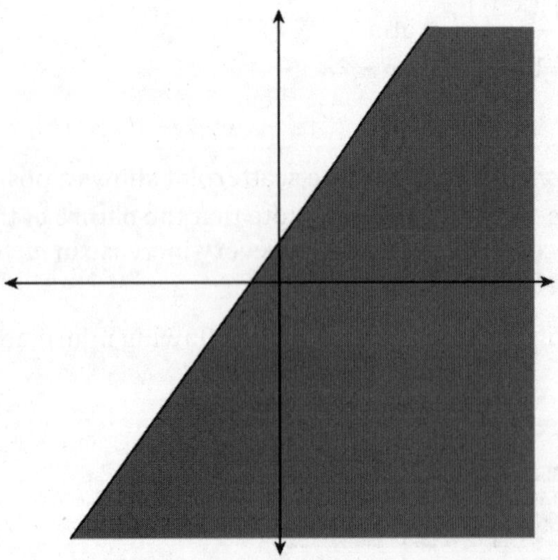

$y > -x + 2$

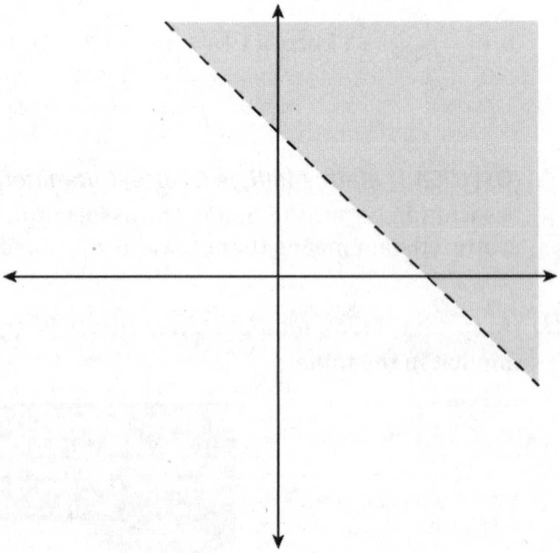

Therefore, the solutions that are common to both inequalities are in Section II of the graph shown in the item stem.

22. (B) (p. 544) ***Math: Multiple-Choice/Coordinate Geometry/Graphs of Linear Equations* and *Graphs of Quadratic Equations and Relations.*** The quickest solution to this item is to quickly sketch the four equations:

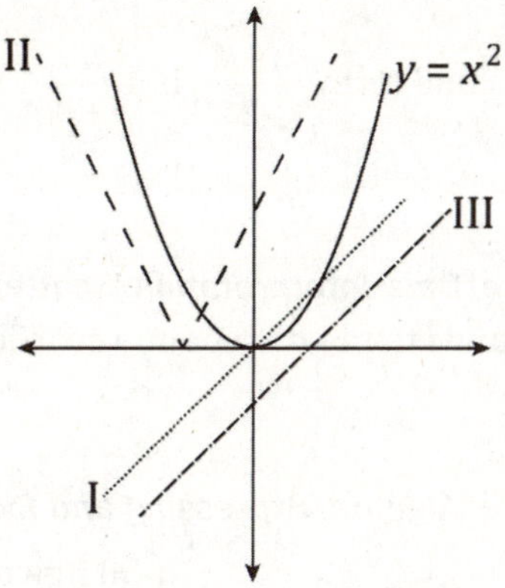

The only equation that does not intersect the equation in the stem is (III). Therefore, (B) is the correct choice.

Note that this item can also be solved using the system of simultaneous equations (by setting each of the three equations equal to the stem equation and determining if there are values for x that make the equality true). However, a sketch of the equations is a much faster solution.

23. (D) (p. 545) ***Math: Multiple-Choice/Geometry/Triangles/Properties of Triangles* and *30°-60°-90° Triangles.*** This problem can be solved with or without trigonometry. First, with trigonometry: ΔPQR is equilateral and therefore equiangular with three 60° angles. And $\angle PQS$ is 30°. Since ΔPQS is a 30°-60°-90° triangle, it has special properties: $PQ = 6$ and $QS = 3\sqrt{3}$. Therefore, the altitude $\overline{QS}$ has a length of $3\sqrt{3}$ and the base $\overline{PR}$ has a length of $(2)(3) = 6$, so the area is $\frac{1}{2}(3\sqrt{3})(6) = 9\sqrt{3}$, which is approximately 15.58.

Note that the cosine relationship can also be used to find the length of $\overline{QS}$: $\cos\angle PQS = \cos 30 = \frac{\overline{QS}}{\overline{PQ}} \Rightarrow \frac{\sqrt{3}}{2} = \frac{QS}{6} \Rightarrow QS = \frac{6\sqrt{3}}{2} = 3\sqrt{3}$. And again, the area is: $\frac{1}{2}(3\sqrt{3})(6) = 9\sqrt{3}$.

Alternatively, solve the problem without trigonometry: $\Delta PQS \cong \Delta RQS$, $\overline{PS} = \overline{SR}$, and $\overline{PQ} = \overline{PR} \Rightarrow PQ = 2PS$. Since $PS = 3$, $PQ = 6$. ΔPQS is a right triangle, so by the Pythagorean theorem: $(PQ)^2 = (PS)^2 + (QS)^2 \Rightarrow 6^2 = 3^2 + (QS)^2 \Rightarrow (QS)^2 = 36 - 9 = 27 \Rightarrow QS = \sqrt{27} = 3\sqrt{3}$. Then, area $= \frac{1}{2} \cdot 6 \cdot 3\sqrt{3} = 9\sqrt{3}$.

24. (B) (p. 545) ***Math: Multiple-Choice/Algebra/Manipulating Algebraic Expressions/Evaluating Expressions*** and ***Problem Solving and Advanced Arithmetic/Common Problem Solving Items/Ratios.*** Using the rule for constructing the sequence, if n is the first term, then, the second term is equal to $\frac{1}{2}(n+4)=\frac{n+4}{2}$. The ratio of the first term, n, to the second term, $\frac{n+4}{2}$, is $\frac{n}{\frac{n+4}{2}}=n\bullet\frac{2}{n+4}=\frac{2n}{n+4}$.

25. (C) (p. 546) ***Math: Multiple-Choice/Data Interpretation/Scatterplots.*** Simply read the graph to find the force value (y-axis) that corresponds to the data point recorded for a distance (x-axis) of 0.5 meters: 50 newtons.

26. (B) (p. 546) ***Math: Multiple-Choice/Algebra/Expressing and Evaluating Algebraic Functions/Functions as Models.*** Plug the given values into the function: $F=\left(\frac{50\text{ newtons}}{\cancel{\text{meter}}}\right)(0.25\ \cancel{\text{meter}})=12.5$ newtons.

27. (C) (p. 546) ***Math: Multiple-Choice/Coordinate Geometry/Slope-Intercept Form of a Linear Equation*** and ***Graphs of Linear Equations*** and ***Data Interpretation/Scatterplots.*** For the linear equation $F=kx$, k is the slope of the line when F is graphed as a function of x. Approximate a line of best fit through the data:

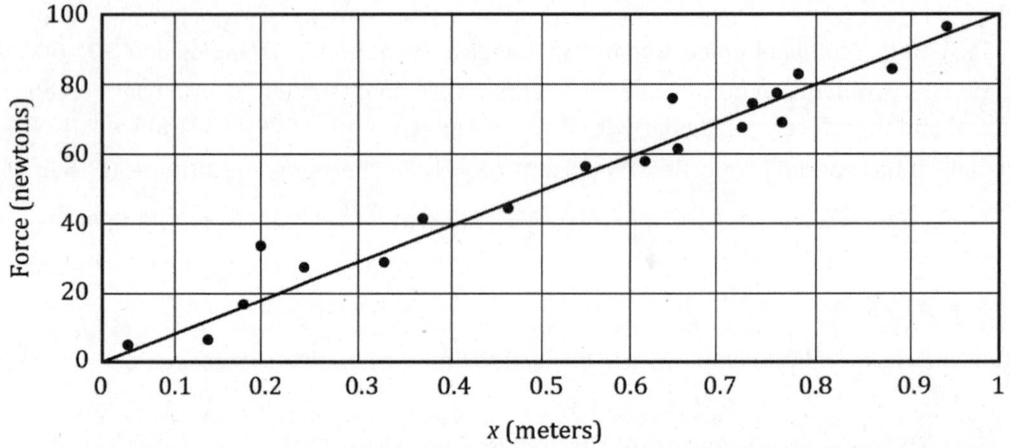

The slope of the line is the change in y divided by the change in x, or approximately $\frac{100-0}{1-0}=100$ newtons per meter. Convert this to dynes per centimeter:

$$\frac{100\ \cancel{\text{newtons}}}{\cancel{\text{meter}}}\times\frac{1\ \cancel{\text{meter}}}{100\text{ centimeters}}\times\frac{1\text{ dyne}}{10\ \cancel{\text{micronewtons}}}\times\frac{10^6\ \cancel{\text{micronewtons}}}{1\ \cancel{\text{newtons}}}=10^5\,\frac{\text{dynes}}{\text{centimeter}}.$$

28. (C) (p. 547) ***Math: Multiple-Choice/Algebra/Creating, Solving, and Interpreting Algebraic Equations and Functions.*** The number of eggs in Basket A after transfer of n eggs from Basket B is $a=n+6$; the number of eggs in Basket B after transfer of n eggs to Basket A is $b=24-n$. The final number of eggs in basket B, b, is at least twice the final number of eggs in Basket A, a, so $2a\le b$.

29. (C) (p. 547) ***Math: Multiple-Choice/Coordinate Geometry/Slope-Intercept Form of a Linear Equation.*** Begin by finding the slope from the two points on the line, $(-1,0)$ and $(2,2)$: $m=\frac{y_2-y_1}{x_2-x_1}=\frac{2-0}{2-(-1)}=\frac{2}{3}$. *b* is the *y* value when the line crosses the y-axis (where *x*=0). The equation of the line is *y=mx+b*; *m* is $\frac{2}{3}$. Plug in a known point on the line and solve for *b*. $0=\frac{2}{3}(-1)+b \Rightarrow b=\frac{2}{3}$. Therefore: $y=\frac{2x}{3}+\frac{2}{3}$.

30. (B) (p. 547) ***Math: Multiple-Choice/Coordinate Geometry/Graphs of Quadratic Equations and Relations.*** Solve the inequality for *y*: $y-2x^2+3x\le 2 \Rightarrow y\le 2x^2-3x+2$. You could graph the inequality, which is a parabolic function, and determine which of the points falls outside of the area represented by the inequality. However, a simpler approach is to test each ordered pair in the inequality:

$(-1,2)$: $2\overset{?}{\le}2(-1)^2-3(-1)+2 \Rightarrow 2\le 7$ ✓

$(1,2)$: $2\overset{?}{\le}2(1)^2-3(1)+2 \Rightarrow 2\le 1$ ✗

$(\frac{3}{2},2)$: $2\overset{?}{\le}2\left(\frac{3}{2}\right)^2-3\left(\frac{3}{2}\right)+2 \Rightarrow 2\le\frac{9}{2}-\frac{9}{2}+2 \Rightarrow 2\le 2$ ✓

$(3,4)$: $4\overset{?}{\le}2(3)^2-3(3)+2 \Rightarrow 4\le 11$ ✓

Therefore, the inequality holds true for three of the four given points. Only one of the given points, (1,2), is not part of the solution set.

31. (1/20, 0.05) (p. 549) ***Math: Student-Produced Responses/Problem Solving and Advanced Arithmetic/Common Problem Solving Items/Percents and Data Interpretation/Bar, Cumulative, and Line Graphs.*** Since all of the data are reported as rates (the number of crimes per 100,000 people), simply deal with the number of crimes. In 1991, there were 6,000 property crimes and 11,000 crimes total; in 2006, there were 4,000 property crimes and 8,000 crimes total. Thus, in 1991, property crimes accounted for $\frac{6}{11}\approx 55\%$ of total crimes; and in 2006, property crimes accounted for $\frac{4}{8}=50\%$ of total crimes. This is a decrease of 5%, or $\frac{1}{20}$.

32. (7) (p. 550) ***Math: Student-Produced Responses/Statistics/Averages and Data Interpretation/Bar, Cumulative, and Line Graphs.*** The number of hurricanes in categories 3, 4, and 5 for each decade is the difference between the total bar length and the number of hurricanes in categories 1 and 2: $19-11=8$, $24-14=10$, $18-9=9$, $14-8=6$, $12-8=4$, $15-11=4$, $14-9=5$, and $19-12=7$. Therefore, the average number of hurricanes in categories 3, 4, and 5 hitting the US mainland per decade since 1931 is $\frac{8+10+9+6+4+4+5+7}{8}=\frac{53}{8}=6.625$. Since the stem asks for the nearest whole number, the correct answer is 7.

33. (2/3, 4/6, 0.66) (p. 551) ***Math: Student-Produced Responses/Algebra/Solving Quadratic Equations and Relations.*** If you remember that for a quadratic equation in the form $ax^2+bx+c=0$, the sum of the roots of the equation is equal to $-\frac{b}{a}$ (the product is equal to $\frac{c}{a}$), this problem is quick to solve. In the given equation, $a=3$, $b=-2$, and $c=-16$, so the sum of the roots is $-\frac{b}{a}=-\frac{-2}{3}=\frac{2}{3}$.

Alternatively, factor the equation: $3x^2-2x-16=0 \Rightarrow (3x-8)(x+2)=0$. Set each factor equal to 0 and solve: $(3x-8)=0 \Rightarrow x=\frac{8}{3}$ and $(x+2)=0 \Rightarrow x=-2$. And the sum of the roots is $\frac{8}{3}+(-2)=\frac{16}{6}+\frac{-12}{6}=\frac{4}{6}=\frac{2}{3}$.

34. (20) (p. 551) ***Math: Student-Produced Responses/Problem Solving and Advanced Arithmetic/Common Problem Solving Items/Percents and Geometry/Solids/Volume.*** Use the equation for the volume of a cylinder, $V=\pi r^2 h$, where *r* is the radius and *h* is the height. If the overall volume increase must be at least 25%, $V'=\frac{5}{4}V=\frac{5}{4}(\pi r^2 h)=\frac{5\pi h}{4}\left(\frac{d}{2}\right)^2=\frac{5\pi h}{16}d^2$. Since the new diameter is to be increased by 50%, $d'=\frac{3}{2}d$, so $V'=\frac{\pi h'}{4}d'^2=\frac{\pi h'}{4}\left(\frac{3}{2}d\right)^2=\frac{9\pi h'}{16}d^2$. Set the two expressions equal to one another and solve for h': $\frac{5\pi h}{16}d^2=\frac{9\pi h'}{16}d^2 \Rightarrow 5h=9h' \Rightarrow h'=\frac{5}{9}h$. Since $h=36$ feet, the new height must be at least $\frac{5}{9}(36)=20$ feet.

35. (7) (p. 551) ***Math: Student-Produced Responses/Algebra/Solving Algebraic Equations or Inequalities with One Variable/Equations Involving Exponents.*** Rewrite the equation so both sides have the same base, 3: $3^{n-4}=27 \Rightarrow 3^{n-4}=3^3$. Set the exponents equal and solve for *n*: $n-4=3 \Rightarrow n=7$.

36. (75) (p. 551) ***Math: Student-Produced Responses/Geometry/Circles*** and ***Problem Solving and Advanced Arithmetic/Common Problem Solving Items/Proportions and Direct-Inverse Variation.*** There are 360 degrees in a circle, so 8 hours is represented by 360 degrees. Set up a direct proportion to determine the size of the sector representing 100 minutes (20 minutes + 20 minutes + 60 minutes):

$$\frac{100 \text{ minutes}}{8\times 60 \text{ minutes}}=\frac{x°}{360°} \Rightarrow x=\frac{100\times 360}{8\times 60}=\frac{100\times 6}{8}=\frac{100\times 3}{4}=75°.$$

37. (1) (p. 551) ***Math: Student-Produced Responses/Problem Solving and Advanced Arithmetic/Common Advanced Arithmetic Items/Complex Numbers.*** Rationalize the denominator in the fraction by multiplying the numerator and the denominator by the conjugate of the denominator (a complex number multiplied by its conjugate results in a real number). Expand the binomials using the FOIL method for multiplying polynomials: $\frac{4+2i}{3-i}\bullet\frac{3+i}{3+i}=\frac{(4+2i)(3+i)}{(3-i)(3+i)}=\frac{12+4i+6i+2i^2}{9+3i-3i-i^2}=\frac{12+10i+2i^2}{9-i^2}$. Since $i=\sqrt{-1}$, $i^2=-1$, so substitute and simplify: $\frac{12+10i+2(-1)}{9-(-1)}=\frac{10+10i}{10}=1+i$. Therefore, $1+i=a+bi$, so $a=1$.

38. **(4)** (p. 551) ***Math: Student-Produced Responses/Creating, Solving, and Interpreting Algebraic Equations and Functions and Solving Simultaneous Equations.*** Create an equation for the total cost under each special as a function of the number of games per bowler. In the first case, $\frac{\$5}{\text{game}} \times x \text{ games} \times 4 \text{ players} = \$20x$ and a discount of \$20 for more than 3 games per bowler. Thus, for $x \leq 3,\ C = 20x$; for $x > 3,\ C = 20x - 20$.

In the second case, $\frac{\$3}{\text{shoes}} \times 4 \text{ players} + \frac{\$3}{\text{game}} \times 4 \text{ players} \times x \text{ games} = 12 + 12x$. For each range of x (integers less than or equal to 3 and greater than 3), set the two equations equal and solve for x games. For $x \leq 3,\ 20x = 12x + 12 \Rightarrow 8x = 12 \Rightarrow x = \frac{3}{2}$; for $x > 3, 20x - 20 = 12x + 12 \Rightarrow 8x = 32 \Rightarrow x = 4$. Since purchasing 1.5 games per bowler is not possible, the correct answer is 4.

Section 5: Writing (p. 552)

Sample Essay Responses and Analyses

Above Average Response

Although we no longer have segregated schools, an argument has been made that educational segregation is "the civil rights issue of our generation." In his speech "Sixty Years After Brown: Where is the Outrage?" Secretary of Education Arne Duncan makes this exact argument, presenting facts and statistics that show certain groups still do not have the same access to high-quality education that white students have. Duncan discusses that, even though we are no longer under the Jim Crow school segregation laws, equal opportunity is still not a reality for many minority, female, disabled, LGBT and disadvantaged students.

Duncan begins his argument by sharing some statistics about modern school segregation. According to the information he presented in his speech, all regions in the US have seen an increased number of African American students attending highly segregated schools (that is, a school where 90 percent or more of the students are students of color). Duncan clarifies that this type of segregation is not by law (which is now unconstitutional after the Brown v. Board of Education decision), but rather by fact. The South sees more than a third of African American students attending this type of school.

While segregation has long been thought of as a "black versus white" issue, Duncan explains that other groups, namely females, disabled students, disadvantaged students, LGBT students, and English-language learners, are not seeing the same educational opportunities as white students. Duncan explains that providing equal educational opportunities for these groups "remains an urgent civil rights issue in ways that would have been unimaginable 60 years ago." However, beyond one small example at the end of the essay regarding students with disabilities, Duncan does little else to address the educational segregation these other groups of students face. Almost all of his examples deal with the segregation of blacks and whites. If Duncan had wanted to show that educational desegregation is truly as universal and current a civil rights issue as he claims it is, he would have provided a more compelling argument if he had added more examples of educational segregation these other groups face.

Another point Duncan makes to persuade his audience into considering education a civil rights issue is the disparity in access to advanced learning courses (AP courses, calculus, etc.). He states that 68 percent of African American students do not have access to calculus courses that are readily available to their 81 percent of their white and 87 percent of their Asian counterparts. Not all families have access to high-quality early learning (pre-kindergarten), which places their children at a disadvantage when it comes time to begin schooling.

While we tend to think that school segregation is an issue of the past, namely because de jure segregation no longer exists, Duncan reminds us that educational segregation is quite possibly the biggest civil rights issue of our time. He is able to make this compelling argument by discussing facts and statistics that clearly show a lack of access to educational opportunities for African American students. However, his argument could be stronger if he had included more facts and statistics about other groups who do not have access to full educational opportunities. While much has been accomplished in the arena of desegregation, there is still much to be done to ensure all students have equal access to a high-quality education.

Analysis of Above Average Response

The writer demonstrates an understanding of the issues presented in the passage, and he/she effectively discusses how the speaker made his argument. The use of textual evidence makes the writer's discussion logical and compelling and shows a solid grasp on the speaker's claims. The writer's choice of vocabulary and sentence structure makes for a response with an appropriate style.

Below Average Response

Since there is no more segregated schools, you would think that we don't have to worry about black people being treated unfairly when it comes to education. But really that is not the case. Even in the modern age there are problems with black students not having as good of an education as white students. This is what Arne Duncan talks about in his speech, the way that education is still segregated in a way, even though there aren't just black schools and white schools. In this essay I am going to talk about how education is still kind of segregated and why according to Arne Duncan's speech.

The first reason Arne Duncan talks about is the fact that black student attend schools with mostly other black students. This means that they don't have access to a lot of the classes that white students have. They also don't have the same opportunities as white students. The reason why this happens is because they can't figure out why there are so many black students all going to the same schools and why it is not more balanced. It is not because of the law because the old laws are gone and you can't make black students go to one school and white students go to another. For some reason this happens and it causes segregation.

The second reason why there is segregation still today is because it includes more than just black students. Female students, disabled students, LGBT students, and students who are still learning English. These students also are sort of separated from the typical white students that have all the educational opportunities open to them without any problem. There needs to be a way to make sure that all students can have access to all the educational opportunities that white students have. This would help with the segregation.

The final reason why schools are still segregated is that there is still discrimination. People like to think that discrimination ended a long time ago but you can still see it a lot of places today. One of the places you find it is in schools. It really is true that there is still discrimination and we need to figure out a way to stop it.

All in all it is surprising that discrimination still exists today. Schools are actually the one place where there might be the most segregation, because there are lots of students and not just black students who are not getting the same education as white students. I think Arne Duncan was right when he talked about this and we need to figure out a way to make sure this segregation and discrimination ends.

Analysis of Below Average Response

While the response follows a somewhat logical sequence, it is clear that the writer does not have a firm grasp on the topic presented in the passage. There are issues of subject-verb agreement and word choice that make the essay difficult to read. The writer does not use much evidence from the text to support his/her argument, and some of the information in the essay may not be accurate. The writer missed the point of the prompt and did not discuss how the speaker developed his argument.

ITEM INDEX

In the following index, all of the numeric references are designed as follows: **Page #**/Item #. The parenthetical information beside each item category refers to the subject-area in which that item category appears.

Cambridge *Victory for ACT® and SAT® Test, 5th Edition*
Error Correction and Suggestion Form

Name/Location: ______________ Day Phone: ______________ E-mail Address: ______________

Part of Materials:
- ☐ Student Text, Specify Subject: ______________ Page: ______ Item: ______
- ☐ Teacher's Guide, Specify Subject: ______________ Page: ______ Item: ______
- ☐ Test Explanations, Specify Code: ______________ Page: ______ Item: ______

Error/Suggestion: ______________

Part of Materials:
- ☐ Student Text, Specify Subject: ______________ Page: ______ Item: ______
- ☐ Teacher's Guide, Specify Subject: ______________ Page: ______ Item: ______
- ☐ Test Explanations, Specify Code: ______________ Page: ______ Item: ______

Error/Suggestion: ______________

Part of Materials:
- ☐ Student Text, Specify Subject: ______________ Page: ______ Item: ______
- ☐ Teacher's Guide, Specify Subject: ______________ Page: ______ Item: ______
- ☐ Test Explanations, Specify Code: ______________ Page: ______ Item: ______

Error/Suggestion: ______________

Part of Materials:
- ☐ Student Text, Specify Subject: ______________ Page: ______ Item: ______
- ☐ Teacher's Guide, Specify Subject: ______________ Page: ______ Item: ______
- ☐ Test Explanations, Specify Code: ______________ Page: ______ Item: ______

Error/Suggestion: ______________

Part of Materials:
- ☐ Student Text, Specify Subject: ______________ Page: ______ Item: ______
- ☐ Teacher's Guide, Specify Subject: ______________ Page: ______ Item: ______
- ☐ Test Explanations, Specify Code: ______________ Page: ______ Item: ______

Error/Suggestion: ______________

Mail form to Cambridge Educational Services, Inc. or fax form to 1-847-299-2933. For teacher's assistance, call 1-800-444-4373 or e-mail solutions@CambridgeEd.com. Visit our website at www.CambridgeEd.com.